Hazards, Vulnerability and Environmental Justice

D1558746

Risk, Society and Policy Series
Series editor: Ragnar E. Löfstedt

Facility Siting
Risk, Power and Identity in Land-Use Planning
Edited by Åsa Boholm and Ragnar E. Löfstedt

The Perception of Risk
Paul Slovic

Risk, Media and Stigma
Understanding Public Challenges to Modern Science and Technology
Edited by James Flynn, Paul Slovic and Howard Kunreuther

Risk, Uncertainty and Rational Action
Carlo C. Jaeger, Ortwin Renn, Eugene A. Rosa and Thomas Webler

The Social Contours of Risk Volume 1
The Social Contours of Risk Volume 2
Jeanne X. Kasperson and Roger E. Kasperson

Social Trust and the Management of Risk
Edited by George Cvetcovich and Ragnar E. Löfstedt

Transboundary Risk Management
Edited by Joanne Linnerooth-Bayer, Ragnar E. Löfstedt and Gunnar Sjöstedt

Hazards, Vulnerability and Environmental Justice

Susan L. Cutter

London • Sterling, VA

First published by Earthscan in the UK and USA in 2006

ISBN-10:   1-84407-311-4   paperback
           1-84407-310-6   hardback
ISBN-13:   978-1-84407-311-5 paperback
           978-1-84407-310-8 hardback

Typesetting by Composition and Design Services
Printed and bound in the UK by Cromwell Press
Cover design by Yvonne Booth

For a full list of publications please contact:

Earthscan
8–12 Camden High Street
London, NW1 0JH, UK
Tel: +44 (0)20 7387 8558
Fax: +44 (0)20 7387 8998
Email: earthinfo@earthscan.co.uk
Web: **www.earthscan.co.uk**

22883 Quicksilver Drive, Sterling, VA 20166-2012, USA

Earthscan is an imprint of James and James (Science Publishers) Ltd and publishes in association
with the International Institute for Environment and Development

A catalogue record for this book is available from the British Library

Library of Congress Cataloging-in-Publication Data:

Cutter, Susan L.
  Hazards, vulnerability and environmental justice / Susan L. Cutter.
    p. cm.
  ISBN-13: 978-1-84407-311-5 (pbk.)
  ISBN-10: 1-84407-311-4 (pbk.)
  ISBN-13: 978-1-84407-310-8 (hardback)
  ISBN-10: 1-84407-310-6 (hardback)
  1. Environmental risk assessment. 2. Environmental degradation. I. Title.
  GE145.C88 2006
  333.71'4--dc22
                              2006001586

Printed on elemental chlorine-free paper

Contents

Part I – Old, New and Familiar Hazards

Part II – Vulnerability to Threats

Part V – From Theory to Practice

List of Figures, Tables and Boxes

Figures

Tables

Boxes

List of Acronyms and Abbreviations

AAAS	American Association for the Advancement of Science
AAG	Association of American Geographers
ACOE	Army Corps of Engineers
ACRID	Airborne Chemical Release Inventory Data set
AHE	Acute Hazardous Events
ALOHA	Areal Locations of Hazardous Atmospheres (model)
AMS	American Meteorological Society
APELL	Awareness and Preparedness for Emergencies at Local Level
ATSDR	Agency for Toxic Substances and Disease Registry
BANANA	build absolutely nothing anywhere near anybody
BLEVE	boiling liquid expanding vapour explosion
BRS	Biennial Reporting System
CAER	Community Awareness and Emergency Response
CAMEO	Computer-Aided Management of Emergency Operations (model)
CBEP	Community-Based Environmental Protection
CERCLA	Comprehensive Environmental Response, Compensation, and Liability Act
CERCLIS	Comprehensive Environmental Response, Compensation, and Liability Information System
CFC	chlorofluorocarbons
CGI	common gateway interface
CHEMTREC	Chemical Transportation Emergency Center
CIMAH	Control of Industrial Major Accident Hazard programme (UK)
CRED	Centre for Research on the Epidemiology of Disasters
DDT	dichloro-diphenyl-trichloroethane
DOT	Department of Transportation
DPT	Diptheria, Pertussis, Tetanus
EPA	Environmental Protection Agency
EPCRA	Emergency Planning and Community Right-to-Know Act
EPZ	emergency planning zone
FEMA	Federal Emergency Management Agency
FSU	Former Soviet Union
GDP	gross domestic product
GI	geographic information
GIF	graphics interchange format
GIS	geographic information systems
GMO	genetically modified organism

GNP	gross national product
GPS	global positioning system
hazmat	hazardous materials
HE/LT	high emissions of lower toxicity
HRS	Hazardous Ranking System
HTML	hypertext markup language
IAEA	International Atomic Energy Agency
IDNDR	International Decade of Natural Disaster Reduction
IPCS	International Programme on Chemical Safety
IRPTC	International Register of Potentially Toxic Chemicals
IUCN	World Conservation Union, formerly known as the International Union for the Conservation of Nature
LE/HT	lower emissions of higher toxicity
LPG	liquid petroleum gas
LULU	locally unwanted land use
MAU	modifiable areal unit
MCD	minor civil division
MIC	methyl isocyanate
MOM	Maximum of Maximum Envelope of High Water (model)
MRE	Meal Ready to Eat
MSA	Metropolitan Statistical Area
NCGIA	National Center for Geographic Information and Analysis
NECMA	New England County Metropolitan Area
NEMA	National Emergency Management Agency
NIMBY	not in my back yard
NOAA	National Oceanic and Atmospheric Administration
NPL	National Priority List (Superfund)
NRC	Nuclear Regulatory Commission
NRT	National Response Team
OAS	Organization of American States
OECD	Organisation for Economic Co-operation and Development
PAD	protective action distance
PAR	pressure and release (model)
PCB	polychlorinated biphenyls
PDSI	Palmer Drought Severity Index
PEMA	Pennsylvania Emergency Management Agency
PMSA	Primary Metropolitan Statistical Area
R&D	research and development
RCRA	Resource Conservation and Recovery Act
RV	recreational vehicle
SARA	Superfund Amendments and Reauthorization Act
SCDOT	South Carolina Department of Transportation
SCTRAP	South Carolina Toxic Risk Atlas Prototype
SIC	Standard Industrial Code
SLOSH	Sea, Lake, Overland Surges from Hurricanes (model)
SMSA	Standard Metropolitan Statistical Area
SoVI	Social Vulnerability Index

TB	tuberculosis
TCDD	Tetrachlorodibenzon-p-dioxin
TCPA	Toxic Catastrophe Prevention Act (New Jersey)
TLV	threshold limit value
TMI	Three Mile Island
TRI	Toxic Release Inventory
TSD	treatment, storage and disposal
TVA	Tennessee Valley Authority
TWA	time-weighted average
UCC	United Church of Christ's Commission for Racial Justice
UK	United Kingdom
UN	United Nations
UNDRO	United Nations Disaster Relief Organization
UNEP	United Nations Environment Programme
US	United States
USAR	Urban Search and Rescue
USC	University of South Carolina
USGS	US Geological Survey
WAT	weighted average toxicity
WHO	World Health Organization
WTEF	waste-to-energy facility

Acknowledgements

This book and the intellectual content within is not a sole effort, but rather a collaborative adventure that has now spanned three decades. My journey has been an interesting one, filled with meanders and abrupt events that facilitated and guided new research domains. The strongest intellectual influences are noted in the introductory chapter, 'Pathways to Disaster', so I won't repeat them here. While not a student of Gilbert F. White, I have benefited from his mentorship, wisdom and encouragement. Similarly, Bob Kates, Roger Kasperson, Tom Wilbanks, Brian Berry and Risa Palm have been excellent sounding boards for professional advice.

Many of the articles in this collection are co-authored. The collaborations on hurricane evacuation behaviour in South Carolina (done with my colleague Kirstin Dow) draw on her long-standing interests in vulnerability and the role of uncertainty, and my interests in evacuation behaviour and public policy. We continue to monitor the hurricane season closely – waiting for the next storm to make landfall in South Carolina so we can gauge the community's response. The co-authors of all the remaining articles were either students or former students of mine at the time the articles were published. This is perhaps the biggest contribution to the field that I have made – mentoring the next generation of hazard and disaster scholars. I have been blessed with articulate, bright, energetic and committed students for most of my career. They work hard; they play hard; and they enjoy what they do and the contributions we collectively make. You can't ask for a better environment in which to flourish.

I would be remiss if I didn't mention some very specific individuals who helped get this project going. The first is Jonathan Sinclair Wilson, who suggested the project in the first place – a project that I wasn't ready for at the time. Jonathan's persistence (and patience) resulted in this book. Amanda Inman helped in the compilation of materials. Lastly, the National Science Foundation, the US Department of Energy, the US Federal Emergency Management Agency and the State of South Carolina have generously supported much of the research in this book.

Finally, Nathaniel and Megan Warner continue to bring me joy as a parent as I watch them embark on their own careers. Max, Hurricane, Lily and Bogotá provide much needed diversions and occasionally 'help' at the keyboard. And my husband, Langdon Warner, is the glue that holds the family together and nurtures us all. Thanks to you all.

October 2005

Introduction
Pathways to Disaster[1]

It was bound to happen. The scenario had been researched, rehearsed and replayed over and over again among emergency managers. It was just a matter of when and where the major hurricane would strike a large American city. Two specific scenarios had been considered: a major hurricane with 20-foot-plus storm surge inundation affecting the Gulf Coast region or a hurricane-induced levee failure in New Orleans. Both captured the imagination of emergency planners designing training scenarios. Hurricane Pam, the fictional emergency exercise for federal, state and local officials in Louisiana encapsulated both scenarios. Hurricane Katrina played them out in real time in the late summer of 2005. Who would have imagined that just a short three weeks later the region would be struck by another major hurricane, prompting more than a million people to evacuate coastal areas from Texas eastward to Louisiana? But these are not the only doomsday or worst-case scenarios that concern disaster experts. There are many disaster hot spots around the world (Dilley et al, 2005). Consider the impacts of a 8.0 Richter magnitude earthquake in Tokyo or Istanbul; a Category 5 typhoon making land-fall near Manila, Taipei or Hong Kong; another tsunami in the Indian Ocean; an explosive volcanic eruption in Central America, South America, or Indonesia from the many active volcanoes that dot the landscape; another prolonged heat-wave in Europe; a dirty bomb in London or Washington DC; or an avian influenza outbreak in China. All are likely and all will produce catastrophic losses of life, or property damage, or both.

Gender, Race, Class and Catastrophe

The revelations of inadequate response to Hurricane Katrina's aftermath are not just about failures in emergency response at the local, state and federal levels or failures in the overall emergency management system. They are also about failures of the social support systems for America's impoverished – the largely invisible inner-city poor. The former can be rectified quickly (months to years) through organizational restructuring or training; the latter requires much more time, more resources, and the political will to redress social inequities and inequalities that have been sustained for more than half a century and show little signs of dissipating. The lessons from this singular event are instructive for cities throughout the world that are equally hazard-prone.

How did the US arrive at the confluence of natural and social vulnerabilities that manifested itself as the Hurricane Katrina disaster? This complex emergency began with geography – the spatial interaction of humans and their environment over time. The original settlement was on the highest ground in the bayou, Vieux Carré (the French Quarter), which later became the heart and soul of the modern city. How prescient for the early settlers to build on the highest ground available. As the settlement grew, New Orleans became a sprawling metropolis sandwiched between, and surrounded by, water. The siting and growth of New Orleans was inevitable given its access to water-borne transportation routes, but that access also contributed to the extremely precarious and peculiar range of environmental risks. The same geographic vulnerability is true for many of the world's megacities.

The human transformation of the physical environment enabled New Orleans to grow and prosper (Colten, 2001, 2004). Levees were built to control the flow of the mighty Mississippi, but they were also built to contain flooding from Lake Pontchartrain, especially useful during the hurricane season. The ideology of conquering and taming nature (that man could actually control nature was an inherited European ideal), rather than living in harmony with it, was (and still is) the driving force in the production of the physical vulnerability of the metropolitan area. Instead of seeing the deposition of alluvium that one expects in a deltaic coastline, the levees channelled the river and its sediment, destroying protective wetlands south and east of the city. With many areas of the city below sea level, even heavy rainfall became a problem, filling the city with water just like a giant punchbowl. An elaborate pumping system was required to keep the city dry during heavy rains, let alone tropical storms. What would happen during a hurricane, a levee failure, or an intentional levee breach used to divert floodwaters away from the city as was done in 1927 (Barry, 1997)?

Concurrent with the physical transformation of the city, a new social geography was being created as well. The American South's segregated past was best seen in the spatial and social evolution of southern cities, including New Orleans. Migration from the rural impoverished areas to the city was followed by white flight from urban areas to more suburban communities. Public housing was constructed to cope with black population influxes during the 1950s and 1960s, and, in a pattern repeated throughout America, the housing was invariably located in the most undesirable areas – along major transportation corridors, on reclaimed land or next to industrial facilities. Employment opportunities were limited for inner-city residents as jobs moved outward from the central city to suburban locations, or overseas as the process of globalization reduced even further the number of low-skilled jobs. The most impoverished lived in squalid conditions concentrated in certain neighbourhoods within cities, with little or no employment, poor education and little hope for the future of their children or grandchildren. It is against this backdrop of the social geography of cities and the differential access to resources that we can best understand the Hurricane Katrina disaster.

Socially created vulnerabilities are largely ignored in the hazards and disaster literature because they are so hard to measure and quantify. Social vulnerability is partially a product of social inequalities – those social factors and forces that create the susceptibility of various groups to harm, and in turn affect their ability to respond and bounce back after the disaster (their resilience). But it is much more than that. Social vulnerability involves the basic provision of health care, the liveability of places, overall indicators of quality of life, and accessibility to lifelines (power, water, emergency response personnel), capital and political representation.

Race and class are certainly factors that help explain the social vulnerability in the American South, while ethnicity plays an additional role in many cities. When the middle classes (both white and black) abandon a city, the disparities between the very rich and the very poor expand. Add to this an increasing elderly population, the homeless, transients (including tourists) and other special needs populations, and the prospects for evacuating a city during times of emergency become a daunting challenge for most American cities. What is a major challenge for other cities became a virtual impossibility for New Orleans. Those that could muster the personal resources evacuated the city. With no welfare cheque (the hurricane struck near the end of the month), little food and no help from the city, state or federal officials, the poor were forced to ride out the storm in their homes or move to the shelters of last resort. This is the enduring face of Hurricane Katrina: poor, black, single mothers, young and old, struggling just to survive, options limited by the ineffectiveness of preparedness and the inadequacy of response.

Disasters also disproportionately affect women and children. According to some initial studies (Oxfam International, 2005), more than four times as many women perished than men in the South Asian tsunami. In some places, the proportion of deaths that were children exceeded 40 per cent. The South Asian tsunami in all probability will result in a 'tsunami generation' in many countries where the death toll among women and children was especially high. For the living, the South Asian tsunami will magnify the existing gender inequalities and the disproportionate consequences of the event. Marriage will occur earlier for young women (and girls), which will compromise their educational opportunities and reproductive health. Women's workloads will increase, as not only are they the first to respond to the emergency, but are also the primary care-givers to the sick, infirm and elderly survivors. There will be an increase in domestic violence and sexual abuse during the recovery and reconstruction as the family structure changes, the pressures to return to normal exceed the capacity to do so, and communities cope with the latent emotional toll of the losses.

In the actual planning for emergencies, social vulnerability is captured under the heading of 'special needs populations'. While small communities can identify their special needs populations, it becomes a daunting task in major cities. What is the homeless population and where are they? How many tourists are in town that may need help in evacuating? How full are the large hospitals, outpatient clinics and mental health care facilities? What about nursing homes? Prisons? The healthy poor are rarely considered as a special needs population, even though they lack the financial resources to respond to emergencies. What about the rural poor?

The US has very little experience with evacuating cities from natural hazards let alone technological failures or wilful acts. This is true in other nations as well. Our collective experience with evacuations is based on chemical spills or toxic releases, planning for nuclear power plant accidents, wildfires and hurricanes. In most cases, but certainly not all, the evacuations have been in rural or suburban places, not a major US city. Florida's hurricane experience during the past few years has been a suburban phenomenon, not an inner-city one, for example.

The potential differences in response are critical and highlight the difficulties in emergency preparedness for major cities. The number of large urban hospitals, the dependence on public transportation and the need for mass sheltering all complicate preparedness efforts in high-density multi-ethnic and multiracial cities. In addition to the sheer number of people at risk, emergency managers have the additional task of identifying those residents who may be the most vulnerable – the poor, the infirm, the elderly, the homeless, women and children. The nescient result is an ever-widening disparity in society's ability to cope with more persistent social and economic problems in urban areas, let alone a potential mass impact event of unknown origin. This is the story of Hurricane Katrina and its aftermath.

Scale, of course, is also an important element to consider. While the terrorist attacks of 11 September 2001 affected two major cities (New York and Washington, DC), the actual damage swath in New York City, for example, was quite small (tens of acres, not thousands of square miles) and involved one local jurisdiction. Hurricane Katrina affected a much larger region, encompassing more than 600 miles of the Gulf coastline stretching from Grand Isle, LA to Gulf Shores, AL; three states; and hundreds of local jurisdictions. The Indian Ocean tsunami covered an even broader geographic area involving many nations. Scale matters: the larger the geographical area of impact, the more complex the response.

Just as there is variation in the physical landscape, the landscape of social inequity has increased the division between rich and poor in America, leading to the increasing social vulnerability of residents, especially to coastal hazards (Heinz Center, 2002). Strained race relations and the seemingly differential response to the Katrina disaster suggest that, in planning for future catastrophes, we need to look not only at the natural environment in the development of mitigation programmes, but the social environment as well. It is the interaction between nature and society that produces the vulnerability of places. While physical vulnerability is reduced through the construction of disaster-resistant buildings, changes in land use and restoration of wetlands and floodways, a marked reduction in social vulnerability will require an improvement in the overall quality of life for the inner-city poor.

A Personal Perspective

Who we are often defines what we do. As I was monitoring the impacts and human toll of the Hurricane Katrina disaster, I began to ask myself 'How did I develop such an interest in environmental hazards and disasters? What is it about these events that piqued my interest? Were there personal events in my own background that pre-ordained my future interest in hazards research?'

I have always been interested in the relationship between human activity and natural processes. The social transformations in the US during the 1960s – the civil rights movement, the rise of social and anti-war protests, and the nascent environmental movement initially inspired this interest. I spent my formative years in the San Francisco Bay area where I was exposed to the rampant social activism of the time. Social change, achieved by peaceful social protest, became my mantra and, coupled with my interest in landscapes, drew me to geography as a discipline. What other discipline afforded the opportunity to examine social conditions, environmental concerns and natural landscapes? In looking back upon my family and social influences, I think I've always been a geographer. At the same time, I also knew that I wanted to change (and improve) the human conditions, so I was drawn to academe.

I didn't have a grand plan to become a professor in a university; it just happened by serendipity. I liked going to school and learning about new things. After two years at a junior college, I transferred to California State University, Hayward (across the San Francisco Bay), where I majored in geography and environmental studies. There were two primary influences on my subsequent career that occurred at Hayward. The first influence was the excellent undergraduate training and education I received in the discipline of geography. I was not only taught the basics but there was a strong orientation to fieldwork – which in many ways is the lifeblood of the discipline. The second major influence was a personal one and that was the encouragement of a geography professor (William L. Thomas) to pursue graduate studies. I was fortunate to work as an undergraduate assistant on one of his funded projects that examined the relationship between herbicidal spraying and changes in settlement patterns in Southeast Asia. This introduced me to the importance of remote sensing in understanding landscape change. I didn't truly appreciate the importance of this project or its impact on my own career until decades later. With encouragement from Thomas, I applied to a number of graduate schools and chose to attend the University of Chicago.

Despite its long tradition in hazards research, by the time I arrived at Chicago (1972), Gilbert White had already relocated to the University of Colorado, Boulder, but his legacy remained. Despite their specialized interests, most faculty members had a keen appreciation for nature–society interactions. For a California girl raised in the suburbs, Chicago was quite a change – socially as well as environmentally. In the early 1970s, the Southside of Chicago was a very interesting place. Hyde Park, where the University is located, was an island, socially segregated from the surrounding communities. I became fascinated with the social geography of the city and this led to working under the direction of Brian J. L. Berry. Berry gave his students considerable latitude in their coursework and programmes of study. My coursework at Chicago, in addition to geography, ranged from urban studies and psychology to ecology and geological sciences. One of Berry's great strengths as a mentor was his insistence on a strong methodological orientation; in this case, spatial analysis. Berry had many advisees working in many subfields of the discipline – urban, economic, spatial analysis. While his students were often unable to chat with one another about the substance of the dissertation problem, we were all bound together by our common methodological approach to research.

It was through Berry's work on land use, environmental quality and urban form (Berry, 1976) and the social burdens of pollution (Berry, 1977) that I discovered the mechanism for combining my personal interests in social change and activism with my research interests in nature–society interactions. My dissertation examined community attitudes toward pollution in Chicago (Caris, 1978). I studied the disparities not only in the social burdens of pollution, but in community perceptions about what could be done to mitigate the impacts. In hindsight, this work provided the intellectual foundation for environmental justice research, a topic I returned to nearly 20 years later.

Responsiveness to Disasters

The core-meltdown incident at Three Mile Island in 1979 occurred during my second year as a faculty member at Rutgers University. Along with my colleague, Ken Mitchell, we conducted field studies of evacuation behaviour in response to the incident. This not only led to my lifelong interest in evacuation behaviour (Chapters 3 and 11–15) and its underlying correlates (cognitions of risk), it also stimulated my interest in emergency response planning (Chapters 22 and 25). It was clear that nuclear power plant failures were low probability events, so if I were to make a career of this I would have to look at other sources of technological hazards in order to develop my emerging theoretical and conceptual interests in vulnerability (Cutter, 1993). Chemical or hazardous material spills seemed to fit nicely with my evolving constructs and they became my 'hazard du jour' in the 1980s (Chapters 2 and 23).

The intensification of the arms race during the mid-1980s provided the context for the paper on 'Geographers and Nuclear War' (Chapter 24). I was particularly frustrated by the discipline's lack of involvement in the debates on 'crisis location planning' and the 'environmental impacts of nuclear winter'. It was here that my social activism was piqued and, knowing that the discipline had much to offer, I wanted to drop the gauntlet and challenge the profession to do something. This same activist agenda for the discipline can be seen in the Association of American Geographers' Geographical Dimensions of Terrorism project (see Chapter 1).

My relocation to the University of South Carolina in 1993 afforded ample opportunities to improve my own spatial analytical tool kit. Working from extensive databases on chemical hazards and incidents, I was able to finally 'marry' social characteristics of places to their hazards using geographic information systems (GIS). The sophistication of the analytical capabilities of GIS allowed us (myself and graduate students) to re-explore the science of spatial inequities as they related to environmental justice (Chapters 16–21).

While at Rutgers, Ken Mitchell and I divided up the hazards domain – he took natural events and I specialized in technological. The move to South Carolina meant that I now had to cover all hazards, not just technological ones. The expansion into an all-hazards perspective was fortuitous. The convergence of my interests in physical processes, social systems, technological systems and GIScience fuelled the theoretical and conceptual development of vulnerability science. My first attempt at articulating a vision for this new interdisciplinary field was the article originally published in *Progress in Human Geography* (Chapter 6 of this book). This was then followed by an actual example of how to conduct place-based vulnerability assessments that are both theoretically sound and methodological robust (Chapter 7). An interesting side benefit of this work was its practical application. The hazards of place model of vulnerability and the methodology for constructing it are now being used as a baseline for all-hazards vulnerability assessments not only in South Carolina but also throughout the US. Tweaking the hazards of place model to focus on social vulnerability resulted in a robust algorithm for assessing changes over time and across space (Chapter 8). Finally, charting the future of vulnerability science and its important unanswered research domains appears in Chapter 9.

The themes of vulnerability to hazards, societal cognitions and responses to threats, the role of disparities (race, class, gender) in impacts, and emergency response planning are woven throughout the book. They identify a research agenda that is now nearing three decades and nowhere near being completed. Opportunistic research is evident throughout my research career (Three Mile Island, various hurricanes in South Carolina, 11 September 2001, Hurricane Katrina), but these case studies build the empirical base and test the broader theories and concepts inherent in vulnerability science. While critics may argue that the research in this volume is overly 'applied', I prefer to label it as socially relevant. As alluded to earlier, the personal is political; why spend an entire research career staring at your navel when you have a chance to make the world a better place for your children and grandchildren by providing sound science in support of public policies? From my perspective, this is the real value of the research that is presented here.

Postscript

Disasters will happen. To lessen their impacts in the future, we need to reduce our social vulnerability and increase disaster resilience with improvements in the social conditions and living standards everywhere. We need to build housing (and rebuild damaged housing) and infrastructure in harmony with nature and design communities in order to be resilient to environmental threats, even if it means smaller, more liveable places and fewer profits for land and urban developers. We need to build redundant social, management, technological systems that are flexible and adaptive so that we can respond to threats regardless of their origins – natural hazards, technological failures or terrorist acts. Disasters are income- and gender-neutral, and colour-blind. Their impacts, however, are not.

Columbia, SC   11 October 2005

Note

1. Portions of this essay appear on the Social Science Research Council's web forum on Hurricane Katrina, under the title 'The social vulnerability of disasters: Race, class, and catastrophe' (online at http://understandingkatrina.ssrc.org/Cutter/).

References

Barry, J. M. (1997) *Rising Tide: The Great Mississippi Flood of 1927 and How it Changed America*, Simon & Schuster, New York
Berry, B. J. L. (1976) *Land Use, Urban Form, and Environmental Quality*, University of Chicago Press, Chicago, IL
Berry, B. J. L. (ed) (1977) *The Social Burdens of Environmental Pollution*, Ballinger Press, Cambridge, MA
Caris (Cutter), S. (1978) *Community Attitudes Toward Pollution*, Department of Geography Research Paper 188, University of Chicago, Chicago, IL
Colten, C. E. (2001) *Transforming New Orleans and its Environs: Centuries of Change*, University of Pittsburgh Press, Pittsburgh, PA
Colten, C. E. (2004) *An Unnatural Metropolis: Wresting New Orleans from Nature*, Louisiana State University Press, Baton Rouge, LA
Cutter, S. L. (1993) *Living with Risk: The Geography of Technological Hazards*, Edward Arnold, London
Dilley, M., Chen, R. S., Deichmann, U., Lerner-Lam, A. L. and Arnold, M. with Agwe, J., Buys, P., Kjekstad, O., Lyon, B. and Yetman, G. (2005) *Natural Disaster Hotspots: A Global Risk Analysis*, The World Bank Hazard Management Unit, Washington, DC
Heinz Center (2002) *Human Links to Coastal Disasters*, The H. John Heinz III Center for Science, Economics and the Environment, Washington, DC
Oxfam International (2005) *The Tsunami's Impact on Women*, Oxfam Briefing Note, March. Available at www.oxfam.org.uk/what_we_do/issues/conflict_disasters/downloads/bn_tsunami_women.pdf

Part I

Old, New and Familiar Hazards

1

The Changing Landscape of Fear

Susan L. Cutter, Douglas B. Richardson
and Thomas J. Wilbanks

In the days following 11 September 2001, all geographers felt a sense of loss – people we knew perished, and along with everyone else we experienced discomfort in our own lives and a diminished level of confidence that the world will be a safe and secure place for our children and grandchildren. Many of us who are geographers felt an urge and a need to see if we could find ways to apply our knowledge and expertise to make the world more secure. A number of our colleagues assisted immediately by sharing specific geographical knowledge (such as Jack Shroder's expert knowledge on the caves in Afghanistan) or more generally by assisting rescue and relief efforts through our technical expertise in geographic information systems (GIS) and remote sensing (such as Hunter College's Center for the Analysis and Research of Spatial Information and various geographers at federal agencies and in the private sector). Still others sought to enhance the nation's research capacity in the geographical dimensions of terrorism (the Association of American Geographers' Geographical Dimensions of Terrorism project). Many of us have given considerable thought to how our science and practice might be useful in both the short and longer terms. One result is the set of contributions to this book.

But, we fail in our social responsibility if we spend our time thinking of geography as the end. Geography is not the *end*; it is one of many *means* to the end. Our concern should be with issues and needs that transcend any one discipline. As we address issues of terrorism, utility without quality is unprofessional, but quality without utility is self-indulgent. Our challenge is to focus not on geography's general importance but on the central issues in addressing terrorism as a new reality in our lives in the United States (although, unfortunately, not a new issue in too many other parts of our world).

The 11 September 2001 events have prompted both immediate and longer-term concerns about the geographical dimensions of terrorism. Potential ques-

Note: Reprinted, with permission, from *The Geographical Dimensions of Terrorism*, Susan L. Cutter, Douglas B. Richardson, and Thomas J. Wilbanks (editors), 'The Changing Landscape of Fear', pp1–5. © Routledge/Taylor and Francis Group, 2003

tions on the very nature of these types of threats, how the public perceives them, individual and societal willingness to reduce vulnerability to such threats, and ultimately our ability to manage their consequences require concerted research on the part of the geographical community, among others. Geographers are well positioned to address some of the initial questions regarding emergency management and response and some of the spatial impacts of the immediate consequences, but the research community is not sufficiently mobilized and networked internally or externally to develop a longer, sustained, and theoretically informed research agenda on the geographical dimensions of terrorism. As noted more than a decade ago, 'issues of nuclear war and deterrence [and now terrorism] are inherently geographical, yet our disciplinary literature is either silent on the subject or poorly focused' (Cutter, 1988, p132). Recent events provide an opportunity and a context for charting a new path to bring geographical knowledge and skills to the forefront in solving this pressing international problem.

Promoting Landscapes of Fear

Terrorists (and terrorism) seek to exploit the everyday – things that people do, places that they visit, the routines of daily living, and the functioning of institutions. Terrorism is an adaptive threat which changes its target, timing and mode of delivery as circumstances are altered. The seeming randomness of terrorist attacks (either the work of organized groups or renegade individuals) in both time and space increases public anxiety concerning terrorism. At the most fundamental level, 11 September 2001 was an attack on the two most prominent symbols of US financial and military power: the World Trade Center and the Pentagon (Smith, 2002; Harvey, 2002). The events represented symbolic victories of chaos over order and normality (Alexander, 2002), disruptions in and the undermining of global financial markets (Harvey, 2002), a nationalization of terror (Smith, 2002) and the creation of fear and uncertainty among the public, precisely the desired outcome by the perpetrators. In generating this psychological landscape of fear, people's activity patterns were and are being altered, with widespread social, political, and economic effects. The reduction in air travel by consumers in the weeks and months following 11 September 2001 was but one among many examples.

What are the Fundamental Issues of Terrorism?

There are a myriad of different ways to identify and examine terrorism issues. Some of these dimensions are quite conventional, others less so. In all cases, geographical understanding provides an essential aspect of the enquiry. There are a number of dimensions of the issues that seem reasonably clear. For instance, one conventional way of looking at the topic is to distinguish four central subject-matter challenges:

1   *reducing threats*, including a) reducing the reasons why people want to commit terrorist acts, thereby addressing root causes, and b) reducing the ability of potential terrorists to accomplish their aims, or deterrence;

2   *detecting threats* that have not been avoided, using sensors and signature detection to spot potential actions before they happen and interrupt them;
3   *reducing vulnerabilities* to threats, focusing on critical sectors and infrastructures, hopefully without sacrificing civil liberties and individual freedoms; and
4   *improving responses* to terrorism, emphasizing 'consequence management', and also attributing causation and learning from experience (for example, forensics applied to explosive materials and anthrax strains).

A different way of viewing terrorism is according to time horizons. Immediately after 11 September 2001, governmental leaders told us that the nation was now engaged in a new 'war on terrorism' that will last several years, and that our existing knowledge and technologies are needed for this war. Early estimates of the overall U.S. national effort are very large – in the range of \$30 to \$40 billion per year – including the formation of a new executive department, the Department of Homeland Security. Early priorities include securing national borders, supporting first responders mainly in the Federal Emergency Management Agency (FEMA) and the Department of Justice, defending against bioterrorism, and applying information technologies to improve national security.

Beyond this, we know that better knowledge and practices should be put to use in the next half-decade or so, as we face a challenge that is more like a stubborn virus than a single serial killer. To address this type of need, attention often is placed on capabilities where progress can be made relatively quickly if resources are targeted carefully. Some of our GIS and GIScience tools are especially promising candidates for such enhancements, which have both positive and negative consequences (Monmonier 2002). The use of such technologies surely will help secure homelands, but at what price, the loss of personal freedoms or invasion of privacy?

There are other dimensions as well. For instance, one dimension concerns boundaries between free exchanges of information and limited ones, between classified work and unclassified work. Another differentiates between different types of threats: physical violence, chemical or biological agents, cyberterrorism, and the like. Still other themes are woven through the material that follows.

The Challenge Ahead

The greatest challenge to geographers and our colleagues in neighbouring fields of study is to stretch our minds beyond familiar research questions and specializations so as to be innovative, even ingenious, in producing new understandings that contribute to increased global security. Clearly, the most serious specific threats to security in the future will be actions that are difficult to imagine now: social concerns just beginning to bubble to the surface, technologies yet to be developed, biological agents that do not yet exist, terrorist practices that are beyond our imagination. A core challenge is to improve knowledge and institutional capacities that prepare us to deal with the unknown and the unexpected, with constant change calling for staying one step ahead instead of always being one step behind.

When research requires, say, three years to produce results and another two years to communicate in print to prospective audiences, we need to be unusually pre-scient as we construct our research agendas related to terrorism issues, and we need to be very perceptive and skillful in convincing non-geographers that these longer-term research objectives are, in fact, truly important.

The topic of combating terrorism is not an easy one. It calls for us to stretch in directions that may be new and not altogether comfortable. It threatens to entangle us in policy agendas that many of us may consider insensitively con-ceived, even distasteful. It may endanger social cohesion in our own community of scholars. On the other hand, how can we turn our backs on a phenomenon that threatens political freedom, social cohesion far beyond our own cohorts, eco-nomic progress, environmental sustainability and many other values that we hold dear, including the future security of our own children and grandchildren?

More fundamentally, geographers are not concerned only with winning the war on terrorism in the next two years or deploying new capabilities in the next five or ten. We are concerned with working toward a secure century, restoring a widespread sense of security in the global society in the longer term without undermining basic freedoms. This is the domain of the research world; assuring a stream of new knowledge, understandings, and tools for the longer term, and looking for policies and practices that – if they could be conceived and used – would make a significant difference in the quality of life.

As we prepare to create this new knowledge and these understandings, what we are trying to do, in fact, is to create the new 21st-century utility – not a hard-ened infrastructure such as for power or water, but rather a geographical under-standing and spatial infrastructure that helps the nation understand and respond to threats. The effort required to create this new utility to serve the nation has a historical analogy in the creation of the Tennessee Valley Authority (TVA), under Franklin Roosevelt's New Deal. The Appalachian region of the southeastern US had a long history of economic depression and was among those areas hardest hit by the Great Depression of the 1930s. The creation of the TVA, a multipurpose utility with an economic development mission, constructed dams for flood con-trol and hydroelectric power for the region in order to:

- bring electricity to the rural areas that did not have it;
- stimulate new industries to promote economic development;
- control flooding, which routinely plagued the region; and
- develop a more sustainable and equitable future for the region's residents.

This 21st-century utility must rely on geographical knowledge and synthesis capabilities as we begin to understand the root causes of insecurity both here and abroad, vulnerabilities and resiliencies in our daily lives and the systems that support them, and our collective role in fostering a more sustainable future, both domestically and globally.

Much of the content of this book is aimed at this longer term, and it is impor-tant for geographers to join with others in the research community to assure that the long term is not neglected as research support is directed toward combating terrorism and protecting homelands in the short run. This is why the Association of American Geographers and some of its members have joined together to produce the perspectives and insights represented in this book. It is only a start, we still have a long way to go, and there are daunting intellectual and political hazards to be overcome. But if many of us keep a part of our professional focus on this global and national issue, we have a chance to make our world better in many tangible ways.

References

Alexander, D. (2002) 'Nature's impartiality, man's inhumanity: Reflections on terrorism and world crisis in the context of historical disaster', *Disasters*, vol 26, no 1, pp1–9

Cutter, S. L. (1988) 'Geographers and nuclear war: Why we lack influence on public policy', *Annals of the Association of American Geographers*, vol 78, no 1, pp132–143 (note that this article has been reprinted as Chapter 24 of the present volume, but the quoted extract comes from the abstract, which has been omitted in the reprint)

Harvey, D. (2002) 'Cracks in the edifice of the empire state' in M. Sorkin and S. Zukin (eds) *After the World Trade Center: Rethinking New York City*, Routledge, New York, pp57–67

Monmonier, M. (2002) *Spying with Maps: Surveillance Technologies and the Future of Privacy*, University of Chicago Press, Chicago, IL

Smith, N. (2002) 'Scales of terror: The manufacturing of nationalism and the war for US globalism' in M. Sorkin and S. Zukin (eds) *After the World Trade Center: Rethinking New York City*, Routledge, New York, pp97–108

2
Chemical Hazards in Urban America

Susan L. Cutter and John Tiefenbacher

The potential for death and injury from exposure to acutely toxic chemicals is greatest in urban settings where industries, transportation networks and people are in the closest contact. But which cities are the most hazardous? How might we explain the frequency and distribution of chemical hazards in urban America? Using one type of chemical hazard, acute airborne releases, this chapter examines the spatial distribution of these releases in metropolitan areas and provides a classification scheme that distinguishes high hazard areas from low hazard ones. We also describe factors that help to differentiate these hazard regions and speculate on some of the public policy implications of the research.

Kirby (1986) suggested that urban history can be viewed as a process of dealing with environmental risk. Both processes and responses are in a constant state of flux as populations and industrial structures change and new technologies with new products increase. Unexpected consequences and hazards emerge as new by-products are produced, many of them extremely toxic. Transportation networks provide the linkages between production and consumption and add yet another dimension to the urban hazard mosaic. This mosaic can ultimately be translated into a hazardscape which is the landscape of hazards that characterize a place or region (Solecki, 1990). Hazardscapes refer to the landscape of many hazards (natural, technological or social in origin) in one place, or to one particular type of hazard, such as airborne toxic releases, among many places. For many technological events, the terms technological hazard and environmental risk are used interchangeably. We prefer a more precise definition where hazard connotes an adverse event or situation, whereas risk is a concept that combines the consequences of the event and its likelihood of occurrence (O'Riordan, 1985). The spatial representation of risk and preparedness levels provides the mechanism for analysing and ultimately mapping hazardscapes.

Historically, geographers have reviewed the relationship between urbanism, environmental quality and risk, but only at a very general level (Berry et al, 1974; Berry and Horton, 1974; Coppock and Wilson, 1974; Detwyler and Marcus,

Note: Reprinted, with permission, from *Urban Geography*, vol 12, no 5, Susan L. Cutter and John Tiefenbacher, 'Chemical Hazards in Urban America', pp 417–430. © V. H. Winston & Son, Inc., 360 South Ocean Boulevard, Palm Beach, FL 33480, 1991. All rights reserved.

1972; Greenberg et al, 1979; Herbert and Johnson, 1978). One of the few detailed studies of the differential impacts of pollution risks in urban areas was conducted by Berry (1977). He examined the spatial relationship between pollution and the population exposed to such risks, and thereby determined the social burdens of pollution or, more precisely, the distributional equity in pollution risks. Using air pollution as an example, Berry concluded that, in metropolitan areas where over-all levels of pollution are low, the poor and minority populations are clustered in the worst polluted areas. In those urban areas where air pollution levels are generally higher, middle-class residents are disproportionately affected because of their willingness to trade off the benefits of proximity to central city locations.

The vulnerability of urban places to technological risk has not been addressed in any systematic fashion, although Liverman (1986) examined the ways in which technological risk and urbanism intersect. A systematic attempt to examine other technological risks in urban places is still lacking, although some preliminary empirical investigations on the historical dimensions of hazardous waste generation and contemporary analyses of specific technological hazards in urban areas are emerging (Colton, 1990a, 1990b; Cutter and Tiefenbacher, 1989). Clearly, more research in this area is needed.

On a more theoretical level, insights on the social construction of risk (Kasperson et al, 1988; Kirby, 1991; Johnson and Covello, 1987) aid in our understanding of how risks are amplified, mediated, and change over time. Risks are embedded in socio-political structures. As these change, so does the level of danger and fear, even though the physical dimension of risk and the human response to it are relatively static. Risks cannot be examined in isolation, but need to be conceived as part of a larger process of societal transformation. The same is true for hazards.

Toxic Clouds as Hazards

The release of acutely toxic chemicals into the atmosphere serves as one type of tech-nological risk that affects people in urban areas. Toxic clouds produce deadly results as in Bhopal, India in 1984 (Everest, 1985; Morehouse and Subramanian, 1986; Brown, 1987; Bogard, 1989). They can also entail the mass evacuation of residents downwind from the release. For example, the Mississauga, Ontario, chlorine release in 1979 involved 250,000 evacuees (Liverman and Wilson, 1981) and the 1986 Miamisburg, Ohio, white phosphorus release resulted in the evacuation of 40,000 people for several days. These incidents, among thousands more, occurred in densely populated areas and severely challenged emergency response managers to provide quick, safe evacuations and emergency medical care to large numbers of people.

Despite federally mandated emergency response planning, the level of emer-gency preparedness for chemical releases is still highly variable in this country (Chapter 23; see also Solecki, 1990). Part of this is due to variations in the cul-ture of planning from state to state, available funds, and changes in the nature of emergency response planning during the last 25 years. Sorenson (1991) noted the increasing complexity and sophistication of emergency planning and the dichot-omy facing planners who often must make decisions on technological choice and the public acceptance of the hazards associated with those choices.

In a preliminary study of chemical hazards, the state scale was judged insufficient in understanding the hazard complexities of chemical releases (Cutter and Solecki, 1989). Two different categories of incidents were identified: rural agricultural and urban industrial. The clustering of industry produces a variety of industrial landscapes that are misleading if generalized under the artificial confines of state boundaries. Because chemicals are used in both agriculture and industry, generalizations about economic activity and transportation at the state level masked important intrastate variations. Moreover, 73 per cent of incidents were in metropolitan areas, thereby necessitating a closer examination at this scale. The use of metropolitan-level data highlights the functional and social interconnectedness of modern urban systems. It also reflects those aspects of chemical production, transportation and use that contribute to the spatial occurrence of releases of acutely toxic chemicals in gaseous and vapour states, the ubiquitous 'toxic cloud'.

The degree of chemical hazard is based on the hazards of place model developed by Cutter and Solecki (1989). This model suggests that the level of hazard at a place is a function of the degree of risk and the amount of mitigation and planning to respond to such risks. The focus here is on the place, and not the people residing in that place, be it a city or state. We can thus distinguish between the vulnerability of the place (hazards) and the people (exposures) who live in those places.

Furthermore, these risks and mitigation efforts do not occur in isolation. The contextual nature of the hazard is equally important (Palm, 1990; Mitchell et al, 1989). The underlying dimensions of a place, including its social institutions, construct and define risks and either enhance or detract from their management. Hazards and risks, then, are more than just the probability of occurrence of an extreme event. They include the underlying factors that contribute to risks in the first place, in addition to factors that constrain the ability of the population to respond, such as demographics, the level of planning and so forth.

The hazards of place model incorporates these contextual characteristics and uses several factors to determine the level of hazard: incident likelihood and industrial structure are measures of risk, while prior experience and planning are indicators of mitigation. As discussed later, these factors show a snapshot of the risk and mitigation characteristics of metropolitan places. This hazards of place model is then used to produce a city-by-city comparison of the levels of chemical hazards associated with urban settings.

Indicators of Chemical Hazards

Chemical incidents data

We have developed a database on acute toxic chemical incidents in the US for the years 1980–1989. Data were compiled from other more specialized databases, newspaper reports, newsletters, and monographs (Table 2.1). Because of the lack of definitive information on the quantity of chemical released, we included any release which resulted in an 'off-site' (beyond plant boundaries) plume of gas or vapour cloud. Specific data on each spill (when available) included city, county, state, date, time, chemical, quantity released, population and area evacuated, inju-

Table 2.1 *Sources for acute toxic release incidents database*

Existing databases	Newspapers
National Response Center	*New York Times*
US Dept. of Transportation	*Chicago Tribune*
Acute Hazardous Events	*Los Angeles Times*
US Environmental Protection Agency	*Wall Street Journal*
Periodicals	*Washington Post*
	Boston Globe
Chemical and Engineering News	*Philadelphia Inquirer*
Chemical Week	*USA Today*
Hazardous Materials Newsletter	*Columbus Dispatch*
Books	*Houston Chronicle*
Cashman (1988)	
Brown (1987)	
Morehouse and Subramanian (1986)	

ries, deaths and contextual information (e.g. fixed site versus transportation such as rail, road or pipeline).

Since these data reflect actual reporting to government or media sources, the evenness of the data is questionable. There may be some bias based on the areal coverage by the sources we used. We do not know, for example, if a zero figure is not an incident or simply a case of no information. We suspect that our data underestimate the actual frequency of incidents, but we have no way of knowing how much and, more importantly, where. Given these caveats, these data provide a preliminary set of analytical measures of urban chemical incidents, and can be used as numerical indicators of the extent of the problem in each urban area.

Defining risk

Incident likelihood is measured by two variables: the number of days with precipitation and the number of days with storms. Both variables index the potential for altering the safe transportation and use of chemicals. The industrial structure of metropolitan areas is another key indicator of risk. Variables under this subheading include the number of chemical wholesalers (Standard Industrial Code (SIC) 516 and 517), number of chemical services establishments (SIC 28), number of agricultural services establishments (SIC 07 and 078) and number of establishments in non-durable agricultural supplies (SIC 5191). In addition, the size and viability of industrialization strongly determines the amount of use and production of materials, which in turn is partially dictated by regional and local economies. A ranking of metropolitan areas according to economic growth in 1989 was also used to examine this association (Table 2.2).

Interstate road and railroad mileage indicate the transportation infrastructure of metropolitan areas. These values were measured from a variety of maps (USGS topographic maps, maps in commercial atlases, and so on) with scales of 1:50,000 or larger. In addition, the number of railyards (defined as complexes of three or more tracks) in each county was obtained from these same maps.

Table 2.2 *Urban chemical hazard variables and their sources*

Variable	Descriptor	Source
AREA	Land area (square miles)	1
POP	Total population, 1986	1
INTERSTA	Number of Interstate miles	2
RAILMILE	Number of rail miles	2
RAILYARD	Number of railyards	2
REVENUE	Total local government expenditures in 1981–82 in $ million	3
PCTPOUC	Percentage of local government finances spent on police and fire	3
GROTHRNK	Economic growth rank	4
AGSERV07	Number of establishments in SIC 07	5
AGSER078	Number of establishments in SIC 078	5
CHEMSERV	Number of establishments in SIC 28	5
NONDURAG	Number of establishments in nondurable agricultural supplies	5
CHEM5 16	Number of chemical wholesalers, 1987	5
CHEM5 17	Number of petroleum and petroleum product wholesalers, 1987	5
STORMDAY	Number of storm days	6
PRECIPDA	Number of days with precipitation	6
AIRQUAL	Percentage of criteria air pollutants that exceed NAASQ standards based on annual means, 1987	7
TOP500	Listed in the top 500 counties on EPA Toxic Release Inventory emissions, 1987 (1 = yes, 0 = no)	8
RELEASE	Total number acute airborne toxic releases	9
FIXED	Total releases from stationary sources	9
TRANS	Total releases from transportation sources	9
TRUCK	Total transportation releases involving trucks	9
RAIL	Total transportation releases involving rail	9

1 – US Bureau of the Census, 1988.
2 – Measured from USGS and other maps with scales greater than 1:50,000.
3 – US Bureau of the Census, 1986.
4 – Kotkin and Baer-Sinott, 1989.
5 – US Bureau of the Census, 1987.
6 – Boyer and Savageau, 1985.
7 – US EPA, 1989a.
8 – US EPA, 1989b.
9 – Collected by the authors.

Measuring mitigation

Prior experience with chemical hazards and emergency response planning are both important aspects of ameliorating the risk (Chapter 23). Prior experience is measured using ambient air quality data and chronic emissions of toxic substances as indicators of the propensity of urban areas to recognize airborne chemicals as a long-standing problem in their area (Table 2.2).

Emergency response preparedness, including the planning for accidental releases, is also important in reducing the environmental and social impact of these risks. Local and state plans for emergency response mandated by the Superfund Amendments and Reauthorization Act (SARA) Title III (Sections 301–303) are completed for many, if not most, metropolitan counties. Plans and training, however, need funding to be effective. This effectiveness is directly correlated with the amount of money spent on preparedness. The availability of money depends on the revenue accrued by local municipalities in addition to the expenditures on emergency response. Thus the per capita wealth of local government and the percentage of that revenue spent on emergency response are reasonable indicators of the level of mitigation for each metropolitan area.

While far from ideal, these risk and mitigation variables are readily available for all metropolitan regions and thus facilitate our comparative analysis. Metropolitan areas are defined using Primary Metropolitan Statistical Areas (PMSAs) and New England County Metropolitan Areas (NECMAs). Incident, risk, and mitigation data are aggregated accordingly.

The Urban Risk Mosaic

There were a total of 1362 chemical incidents between 1980 and 1989 in the 317 designated metropolitan areas. Nearly one-third of the PMSAs had no accidents, while 10 per cent of them had more than ten, or one accident per year. The majority of incidents were from stationary sources such as industrial sites (72 per cent). Of those transportation-related incidents (28 per cent of the total), 61 per cent involved railroads and railyards, 35 per cent involved trucks, and a small minority involved pipelines and barges (4 per cent). The most frequently released chemicals included ammonia, chlorine and hydrochloric acid.

Injuries and deaths

There were 6100 known injuries and 44 deaths as a result of these 1362 releases. While most of these involved people directly handling the chemicals (occupational exposures), particularly the mortality figures, the potential for injury to local residents is enormous. Whereas we might expect that most injuries occurred in those metropolitan areas with the most accidents, this is not always true (Table 2.3). The highest number of injuries were found in Los Angeles (658), Boston (470), Muncie (400), Newark (357) and Dayton (310).

The relationship between incident frequency and injuries is also not well established, as one may have relatively frequent incidents (high probability) with no injuries or deaths (low consequence) or few incidents (low probability) with many injuries (high consequence). This probability–consequence concept helps to partially explain why Muncie, Indiana, is listed in the top five places based on injury; only one incident during the decade (a 1985 train tank car leak) resulted in the forced evacuation of 400 people, all of whom were exposed to the vinyl acetate fumes. All injuries in Dayton were related to one incident, the 1986 Miamisburg white phosphorus release, while 85 per cent of the injuries in Boston were also related to a single incident, the 1980 Somerville rail spill of phosphoric trichloride and hydrochloric acid. Conversely, the 39 incidents in Brazoria, Texas, resulted in only seven injuries, while Cleveland had two injuries and 26 incidents.

It is problematic to rely on injury data in any meaningful way, since there is a wide range in how these are reported to regulatory and media organizations. Furthermore, injury data do not tell us how many people were exposed to the fumes but not hurt seriously enough to require medical attention.

Spatial distribution

New Orleans had the most incidents during the decade (71), closely followed by Houston (68). Los Angeles (49), Chicago (46), and Charleston, Baton Rouge and Brazoria (each with 39) complete the top five metropolitan areas (Table 2.3). The majority of incidents in each of these metropolitan areas occurred at industrial sites, with the exception of Chicago, which had a majority of incidents involving the transport of materials by rail.

Some strong regional differences in the distribution of incidents are apparent (Figure 2.1). It is clear that the pattern of incidents coincides with older and well-established industrial centres located primarily in the eastern half of the US. The Northeast 'chemical corridor' and petrochemical complexes on the Gulf Coast are clearly highlighted. Regions with less than one incident per year are those that generally use the chemicals or transport them rather than places that produce them. Such metropolitan areas are clustered along the major Interstate and rail transportation systems. Metropolitan areas with no incidents are smaller and more isolated communities such as Chico, CA, Appleton, WI, and Panama City, FL.

Obviously, the history of industrial siting and the initial formation of the industrial landscape is important in determining the urban risk mosaic. Lax environmental regulations and locational policies at the city or state level that attract

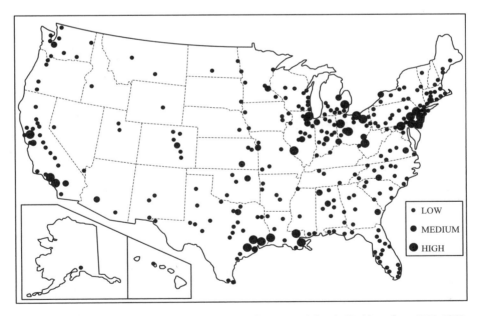

Metropolitan areas (n = 317) are classified based on the frequency of chemical incidents from 1980–1989. High (15+), medium (7–14) and low (0–6) hazard cities are shown.

Figure 2.1 *The urban hazardscape*

Table 2.3 *Worst urban areas (more than 20 incidents, 1980–1989)*

Place	Number of releases			Total injuries
	Industrial	Transport[a]	Total	
New Orleans, LA	55	16	71	103
Houston, TX	61	7	68	70
Los Angeles, CA	37	12	49	658
Chicago, IL	17	29	46	260
Baton Rouge, LA	32	7	39	171
Brazoria, TX	36	3	39	7
Charleston, WV	30	9	39	189
Newark, NJ	31	4	35	357
Wilmington, DE	29	1	30	9
Cleveland, OH	19	7	26	2
Lake Charles, LA	25	0	25	5
Philadelphia, PA	19	6	25	31
Columbus, OH	19	4	23	33
Akron, OH	18	2	20	98
Oakland, CA	15	5	20	107

[a] Includes railroad, pipeline, barge, truck and railyards.

industry and storage facilities may also contribute to the underlying industrial structure which enhances the hazardscape in places. The converse is also true. However, industry is not the only source of incidents. Municipal facilities such as community swimming pools, sewage treatment plants, and water treatment plants are all potential sources of chemicals. Finally, chemicals are often stored (warehoused) and transported through areas with or without the presence of industrial users. All of these provide a potential source for release.

Differentiating Hazard Regions

What characteristics distinguish low-hazard from high-hazard regions? Based on the frequency distribution of incidents (mean = 4.3, std. dev. = 8.7), urban areas were classified into low-, medium- and high-hazard categories. Low-hazard areas have 0–6 incidents, medium-hazard metropolitan areas have 7–14 incidents and high-hazard urban areas have 15 or more.

Table 2.4 shows the mean values for each of the characteristics of metropolitan areas based on hazard classification. High-hazard areas have greater transportation risk conditions (Interstate miles, railroad miles), although not dramatically different from the medium hazard group. What is significant is the number of chemical services (another measure of risk conditions), which is three times greater in the high-hazard group than in the medium one, and more than eight times greater than the low-hazard cities. Mitigation factors also vary. There is little difference in support for emergency preparedness between hazard groups. On the other hand, there are significant differences in prior experience with airborne contaminants between low and medium hazard places (Table 2.4). The overall nature of airborne

Table 2.4 *Metropolitan characteristics by hazard grouping*

Characteristic	Low (0–6) (mean)	Medium (7–14) (mean)	High (15+) (mean)	Difference (F-value) L/M	Difference (F-value) M/H
Interstate miles	54.4	133.4	159.1	5.65***	1.61
Rail miles	155.2	362.0	387.2	6.79***	1.06
Railyards	8.7	20.2	35.5	3.46***	3.34**
% Funding police/fire	8.0	7.8	8.8	6.12***	1.06
Growth rank	133.0	106.8	107.3	1.11	1.4 8
# Chemical firms	19.5	56.8	162.5	2.48***	7.54***
# Nondurable agr. suppliers	16.2	25.7	36.7	5.09***	1.19
# Storm days	39.3	40.1	40.0	1.21	1.50
# Precipitation days	109.2	113.8	111.6	1.28	1.09
% Poor air quality	8.8	16.6	22.4	1.25	1.78
Population density	350.7	484.6	930.1	2.58**	2.30
Local govt. expenses per capita ($)	1080.8	1093.8	1189.7	9.87***	1.17
Top 500 (1 = yes)	.5	.9	1.0	2.15*	0.00

*** significant at $p>0.001$
** significant at $p>0.01$
* significant at $p>0.05$

chemical hazards is greater in medium- and high-risk areas. Low-hazard areas are characterized as places with little transportation infrastructure, few chemical and allied industries, good ambient air quality, and not among the top 500 counties in the country in terms of chronic toxic emissions from industry.

In order to test the validity of our hazard classification scheme, a discriminant analysis was used to elicit those combinations of variables that differentiate places based on the frequency of incidents. Because of collinearity problems among the independent variables, a number of them were subsequently deleted from the analysis (number of agricultural services SIC 07 and 078, number of chemical wholesalers and number of petroleum wholesalers). For the same reason, population density was used in place of population (the correlation between population and incidents is 0.51, s = 0.0000) and area, and a per capita measure for local government expenditures was calculated.

Relying on our three hazard categories (low 0–6, medium 7–14, and high 15+), we were able to correctly classify 81% of the 317 metropolitan regions. Not surprisingly, the most important discriminating variables are the number of chemical services, rail miles, number of establishments in nondurable agricultural supplies, population density, and number of railyards (Table 2.5).

The discriminant analysis was much better at predicting low- and medium-hazard areas than high-hazard urban areas. In fact, the greatest discrepancies between actual and predicted groupings are in the high hazard category. An examination of the outliers shows that two metropolitan areas, Boston and Atlanta, have fewer incidents than predicted based on their hazard conditions (number of chemical services and transportation infrastructure). Conversely, twelve urban

Table 2.5 *Classification of low-, medium- and high-hazard metropolitan areas using discriminant analysis*

Classification Results

Actual Group	No. Cases	Predicted Group Memberships		
		1	2	3
1 Low Risk	264	231	30	3
(0–6)		87.5%	11.4%	1.1%
2 Medium Risk	31	13	16	2
(7–14)		41.9%	51.6%	6.5%
3 High Risk	22	7	4	11
(15+)		31.8%	18.2%	50.0%

% Grouped correctly classified: 81.4%

Discriminators

Step	Variable	Wilks' Lambda	Significance
1	# Chemical services	0.611	0.000
2	# Rail miles	0.541	0.000
3	# Nondurable agr. services	0.487	0.000
4	Population density	0.476	0.000
5	# Railyards	0.469	0.000

areas (Akron, Baltimore, Baton Rouge, Beaumont, TX, Brazoria, TX, Charleston, WV, Columbus, OH, Lake Charles, LA, Lima, OH, New Orleans, and Wilmington, DE) had significantly more incidents than predicted.

Baton Rouge, Charleston, Brazoria, and Lake Charles are highly industrialized areas with significant chemical industries. Although they have fewer establishments, the facilities that are present are large, both in area and production. In these areas, the volume of chemicals used, rather than the actual number of establishments, may be the de facto indicator of the hazard. Baltimore's role as a dense transportation hub probably accounts for the lack of a correct classification; more than half of its accidents, for example, were transportation-related. The appearance of Akron, Lima, and Columbus as underclassified can be partially attributed to the strong environmental reporting mandated in Ohio, which has detailed records of incident frequencies from 1978 to the present. We may, in fact, be seeing accurate reporting of incidents in Ohio, with under-reporting taking place in other metropolitan areas.

Discussion

There is a discernible pattern to these chemical incidents: the presence of risk conditions, particularly the number of chemical services, is one of the best parameters to differentiate high-risk from low-risk regions. Mitigation measures have little impact on the classification.

Whereas we can define high-, medium- and low-hazard metropolitan areas with some success, there is still 20 per cent of metropolitan areas that exhibit some degree of randomness in the frequency of chemical incidents that is not associated with our existing measures of risk and mitigation. To illustrate, there are a number of important indicators only partially addressed in this analysis. The number of chemical services is the key indicator of prevailing risk conditions, yet this number says nothing about the size of the establishment or the volume of chemicals used. In Charleston, West Virginia, for example, there are only 23 chemical establishments (three more than the mean for the low-risk group), yet the density of industry and the sheer size and volume of production play an important role in creating the hazard in this area. Similarly, in Chicago 471 establishments are present, yet the largest single source of incidents is transportation. The total number of releases in each place is comparable (46 in Chicago, 39 in Charleston).

Subsequent analyses by county or community should help to elucidate intra- and intermetropolitan variations in the degree of chemical hazards. In order to determine the chemical hazardscape, a range of contaminants (chronic toxic emissions, criteria pollutants, pesticides) and different media of exposure (air, water, land) must be determined for each place. We could conceivably go so far as to determine the overall 'toxic quality of life' of places by extending the range of technological hazards to more than just chemical contaminants to include hazardous waste and other toxic substances: metals, radiation, and pollution.

This analysis has focused only on the hazards of a place, not the vulnerability of people to such hazards. Questions regarding the total population at risk, levels of exposure, who is more at risk, and socio-spatial inequities in the distribution of risks are all important issues awaiting future analyses.

Our findings have a number of implications for public policy. Since risk factors largely, though not exclusively, determine the chemical hazardscape, their spatial isolation may help to reduce the human consequences of airborne toxic releases. The creation of extensive buffer zones around stationary facilities and transportation corridors is one alternative. The creation of chemical-free zones is another. This concept is now aggressively being pursued by Dow Chemical Company, which is purchasing 220 acres (at a cost of $10 million) and relocating residents away from its Plaquemine, Louisiana, facility (Schneider, 1990; Sternberg, 1989). The company is following the trend of other chemical producers in the Baton Rouge–New Orleans corridor that are in the process of constructing 'green belts' around their facilities by physically removing residents, thereby reducing their corporate liability when that accidental release occurs. This large-scale removal of entire communities has both positive and negative elements.

Improved modelling of the potential movement of the plume coupled with a detailed analysis of the population at risk (the beginnings of a population vulnerability assessment) is also required. This could be incorporated into a more careful analysis of emergency preparedness and may yield better predictions on the role of mitigation in reducing risk. SARA Title III planning only covers stationary facilities. Community-based information on the transportation of chemicals by rail and by truck is needed to complete the planning process. Finally, residents must be educated as to the nature of the risk in their community and to an appropriate level of response (such as closing windows, turning off air conditioners, wearing protective masks). Improved levels of risk communication will certainly help reduce some of the health and safety impacts of these events.

Perrow (1984) suggested there will always be some degree of uncertainty due to human-induced factors and the sheer complexity of many of these technological systems that result in normal accidents (such as releases of toxic chemicals). Despite this, we can still define a set of conditions that might lead to such events. The mere presence or absence of the chemical industry or its subsidiaries, however, does not directly translate into high- or low-hazard regions. Rather, it is a combination of risk conditions and mitigation set within the larger metropolitan context that help us to delineate and explain the urban chemical hazardscape.

References

Berry, B. J. L. (ed) (1977) *The Social Burdens of Environmental Pollution: A Comparative Metropolitan Data Source*, Ballinger, Cambridge, MA

Berry, B. J. L., Bruzewicz, A. J., Cargo, D. B., Cummings, J. B., Dahmann, D. C., Goheen, P. G., Kaplan, C. P., Koopman, D. B., Lamb, R. F., Margerum, L. F., Mikesell, M. W., Morgan, D. J., Mrowka, J. P., Piccininni, J. P. and Soisson, J. A. (1974) *Land Use, Urban Form, and Environmental Quality*, Department of Geography Research Paper 155, University of Chicago, Chicago, IL

Berry, B. J. L. and Horton, F. T. (1974) *Urban Environmental Management: Planning for Pollution Control*, Prentice Hall, Englewood Cliffs, NJ

Bogard, W. (1989) *The Bhopal Tragedy: Language, Logic, and Politics in the Production of Hazard*, Westview Press, Boulder, CO

Boyer, R. and Savageau, D. (1985) *Places Rated Almanac*, Rand McNally, Chicago, IL

Brown, M. H. (1987) *The Toxic Cloud*, Harper and Row, New York

Cashman, J. R. (1988) *Hazardous Materials Emergencies: Response and Control*, Technomic Publishing Inc, Lancaster, PA

Colton, C. E., (1990a) 'Environmental development in the East St. Louis Region, 1890–1970', *Environmental History Review*, vol 14, no 1–2, pp93–114

Colton, C. E., (1990b) 'Historical hazards: The geography of relict industrial wastes', *Professional Geographer*, vol 42, no 2, pp143–156

Coppock, J. T. and Wilson, C. B. (1974) *Environmental Quality with Emphasis on Urban Problems*, John Wiley, New York

Cutter, S. L. and Solecki, W. D. (1989) 'The national pattern of airborne toxic releases', *Professional Geographer*, vol 41, no 2, pp149–161

Cutter, S. L. and Tiefenbacher, J. (1989) 'Plume and doom', *American Demographics*, November, pp44–46

Detwyler, T. R. and Marcus, M. G. (1972) *Urbanization and the Environment*, Duxbury, Belmont, CA

Everest, L. (1985) *Behind the Poison Cloud: Union Carbide's Bhopal Massacre*, Banner Press, Chicago, IL

Greenberg, M. R., Belnay, G., Cesanek, W., Neuman, N. and Shepherd, G. (1979) *A Primer on Industrial Environmental Impact*, Center for Urban Policy Research, Rutgers University, New Brunswick, NJ

Herbert, D. I. and Johnson, R. J. (eds) (1978) *Geography and the Urban Environment: Progress in Research and Applications, Volume I*, John Wiley, New York

Johnson, B. B. and Covello, V. T. (1987) *The Social Construction of Risk*, D. Reidel Publishing, Dordrecht

Kasperson, R. E., Renn, O., Slovic, P., Brown, H., Emel, J., Goble, R., Kasperson, J. X. and Ratick, S. (1988) 'The social amplification of risk: a conceptual framework', *Risk Analysis*, vol 8, no 2, pp177–187

Kirby, A. (1986) 'Technological risk in urban areas', *Cities*, May, pp137–141

Kirby, A. (ed) (1991) *Nothing to Fear: Risks and Hazards in American Society*, University of Arizona Press, Tucson, AZ

Kotkin, J. and Baer-Sinott, S. (1989) 'Metro report: Hot spots', *Inc. Magazine*, March, pp90–92

Liverman, D. (1986) 'The vulnerability of urban areas to technological risks', *Cities*, May, pp142–147

Liverman, D. and Wilson, J. P. (1981) 'The Mississauga train derailment and evacuation, November 10–16, 1979', *Canadian Geographer*, vol 25, pp365–375

Mitchell, J. K., Devine, N. and Jagger, K. (1989) 'A contextual model of natural hazard', *Geographical Review*, vol 79, no 4, pp391–409

Morehouse, W. S. and Subramanian, M. A. (1986) *The Bhopal Tragedy*, Council on International and Public Affairs, New York

O'Riordan, T. (1985) 'Coping with environmental hazards' in R. W. Kates and I. Burton (eds) *Geography, Resources, and Environment, Volume II: Themes from the Work of Gilbert F. White*, University of Chicago Press, Chicago, IL, pp272–309

Palm, R. (1990) *Natural Hazards: An Integrative Framework for Research and Planning*, Johns Hopkins University Press, Baltimore, MA

Perrow, C. (1984) *Normal Accidents: Living with High-Risk Technologies*, Basic Books, New York

Schneider, K. (1990) 'Safety fears prompt plants to buy out neighbors', *The New York Times*, 28 November, pA1

Solecki, W. D. (1990) 'Acute chemical disasters and rural United States hazardscapes', PhD dissertation, Department of Geography, Rutgers University, New Brunswick, NJ

Sorenson, J. H. (1991) 'Society and emergency preparedness: Looking from the past into the future' in A. Kirby (ed) *Nothing to Fear: Risks and Hazards in American Society*, University of Arizona Press, Tucson, AZ, pp241–260

Sternberg, K. (1989) 'Neighbors spurn Dow's embrace', *Chemical Week*, 1 November, pp22–23

US Bureau of the Census (1986) *State and Metropolitan Area Data Book*, US Government Printing Office, Washington, DC

US Bureau of the Census (1987) *County Business Patterns*, US Government Printing Office, Washington, DC

US Bureau of the Census (1988) *County and City Data Book*, US Government Printing Office, Washington, DC

USEPA (US Environmental Protection Agency) (1989a) *National Air Quality: An Emissions Trends Report 1987*, USEPA, EPA-450/4-89-001, Research Triangle Park, NC

USEPA (1989b) *The Toxics Release Inventory*, Government Printing Office, EPA 560/4-89-005, Washington, DC

3

Fleeing from Harm: International Trends in Evacuations from Chemical Accidents

Susan L. Cutter

The 1984 methyl isocyanate release at Bhopal, India reinvigorated chemical hazards research within the disaster community. Yet, much of this work remains in case study form examining the causes, consequences, and policy implications of discrete failures such as Bhopal (Bowonder et al, 1985; Shrivastava, 1987a, b, c; Bogard, 1987, 1989), Seveso (Whiteside, 1979), and other smaller releases of chemicals (Cutter et al, 1980; Hazen et al, 1980; Tierney, 1980; Timmerman, 1980; USFEMA, 1980; Whyte et al, 1980; Liverman and Wilson, 1981; Quarantelli et al, 1984; Johnson, 1985). While case studies are instructive, a much broader view of chemical hazards is now warranted. As Kirby (1990) suggests, hazards theory needs to refocus to incorporate the social construction of hazards, their historical antecedents, and the institutions that govern the management of hazards. In other words, hazards need to be placed in their historical, social, and political contexts (Palm, 1990). The need to examine these issues is most relevant to hazards resulting from technological failures because of the ways in which society governs and responds to the use and misuse of technology.

This chapter examines chemical accidents from 1900–1989 and one mitigating response to them, evacuations, during the same time period. The purpose is to identify the historical context for such hazards to better understand their management. Specifically, are there any links between these chemical events? What is the overall pattern of chemical incidents and how have these patterns changed over time and space? Are we becoming more aware of chemical hazards or is the actual level of risk increasing? How effective are evacuations as a mitigation response to such industrial failures? Has the pattern of evacuations changed over time as well? These last two questions provide the focal point for this chapter.

Note: Reprinted, with permission, from *International Journal of Mass Emergencies and Disasters*, vol 9, no 2, Susan L. Cutter, 'Fleeing from harm: International trends in evacuations from chemical accidents', pp267–285. © Research Committee on Disasters, International Sociological Association, 1991

Community responses to chemical emergencies are highly varied. They involve pre-impact community preparation, mobilization of first responders, lack of coordination among responders, behavioural uncertainty by residents, and problems of convergence (Gray, 1981; Gray and Quarantelli, 1981; Fawcett, 1981; Quarantelli, 1981; Ikeda, 1982). Evacuations themselves are often problematic because of the rapidity of the onset of the emergency; uncertainty regarding the nature, quantity and toxicity of the substances released; the catastrophic potential of such releases; and the mode (a stationary source such as a production facility or some form of transportation such as rail or truck) and medium (air, water, land) of release (see Chapter 23; also Bogard, 1987). Yet, evacuation might be the most appropriate form of response. Since we have little historical information on evacuations in response to airborne releases of chemicals, it is hard to measure their effectiveness as a mitigation alternative; hence the need to examine evacuation responses to chemical hazards more thoroughly. Evacuations from chemical accidents involving an airborne release such as a toxic cloud, BLEVE (boiling liquid expanding vapour explosion), fume or explosion are examined for the period 1900–1989 at the international level to assess changes in the frequency of incidents and the prevalence of evacuations over time. I have purposely not included the US in this analysis since the availability of data is greater and thus skews the global distribution of these events. In addition, the pattern of incidents in the US is described elsewhere (see Chapter 2; also Cutter and Solecki, 1989; Cutter, 1991; Industrial Economics, 1989).

Trends in Industrial Accidents

The pervasive use of chemicals ranging from ammunition and fireworks to the more recent innovations in the plastics industries has had a profound effect on modern society. Along with the conveniences associated with these chemical products, the increased toxicity of many synthetic substances, as well as their ultimate disposal, has created a form of chemophobia that pervades American society, if not the entire globe. In the US for example, the hazards posed by chemical manufacturing and transport since the early 1900s have increased (Cutter, 1991). Despite one of the better occupational safely records in US manufacturing, there were still about 240 chemical accidents between 1900–1979 in this country, 41 percent of which released acutely toxic substances as classified by the US Environmental Protection Agency under Superfund Amendments and Reauthorization Act (SARA) Title III legislation (USEPA 1988). More recently, a staggering number of chemical accidents were recorded during the 1980s with estimates ranging from 295 for the 1930–1984 period (Sorenson, 1987) to 10,933 for the entire decade (Industrial Economics, 1989).

At the international level, Shrivastava (1987c) examined major industrial crises, defined as incidents with 50 or more fatalities. He found that of the 28 major accidents, half of them occurred since 1979, with four happening in one year, 1984, all in the developing countries. Most involved chemicals and could be classified as chemical accidents, though not all. One conclusion that Shrivastava draws is that industrial crises are more common in developing nations because they lack the prerequisite industrial structure and safety mechanisms to cope with accidents (1987c, p9). Does this conclusion hold true when longer time periods are examined with lower thresholds of accidents (e.g. those with less than 50 fatalities)? In a different review of industrial accidents, again not strictly limited to chemical ones, the Organisation for Economic Co-operation and Development (OECD, 1991) found a decline in accidents since 1975 and attributes this to better prevention and mitigation, especially evacuations. Finally, roughly 200 serious chemical accidents occur annually in OECD countries (UNEP, 1989). During the last decade, for example, estimates suggest that roughly 5000 deaths, 100,000 injuries and poisonings, and 620,000 evacuees resulted from major chemical accidents (UNEP, 1989). Nearly half of the fatalities and evacuees, however, stemmed from one incident, Bhopal in 1984.

One of the problems with many of these statistics is their lack of comparability. There is rarely any differentiation in the term industrial, often it merely connotes chemical accidents, and other times it encompasses a wide range of technological failures. In addition, the statistics aggregate the medium of exposure (e.g. water, land, air) to one measure, and the time period covered is limited (5, 10 or 20 years). Finally, it is extremely likely that only larger accidents or those with larger numbers of injuries and fatalities are reported resulting in an underestimate of the actual frequency of chemical accidents and the hazards they produce. Currently, there is fragmented and unconsolidated data on industrial accidents during the 19th century. While there are a number of efforts underway to create national and international databases, these are as yet incomplete. The development of a comprehensive database was stimulated, in part, by legislation in the aftermath of Bhopal (especially in the US with the SARA Title III and the Community Right-to-Know law), and earlier in the European Community as a result of the Seveso disaster (the European Community's Seveso Directive, the UK's Control of Industrial Major Accident Hazard (CIMAH) programme). Thus far, these programmes have not been integrated nor expanded to include other world regions, or to include more historical data.

Hazards from Chemical Accidents

There are many types of hazards that are associated with the chemical industry ranging from explosions, BLEVEs (boiling liquid expanding vapour explosions), toxic clouds and fumes, to hazardous waste generation and disposal, to chronic exposures (Marshall, 1987; Vilain, 1989). While all are important, the rapid-onset events such as explosions, fires and vapour releases are more likely to entail an evacuation as a precautionary measure.

A number of compendiums are available that provide historical documentation of chemical accidents outside the US (Nash, 1976; Ikeda, 1982; Marshall, 1987; Lagadec, 1982; Withers, 1988; Smets, 1987; Shrivastava, 1987a, b, c; OECD, 1987, 1989, 1991; UNEP, 1989; Davenport, 1977; Weir, 1987; Hay, 1982; Oberg, 1988, Morehouse and Subramanian, 1986). Most of these, however, focus on a wide range of technological failures, not just industrial or chemical accidents. Very few provide data on evacuations, or if they do it is often sketchy.

Working from these sources gives a conservative estimate of the number, location and type of chemical accident. To further focus on acute events necessitating possible evacuations, only releases into the air were examined. While these data are certainly incomplete, they can be used to illustrate general trends in chemical hazards. We must also assume that the data under-represent the magnitude of chemical accidents during the 20th century because of lack of reporting or governmental suppression of information.

Toxic Plumes, Explosions and BLEVEs

A total of 333 international chemical accidents involving airborne releases were found for the 1900–1989 period. Not surprisingly, the number of incidents per decade has significantly increased since the turn of the century (Table 3.1). The steady rise in incidents from 1900–1969 parallels the development of the modern chemical industry and its transformation from heavy inorganics to more diversified commodities such as petrochemicals, plastics, and speciality chemicals used in electronics. There is an abrupt rise in the accident frequency in the 1970s as a result of the two factors. Larger production facilities were built to handle increased volumes of chemicals, and overseas production facilities were increased both in size and quantity as many of the multinational chemical corporations sought fewer environmental regulations and cheaper sources of labour (*Chemical Week*, 1983). During the 1970s, globalization of the chemical industry took place at an accelerated rate largely reflecting international demands driven by the global oil-based economy.

Table 3.1 *Chemical accidents, 1900–1989*

| Decade | No. | | Source | | | |
	Total	Acute[1]	Stationary[2]	Transport[3]	Pipeline	Unknown
1980–89	97	38	45	16	9	27
1970–79	89	41	42	19	3	25
1960–69	36	14	24	6	0	6
1950–59	27	8	23	2	0	2
1940–49	25	4	19	6	0	0
1930–39	20	2	18	1	0	1
1920–29	18	3	15	1	0	2
1910–19	19	0	14	5	0	0
1900–09	2	0	2	0	0	0
Totals	333	110	202	56	12	63

[1] Defined as posing serious health impairments within minutes to hours of exposure (USEPA, 1988). Also includes radiation exposures.
[2] Includes industrial site, off-loading at a plant to a truck or railroad car.
[3] Truck, railroad, or ship.

Table 3.2 *Types of chemicals involved in reported accidents, 1900–1989*

Class	No. of incidents	% of total
Acutely toxic	94	28.2
Ammonia	*20*	*6.0*
Chlorine	*22*	*6.6*
Dioxin	*5*	*1.5*
Ethylene	*9*	*2.7*
SARA[1] (misc.)	*33*	*9.9*
CERCLA[2] (misc.)	*5*	*1.5*
Ammunition and Explosives	105	31.5
Oil and Gas	73	21.9
Radiation	16	4.8
Other (identified[3])	37	11.1
Unknown	8	2.4
Totals	333	100.0

[1] Defined by the U.S. Superfund Amendments and Reauthorization Act Title III (USEPA1988).
[2] Hazardous chemicals regulated under the Superfund legislation (Comprehensive Environmental Responsibility, Cleanup, and Liability Act) (USEPA 1988).
[3] Includes pesticides and fertilizers.

Frequency and type

Historically, the largest proportion of accidents (31.5 per cent) involved explosives of one sort or another such as dynamite, ammunition, and fireworks (Table 3.2). An additional 21.9 per cent of the accidents involved an explosion or fire from natural gas, gasoline, petroleum, butane, propane, liquid petroleum gas (LPG) or other types of liquid fossil fuels. Acutely toxic chemicals (those causing serious health impairments within minutes to hours after exposure) constitute 28.2 per cent of the accidents on record. SARA is the most prevalent of these followed by chlorine and ammonia. Less than 3 per cent of the accidents had unknown types of chemicals or no information about the substances released.

The earliest accidents (1906 in Witten, UK, and 1907 in Canton, China) involved ammunition, a trend that continued into the 1920s. Between 1910–1919, nineteen accidents were found, all but one involving ammunition. Most of these occurred at storage facilities (Table 3.1). During the 1920s, the number of incidents remained about the same, with ammunition the most prevalent chemical class. However, it is during this decade that we see the first instances of acutely-toxic chemical accidents. These occurred in 1921 in Oppau (Ludwigshafen), Germany, with a release of ammonium nitrate, in 1926 in St Auban, France, involving chlorine, and in 1928 in Hamburg, Germany, involving a release of phosgene.

The war decades (1930–1950) were also characterized by accidents involving ammunition, again largely from stationary sources such as ammunition depots and dumps (Table 3.1). Geographically, accidents during these decades were concentrated in China and Europe. Acute releases occurred twice in Romania (Brachto and Zarnesti) in 1939, both involving chlorine, and once each in Norway in 1940 (chlorine at Mjondalen), Belgium in 1942 (ammonium nitrate at Tessenderloo), Germany in 1943 (butadiene at Ludwigshafen) and Finland in 1947 (chlorine at Rauma).

The post-war decade had more diversity in the types of chemicals involved in accidents. There were a few ammunition accidents, but fireworks, natural gas and petroleum accidents were also numerous. A chlorine release in Walsum, Germany, in 1952 was the only instance of an acutely toxic chemical accident. More significant, however, were the first reported accidental releases of radionuclides due to nuclear reactor failures and meltdowns. The most important of these occurred in Chalk River, Canada (1952), Windscale, UK (1957), and Kyshtym and Troisk, USSR (1958).

The number of incidents rose in the 1960s by about a third. Whether this is due to a net increase in chemical use, changes in production techniques, reduced safety concerns, better reporting, or some combination of factors is unclear. Again, a great diversity of chemicals were involved ranging from ammunition and, fireworks, to natural gas and petroleum. Fourteen instances of acutely toxic releases were recorded, mostly from stationary sources, with all but three located in European countries. Ten of the fourteen releases involved four chemicals: ammonia (four), chlorine (two), dioxin (two) and cyclohexane (two).

A dramatic increase in accidents occurred during the 1970s and 1980s as a result of heightened awareness and intensified use of chemicals in all aspects of modern living. More than half of the accidents in the data set occurred during this 20-year period. As the frequency of accidents increased, so did their hazard potential. For example, the number of acutely toxic releases increased threefold from previous decades (Figure 3.1). Geographically, the majority of toxic releases occurred in the industrialized nations of Europe, but during the 1970s instances were recorded in developing nations such as Mexico (two ammonia in 1977, two

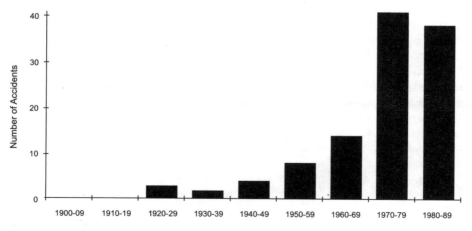

Figure 3.1 *Acutely toxic chemical accidents, 1900–1989*

vinyl chloride in 1977), Tunisia (ammonia in 1978), and Colombia (two ammonia, one each in 1976 and 1977). There was another watershed release during this decade as well – dioxin (TCDD) in Seveso, Italy, in 1976.

By the 1980s, the number of accidents continued to rise, as did the number of incidents involving acutely toxic chemicals (Figure 3.1). It was during this decade that the now famous Bhopal accident occurred involving the release of the potent methyl isocyanate (a chemical compound used to produce pesticides). It was also during this period, that the world's worst nuclear power plant accident took place at the Chernobyl facility in the USSR in 1986 releasing radionuclides and contaminating a vast area in the Ukraine and parts of Europe.

Location

The distribution of accidents by country highlights the dichotomy between industrialized and non-industrialized nations. While accidents occurred in 55 different countries, most of these were in the industrialized world. France had the most (31) followed by the UK (26) and Germany and the Soviet Union who each had 25. This is not surprising given the historical development of the chemical industry in France, England and Germany. What is surprising, however, is the number of incidents in less industrialized countries such as Mexico (20) and India (17). Nearly 36 per cent of all incidents during the century took place in developing countries primarily in Latin America and Asia. Since many African nations are less dependent on the chemical industry for consumer goods and energy, the relative absence of accidents on this continent comes as no surprise.

The distribution of acutely-toxic chemical accidents follows a similar pattern with France having the most (13) followed by the UK (10), Germany (9), Canada (9), Mexico (8), and the Soviet Union (8). It is interesting to note that seven out of the eight incidents in the USSR involved radioactive materials.

Severity

It is difficult to measure the severity of a chemical accident when it happens in the present, let alone in the past. Attempts to determine severity based on monetary damages and insurance claims, injuries and fatalities, or evacuations are dubious because of the subjective and often anecdotal nature of the reported data. An aggregate measure is virtually impossible because of inconsistencies as well. Likewise, the development of longitudinal or time series data sets are extremely difficult and fraught with errors. Therefore, to say with any precision that society is becoming more vulnerable to these types of chemical hazards is impossible. What we can observe, though, is the historical pattern of incidents, using injuries and fatalities as one indicator and evacuations as another. The rationale for doing so involves the type of chemical involved. Explosions involving ammunition, natural gas, or some other type of explosive or flammable substance may cause great immediate injury because of the blast or fire. On the other hand, the evacuations are normally ordered in response to releases of chemicals that are generally less volatile, but are lethal when inhaled or when exposed to the skin. Injuries, fatalities and evacuations all provide useful measures of the seriousness of an accident.

Table 3.3 *Most serious chemical accidents*
(greater than 100 immediate fatalities or 1000 injuries)

Date	Location	Deaths	Injuries[1]	Chemical	Source[2]
1984	Bhopal, India	2750	102,500	methyl isocyanate	F
1935	Lanzhow, China	2000	– *	ammunitions	F
1918	Hamont, Belgium	1750	– *	ammunitions	T
1917	Halifax, Can.	1725	8000	picric acrid	T
1982	Salang Pass, Afg.	1550	400	carbon monoxide	T
1917	Archangle, USSR	1500	3000	ammunitions	T
1941	Ft. Smederevo, Yugo.	1500	200	ammunitions	F
1944	Bombay, India	1376	3000	ammunitions	T
1956	Cali, Colombia	1200	2000	ammunitions	T
1958	Kyshtym, USSR	1118	– *	radiation	F
1916	La Satannaya, USSR	1000	– *	ammunitions	F
1917	Bloeweg, Czech.	1000	– *	ammunitions	F
1921	Ludwigshafen, Germ.	561	1700	ammonium nitrate	F
1984	Cubatao, Brazil	508	50	gasoline	F
1989	Asha, USSR	500	723	LPG	F
1984	St. J. Ixhautepec, Mex.	478	5624	gas	F
1918	Wolfersdorf, Aust.	382	– *	ammunitions	F
1983	Nile River, Egypt	317	44	gas	U
1917	Henningsdorf, Germ.	300	– *	ammunitions	F
1979	Novosibirsk, USSR	300	– *	biochem war agents	F
1925	Beijing, China	300	– *	ammunitions	F
1917	Silvertown, UK	300	– *	ammunitions	F
1934	La Libertad, Salv.	250	– *	dynamite	F
1948	Ludwigshafen, Germ.	220	4909	dimethyl ether	F
1978	San Carlos, Spain	215	133	LPG	T
1942	Tessenderloo, Belg.	200	1000	ammonium nitrate	F
1984	Severomorsk, USSR	200	200	ammunitions	F
1916	Skoda, Austria	195	– *	ammunitions	F
1935	Shanghai, China	190	– *	ammunitions	F
1944	Burton-on-Trent, UK	170	– *	ammunitions	F
1916	Kent, UK	170	– *	ammunitions	F
1925	Harput, Turkey	160	– *	ammunitions	F
1947	Cadiz, Spain	149	– *	ammunitions	F
1982	Tacao, Ven.	145	1000	hydrocarbons	F

Table 3.3 *Most serious chemical accidents*
(greater than 100 immediate fatalities or 1000 injuries)

Date	Location	Deaths	Injuries[1]	Chemical	Source[2]
1981	Tacao, Ven.	145	1000	oil	U
1948	Hong Kong	135	– *	asst. chemicals	F
1924	Otaru, Japan	120	– *	ammunitions	T
1982	Caracas, Ven.	115	828	explosives	U
1915	Havre, Belg.	110	1000	ammunitions	F
1937	Chunking, China	110	300	ammunitions	F
1958	Rio de Janiero, Bra.	110	– *	fireworks	U
1988	Islamabad, .	100	3000	explosives	F
1978	Xiutepec, Mex.	100	150	LPG	T
1984	Romania	100	100	asst. chemicals	U
1960	Havana, Cuba	100	– *	ammunitions	T
1921	Hiroshima, Japan	100	– *	ammunitions	U
1986	Leninsk-Kuznetskiy, USSR	100	– *	ammunitions	F
1938	Madrid, Spain	100	– *	ammunitions	F
1932	Nanking, China	100	– *	ammunitions	F
1931	Niteroi, Brazil	100	– *	ammunitions	F
1917	Petrograd, USSR	100	– *	unknown	F
1921	Saarlous, Germ.	100	– *	oil	F
1984	Tbilisi, USSR	100	– *	natural gas	F
1977	Seoul, S. Korea	58	1300	explosives	T
1986	Chernobyl, USSR	31	thousands	radionuclides	F
1962	Rotterdam, Neth.	2	3500	gas	F
1976	Seveso, Italy	0	22,000	dioxin	F
1978	Pierre Benite, Fr.	0	thousands	acrolein	F
1978	Pierre Benite, Fr.	0	2000	acrolein	F
1987	Shangsi, China	0	1500	fertilizer	U
1981	Sao Joao, Brazil	0	1100	chlorine	U
1982	Melbourne, Australia	0	1000	butadiene	T

*unknown number of injuries
[1]If ranges of figures were given from one source or different numbers from multiple sources for fatalities and/or deaths, an average figure was calculated.
[2]Abbreviations for sources are F = fixed site such as chemical plant, industrial complex, warehouse; T = transportation by rail, truck, or ship; P = pipeline; U = unknown source.

Those accidents involving more than 100 fatalities or 1000 injuries are listed in Table 3.3. Sixty-two accidents are identified, representing 19 per cent of the total number of accidents. The majority of fatalities and injuries result from accidents at stationary facilities. Most of the fatalities involved ammunition explosions. These include the 1935 ammunition dump explosion at Lanzhow, China, killing 2000 and the ammunition explosions at Archangle, Russia (1917), Bombay, India (1944), Bloeweg, Czechoslovakia (1917), Cali, Colombia (1956), Ft. Smederevo, Yugoslavia (1941), Hamont, Belgium (1918) and La Satannaya, Russia (1916), each resulting in 1000 or more fatalities.

The most serious accident involving fatalities occurred in 1984 in Bhopal, India, with the release of methyl isocyanate (MIC) resulting in 2500–3000 immediate fatalities and 5000–20,000 injuries. Another high mortality accident occurred in 1982 in the Salang Pass, Afghanistan, where 1100–2000 people (mostly Soviet troops) died as a result of asphyxiation from car exhaust fumes (carbon monoxide) when their vehicles became trapped in a road tunnel because of heavy traffic.

In terms of injuries, the most significant accidents involved releases of acute toxins such as MIC, and the dioxin release at Seveso injuring 22,000. Only 10 of the 62 accidents resulting in high numbers of fatalities and injuries involved acute toxins and radiation, although these were in fact the most deadly and injurious accidents (Table 3.4).

Thus, while fatalities and injuries are somewhat commonplace with industrial processes and the handling of explosive chemicals like ammunition, the potential for large-scale injury and death is also a likely outcome of releases of acutely toxic substances. While these were less frequent during the beginning of the 20th century, the probability of occurrence has increased during the last 20 years, and with it, a greater potential for adverse public health impacts. As seen in Table 3.5, there is a periodicity to the number of deaths and injuries. The greatest number of fatalities happened between 1910–1919 as a result of ammunition explosions. The next highest decade, 1980–1989 is unique as a result of the disaster at Bhopal that accounts for nearly half of the fatalities and injuries. The number of injuries,

Table 3.4 *Most severe chemical accidents involving acutely toxic chemicals*

Date	Location	Deaths	Injuries	Chemical
1921	Ludwigshafen, Germ.	561	1900	ammonium nitrate
1942	Tessenderloo, Bel.	200	1000	ammonium nitrate
1976	Seveso, Italy	– *	22,000	dioxin
1978	Pierre Benite, Fr.	0	1000s	acrolein
1978	Pierre Benite, Fr.	0	2000	acrolein
1981	Montanas, Mex.	29	750	chlorine
1981	Sao Joao, Bra.	0	1100	chlorine
1982	Melbourne, Aust.	0	1000	butadiene
1984	Bhopal, India	2750	102,500	MIC
1986	Chernobyl, USSR	31	1000s	radiation

* unknown

Table 3.5 *Deaths and injuries*

Years	Deaths	Injuries	No. evacuation events	No. evacuees
1900–09	48	200	0	0
1910–19	8827	12,000	0	0
1920–29	1673	2403	1	350
1930–39	3432	1392	0	0
1940–49	4313	10,167	0	0
1950–59	2990	2755	1	10,000
1960–69	550	4660	1	5000
1970–79	1925	30,954	15	300,710
1980–89	8357	193,788	38	1,461,160
Totals	32,115	258,319	56	1,777,220

however, has continued to escalate over time. As a consequence of the increased risk, evacuations are increasingly used as a precautionary measure to remove or significantly reduce the likelihood of exposure to chemical hazards, as shown in Table 3.5.

Evacuations

Large-scale evacuations (defined here as more than 5000 evacuees) are one indication of the seriousness of the chemical release and its potential effect on the public's health and welfare. Only 17 per cent of the total number of accidents involved any type of an evacuation, regardless of size. Forty-eight accidents entailed evacuations of 1000 or more people, and 30 of these had more than 5000 evacuees (Table 3.6). More than half of the accidents involved an acutely toxic substance. The remainder involved an assortment of volatile chemicals. The largest evacuation took place in Mississauga, Canada, in response to a 1979 train derailment and release of chlorine. Other evacuations involving more than 100,000 people occurred in Tours, France; Guadalupe and St Juan Ixhuatec, Mexico; Bhopal, India; Chernobyl, USSR; and New Delhi, India. Most of the large-scale evacuations took place during the 1980s, and involved an acutely toxic chemical release such as chlorine or ammonia with the exception of the Mexico evacuations resulting from oil and natural gas explosions.

Very few accidents have both large numbers of fatalities and/or injuries at large evacuations. By comparing accidents in Tables 3.4 and 3.6 there are only four that appear on both lists and all of these involve acute toxins (Montanas with chlorine, Bhopal with MIC, Melbourne with butadiene, and Chernobyl with radiation).

A closer examination of evacuation events by size illustrates the highest frequency of evacuations involved between 1000–6000 people. While there were

Table 3.6 *Large evacuations from chemical accidents (≥5000 evacuees)*

Data	Place	No. evacuated	Chemical	Source[1]
1979	Mississauga, Can.	250,000	chlorine	T
1984	St. J. Ixhuatepec, Mex.	250,000	natural gas	F
1988	Tours, France	200,000	misc. chemicals	U
1989	Guadalupe, Mex.	200,000	crude oil	F
1984	Bhopal, India	200,000	MIC	F
1986	Chernobyl, USSR	116,000	radionuclides	F
1985	New Delhi, India	100,000	sulphur trioxide	F
1988	Arzamas, USSR	90,000	explosives	T
1988	Sibanik, Yugo.	60,000	fertilizers	F
1982	Tacao, Ven.	40,000	hydrocarbons	F
1987	Shangsi, China	30,000	fertilizers	U
1987	Nantes, France	25,000	fertilizers	U
1983	Corinto, Nicar.	23,000	oil	U
1986	Cardenas, Mex.	20,000	natural gas	P
1985	Priolo, Italy	20,000	propylene	U
1978	Manfredonia, Italy	10,000	ammonia	F
1975	Helmstedt, Germ.	10,000	nitrogen oxides	F
1958	Kyshtym, USSR	10,000	radionuclides	F
1977	El Pueblo, Mex.	10,000	vinyl chloride	U
1984	Ontario, Can.	9000	chlorine	U
1980	Ohbu City, Japan	8000	chlorine	F
1978	Melbourne, Austl.	6000	butadiene	T
1982	Sakai, Japan	5000	acrylonitrile	U
1985	Cubatao, Braz.	5000	ammonia	P
1984	Cubatao, Braz.	5000	gasoline	P
1979	North York, Can.	5000	gasoline	F
1986	Ontario, Can.	5000	petroleum	T
1969	Repesa, Spain	5000	LPG	U
1985	Guadalajara, Mex.	5000	sulphuric acid	F
1981	Montanas, Mex.	5000	chlorine	T

[1]Abbreviations for sources are F = fixed site such as chemical plant, industrial complex, warehouse; T = transportation by rail, truck, or ship; P = pipeline: U = unknown source.

some massive evacuations (over 50,000 people) there were an almost equal number of smaller ones (less than 1000) (Table 3.7). The majority of evacuations (48 per cent) were in response to accidental releases from stationary facilities. Nearly 38 per cent of the evacuation events had no deaths or injuries recorded. On the

Table 3.7 *Evacuation size, incident frequency and injuries*

Evacuation size	No. of deaths	No. of injuries	No. of incidents						
			In each chemical class*						Total
			1	2	3	4	5	6	
1–1000	156	567	3	0	2	2	1	0	8
1001–5999	626	26,331	16	0	1	6	2	1	26
6000–19,999	1118	0	4	1	0	1	1	0	7
20,000–49,999	145	2526	1	0	0	3	2	0	6
50,000–100,000	74	1065	1	0	1	0	1	0	3
> 100,000	3278	108,777	2	1	0	2	1	0	6
Totals	5397	139,266	27	2	4	14	8	1	56

* Chemical classes defined as: 1 = acute chemicals; 2 = radiation; 3 = ammunitions and explosives; 4 = oil and gas; 5 = other; 6 = unknown

other hand, there were roughly 5400 fatalities with more than 139,000 injuries, the majority of which were caused by one incident – Bhopal (average estimates of 2750 fatalities, 102,500 injuries). Slightly less than half of the evacuation events were ordered because of the release of acutely toxic chemicals (Table 3.7).

Conclusions

Chemical hazards are not new events that suddenly emerged with the Seveso or Bhopal disasters. As illustrated here, there is a long history of accidents involving chemical explosions and/or the airborne release of acutely toxic substances. The historical context is crucial in assessing the hazard itself in addition to the risks of chemical use (the likelihood that the hazard potential will be realized during a given time span).

While there has been a steady rise in accident frequency since 1900, the relative severity (measured by deaths and injuries) has declined. Bhopal, however, is the exception and illustrates how one catastrophic event can alter the temporal trends. Yet, the potential for harm has increased as a result of the increased toxicity of substances as measured by the number of evacuations that occurred over time. Earlier decades were characterized by highly volatile ammunition and natural gas explosions with numerous fatalities and injuries but no evacuations. It was not until the 1960s that these chemicals waned in importance. Beginning in the 1960s, acutely toxic chemicals were involved in 38 per cent of all accidents and increased to 46 per cent during the 1970s and then dropped to 39 per cent the following decade. While the total number of chemical accidents increased slightly between the 1970s and 1980s, the potential for catastrophe has escalated.

Better safety measures in the aftermath of large chemical disasters have helped to reduce the risks. Clearly the efforts of the United Nations through its International Programme on Chemical Safety (IPCS) is one example. In addition to providing international cooperation on chemical emergencies, the programme also assists in the development of national prevention programmes. The United Nations Environment Programme (UNEP), for example, provides a community-based programme aimed at promoting response strategies at the local level through the Awareness and Preparedness for Emergencies at Local Level (APELL) initiative run though the Industry and Environment Office. UNEP also provides technical assistance on dangerous chemicals through its International Register of Potentially Toxic Chemicals (IRPTC). This registry includes data on chemical production, trade, profiles of individual chemicals, their toxic effects and controls, and environmental fate. Nearly 110 United Nations member countries have a scientific or civil servant representative that assists with IRPTC information gathering and dissemination. The usefulness of such a registry has already been proven with 450 requests involving 1799 chemicals in 1989 alone (UNEP 1990). Regional programmes like the European Community's Seveso Directive, and the UK's CIMAH programme are also helping to mitigate the losses from these hazards.

As a mitigating response to chemical hazards, evacuations have been extremely successful in reducing fatalities and injuries. This is especially true during the last decade when very large evacuations were ordered in response to acute airborne releases of chemicals. Fleeing from harm just might be one of the best responses when that toxic plume drifts your way.

References

Bogard, W. (1987) 'Evaluating chemical hazards in the aftermath of the Bhopal tragedy', *International Journal of Mass Emergencies and Disasters*, vol 5, no 3, pp223–241

Bogard, W. (1989) *The Bhopal Tragedy: Language, Logic, and Politics in the Production of a Hazard*, Westview Press, Boulder, CO

Bowonder, B., Kasperson, J. X. and Kasperson, R. E. (1985) 'Avoiding future Bhopals', *Environment*, vol 27, no 7, pp6–13, 31–37

Chemical Week (1983) 'Restructuring: How the chemical industry is building its future', *Chemical Week*, 26 October, pp26–62

Cutter, S. L. (1991) *The Transformation of the Chemical Industry and US Industrial Disasters 1900–1970*, Department of Geography, Rutgers University, New Brunswick, NJ

Cutter, S. L., Decter, S., Brosius, J. and Kelly, C. (1980). 'Institutional and individual responses to toxic chemical fires: The Chemical Control Corp. Fire, April 21, 1980, Elizabeth, New Jersey', Department of Geography Discussion Paper No. 17, Rutgers University, New Brunswick, NJ

Cutter, S. L. and Solecki, W. D. (1989) 'The national pattern of airborne toxic releases', *The Professional Geographer*, vol 41, no 2, pp149–161

Davenport, J. A. (1977) 'A survey of vapor cloud incidents', *Chemical and Engineering Process*, vol 73, no 9, pp54–63

Fawcett, H. H. (1981) 'The changing nature of acute chemical hazards: A historical perspective', *Journal of Hazardous Materials*, no 4, pp313–319

Gray, J. K. (1981) 'Characteristic Patterns of and Variations in Community Response to Acute Chemical Emergencies.' *Journal of Hazardous Materials*, no 4, pp357–366

Gray, J. K. and Quarantelli, E. L. (1981) 'An editorial introduction to the issue: Social aspects of acute chemical emergencies', *Journal of Hazardous Materials*, no 4, pp309–311

Hay, A. (1982) *The Chemical Scythe*, Plenum, New York

Hazen, S., Myers, H. and Timmerman, P. (1980) 'The North York gasoline leak, February 21, 1979: Emergency response and impact assessment', Working Paper ERR-5, Institute for Environmental Studies, University of Toronto, Canada

Ikeda, K. (1982) 'Warning of disaster and evacuation behavior in a Japanese chemical fire', *Journal of Hazardous Materials*, no 7, pp51–62
Industrial Economics (1989) *Acute Hazardous Events Data Base, Final Report,* Industrial Economics Inc., Cambridge, MA
Johnson, K. (1985) 'State and community during the aftermath of Mexico City's November 19, 1984 gas explosion', Special Publication No. 13, Natural Hazards Research and Applications Information Center, Boulder, CO
Kirby, A. (1990) *Nothing to Fear: Risks and Hazards in American Society,* University of Arizona Press, Tucson, AZ
Lagadec, P. (1982) *Major Technological Risk: An Assessment of Industrial Disasters,* Pergamon, Oxford
Liverman, D. and Wilson, J. P. (1981) 'The Mississauga Train Derailment and Evacuation, 10–16 November 1979', *Canadian Geographer,* no 25, pp365–375
Marshall, V. C. (1987) *Major Chemical Hazards,* Halstead, New York
Morehouse, W. and Subramanian, M. A. (1986) *The Bhopal Tragedy,* Council on International and Public Affairs, New York
Nash, J. R. (1976) *Darkest Hours,* Nelson-Hall, Chicago
Oberg, J. (1988) *Uncovering Soviet Disasters,* Random House, New York
OECD (Organisation for Economic Co-operation and Development) (1987) *Environmental Data Compendium,* OECD, Paris
OECD (1989) *Environmental Data Compendium,* OECD, Paris
OECD (1991) *Environmental Indicators,* OECD,Paris
Palm, R. (1990) *Natural Hazards: An Integrative Framework for Research and Planning,* Johns Hopkins University Press, Baltimore, MD
Quarantelli, E. L. (1981) *Sociobehavioral Responses to Chemical Hazards,*
Quarantelli, E. L., Hutchinson, D. C. and Phillips, B. (1984) *Evacuation Behavior: Case Study of the Taft, Louisiana Chemical Tank Explosion,* Miscellaneous Report 34, Disaster Research Center, Ohio State University, Columbus, OH
Shrivastava, P. (1987a) 'Preventing industrial crises: The challenges of Bhopal', *International Journal of Mass Emergencies and Disasters*, vol 5, no 3, pp199–221
Shrivastava, P. (1987b) 'A cultural analysis of conflicts in industrial disaster.' *International Journal of Mass Emergencies and Disasters,* vol 5, no 3, pp243–264
Shrivastava, P. (1987c) *Bhopal: Anatomy of a Crisis,* Ballinger, Cambridge, MA
Smets, H. (1987) 'Compensation for exceptional environmental damage' in P. R. Kleindorfer and H. C. Kunreuther (eds) *Insuring and Managing Hazardous Risks: From Seveso to Bhopal and Beyond,* Springer Verlag, Berlin, pp79–114
Sorenson, J. H. (1987) 'Evacuations due to off-site releases from chemical accidents: Experience from 1980 to 1984', *Journal of Hazardous Materials,* no 14, pp247–257
Tierney, K. (1980) *A Primer for Acute Chemical Emergencies,* Book and Monograph Series No. 14, Disaster Research Center, Ohio State University, Columbus, OH
Timmerman, P. (1980) 'The Mississauga train derailment and evacuation, November 10–17, 1979: Event reconstruction and organizational response', Working Paper EER-6, Institute for Environmental Studies Emergency and Risk Research, University of Toronto, Canada
UNEP (United Nations Environment Programme) (1989) *Environmental Data Report,* Blackwell, London
UNEP (1990) 'The UNEP guide to dangerous chemicals', *Our Planet,* vol 2, no 4, p15
USEPA (United States Environmental Protection Agency) (1988) *Title III List of Lists. Consolidated List of Chemicals Subject to Reporting under Title III of the Superfund Amendments and Reauthorization Act (SARA) of 1986,* Office of Toxic Substances, USEPA, Washington, DC
USFEMA (United States Federal Emergency Management Agency) (1980) *Case Study: Hazardous Material Spill Somerville, MA, April 3, 1980,* USFEMA, Boston, MA
Vilain, J. (1989) 'The nature of chemical hazards, their accident potential and consequences', in P. Bourdeau and G. Green (eds) *Methods for Assessing and Reducing Injury from Chemical Accident,* SCOPE 40, IPCS Joint Symposia 11, SGOM-SEC6, John Wiley, New York, pp251–290
Weir, D. (1987) *The Bhopal Syndrome,* Sierra Club Books, San Francisco, CA

Whiteside, T. (1979) *The Pendulum and the Toxic Cloud: The Course of Dioxin Contamination*, Yale University Press, New Haven, CT

Withers, J. (1988) *Major Industrial Hazards: Their Appraisal and Control*, Halstead, New York

Whyte, A. V. T., Liverman, D. M. and Wilson, J. P. (1980) 'Preliminary survey of households evacuated during the Mississauga chlorine gas emergency, November 10–16, 1979', Working Paper ERR-7, Institute for Environmental Studies, University of Toronto, Canada

4

Ecocide in Babylonia

Susan L. Cutter

The immense environmental ramifications of operations Desert Shield and Desert Storm are just now coming into view. The images of oil-soaked birds and the towering infernos in the Kuwaiti oil fields held the world's attention for a brief time, but long after the hostilities cease and media reports diminish, the environmental degradation caused by the conflict remains. It will take decades to restore the environment to its pre-war condition, assuming this restoration is even possible. Short-term problems have been replaced by longer-term ones with regional and possibly global repercussions.

As far back as the 7th century BC, social codes were constructed to prevent military disruption of the environment by means of scorched earth policies. For example, Biblical law states 'When you besiege a city for a long time, making war against it in order to take it, you shall not destroy its trees by wielding an axe against them' (Deuteronomy 20:19–20).

More recently, UN member nations have enacted a number of multilateral treaties governing environmental disruption. The Environmental Modification Convention of 1977 – ratified by 50 countries, including the US, but not Iraq – is one example. This treaty prohibits signatory nations from engaging in military or other hostile use of the environment or using environmental modification techniques in warfare that have widespread, long-lasting, or severe effects. There are also the 1977 Bern Protocols (I and II), addenda to the 1949 Geneva Conventions, that prohibit the use of military actions that are intended, or may be expected to cause wide-spread, long-term, and severe damage to the natural environment, including damage to agricultural areas, water installations, and nuclear generating stations. Neither the US nor Iraq are signatories to the Bern Protocols.

In 1982, the United Nations General Assembly passed the World Charter for Nature which proclaims that military activities damaging to nature are to be avoided; nature should be protected against degradation cased by warfare or hostile activities; and special care must be taken to prevent discharges of toxic or

Note: Reprinted, with permission, from *Focus*, vol 41, no 2, Summer, Susan L. Cutter, 'Ecocide in Babylonia', pp26–31. © American Geographical Society, 1991

radioactive waste into the natural environment. Iraq voted in favour of this charter, along with 111 other nations. The US was the only country to vote no.

It is clear that during the Persian Gulf War these treaties and declarations were
not honoured; a scorched earth policy was the norm. The environment has become
one of the many casualties of the war. Two processes contributed to ecocide in the
region: ecoterrorism, the specific use of the environment as a strategic or tactical
weapon; and the actual use of military force, including support activities.

Ecoterrorism

Ecoterrorism is not a new weapon among the world's military arsenals. In the
1960s and 1970s, the US military undertook ecoterrorist activities by unleashing
its Agent Orange (2,4,5-T 2,4-D) defoliation campaign on the South Vietnamese
countryside. More than 20,000 flights between 1962–1971 dumped an estimated
19–23 million gallons of herbicides on more than 4 million acres. Nearly 10
per cent of the total land mass in South Vietnam was affected by the herbicide
spraying; 500,000 crop acres destroyed, and thousands more acres destroyed by
the napalm firestorms. The inland forests in the north were especially hard hit with
64 per cent of the area sprayed. The mangrove forests in the south were also targeted, with 36–50 per cent of them permanently destroyed. These forests are coastal
transition zones that help in maintaining a stable coastline. Mangroves also serve
as primary producers in the food chain, and their destruction led to the collapse
of this ecosystem. As dioxin (the most toxic ingredient in Agent Orange) made its
way into the soil and biota, the contamination spread over even larger areas. On the
human side, latent cancers – slow-developing, long-term ones – are now beginning
to appear among the Vietnamese people and US armed forces veterans.

The use of oil as an environmental weapon initially appeared in the 1980–
1988 Iran–Iraq war. Refineries were intentionally targeted to create oil spills that
would disrupt our global hydrocarbon society. The Iraqi military bombed the
Abadan refinery, the world's largest, on the second day of the conflict (September
23, 1980). They continued their ecoterrorist offensive by targeting all Iranian oil
ports and cities. A 1983 military attack on Iran's Nawruz drilling platform resulted
in a 21 million gallon spill that lasted for eight months, while another attack in
1986 on oil terminals at Surri Island resulted in another massive spill. Routine
spills by supertankers cleaning their bilges, and from platforms, loading docks,
and pipelines, contributed another 150,000 metric tons of oil spilled in the Gulf
during the decade. By the end of the eight-year conflict, the Persian Gulf was
already severely polluted.

In addition to petroleum, naval debris from the conflict, along with rapid
industrialization during the previous decades, contributed to the Gulf's degradation. In an attempt to clean up the results of the ecoterrorism of the Iran–Iraq
war, the Persian Gulf became part of the UN Regional Seas programme in 1988.
This programme is designed to foster cooperation in the restoration of a regional
common property resource such as the sea. The Kuwait Action Plan called for
cooperative proposals by all Gulf nations (Iran, Iraq, Kuwait, Saudi Arabia, Bahrain, Qatar, United Arab Emirates, Oman) for coastal zone management, envi-

ronmental monitoring and public awareness in an attempt to clean up the Gulf. All Gulf nations signed the agreement.

Ecosystem Disruption

During the Persian Gulf War in early 1991, the Iraqi bombing of Sea Island terminals at Mina' al Ahmadi, and Mina' al Bakr resulted in a series of oil spills. Estimates on the volume spilled range from 42 to 462 million gallons. Despite this uncertainty, all agree this is the largest oil spill in history.

The slick reached a maximum size of 100 by 40 miles, and was 4 inches thick. Depending on whose estimates you believe, the spill is 5 to 27 times the size (in gallons spilled) of the *Exxon Valdez*, and more than twice the size of the 1979 IXTOC-1 blow-out in the Bay of Campeche in the Gulf of Mexico that did enormous damage to the Mexican and Texan shorelines. While much of the Kuwaiti light crude oil evaporated, the slick continues on its coastal journey south from Mina' al Ahmadi, threatening the massive desalination plants on the Saudi Arabian coast.

The immediate ecosystem impacts are well known to American television viewers. There are 113 bird species that migrate from Africa to Eurasia spending the winter in the Gulf. Many of these have been severely depleted as a result of these oil spills, including one endangered species, the Caspian tern. Cormorants and grebes were especially hard hit. As the annual northern migration continues, more birds will be lost. Turtles, shrimp, marine mammals and other marine species are threatened, as are their feeding, nesting and breeding sites. One of the largest prawn breeding areas in the Gulf is seriously affected, as is Abu Ali Island, a wildlife sanctuary. The mangrove regions (preserved under Saudi royal decree), coral reefs, and algal flats south of Khafji are decimated to such an extent that they may take years or decades to recover. The abundance and diversity of marine life (180 species of mollusks and 106 species of fish) once found in the Gulf are now in serious jeopardy.

Longer-term impacts of the oil spill are becoming apparent. The Gulf is a shallow body of water (average depth 110 feet) with a restricted access point at the Straits of Hormuz, to the south. It takes between 3–5 years to completely flush the Gulf, or recirculate its waters, compared to the 28-day cycle for Alaska's Prince William Sound, the site of the *Exxon Valdez* spill. As a result, dilution, a plausible natural method to reduce contaminants, will not work in the Gulf. Cleansing by wave action, another possible natural way to reduce contaminants, is also ineffective. The Gulf's fetch, or area of water over which wind blows in a constant direction, is small resulting in low wind-driven wave energy. Much of the oil will remain in the ecosystem particularly in the bottom sediments. Phytoplankton and other species dwelling on the bottom will be affected by the oil itself and by the possible reduction in sunlight penetrating through the oil sheen. Thus, the feeding grounds for a thriving shrimp industry and other marine fisheries have been destroyed. Between 1985–1987, for example, the Gulf nations (Bahrain, Iran, Iraq, Kuwait, Qatar, UAE) caught 215,000 metric tons of fish, a primary source of protein for the region. Commercial marine fisheries will take decades to recover.

Clean up efforts are underway and more than 21 million gallons, twice the volume of oil spilled by the *Exxon Valdez*, have been recovered, although some terminals and tankers are still releasing oil, albeit at a trickle into the Gulf. A holding pond, 8 feet deep and the size of two football fields, has been dug in the sandy desert and lined with plastic to store the recovered oil until eventual reprocessing into fuel. The first of these is now full, and another is being dug – and so oil lakes have been created, and now dot the landscape. Although our oil-based, oil-biased US view has focused on the spills, water is the most precious resource in this arid region. The oil spill has harmed some and threatens many more desalination plants in Kuwait and Saudi Arabia, particularly the one at Jubail that produces almost half of the potable water in Saudi Arabia. Seventy per cent of the potable water in Kuwait comes from desalination plants farther up the coast. In addition to the oil itself, toxic chemicals such as benzene, often found in crude oil, might remain in the water column for years, possibly further contaminating the drinking water of the region long after the tar balls are removed. Finally, Gulf water provides coolant for the petrochemical facilities that line the western shore. Loss of this supply, even if temporary, could lead to a further reduction in the region's economic base. As of mid-April 1991, the oil slick was 50 miles north of Jubail, but many experts think it will not reach the facility; instead the oil appears caught in a pocket formed by Abu Ali island and the causeway that connects it to the mainland.

During and after the Persian Gulf War, the desert itself suffered from heavy armour movements, strategic fortifications, carpet bombing, and the construction of support bases and roads. Most desert ecosystems take decades to recover from human activities and abuses. For example, the Southern California deserts still bear scars from the World War II tank manoeuvres directed by General George Patton. Despite the intervening 50 years, only 35% of the vegetation has recovered. Remnant war landscapes from World War II and the Arab–Israeli wars of 1948, 1956, 1967 and 1973 among others still persist, especially in the Libyan and Negev deserts.

In addition to the loss of desert flora (perennial shrubs and quick-germinating annuals) and fauna (insects, rodents and small mammals) as a result of the war, the heavy armour and road construction, the basic geomorphology of the desert has been altered by the mass movement of sand. Iraqi military defensive fortifications were constructed all along the 175 mile Kuwait–Saudi Arabia border. This created a series of berms, from 12 to 40 feet in height, and trenches that were later filled with oil. These actions and the accompanying loss of vegetation could lead to an increased amount of sand on the move. Sandstorms that already afflict the region could intensify since more sand is now freely available. A lower wind velocity would be needed to move sand, resulting in more sandstorms as well. Soil disturbance also results from the tank and vehicular traffic, and bombing. Once disturbed, sparsely vegetated areas may not recover, accelerating the process of desertification.

Petroleum Winter? Spring? Fall?

Will a worldwide 'petroleum winter' develop? Probably not, yet we are still uncertain about the global significance of the 700 burning oil fires, another ecoterrorist act. Current estimates place the volume of burning oil at 3 million barrels per day, or half the total daily output of the US. This *could* result in a global increase in carbon dioxide in the order of 3 to 5 per cent per year, which could ultimately contribute to global warming, although these have not had any appreciable effect as yet. On the other hand, climate modellers initially concluded that a local chill might be triggered because of the smoke from the fires, though there was little likelihood of global cooling. Unfortunately, this preliminary modelling underestimated the length of time of the burning, using a figure of one month, not the current estimate of two years. Because it will take at least two years to extinguish most of the fires, some significant effects on the global climate may emerge in the near future. These may not be as dramatic as the 'petroleum winter' prediction of an immediate decline in global temperatures, but we might see a more rapid emergence of the greenhouse effect, with global temperatures rising sooner than predicted.

The immediate risks are at the local and regional levels. Darkness reigns at noon, particularly near the Greater Burgan oil fields, 25 miles south of Kuwait City. Temperatures there are at least 25°F cooler than in Kuwait City, which is now averaging 10°F below normal. These lower surface temperatures are a result of the smoke that effectively blocks incoming sunlight. The toxic smoke includes not only soot, but also carbon dioxide, carbon monoxide, sulfur dioxide, hydrocarbons, benzene and other carcinogens. The immediate smog problems are enormous, impairing visibility in many parts of the region. Human health is also affected, with children and the elderly first reporting respiratory problems. Greater health problems for all residents and the occupying forces are expected during the summer months when winds diminish and atmospheric inversions trap the pollutants. Pollution concentrations of sulphur dioxide, particulates and nitrogen oxides are 10 to 30 times higher than what you might find in a heavily polluted city, forcing many returning Kuwaitis to flee yet again. In addition to the burning oil fields, the napalming of oil-filled trenches by the Coalition forces before the ground campaign began initially contributed to the toxic smoke plume. Currently, the smoke plume is clearly visible thousands of miles from the source on satellite imagery. If it takes another three to six months just to clear the minefields before the specialized oil fire teams can begin extinguishing any of the fires, this situation will worsen. As of late April 1991, for example, around 200 well fires had been extinguished or capped.

Black rain has fallen locally in Kuwait and Iraq, and regionally as far away as Turkey, the Black Sea region and the Himalayan slopes of Kashmir. Produced from the high-sulphur content of the oil, the acid rain is perhaps the most significant of the regional impacts. The effects of acid rain on forests and vegetation are well known and will surely pose problems in downwind regions, many of which have marginal agricultural resources to begin with. For example, the agricultural regions of Iran and Iraq are particularly at risk from highly acidic rainfall.

Oil fires could alter the monsoon – rainy – season on the Indian subcontinent and perhaps across Southeast Asia. Increased particulate matter (soot) will have a large impact on the amount of sunlight reaching the earth's surface, especially in Eurasia. The soot could help alter temperature, atmospheric pressure and air circulation patterns. This could delay or shorten the monsoon, reduce its intensity, or some combination of these. Because of the initial time of the fires (February to March 1991), there will be no dramatic decline in temperatures on the Indian subcontinent this year. For example, March temperatures in Karachi hover around 76°F while in Ahmadabad, India, they reach 81°F during the month. April and June are even warmer (89–91°F in Ahmadabad, 82–88°F in Karachi). Even with a 20°F drop, as has happened in Kuwait, temperatures would still be warm enough that a cold wave would not materialize during India's 1991 summer. To the contrary, we may see a 'petroleum spring or fall' where daytime temperatures are lower than normal, but evening temperatures are higher because of the increased cloud cover which keeps the warmer air nearer the surface. Over the next year, we may see an intensification of rainfall from Kuwait to the Indian subcontinent. This speculation is highly controversial at the moment, but we do know that particulates often act as seeding agents. Unusually high rainfall in Bangladesh and Kuwait might be linked to the pollutants from the oil fires.

Energy Use and Air Pollution

Before 1991, hydrocarbon air pollution was already a problem in the Gulf region. Smog from the industrial emissions of refineries and petrochemical plants was a necessary environmental compromise in exchange for development, and oil and gas export. The deployment of Coalition forces simply compounded the local air pollution problem.

In peacetime, the world's military forces use about 4 per cent of the world's petroleum, or what Japan uses for all its energy needs. The military is the single largest domestic user of oil in the US, consuming about 2 to 3 per cent of our total energy demand. In fact, the military uses enough energy in one year to run the entire US mass transit system for 14 years.

During war, petroleum use increases by 15 to 20 per cent. For example, before World War II, the US military used about 1 per cent of the country's petroleum; by 1945 this had increased to 29 per cent. According to a 23 February 1991 CBS News report, the US military used 3 billion gallons of fuel in one week, just to move the front lines nearer to the Iraq border in preparation for the ground campaign. This equals 2 per cent of the US yearly use for all motor vehicles, or what we use in 10 days for our cars, buses and trucks. One armoured division (348 tanks) uses about 600,000 gallons of fuel in just one day! Armour is so petroleum-intensive that fuel efficiency is a misnomer; its fuel consumption is measured in gallons per mile rather than miles per gallon. The six divisions that took part in the ground campaign, plus support vehicles, consumed 8 million gallons of fuel during the 100-hour war.

The extensive air campaign has also used an enormous amount of jet fuel. An F-4 fighter, for example, uses 1680 gallons per hour, while a B-52 uses around 3600. Taking an average of 2640 gallons (the average of B-52 and F-4 flights), an average time of three hours per sortie, times 80,000 sorties, we see that Coalition forces used a total of 634 million gallons of jet fuel just for the air campaign up to the end of January 1991, or 58 times the volume of oil spilled from the *Exxon Valdez* in Prince William Sound. These numbers are very conservative, considering that the majority of B-52 flights originated from bases in Diego Garcia (about 3100 miles away from the theatre of war) or Fairford, England (2750 miles or a 16-hour round trip). These figures do not include the massive airlifts into or out of the region, nor the fuel used by the ground forces during the same two-week period.

Fuel use produces emissions. During peacetime, carbon dioxide, hydrocarbon, nitrogen oxide and sulphur dioxide emissions average 640,000 tons annually just from the world's military alone. If we estimate a wartime increase in fuel usage in the order of 15 to 20 per cent, then we can expect a similar rise in emissions. A high-tech conflict with an extensive air campaign, such as in the Gulf War, may involve even greater fuel use – thus producing even higher emissions. The effect of local emissions on the global carbon budget and the greenhouse effect is unknown at the moment, but we do know that in peacetime annual carbon emissions from the military are around 3 per cent of the global total, or roughly the equivalent to the total carbon emissions of the UK. Carbon dioxide emissions from fuel consumption during the 100-hour ground war were about 80,000 tons or roughly the same amount as the total emissions from all fossil fuels from Uganda for an entire year.

Finally, the US military also uses ozone-depleting substances such as CFC-113 and Halon 1211. The particular applications are classified, but CFCs are included as fuel additives (primarily in stealth bombers) to reduce particulate emissions that might be detected. How many CFCs are used, and where, remains a military secret.

Agricultural Systems and Land Degradation

Iraq is slightly larger than the state of California, but only 13 per cent arable land, a third of it irrigated. The alluvial plains of the Tigris and Euphrates River valleys host one of the major agricultural regions in Iraq with major crops such as dates, rice and cotton. The northern grain-growing region is expected to have a bumper harvest in 1991, for farmers put in vast acreages, double the previous year, at the start of the 1990 trade embargo. Other regions, especially southern Iraq, endured heavy bombing. Food shortages seem likely because of fuel shortages for power for irrigation pumps, grain mills, and other machinery that would have been used to harvest the crops. Bombed-out roads and bridges will hamper food distribution.

Kuwait is slightly smaller than New Jersey, has only 1 per cent arable land, and so is totally dependent on food imports. Irrigated agriculture is concentrated on the coast south of Kuwait City, with vegetables, dates and fodder the primary crops. Most of the irrigation water comes from desalinization plants, many now closed because of the oil spill or damaged by the retreating Iraqi forces.

We can only speculate at this time on the soil and water damage that will result from the black rain and the hydrocarbon pollution. The reduction in sunlight and reduced temperatures below the smoke clouds may affect agricultural activity, especially during the early planting season when seedlings are most vulnerable to sunlight and temperature changes.

Land is always a casualty of war. Oil spills from the destruction of refineries, oil burning in trenches, and miscellaneous leakages all contaminate land. Rivers of oil from burning and uncapped wells run unchecked through the desert, eroding channels in the sand, and ponding in low-lying areas. The precision of Coalition bombing of Iraq's chemical and biological weapons factories must have released toxic substances into nearby areas. It is likely that soil and surface waters were and possibly still are contaminated with mustard gas and the nerve agents tabun and sarin, or some of the toxic chemicals used to manufacture them such as ethylene, hydrochloric acid, phosphoric acid, sulphur, and chlorine. While there is no definite evidence at this time of radioactive, biological, or chemical contamination, the stockpiles of these weapons of mass destruction may still exist in Iraq with estimates ranging from 2000 to 4000 metric tons.

Toxic wastes produced by the Coalition forces also degrade the land. The heat and sand of the desert magnify machinery maintenance problems, requiring heavier weight oil and other lubricants. The production of toxic wastes is greater than normal because of the desert environment.

Remnant landmines create a hazardous landscape as well. Unexploded mines from World Wars I and II are present in Europe to this day. The continuing explosion of Gulf mines will create a pock-marked landscape that in an arid environment will take decades to recover. In addition to the bomb craters, metal fragments from the explosions litter the landscape as does the barbed wire used in defensive fortifications. Military personnel continue to clear mines from the heavily fortified Kuwaiti beaches, but other mined areas have yet to be cleared. The minefields may keep people and their grazing animals out allowing the desert ecosystem to recover more quickly than normal. More likely, however, is the loss of life and limb as herders lead their animals through the desert in search of food.

Then there is the problem of solid waste disposal. The build-up of Coalition forces involved more than 525,000 troops, about half the size of each of Saudi Arabia's two largest cities, Riyadh and Jedda. US personnel daily consumed two hot meals encased in plastic – no longer termed C-rations, but Meals Ready to Eat (MREs) – thus generating 6 million used bags per week. This figure does not include plastic water containers, nor other debris such as mail and packages. All the waste, estimated at 250,000 tons per year, must be put in a landfill or incinerated. There is also the problem of human waste, about 10 million gallons per day. Finally, there is the vast amount of military debris, for instance bombed-out tanks, cars and buildings that will need to be disposed of along with the demolition debris generated during reconstruction These are challenging tasks under normal circumstances, and even more daunting in an arid and post-war setting.

Lastly, and perhaps most poignantly, the Saudi government dug 50,000 graves facing Mecca in anticipation of the ground campaign. Since casualties were low, it is not known if these have been refilled. In southern Iraq, Coalition forces dug mass graves and buried tens of thousands of victims in plastic body bags, manufactured of course from oil.

Uncertain Futures

Warfare creates environmental destruction not only in the theatre of conflict but also closer to home. Toxic wastelands developed by the US military now cover vast sections of this country. In the US, military bases and associated facilities produce biological, chemical, conventional and nuclear weapons, and are so polluted that 96 are now on the Superfund list of critically polluted places in most urgent need of immediate clean-up. In August 1990, just after Iraq's invasion of Kuwait, the US military – with White House approval – began to claim exemption from producing environmental impact statements, even though this is required by federal law, about its domestic activities. The military's toxic past and present will remain top secret. The Bush administration's war-inspired energy policy calls for the increased use of oil and natural gas, emphasizes new drilling in Alaska and along the outer continental shelf, and promotes a heavier reliance on nuclear power. The perpetuation of the hydrocarbon society's toxic middens is just a part of the domestic ramifications of the Gulf War.

But back to the Persian Gulf and the ecocide ravaging the region. Because of military censorship, much of the scientific discussion on the environmental effects of the Gulf War is rather speculative at this time. As data become available to the international research community and subject to independent verification, the true extent of the environmental catastrophe will become known. We do know for certain, however, that warfare and war preparation annihilates places and renders the natural environment unproductive for decades. I close with the haunting question of what type of environment is left in Kuwait and especially in Iraq, where 46 per cent of the Iraqi population is under 15 years of age? What environmental legacy is left for their children?

References

Brawer, M. (ed) (1988) *Atlas of the Middle East*, Macmillan, New York

Canby, T. Y. (1991) 'After the storm', *National Geographic*, vol 180, no 2, pp2–35

Chynoweth, E. and Alperowicz, N. (1991) 'Chemical weapons under fire', *Chemical Week*, vol 148, no 6, pp12

Earth Island Institute (1991) 'Gulf War reports', *Earth Island Institute Journal*, vol 6, no 2, pp43–50

Environmental Action (1991) 'Waging war on the Earth', *Environmental Action*, vol 22, no 5, pp20–24

Hay, J. R. (1982) *The Chemical Scythe*, Plenum, New York

Hoffman, M. (1991) 'Taking stock of Saddam's fiery legacy in Kuwait', *Science*, vol 253, pp971

Horgan, J. (1991) 'Up in flames', *Scientific American*, May, pp17–24

Marshall, E. (1991) 'Nuclear winter from Gulf War discounted', *Science*, vol 251, p372

Monroe, F. (1991) 'Persian Gulf: Winter weather and desert storm', Geographic Notes no 13, Bureau of Intelligence and Research, US Department of State, pp8–10

Political Ecology Group (1991) *War in the Gulf: An Environmental Perspective*, Action Paper No 1, Alonzo Press, San Francisco, CA

Renner, M. (1991) 'Assessing the military's war on the environment' in L. Brown (ed) *State of the World*, Worldwatch Institute, Washington, DC

Seager, J. (1990) *State of the Earth Atlas*, Simon and Schuster, New York

SIPRI (Stockholm International Peace Research Institute) (1980) *Warfare in a Fragile Environment: Military Impact on the Human Environment*, Taylor and Francis, London

Smith, G. (1991) 'Cradle to grave', *Earth Island Journal*, Winter, pp36–40

United Nations (1982) *Yearbook of the United Nations*, United Nations, New York

Warner, F. (1991) 'The environmental consequences of the Gulf War', *Environment*, vol 33, no 5, pp7–9, 25–26

Westing, A. H. (1984) 'Herbicides in war: Past and present' in A. H. Westing (ed) *Herbicides in War: The Long-term Ecological and Human Consequences*, Taylor and Francis, London, pp3–24

Westing, A. H. (ed) (1988) *Cultural Norms, War and the Environment*, Oxford University Press for SIPRI and UNEP, New York

Westing, A. H. (ed) (1991) *Environmental Hazards of War: Releasing Dangerous Forces in an Industrialized World*, Sage Publications, London

Wood, W. B. and Mofson P. (1991) 'Persian Gulf: Oil as an "eco-weapon"', Geographic Notes no 13, Bureau of Intelligence and Research, US Department of State, pp7–8

World Resources Institute (1990) *World Resources 1990–91*, Oxford University Press, New York

Yergin, D. (1991) *The Prize: The Epic Quest for Oil, Money and Power*, Simon and Schuster, New York

5

The Forgotten Casualties: Women, Children and Environmental Change

Susan L. Cutter

One of the continuing criticisms of the human dimensions of global change litera-ture is the paucity of research on topics other than global warming or tropical defor-estation, a point reiterated recently by the editors of this journal (Parry et al, 1993). Global change is not simply climate change. Global change recognizes that environ-mental processes are inextricably linked to other global transformations underway in governments, economies, technologies, populations and culture (Kates, 1994). Furthermore, the integration of earth systems processes, anthropogenic sources of environmental change, cumulative and systemic impacts on social systems, and human vulnerability and responses (prevention and adaptation) is necessary and merits high priority in policy-relevant studies of global change (Turner et al, 1990; Committee on the Human Dimensions of Global Change, 1994).

Of equal importance in the policy debates is the principle of equity or fair-ness (Kasperson and Dow, 1991). We know that natural resources are unevenly distributed over the Earth's surface, and their utilization is governed by diverse economic, political and social forces (Cutter, 1994). Variations in technology and economic capability set the stage for political confrontations over resources, just as differential adaptive abilities set the stage for political confrontations over envi-ronmental protection at local, regional, and global scales. Since environmental resources underpin the material welfare of all societies, threats to environmental security create political instability and turmoil that further exacerbate inequalities between regions and peoples (Myers, 1993; Chen and Kates, 1994).

This chapter examines the concept of environmental equity and its utility in highlighting the socio-spatial impacts of environmental change and the differen-tial adjustments to such changes by women and children. These subpopulations are continually overlooked in the global change literature, yet as a group, they

Note: Reprinted, with permission, from *Global Environmental Change: Human and Policy Dimen-sions*, vol 5, no 3, Susan L. Cutter, 'The forgotten casualties: Women, children, and environmental change', pp181–194. © Elsevier, 1995.

often have the greatest social and biophysical vulnerability to local, regional and global environmental disturbances.

The Equity Principle

In its broadest sense, equity means freedom from bias or favouritism.[1] In an environmental context, equity refers to the equal access to resources, equal allocation and treatment of societal risk, and the equal consideration of competing interests. Environmental equity manifests itself in two ways: as an outcome and as a process (Greenberg, 1993; Kasperson, 1994). Outcome equity is the distributional pattern of social benefits and environmental risks. Process equity is the underlying social, economic, political or institutional causes of these uneven distributions. To rectify past inequities, governmental intervention in social programmes or in the marketplace is required. These interventions are variously referred to as social or environmental justice.

The terms equity and fairness are often used interchangeably, which is the case here, although there are subtle distinctions between them. Environmental risks, for example, can be distributed evenly across society, but their distribution may not be fair as some subpopulations (e.g. women, children, the elderly) might be more vulnerable or susceptible to their impact than others.

The broad framework for global environmental equity was set forth in the United Nation's 1992 Rio Declaration on Environment and Development. The action plan, *Agenda 21*, provides the framework for implementing the fairness doctrine and outlines 27 specific principles (UN, 1992). Close to half of the stated principles directly address some form of equity (Table 5.1). For this discussion, three broad forms of equity are reviewed (social, generational and procedural) as these have the greatest relevance to the health and well-being of the world's women and children.

Social equity

Social equity refers to the role of social, economic, and political forces in resource consumption and environmental degradation. It also means the differential impact of environmental degradation on social groups such as those defined by class, age, race, political, or gender distinctions. Locally unwanted land uses (LULUs) such as landfills, noxious industries, or highways often coincide with poorer neighbourhoods or communities, especially in the developed world. The juxtaposition of economic activities, largely determined by locational criteria (such as cheap land or transportation access) and the social geography of places creates the landscape of risk. These landscapes distinguish beneficiary from host communities, populations at risk, and relative levels of vulnerability for both people and places.

The hazardous waste issue is a prime example of social equity problems. Unfortunately, there are no reliable estimates on industrial waste generation and waste flows at the global level, let alone information on the subcategory of waste labelled 'hazardous'. Whereas more than 2 billion metric ton of industrial waste are generated annually, only 16 per cent is estimated to be hazardous (OECD,

Table 5.1 *Equity principles embodied in the Rio Declaration on Environment and Development*

Generational
Principle 3: right to development to meet environmental needs of present and future generations
Social
Principle 5: decrease the disparities in standards of living and better meet the needs of the majority of the people of the world
Principle 6: special needs of developing countries especially the least developed and most environmentally vulnerable
Principle 10: equal access to information and decision-making processes
Principle 12: reduce discrimination and restrictions on trade policies and trans-boundary problems
Principle 14: discourage toxic transfers
Principle 20: full participation of women in environmental management and development
Principle 21: mobilize youth
Principle 22: recognize the rights of indigenous people and communities
Principle 23: environment and natural resources of people under oppression are protected
Procedural
Principle 11: environmental standards reflect the context within which they apply
Principle 13: national liability for environmental damages

Source: UN, 1992, pp 9–11

1991). The largest *known* hazardous waste generator in the world is the US, contributing about 180 million tonnes, or 80 per cent of the total (OECD, 1993). Where does this waste go? More importantly, whose backyard does it end up in?

In the US, hazardous waste-generating facilities are located in the densely populated and industrialized Northeast and Midwest stretching from New York–New Jersey westward along the Great Lakes to Illinois. Other states with large numbers of generators include portions of the South (Virginia, North Carolina, and Tennessee), Texas and California. On a per capita basis, the 13 Southern states have the highest hazardous waste generation rates in the country, averaging more than 960 pounds per person per year. The American South is also the poorest region in the nation, and the one with the highest percentage of African American residents. States in the American South spend the least on the management of hazardous wastes, averaging less than US$ 0.44 for every metric ton generated (Hall and Kerr, 1991).

Thus far I have described the locational patterns of hazardous generating facilities. But what about those sites that have ceased operation or where hazardous materials were intentionally dumped during the last 40 years? In the US, the federal Superfund law prioritizes site remediation based on the seriousness of potential health impacts to surrounding communities. Currently, more than 1200 sites are identified on this National Priority List and as many as 35,000 are awaiting review (Cutter, 1993). Many of these sites are located in African American and Hispanic communities in Northern urban areas or in the South (Bryant and Mohai, 1992; Bullard, 1990). In fact, a recent study concluded that African

Americans are 50 per cent more likely to live in a community with a hazardous waste site than the population at large (Zimmerman, 1993).

As a political movement, environmental justice has gathered considerable momentum within the US, yet the empirical support for environmental racism claims is quite mixed (Chapter 16; see also Goldman and Fitton, 1994; Zimmerman, 1994). Most studies only focus on the geographical distribution (or outcome) of hazardous waste facilities and the social characteristics of host communities at a single point in time. The literature is confounded by researchers using different measurement scales (states, counties, census tracts) and a diverse set of indicators (abandoned hazardous waste sites, landfills, facilities currently releasing toxic emissions). Clearly, more empirical evidence is needed on the underlying processes contributing to these distributions to fully test whether communities of colour are intentionally targeted for such noxious facilities.

On the international level, the trans-boundary movement of hazardous waste is a serious concern as data on the type and amount of waste exports, country of origin, and country of destination are not widely available. The issue is further complicated by lack of agreement on definitions of hazardous waste in the first place. Greenpeace documented more than 1000 cases of exporting hazardous waste from industrialized nations, mostly to unsuspecting developing countries (Valette and Spalding, 1990). Developing countries on the receiving end of the toxic waste trade include Brazil, Mexico, Nigeria, Lebanon, Syria, Venezuela, Zimbabwe and South Korea.

Trade merchants in the US knowingly export hazardous waste to developing countries, more than 200,000 metric tons were exported in 1988, for example. The European Community's record is no better, as it generates three times the amount of hazardous waste than it has the capacity to handle. It is estimated that 700,000 metric tons of European hazardous waste are exported annually to countries other than the country of origin (Tolba et al, 1992). A good proportion of it is sent to Central and Eastern European nations especially Poland, Romania, and the former East Germany. As part of reunification, Germany (the largest exporter during the 1980s) must now pay for the decades of dumping on its eastern neighbour as it spends millions of dollars to clean up hazardous waste sites in the former East German Republic.

Whether dumping in Dixie or dumping on the developing world, the root cause is the same: uneven power – one of the defining elements in social equity problems. As trans-boundary problems become more severe, social inequities will intensify and threaten the environmental security of rich and poor nations alike.

Generational equity

Generational equity is the principle of fairness to future generations. We benefit from the stewardship of the Earth's natural and cultural resources by previous generations (our parents and grandparents). In return, we become the trustees and custodians of those resources for future generations (our children and grandchildren). We have, according to the generational equity code, certain obligations that require us to care for this environmental legacy, to ensure its maintenance and survival, and to pass it on to future generations in the same or better condition than when it was received.

Generational equity has both outcome and process elements. We can see generational outcomes in the issue of permanent radioactive waste disposal, where the narrow self-interests of one generation (the beneficiaries of commercial nuclear power) could cause irreparable harm to another future generation (inequities in risks and benefits). As Shrader-Frechette suggests, 'Analogous to racism and sexism, the narrow self-interest of this generation might be called "generationism" ... Likewise, our power over future persons does not give us the right to do to them whatever we wish. Might does not make right' (Shrader-Frechette, 1993, p212).

Generational equity is also a process that provides a framework of ethical considerations and legal norms intended to bring justice to future generations from current and past practices (Weiss, 1989, 1990). It encourages contemporary public policy-makers to consider fairness to future generations as part of their environmental decision-making. In implementing generational equity, three strategies are important:

1 the maintenance of natural and cultural diversity;
2 a reduction in environmental degradation attendant on
   economic development; and
3 the provision of equal access to resources (Weiss, 1989, 1990).

The most obvious example of achieving generational equity is the preservation of natural areas, one approach for conserving biodiversity. In the US, the National Park Service's mission is to protect America's natural heritage for future generations. Nearly 80 million acres of America's public lands are preserved in more than 350 geographic locales, mainly in the western states. Other nations replicated this preservation strategy, developing their own system of national parks. Although the concept is a good one, encroachment on these preserves is a continual problem in both the developed and developing world.

Globally, there are more than 14,000 protected areas covering about 13 per cent of the Earth's land surface (Table 5.2). International treaties protect habitats as well as individual species. Large acreages in international protection systems are found in North and Central America, Oceania and Africa. Nationally based protection strategies are also most pronounced in North and Central America (263 million hectares) representing close to 12 per cent of its total land area. Nations in the Former Soviet Union (FSU) have the least amount of national parks (24 million hectares, representing around 1 per cent of their total land area).

A less obvious example of generational equity involves the health and welfare of the next generation. Mutagenic and teratogenic substances such as radioactivity and heavy metals impair human physiology, often resulting in diminished mental and physical capabilities. Poor health and nutrition also impede women's capacity to bear healthy children and nurture these children to adulthood. Women's lack of access to health services and lack of reproductive freedom ensures the continuation of high child mortality rates in many parts of the world. High mortality and morbidity rates affect many of the world's children, especially those children living in sub-Saharan Africa where the average mortality rate for children under five is 2.5 times the world average (UNICEF, 1993). A recent United Nations report claims that the issue of intergenerational equity is one of 'concern for the

Table 5.2 *Environmental protection systems*

	Number	Acreage (000 hectares)
International		
Biosphere reserves	312	171,241
World heritage sites	100	100,980
Wetlands	590	36,695
Marine and coastal environments	977	211,406
National		
World Conservation Union protected areas (I–V)	8619	792,266
Resource and anthropological reserves	3868	358,848
Totals	14,466	1,671,436

Source: World Resources Institute, 1994b

growing population of children and the deteriorating environment that hampers their development' (Tolba et al, 1992, p482).

Procedural equity

The last form of equity, procedural, is the extent to which governmental rules and regulations, enforcement, and international treaties and sanctions are applied in a fair way. Systematic biases in environmental protection are found worldwide. In the US, these biases are collectively labelled environmental racism by activists who claim that people of colour are affected by industrial pollution more than white residents, and that people of colour also can expect different treatment from the government (Bullard, 1994). While the evidence of unjust pollution burdens is not definitive as noted earlier, there is some truth to the claims of procedural inequities. For example, between 1985 and 1991, violators of the federal hazardous waste laws paid restitution that was 500 per cent higher if they polluted a white community than if they polluted a minority one. It also took minority communities 20 per cent longer to get sites placed on the National Priority List (World Resources Institute, 1994a).

In an attempt to rectify these procedural inequities, President Clinton signed an executive order in February 1994 that requires each federal agency to make the principle of environmental justice part of its mission. US federal agencies are now required to identify and address the adverse human health or environmental effects of their programmes, policies and activities on minority and low-income populations (Bullard, 1994). In addition to data collection and monitoring, all federal agencies must develop strategies for reducing and preventing environmental inequities in their programmes.

The exploitation of environmental regulations in the developing world by multinational corporations produces an export economy in toxic production facilities. On the surface, these arrangements seem profitable for both the host country and the multinational corporation, but accidents can and do happen. Many countries have a limited capacity to enforce environmental regulations (lack of staff, overlapping jurisdictions, lack of monitoring equipment, lack of data) even though these regulations exist on paper. Countries in transition to market economies are also susceptible to the exploitation of environmental regulations as they strive for privatization and investment opportunities for industrial modernization, making social choices that often place immediate materialism over longer-term environmental protection goals (Manser, 1994).

The implementation of international environmental accords also illustrates procedural equity concerns. For example, the trans-boundary shipments of hazardous waste were so numerous that international restrictions and controls on the trade were put in place in 1989 and the treaty became effective in 1992. Unfortunately, the Basel Convention did not ban exports outright, due ostensibly to pressure from the industrialized nations, and many developing countries had to impose their own import bans to stem the waste trade. The Lome Convention bans hazardous and radioactive waste imports from EC countries to developing nations. The Bamako Convention bans hazardous waste (including radioactive waste) imports and trans-boundary movements of hazardous waste in 17 African countries (Cutter, 1993). The success of these treaties in stemming the waste trade is debatable. More significantly, industrialized nations are now offering to construct waste-to-energy plants in the developing world (the new euphemism for hazardous waste incinerators) as a solution to local energy needs.

The equity framework provides a useful mechanism for examining the differential impacts and responses to global environmental changes, especially those that effect the health and well-being of women and children. Before we consider some specific applications, however, a brief review of where women and children live and work is required.

Demographic Patterns of Women and Children

In 1990, slightly less than half (49.6 per cent) of the world's population were women. Even though women generally live longer, there are simply fewer women than men. In many regions, women significantly outnumber men, but not in all (Table 5.3). In Asia, female mortality rates at all ages are often higher than males contributing to a regional lowering of female/male ratios.[2] Most of the world's women now live in Asia (55.6 per cent), with 24 per cent residing in the developed countries (Manser, 1994).

One-third of the world's population are children under age 15 based on 1995 estimates and 85 per cent of them live in developing nations. Within the decade, demographers expect another 1.5 billion births in the developing regions with a majority of these in Asia. Perhaps the most striking demographic pattern is the child dependency ratio, the number of children under 15 per 100 people aged 15–64 in the work force. In 1990 it was 60 children per 100 people aged 15–64 in the developing regions (30 children per 100 people in the developed countries). The child dependency ratio is expected to drop somewhat by the turn of the century (57/100 in developing countries, 30/100 in developed countries). However,

Table 5.3 *Gender ratios*

Region	Number of females per 100 males
Developed countries	106
Africa	
North Africa	98
Sub-Sahara	102
Latin America/Caribbean	100
Asia/Pacific	
East Asia	95
Southeast Asia	101
Southern Asia	94
Western Asia	94

Source: UN, 1991

the flip side, the elderly dependency ratio (number of people 65 and over per 100 people aged 15–64) is expected to increase to 12/100 by the year 2000 (Manser, 1994). Elderly women outnumber elderly men everywhere, with the highest elderly female/male ratio (152/100) found in the developed countries (UN, 1991).

Lastly, just as the world's settlement patterns are becoming more urbanized, so are women and children. It is estimated that 45 per cent of the world's population lives in urban settings, with 17 per cent of the people living in cities with more than 750,000 inhabitants (Table 5.4). In 1990, 61 per cent of urbanites lived in

Table 5.4 *World urbanization trends*

	Percentage of population living in:				No. of cities with population over 750,000	No. of cities with population over 10 million (estimate)
	Urban areas		Cities of over 750,000			
Region	1965	1995	1965	1995	1990	2000
World	35.5	45.2	14.7	17.4	376	21
Africa	20.6	34.7	6.9	10.9	34	2
Asia	22.2	34.0	9.6	13.3	149	13
North/Central America	67.4	74.0	36.0	38.6	66	3
South America	55.9	78.0	26.0	36.8	35	3
Europe	63.8	75.0	23.0	24.0	56	0
Former Soviet Union	52.8	68.1	14.6	17.9	30	0
Oceania	68.6	71.0	39.2	41.3	6	0

Source: World Resources Institute, 1994b

the developing countries and this will escalate to 73 per cent in 2010, when 2.7 billion people are expected to live there. By the end of the 20th century, 21 cities in the world are expected to reach more than 10 million in population, 18 of these will be in the developing world (Table 5.4). Mexico City, Sao Paulo, and the metropolitan complex of Tokyo-Yokohama will top the list. The percentage of women living in urban areas ranges from 70 per cent in developed countries to 26 per cent in Africa, 57 per cent in Latin America and the Caribbean, and 40 per cent in Asia and the Pacific region (UN, 1991). The locational pattern for children is similar.

Environmental Burdens on Women and Children

Given the brief demographic profile of the world's women and children, just how significant are their environmental burdens and how well can they adjust to environmental disturbances? Three sources of hazards are used to illustrate the specific vulnerability of women and children to environmental changes, each reflecting one of the types of equity described earlier.

Environmental contaminants

The first example is an indicator of intergenerational equity. The world is becoming a more toxic place in which to live. The industrial and military excesses of the previous four decades haunt us daily with discoveries of new toxic legacies – Love Canal, Chelyabinsk, or ones we have yet to discover. In the US alone this toxic legacy includes 14,401 military hot spots at 1600 facilities (Seigel et al, 1991; Seager, 1993). Since the mid-1980s, more than 113 major chemical accidents/incidents from transportation or industrial facilities have occurred worldwide (UNEP, 1991). More than 8000 deaths were reported along with about 190,000 known injuries. Preliminary data by World Resources Institute and the World Bank estimated the amount of toxic releases during the mid-1980s and found the US contributes 18 million metric tons, while Japan (a close second) releases around 13 million metric tons annually (World Resources Institute, 1994b).

While we have considerable knowledge on the impact of pollution on adult health we know less about the effects of environmental toxins on sperm, eggs and young bodies. Children are especially susceptible to environmental contaminants because their organs are still developing, their immune systems are not as fully developed as adults, and they have smaller body weights and thus absorb more pollutants per body weight than adults (Kane and Kates, 1985). Foetuses, for example, are highly vulnerable to industrial toxins such as PCBs, organic solvents, mercury, and pesticides, as well as to self-administered toxins such as alcohol, tobacco, cocaine, and heroin (Timberlake and Thomas, 1990). Breast-fed infants continue their exposure to PCBs, dioxin, and even DDT from the bioaccumulation of toxins in their mother's milk. Children who play in the streets, next to streets, near highways, in garbage dumps or in abandoned lots are constantly exposed to a wide array of contaminants, especially pesticides and heavy metals. The water children drink, the food they eat and even the air they breathe create a mysterious toxic cocktail. Although a long-standing concern exists over the role of environmental contaminants in causing cancers, more recent studies suggest an even greater role for these environmental toxins: their ability to disrupt hormonal systems, especially those hormonal systems that govern reproduction (Sexton, 1994; Swanston, 1994; Lemonick, 1994). Screening chemicals for their effects on reproductive systems, embryos and children is a clear recognition of fairness to future generations.

Environmental contaminants from industrial sources most often affect children in the developed world. For example, in the Czech Republic town of Most located in the heart of the Bohemian industrial region, pollution from burning brown coal, coupled with winter inversions, creates a situation so bad that children are routinely taken out of the city for weeks at a time, nominally on 'green' vacations, to partially restore pulmonary functions. This pattern is replicated elsewhere in Central and Eastern Europe.

Air pollution poses additional risks for children, whether they live in industrialized or developing countries. High carbon monoxide levels, especially in crowded cities, result in decreased foetal weights and increased likelihood of *in utero* brain damage after periods of prolonged exposure by pregnant women. Children are more susceptible to carbon monoxide poisoning than adults (Christiani, 1993). Particulates are a contributing cause of the acute respiratory infections, which claim 4.3 million childhood deaths annually (World Resources Institute, 1992). In developing countries, the burning of wood and dung in traditional stoves with poor ventilation in rural areas releases 2–100 times the particulate level safety standard recommended by the World Health Organization (WHO). Carbon monoxide poisoning is also a threat. Women and girls are particularly vulnerable to these indoor contaminants since they spend long hours preparing and cooking food and maintaining the indoor environment. It is estimated that 700 million women and children are at risk from chronic respiratory diseases from indoor air pollution (Tolba et al, 1992).

In urban areas, particulates are the most threatening air pollutant in the world's megacities, 12 of which exceed WHO guidelines by more than a factor of two (UNEP, 1994). Air pollution levels in many of the developing world's cities are at crisis levels. Mexico City exceeds all WHO standards for the six pollutants measured, and ozone levels have tripled since 1986 now registering more than 60 per cent higher than WHO safety standards. For children, just breathing the air in Mexico City is as bad as smoking two packs of cigarettes a day since birth (World Resources Institute, 1991). Blends of particulates and sulphur dioxide render the air in Beijing, Mexico City, Rio de Janeiro, Seoul and Shanghai extremely hazardous. Elsewhere, Cairo, Jakarta, Sao Paulo, Moscow, and Los Angeles fail to meet more than half the standards for WHO criteria pollutants (sulphur dioxide, suspended particulate matter, lead, carbon monoxide, nitrogen oxides and ozone).

Lead is an ancient toxin of particular concern as it poses significant problems for children, contributing to neuropsychological impairments that often result in learning disabilities. Lead-based paint, mostly ingested by African American infants and toddlers from the deteriorating walls of tenements in US inner-city neighbourhoods, led to the reformulation of paint in the US in 1971. As more affluent couples gentrify inner-city housing, lead exposure from this pre-1971 paint is now affecting affluent white children as well. Exhaust fumes from leaded gasoline also contributed to high levels of lead found in children's blood, with more than 17 per cent of children in American metropolitan areas (the majority of whom are African American) recording higher than normal levels. In 1975, lead was banned in gasoline in the US resulting in declining lead levels here and elsewhere in the industrialized world. Despite this, about one-sixth of American children have excess lead levels in their systems, enough to impair their health and interfere with learning (Bowen and Hu, 1993).

Global industrial emissions of lead average 330,000 metric tons per year, of which 76 per cent come from leaded gasoline (Nriagu, 1994). Lead contamination is on the rise in the developing world as cities grow and the use of motor vehicles and leaded fuel increases. In Mexico City, for example, seven out of ten babies have blood lead levels in excess of the WHO standards (World Resources Institute, 1992). In Cairo and Karachi ambient lead levels in the air exceed the WHO standards by a factor of two. Lead fallout from motor vehicles and industries accumulates in the soil, contaminating crops for human and livestock consumption. Ingestion of contaminated soil and food (leafy green vegetables, for example, bioaccumulate lead), occupational exposures and use of lead in folk remedies all are contributing to an entire generation of developmentally disabled people.

Pesticides are another group of environmental contaminants that disproportionately affect children, ranging from acute exposures to the insidious contamination found in the fields where children play and on the food they eat and the water they drink. In addition to the increased likelihood of cancer, many pesticides suppress the human immune system rendering children and the elderly more susceptible to infectious agents. Pesticides represent an occupational hazard for close to 3.8 million agricultural workers and their dependents in the developing world alone (World Resources Institute, 1994b).

The poverty–population–environmental degradation spiral

As bad as these pollution statistics are, other environmental threats compromise women and children's health and well-being and impede their ability to adjust or adapt to changing environmental conditions. These threats come about as a result of the intertwining of poverty, development and urbanization and the social inequities that arise from these driving forces (Mellor, 1988; Kates and Haarmann, 1992). Environmental degradation is felt more acutely in developing nations where most of the world's 1.7 billion children currently live and where 98 per cent of them die (UNICEF, 1993). The economic, social and environmental conditions in the developing world already place women and children at risk from malnutrition, disease, life-long physical and mental disabilities, domestic violence, war and death at an early age.

Environmental degradation makes a bad situation worse. Infant mortality rates hover around 78 deaths per 1000 live births in the developing world compared to the industrialized world's 13 per 1000 (UNICEF, 1993). In 1990, 914,000 Latin American and Caribbean children died before they reached the age of five; worldwide 12.9 million died (World Resources Institute, 1992), many from diseases for which we have preventive measures. A baby born in the develop-

Table 5.5 *Gender differences in children's mortality rates in selected countries*

Country	Deaths per year per 1000 population aged 2–5	
	Girls	Boys
Pakistan	54.4	36.9
Haiti	61.2	47.8
Bangladesh	68.6	57.7
Thailand	26.8	17.3
Syria	15.6	9.3
Colombia	24.8	20.5
Costa Rica	8.1	4.8
Nepal	60.7	57.7
Dominican Republic	20.2	17.2
Philippines	21.9	19.1
Sri Lanka	18.7	16.3
Peru	30.8	28.8
Mexico	16.7	14.7
Panama	8.7	7.6
Turkey	19.5	18.4
Republic of Korea	12.7	11.8
Venezuela	8.4	7.6

Source: UN, 1991

ing world is seven times more likely to die in her/his first year of life than a baby born in the North. Even within the developing world there are social inequalities. Historical patterns of gender discrimination manifest themselves in the differentials between male and female child mortality rates. In a recent study, female child mortality rates are consistently higher than for males (Table 5.5). If you include female infanticide and female foetal abortions, the gender biases are even more pronounced (Holloway, 1994).

The leading causes of childhood death in the developing world are acute respiratory infections and diarrhoea, the latter accounting for 3.2 million children's deaths annually (World Resources Institute, 1992). Both can be drastically reduced with improvements in environmental quality. Contaminated water and food as well as contact with faecal matter (farm animals, human waste in local streams and play areas) contribute to bacterial, viral, and parasitic infestations resulting in acute diarrhoeal episodes and gastroenteritis. Infants are the most susceptible since they require more fluids. There is some mixed evidence of an increased tendency away from breast-feeding especially in urban areas in some parts of the developing world (Millman, 1986). Yet formula-based substitutes often require mixing with the local water (often highly contaminated), thus prolonging the diarrhoeal cycle. Epidemics of cholera in Latin America in

Table 5.6 *Meeting basic needs*

	Least developed countries			Developing countries		
	Total	Urban	Rural	Total	Urban	Rural
A. Services						
% access to safe drinking water	47	61	42	72	84	65
% access to adequate sanitation	29	57	22	39	71	22
% population below absolute poverty level	–	55	70	–	27	31
% with access to health services	45	–	–	75	–	–

	Least developed	Developing	Developed
B. Health and well-being			
% one-year-old children immunized against TB	68	84	82
% one-year-old children immunized against DPT	51	78	82
% one-year-old children immunized against polio	51	79	84
% one-year-old children immunized against measles	48	76	80
% oral rehydration therapy use	35	40	–
% of first grade enrolment reaching final grade of primary school	52	64	94
% contraceptive use	12	50	72
daily per capita calorie supply as a % of requirements	90	107	133
Total adult literacy rate (%)	47	65	–

Source: UNICEF, 1993

1992 affected 300,000 people, with 4000 deaths, many of them children (Brooke, 1992). Public awareness about the cholera outbreak prompted the use of the simplest form of preventive measures – boiling water and better sanitation practices – and it actually saved nearly 100,000 children who otherwise would have died from acute diarrhoea. Nearly 396 million children under five experienced acute diarrhoea episodes in 1988 necessitating oral rehydration therapy (UNEP, 1991), mostly in India, China and Africa.

During the next few decades, these conditions will worsen as civil strife escalates and the pace of urbanization accelerates in the developing countries putting even greater stresses on basic services such as potable water and sanitation services (Table 5.6). As urbanization continues unabated, the human condition worsens as the poor become concentrated in the squatter settlements, barrios or slums that ring most of the world's large cities. These temporary settlements provide little in the way of housing, water and sanitation. Governments try in vain to provide the basic elements of human survival – clean water, sanitation, housing – to the urban populations now, but with limited success (Easterbrook, 1994; McGranahan and Songsore, 1994). Household behaviour patterns need to change to include better hygiene, sanitation and food preparation practices. Behavioural modifications along with efforts to address the underlying causes of rapid urbanization, such as poverty, migration, development or women's status, will be required if there is to be hope for the children, or their parents for that matter.

The links between poverty and environmental degradation are important especially for countries caught in the poverty, population, environmental degradation spiral. Not only will the impacts of environmental change be greater for selected regions or people, differential adjustments to these changing conditions will take place with varying social costs and benefits. Wealth plays a role in fostering opportunities for human adjustments to environmental conditions, especially in response to changes in basic resources such as food (Kates and Haarmann, 1992; Bohle et al, 1994). Poor people simply get displaced from marginal agricultural lands often becoming environmental refugees.

Gender inequalities are an important driving force behind overpopulation in poor countries where women are caught in a vicious cycle of patriarchal societies (Dankelman and Davidson, 1988; Shiva, 1989; Rodda, 1993; Braidotti et al, 1994). A woman's worth is often measured by her ability to bear healthy children. Maternal health is compromised because of malnutrition, cultural taboos during pregnancy, anaemia and maternal mortality (UN, 1991; Holloway, 1994). Maternal mortality is still high in developing countries (420 deaths per 100,000 births compared to 15 deaths per 100,000 births in developed nations). Between 25–40 per cent of these maternal deaths are caused by unsafe abortions (Holloway, 1994). Children born to these malnourished women are underweight and often undernourished. In 1990, 43 per cent of all the infants born to women in the developing world had extremely low birth weights (less than 2500 grams) and close to 50 per cent of the children showed evidences of stunted growth at ages two to five (UNICEF, 1993). Women have more difficult pregnancies, are often less able to produce healthy children, thus their value declines even further (Jacobson, 1991).

Equal rights for women

Improving women's reproductive health and their status, in addition to reducing poverty, may help break the unsustainability cycle. However, there are many barriers that must be overcome, many that reflect procedural equity considerations. In December of 1979, the Convention on the Elimination of all Forms of Discrimination Against Women was adopted by the United Nations General Assembly. The treaty went into effect in September 1981 thereby creating an international bill of rights for women. By 1990, 102 nations had ratified the treaty, yet because of cultural and religious attitudes and mores, equal rights for women are still not a reality. Discriminatory laws against women persist in many parts of the world. Women are unable to own land or the resources on it, to obtain their own credit, and they are often legally powerless to stop domestic violence against themselves or their children. Elsewhere, there are fewer opportunities for women to achieve economic self-sufficiency. Domestic unpaid labour (most of it performed by women) is not included in national gross domestic product (GDP) calculations, in employment statistics or in financial transactions. Instead, women are most visible in the informal labour sector, where compensation is derived via bartering for goods and services not in hard currency. In the formal sector, enormous wage differentials exist between female and male workers. Segregation in the workplace still endures with women facing glass ceilings and barriers to positions that are colloquially viewed as 'men's jobs'. Female labour participation in the formal economic sector is highest in urban areas in Latin America, the Caribbean, and in the developed world. Female labour participation in the agricultural sector is highest in Africa and Asia, yet is rarely paid work. As a result of these economic barriers, there is an increasing global trend towards the feminization of poverty (World Resources Institute, 1994b).

Educationally, women lag behind men in illiteracy rates (34 per cent female illiteracy rate in 1990 compared to 19 per cent for males), despite rapid improvements during the last two decades. Generally speaking, females get less years of formal education than males, unless they come from wealthy families. Reproductive freedom and access to health services help reduce high fertility rates, reducing demands on the environmental resource base, yet these basic rights are unavailable to many women because of cultural norms or taboos, or economic limitations.

Women have the right to vote in most nations, yet they are not well represented in decision-making bodies that oversee economic development and environmental management. For example, in 1987 only 45 nations had more than 10 per cent of their parliamentary seats held by women (UN, 1991). In nearly 100 countries, women held no ministerial positions at all. Women are much more politically active at the grass roots level where they have achieved localized successes in improving environmental conditions and the health and well-being of their families.

There are still structural barriers to women's full participation in development and environmental management. In order to achieve the goal of sustainability, women must become full and equal partners. They are the bearers of children and in many instances are the primary managers of essential natural resources such as food, where they account for more than half of the food production activities in the developing world (Tolba et al, 1992, p495). As Gro Brundtland remarked in her keynote address to the International Conference on Population and Development last year, 'Women will not become more empowered merely because we want them to be, but through legislative changes, increased information, and redirection of resources' (Brundtland, 1994, p18).

Equity Reconsidered

While the 1992 Earth Summit did not provide all the answers, it ushered in the acceptance of an equity code that ensures the future viability and integrity of the Earth's environment. The linking of women's reproductive health, children's well-being, poverty, hunger, human rights and environmental degradation is the first step in this long process of achieving social, generational and procedural equity as we cope with global environmental changes. Geography matters, for it helps us see the connections between our role as agents of environmental change, the likely impacts of such changes on the physical environment and society, and how our institutions and collective behaviours can and must respond to alterations of our physical, social and psychological worlds.

As I have suggested, women and children currently bear a disproportionate burden of environmental degradation in both the developed and developing countries, yet have restricted abilities to adjust to or mitigate the consequences of these deteriorating environmental conditions. As the driving forces behind environmental change become better documented, more reliable data on the differential impacts on women and children will be available. When we can adequately document impacts, then we can address likely individual and societal adjustment strategies for these subpopulations, strategies that will no longer marginalize women and children, placing them in the *terra incognita* of forgotten casualties. Clearly, this is an urgent research need if we are going to implement equity and fairness in our policy responses to environmental change. My own bias is that the most salient issue continues to be the health and well-being of children, the next generation of environmental stewards. If our actions today prevent us from conceiving and rearing healthy offspring and providing a sustainable environmental base within which they can prosper, then we clearly have failed to achieve the ambitious equity goals set forth during the Earth Summit and reaffirmed by the Cairo Conference on Population and Development. We may never achieve this illusive goal because of our collective biases (gender, race, class, generational), but it is a goal with pursuing.

Notes

1   There are many theoretical issues in the definition of equity. Philosophical arguments focus on egalitarian views – equal rights, equal protection and the creation of a just and fair society (see Rawls, 1971, 1985; Smith, 1994). Economic arguments frame the equity issue as the monetary value of property or an ownership interest in a property. From this perspective, equity is the efficient or utilitarian allocation of resources or risk (Rees, 1990). The application of both perspectives to equity issues is best seen in the area of radioactive waste/disposal (see Kasperson, 1983; Shrader-Frechette, 1993).

2   See UN, 1991. The lower female/male ratios are partially explained by social forces that deny nutritional and health care access to females resulting in higher mortality rates. Female infanticide, abortions on the basis of male preference, widow burning and dowry deaths still persist in many regions.

References

Bohle, H. G., Downing, T. E. and Watts, M. J. (1994) 'Climate change and social vulnerability: Towards a sociology and geography of food insecurity', *Global Environmental Change*, vol 4, no 1, pp37–46

Bowen, E. L. and Hu, H. (1993) 'Food contamination due to environmental pollution' in E. Chivian, M. McCally, H. Hu and A. Haines (eds) *Critical Condition: Human Health and the Environment*, MIT Press, Cambridge, MA, pp49–70

Braidotti, R., Charkiewicz, E., Hausler, S. and Wieringa, S. (1994) *Women, the Environment and Sustainable Development*, Zed Books, London

Brooke, J. (1992) 'How the cholera scare is waking Latin America', *The New York Times*, 8 March, pE4

Brundtland, G. H. (1994) 'Empowering women: The solution to a global crisis', *Environment*, vol 36, no 10, pp16–20 (quote is from p18)

Bryant, B. and Mohai, P. (eds) (1992) *Race and the Incidence of Environmental Hazards*, Westview Press, Boulder, CO

Bullard, R. D. (1990) *Dumping in Dixie: Race, Class, and Environmental Quality*, Westview Press, Boulder, CO

Bullard, R. D. (1994) 'Overcoming racism in environmental decision-making', *Environment*, vol 36, no 4, pp10–20, 39–44

Chen, R. S. and Kates, R. W. (1994) 'World food security: Prospects and trends', *Food Policy*, vol 19, no 2, pp192–208

Christiani, D. C. (1993) 'Urban and transboundary air pollution: Human health consequences' in E. Chivian, M. McCally, H. Hu and A. Haines (eds) *Critical Condition: Human Health and the Environment*, MIT Press, Cambridge, MA, pp13–30

Committee on the Human Dimensions of Global Change (1994) *Science Priorities for the Human Dimensions of Global Change*, National Academy Press, Washington, DC

Cutter, S. L. (1993) *Living with Risk: The Geography of Technological Hazards*, Edward Arnold, London

Cutter, S. L. (1994) 'Exploiting, conserving, and preserving natural resources' in G. J. Demko and W. B. Wood (eds) *Reordering the World: Geopolitical Perspectives on the 21st Century*, Westview Press, Boulder, CO, pp123–140

Dankelman, I. and Davidson, J. (1988) *Women and Environment in the Third World*, Earthscan, London

Easterbrook, G. (1994) 'Forget PCBs, radon, alar; the world's greatest environmental dangers are dung smoke and dirty water', *The New York Times Magazine*, 11 September, pp 60–63

Goldman, B. A. and Fitton, L. (1994) *Toxic Wastes and Race Revisited*, Center for Policy Alternatives, New York

Greenberg, M. R. (1993) 'Proving environmental inequity in siting locally unwanted land uses', *4 Risk-Issues in Health and Safety*, no 235 (Summer), pp235–252

Hall, B. and Kerr, M. L. (1991) *1991–92 Green Index*, Island Press, Washington, DC

Holloway, M. (1994) 'Trends in women's health: A global view', *Scientific American*, vol 271, no 2, pp76–83

Jacobson, J. L. (1991) 'Women's reproductive health: The silent emergency', *Worldwatch Paper 102*, Worldwatch Institute, Washington, DC

Kane, D. N. and Kates, R. W. (1985) 'Environmental hazards and the lives of children' in D. N. Kane (ed) *Environmental Hazards to Young Children*, Oryx Press, Phoenix, AZ, pp1–9

Kasperson, R. E. (ed) (1983) *Equity Issues in Radioactive Waste Management*, Oelgeschlager, Gunn and Hain, Cambridge, MA

Kasperson, R. E. (1994) 'Global environmental hazards: Political issues in societal responses' in G. J. Demko and W. B. Wood (eds) *Reordering the World: Geopolitical Perspectives on the 21st Century*. Westview Press, Boulder, CO, pp141–166

Kasperson, R. E. and Dow, K. (1991) 'Developmental and geographical equity in global environmental change: A framework for analysis', *Evaluation Review*, vol 15, no 1, pp149–171

Kates, R. W. (1994) 'Extending human dimension', *Human Dimensions Quarterly*, vol 1, no 1, Winter 1994, pp1–5

Kates, R. W. and Haarmann, V. (1992) 'Where the poor live, are the assumptions correct?', *Environment*, vol 34, no 4, pp4–11, 25–28

Lemonick, M. D. (1994) 'Not so fertile ground', *Time*, 19 September, pp68–70

Manser, R. (1994) 'Going West: Market reform and the environment in Eastern Europe: The first three years', *The Ecologist*, vol 24, no 1, pp27–32

McGranahan, G. and Songsore, J. (1994) 'Wealth, health, and the urban household: Weighing environmental burdens in Accra, Jakarta, and Sao Paulo', *Environment*, vol 36, no 6, 1994, pp4–11, 49–45

Mellor, J. W. (1988) 'The intertwining of environmental problems and poverty', *Environment*, vol 30, no 9, pp8–13, 28–30

Millman, S. (1986) 'Trends in breastfeeding in a dozen developing countries', *International Family Planning Perspectives*, vol 12, no 3, pp91–95

Myers, N. (1993) *Ultimate Security: The Environmental Basis of Political Stability*, W. W. Norton, New York

Nriagu, J. (1994) 'Industrial activity and metal emissions' in R. Socolow, C. Andrews, F. Berkhout, and V. Thomas (eds) *Industrial Ecology and Global Change*, Cambridge University Press, Cambridge, MA, pp277–285

OECD (Organisation for Economic Co-operation and Development) (1991) *Environmental Data Compendium 1991*, OECD, Paris

OECD (1993) *Environmental Data Compendium 1993*, OECD, Paris

Parry, M., Goudie, A. and Williams, M. (1993) 'Editorial', *Global Environmental Change*, vol 3, no 3, pp226–227

Rawls, J. (1971) *A Theory of Justice*, Harvard University Press, Cambridge, MA

Rawls, J. (1985) 'Justice as fairness: Political not metaphysical', *Philosophy and Public Affairs*, vol 14, pp223–252

Rees, J. (1990) *Natural Resources: Allocation, Economics, and Policy*, Routledge, New York

Rodda, A. (1993) *Women and the Environment*, Zed Books, London

Seager, J. (1993) *Earth Follies: Coming to Feminist Terms with the Global Environmental Crisis*, Routledge, New York

Seigel, L., Cohen, G. and Goldman, B. (1991) *The US Military's Toxic Legacy*, National Toxic Campaign Fund, Boston, MA

Sexton, S. (1994) 'Reproductive hazards of industrial chemicals: The politics of protection', *The Ecologist*, vol 23, no 6, pp212–218

Shiva, V. (1989) *Staying Alive: Women, Ecology, and Development*, Zed Books, London

Shrader-Frechette, K. S. (1993) *Burying Uncertainty*, University of California Press, Berkeley, CA

Smith, D. M. (1994) *Geography and Social Justice*, Blackwell, Oxford

Swanston, S. F. (1994) 'Race, gender, age, and disproportionate impact: What can we do about the failure to protect the most vulnerable?' *Fordham Urban Law Journal*, vol 21, pp577–604

Timberlake, L. and Thomas, L. (1990) *When the Bough Breaks ... Our Children, Our Environment*, Earthscan, London

Tolba, M. K., El-Kholy, O. A., El-Hinnawi, E., Holdgate, M. W., McMichael, D. F. and Munn, R. E. (eds) (1992) *The World Environment 1972–1992*, Chapman and Hall, London

Turner, B. L. (1990) 'Two types of global environmental change: Definitional and spatial scale issues in their human dimensions', *Global Environmental Change*, vol 1, no 1, 1990, pp14–22

UN (United Nations) (1991) *The World's Women 1970–1990: Trends and Statistics*, United Nations, New York

UN (1992) *Agenda 21: Programme of Action for Sustainable Development*, United Nations, New York, NY

UNEP (United Nations Environment Programme) (1991) *Environmental Data Report*, 3rd Edition, Blackwell, Oxford

UNEP (1994) 'Air pollution in the world's megacities', *Environment*, vol 36, no 2, pp4–13, 25–37

UNICEF (1993) *The State of the World's Children, 1993,* Oxford University Press, Oxford

Valette, J. and Spalding, H. (eds) (1990) *The International Trade in Wastes: A Greenpeace Inventory,* Greenpeace USA, Washington, DC

Weiss, E. B. (1989) *In Fairness to Future Generations: International Law, Common Patrimony, and Intergenerational Equity,* Transnational Publishers and the United Nations University, New York

Weiss, E. B. (1990) 'In fairness to future generations', *Environment,* vol 32, no 3, pp6–11, 30–31

World Resources Institute (1991) *World Resources 1990–91,* Oxford University Press, New York

World Resources Institute (1992) *World Resources 1992–93,* Oxford University Press, New York

World Resources Institute (1994a) *The 1994 Information Please Environmental Almanac,* Houghton Mifflin, Boston, MA

World Resources Institute (1994b) *World Resources 1994–95,* Oxford University Press, New York

Zimmerman, R. (1993) 'Social equity and environmental risk', *Risk Analysis,* vol 13, no 6, pp649–666

Zimmerman, R. (1994) 'Issues of classification in environmental equity: How we manage is how we measure', *Fordham Urban Law Journal,* vol 21, pp633–669

Part II

Vulnerability to Threats

6

Vulnerability to Environmental Hazards

Susan L. Cutter

For over 50 years, hazards researchers have focused on a series of fundamental questions:

- What is the human occupancy of hazard zones?
- How do people and societies respond to environmental hazards and what factors influence their choice of adjustments?
- How do you mitigate the risk and impact of environmental hazards?

Within the last decade or so, another question was added to our ongoing list of imponderables: are societies becoming more vulnerable to environmental hazards?

Vulnerability, broadly defined as the potential for loss, is an essential concept in hazards research and is central to the development of hazard mitigation strategies at the local, national and international level. Within the framework of the UN's International Decade of Natural Disaster Reduction (IDNDR), for example, vulnerability assessments are used to determine the potential damage and loss of life from extreme natural events. They are important as well in proposing hazard reduction alternatives where mitigation normally takes the form of structural (engineered) approaches to hazard reduction (Coburn and Spence, 1992; Clayton, 1994). Rarely mentioned are the underlying causes of increased social vulnerability to hazards or disaster events. Yet, vulnerability now forms the cornerstone of international efforts aimed at reversing the poverty, population, development and environmental degradation downwards spiral. This developmental-based approach to vulnerability reduction is best seen in Cuny's (1983) classic work on *Disasters and Development*. Despite these noteworthy efforts, we still lack a common conceptualization of vulnerability.

This progress report reviews the recent research on vulnerability in the hazards field. This critical evaluation focuses on three thematic areas: the confusion and contradiction on the meaning of the term; measurement; and the causes of spatial outcomes associated with vulnerability studies. A new conceptual model of vulnerability is then proposed, the hazards of place, which clarifies many of the discrepancies found in the existing literature.

Note: Reprinted, with permission, from *Progress in Human Geography*, vol 20, no 4, Susan L. Cutter, 'Vulnerability to environmental hazards', pp529–539. © Hodder Arnold Journals, 1996

Fuzzy Definitions and Divergent Themes

To begin the discussion we need to distinguish between the origins of vulnerability, for this is often the initial point of disagreement. While the broad definition of vulnerability infers a potential for loss, it never clearly articulates what type of loss and whose loss we are describing. There is personal or individual potential for, or sensitivity to, losses (or harm) that have both spatial and non-spatial domains. This is termed individual vulnerability. Social vulnerability includes the susceptibility of social groups or society at large to potential losses (structural and non-structural) from hazard events and disasters. It has distinct spatial outcomes and varies over time. Finally, there is a potential for loss derived from the interaction of society with biophysical conditions which in turn affect the resilience of the environment to respond to the hazard or disaster, as well as influencing the adaptation of society to such changing conditions. The biophysical vulnerability also has explicit spatial outcomes. For this chapter, I will focus more on those sources of vulnerability that produce explicit spatial outcomes, social and biophysical, and describe their origins and common usage within the social science hazards literature.

Vulnerability is frequently used in the risk, hazards and disasters literature (Gilbert, 1995; Hewitt, 1983, 1995), but is becoming more prominent in the areas of global change and environment and development studies (Liverman, 1990a; Dow, 1992; Dow and Downing, 1995). Within geography, the vulnerability concept has been in use for more than a decade with one of the best conceptualizations written in the early 1980s (Timmerman, 1981). Despite more than a decade's worth of collective research experience on the concept, vulnerability still means different things to different people (Table 6.1).

Table 6.1 *Selected definitions of vulnerability*

Source	Definition
Gabor and Griffith (1980)	Vulnerability is the threat (to hazardous materials) to which people are exposed (including chemical agents and the ecological situation of the communities and their level of emergency preparedness). Vulnerability is the risk context.
Timmerman (1981)	Vulnerability is the degree to which a system acts adversely to the occurrence of a hazardous event. The degree and quality of the adverse reaction are conditioned by a system's resilience (a measure of the system's capacity to absorb and recover from the event).
UNDRO (1982)	Vulnerability is the degree of loss to a given element or set of elements at risk resulting from the occurrence of a natural phenomenon of a given magnitude.
Susman et al (1984)	Vulnerability is the degree to which different classes of society are differentially at risk.
Kates (1985)	Vulnerability is the 'capacity to suffer harm and react adversely'.
Pijawka and Radwan (1985)	Vulnerability is the threat or interaction between risk and preparedness. It is the degree to which hazardous materials threaten a particular population (risk) and the capacity of the community to reduce the risk or adverse consequences of hazardous materials releases.

Table 6.1 *Selected definitions of vulnerability*

Source	Definition
Bogard (1989)	Vulnerability is operationally defined as the inability to take effective measures to insure against losses. When applied to individuals, vulnerability is a consequence of the impossibility or improbability of effective mitigation and is a function of our ability to detect the hazards.
Mitchell (1989)	Vulnerability is the potential for loss.
Liverman (1990a)	Distinguishes between vulnerability as a biophysical condition and vulnerability as defined by political, social and economic conditions of society. She argues for vulnerability in geographic space (where vulnerable people and places are located) and vulnerability in social space (who in that place is vulnerable).
Downing (1991b)	Vulnerability has three connotations: it refers to a consequence (e.g. famine) rather than a cause (e.g. drought); it implies an adverse consequence (e.g. maize yields are sensitive to drought; households are vulnerable to hunger); and it is a relative term that differentiates among socio-economic groups or regions, rather than an absolute measure of deprivation.
Dow (1992)	Vulnerability is the differential capacity of groups and individuals to deal with hazards, based on their positions within physical and social worlds.
Smith (1992)	Risk from a specific hazard varies through time and according to changes in either (or both) physical exposure or human vulnerability (the breadth of social and economic tolerance available at the same site).
Alexander (1993)	Human vulnerability is a function of the costs and benefits of inhabiting areas at risk from natural disaster.
Cutter (1993)	Vulnerability is the likelihood that an individual or group will be exposed to and adversely affected by a hazard. It is the interaction of the hazards of place (risk and mitigation) with the social profile of communities.
Watts and Bohle (1993)	Vulnerability is defined in terms of exposure, capacity and potentiality. Accordingly, the prescriptive and normative response to vulnerability is to reduce exposure, enhance coping capacity, strengthen recovery potential and bolster damage control (i.e. minimize destructive consequences) via private and public means.
Blaikie et al (1994)	By vulnerability we mean the characteristics of a person or group in terms of their capacity to anticipate, cope with, resist and recover from the impact of a natural hazard. It involves a combination of factors that determine the degree to which someone's life and livelihood are put at risk by a discrete and identifiable event in nature or in society.
Bohle et al (1994)	Vulnerability is best defined as an aggregate measure of human welfare that integrates environmental, social, economic and political exposure to a range of potential harmful perturbations. Vulnerability is a multi-layered and multidimensional social space defined by the determinate, political, economic and institutional capabilities of people in specific places at specific times.
Dow and Downing (1995)	Vulnerability is the differential susceptibility of circumstances contributing to vulnerability. Biophysical, demographic, economic, social and technological factors such as population ages, economic dependency, racism and age of infrastructure are some factors which have been examined in association with natural hazards.

Many of the discrepancies in the meanings of vulnerability arise from different epistemological orientations (political ecology, human ecology, physical science, spatial analysis) and subsequent methodological practices. Also, there is considerable variation in the choice of hazards themselves (famine, floods, drought, seismic events, technology) and in the regions chosen for examination (developed versus developing countries). Fundamental conceptual differences exist, as well, visions that either focus research on the likelihood of exposure (biophysical/technological risk), the likelihood of adverse consequences (social vulnerability) or some combination of the two. The result is a confused lexicon of meanings and approaches to understanding vulnerability to environmental hazards. At the very least, some form of clarification or consistency in our use of vulnerability would be helpful if we are to advance our theoretical and practical understanding of how and why places and people are vulnerable to environmental hazards. At this juncture, one can find three distinct themes in vulnerability studies, although others-have suggested alternative categorizations (Liverman, 1990a; Dow, 1992). They are vulnerability as risk/hazard exposure; vulnerability as social response; and vulnerability of places. While not mutually exclusive nor exhaustive, this typology helps to distinguish between the theoretical and methodological orientations of the current research.

Vulnerability as pre-existing condition

The first research theme examines the source (or potential exposure or risk) of biophysical or technological hazards. These studies are characterized by a focus on the distribution of some hazardous condition, the human occupancy of this hazardous zone (e.g. floodplains, coastal areas, seismic zones) and the degree of loss (life and property) associated with the occurrence of a particular event (flood, hurricane, earthquake). Magnitude, duration, impact, frequency and rapidity of onset all characterize these exposure or biophysical vulnerability studies (Chapter 2; see also Hewitt and Burton, 1971; Gabor and Griffith, 1980; Ambraseys and Jackson, 1981; Gabor and Pelanda, 1982; UNDRO, 1982; Pijawka and Radwan, 1985; Cutter and Solecki, 1989; Heyman et al, 1991; Burton et al, 1992; Haque and Blair, 1992; Quarantelli, 1992; Swearingen, 1992; Alexander, 1993; Parrish et al, 1993). A subset of studies examines the distribution of structural losses and vulnerability reduction in the built environment associated with natural disasters events (Harlan, 1988; Coburn and Spence, 1992; Corsanego et al, 1993; Tavakoli and Tavakoli, 1993; Solway, 1994).

Vulnerability as tempered response

The second group of vulnerability studies focuses on coping responses including societal resistance and resilience to hazards. The nature of the hazardous event or condition is usually taken as a given, or at the very minimum viewed as a social construct not a biophysical condition. Much of the research examines chronic disturbances such as drought, famine, hunger, climate change or environmental change (Susman et al, 1984; Bogard, 1989; Chambers, 1989; Anderson and Woodrow, 1991; Downing, 1991a, b; 1992; Watts and Bohle, 1993; Blaikie et al,

1994; Bohle et al, 1994; Chen, 1994; Yarnal, 1994). This perspective highlights the social construction of vulnerability, a condition rooted in historical, cultural social and economic processes that impinge on the individual's or society's ability to cope with disasters and adequately respond to them.

Vulnerability as hazard of place

While vulnerability as potential exposure or social response pervades the literature, a third direction is emerging that combines elements of the two, but which is inherently more geographically centred. In this perspective, vulnerability is conceived as both a biophysical risk as well as a social response, but within a specific areal or geographic domain. This can be geographic space, where vulnerable people and places are located, or social space, who in those places are most vulnerable. Recently, a number of researchers have used this integrative approach in a wide array of spatial contexts or places (local, regional, national) (Blaikie and Brookfield, 1987; Wilhite and Easterling, 1987; Mitchell et al, 1989; Lewis, 1987, 1990; Liverman, 1986, 1990b; Palm and Hodgson, 1992a, b; Degg, 1993; Longhurst, 1995).

Measurement and Assessment Techniques

While the three theoretical streams run parallel courses, the methodological approaches to vulnerability are highly varied. Since there is little consistency in the definitions of vulnerability, we would expect it to be quite difficult to operationalize the concept using specific variables or indicators. Remarkably, the measurement task is somewhat easier than the definitional one. Variables related to exposure normally include proximity to the source of threat, incident frequency or probability, magnitude, duration or spatial impact. Social impact and response are often measured by threats to lifelines or infrastructure to support basic needs (Gasser and Snitofsky, 1990; Platt, 1991), special needs populations (children, elderly, infirm), poverty/wealth indicators, gender, race and so forth. Often, the vulnerability indicators are single variables but multidimensional factors such as food aid, institutional development, social relations or political power have been employed as well (Watts and Bohle, 1993; Blaikie et al, 1994).

Geographic scale poses another measurement difficulty for vulnerability with applications ranging from local to global scales. Detailed vulnerability assessments are conducted most often at the micro or local level (Colten, 1986; 1991; OAS, 1991) with an occasional regional application (Downing, 1992; Lowry et al, 1995). Methodological decisions often mean sacrificing localized detailed case-study approaches for more broadly based patterns and distributions. The choice of areal unit within local studies also ranges from individual household level to geopolitical census units.

The time dimension poses other problematic issues for vulnerability studies. There are relatively few historical treatments of vulnerability with the exception of Colten's (1988, 1993) work on hazardous waste in Illinois. The temporal context of vulnerability is crucial, as alluded to elsewhere (Cutter, 1993), yet the temporal dimension remains one of the least studied aspects of vulnerability. It is unclear, at this time, why this is so.

Lastly, the techniques used in vulnerability studies are diverse as well. The analytical approaches closely follow research paradigms and run the gamut from historical narratives (Colten, 1991), contextual analyses (Mitchell et al, 1989), case studies (Liverman, 1990b), to statistical analyses, GIS and mapping techniques (McMaster and Johnson, 1987; McMaster, 1988; Burke, 1993; Parrish et al, 1993; von Braun, 1993; Wadge et al, 1993; Hepner and Finco, 1995).

Causal Linkages and Spatial Outcomes

The vulnerability literature is bifurcated when it comes to an understanding of causes of vulnerability, which is not a surprise considering the different theoretical orientations. The vast majority of vulnerability studies take a political-economic perspective and suggest a causal structure that concentrates on the differential social impacts and abilities to cope with the crisis at hand. Causal explanations of the vulnerability arise from underlying social conditions that often are quite remote from the initiating event itself (e.g. a natural event, technological failure). Others contend that vulnerability is locationally driven and is a function of the proximity to the source of the threat.

Causal structure

The causes of social vulnerability are explained by the underlying social conditions that are often quite remote from the initiating hazard or disaster event. For example, Watts and Bohle (1993) propose one such explanatory model in their analysis of hunger and famine. In their view, vulnerability is defined by three processes: entitlement (or economic capability), empowerment (political/social power) and political economy (historical/structural class-based patterns of social reproduction). They suggest that the intersection of these tripartite processes produces the social space of vulnerability. This model is then applied to a comparative study of south Asia and sub-Saharan Africa to examine famine vulnerability over space and time. In a subsequent analysis (Bohle et al, 1994), the model is used to explain the social context of hunger and famine and vulnerability to climate change in Zimbabwe.

In another formulation, Blaikie et al, (1994) examine causality using two alternative models: the pressure and release model (PAR) and the access to resources model. The PAR model provides an explanation of the relationship between processes that give rise to 'unsafe conditions' (e.g. exposure) and their intersection with some type of hazard or disaster event, thus creating a form of social vulnerability. The focus is clearly on the dynamic pressures and underlying driving forces that give rise to vulnerability in the first place. The access to resources model is a more refined explanation of the role of political and economic forces as the root cause of the unsafe conditions.

Vulnerability/exposure assessments

Another approach to understanding causality found in the literature explains the out-come by modelling the potential exposure to hazards. The assumption, of course, is that vulnerability is primarily a function of the proximity to the source of the risk or hazard in question (Alexander, 1993). A simple mapping of the biophysical risk should result in a simplistic delineation of the likely exposure or biophysical vulnerability. Palm and Hodgson's (1992a) work on seismic mapping in relation to earthquake insurance purchase is a good example of this approach.

Within the hazards management community, vulnerability assessments are extensively used to delineate, characterize and assess the hazard with an eye towards the development of some mitigation strategy. The US Federal Emergency Management Agency's (FEMA's) floodplain maps are one example of simple vulnerability assessments. The Organization of American States (OAS, 1991) also developed a series of multi-hazard maps that incorporate vulnerability assessments into their pre-impact planning and mitigation efforts. These assessments include human populations, critical facilities and lifelines, economic production facilities, and differences in vulnerability among economic sectors. All these are mapped to illustrate both the biophysical/technological risk as well as the impact of this risk on these vulnerable indicators (population, economic activity, lifelines).

More recently, governmental agencies are using computer-assisted emergency information systems that incorporate some vulnerability indicators into them. For example, the USNOAA's Areal Locations of Hazardous Atmospheres (ALOHA) provides a plume dispersion model designed for airborne toxic releases to ascertain the risk to populations from potential chemical exposure. The US Environmental Protection Agency's (EPA's) Computer-Aided Management of Emergency Operations (CAMEO) focuses more on preimpact planning and during-hazard event responses, again utilizing exposure indicators and populations at risk. The same is true of the National Response Team's manual for hazardous material spills (NRT, 1987). Included in these documents are potential scenarios on likely exposures and some indicators of demographic distributions and critical facilities, all indicators of social and biophysical vulnerability. Commercial emergency information systems vendors also provide software for exposure and vulnerability assessments from a wide range of hazards. This increased use of geographic information systems (GIS) and related technologies by researchers, managers, governmental agencies and non-governmental groups interested in hazards and disasters is prompting us to reconsider our understanding of vulnerability, both in theoretical and applied ways.

Towards a New Synthesis: The Hazards of Place Revisited

In struggling with these issues for many years, it became necessary to clarify my own thinking and interest in vulnerability. Largely working within the North American context and with a category of hazards that arose from the interaction between nature, society and technology, it was clear to me that many of the existing theoretical constructs were either too limiting or too diffuse to be of practical use to the problems I examined. Out of a sense of intellectual continuity,

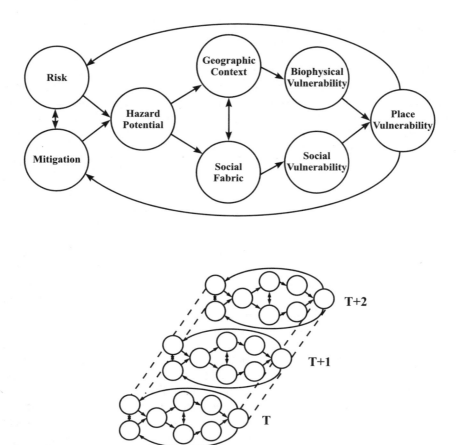

Note: The various elements that constitute vulnerability interact to produce the vulnerability of specific places and the people who live there (top). This vulnerability can change over time (bottom) based on changes in the risk, mitigation and contexts within which environmental hazards occur.

Figure 6.1 *The hazards of place model of vulnerability*

I returned to the original work of Hewitt and Burton (1971) on the hazardousness of places where they attempted a multi-hazard mapping exercise to delineate a regional ecology of natural hazards events. Borrowing from them, the initial hazards of place model was proposed (Cutter and Solecki, 1989), and then tested with other hazards (Solecki, 1990; Tiefenbacher, 1992; Cutter, 1993).

The model of vulnerability in Figure 6.1 is the culmination of this journey coupled with inputs from the recent literature. It is exploratory in nature, but serves as a useful heuristic in understanding the diverse elements that contribute to our understanding of the vulnerability of places. There is an explicit focus on locality within this conceptual framework, for it is place that forms the fundamental unit of analysis for any geographer. The model is simplistic in its presentation, yet we must understand that all the parameters change over time (as shown on the bottom half of the diagram). Also, each of the major indicators consists of a series of nested or contextual arrangements that influence it, which could easily be expanded but are not in this review.

Risk is the likelihood of occurrence (or probability) of the hazard. Risk has two domains: it includes the potential sources of risk (industrial, flooding, transportation) and the contextual nature of the risk itself (high consequence, low consequence). The second domain is a simple probabilistic estimate based on the frequency of occurrence (100-year flood, 5 per cent risk). Risks combine with mitigation (efforts to reduce risks such as planning, prior experience) to create an overall hazard potential. Risks can be attenuated with good mitigation or they can be amplified by poor or non-existent mitigation practices. The hazard potential is filtered through the social fabric of society (socio-economic indicators, cognition of risk, individual/societal ability to respond) to determine the overall social vulnerability of the place. The hazard potential is also filtered through its geographic context (site and situation, proximity) to determine biophysical/technological vulnerability. It is the intersection and interaction of both the social vulnerability and biophysical/technological vulnerability that create the vulnerability of places. The place vulnerability provides a feedback loop to both the risk and mitigation, which in turn further reduces or enhances both risk and mitigation.

The hazards of place model is a useful construct for examining vulnerability and incorporates the range of theoretical and conceptual issues outlined in this chapter. As was illustrated, vulnerability was traditionally viewed as either a pre-existing condition or potential exposure to a risk (biophysical) or as a social condition predisposing some response to an environmental threat (social vulnerability). The merger of these permits an examination of both the biophysical and social vulnerabilities as they affect places. The hazards of place model can facilitate a single or multihazards approach with differing hazard characteristics (chronic and acute), contrasting contexts (social, political, economic) and diverse methodological approaches (historical, GIS, descriptive, empirical). While empirical verification is still at a nascent stage, the simplicity of the hazards of place model suggests wide application in our comparative understanding of vulnerable places and the people who live there.

References

Alexander, D. (1993) *Natural Disasters*, Chapman & Hall, New York

Ambraseys, N. N. and Jackson, J. A. (1981) 'Earthquake hazard and vulnerability in the northeastern Mediterranean: The Corinth earthquake sequence of February–March 1981', *Disasters*, vol 5, pp355–368

Anderson, M. B. and Woodrow, P. J. (1991) 'Reducing vulnerability to drought and famine: Developmental approaches to relief', *Disasters*, vol 15, pp43–54

Blaikie, P. and Brookfield, (1987) *Land Degradation and Society*, Methuen, London

Blaikie, P., Cannon, T., Davis, I. and Wisner, B. (1994) *At Risk: Natural Hazards, People's Vulnerability, and Disasters*, Routledge, London

Bogard, W. C. (1989) 'Bringing social theory to hazards research: Conditions and consequences of the mitigation of environmental hazards', *Sociological Perspectives*, vol 31, pp147–168

Bohle, H. G., Downing, T. E. and Watts, M. J. (1994) 'Climate change and social vulnerability: The sociology and geography of food insecurity', *Global Environmental Change*, vol 4, pp37–48

Burke, L. (1993) 'Race and environmental equity: A geographic analysis in Los Angeles', *GeoInfo Systems*, October, pp44–50

Burton, I., Kates, R. W. and White, G. F. (1992) *The Environment as Hazard*. Oxford University Press, New York

Chambers, R. (1989) 'Vulnerability, coping and policy', *IDS Bulletin*, vol 20, pp1–7

Chen, R. S. (1994) 'The human dimension of vulnerability' in R. Socolow, C. Andrews, F. Berkhout and V. Thomas (eds) *Industrial Ecology and Global Change*, Cambridge University Press, Cambridge, UK, pp85–105

Clayton, A. (1994) 'IDNDR conference: Protecting vulnerable communities', the Royal Society and the Institution of Civil Engineers, London, 13–15 October 1993, *Disasters*, vol 18, pp89–90

Coburn, A. and Spence, R. (1992) *Earthquake Protection*, John Wiley, New York

Colten, C. E. (1986) 'Industrial wastes in southeast Chicago: Production and disposal 1870–1970', *Environmental Review*, vol 10, pp92–105

Colten, C. E. (1988) 'Historical questions in hazardous waste management', *Public Historian*, vol 10, pp7–20

Colten, C. E. (1991) 'A historical perspective on industrial wastes and groundwater contamination', *Geographical Review*, vol 81, pp215–228

Colten, C. E. (1993) 'The historical hazard GIS', *Illinois GIS and Mapnotes*, summer, pp48–49

Corsanego, A., Giorgini, G. and Roggeri, G. (1993) 'Rapid evaluation of an indicator of seismic vulnerability in small urban nuclei', *Natural Hazards*, vol 8, pp109–120

Cuny, F. C. (1983) *Disasters and Development*, Oxford University Press, New York

Cutter, S. L. (1993) *Living with Risk*, Edward Arnold, London

Cutter, S. L. and Solecki, W. D. (1989) 'The national pattern of airborne toxic releases', *The Professional Geographer*, vol 41, pp149–161

Degg, M. (1993) 'Earthquake hazard, vulnerability and response', *Geography*, vol 78, pp165–170

Dow, K. (1992) 'Exploring differences in our common future(s): The meaning of vulnerability to global environmental change', *Geoforum*, vol 23, pp417–436

Dow, K. and Downing, T. E. (1995) 'Vulnerability research: Where things stand', *Human Dimensions Quarterly*, vol 1, pp3–5

Downing, T. E. (1991a) *Assessing Socio-economic Vulnerability to Famine. A Report to the US Agency for International Development (AID), Famine Early Warning System (FEWS) Project*, AID/FEWS, Washington, DC, and Alan Shawn Feinstein Hunger Program, Brown University, Providence, RI

Downing, T. E. (1991b) 'Vulnerability to hunger and coping with climate change in Africa', *Global Environmental Change*, vol 1, pp365–380

Downing, T. E. (1992) *Climate Change and Vulnerable Places: Global Food Security and Country Studies in Zimbabwe, Kenya, Senegal and Chile. Research Report 1*, Environmental Change Unit, University of Oxford, Oxford

Gabor, T. and Griffith, T. K. (1980) 'The assessment of community vulnerability to acute hazardous materials incidents', *Journal of Hazardous Materials*, vol 8, pp323–333

Gabor, T. and Pelanda, C. (1982) 'Assessing differences in chemical disaster-proneness: The community chemical hazard vulnerability inventory', *Disasters*, vol 6, pp215–221

Gasser, J. and Snitofsky, E. (1990) 'Vulnerability analyses plan for wastewater emergencies', *American City and County*, vol 105, pp81–82

Gilbert, C. (1995) 'Studying disaster: A review of the main conceptual tools'. *International Journal of Mass Emergencies and Disasters*, vol 13, pp231–240

Haque, C. E. and Blair, D. (1992) 'Vulnerability to tropical cyclones: Evidence from the April 1991 cyclone in coastal Bangladesh', *Disasters*, vol 16, pp217–229

Harlan, M. (1988) *An Earthquake Vulnerability Analysis of the Charleston, South Carolina Area: Final Report*, The Citadel, Department of Civil Engineering, Charleston, SC

Hepner, G. F. and Finco, M. V. (1995) 'Modeling dense gaseous contaminant pathways over complex terrain using a geographic information system', *Journal of Hazardous Materials*, vol 42, pp187–199

Hewitt, K. (ed) (1983) *Interpretations of Calamity*, Allen & Unwin, Winchester, MA

Hewitt, K. (1995) 'Excluded perspectives in the social construction of disaster', *International Journal of Mass Emergencies and Disasters*, vol 13, pp317–339

Hewitt, K. and Burton, I. (1971) *The Hazardousness of a Place: A Regional Ecology of Damaging Events*, Research Publication 6, Department of Geography, University of Toronto, Canada

Heyman, B. N., Davis, C. and Krumpe, P. F. (1991) 'An assessment of worldwide disaster vulnerability', *Disaster Management*, vol 4, pp3–14

Kates, R. W. (1985) 'The interaction of climate and society' in R. W. Kates, J. H. Ausubel, and M. Berberian (eds) *Climate impact assessment*, SCOPE 27, John Wiley, New York, pp3–36

Lewis, J. (1987) 'Risk, vulnerability, and survival: Some post-Chernobyl implications of people, planning, and civil defence', *Local Government Studies*, July/August, pp75–93

Lewis, J. (1990) 'The vulnerability of small island states to sea level rise: The need for holistic strategies', *Disasters*, vol 14, pp241–249

Liverman, D. (1986) 'The vulnerability of urban areas to technological risks', *Cities*, May, pp142–147

Liverman, D. (1990a) 'Vulnerability to global environmental change' in R. E. Kasperson, K. Dow, D. Golding and J. X. Kasperson (eds) *Understanding Global Environmental Change: The Contributions of Risk Analysis and Management*, The Earth Transformed Program, Clark University, Worcester, MA, pp27–44

Liverman, D. (1990b) 'Drought in Mexico: Climate, agriculture, technology and land tenure in Sonora and Puebla', *Annals of the Association of American Geographers*, vol 80, pp49–72

Longhurst, R. (1995) 'The assessment of community vulnerability in hazard prone areas', Conference report, *Disasters*, vol 19, pp269–270

Lowry, J. H., Miller, H. J. and Hepner, G. F. (1995) 'A GIS-based sensitivity analysis of community vulnerability to hazardous contaminants on the Mexico/US border', *Photogrammetric Engineering and Remote Sensing*, vol 61, pp1347–1359

McMaster, R. B. (1988) 'Modeling community vulnerability to hazardous materials using geographic information systems' in *Proceedings, Third International Symposium on Spatial Data Handling, Sydney*, pp143–156

McMaster, R. B. and Johnson, J. H., jr (1987) 'Assessing community vulnerability to hazardous materials with a geographic information system' in N. R. Chrisman (ed) *AutoCarto 8 Proceedings*, American Society for Photogrammetry and American Congress on Surveying and Mapping, Falls Church, VA, pp471–480

Mitchell, J. K. (1989) 'Hazards research' in G. L. Gaile and C. J. Willmott (eds) *Geography in America*, Merrill, Columbus, OH, pp410–424

Mitchell, J. K., Devine, N. and Jagger, K. (1989) 'A contextual model of natural hazard', *Geographical Review*, vol 79, pp391–409

NRT (National Response Team) (1987) *Hazardous Materials Emergency Planning Guide (NRT–1)*, National Response Team, Washington, DC

OAS (Organization of American States) (1991) *Primer on Natural Hazard Management in Integrated Regional Development Planning*, Department of Regional Development and Environment, Executive Secretariat for Economic and Social Affairs, OAS, Washington, DC

Palm, R. I. and Hodgson, M. E. (1992a) 'Earthquake insurance: Mandated disclosure, and homeowner response in California', *Annals of the Association of American Geographers*, vol 82, pp207–222

Palm, R. I. and Hodgson, M. E. (1992b) *After a California Earthquake: Attitude and Behavior Change*, Geography Research Paper no 233, University of Chicago Press, Chicago, IL

Parrish, D. A., Townsend, L., Saunders, J., Carney, G. and Langston, C. (1993) 'US EPA Region 6 comparative risk project: Evaluating ecological risk' in M. F. Goodchild, B. O. Parks and L. T. Steyaert (eds) *Environmental modeling with GIS*, Oxford University Press, New York, pp348–352

Pijawka, K. D. and Radwan, A. E. (1985) 'The transportation of hazardous materials: Risk assessment and hazard management', *Dangerous Properties of Industrial Materials Report*, September/October, pp2–11

Platt, R. (1991) 'Lifelines: An emergency management priority for the United States in the 1990s', *Disasters*, vol 15, pp172–176

Quarantelli, E. L. (1992) *Urban Vulnerability and Technological Hazards in Developing Societies. Article 236*, Disaster Research Center, University of Delaware, Newark, DE

Smith, K. (1992) *Environmental Hazards: Assessing Risk and Reducing Disaster*, Routledge, London

Solecki, W. D. (1990) 'Acute chemical disasters and rural United States hazardscapes', unpublished PhD dissertation, Department of Geography, Rutgers University

Solway, L. (1994) 'Urban developments and megacities: Vulnerability to natural disasters', *Disaster Management*, vol 6, pp160–169

Susman, P., O'Keefe, P. and Wisner, B. (1984) 'Global disasters: A radical interpretation' in K. Hewitt (ed) *Interpretations of Calamity*, Allen & Unwin, Boston, MA, pp264–283

Swearingen, W. D. (1992) 'Drought hazard in Morocco', *Geographical Review*, vol 82, pp401–412

Tavakoli, B. and Tavakoli, S. (1993) 'Estimating the vulnerability and loss functions of residential buildings', *Natural Hazards*, vol 7, pp155–171

Tiefenbacher, J. P. (1992) 'Pesticide drift and the hazards of place in San Joaquin County, California', unpublished PhD dissertation, Department of Geography, Rutgers University

Timmerman, P. (1981) *Vulnerability, Resilience and the Collapse of Society*, Environmental Monograph 1, Institute for Environmental Studies, Toronto, Canada

UNDRO (United Nations Disaster Relief Organization) (1982) *Natural Disasters and Vulnerability Analysis*, Office of the United Nations Disaster Relief Coordinator, Geneva, Switzerland

von Braun, M. (1993) 'The use of GIS in assessing exposure and remedial alternatives at Superfund sites' in M. F. Goodchild, B. O. Parks and L. T. Steyaert (eds) *Environmental Modeling with GIS*, Oxford University Press, New York, pp339–347

Wadge, G., Wislocki, A. P. and Pearson, E. J. (1993) 'Spatial analysis in GIS for natural hazard assessment' in M. F. Goodchild, B. O. Parks and L. T. Steyaert (eds) *Environmental Modeling with GIS*, Oxford University Press, New York, pp332–338

Watts, M. J. and Bohle, H. G. (1993) 'The space of vulnerability: The causal structure of hunger and famine', *Progress in Human Geography*, vol 17, pp43–67

Wilhite, D. and Easterling, W. (eds) (1987) *Planning for Drought: Toward a Reduction of Societal Vulnerability*, Westview Press, Boulder, CO

Yarnal, B. (1994) 'Socioeconomic restructuring and vulnerability to environmental hazards in Bulgaria', *Disasters*, vol 18, pp95–106

7

Revealing the Vulnerability of People and Places: A Case Study of Georgetown County, South Carolina

Susan L. Cutter, Jerry T. Mitchell and Michael S. Scott

A profound change in governmental disaster management has occurred during the last two decades. Gone are the days of 'hunkering down' and riding out the hazard event with a command and control mentality that only focused on clean-up and the rescue of survivors. In its place is an emphasis on the reduction of loss of life and property through mitigation, preparedness, response and recovery. The impetus for change was spurred largely by the costly disasters of the last decade: the Loma Prieta earthquake and Hurricane Hugo (1989), Hurricane Andrew (1992), the Midwest floods (1993 and 1995), the Northridge earthquake (1994) and, most recently, Hurricane Floyd (1999). Pressed by Congress, the Federal Emergency Management Agency (FEMA) reprioritized its mission toward reducing future hazard impacts by implementing the National Mitigation Strategy (FEMA, 1995).

One core element of the National Mitigation Strategy is hazard identification and risk assessment. A guiding principle behind this element is that risk reduction measures for one hazard should be compatible with risk reduction measures for other hazards. This eliminates the possible substitution of one risk for another, such as relocating people from a floodplain to higher ground, which turns out to be a landslide-prone hillside. Mitigating against the effects of potential disasters and having the appropriate infrastructure in place for response requires detailed knowledge on the vulnerability of the places to a wide range of environmental hazards. To assist in developing such an 'all-hazards' assessment, FEMA and the National Emergency Management Association (NEMA) unveiled a *State Capability Assessment for Readiness*, which provides an objective way to gauge hazard

Note: Reprinted, with permission, from *Annals of the Association of American Geographers*, vol 90, no 4, Susan L. Cutter, Jerry T. Mitchell, and Michael S. Scott, 'Revealing the vulnerability of people and places: A case study of Georgetown County, South Carolina', pp713–737. © Blackwell Publishing, 2000

mitigation and preparedness (FEMA and NEMA, 1997). This publication was supplemented with a primer on hazard identification and assessment at the state level only (FEMA, 1997). While laudatory in scope, the FEMA guidelines defined hazard vulnerability as the mere presence or absence of a source of risk such as earthquake faults, coastal areas or rivers.

The degree to which populations are vulnerable to hazards is not solely dependent on proximity to the potential source of the threat. Social factors such as wealth and housing characteristics can contribute to greater vulnerability on the part of some population subgroups. As White and Haas (1975, p8) noted almost 25 years ago, the following factors contribute to the nation's vulnerability to hazards:

- Population shifts from rural to urban to suburban and exurban result in more people living in seismic risk areas, unregulated floodplains, and exposed coastal locations.
- Increased mobility means that more people live in new surroundings and are unfamiliar with the risks in their area and how to respond to them.
- Economies of scale in industries result in plants being located in high-risk areas, since industry can often absorb the costs. When the plants locate in hazardous areas, so do employees and their families, thus increasing vulnerability.
- The increase in new housing starts from manufactured housing (mobile homes) means that more people are living in dwellings that are likely to be damaged by natural hazards.

These factors are just as germane now as they were in the 1970s. More important, the density of infrastructure, the sheer number of people living in riskier areas, and the increasing disparities in wealth and socio-economic status increase the potential for greater human losses to hazards in the future (Mileti, 1999). Yet a discussion on the role of social indicators in enhancing or reducing vulnerability is non-existent in the FEMA guidance.

This chapter uses a conceptual model of vulnerability that incorporates both biophysical and social indicators to provide an all-hazards assessment of vulnerability at the local level. The descriptive approach is designed to aid in our understanding of the complexities of vulnerability and to see how it plays out in a real-world setting. We selected the county scale and used sub-county social and hazard indicators as much as possible. The selection of Georgetown County, South Carolina as our study site was driven by three considerations. First, the research team has extensive experience and knowledge of the area. Second, the county has a vast array of different types of hazards and a broad socio-demographic profile. Last, our ability to construct and enhance the contextual nature of the data is facilitated by this geographic scale of analysis.

Rediscovering Geography as Human Ecology

The initial birth of hazards research in geography is attributed to Harlan Barrows and his presentation of 'geography as human ecology' (Barrows, 1923). Employing the human ecological approach, Barrows and his students delved into the study of how people and society adjust to environmental extremes, most notably floods (Kates and Burton, 1986). The research was driven not only by intellectual curiosity, but also by a desire to solve a practical problem. Gilbert White's work (1945, 1964), in particular, was significant in rethinking and reshaping national flood-management policy. Decades later, another geographer, Gerry Galloway, had a similar impact on national flood policy following the disastrous 1993 Midwest floods (Interagency Floodplain Management Review Committee, 1994).

White and his students (first at the University of Chicago and later at the University of Colorado) formed the core of natural-hazards researchers well into the 1970s. This ensemble of researchers focused on:

- the identification and distribution of hazards;
- the range of adjustments that are available to individuals and society; and
- how people perceive and make choices regarding hazard events.

The culmination of much of this research was presented in *The Environment as Hazard* (Burton et al, 1978). The traditional natural hazards approach soon evolved into a pragmatic geographic response to broader societal issues.

The historic emphasis in hazards research on solving practical problems produced a number of critiques among the research community during subsequent decades, which expounded on the lack or narrowness of theory underpinning hazards research (Hewitt, 1983, 1997; Watts, 1983; Oliver-Smith, 1986; Alexander, 1991, 1997; Lindell, 1997). In addition to the narrowness of the theory and the singular focus on extreme natural events, criticisms included a lack of international research sources, an ignorance of the anthropological literature on human–environment relations (Torry, 1979), and the more contemporary view that natural hazards are socially and culturally constructed (O'Keefe et al, 1976; Douglas and Wildavsky, 1982; Susman et al, 1983; Johnson and Covello, 1989; Krimsky and Golding, 1992; Blaikie et al, 1994; Palm and Carroll, 1998).

Although extreme natural events have long been the primary research focus, the recognition that hazards are not just physical events, but also include socially constructed situations, has broadened both the definition of hazard and geographers' approaches toward understanding and ameliorating them. Technological failures and risk management received considerable attention by geographers (Kates et al, 1985; Sorenson et al, 1987; Cutter, 1993; Mitchell, 1998). The extensive occurrence of these types of hazards and their rising attention level among the public and decision-makers are driving this current research focus much like the pragmatic concerns of the Cold War era defined disaster research from 1950–1980 (Quarantelli, 1988). Indeed, the distinction between natural and technological hazards is now blurred, with hazards viewed as a continuum of interactions among physical, social and technological systems. In fact, global environmental change and awareness of technological hazards caused by natural events contributed to this reconceptualization.

Acknowledging the critiques of the natural hazards paradigm, especially from the political economy perspective, hazards research now considers not only the hazards themselves, but the particular contexts in which they are embedded. This context includes the geography of the event and the physical properties of the hazards (physical geography), as well as aspects of the social, political, spatial, temporal, organizational and economic milieu within which the hazard takes place. One approach, *hazards in context,* is best embodied in the work of Mitchell et al (1989) and Palm (1990). This research methodology uses both empirical and social analyses and recognizes that hazards are inherently complex physical and social phenomena. Geographic scale is a central component in this perspective.

Another approach is derived from the risk research community. In their pioneering work, Kasperson et al (1988) suggest that risks (the term hazards easily could be substituted) interact with cultural, social and institutional processes in such a way as to either temper public response or heighten it. This *social amplification of risk* model helps us to interpret public perceptions and, ultimately, policy responses to risk and hazards in contemporary society.

A third perspective examines vulnerability – its causal structure, spatial variability and methods for reduction. Broadly defined, vulnerability is the potential for loss of property or life from environmental hazards, although there are many competing and contradictory definitions of the concept, as pointed out elsewhere (Chapter 6). Individual vulnerability, for example, refers to a specific individual or structure and is most often examined by the health and engineering sciences respectively. Social and biophysical vulnerability are broader in scope and refer to social groups and landscapes that have the potential for loss from environmental hazards events. Most of the hazards literature examines vulnerability as a preexisting condition (e.g. potential exposure), largely describing the biophysical forces that produce risks and hazards (Chapter 2; see also Burton et al, 1993). The geographical manifestation of this perspective is a locationally dependent analysis based on proximity to the source of the threat. Other research suggests, however, that the causal structure of vulnerability may be dependent upon the underlying social conditions that are often temporally and geographically remote from the initiating hazard event. The term *social vulnerability* is used to define the susceptibility of social groups to potential losses from hazard events or society's resistance and resilience to hazards (Blaikie et al, 1994; Hewitt, 1997). The nature of the hazard event itself is usually taken as a given, for this research normally highlights the historical, cultural, social and political processes that give rise to 'unsafe' conditions in the first place. Most of the social-vulnerability literature examines slow onset or chronic types of hazards, such as industrial pollution (Yarnal, 1994), global environmental change (Dow, 1992), or drought and famine (Bohle et al, 1994).

While the notion of vulnerability as potential exposure or social resilience is most prevalent in the literature, the integration of the two is occurring with a more pronounced focus on specific places or locations. The concepts of vulnerability and multiple hazards in a place *(hazard of place)* encompass both biophysical and social vulnerability, and are applied to many geographic domains ranging from the local to the global. Examples of the integration of biophysical and social vulnerability in understanding hazards and societal responses to them can be found in studies on the causes and consequences of land degradation (Blaikie and Brookfield, 1987), drought (Wilhite and Easterling, 1987; Liverman, 1990a, b), and severe environmental degradation in selected world regions (Kasperson et al, 1995).

The interplay of social, political, and economic factors – interacting separately, in combination with one another, and with the physical environment – creates a mosaic of risks and hazards that affect people and the places they inhabit *(riskscapes* or *hazardscapes).* Cutter and Solecki (1989) proposed the hazards of place concept to examine the distributive patterns of hazards and the underlying processes that give rise to them. The study of the hazards of place has its roots in Hewitt and Burton's (1971) regional ecology of damaging events. They maintain that considering the threat from all hazards provides an opportunity to mitigate several hazards simultaneously. Yet previous work has rarely attempted to characterize the risk from all hazards or the intersection they share with vulnerable populations. A notable exception is FEMA's (1997) publication, *Multi-Hazard Identification and Risk Assessment.* Curiously, however, this report provides a hazard-by-hazard analysis (at the state level), including natural and technological hazards, but there is no overall summary of cumulative hazards within the states, so it is impossible to ascertain the relative hazardousness of states. There is also no mention of the social vulnerability of residents living in these places.

In this chapter, we further extend this research methodology by incorporating biophysical and social indicators with location for all hazards in a particular area, in this instance, a county. In this way, we extend some of the theoretical, conceptual, and technological advancements in hazards research to a real-world application, including the use of GIS in hazard mapping (Monmonier, 1997).

Conceptual Model and Practical Implementation

To organize and combine both the traditional view of vulnerability (biophysical risk) with the more recent ideas on social vulnerability, Cutter developed a hazards of place model of vulnerability (Figure 6.1, page 78). While exploratory in nature, it seeks to integrate the two aspects of vulnerability by tying them both to particular places. The focus on place provides an opportunity to examine some of the underlying social and biophysical elements that contribute to vulnerability, as well as to assess their interaction and intersection. Place vulnerability can change over time based on alterations in risk, mitigation and the variable contexts within which hazards occur.

Risk and mitigation interact to create an initial hazard potential. Risk is the likelihood of the event occurring and includes three sub-elements: the potential source of the risk (e.g. industrial accident, riverine flooding), the impact of the risk itself (high-consequence, low-consequence event) and an estimate of its frequency of occurrence (500-year flood, 2 per cent chance of a valve failure). Risk interacts with mitigation (a whole suite of efforts to reduce risks or lessen their impacts such as planning or structural improvements in buildings) to produce the hazard potential. Following from the social amplification model, risks can either be reduced through good mitigation policy, or amplified by poor or non-existent mitigation policies and practices. The hazard potential interacts with the underlying social fabric of the place to create the social vulnerability. The social fabric includes socio-demographic characteristics, perception of and experience with risks and hazards, and overall capacity to respond to hazards. The geographic filter includes the site and situation of the place and the proximity to hazard sources and events, and interacts with the hazard potential to produce the biophysical vulnerability. The social and biophysical vulnerability elements mutually relate and produce the overall vulnerability of the place. Notice that the place vulnerability has a feedback loop to the initial risk and mitigation inputs, allowing for the enhancement or reduction of both risk and mitigation, which in turn would lead to increased or decreased vulnerability. To operationalize the conceptual model, we focused only on the last three elements: biophysical, social, and place vulnerability. Three outcome indicators were used to measure the relative hazardousness of Georgetown County: biophysical vulnerability (measured by event frequency and delineation of hazard zones), social (measured by socio-demographic characteristics) and overall place vulnerability (the interchange of the two).

A key component of any vulnerability assessment is the acquisition of systematic baseline data, particularly at the local level. These data provide inventories of hazard areas and vulnerable populations – information that is essential for preimpact planning, damage assessments, and post-disaster response. One ancillary goal of this research is to create a method for identifying the risk posed by multiple hazards in order to promote mitigation at the local level. A vulnerability assessment requires not only an audit of all potential hazards, but also an understanding of the human dimensions involved.

The fundamental causes of human vulnerability include a lack of access to resources, information and knowledge, and limited access to political power and representation (Blaikie et al, 1994; Institution of Civil Engineers, 1995). Certain demographic factors are prominent when establishing social vulnerability. Age is an important consideration in evacuations, specifically the elderly and young who are more difficult to move and subject to health complications from certain hazard events (McMaster, 1988; O'Brien and Mileti, 1992). The poor are more susceptible to certain hazards due to lack of resources, poor-quality housing, and the inability to recover quickly (Burton et al, 1993; Dasgupta, 1995). Conversely, the richest households may experience greater material losses during a hazard event, but that same wealth also enables them to absorb those losses through insurance, social safety nets and entitlements, and thus to more quickly recover from the hazard's impact. Gender can also be an indicator of a more vulnerable population due to a lack of access to resources and differential exposures (see Chapter 5; also Liverman, 1990a; Fothergill, 1996; Enarson and Morrow, 1998). The environmental equity literature also supports race and ethnicity as factors in vulnerability to certain hazards (Perry and Lindell, 1991; Pulido, 2000; USGAO, 1995). Finally, population distribution and density further serve as vulnerability indicators, since higher concentrations of people present further evacuation difficulties (Johnson and Zeigler, 1986; McMaster, 1988; Cova and Church, 1997).

Place vulnerability, while largely shaped by biophysical and social factors, is also compounded by a population's reliance on infrastructure that includes roads, utilities, bridges, dams, airfields, railroads and emergency response facilities. According to Platt, many of these infrastructure components fall under the definition of 'lifeline,' the networks that 'provide for the circulation of people, goods, services, and information upon which health, safety, comfort, and economic activity depend' (1995, p173). 'Special needs' locations or populations also exist that require careful consideration for hazard and emergency response due to the requirement for advanced evacuation lead time and the difficulty in relocation. Examples of special needs facilities include daycare centres, nursing homes, hospitals and schools.

The use of Geographic Information Systems (GIS) is growing in emergency planning and management, and FEMA recently embraced the technology, especially for monitoring responses and estimating losses (Marcello, 1995; FEMA, 1997). Within the research community, GIS-related studies have been used in hazard identification (Chou, 1992; Wadge et al, 1993; Jones, 1995; Brainard et al, 1996; Carrara and Guzzetti, 1996) and in social response (Hodgson and Palm, 1992; Sorenson et al, 1992). Relatively few researchers have used GIS as a tool for understanding both biophysical *and* social vulnerability. There are some notable exceptions, including the work of Emani et al (1993), who investigated vulnerability to extreme storm events and sea-level rise, and the work of Lowry et al (1995), who examined vulnerability to hazardous chemicals releases. Clearly, there is a void in the literature on the spatial analytic approach to vulnerability, a shortcoming that this present chapter addresses.

Georgetown County, South Carolina

Georgetown County is located along the South Carolina coast between Myrtle Beach, a high-volume tourist destination to the north, and the historic city of Charleston to the south (Figure 7.1). The county is diverse in both its physical landscape and social structure. The Sampit, Black, Great Pee Dee and Waccamaw Rivers converge upon the city of Georgetown and empty into Winyah Bay. The southern border of the county is formed by the Santee River. This low-lying, poor-draining area contrasts with the quasi-barrier island landscape of the so-called Waccamaw Neck region, which is separated from the mainland by the Waccamaw River and the Intracoastal Waterway and is accessible by bridge from Georgetown.

The county is about 815 square miles (eighth largest in the state). Its population density (63.3 persons per square mile) is lower than the state average but ranks in the middle of all South Carolina counties. More than 60 per cent of the county's tax base is derived from the Waccamaw Neck beachfront communities of Murrells Inlet, Pawleys Island, Litchfield Beach, and Debordieu Colony (Cutter et al, 1997). Pawleys Island and Debordieu are among the state's more elite beach enclaves (Edgar, 1998). The county seat, Georgetown, was one of the earliest port cities in South Carolina. Agriculture, especially the cultivation of indigo and rice, dominated the colonial and antebellum economy. During the 1840s, nearly half of the rice produced in the US was grown in Georgetown County (Rogers, 1970). Traces of the rice plantations and the tenant housing for the slaves that worked them are still visible in the landscape.

Today, the county has a diverse economic base, with two of the state's largest manufacturers, Georgetown Steel and International Paper, located in the city

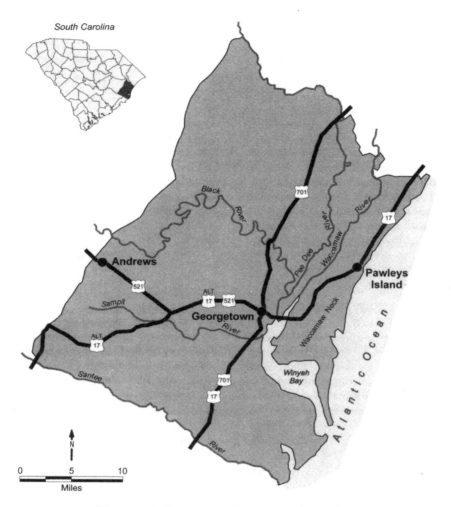

Figure 7.1 *Georgetown County, South Carolina*

itself. The paper and pulp industry also owns 28 per cent of the county's forested land. Tourism doubles the population during the summer months and generates more than $115 million in annual sales (Waccamaw Regional Planning and Development Council, 1997).

The county is stratified both racially and economically. In the county as a whole, the percentage of minority population is 44 per cent, compared to the state average of 31 per cent. Per capita income is lower than the state average. The percentage of families living in poverty (15.8 per cent) exceeds the state average as well (11.9 per cent) (South Carolina Budget and Control Board 1997). Mean housing values are greatest along the coast, where most residents are white. As one travels inland, the housing value drops and the population becomes more racially mixed, especially in the city of Georgetown. In the rural areas, the population is predominantly black and poor. The majority of housing is single-family detached houses. Due to increased housing demand, land costs, and construction costs, one-quarter of the county's housing stock now consists of mobile homes. Finally, the cultural diversity of the county ranges from a year-round tourist-based population to one of the few remaining Gullah communities (Sandy Island) along the southeast coast[1] (Winberry 1996).

Georgetown County historically has been exposed to several recurring types of natural hazards. Primarily meteorological and hydrometeorological in nature, these include hurricanes, tornadoes, hail, floods, severe thunderstorms and wind events. Forty-six deaths have been attributed to natural events, forty-one before 1900 and five in one incident in 1974 (Cutter et al, 1997). The majority of damage caused by natural hazards at the start of the 20th century were crop losses. Although the amount of rice grown in the county decreased after the Civil War, rice remained the primary agricultural commodity until the early 1900s. As a consequence of both the hazards that occurred (hurricanes) and the physical location of the fields (coastal riverine), rice-crop failures were commonplace. Crop losses have varied from a 25 per cent loss in 1893 to a 90 per cent loss in 1928, both due to hurricanes (Rogers, 1970).

The shift from an agricultural to an industrial and tourism-oriented economy, beginning in the 1950s, fundamentally changed the nature of Georgetown County's exposure to hazards. Where a hurricane once washed out a rice field, it now has the potential to wipe out vacation condominiums (Schneider, 1995) or spur the release of hazardous chemicals from an industrial facility. The transportation of chemicals used in manufacturing and the hazardous wastes generated at similar facilities have added to the hazard mosaic of the county.

Determining Biophysical Vulnerability

The identification of potential hazards, their frequency, and their locational impacts are essential components in describing biophysical vulnerability. The hazards we analysed represent more acute events (e.g. hazardous materials (hazmat) spills, hurricanes) – situations that local emergency managers must respond to during an emergency situation – rather than the entire array of hazards that potentially affect areas (e.g. pollution). Three sets of information were required for the analysis: identification of hazards, hazard frequency, and hazard-zone delineation.

Hazard identification and frequency

The first step was to determine what hazard events occurred in the study area (Kates and Kasperson, 1983; National Research Council, 1991; FEMA, 1997) and the estimated rate of occurrence based on the historical frequency of hazard events. The hazard history of the county was compiled from archival materials (especially the local newspaper, the *Georgetown Times,* which began publishing in 1798) and existing longitudinal hazards databases.[2]

The frequency of occurrence is a straightforward calculation from the historical data and the length of that record in years. The number of hazard occurrences divided by the number of years in the record yields the rate of the event occurring

Table 7.1 *Annual rate of occurrence of identified hazards
for Georgetown County, South Carolina*

Hazard	Number of events	Years in record	Hazard frequency (% chance/ year)	Data source
Chemical release *fixed*	41	10	410	Toxic Release Inventory; EPCRA Tier 2; Emergency Response Notification System; US DOT
Chemical release *railroad*	6	10	60	Emergency Response Notification System; US DOT
Chemical release *roadway*	4	10	40	Emergency Response Notification System; US DOT
Drought (no. drought months)	25	101	24.75	Palmer Drought Severity Index, 1895–1995
Earthquake (no. felt)	9–12	298	3.02–4.03	South Carolina Seismic Network, 1698–1995
Floods			1.0/0.2	FEMA, 1995
Hail	10	41	24.39	National Severe Storms Lab, 1955–1995
Hurricane *surge-cat. 1*	19	111	17.12	SLOSH; National Hurricane Center, 1886–1996
Hurricane *surge-cat. 2*	18	111	16.22	SLOSH; National Hurricane Center, 1886–1996
Hurricane *surge-cat. 3*	3	111	2.7	SLOSH; National Hurricane Center, 1886–1996
Hurricane *surge-cat. 4*	4	111	3.6	SLOSH; National Hurricane Center, 1886–1996
Hurricane *surge-cat. 5*	0	111	0.01	SLOSH; National Hurricane Center, 1886–1996
Hurricane *wind*	1–4	111	0.9–3.6	National Hurricane Center, 1886–1996
Thunderstorm *wind*	48	41	117.07	National Severe Storms Lab, 1955–1995
Tornado	7	46	15.22	National Severe Storms Lab, 1950–1995
Wildfire	3213	15	21,420	South Carolina Forestry Commission, 1981–1996

in any given year. For instance, if a hypothetical hazard, A, occurred 17 times in the county over the past 23 years, the rate of occurrence for that hazard in any given year is 17/23 (0.739, or 73.9 per cent), or less than once per year.

Table 7.1 provides the hazard frequencies for each of the primary hazards affecting Georgetown County, as well as the source of the data. While emergency preparedness officials are most concerned with hurricanes, it is clear that wildfires and chemical releases from stationary facilities are the more common hazard events in the county.

In some instances, the calculation of an occurrence rate required more detail than the number of events per some unit of time. For example, drought hazard occurrence was calculated using data from the Palmer Drought Severity Index (PDSI). The PDSI is calculated from the weighted differences between actual precipitation and evapotranspiration (Palmer, 1965), with a scale typically ranging from +4.0 (very moist spell) to zero (near normal) to −4 (extreme drought). Data for Georgetown County were acquired from the Southeast Regional Climate Center. We defined a drought year as being any year in which the PDSI exceeded the moderate drought level of −2.0 for any three consecutive months. Unfortunately, since a true definition of drought should include both physical and human systems, this method still is deficient in assessing the impacts of drought accurately. Georgetown County had 25 years of at least moderate drought between 1895 and 1995, or roughly the equivalent of 300 drought months.

Hazard Zone Delineation

The next stage in the process was to delineate each hazard zone and assign the rate of occurrence. Some hazards have well-defined spatial impact areas within the county (e.g. floodplains). Likewise, chemical spills from train accidents normally are confined to those areas surrounding the rail lines, not the entire county. Other hazards are less spatially concentrated. Based on their infrequent occurrence, these hazards often appear to have a random spatial distribution at the county level. For these hazard events (tornadoes, wind events, hail, severe storms), we assumed the hazard zone encompassed the entire county.

Spatially concentrated hazards were approached similarly but first required the delineation of those areas potentially affected. Flooding is perhaps most illustrative. Flood-hazards zones were based on FEMA's Q3 flood data using 100-year and 500-year flood zones[3] (Figure 7.2). Thus, the rates of occurrence are implied in these geographic delineations (1 per cent chance per year in the 100-year flood zone; 0.25 per cent chance per year in the 500-year flood zone).

Hurricane hazards have two primary components, storm surge and wind, both requiring spatial delineation. We used the output from the National Hurricane Center's SLOSH[4] model to define hurricane storm-surge hazard areas. The National Hurricane Center uses this model to calculate the areas that potentially will be inundated by storm surge in each Saffir-Simpson[5] scale category. These hazard zones represent the worst-case scenario for each hurricane category (Figure 7.3a).

Hurricane windfields were derived from modelling historic storm winds using estimated wind speed, direction, duration and the geographic area affected by the storm (Ramsey et al, 1998). The model used 44 historic hurricanes to determine the spatial extent of windfields (>70 mph sustained winds) (Figure 7.3b). The duration of wind speeds greater than 70 mph (reported in minutes) provides an estimate of the occurrence rate on a yearly basis.

Hazard zones for hazardous materials releases also had to be constructed (Figure 7.4). A buffer of one-half mile was created around each railroad and arterial highway segment. This distance is the default isolation distance recommended

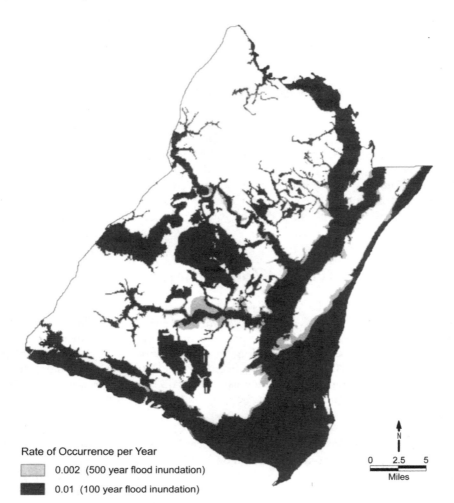

Rate of Occurrence per Year

☐ 0.002 (500 year flood inundation)

■ 0.01 (100 year flood inundation)

Figure 7.2 *Flood zones in Georgetown County based on the 100-year and 500-year flood inundation zones derived from FEMA Q3 data*

by the US Department of Transportation (DOT) for a fire involving hazardous chemicals (USDOT, 1993). For fixed sites, a buffer was created equal to the largest protective action distance (PAD) for all chemicals at a given facility. Industrial facilities are required to report annual releases of toxic chemicals through the Toxic Release Inventory that provides data by specific chemical and quantity released (in pounds). These protective action distances range from 0.2 to 5.0 miles, depending on the toxicity of the chemical involved.

More problematic in geographic delineation is the earthquake hazard. Georgetown County has no recorded earthquake epicentres from 1698 to 1995, but 23 earthquakes were felt within the county during this time period (South Carolina Seismic Network 1996). Using 'felt earthquakes' as our indicator, the hazard zone

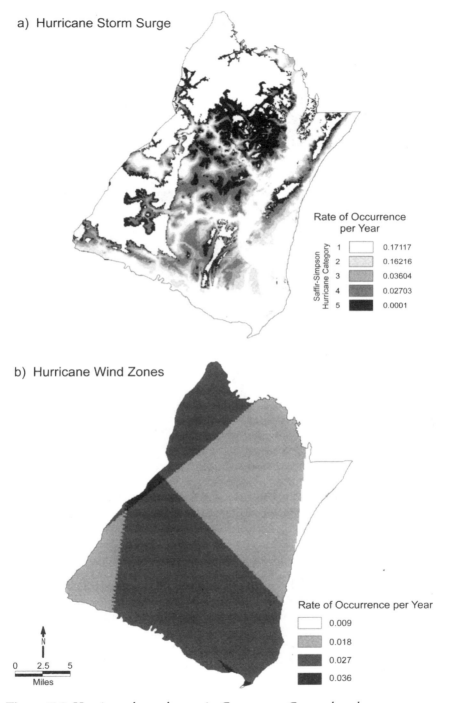

Figure 7.3 *Hurricane hazard zones in Georgetown County based on storm-surge inundation* (a) *and wind-impact zones* (b)

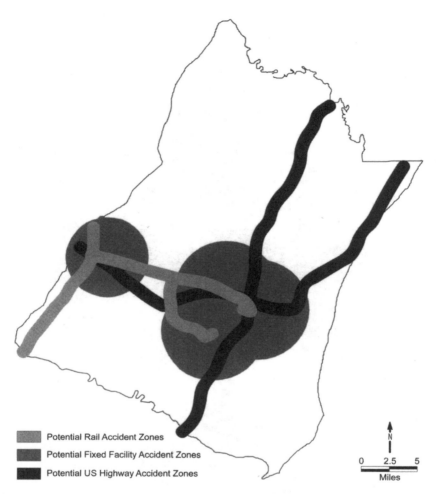

Figure 7.4 *Rail, highway and fixed-facility chemical accident zones in Georgetown County*

was constructed by first entering the epicentre latitude and longitude into a GIS. The South Carolina Seismic Network provides the total area (in square miles) that felt the earthquake. Given the fairly uniform soils and geology of the county, we created a circular buffer around the epicentre to approximate the 'felt area.' Using GIS, each of the 'felt areas' for the 23 earthquakes was overlaid and aggregated into a 'felt earthquake layer' for the county (Figure 7.5).

Data integration

In all, more than 25 different data layers were created in the GIS. Each hazard zone, along with their rate of occurrences, was stored as an individual GIS layer. To assess the total biophysical vulnerability, all the layers were combined into a

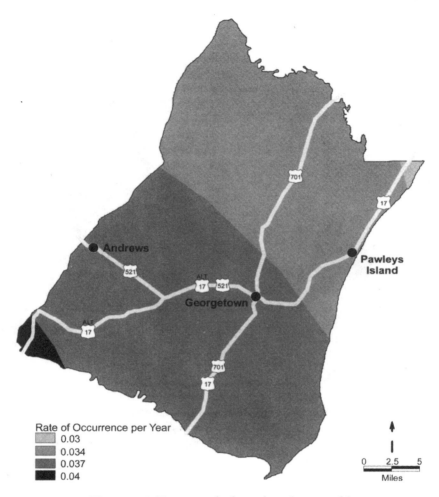

Figure 7.5 *Zones in which earthquakes were felt based on frequency of occurrence per year*

single composite of intersecting polygons. A biophysical hazard score (based on the rate of occurrence) was assigned to each polygon; these scores were subsequently classed into deciles and mapped to produce a visual display of biophysical vulnerability. A simplified map (using quintiles) shows those portions of the county with the greatest biophysical vulnerability (Figure 7.6).

Hazardous material risks are clearly visible on the composite hazards map, represented by the potential evacuation zones surrounding the major facilities, railroads, and highways. Not only is their areal dimension great, but they also have a higher rate of occurrence. The effects of storm surge and flooding are also noticeable, especially within the city of Georgetown and in the coastal portions of the Waccamaw Neck area. Those more geographically diffuse hazards, such as earthquakes, or those that encompass the entire county, such as tornados, are not

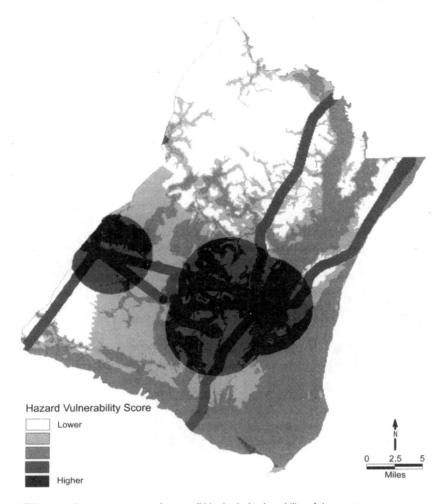

Note: This composite map represents the overall biophysical vulnerability of the county

Figure 7.6 *Zones of biophysical hazard vulnerability on a 1–5 scale*

individually recognizable. They all contribute, however, to the overall biophysical vulnerability of the county.

Defining Social Vulnerability

Social vulnerability 'derives from the activities and circumstances of everyday life or its transformations' (Hewitt 1997, p26). Those broad factors that influence many of the fundamental causes of social vulnerability include the following (Blaikie et al, 1994; Institution of Civil Engineers, 1995; Cutter et al, 1997; Mileti, 1999):

- lack of access to resources, including information and knowledge;
- limited access to political power and representation;
- certain beliefs and customs;
- weak buildings or weak individuals; and
- infrastructure and lifelines.

While these fundamental causes are quite variable in time and space, most research demonstrates that certain demographic and housing characteristics – age, race/ ethnicity, income levels, gender, building quality, public infrastructure – are influential in amplifying or reducing overall vulnerability to hazards (Blaikie et al, 1994; Hewitt, 1997; Tobin and Montz, 1997). Based on the existing literature, we chose to examine those characteristics of the population and their residential environment that contribute to social vulnerability. While not fully explaining the underlying causes of the social vulnerability, these variables do provide an initial metric for operationalizing the concept. The indicators listed in Table 7.2 were selected to characterize vulnerable populations. All of the social data were taken from the 1990 US Census block statistics, the most recent data available.

Rather than using simple percentages, each social variable was standardized by first determining the ratio of that variable in each census block to the total number of that variable in the county.[6] In Table 7.3, for example, the number of

Table 7.2 *Measures of socially vulnerable populations*

Characteristic	Variable
Population and structure	Total population Total housing units
Differential access to resources/greater susceptibility to hazards due to physical weakness	Number of females Number of nonwhite residents Number of people under age 18 Number of people over age 65
Wealth or poverty	Mean house value
Level of physical or structural vulnerability	Number of mobile homes

Table 7.3 *Example of Social Vulnerability Index: Number of mobile homes*

Census block	No. of mobile homes in block	No. of mobile homes in county	Ratio of block to county (X)	Mobile home vulnerability index (X/maximum X)
A	125	3500	0.036	1.00
B	76	3500	0.022	0.61
C	4	3500	0.001	0.03
D	21	3500	0.006	0.17

Table 7.4 *Calculation of Social Vulnerability Index: Mean house value*

Census block	Mean house value ($) in block	Mean house value ($) in county	Value difference ($) of county and block (X)	X + absolute value of maximum X (Y)	Mean house value vulnerability score (Y/maximum Y)
A	41,286	75,000	33,714	69,364	1.00
B	110,650	75,000	−35,650	0	0.00
C	76,776	75,000	−1776	33,874	0.49
D	64,900	75,000	5100	40,750	0.58

mobile homes in each census block was tabulated (column 2), as was the number of total mobile homes in the county (column 3). The ratio of the number of mobile homes to the total for the county was computed (column 4). This value (X) was then divided by the maximum value (X) to create an index that ranges from 0 to 1.00. Higher index values indicate greater vulnerability, as in Block A (Table 7.3). All the social variables were standardized in this manner with the exception of mean house value. In this case, negative numbers were possible, so the absolute value of the difference between block and county values was added (Table 7.4). The difference between county and block housing was computed (column 4) by taking the county average of mean house value and subtracting the mean house value for each census block. In order to remove negative values, the absolute value of the maximum X (column 4) was added to create Y (column 5). Finally, the ratio of the new value (Y) to the maximum Y generated the mean house value index (column 6). Again, higher values indicate greater vulnerability. As shown in Table 7.4, Block A is the most vulnerable, followed by Block D, Block C, and then Block B. Once the index values were computed, they were assigned to each block and entered into a GIS as a data layer. It must be reiterated that mean house value is serving as a surrogate for wealth and, thus, resilience. Mean house value is not used to infer that higher priced homes are necessarily less structurally vulnerable. Although those homes may have safety features lacking in homes of lesser value, they are often located in areas that make them more susceptible to damage (e.g. expensive beachfront homes). They also are more likely to be adequately insured.

The same procedure used to develop the composite biophysical vulnerability map was replicated for the social vulnerability mosaic. The index values for each variable were summed to arrive at a composite index score for each block, which represents an aggregate measure of social vulnerability. These values were also placed into deciles, but are visually displayed as five categories on the map (Figure 7.7). As is the case with the biophysical indicators, each individual indicator of social vulnerability can be examined independently; however, it is the summary of all the measures that produces a broad overview of the spatial distribution of social vulnerability within the county. This broad overview has greater functionality for the emergency-management community, who need both the generalized

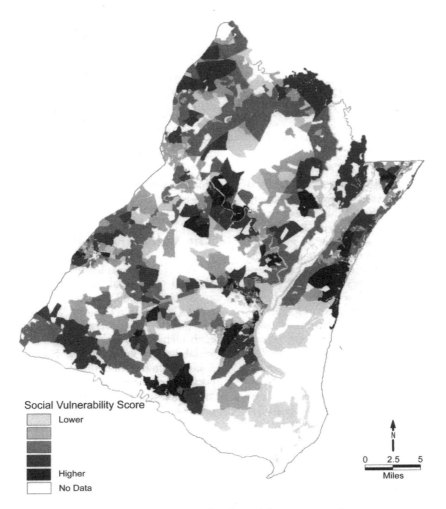

Figure 7.7 *Composite social vulnerability zones in the county*

information as well as the specifics. Two of the most socially vulnerable areas in Georgetown County are near its southern boundary and near the county center, both depicting poor minority areas. Pawleys Island (on Waccamaw Neck) is relatively wealthy and stands out because of the large number of people (both retirees and families with young children) and a higher density of housing units. The vulnerable block near the northern border of the county (Murrells Inlet) is a result of a relatively large elderly population living in mobile home parks. The county's rural regions are less vulnerable because of lower population and housing densities.

The Vulnerability of Places

The components leading to hazard loss (biophysical and social vulnerability) intersect to produce an overall assessment of the vulnerability of Georgetown County. We have intentionally taken a descriptive approach in presenting each element in order to highlight the spatial variability in vulnerability. Since there is no common metric for determining the relative importance of the social vis-à-vis biophysical vulnerability, nor the relative importance of each individual variable (or GIS layer) to the composite picture, this seemed like a prudent course of action.

As the conceptual model suggests, the overlap of hazard zones and social vulnerability produces the spatial variation in overall vulnerability for the county. To achieve the final place vulnerability, the social vulnerability layer was combined with the biophysical vulnerability layer within the GIS. No a priori weights were assigned to the individual layers within the GIS or in the composite social and biophysical indices. Instead, all indicators were treated equally, and we assumed that each had the same relative importance in their contributions to overall vulnerability.[7] Some may argue the appropriateness of this approach, suggesting a weighting scheme based on property at risk or other measures of economic losses. No reliable statistics, however, are available at the present time on annual losses from natural disasters at the national level, let alone at the county level (Mileti, 1999). The product of the two index scores (social and biophysical vulnerability) was then reclassified into five categories and mapped.

As can be seen in Figure 7.8, the most vulnerable areas – the cities of Georgetown and Andrews, and the communities of the Waccamaw Neck – include a moderate level of both hazards and social indicators. Most of the areas of high biophysical vulnerability do not overlap with areas of high social vulnerability. Rather, the overall hazard vulnerability of Georgetown County is a function of medium levels of biophysical risk coupled with medium-to-high levels of social vulnerability. The less vulnerable areas are inland, located away from the county's major industries, transportation corridors, and major waterways. They are also sparsely populated.

Numerical estimates of vulnerability

In addition to the spatial representation of place vulnerability using the GIS, we can also estimate the number of people and structures in each hazard zone utilizing areal interpolation techniques. In this way, we can produce an empirical 'estimate' of the potential population or structures at risk either from a singular hazard (Table 7.5) or from all hazards combined (Table 7.6). For example, a Category 1 hurricane (on the Saffir-Simpson Scale) would affect 26 per cent of the county area, 22 per cent of its housing units (single family and mobile homes) but only 8 per cent of its population. The mean house value ($71,213), however, is greatest in this Category 1 hurricane hazard zone, so we would anticipate considerable economic loss should a hurricane strike this area. Chemical releases from fixed sites could affect 22 per cent of the county area, nearly half of its total population and 42 per cent of its housing units. These same releases would also dispropor-

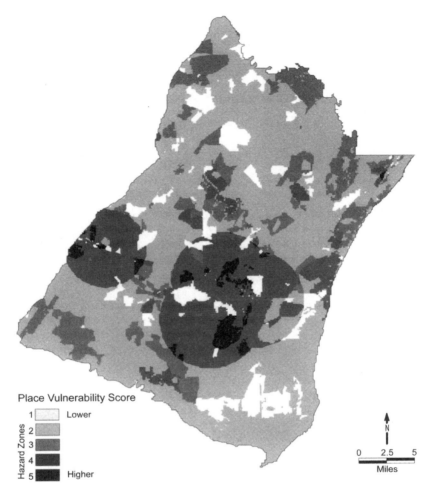

Figure 7.8 *The spatial distribution of overall hazard vulnerability in Georgetown County*

tionately affect children, the elderly, minorities and women (approximately half of whom live in the affected areas) (Table 7.5).

We also examined the individual components of social vulnerability based on hazard subregion (Figure 7.8, Table 7.6). For example, the most vulnerable area (Hazard Zone 5) contains about 17,000 people, or 41 per cent of the county's total population, but only 15 per cent of the land area. Similarly, this highly vulnerable region includes 36 per cent of the county's housing units, or an estimated $369 million in housing stock that is at risk. As population and development increase in this coastal county, some estimates project a 32 per cent population increase by 2005 from 1990 levels, Georgetown County's vulnerability to hazards will surely increase. It is important to anticipate where this vulnerability might be the greatest and whom it might affect the most.

Table 7.5 *Percentage of each social indicator per specific hazard zone*

Hazard zones	% Total population	% Housing units	% Mobile homes	% Age <18	% Age >65	% Non-white	% Female	% Area	Average mean house value ($)
Chemical release – fixed	49.23	42.09	34.34	51.67	48.41	48.90	49.81	21.97	55,402
Chemical release – rail	19.48	16.88	14.98	21.03	20.26	25.92	20.01	4.75	47,726
Chemical release – road	46.49	49.18	45.37	43.42	55.87	42.88	47.36	9.10	71,421
Drought	100.00	100.00	100.00	100.00	100.00	100.00	100.00	100.00	62,956
Earthquake – low	2.19	4.56	4.56	1.24	2.70	0.17	2.09	0.38	100,510
Earthquake – low/med	36.97	46.53	46.53	33.42	41.06	34.29	36.67	41.09	69,429
Earthquake – med/high	60.59	48.55	48.55	65.05	56.02	65.27	61.02	57.32	48,298
Earthquake – high	0.16	0.34	0.34	0.20	0.12	0.26	0.14	1.21	10,627
Flood – 100 year	16.00	13.65	13.65	14.36	19.50	11.40	15.75	42.12	62,506
Flood – 500 year	6.29	4.23	4.23	5.79	7.10	3.65	6.26	2.95	78,998
Hail	100.00	100.00	100.00	100.00	100.00	100.00	100.00	100.00	62,956
Hurricane cat. 1	8.12	4.60	4.60	6.39	11.44	4.32	7.95	25.95	71,213
Hurricane cat. 2	8.85	7.07	7.07	7.51	10.52	5.93	8.75	9.65	69,871
Hurricane cat. 3	16.07	15.11	15.11	15.68	17.74	15.17	16.28	8.56	69,124
Hurricane cat. 4	25.12	23.30	23.30	26.32	26.18	30.81	25.61	13.39	61,087
Hurricane cat. 5	13.21	19.79	19.79	13.02	12.30	12.91	12.89	14.06	64,273
Hurricane wind – low	15.33	24.97	24.97	9.80	23.83	6.21	15.15	4.32	116,338
Hurricane wind – low/med	32.76	30.52	30.52	34.43	27.57	36.03	32.66	40.36	57,805
Hurricane wind – med/high	51.47	43.91	43.91	55.33	48.25	57.61	51.76	54.41	42,849
Hurricane wind – high	0.36	0.58	0.58	0.38	0.27	0.14	0.35	0.89	26,600
Severe wind	100.00	100.00	100.00	100.00	100.00	100.00	100.00	100.00	62,956
Tornado	100.00	100.00	100.00	100.00	100.00	100.00	100.00	100.00	62,956
Wildfire	100.00	100.00	100.00	100.00	100.00	100.00	100.00	100.00	62,956

Table 7.6. *Social vulnerebility for each hazard zone*

Hazard zone*	Total population	Housing units	Mobile homes	Age <18	Age >65	Non-white	Female	Area (%)	Average mean house value ($)	Total housing value ($ millions)
1	6421	2267	498	1849	450	3154	3217	23.00	42,968	97
2	5571	1817	446	1621	353	3316	2703	18.00	44,729	81
3	3230	2424	147	753	268	1532	1503	30.50	49,715	120
4	9973	5212	1381	2236	1173	2655	4879	13.50	63,174	329
5	17,806	6591	777	5055	1947	7746	9177	15.00	56,062	369
Total	43,001	18,311	3249	11,514	4191	18,403	21,479	100.00	n/a	996

* In order of vulnerability, from lowest (1) to highest (5)

Establishing the social and infrastructure context

The simple overlap of hazard and social-vulnerability zones does not complete the hazard scenario for Georgetown County. The social and infrastructure context must also be established. There are certain elements of each that can contribute to the attenuation or amplification of the vulnerable areas. For instance, vulnerable groups that are distant from evacuation routes or downstream from a dam will be at greater risk. Overlaying the infrastructure over the place vulnerability may yield valuable information for mitigation planning. For example, an area ranking high in place vulnerability may contain two daycare centres and be near a known traffic 'choke' point on an evacuation route. This information would alert emergency managers that a vulnerable population, such as children, may need to be evacuated, and special steps taken to avert the congestion associated with that particular evacuation route.

Two procedures are involved in establishing the infrastructure context:

1 the identification and collection of special needs population data; and
2 the determination of key infrastructure and lifelines.

Special needs locations include daycare centres, nursing homes, health centres, hospitals and schools. These locations were determined through the use of a digital phonebook, a conventional phonebook and by contacting the local US Post Office. Some facilities were also accurately located by using address-matching software or a global positioning system (GPS). Infrastructure includes roads, structures, utilities, railroads, bridges, dams, airfields, ports and evacuation/response facilities. These locations were determined in the same manner. The infrastructure, lifelines and special needs locations were entered into the GIS and then added to the place vulnerability layer to create our contextualized place vulnerability (Figure 7.9). The mapped presentation of these data illustrate that many of the lifelines are located in highly vulnerable areas, notably evacuation shelters, police/fire stations and schools. The latter are important from an emergency response perspective. If a hazard event occurs during the day, additional resources may be needed to relocate a population out of harm's way (time permitting) or to assist in immediate

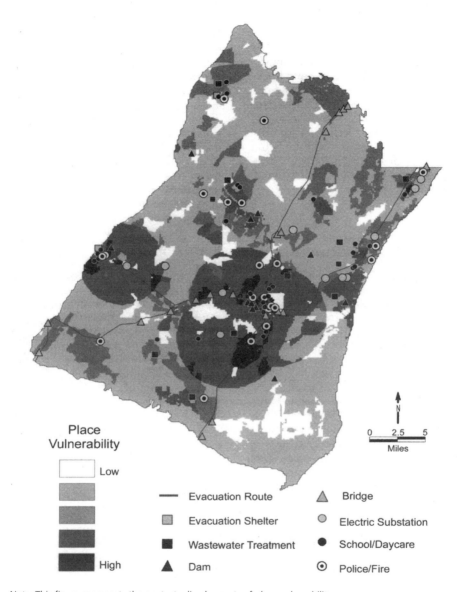

Place
Vulnerability

Low

High

— Evacuation Route △ Bridge

▦ Evacuation Shelter ◎ Electric Substation

■ Wastewater Treatment ● School/Daycare

▲ Dam ⊙ Police/Fire

Note: This figure represents the contextualized aspects of place-vulnerability.

Figure 7.9 *Place vulnerability, lifelines and infrastructure*

recovery operations. In this respect, the infrastructure amplifies the information on hazard vulnerability. For those slower-onset hazard events that strike the area, severely damaged schools may increase the amount of time it takes the community to return to normal, as parents will not leave school-aged children unattended while they return to work.

It is unlikely that all multiple-hazard events would occur simultaneously, thereby achieving the level of biophysical vulnerability depicted here. There have been instances, however, where natural events such as floods, earthquakes and hurricanes have ruptured pipelines and damaged facilities, resulting in hazardous materials releases. Knowledge of the spatial distribution of biophysical and social vulnerability, coupled with a geographic understanding of lifelines, can help counties to better prepare for disasters and to develop mitigation strategies to reduce future losses.

Conclusions

The multifaceted nature of vulnerability demands a thorough consideration of both the biophysical and social systems that give rise to hazards. To understand the potential for loss of property or life from environmental hazards, we also must consider the particular context in which the hazard takes place. Physical hazard exposure and social susceptibility to hazards must be understood within a geographic framework, that is, the hazardousness of a specific place. This uniquely geographical concept considers the threat from all hazards in a given place and provides the opportunity to mitigate several hazards concurrently. By harnessing geographic innovations such as GIS, we have the ability to investigate the spatial nature of multiple hazards and the specific subpopulations that are differentially affected. In this chapter, we have presented a conceptual model of vulnerability that includes both biophysical and social dimensions. The usefulness of this descriptive approach and its implementation, using a geographic information system, was explored for Georgetown County, South Carolina.

To determine biophysical vulnerability, we analysed those hazardous events, both natural and technological, that are likely to occur within a specific geographic area. To do this required an examination of the past history of nine hazards that affected the county, ranging from hurricanes to chemical releases. The likely rate of occurrence for each hazard was assigned within a GIS to the appropriate hazard zone, enabling us to examine the geography of individual hazard zones, as well as those areas that are vulnerable to multiple hazards. In a similar fashion, socially vulnerable areas were identified through a comparative analysis using eight socio-economic characteristics.

In combining biophysical and social vulnerability, we found a high degree of spatial variability in overall hazard vulnerability within Georgetown County. The most vulnerable places (from a biophysical standpoint) do not always overlap with the most vulnerable populations. Rather, it is the combination of medium levels of biophysical vulnerability coupled with medium-to-high levels of social vulnerability that characterize the overall hazard vulnerability of Georgetown County. This is an important finding as it reflects the likely 'social costs' of hazard events to the region. While economic losses would be great for residents in areas delineated in high-risk biophysical hazard zones, their recovery will be facilitated by greater wealth and access to resources. On the other hand, it would take only a moderate hazard event to disrupt the livelihoods and well-being of the majority of county residents and retard their longer-term recovery from disasters.

The research methodology and theoretical conceptualization of hazard vulnerability presented in this chapter highlights relevant data for local and state emergency management planners. It is the first step toward developing a baseline all-hazards assessment for places that can be used to evaluate the effectiveness of future mitigation or hazard reduction plans. The paper illustrates the utility of considering both physical exposure and social susceptibility when determining the hazardousness of places and, as such, provides a template for other integrated place-based hazard studies. The research demonstrates how geographers can and do make significant contributions in the public policy arena. Further, the chapter demonstrates the importance of joining the technical aspects of our discipline with theoretical partners in illustrating the power of geographic explanation and its relevance to nature–society interactions.

It is appropriate at this juncture to pose a number of questions. First, how might data issues be resolved to strengthen the analysis? There are some obvious concerns and caveats regarding the difficulty of data acquisition, data coverage, and data representation. Some of the data had good spatial resolution, other data sets less so. A concentrated effort to collect more detailed and geographically referenced data by all those involved in hazard reduction and management will go far in eliminating several of the data difficulties we experienced. In fact, this is one of the primary conclusions of a recently released report assessing the state of the knowledge in hazard research and management (Mileti, 1999). There is also a temporal dimension to hazard events that make some months more disaster-prone than others. The issue of seasonal variability in biophysical vulnerability was not addressed here, but could be incorporated into subsequent research that builds upon the approach we suggested. Despite these data concerns, this chapter demonstrates that the conceptual model can be successfully implemented and therefore contribute to our understanding of the complexities in determining what makes people and places vulnerable to hazards.

Keeping within the spirit of traditional hazards research, what real-world relevance does this research contribute to a state or local emergency manager? At a county scale, this chapter provides local-level emergency managers with a methodology and analytical tool for identifying those areas most vulnerable to hazards within their counties. The chapter highlights the importance of identifying hazards with the greatest potential to affect the county, and those geographic areas (hazard zones) most likely to suffer when the hazard event does occur. The approach enables the practitioner to view the relative importance of the social aspect of hazards by identifying those social groups who are differentially vulnerable, and to plan accordingly. The greatest challenge to the implementation of this approach to hazard planning and management at the local level is the availability of funds for training and data acquisition. Nevertheless, the usefulness of this methodology as a planning and training tool for emergency preparedness and response is evident.

Last, some might argue whether the county is the most appropriate or useful scale for this type of hazard analysis. While we used the county as the study area, with census blocks as sub-units for the social data, the analysis easily could have been conducted at another scale. Given that most hazard mitigation is local, the county seemed like a prudent choice, especially when the significance of county-wide land use and zoning decisions and emergency preparedness operations are taken into consideration. Caution should be exercised in reducing the size of geographic units, as differences in hazard occurrence rates between enumeration units may be so negligible that it would be difficult to undertake hazards assessments at the sub-county level. Additional research on the spatial vulnerability of urban areas might prove useful. For example, a metropolitan area-level analysis might be used to determine the regional variation in social vulnerability and biophysical risk in order to develop coordinated responses to hazard events that affect multiple jurisdictions.

The application of the theoretical understanding of human–environment relations, the conceptualization of hazard vulnerability and its complexities, and the use of geographical techniques to spatially represent vulnerability provide powerful selling points for the salience of the discipline to public policy. The research presented here demonstrates the need for and value of broadly trained geographers with a knowledge of both physical and human systems and geographic techniques – skills that are increasingly necessary to solve contemporary problems such as those posed by environmental hazards.

Acknowledgements

The South Carolina Emergency Preparedness Division, Office of the Adjutant General, provided funding for this research. The authors wish to acknowledge the assistance of the following persons and agencies: Lewis Dugan at the Georgetown County Office of Emergency Preparedness, Chip Balthis at the Georgetown County GIS Center, and Joe Burch at the Waccamaw Regional Planning and Development Council. We also thank Patrice Burns, Arleen Hill, Kirstin Dow, Charmel Menzel, and Deborah Thomas, as well as the anonymous reviewers, for their helpful comments. Deborah Thomas deserves special thanks for her assistance in the production of graphics for publication. The authors take full responsibility for errors of commission or omission.

Notes

1. South Carolina's Gullah community is descendent from West African slaves brought over to work the indigo and rice plantations. The Gullah language, partially derived from the slave era, is still spoken by many rural blacks along the coast. Gullah culture has distinctive music, foods, and crafts. Blacksmithing that created much of Charleston's ornamental iron-work and the Gullah baskets made of marsh grass and sold in Charleston's Historic City Market are examples of the Gullah material culture that can be seen today (Winberry, 1996; Edgar, 1998).
2. For a more detailed discussion of data sources and caveats, see Cutter et al (1997) and Mitchell et al (1997).
3. FEMA's so-called Q3 flood data is primarily used for planning purposes and not for strict determination of floodways, as is the case for Federal Insurance Rate Maps (FIRM). The Q3 maps are digital generalizations of the FIRM normally done at the county scale (1:24,000). The Q3 maps show floodways for both coastal and riverine environments and represent them as the 100-yr and 500-yr flood inundation zones, but the Q3 data do not have the level of accuracy required for enforcing the National Flood Insurance Program and cannot be used as such.

4. Storm surge is the elevation of the ocean surface resulting from the compound effects of water being pushed shoreward by wind across decreasing depths on a continental shelf, low pressure at the sea surface, tides raising the water level, and winds raising the ocean surface. The SLOSH model (Sea, Lake, Overland Surges from Hurricanes) is a computer simulation developed by the National Weather Service and is used to predict the height of hurricane storm surge. The US Army Corps of Engineers and FEMA contracted with the NOAA National Hurricane Center to calculate the worstcase inundation zones for coastal South Carolina using SLOSH model output. These zones are based upon the Saffir-Simpson hurricane scale. The SLOSH model output has been run for all of the coastal counties (Horry, Georgetown, Charleston, Colleton, Jasper and Beaufort).

5. The Saffir-Simpson scale is a measure of hurricane intensity and magnitude based on central pressure (millibars), windspeed (knots), storm surge and potential damage. Categories range from 1 (minimal) to 5 (catastrophic). The SLOSH model described previously is run multiple times, and its output is combined into the Maximum of Maximum Envelope of High Water (MOMs) for all storms from various directions of the same Saffir-Simpson scale. Depending on the specifications or parameters used in developing the 'idealized' storm, there may be subtle changes in the inundation contours. The MOMs used in the Georgetown study were for a fast-moving storm (>25 mph).

6. The social data were standardized by the total count for the entire county (similar to z-scores). This enables us to compare (and thus map) variations from the county-wide average. The social variables are thus transformed from spatially extensive data (simple counts such as the number of mobile homes) to spatially intensive data (proportions or ratios such as the number of mobile homes per block/total number of mobile homes in the county). By keeping the social variables on the same scale (0–1.0), we can spatially compare blocks with higher or lower values and develop composite indices of social vulnerability.

7. We recognize that all indicators of biophysical risk and social vulnerability are not equal. Nonetheless, the lack of reliable damage estimates (local, state, or national) to use as weights, and the need for simplification, forced us to consider all indicators as making equal contributions to vulnerability. Clearly, additional research is needed to develop weighting schemes for the social and biophysical indicators and to test their relative importance in statistically predicting vulnerability. This, however, is beyond the scope of the present chapter.

References

Alexander, D. (1991) 'Natural disasters: A framework for research and teaching', *Disasters*, vol 15, pp209–226

Alexander, D. (1997) 'The study of natural disasters, 1977–1997: Some reflections on a changing field of knowledge', *Disasters*, vol 21, pp284-304

Barrows, H. (1923) 'Geography as human ecology', *Annals of the Association of American Geographers*, vol 13, pp1–14

Blaikie, P. and Brookfield, H. (1987) *Land Degradation and Society*, Methuen, London

Blaikie, P., Cannon, T., Davis, I. and Wisner, B. (1994) At *Risk: Natural Hazards, People's Vulnerability, and Disasters*, Routledge, London

Bohle, H. G., Downing, T. E. and Watts, M. J. (1994) 'Climate change and social vulnerability: The sociology and geography of food insecurity', *Global Environmental Change*, vol 4, pp37–48

Brainard, J. S., Lovette, A. and Parfitt, J. P. (1996) 'Assessing hazardous waste transport risks using a GIS', *International Journal of Geographical Information Systems*, vol 10, pp831–849

Burton, I., Kates, R. and White, G. F. (1978) *The Environment as Hazard*, Oxford Univeristy Press, New York

Burton, I., Kates, R. and White, G. F. (1993) *The Environment as Hazard*, 2nd edition, Guilford Press, New York

Carrara, A. and Guzzetti, E. (eds) (1996) *Geographical Information Systems in Assessing Natural Hazards*, Kluwer, Dordrecht

Chou, Y. H. (1992) 'Management of wildfires with a geographical information system', *International Journal of Geographical Information Systems*, vol 6, pp123–140

Cova, T. J. and Church, R. L. (1997) 'Modeling community evacuation vulnerability using GIS', *International Journal of Geographical Information Science*, vol 11, pp763–784

Cutter, S. L. (1993) *Living with Risk: The Geography of Technological Hazards*, Edward Arnold, New York

Cutter, S. L. and Solecki, W. D. (1989) 'The national pattern of airborne toxic releases', *The Professional Geographer*, vol 41, pp149–161

Cutter, S. L., Mitchell, J. T. and Scott, M. S. (1997) *Handbook for Conducting a GIS-Based Hazards Assessment at the Local Level*, South Carolina Emergency Preparedness Division and Hazards Research Laboratory, Department of Geography, University of South Carolina, Columbia, SC

Dasgupta, P. (1995) 'Population, poverty, and the local environment', *Scientific American*, vol 272, pp40–45

Douglas, M. and Wildavsky, A. (1982) *Risk and Culture: An Essay on the Selection of Technological and Environmental Dangers*, University of California Press, Berkeley

Dow, K. (1992) 'Exploring differences in our common future(s): The meaning of vulnerability to global environmental change', *Geoforum*, vol 23, pp417–436

Edgar, W. (1998) *South Carolina: A History*, University of South Carolina Press, Columbia, SC

Emani, S., Ratick, S. J., Clarke, G. E., Dow, K., Kasperson, J. X., Kasperson, R. E., Moser, S. and Schwarz, H. E. (1993) 'Assessing vulnerability to extreme storm events and sea-level rise using geographical information systems (GIS)', *GIS/LIS '93 Proceedings*, ACSM, ASPRS, AM/FM, AAG, URISA, Bethesda, MD, pp201–209

Enarson, E. and Morrow, B. (1998) *The Gendered Terrain of Disaster*, Praeger, New York

FEMA (Federal Emergency Management Agency) (1995) *National Mitigation Strategy: Partnerships for Building Safer Communities*, Government Printing Office, Washington, DC

FEMA (1997) *Multi-Hazard Identification and Risk Assessment*, Government Printing Office, Washington, DC

FEMA and NEMA (National Emergency Management Association) (1997) *State Capability Assessment for Readiness (CAR)*, report version 1, Government Printing Office, Washington, DC

Fothergill, A. (1996) 'Gender, risk, and disaster', *International Journal of Mass Emergencies and Disasters*, vol 14, no 1, pp33–56

Hewitt, K. (ed) (1983) *Interpretations of Calamity*, Allen and Unwin, Winchester, MA

Hewitt, K. (1997) *Regions of Risk: A Geographical Introduction to Disasters*, Longman, Essex

Hewitt, K. and Burton, I. (1971) The *Hazardousness of a Place: A Regional Ecology of Damaging Events*, Department of Geography, University of Toronto, Toronto

Hodgson, M. E. and Palm, R. (1992) 'Attitude and response to earthquake hazards: A GIS design for analyzing risk assessment', *GeoInfoSystems*, vol 2, no 7, pp 40–51

Institution of Civil Engineers (1995) *Megacities: Reducing Vulnerability to Natural Disasters*, Thomas Telford Press, London

Interagency Floodplain Management Review Committee (1994) *Sharing the Challenge: Floodplain Management into the 21st Century*, Government Printing Office, Washington, DC

Johnson, B. B. and Covello, V. T. (1989) *The Social and Cultural Construction of Risk: Essays on Risk Selection and Perception*, D. Reidel Publishing, Dordrecht

Johnson, J. and Zeigler, D. (1986) 'Evacuation planning for technological hazards: An emerging imperative', *Cities*, vol 3, pp148–156

Jones, A. C. (1995) 'Improvement of volcanic hazard assessment techniques using GIS: A case study of Mount Etna, Sicily' in P. Fisher (ed) *Innovations in GIS 2*, Taylor and Francis, London, pp223–231

Kasperson, J. X., Kasperson, R. E. and Turner III, B. L. (eds) (1995) *Regions at Risk: Comparisons of Threatened Environments*, United Nations University Press, Tokyo

Kasperson, R. E., Renn, O., Slovic, P., Brown, H. S., Emel, J., Goble, R., Kasperson, J. X. and Ratick, S. (1988) 'The social amplification of risk: A conceptual framework', *Risk Analysis*, vol 8, pp177–187

Kates, R. and Burton, I. (eds) (1986) *Geography, Resources, and Environment*, vol 1, University of Chicago Press, Chicago

Kates, R. and Kasperson, J. X. (1983) 'Comparative risk analysis of technological hazards (a review)', *Proceedings of National Academy of Science USA*, vol 80, pp7027–7038

Kates, R., Hohenemser, C. and Kasperson, J. X. (1985) *Perilous Progress: Managing the Hazards of Technology*, Westview Press, Boulder, CO

Krimsky, S. and Golding, D. (eds) (1992) *Social Theories of Risk*, Praeger, Westport, CT

Lindell, M. K. (ed) (1997) 'Adoption and implementation of hazard adjustments', *International Journal of Mass Emergencies and Disasters*, vol 15, pp323–453

Liverman, D. (1990a) 'Vulnerability to global environmental change', in Kasperson, R. et al (eds) *Understanding Global Environmental Change*, Clark University, Worcester, MA

Liverman. D. (1990b) 'Drought in Mexico: Climate, agriculture, technology and land tenure in Sonora and Puebla', *Annals of the Association of American Geographers*, vol 80, pp49–72

Lowry, J. L. jr, Miller, H. J. and Hepner, G. F. (1995) 'A GIS-based sensitivity analysis of community vulnerability to hazardous contaminants on the Mexico/U.S. Border', *Photogrammetric Engineering and Remote Sensing*, vol 61, pp1347–1359

McMaster, R. (1988) 'Modeling community vulnerability to hazardous materials using geographic information systems', *Proceedings, 3rd International Symposium on Spatial Data Handling*, Ohio State University, Columbus, OH, pp143–156

Marcello, B. (1995) 'FEMA's new GIS reforms emergency response efforts', *GIS World*, vol 8, no12, pp70–73

Mileti, D. (1999) *Designing Future Disasters: An Assessment and Bolder Course for the Nation*, Joseph Henry Press, Washington, DC

Mitchell, J. K. (ed) (1998) *The Long Road to Recovery: Community Responses to Industrial Disaster*, United Nations University Press, Tokyo

Mitchell, J. K., Devine, N. and Jagger, K. (1989) 'Contextual model of natural hazard', *The Geographical Review*, vol 79, pp391–409

Mitchell, J. T., Scott, M. S., Thomas, D. S. K., Cutler, M., Putnam, P. D., Collins, R. F. and Cutter, S. L. (1997) 'Mitigating against disaster: Assessing hazard vulnerability at the local level', *GIS/LIS '97 Proceedings*, ACSM, ASPRS, AM/FM, AAG, URISA, Bethesda, MD, pp563–571

Monmonier, M. (1997) *Cartographies of Danger: Mapping Hazards in America*, University of Chicago Press, Chicago

NRC (National Research Council) (1991) *A Safer Future: Reducing the Impacts of Natural Disasters*, National Academy Press, Washington DC

O'Brien, P. and Mileti, D. (1992) 'Citizen participation in emergency response following the Loma Prieta earthquake', *International Journal of Mass Emergencies and Disasters*, vol 10, pp71–89

O'Keefe, P., Westgate, K. and Wisner, B. (1976) 'Taking the naturalness out of natural disasters', *Nature*, vol 260, pp566–567

Oliver-Smith, A. (1986) 'Disaster context and causation: An overview of changing perspectives in disaster research', *Natural Disasters and Cultural Responses: Studies in Third World Societies*, vol 36, pp1–34

Palm, R. (1990) *Natural Hazards: An Integrative Framework for Research and Planning*, Johns Hopkins University Press, Baltimore

Palm, R. and Carroll, J. (1998) *Illusions of Safety: Culture and Earthquake Hazard Response in California and Japan*, Westview Press, Boulder, CO

Palmer, W. (1965) *Meteorological Drought*, Research Paper 45, US Weather Research Bureau, Washington, DC

Perry, R. and Lindell, M. (1991) 'The effects of ethnicity on evacuation decision making', *International Journal of Mass Emergencies and Disasters*, vol 9, pp47–68

Platt, R. H. (1995) 'Lifelines: An emergency management priority for the United States in the 1990s', *Disasters*, vol 15, pp172–176

Pulido, L. (2000) 'Rethinking environmental racism: White privilege and urban development in Southern California', *Annals of the Association of American Geographers*, vol 90, pp12–40

Quarantelli, E. L. (1988) 'Disaster studies: An analysis of the social historical factors affecting the development of research in the area', *International Journal of Mass Emergencies and Disasters*, vol 5, pp285–310

Ramsey III, E. W., Hodgson, M. E., Sapkota, S. K., Laine, S. C., Nelson, G. A. and Chappell, D. K. (1998) 'Forest impact estimated with NOAA AVHRR and landsat TM data related to a predicted hurricane wind field distribution', unpublished manuscript, subsequently published in 2001 in *Remote Sensing of the Environment*, vol 77, no 3, pp279–292

Rogers, G. C. jr (1970) *The History of Georgetown County, South Carolina*, University of South Carolina Press, Columbia, SC

Schneider, S. K. (1995) *Flirting with Disaster: Public Management in Crisis Situations*, M.E. Sharpe, Armonk, NY

Sorenson, J. H., Carnes, S. A. and Rogers, G. O. (1992) 'An approach for driving emergency planning zones for chemical munitions emergencies', *Journal of Hazardous Materials*, vol 30, pp223–242

Sorenson, J. H., Soderstrom, J., Copenhaver, E., Carnes, S. and Bolin, R. (1987) *Impacts of Hazardous Technology: The Psycho-social Effects of Restarting TMI-1*, State University of New York Press, Albany, NY

South Carolina Budget and Control Board (1997) *South Carolina Statistical Abstract*, South Carolina Budget and Control Board, Columbia, SC

South Carolina Seismic Network (1996) *South Carolina Earthquakes, 1698–1995*, University of South Carolina, Columbia, SC

Susman, P., O'Keefe, P. and Wisner, B. (1983) 'Global disasters, a radical interpretation' in K. Hewitt (ed) *Interpretations of Calamity*, Allen and Unwin, Boston, MA, pp263–283

Tobin, G. and Montz, B. (1997) *Natural Hazards: Explanation and Integration*, New York, Guilford Press

Torry, W. (1979) 'Hazards, hazes, and holes: A critique of *The Environment as Hazard* and general reflections on disaster research', *Canadian Geographer*, vol 23, pp368–383

USDOT (US Department of Transportation) (1993) *Emergency Response Guidebook*, Government Printing Office, Washington, DC

USGAO (US General Accounting Office) (1995) *Hazardous and Nonhazardous Waste: Demographics of People Living Near Waste Facilities*, Government Printing Office, Washington, DC

Waccamaw Regional Planning and Development Council (1997) *Georgetown County Comprehensive Plan*, Georgetown, SC

Wadge, G., Wislocki, A. and Pearso, E. J. (1993) 'Spatial analysis in GIS for natural hazard assessment' in M. F. Goodchild, B. O. Parks and L. T. Steyaert (eds) *Environmental Modelling with GIS*, Oxford University Press, Oxford, pp332–338

Watts, M. (1983) 'On the poverty of theory' in K. Hewitt (ed) *Interpretations of Calamity*, Allen and Unwin, Boston, MA, pp231–262

White, G. F. (1945) *Human Adjustments to Floods*, Department of Geography Research Paper 29, University of Chicago Press, Chicago

White, G. F. (1964) *Choice of Adjustments to Floods*, Department of Geography Research Paper 93, University of Chicago Press, Chicago

White, G. F. and Haas, J. E. (1975) *Assessment of Research on Natural Hazards*, MIT Press, Cambridge, MA

Wilhite, D. and Easterling, W. (eds) (1987) *Planning for Drought: Toward a Reduction of Societal Vulnerability*, Westview Press, Boulder, CO

Winberry, J. (1996) 'Gullah: People, language, and culture of South Carolina's sea islands' in G. G. Bennett (ed) *Snapshots of the Carolinas: Landscapes and Cultures*, Association of American Geographers, Washington, DC, pp11–16

Yarnal, B. (1994) 'Socioeconomic restructuring and vulnerability to environmental hazards in Bulgaria', *Disasters*, vol 8, pp95–106

8

Social Vulnerability
to Environmental Hazards

Susan L. Cutter, Bryan J. Boruff and W. Lynn Shirley

Generally speaking, vulnerability to environmental hazards means the potential for loss. Since losses vary geographically, over time, and among different social groups, vulnerability also varies over time and space. Within the hazards literature, vulnerability has many different connotations, depending on the research orientation and perspective (see Chapter 6; also Dow, 1992; Cutter, 2001a). There are three main tenets in vulnerability research: the identification of conditions that make people or places vulnerable to extreme natural events, an exposure model (Burton et al, 1993; Anderson, 2000); the assumption that vulnerability is a social condition, a measure of societal resistance or resilience to hazards (Blaikie et al, 1994; Hewitt, 1997); and the integration of potential exposures and societal resilience with a specific focus on particular places or regions (see Chapter 7; also Kasperson et al, 1995).

The Vulnerability Paradox

Although considerable research attention has examined components of biophysical vulnerability and the vulnerability of the built environment (Mileti, 1999), we currently know the least about the social aspects of vulnerability. Socially created vulnerabilities are largely ignored, mainly due to the difficulty in quantifying them, which also explains why social losses are normally absent in after-disaster cost/loss estimation reports. Instead, social vulnerability is most often described using the individual characteristics of people (age, race, health, income, type of dwelling unit, employment). Social vulnerability is partially the product of social inequalities – those social factors that influence or shape the susceptibility of various groups to harm and that also govern their ability to respond. However,

Note: Reprinted, with permission, from *Social Science Quarterly*, vol 84, no 1, Susan L. Cutter, Bryan J. Boruff, and W. Lynn Shirley, 'Social vulnerability to environmental hazards', pp242–261. © Blackwell Publishing, 2003

it also includes place inequalities – those characteristics of communities and the built environment, such as the level of urbanization, growth rates and economic vitality, that contribute to the social vulnerability of places. To date, there has been little research effort focused on comparing the social vulnerability of one place to another. For example, is there a robust and consistent set of indicators for assessing social vulnerability that facilitates comparisons among diverse places, such as eastern North Carolina and southern California? How well do these indicators differentiate places based on the level of social vulnerability and how well do these factors explain differences in economic losses from natural hazards? This chapter examines these questions through a comparative analysis of social vulnerability to natural hazards among US counties.

This chapter utilizes the hazards of place model of vulnerability (see Chapters 6 and 7; also Heinz Center for Science, Economics, and the Environment, 2002) to examine the components of social vulnerability. In this conceptualization (Figure 6.1, page 78), risk (an objective measure of the likelihood of a hazard event) interacts with mitigation (measures to lessen risks or reduce their impact) to produce the hazard potential. The hazard potential is either moderated or enhanced by a geographic filter (site and situation of the place, proximity) as well as the social fabric of the place. The social fabric includes community experience with hazards and community ability to respond to, cope with, recover from and adapt to hazards, which in turn are influenced by economic, demographic and housing characteristics. The social and biophysical vulnerabilities interact to produce the overall place vulnerability. In this chapter we examine only the social vulnerability portion of the conceptual model.

Redirecting Social Indicators Research

In the 1960s and 1970s, social indicators research was a thriving topic within the social sciences with volumes written on theoretical and methodological issues (Duncan, 1969, 1984; Land, 1983; Land and Spilerman, 1975; Smith, 1973; Smith, 1981), and applications to social policy formation (Rossi and Gilmartin, 1980). The development of environmental indicators followed shortly thereafter, with quality-of-life studies emerging as an amalgam of the two (Cutter, 1985).

As a current research endeavour, social indicators and quality-of-life studies have lost some of their original lustre, although specialized journals (e.g. *Social Indicators Research*) remain as outlets for focused empirical research on the topic. Much of the contemporary work on social and quality-of-life indicators is relegated to popular rating places guides such as the *Places Rated Almanac* (Savageau, 2000), *America's Top-Rated Cities* (Garoogian, 1999), or comparative rankings of environmental quality (*Green Metro Index* by World Resources Institute, 1993; *Green Index* by Hall and Kerr, 1991). Also, there are a few examples of comparative measures of community health at the county level (Miringhoff, 1999; Shaw-Taylor, 1999; US Health and Human Services Administration, 2001). One of the best national assessments that integrates demographic, public health and environmental quality indicators is now more than a decade old, however (Goldman, 1991).

Social and environmental indicators research is experiencing a renaissance at present, especially in the arena of sustainability science. For example, the United Nations Development Programme's Human Development Index (UNDP, 2000) provides a composite indicator of human well-being, as well as indicators of gender disparity and poverty among nations – measures that have been used for more than a decade. Similarly, the World Bank (2001) provides data on the links between environmental conditions and human welfare, especially in developing nations, to monitor national progress toward a more sustainable future. An index has been developed to measure the environmental sustainability of national economies (World Economic Forum, 2000, 2002; Esty and Cornelius, 2002). Meanwhile, a set of indicators to monitor and assess ecological conditions for public policy decisions has been proposed (National Research Council, 2000). Similarly, the US Environmental Protection Agency (USEPA, 2002) is using a small set of environmental indicators to track progress in hazardous waste remediation. Finally, the social capital embodied in various communities has been surveyed in selected communities to determine a baseline and comparative assessment of American social and civic engagement at the local level (Social Capital Community Benchmark Survey, 2002). Despite these efforts, there still is no consistent set of metrics used to assess vulnerability to environmental hazards, although there have been calls for just such an index (Comfort et al, 1999; Cutter, 2001b).

Factors Influencing Social Vulnerability

There is a general consensus within the social science community about some of the major factors that influence social vulnerability. These include: lack of access to resources (including information, knowledge and technology); limited access to political power and representation; social capital, including social networks and connections; beliefs and customs; building stock and age; frail and physically limited individuals; and type and density of infrastructure and lifelines (Cutter, 2001a; Tierney et al, 2001; Putnam, 2000; Blaikie et al, 1994). Disagreements arise in the selection of specific variables to represent these broader concepts.

Those characteristics that influence social vulnerability most often found in the literature are listed in Table 8.1, along with the relevant research that identified them. Among the generally accepted are age, gender, race, and socio-economic status. Other characteristics identify special needs populations or those that lack the normal social safety nets necessary in disaster recovery, such as the physically or mentally challenged, non-English-speaking immigrants, the homeless, transients and seasonal tourists. The quality of human settlements (housing type and construction, infrastructure and lifelines) and the built environment are also important in understanding social vulnerability, especially as these characteristics influence potential economic losses, injuries and fatalities from natural hazards. Given their general acceptance in the literature, can we empirically define a robust set of variables that capture these characteristics, which then allows us to monitor changes in social vulnerability geographically and over time?

Table 8.1 *Social vulnerability concepts and metrics*

Concept	Description	Increases (+) or decreases (−) social vulnerability
Socio-economic status (income, political power, prestige)	The ability to absorb losses and enhance resilience to hazard impacts. Wealth enables communities to absorb and recover from losses more quickly due to insurance, social safety nets and entitlement programmes. *Sources*: Chapter 7; see also Burton et al (1993), Blaikie et al (1994), Peacock et al (1997), Hewitt (1997), Puente (1999) and Platt (1999).	High status (+/−) Low income or status (+)
Gender	Women can have a more difficult time during recovery than men, often due to sector-specific employment, lower wages, and family care responsibilities. *Sources*: Chapter 6; see also Blaikie et al (1994), Enarson and Morrow (1998), Enarson and Scanlon (1999), Morrow and Phillips (1999), Fothergill (1996), Peacock et al (1997) and Hewitt (1997).	Gender (+)
Race and ethnicity	Imposes language and cultural barriers that affect access to post-disaster funding and residential locations in high hazard areas. *Sources*: Pulido (2000), Peacock et al (1997), Bolin with Stanford (1998) and Bolin (1993).	Non-white (+) Non-Anglo (+)
Age	Extremes of the age spectrum affect the movement out of harm's way. Parents lose time and money caring for children when daycare facilities are affected; elderly may have mobility constraints or mobility concerns increasing the burden of care and lack of resilience. *Sources*: Chapter 7; see also O'Brien and Mileti (1992), Hewitt (1997) and Ngo (2001).	Elderly (+) Children (+)
Commercial and industrial development	The value, quality and density of commercial and industrial buildings provides an indicator of the state of economic health of a community, potential losses in the business community and longer-term issues with recovery after an event. *Sources*: Heinz Center for Science, Economics, and the Environment (2000) and Webb et al (2000).	High density (+) High value (+/−)
Employment loss	The potential loss of employment following a disaster exacerbates the number of unemployed workers in a community, contributing to a slower recovery from the disaster. *Source*: Mileti (1999).	Employment loss (+)

Rural/urban	Rural residents may be more vulnerable due to lower incomes and more dependent on locally based resource extraction economies (e.g. farming, fishing). High-density areas (urban) complicate evacuation out of harm's way. *Sources:* Chapter 7; see also Cova and Church (1997) and Mitchell (1999).	Rural (+) Urban (+)
Residential property	The value, quality and density of residential construction affects potential losses and recovery. Expensive homes on the coast are costly to replace; mobile homes are easily destroyed and less resilient to hazards. *Sources:* Chapter 7; see also Heinz Center for Science, Economics, and the Environment (2000) and Bolin and Stanford (1991).	Mobile homes (+)
Infrastructure and lifelines	Loss of sewers, bridges, water, communications and transportation infrastructure compounds potential disaster losses. The loss of infrastructure may place an insurmountable financial burden on smaller communities that lack the financial resources to rebuild. *Sources:* Heinz Center for Science, Economics, and the Environment (2000) and Platt (1995).	Extensive infrastructure (+)
Renters	People that rent do so because they are either transient or do not have the financial resources for home ownership. They often lack access to information about financial aid during recovery. In the most extreme cases, renters lack sufficient shelter options when lodging becomes uninhabitable or too costly to afford. *Sources:* Heinz Center for Science, Economics, and the Environment (2000) and Morrow (1999).	Renters (+)
Occupation	Some occupations, especially those involving resource extraction, may be severely impacted by a hazard event. Self-employed fisherman suffer when their means of production is lost and may not have the requisite capital to resume work in a timely fashion and thus will seek alternative employment. Those migrant workers engaged in agriculture and low-skilled service jobs (housekeeping, childcare, and gardening) may similarly suffer as disposable income fades and the need for services declines. Immigration status also affects occupational recovery. *Sources:* Heinz Center for Science, Economics, and the Environment (2000), Hewitt (1997) and Puente (1999).	Professional or managerial (–) Clerical or labourer (+) Service sector (+)
Family structure	Families with large numbers of dependents or single-parent households often have limited finances to outsource care for dependents, and thus must juggle work responsibilities and care for family members. All affect the resilience to and recovery from hazards. *Sources:* Blaikie et al (1994), Morrow (1999), Heinz Center for Science, Economics, and the Environment (2000) and Puente (1999).	High birth rates (+) Large families (+) Single-parent households (+)

Table 8.1 *continued*

Concept	Description	Increases (+) or decreases (−) social vulnerability
Education	Education is linked to socio-economic status, with higher educational attainment resulting in greater lifetime earnings. Lower education constrains the ability to understand warning information and access to recovery information. *Source:* Heinz Center for Science, Economics, and the Environment (2000).	Little education (+) Highly educated (−)
Population growth	Counties experiencing rapid growth lack available quality housing, and the social services network may not have had time to adjust to increased populations. New migrants may not speak the language and not be familiar with bureaucracies for obtaining relief or recovery information, all of which increase vulnerability. *Sources:* Chapter 7; see also Heinz Center for Science, Economics, and the Environment (2000), Morrow (1999) and Puente (1999).	Rapid growth (+)
Medical services	Health care providers, including physicians, nursing homes, and hospitals, are important post-event sources of relief. The lack of proximate medical services will lengthen immediate relief and longer-term recovery from disasters. *Sources:* Heinz Center for Science, Economics, and the Environment (2000), Morrow (1999) and Hewitt (1997).	Higher density of medical (−)
Social dependence	Those people who are totally dependent on social services for survival are already economically and socially marginalized and require additional support in the post-disaster period. *Sources:* Morrow (1999), Heinz Center for Science, Economics, and the Environment (2000), Drabek (1996) and Hewitt (2000).	High dependence (+) Low dependence (−)
Special needs populations	Special needs populations (infirm, institutionalized, transient, homeless), while difficult to identify and measure, are disproportionately affected during disasters and, because of their invisibility in communities, mostly ignored during recovery. *Sources:* Morrow (1999) and Tobin and Ollenburger (1993).	Large special needs population (+)

Source: Cutter et al (2001); Heinz Center for Science, Economics, and the Environment (2002).

Methods

To examine the social vulnerability, socio-economic data were collected for 1990 for all 3141 US counties, our unit of analysis. Using the US Census (City and County Data Books for 1994 and 1998), specific variables were collected that characterized the broader dimensions of social vulnerability identified in Table 8.1. Originally, more than 250 variables were collected, but after testing for multicollinearity among the variables, a subset of 85 raw and computed variables was derived. After all the computations and normalization of data (to percentages, per capita or density functions), 42 independent variables were used in the statistical analyses (Table 8.2). The primary statistical procedure used to reduce the data was factor analysis, specifically, principal components analysis.[1] The use of a reductionist technique such as factor analysis allows for a robust and consistent set of variables that can be monitored over time to assess any changes in overall vulnerability. The technique also facilitates replication of the variables at other spatial scales, thus making data compilation more efficient. A total of 11 factors was produced, which explained 76.4 per cent of the variance among all counties.[2]

Empirically Defining the Underlying Dimensions of Social Vulnerability

Eleven composite factors were found that differentiated US counties according to their relative level of social vulnerability in 1990 (Table 8.3). Each of these is briefly described below.

Personal wealth

The first factor identified the individual personal wealth of counties as measured by per capita income, percentage of households earning more than $75,000 per year, median house values and median rents. The wealth variables loaded positively on this factor and the lack of wealth (poverty) variables, negatively. The wealth factor explains 12.4 percent of the variance. Wealth enables communities to quickly absorb and recover from losses, but it also means that there may be more material goods at risk in the first place. On the other hand, there is more agreement that lack of wealth is a primary contributor to social vulnerability as fewer individual and community resources for recovery are available, thereby making the community less resilient to the hazard impacts.

Age

The two demographic groups most affected by disasters, children and the elderly, are identified in the second factor, which explains 11.9 per cent of the variation among counties, an empirical finding also consistent with the literature. The preponderance of children in the community and high birth rates both load

Table 8.2 *Variable names and descriptions*

Name	Description
MED_AGE90	Median age, 1990
PERCAP89	Per capita income (in dollars), 1989
MVALOO90	Median dollar value of owner-occupied housing, 1990
MEDRENT90	Median rent (in dollars) for renter-occupied housing units, 1990
PHYSICN90	Number of physicians per 100,000 population, 1990
PCTVOTE92	Vote cast for president, 1992 – per cent voting for leading party (Democratic)
BRATE90	Birth rate (number of births per 1000 population), 1990
MIGRA_97	Net international migration, 1990–1997
PCTFARMS92	Land in farms as a percentage of total land, 1992
PCTBLACK90	Per cent African American, 1990
PCTINDIAN90	Per cent Native American, 1990
PCTASIAN 90	Per cent Asian, 1990
PCTHISPANIC90	Per cent Hispanic, 1990
PCTKIDS90	Percentage of population under five years old, 1990
PCTOLD90	Percentage of population over 65 years, 1990
PCTVLUN91	Percentage of civilian labour force unemployed, 1991
AVGPERHH	Average number of people per household, 1990
PCTHH7589	Percentage of households earning more than $75,000, 1989
PCTPOV90	Percentage living in poverty, 1990
PCTRENTER90	Percentage renter-occupied housing units, 1990
PCTRFRM90	Percentage rural farm population, 1990
DEBREV92	General local government debt to revenue ratio, 1992
PCTMOBL90	Percentage of housing units that are mobile homes, 1990
PCTNOHS90	Percentage of population 25 years or older with no high school diploma, 1990
HODENUT90	Number of housing units per square mile, 1990
HUPTDEN90	Number of housing permits per new residential construction per square mile, 1990
MAESDEN92	Number of manufacturing establishments per square mile, 1992
EARNDEN90	Earnings (in $1000) in all industries per square mile, 1990
COMDEVDN92	Number of commercial establishments per square mile, 1990
RPROPDEN92	Value of all property and farm products sold per square mile, 1990
CVBRPC91	Percentage of the population participating in the labour force, 1990
FEMLBR90	Per cent females participating in civilian labour force, 1990
AGRIPC90	Per cent employed in primary extractive industries (farming, fishing, mining, and forestry), 1990
TRANPC90	Per cent employed in transportation, communications and other public utilities, 1990
SERVPC90	Per cent employed in service occupations, 1990
NRRESPC91	Per capita residents in nursing homes, 1991
HOSPTPC91	Per capita number of community hospitals, 1991
PCCHGPOP90	Per cent population change, 1980/1990
PCTURB90	Per cent urban population, 1990
PCTFEM90	Per cent females, 1990
PCTF_HH90	Per cent female-headed households, no spouse present, 1990
SSBENPC90	Per capita Social Security recipients, 1990

Table 8.3 *Dimensions of social vulnerability*

Factor	Name	Per cent variation explained	Dominant variable	Correlation
1	Personal wealth	12.4	Per capita income	+0.87
2	Age	11.9	Median age	−0.90
3	Density of the built environment	11.2	No. commercial establishments/mi^2	+0.98
4	Single-sector economic dependence	8.6	% employed in extractive industries	+0.80
5	Housing stock and tenancy	7.0	% housing units that are mobile homes	−0.75
6	Race – African American	6.9	% African American	+0.80
7	Ethnicity – Hispanic	4.2	% Hispanic	+0.89
8	Ethnicity – Native American	4.1	% Native American	+0.75
9	Race – Asian	3.9	% Asian	+0.71
10	Occupation	3.2	% employed in service occupations	+0.76
11	Infrastructure dependence	2.9	% employed in transportation, communication, and public utilities	+0.77

positively on this dimension. Median age, on the other hand, loads negatively. The other demographic group, the elderly, is measured by the percentage of the population over 65 and percentage receiving Social Security benefits. These variables load negatively on this dimension.

Density of the built environment

The third factor also confirms findings in the literature and describes the degree of development of the built environment. As measured by the density of manufacturing and commercial establishments, housing units and new housing permits, this factor highlights those counties where significant structural losses might be expected from a hazard event. Eleven per cent of the variation in counties is captured by this factor.

Single-sector economic dependence

A singular reliance on one economic sector for income generation creates a form of economic vulnerability for counties. The boom and bust economies of oil development, fishing or tourism-based coastal areas are good examples – in the heyday of prosperity, income levels are high, but when the industry sees hard times or is affected by a natural hazard, the recovery may take longer. The agricultural sector is no exception and is, perhaps, even more vulnerable given its dependence on climate. Any change in weather conditions or increases in hydrometeorological hazards, such as flooding, drought or hail, can affect annual and decadal incomes and the sustainability of the resource base. This fourth factor explains 8.6 per cent of the variation, with percentage rural farm population and percentage employment in extractive industries having the highest correlations.

Housing stock and tenancy

The quality and ownership of housing is an important component of vulnerability. The fifth factor explains 7 per cent of the variance, with the most dominant variables including mobile homes, renters and urban living. The nature of the housing stock (mobile homes) and the nature of ownership (renters) and the location (urban) combine to produce the social vulnerability depicted in this factor. The displacement of affected populations from damaged dwellings is potentially greater in urban areas than rural ones, while the destruction of mobile homes is potentially greater in rural areas (where they are often the dominant form of housing).

Race

Race contributes to social vulnerability through the lack of access to resources, cultural differences and the social, economic and political marginalization that is often associated with racial disparities. Our sixth factor identifies race, specifically African American, as an indicator of social vulnerability. This factor also correlates highly with percentage female-headed households, noting that counties with high percentages of African American female-headed households are among the most vulnerable. This factor explains 6.9 per cent of the variation among US counties. Factor 9 identifies another racial group, Asians, and accounts for 3.9 per cent of the variability among counties.

Ethnicity

Like race, ethnicity also is a clearly defined factor contributing to vulnerability and this factor is mostly correlated with Hispanic in Factor 7 and Native American in Factor 8. These factors explain 4.2 per cent and 4.1 per cent of the variation among US counties, respectively.

Occupation

The literature suggests that occupation is an important dimension of vulnerability. The tenth factor, in fact, distinguishes counties based on occupations – primarily lower-wage service occupations such as personal services. As might be expected, counties heavily dependent on this employment base might suffer greater impacts from natural hazards and face slower recovery from disasters. This factor explains 3.2 per cent of the variance among counties.

Infrastructure dependence

The 11th factor (explaining 2.9 per cent of the variance) is a hybrid one that loads highly on two individual indicators – large debt to revenue ratio and percentage employed in public utilities and other infrastructure (transportation and communications). The economic vitality and revenue-generating capability of a county is a good indicator of its ability to divert resources to hazard mitigation and, ultimately, recovery should the disaster occur. Those counties with high debt to revenue ratio and primary dependence on infrastructure employment have fewer localized resources for recovery, thereby affecting their ability to successfully recover from a disaster.

The Social Vulnerability Index (SoVI)

The factor scores were added to the original county file as 11 additional variables and then placed in an additive model to produce the composite Social Vulnerability Index score (SoVI) for each county. The SoVI is a relative measure of the overall social vulnerability for each county. We selected an additive model, thereby making no a priori assumption about the importance of each factor in the overall sum. In this way, each factor was viewed as having an equal contribution to the county's overall vulnerability. In the absence of a defensible method for assigning weights, we felt this was the best option. Further, all factors were scaled so that positive values indicated higher levels of vulnerability; negative values decreased or lessened the overall vulnerability. In those instances where the effect was ambiguous (both increased and decreased vulnerability), we used the absolute value. To determine the most and least vulnerable of the counties (e.g. the outliers based on a normal curve), the SoVI scores were mapped based on standard deviations from the mean into five categories ranging from −1 on the lower end to +1 on the upper end.

The Geography of Social Vulnerability

As expected, the vast majority of US counties exhibit moderate levels of social vulnerability. The SoVI ranges from −9.6 (low social vulnerability) to 49.51 (high social vulnerability) with mean vulnerability score of 1.54 (std. dev. = 3.38) for all US counties. With some notable exceptions, the most vulnerable counties appear in the southern half of the nation (Figure 8.1), stretching from south Florida to California – regions with greater ethnic and racial inequalities as well as rapid population growth.

Counties with SoVI scores greater than +1 standard deviations are labelled as most vulnerable. They include a geographic mix of highly urbanized counties, large Hispanic and/or Native American populations, and socially dependent populations (those in poverty and lacking in education). A total of 393 counties (12.5 per cent of the total) were classified in the most vulnerable category. The most socially vulnerable county in the nation is Manhattan Borough (part

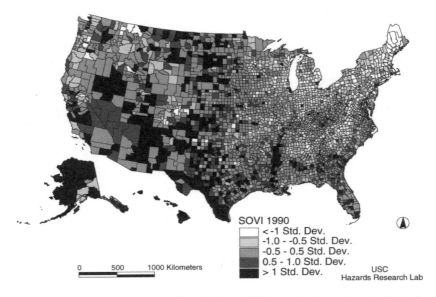

Figure 8.1 *Comparative vulnerability of US counties based on the Social Vulnerability Index (SoVI)*

of New York City), largely based on the density of the built environment. This factor accounts for the placement of San Francisco County and Bronx County (New York City) among the top five most vulnerable counties as well. Two other counties complete the top five, but their vulnerability is derived entirely from different indicators. Kalawao, Hawaii is ranked second in overall social vulnerability based on three factors: age of residents (elderly), race/ethnicity (Asian and Native Hawaiian), and personal wealth (poverty). This is not surprising given the county's history as a former leper colony. In 1990, there were fewer than 200 residents of this county. Benton, Washington's social vulnerability is defined by its large debt to revenue ratio and reliance on high percentage employment in utilities. Again, this is not surprising when one considers that Benton County is home to Hanford Nuclear Reservation, a Department of Energy facility. A lower tax base (most of the county is in federal land ownership) coupled with the need to provide services helps to account for the relatively high debt to revenue ratio, thus increasing its social vulnerability.

Counties labelled as the least vulnerable (more than –1 standard deviation from the mean) are clustered in New England, along the eastern slopes of the Appalachian Mountains from Virginia to North Carolina, and in the Great Lakes states. Topping the list of least vulnerable counties are Yellowstone National Park, MT; Poquoson, VA; Los Alamos, NM; Tolland, CT; and Moore, TN. The low social vulnerability score for Yellowstone National Park County is not a surprise given that the county is mostly in a protected status with a very small population that has little ethnic, racial or gender diversity. The remaining counties are all relatively homogeneous – suburban, wealthy, white and highly educated – characteristics that lower the level of social vulnerability. The exception is Moore County, TN, located in the south central portion of the state. The county is also homogeneous, with predominately white, middle-class residents living in owner-occupied housing who are employed in technical, sales or executive positions. The county has relatively low unemployment as it is home to the Jack Daniel's Distillery, the primary source of employment in the area.

Using SoVI to Predict Disaster Impacts

To initially test the reliability and usefulness of the SoVI, we examined the number of presidential disaster declarations by county for the 1990s. We recognize that these declarations represent larger, singular events rather than smaller, more chronic losses, and are often seen as political rewards rather than risk or impact-driven responses (Downton and Pielke, 2001). However, as a proof of concept, the relationship between the frequency of disaster declarations per county and its level of social vulnerability (as measured by the SoVI) might yield some useful insights.

We conducted a simple correlation between the frequency of presidential disaster declarations by county (during the 1990s) and the SoVI index score. There is a weak but negative relationship ($r = -0.099$, $s = 0.000$) between the number of disaster declarations and higher SoVI scores. This initially suggests no discernible trend in the relationship between presidential declarations and the degree of social vulnerability. Nationally, the average number of presidential disaster declarations per county is 2.4, yet among the most vulnerable counties (Figure 8.1), the mean is 1.97, while for the least vulnerable the mean number of disaster declarations is 2.52. These differences, however, are not statistically significant.

Conclusions

There is no consensus within the social science community about social vulner-ability or its correlates. Using the hazards of place model of vulnerability, we suggest that social vulnerability is a multidimensional concept that helps to identify those characteristics and experiences of communities (and individuals) that enable them to respond to and recover from environmental hazards. The correlates are largely derivative from local case studies of disasters and community responses. There have been few, if any, attempts to develop larger theoretical or conceptual understandings of comparative indicators of social vulnerability, despite the clear need to develop such a robust and replicable set.

The factors identified in the statistical analysis are consistent with the broader hazards literature and not only demonstrate the geographic variability in social vulnerability, but also the range in the underlying causes of that vulnerability. As a comparative measure, this methodology works quite well, explaining about 76 per cent of the statistical variance in US counties, using 11 independent factors. Having said this, we realize that the SoVI is not a perfect construct and more refinements are necessary. This is very clear based on the lack of correlation with presidential disaster declarations, which may be a function of the SoVI, but is more likely a function of the frequency and location of disaster events as well as the political process involved in the declaration process itself.

The SoVI can be coupled with hazard event frequency (number of natural hazards events, for example) and economic loss data to further examine those individual factors that are the most important contributors to dollar losses. This could be done on an individual hazard basis (e.g. floods, hurricanes) or by specific time period for all hazards. Not all factors are equal, and the need to develop a defensible weighting scheme is important. But what should determine those relative weights?

The next step is to examine how the overall social vulnerability as measured by the SoVI has changed over time and space. To do that requires a historical reconstruction of the variables used in this analysis. In this way, one can monitor changes in the total social vulnerability score as well as its underlying dimensions from a set period, 1960 onward, for example. Further, the analysis can be projected into the future (in this case using Census 2000 and beyond) using this analogue data to develop realistic scenarios of potential future vulnerabilities.

This methodology also can support specific subsetting of counties, such as coastal or riverine counties, to ascertain similarities and differences in relative levels of social vulnerability. The relationship between the level of social vulnerability and biophysical risk is the obvious next step. How well do the counties match up? Are those counties most exposed (higher hazard potential or greater biophysical risk) also the most socially vulnerable? In adding a physical component, vulnerability can be examined not just as a social or a biophysical phenomenon, but as a complex interaction of the two. This integrative step will help advance our understanding of vulnerability science at the local, regional and national scales. The SoVI can assist local decision-makers in pinpointing those factors that threaten the sustainability and stability of the county (or community). Using this index in conjunction with biophysical risk data, means that mitigation efforts can be targeted at the most vulnerable groups or counties. The development and integration of social, built environment, and natural hazard indicators will improve our hazard assessments and justify the selective targeting of communities for mitigation based on good social science, not just political whim.

Acknowledgements

This research was supported by a grant from the National Science Foundation (CMS9905352). We would like to thank Dennis Mileti, Lori Peek, and Arleen A. Hill for their thoughtful comments on earlier drafts of this chapter, and Katie Field and Jeffrey Vincent who helped compile some of the original data. Preliminary versions of this chapter were presented at the annual meetings of the Association of American Geographers and the annual Natural Hazards Workshops. We will readily share all data and coding information with those researchers who wish to replicate the study. The authors are responsible for any errors of omission or commission as well as the interpretations and conclusions made in this chapter.

Notes

1. This procedure cannot be performed with missing values, so in these cases a value of zero was substituted. We recognize that assigning a value of zero for a missing variable for a case may not accurately represent the true vulnerability based on that one variable, and that in all likelihood it would underestimate the level of vulnerability for those affected counties. From our perspective, it was more important to include all US counties in the analysis (a spatial decision), rather than dropping them (the majority of which were in Alaska and Hawaii).
2. To simplify the structure of underlying dimensions and produce more independence among the factors, a varimax rotation was used in the factor analysis. The varimax rotation minimizes the number of variables that load high on a single factor, thereby increasing the percentage variation between each factor. Eigenvalues greater than 1.00 were used to generate the 11 factors and were based on a scree diagram showing a distinct break in the values.

References

Anderson, M. B. (2000) 'Vulnerability to disaster and sustainable development: A general framework for assessing vulnerability' in R. Pielke, jr and R. Pielke sr (eds) *Storms (vol. 1)*, Routledge, London, pp11–25

Blaikie, P., Cannon, T., Davis, I. and Wisner, B. (1994) *At Risk: Natural Hazards, People's Vulnerability, and Disasters*, Routledge, London

Bolin, R. (1993) *Household and Community Recovery After Earthquakes*, Institute of Behavioral Science, University of Colorado, Boulder, CO

Bolin, R. and Stanford, L. (1991) 'Shelter, housing and recovery: A comparison of US disasters', *Disasters*, vol 15, no 1, pp24–34

Bolin, R. with Stanford, L. (1998) *The Northridge Earthquake: Vulnerability and Disaster*, Routledge, London:

Burton, I., Kates, R. W. and White, G. F. (1993) *The Environment as Hazard* (2nd edition), Guildford, New York

Comfort, L., Wisner, B., Cutter, S., Pulwarty, R., Hewitt, K., Oliver-Smith, A., Wiener, J., Fordham, M., Peacock, W. and Krimgold, F. (1999) 'Reframing disaster policy: The global evolution of vulnerable communities', *Environmental Hazards*, vol 1, no 1, pp39–44

Cova, T. J. and Church, R. L. (1997) 'Modeling community evacuation vulnerability using GIS', *International Journal of Geographical Information Science*, vol 11, pp763–784

Cutter, S. L. (1985) *Rating Places: A Geographer's View on Quality of Life*, Association of American Geographers, Washington, DC

Cutter, S. L. (ed) (2001a) *American Hazardscapes: The Regionalization of Hazards and Disasters*, Joseph Henry Press, Washington, DC

Cutter, S. L. (2001b) 'A research agenda for vulnerability science and environmental hazards', *IHDP Update* (Newsletter of the IHDP), vol 2, pp8–9

Cutter, S. L., Boruff, B. and Shirley, W. L. (2001) 'Indicators of social vulnerability to hazards', unpublished paper, University of South Carolina, Hazards Research Lab, Columbia, SC

Dow, K. (1992) 'Exploring differences in our common future(s): The meaning of vulnerability to global environmental change', *Geoforum*, vol 23, no 3, pp417–436

Downton, M. W. and Pielke, R. A. (2001) 'Discretion without accountability: Politics, flood damage, and climate', *Natural Hazards Review*, vol 2, no 4, pp157–166

Drabek, T. E. (1996) *Disaster Evacuation Behavior: Tourists and Other Transients*, Program on Environment and Behavior Monograph No. 58, Institute of Behavioral Science, University of Colorado, Boulder, CO

Duncan, O. D. (1969) *Towards Social Reporting: New Steps*, Russell Sage Foundation, New York

Duncan, O. D. (1984) *Notes on Social Measurement, Historical and Critical*, Russell Sage Foundation, Beverly Hills, CA

Enarson, E. and Morrow, B. (1998) *The Gendered Terrain of Disaster*, Praeger, New York

Enarson, E. and Scanlon, J. (1999) 'Gender patterns in flood evacuation: A case study in Canada's Red River Valley', *Applied Behavioral Science Review*, vol 7, no 2, pp103–124

Esty, D. and Cornelius, P. K. (eds) (2002) *Environmental Performance Measurement: The Global Report 2001–2002*, Oxford University Press, New York

Fothergill, A. (1996) 'Gender, risk, and disaster', *International Journal of Mass Emergencies and Disasters*, vol 14, no 1, pp33–56

Garoogian, D. (1999) *2000 America's Top-Rated Cities: A Statistical Handbook* (7th edition), Grey House Publishing, Lakeville

Goldman, B. A. (1991) *The Truth About Where You Live. An Atlas for Action on Toxics and Mortality*, Random House, New York

Hall, B. and Kerr, M. L. (1991) *1991–1992 Green Index*, Island Press, Washington, DC

Heinz Center for Science, Economics, and the Environment (2000) *The Hidden Costs of Coastal Hazards: Implications for Risk Assessment and Mitigation*, Island Press, Covello, CA

Heinz Center for Science, Economics, and the Environment (2002) *Human Links to Coastal Disasters*, The H. John Heinz III Center for Science, Economics and the Environment, Washington, DC

Hewitt, K. (1997) *Regions of Risk: A Geographical Introduction to Disasters*, Longman, Essex

Hewitt, K. (2000) 'Safe place or 'catastrophic society'? Perspectives on hazards and disasters in Canada', *Canadian Geographer*, vol 44, no 4, pp325–341

Kasperson, J. X., Kasperson, R. E. and Turner, B. L. (eds) (1995) *Regions at Risk: Comparisons of Threatened Environments*, United Nations University Press, Tokyo

Land, K. C. (1983) 'Social Indicators', *Annual Review of Sociology*, vol 9, pp1–26

Land, K. C. and Spilerman, S. (1975) *Social Indicator Models*, Russell Sage Foundation, New York

Mileti, D. (1999) *Disasters by Design: A Reassessment of Natural Hazards in the United States*, Joseph Henry Press, Washington, DC

Mitchell, J. K. (ed) (1999) *Crucibles of Hazard: Mega-Cities and Disasters in Transition*, United Nations University Press, Tokyo

Miringhoff, M. L. (1999) *The Social Health of the Nation: How America Is Really Doing*, Oxford University Press, New York

Morrow, B. H. (1999) 'Identifying and mapping community vulnerability', *Disasters*, vol 23, no 1, pp11–18

Morrow, B. H. and Phillips, B. (1999) 'What's gender "got to do with it"?', *International Journal of Mass Emergencies and Disasters*, vol 17, no 1, pp5–11

Ngo, E. B. (2001) 'When disasters and age collide: Reviewing vulnerability of the elderly', *Natural Hazards Review*, vol 2, no 2, pp80–89

National Research Council (2000) *Ecological Indicators for the Nation*, National Academy Press, Washington, DC

O'Brien, P. and Mileti, D. (1992) 'Citizen participation in emergency response following the Loma Prieta earthquake', *International Journal of Mass Emergencies and Disasters*, vol 10, pp71–89

Peacock, W., Morrow, B. H. and Gladwin, H. (eds) (1997) *Hurricane Andrew and the Reshaping of Miami: Ethnicity, Gender, and the Socio-Political Ecology of Disasters*, University Press of Florida, Gainsville, FL

Platt, R. H. (1995) 'Lifelines: An emergency management priority for the United States in the 1990s', *Disasters*, vol 15, pp172–176

Platt, R. H. (1999) *Disasters and Democracy: The Politics of Extreme Natural Events*, Island Press, Washington, DC

Puente, S. (1999) 'Social vulnerability to disaster in Mexico City' in Mitchell, J. K. (ed) *Crucibles of Hazard: Mega-Cities and Disasters in Transition*, United Nations University Press, Tokyo, pp295–334

Pulido, L. (2000) 'Rethinking environmental racism: White privilege and urban development in Southern California', *Annals of the Association of American Geographers*, vol 90, pp12–40

Putnam, R. D. (2000) *Bowling Alone: Collapse and Revival of the American Community*, Simon and Schuster, New York

Rossi, R. J. and Gilmartin, K. J. (1980) *The Handbook of Social Indicators: Sources, Characteristics and Analysis*, Garland STPM Press, New York

Savageau, D. (2000) *Places Rated Almanac*, IDG Books, Foster City, CA

Shaw-Taylor, Y. (1999) *Measurement of Community Health: The Social Health Index*, University Press of America, Lanham, MD

Smith, D. (1973) *Geography of Social Well Being*, McGraw Hill, New York

Smith, T. W. (1981) 'Social indicators: A review essay', *Journal of Social History*, vol 14, pp739–747

Social Capital Community Benchmark Survey (2002) *Social Capital Community Benchmark Survey*, www.cfsv.org/communitysurvey/results.html

Tierney, K. J., Lindell, M. K. and Perry, R. W. (2001) *Facing the Unexpected: Disaster Preparedness and Response in the United States*, Joseph Henry Press, Washington, DC

Tobin, G. A. and Ollenburger, J. C. (1993) *Natural Hazards and the Elderly*, University of Colorado, Natural Hazards Research and Applications Information Center, Boulder, CO

UNDP (United Nations Development Programme) (2000) *Human Development Report 2000*, Oxford University Press, New York

USEPA (US Environmental Protection Agency) (2002) *Environmental Indicators*, www.epa.gov/epaoswer/hazwaste/ca/eis.htm

US Health and Human Services Administration (2001) *Community Health Status Report*, www.communityhealth.hrsa.gov

Webb, G. R., Tierney, K. J. and Dahlhamer, J. M. (2000) 'Business and disasters: Empirical patterns and unanswered questions', *Natural Hazards Review*, vol 1, no 2, pp83–90

World Bank (2001) *World Development Indicators: Environmental Indicators*, www.worldbank.org/wdi2001/environment.htm

World Economic Forum (2000) *Pilot Environmental Sustainability Index*, Yale Center for Environmental Law and Policy, New Haven

World Economic Forum (2002) *Environmental Sustainability Index*, www.ciesin.columbia.edu/indicators/ESI/downloads.html

World Resources Institute (1993) *Green Metro Index: The 1993 Information Please Environmental Almanac*, Houghton Mifflin, Boston, MA

9

The Science of Vulnerability
and the Vulnerability of Science

Susan L. Cutter

> *The organized complexity of modern existence is a new phenomenon in [hu]man's experience. Considering what has happened in the United States during the last century, one is tempted to ask whether we are living in a moment of great progress or of great aberration in the human adventure.*
>
> (Thomas, 1956, ppxxxv–xxxvi)

Watching the tragedy of 11 September 2001 unfold on television highlighted the instantaneous globalization of an essentially local hazard event (albeit with national and international repercussions), an event similar to other rapid-onset hazards, such as major earthquakes. The terrorist hijackings, the collapse of the World Trade Centers, and the attack on the Pentagon resulted in the most costly disaster in the nation's history, yet the immediate disaster response employed the same procedures and activated the same emergency response plans that were already in place at the local, state and federal levels for natural disasters.

Immediately following the initial rescue and relief phases of the emergency (after the first month or so) the questions began. Why did we not foresee this type of attack as a real threat? Why was the nation not more prepared for these types of terrorist attacks? When and where will this type of action occur again? How should the nation prepare for and respond to potential threats such as those manifested by the 11 September events? What constraints are there on such responses, both domestically and internationally?

The events of 11 September illustrate some of the shortcomings in our knowledge about the world we live in. Despite some of the most sophisticated models, monitoring systems and science in the world, we were unable to effectively anticipate and predict the series of cascading impacts rendered by the attacks, nor were

Note: Reprinted, with permission, from the *Annals of the Association of American Geographers*, vol 93, no 1, Susan L. Cutter, 'AAG Presidential Address: The science of vulnerability and the vulnerability of science', pp1–12. © Blackwell Publishing, 2003

we able to completely understand and articulate the root causes of such actions. This chapter examines the twin issues of the inadequacies in our current modes of understanding (the vulnerability of science) and the need for more integrative approaches in understanding and responding to environmental hazards (vulnerability science).

Why Is Science Vulnerable?

According to *Webster's Dictionary*, one of the definitions of vulnerable is 'open to or easily hurt by criticism or attack'. There are many ways in which science is vulnerable. I will only focus on a few that are most relevant to understanding environmental threats: assumptions of rationality and objectivity; expert versus lay judgements; inability to capture surprise; and the social construction of scientific practice.

Objectivity and rationality

The US public readily turns to science for inputs relevant to hazards such as hurricane tracking or tornado monitoring. One of the primary values of science is its power of explanation, which is then tested by prediction. The problem, from a hazards or risk perspective, is one of bounding. How can one calculate *all* the probabilities and contingencies associated with dangers and dangerous activities? This is impossible, for people are constrained both by the sheer volume of available information and by human cognitive abilities to process all of it. Therefore, the evaluation of risks (and dangers) is based on a narrower set of information and becomes a subjective process based on value judgements (Shrader-Frechette, 1991) and other simplifying criteria. Decisions on what risks are acceptable (and to whom) often lead to the contested nature of risk assessment (as a formal process and practice) and the politicization of public policies to reduce or manage them (Cutter, 1993). How do individuals and societies choose what risks to ignore and which ones to manage?

The rational-actor paradigm that is so prevalent in modern science is a Western worldview, one that presumes that humans are rational beings motivated by self-interest who consciously evaluate alternative courses of action to maximize individual reward (Jaeger et al, 2001, p23). As a theoretical starting point, this paradigm alone appears insufficient to explain the seemingly non-rational (at least from a Western perspective) behaviour of suicide bombers and terrorists in the Middle East and elsewhere. On the other hand, if rational choice is construed in relative terms, then the context or framing perspective becomes important (Smelser, 1998) and helps to explain the 'irrational' outcome. For example, the same risky behaviour (e.g. suicide bomber) would seem like a perfectly rational choice in one setting (disenfranchisement of Palestinian youth), but appear as totally irrational in another (American mass media). How does science explain this seeming contradiction?

Expert versus lay judgements: How safe is safe enough?

Another aspect of science's vulnerability is the notion that scientific judgements about threats are always correct, while public perceptions of threats are misguided because they are fostered by the mass media and therefore are largely emotional. The result is conflict between what is termed actual or 'real' risk based on some type of quantitative metric (normally measured by expected fatalities from the activity or technology in question) and 'perceived' risk based on more qualitative assessments using a set of more expansive factors than just expected fatalities (Freudenburg, 1988). The former often are called 'expert views', the latter 'lay judgements'. Historically, risk assessments and judgements were left up to experts, the so-called risk professionals (Starr, 1969; Dietz and Rycroft, 1987). The communication of such risks to the public was hierarchical (from the top down), with the risk assessors telling the public what technology or activity was risky, not the other way around (National Research Council, 1989).

With advancements in risk perception research spearheaded by the psychology community (Slovic, 1987, 2001) a new understanding emerged. First, both expert and lay judgements are subject to cognitive biases based on human inabilities to process all the required information needed for a decision. Instead, decision-making relies on a series of heuristics (or decision tools) that enable people to simplify the information and cognitively process it more effectively. The availability heuristic, for example, suggests that when hazard or risk incidents are easily recalled from memory (such as media coverage of tornado damage or airplane crashes), people develop biased probability estimates and tend to overestimate the actual frequency of tornadoes or airplane crashes. Another example is the affect heuristic (Slovic et al, 2002). This simplifying rule states that activities or technologies that are disliked or feared (an emotional response) influence both the perception of the risk (high) and the perceptions of the benefits of that technology or activity (low).

Second, risk perception research found that public understanding of risk was not flawed or wrong; rather, risks were more broadly defined by the public, who took into account some of the societal implications of accepting the risks in their acceptability/unacceptability judgements (National Research Council, 1996). In other words, societal selection of what risks or hazards to emphasize and which ones to ignore often reflected moral, political, and economic choices that were themselves value-laden and socially constructed (Douglas and Wildavsky, 1982). Increasingly, the technical or scientific view of risk is being supplanted by issues of feelings, trust, social equity, values and ambiguities in determining what risks are acceptable by the public and which ones are not. Who is more correct? Which view should be the basis for public policies? Clearly, the politicization of risk and the necessity for public debates on the social tolerance of risk are important. Equally important, however, is to consider how societal processes amplify or attenuate public risk judgements.

In their pioneering study, Kasperson and colleagues (1988) posit that risks interact with social, cultural, economic, psychological and institutional processes in ways that either amplify or dampen public responses. Using the analogy of throwing different-sized stones into a pond and watching the ripples emerge, some products, activities, or technologies have relatively minor risks (as defined by technical experts), yet they produce massive public reactions. The anthrax episode following the 11 September terrorist attack is a classic example of the social amplification of risk. Anthrax (*Bacillus anthracis*) is not a new hazard. Anthrax spores have been around for centuries, and human cases of inhalation exposure were most often associated with people who had close contact with animals or animal products, such as those in the tanning and textile industries (Jernigan et al, 2001). The first instance of a large-scale public exposure to weaponized anthrax occurred in 1979 in Sverdlovsk, Russia, when an explosion at a military research facility accidentally released dried spores into the atmosphere, resulting in more than 1000 immediate fatalities (Oberg, 1988; Meselson et al, 1994; Alibek, 1999; Guillemin, 1999; Miller et al, 2001).

As the social amplification of risk model hypothesizes, large volumes of information about the risk or an event from the media, disputes over factual information (arguments among technical or scientific experts challenging data, assumptions, findings) and the visual dramatization of the event all lead to the amplification of the risk (or risk event) along with its attendant impacts and management challenges (Kasperson and Kasperson, 1996). So, did the public fear anthrax because it was inherently dangerous, or were they responding to the sensational media coverage that exaggerated the individual threat potential at the time, which in turn affected the over-response of management institutions and decision-makers?

Capturing surprise and unintended consequences

The increasing interconnectedness of human, natural and engineered systems necessitates greater understanding of all the likely causes and consequences of failures in technological systems. The technological complexity and interdependence of many of our transportation, power, utility and economic systems means that a failure in one cascades to disruptions and failures in others. For example, the delays (often weeks to months) in factory shipments to consumers (especially computers) from the grounding of commercial aviation in the wake of 11 September was an unanticipated consequence of the collapse of the World Trade Center and Pentagon attacks. As Perrow argued in 1984, the increasing complexity of these tightly coupled and interdependent systems could result in catastrophic failures, as multiple subsystems (and their back-ups) fail (Perrow, 1984). Invariably, a seemingly insignificant problem such as a malfunctioning instrument gauge, coupled with human error, escalates into a full-blown systems failure, such as the nuclear power plant accident at Three Mile Island (Perrow, 1984).

Many examples exist of science's inability to capture 'imaginable' surprise (Schneider et al, 1998) and anticipate unintended consequences (Tenner, 1996).[1] Not only did the overuse of DDT starting in the 1950s affect bird populations (especially the bald eagle) and ecosystems, as noted by Carson (1962), but environmental persistence and pest resistance to these chlorinated pesticides ushered in a new generation of synthetic pesticides and other industrial chemicals (organochlorines) that are now bioaccumulating in the environment and affecting human health (Wargo, 1996; Thornton, 2000). Some of these synthetic compounds mimic natural hormones and disrupt developmental and reproductive processes, which in turn lead to increases in birth defects, hormonal disorders and reproductive failures in many species (amphibians and mammals, including humans) (Colborn et al, 1996; Schettler et al, 1999). The environmental endocrine hypothesis, as it is known, was initially greeted with scepticism by the scientific community, but it has now become a central focus of environmental health research and policy agendas (Krimsky, 2000).

There are historical analogues as well. The most obvious example was the implementation of the 'Atoms for Peace' programme in the Eisenhower administration, policies that promoted the peaceful use of atomic power, especially for electrical power generation. The nation embarked on a commercial nuclear power programme without fully realizing the necessity for, or the technological specifications of, managing the long-term disposal of high-level nuclear wastes. The consequence is the lack of a permanent national repository and the ongoing controversy over the selection of Yucca Mountain as the site for high-level radioactive waste disposal (Jacob, 1990; Shrader-Frechette, 1993).

What emergent risks are awaiting us and how might they manifest themselves (Erikson, 1994)? The widespread use of antibiotics during the past decades for bacterial infections (an effective treatment) and viruses such as common colds, flu or sore throats (an ineffective treatment) has resulted in antibiotic-resistant bacteria (CDC, 2002). Infectious diseases and bacterial infections that were once easily treatable (such as children's ear infections) are now more difficult and costly to care for, and the re-emergence of drug-resistant forms of tuberculosis and bacterial pneumonias foreshadows one of the most pressing health problems for the nation and the world (Smith, 2001). The increasing role of genetically modified organisms (GMOs) will have unintended consequences, many that are only imaginable in the fertile minds of science-fiction authors (Clement, 2001; Sherbaniuk, 2001). Who really knows when, where and under what conditions these risks might emerge?

The world is not static, and we discover new threats daily. A case in point is the recent analysis of the nation's water quality, which provided a detailed assessment of the occurrence of organic wastewater contaminants (pharmaceuticals, medications, personal care products) excreted by livestock and humans (Revkin, 2002). The researchers found that 80 per cent of the streams sampled had organic wastewater contaminants. The most frequently detected substances included steroids, insect repellants, non-prescription drugs and disinfectants (Kolpin et al, 2002). This research illustrates another potential source of hormonally active chemicals into the environment, many of them with unknown effects on humans and aquatic ecosystems. As Kates (1985, p47) so eloquently stated nearly two decades ago, 'The shift from better-understood hazards to less-understood hazards has placed an enormous burden on science to identify hazards and assess their risks.' Kates (1985, pp56–57) reminds us further that 'New products will bring new hazards problems. Old products and processes in new locales will bring new hazard problems ... Finally, there will be surprises – surprises that in turn will generate new concerns and activities.' The question becomes: is science up to the job?

Social construction of science and scientific practice

Attempts to explain the intrinsic order of nature often fall into polarizing extremes. In the 19th century, for example, it was science versus religion. In the latter half of the 20th century, C. P. Snow (1993) labelled the dichotomy the 'two cultures' in 1959, highlighting the growing schism in modes of language and explanation between science on the one hand and the humanities on the other. More recently, the new 'science wars' pit realists against relativists (Gould, 2000). Realists uphold the objective nature of science and its empirical adequacy, while relativists argue that science is but one set of beliefs where universality or scientific truth is socially conditioned, not absolute.

The contending visions of science are rarely complementary, but more often than not, they are mutually exclusive (see Turner, 2002). For some, science is a lens through which we view the world. It is not the only way of viewing it, of course, but science has been the dominant perspective in the 20th century and beyond. Another view of science is that it is a process for understanding and making sense of the world, largely reflected in its methods. Finally, there is a pragmatic vision of science, which is to support public policy, to offer 'objectivity' in a sea of political waves. These competing visions of science by various stakeholders result in a less than satisfying understanding of the causes and consequences of and responses to environmental threats, including terrorism.

One critique of science, from the perspective of standpoint theory, argues that the acquisition of knowledge is partially determined by adopting different views about the natural world. These perspectives are influenced by gender, race, social and cultural differences (Haraway, 1988; Harvey, 1996; Schiebinger, 1999), and translate into privileged or unprivileged positions within society (Pulido, 2000). Inasmuch as the belief of science and the acquisition of knowledge are socially influenced, the practice of science also is socially constructed (Harding, 1991). The social construction of science helps to explain why some scientific results are not always replicable – different labs working on the same 'problem,' using the same protocols, and coming up with different results, the discrepancy attributed to the social organization within the lab itself. Scientific problems and hypotheses themselves can be defined and structured differently depending on one's perspective and agenda.

The under-representation of women and people of colour in science is a perennial problem, one that affects the nature of scientific enquiry and the practice of science. Work-force diversity leads to new scientific discoveries by challenging existing norms and research paradigms (Rosser, 2000). The under-representation of women, children and people of colour in clinical trials – a peculiar omission given the age, race and gender-specific pattern of major debilitating diseases such as asthma, breast cancer, osteoporosis or hypertension – also highlights the social construction of scientific practice. Formal federal recognition of the latter occurred in 1991 when the National Institutes of Health established its 15-year, multi-million-dollar Women's Health Initiative. Designed to identify gaps in biomedical research on the common causes of mortality, disease and impaired quality of life in post-menopausal women, clinical trials involving more than 167,000 women began. Similarly, more environmental-health science research is now focused on the differential susceptibility of children to environmental toxicants through a comparable Children's Health Initiative. Paediatric environmental disease (lead poisoning, asthma, cancer, neurobehavioural disorders) averages around 3 per cent of the US total health care costs (Landrigan et al, 2002), an unacceptable level for many health professionals.

The Role of 11 September

Science-conditioned expectations defined pre-11 September dangers, especially from a national security perspective. American national-defence policy was oriented towards advanced technology and exotic missile defence systems. The likely source of the threat, based on prevailing Cold War ideologies, was strategic nuclear warheads. In many ways, the low-technology simple weapons (the use of a fully loaded jet airliner) were not part of the collective perception of national security concerns. The events of 11 September highlighted the vulnerability in the nation's information gathering – an over-reliance on technologically sophisticated surveillance assets at the expense of additional, on-the-ground human intelligence – and contributed to our surprise and general lack of understanding about some of the root causes (precursors) of international terrorism. The American public was left without sufficient explanations about why this group (al Qaeda), why now, and why the World Trade Center and Pentagon as targets.

With the collapse of the World Trade Center towers, there was and continues to be an underestimation of the impacts of this failure at all spatial scales. There is inadequate prediction and understanding of the cascading impacts of the 11 September events on local, regional, national and global economies – impacts that we still are discovering nearly a year and a half after the event. Finally, the events of 11 September illustrated in very private ways the interconnectedness of modern society, and painfully and publicly exposed the extent of our societal vulnerabilities. As noted in the National Research Council's (2002, pES-1) *Making the Nation Safer* report:

> *The vulnerability of societies to terrorist attacks results in part from the proliferation of chemical, biological, and nuclear weapons of mass destruction, but it also is a consequence of the highly efficient and interconnected systems that we rely on for key services such as transportation, information, energy, and health care. The efficient functioning of these systems reflects great technological achievements of the past century, but interconnectedness within and across systems also means that infrastructures are vulnerable to local disruptions, which could lead to widespread or catastrophic failures.*

The Need for a Geographical Response: Personal Reflections

My formative intellectual years were in the San Francisco Bay Area during the mid- to late 1960s, where my social and environmental activism was nurtured first in high school and later as an undergraduate at California State University, Hayward. My first research experience was as an undergraduate, examining defoliant spraying in Vietnam (Agent Orange) and its effects on human settlement patterns in the region (Thomas, 1975). Initially trained in qualitative approaches (the Berkeley School) with a strong emphasis on fieldwork, my graduate studies at the University of Chicago were just the opposite (spatial analysis and quantitative methods). By the time I reached Chicago, Gilbert White had already left for the University of Colorado, but the rich human environmental tradition remained. I maintained my interest in environmental issues and was fortunate enough to work on one of Brian Berry's funded research projects at the time (Berry, 1977). This comparative metropolitan assessment of the social burdens of pollution was one of the first environmental-justice research projects and fostered my ongoing concern about the relationship between race, class and environmental quality in urban areas. My dissertation (directed by Berry) examined community attitudes towards pollution in Chicago (Caris, 1978) and added additional methodological skills in survey research to my tool kit. In hindsight, I am convinced that my interests in environmental activism, social justice, methodological pluralism, nature–society interactions and – yes – tacky landscapes (especially the ubiquitous plastic pink flamingo) all had their origins in my experiences as a formal student.

As I embarked on my professional career, first as a visiting assistant professor in geography and environmental studies at the University of Washington, and then in a tenure-track appointment at Rutgers (surprisingly enough, not in geography, at first), I was able to foster my intellectual curiosity in all aspects of environmental science and policy by working in these multidisciplinary contexts. It was clear to me that geography, instead of being at the core of environmental studies (where it rightfully belonged), was instead on the periphery. With such a rich tradition in nature–society themes, how could this have happened?

As I watched the 11 September events unfold on television, it was obvious that the discipline could assist in the disaster response and recovery efforts, but more importantly, that it *should* take a lead role in guiding public policy in understanding what made people and places vulnerable to these and other environmental threats. I did not want the discipline to be a tertiary player in guiding public-policy response, as it was in the formative stages of the early environmental movement (harkening back to my frustrations as a student). The combination of geography's technical sophistication, regional expertise, understanding of the relationships between physical systems and social systems, methodological diversity and history of well-received pragmatic research gave us an advantage over other social science and natural science disciplines. My activist response was to spearhead a collaborative research and action agenda on the geographical dimensions of terrorism on behalf of the Association of American Geographers (AAG) (Cutter et al, 2002).[2] It is too soon to gauge the effectiveness of this effort, but the discipline has been recognized by federal policy, mission and funding agencies for the thoughtfulness and rapidity of its response.

Vulnerability Science

Society expects science to help reduce uncertainty, yet for many environmental controversies and some environmental threats, science has actually increased ambiguity. While uncertainty is a part of reality, especially when describing environmental threats such as climate change (National Research Council, 1999a), often the only socially responsible thing for science to do is to highlight it and talk about the consequences of doing something or doing nothing about the threat. Within the hazards arena, the precautionary principle (e.g. evacuations from hurricanes, vaccinations for communicable diseases) is one way that uncertainty is handled.

One of the great challenges for the environmental sciences is to live up to their policy potential and address questions that are of interest to policy-makers, instead of narrowly focused research questions that appeal only to environmental scientists (National Research Council, 2001). Vulnerability science is one such approach. Vulnerability science helps us understand those circumstances that put people and places at risk and those conditions that reduce the ability of people and places to respond to environmental threats. Vulnerability science provides a basis for risk, hazard and disaster reduction policies. It integrates the constructs of risk (exposure), hazard, resilience, differential susceptibility and recovery/mitigation. It parallels sustainability science (National Research Council, 1999b; Kates et al, 2001) and employs many of the same concepts (susceptibility, resistance, resilience and adaptation), but applies them more locally in trying to understand environmental risks and hazards and their adverse impacts. The current research trends in hazard vulnerability, however, are too focused on local social dynamics or identification of physical exposures (FEMA, 1997), too broad in their applications (models of physical processes and their attendant regional to global human impacts) (Downing, 1991; Blaikie et al, 1994; Clark et al, 2000), or examine only individual risks, not multi-hazard or multiple risks (Chapter 6).

Vulnerability science requires an integrative approach to explain the complex interactions among social, natural and engineered systems. It requires a new way of viewing the world, one that integrates perspectives from the sciences, social sciences and humanities. Since vulnerability can refer to individuals (person, housing structure), groups, systems or places, scalar differences and the ability to articulate between geographic scales are important components. Vulnerability manifests itself geographically in the form of hazardous places (floodplains, remnant waste sites); thus, spatial solutions are required, especially when comparing the relative levels of vulnerability between places or between different groups of people who live or work in those places. Last, methodological diversity in the examination and explanation of those circumstances that give rise to vulnerability and those factors that influence resistance and resilience to harm are essential.

Vulnerability science builds on the integrated and multidisciplinary tradition of hazards research (see Chapter 7; also Mileti, 1999; Cutter, 2001a; Montz et al, 2003). It uses qualitative and quantitative approaches, employs historic to future time perspectives, and incorporates pragmatic problem selection and problem solving. In addition to the obvious and considerable contributions from the nature–society interaction perspectives within the discipline (which gave rise to hazards research in the first place), geography has added a technological sophistication to hazards research that is unrivalled among the social sciences. The discipline is rapidly becoming the driving force behind vulnerability science, in much the same way that it was the driving force behind human dimensions of global change science (Turner et al, 1990) and, more recently, sustainability science.

Embedded throughout the discussion on the science of vulnerability is the requirement to anticipate surprise, capture uncertainty and accept change in our science and understanding. But how to do that poses one of the greatest challenges to the discipline. In advocating this new approach, the science of vulnerability, one must be mindful of how vulnerability science is affected by some of the vulnerabilities of science itself – rationality, expert versus lay judgements, uncertainty.

A research agenda for vulnerability science has been suggested elsewhere (Cutter, 2001b), but it bears re-examination in light of the events of 11 September. A number of the most significant themes for the discipline of geography are described briefly below.

Driving forces that amplify or attenuate vulnerability

We need to identify, delineate, and understand those driving forces that increase or decrease vulnerability at all scales. There was some initial work on this topic at the global scale (Blaikie et al, 1994; Kasperson et al, 1995; Mitchell, 1999; Clark et al, 2000; Kasperson and Kasperson, 2001) and regionally (Heinz Center, 2002), but much more research is required to answer the important questions. What makes megacities such as Caracas or Tokyo increasingly vulnerable to natural hazards or economic disruptions? How do the processes and patterns of urbanization affect developing countries' susceptibility to disease and increased mortality among their youth? How do the patterns of resource exploitation (or crop conversion) lead to environmental degradation, which in turn produces environmental refugees, which in turn increases ethnic tensions, ultimately creating more civil strife and armed conflict? What are some of the root causes of terrorism and terrorist acts, and what is the geographical linkage between the sources of financing and potential targets?

Risk relocation

What is the role of our current practices and public policies in fostering the relocation of risk (Etkin, 1999)? In what ways do our current policies transfer the risk burden from one individual to another or from one place to another? A case in point is the increase in car insurance rates in some areas among current policy-holders to compensate for the large pool of motorists without insurance, or the reduction in the choice of insurance companies for purchasing homeowners' insurance in post-Hurricane Andrew, Florida. How do federal policies, initially aimed at risk and hazard reduction, inadvertently put more people and places at risk? Despite some successes in relocating structures out of riverine floodplains, the National Flood Insurance Program is not particularly adept overall at reducing development in flood-prone barrier-island locations, ultimately encouraging coastal development rather than deterring it (Platt, 1999; Heinz Center, 2000). Many of our public policies transfer the risk to future generations through a 'use now, pay for the impacts later' mentality. The most obvious examples are the lack of a secure repository for high-level nuclear waste and controls on greenhouse gas emissions. How can we prevent this in the future? Vulnerability science can help guide us to answers on the temporal and spatial transference of risk.

Forecasting losses and their impact

As a nation, we lack the most elemental data on what hazard events cost the US on an annual basis. It may come as a surprise to many, but there is inconsistent and incomplete data on hazards events and losses (Mileti, 1999; Thomas, 2001) for the US. Often, events that are recorded (many are not) have incomplete information (cover only a certain time period), include only a few selected hazards (earthquakes or meteorological events), and define and measure losses in so many different and inconsistent ways that the development of a standardized national baseline of hazard events and losses is problematic at best. In addition to data, we lack the predictive capability to forecast future losses based on these historical analogues. Furthermore, the lack of data hampers any type of analysis of the effectiveness of risk and hazard reduction programmes, since we do not really know what the temporal and spatial patterning of losses were before the programme or policy was implemented and certainly do not know them 20 years later. We have failed as a nation in developing audits of hazard and risk reduction programmes, preferring instead to continue with disaster business as usual. At a minimum, loss estimation needs to be more scientifically based and less politically driven if we are to advance our understanding of vulnerability, especially at the sub-national level.

Better integrative models

One of the areas in vulnerability science that requires significant development is the modelling community. We need dynamic – not static – models that integrate risk exposures with place-based biophysical and social indicators. While there are very sophisticated and advanced risk models in the natural, engineering and health sciences, most of these are hazard-specific, and they rarely incorporate a spatial dimension (Hill and Cutter, 2001). There is an enormous potential for the discipline to be in the forefront in the development of spatially integrated all-hazards assessment models, an opportunity that should not be squandered. Contributions from the geographical information science field, among others, are required.

Comparative indicators

From the perspective of the policy community, there is a real need to develop a set of metrics to measure and compare the relative vulnerability of one place to another. Indices such as the UN Human Development Index (UNDP, 2000) or the disaster risk index (Cardona et al, 1999), while imperfect, do enable this type of comparative assessment of environmental and social conditions. The renewed interest in ecological and sustainability indicators (National Research Council, 2000; World Economic Forum, 2000; World Bank, 2001) and social vulnerability indicators (see Chapter 8; also Heinz Center, 2002) are recent examples. In many instances, the tools and techniques are available if adapted properly, but we lack the conceptual development on the most appropriate metrics and scale, as well as the minimum subset of indicators that will provide the foundation for comparisons.

Visualization and representation

Geography is a visual discipline and should be the leading intellectual force in developing visual representations of dynamic phenomena such as vulnerability. The use of geographic information systems (GIS) in hazards mapping and emergency response has increased during the past decade (Monmonier, 1997; Radke et al, 2000; Hodgson and Cutter, 2001). GIS certainly became a focal point for the 11 September rescue and relief operations (Cahan and Ball, 2002; Thomas et al, 2002). Better representations in three and four dimensions are required for real-time response, yet we need to be cognizant of how emergency managers (and the public for that matter) respond to, process and use such visualizations. The goal should be to develop an accurate and easily understandable visualization of risks, hazards and vulnerability. This will require enhanced linkages between the research community in GIScience (visualization and modelling) and the practitioner community in emergency preparedness and response and is absolutely essential if we are to advance vulnerability science.

Decision-making in response to threats

How individuals estimate risk, the role of uncertainty in risk judgements, and how risk cognition translates into overt action is another potential research area for our community. Within geography, natural-hazard perception research originated through collaborations with psychologists in trying to understand individual and collective decision-making in response to extreme threats (Sims and Baumann, 1972; White, 1974; Burton et al, 1993). There is considerable work within the discipline on evacuation behaviour (see Chapters 3, 14, 15 and 25; also Baker, 1991; Cova and Church, 1997) and the adoption of hazard mitigation options (e.g. insurance) in response to risk perceptions (Palm and Hodgson, 1992; Palm, 1994). Behavioural geographers have not focused as much attention on hazards as they could, preferring instead to focus on urban spatial behaviour (travel, transportation) and cognitive processes in understanding maps and spatial information (Golledge and Stimson, 1997; Golledge, 2002). One of the most perplexing questions presently confronting the social-science community is, why do people place themselves at risk and increase their vulnerability to environmental threats? More importantly, what contextual factors (e.g. institutions, market forces, social status) decrease individual responsibility for the consequences of stupid locational decisions?

Geography's Science and Practice

It is clear that vulnerability science has contributed to some of the increased vulnerabilities in science during the past few decades. As it evolves into a more robust field, however, vulnerability science is in a position to help reduce some of the inherent vulnerability of science and scientific explanations. But it will require transdisciplinary linkages, methodological pluralism, place-based knowledge and a continued practical focus on policy relevancy.

The science of vulnerability seeks to understand the range of possible effects of unlikely but possible events, their unintended consequences (on people and places and in scientific and technological research and development).[3] Further, vulnerability science is reflexive (Beck, 1999), learning from experience and anticipating how future vulnerability will change. In many ways, vulnerability science is the most intrinsically anticipatory branch of science and the one to turn to in times of crisis and response. Ultimately concerned with the pragmatic, vulnerability science has the response knowledge, supporting data, and tools and techniques for contingency analysis and is certainly ready to help understand unlikely and unanticipated eventualities. Vulnerability science links geography's research and application communities, providing a common and important ground for interaction. But it does more than that: it provides a critical linkage between geography and other social, natural, engineering and health sciences.

One challenge we face is to produce the next generation of researchers who will further advance the development of new conceptual models, tools and techniques for understanding vulnerability. It is imperative that we move beyond the hazard du jour approach in our current scholarship and seek funding and reward mechanisms that enable an all-hazards approach to vulnerability science.

The discipline of geography is at the core of vulnerability science, and we should not be bashful about this claim. As Harlan Barrows (1923, p1) stated more than a century ago, '[G]eography ... properly can claim the title of Mother of the Sciences.' Let us use this to our advantage. The importance and relevance of geography to public policy is also vital and has been a consistent theme echoed by past presidents as well, including White (1962, p279), who wrote: 'The contributions which geographic thought can make to the advancement of society are ... so powerful that failure to recognize them jeopardizes the ability of citizens to deal intelligently with a rapidly changing and increasingly complex world.' This statement is applicable now more than ever, as we seek information about terrorism and terrorist threats, root causes, and our collective vulnerabilities to them. However, we cannot be mired by philosophical debates and ruminations about cause and effects, nor can we be so eager to blissfully apply all of the geographical techniques to these pressing problems without questioning the repercussions of their use on privacy and personal freedoms. We must find the balance between theoretical and the applied perspectives to more fully engage the pragmatic and public policy dimensions of vulnerability. This is not a new admonition either, as many past presidents have made similar remarks. For example, Brian Berry (1980, p454) wrote:

Many of the concepts employed by practitioners do have their origin in scholarly work, but even larger numbers of such concepts have been applied and found wanting, misguided, or irrelevant. Such practical assessments should be the source of change in academia, for a scholarly agenda developed in isolation can quickly become scholastic, misdirected, or just plain wrong.

We need to take the road still beckoning (Kates, 1987) and provide the theory and practical understanding of human environmental science and to make it more spatially informed. Vulnerability science is one path that leads to understanding what makes people, places and societies vulnerable to a range of environmental threats. With geography as the intellectual and integrative driving force behind vulnerability science, the goal – and thus grand challenge – is to improve our public policies to lessen the vulnerability of our own children and the world's children, all of whom deserve and demand the right to a healthy environment and a peaceful future. If our science and practice can achieve this, then we will have truly made a difference.

Acknowledgements

I am grateful to Brian Berry, Risa Palm, Billie Turner and Tom Wilbanks for thoughtful comments on earlier drafts of this chapter. Tom and Billie were especially critical and extremely helpful in clarifying some of the themes. As is evident in the text, I was fortunate to have excellent mentors along my academic journey and many strong influences that were too numerous to cite in the text. My students (past and present) provide a constant source of inspiration and interaction and stretch and enhance my knowledge base in innumerable ways. I cannot possibly thank them all publicly, but you know who you are! There are four individuals, however, who played important roles in my intellectual development and in my career who are unable to read this chapter and whom I shall remember with great fondness: William L. Thomas, Jeanne X. Kasperson, Jack Mwroka and Jim Allen.

Notes

1. I am grateful to B. L. Turner II for his insistence that imaginable surprise is a better way of stating this and for pointing me towards the Schneider, Turner, and Morehouse Garriga (1998) contribution.
2. The principal investigators on behalf of the AAG included myself, Douglas B. Richardson, and Thomas J. Wilbanks. The project was supported through funding from the National Science Foundation's Geography and Regional Science Program (BCS-0200619).
3. I am indebted to Tom Wilbanks for suggesting the ideas in this paragraph.

References

Alibek, K. (1999) *Biohazard*, Random House, New York
Baker, E. J. (1991) 'Hurricane evacuation behavior', *International Journal of Mass Emergencies and Disasters*, vol 9, no 2, pp287–310
Barrows, H. H. (1923) 'Geography as human ecology', *Annals of the Association of American Geographers*, vol 13, no 1, pp1–14

Beck, U. (1999) *World Risk Society*, Polity Press, Oxford

Berry, B. J. L. (1977) *The Social Burdens of Environmental Pollution*, Ballinger, Cambridge, MA

Berry, B. J. L. (1980) 'Creating future geographies', *Annals of the Association of American Geographers*, vol 70, no 4, pp449–458

Blaikie, P., Cannon, T., Davis, I. and Wisner, B. (1994) *At Risk: Natural Hazards, People's Vulnerability, and Disasters*, Routledge, London

Burton, I., Kates, R. W. and White, G. F. (1993) *The Environment as Hazard*, 2nd edition, Guildford Press, New York

Cahan, B. and Ball, M. (2002) 'GIS ground zero: Spatial technology bolsters World Trade Center response and recovery', *GEOWorld* online, www.geoplace.com/gw/2002/0201/0201wtc.asp accessed in October 2002

Cardona, C., Davidson, R. and Villacis, C. (1999) 'Understanding urban seismic risk around the world' in J. Ingleton (ed) *Natural Disaster Management*, Tudor Rose, Leicester, pp262–263

Caris (Cutter), S. L. (1978) *Community Attitudes Toward Pollution*, Department of Geography Research Paper no 188, University of Chicago, Chicago

Carson, R. (1962) *Silent Spring*, Houghton Mifflin, Boston

CDC (Centers for Disease Control) (2002) 'Background on antibiotic resistance', www.cdc.gov/drugresistance/community/accessed in October 2002

Clark, W. C., Jager, J., Corell, R., Kasperson, R., McCarthy, J. J., Cash, D., Cohen, S. J., Desanker, P., Dickson, N. M., Epstein, P., Guston, D. H., Hall, J. M., Jaeger, C., Janetos, A., Leary, N., Levy, M. A., Luers, A., MacCracken, M., Melillo, J., Moss, R., Nigg, J. M., Parry, M. L., Parson, E. A., Ribot, J. C., Schrag, D. P., Seielstad, G. A., Shea, E., Vogel, C. and Wilbanks, T. J. (2000) *Assessing Vulnerability to Global Environmental Risks*, Belfer Center for Science and International Affairs (BCSIA) Discussion Paper 2000–12, Environment and Natural Resources Program, John F. Kennedy School of Government, Harvard University, Cambridge, MA, http://ksgnotes1.harvard.edu/BCSIA/sust.nsf/pubs/pub1 accessed in October 2002

Clement, P. (2001) *Mutant*, Fawcett Books, New York

Colborn, T., Dumanoski, D. and Myers, J. P. (1996) *Our Stolen Future*, Dutton, New York

Cova, T. J. and Church, R. L. (1997) 'Modeling community evacuation vulnerability using GIS', *International Journal of Geographical Information Science*, vol 11, pp763–784

Cutter, S. L. (1993) *Living With Risk: The Geography of Technological Hazards*, Edward Arnold, London

Cutter, S. L. (ed) (2001a) *American Hazardscapes: The Regionalization of Hazards and Disasters*, The Joseph Henry Press, Washington, DC

Cutter, S. L. (2001b) 'A research agenda for vulnerability science and environmental hazards', *IHDP Update. Newsletter of the International Human Dimensions Programme on Global Environmental Change*, vol 2, no 1, pp8–9

Cutter, S. L., Richardson, D. B. and Wilbanks, T. J. (2002) *The Geographical Dimensions of Terrorism: A Research and Action Agenda*, Association of American Geographers, Washington, DC

Dietz, T. and Rycroft, R. (1987) *The Risk Professionals*, Russell Sage Foundation, New York

Douglas, M. and Wildavsky, A. (1982) *Risk and Culture: An Essay on the Selection of Technological and Environmental Dangers*, University of California Press, Berkeley

Downing, T. E. (1991) 'Vulnerability to hunger and coping with climate change in Africa', *Global Environmental Change*, vol 1, pp365–380

Erikson, K. (1994) *A New Species of Trouble: Explorations in Disaster, Trauma, and Community*, W. W. Norton and Co., New York

Etkin, D. (1999) 'Risk transference and related trends: Driving forces toward more mega-disasters', *Environmental Hazards*, vol 1, no 2, pp69–75

FEMA (Federal Emergency Management Agency) (1997) *Multihazard Identification and Risk Assessment*, US Government Printing Office, Washington, DC

Freudenburg, W. R. (1988) 'Perceived risk, real risk: Social science and the art of probabilistic risk assessment', *Science*, vol 39, pp44–49

Golledge, R. G. (2002) 'The nature of geographic knowledge', *Annals of the Association of American Geographers*, vol 92, no 1, pp1–14

Golledge, R. G. and Stimson, R. J. (1997) *Spatial Behavior: A Geographic Perspective*, Guilford Press, New York

Gould, S. J. (2000) 'Deconstructing the "science wars" by reconstructing an old mold', *Science*, vol 287, pp253–261

Guillemin, J. (1999) *Anthrax: The Investigation of a Deadly Outbreak*, University of California Press, Berkeley, CA

Haraway, D. (1988) 'Situated knowledges: The science question in feminism and the privilege of partial perspective', *Feminist Studies*, vol 14, pp575–599

Harding, S. (1991) *Whose Science Whose Knowledge? Thinking from Women's Lives*, Cornell University Press, Ithaca, NY

Harvey, D. (1996) *Justice, Nature, and the Geography of Difference*, Blackwell, Malden, MA

Heinz Center (2000) *The Hidden Costs of Coastal Hazards: Implications for Risk Assessment and Mitigation*, Island Press, Covelo, CA

Heinz Center (2002) *Human Links to Coastal Disasters*, Heinz Center for Science, Economics, and the Environment, Washington, DC

Hill, A. A. and Cutter, S. L. (2001) 'Methods for determining disaster-proneness' in S. L. Cutter (ed) *American Hazardscapes: The Regionalization of Hazards and Disasters*, The Joseph Henry Press, Washington, DC, pp13–36

Hodgson, M. E. and Cutter, S. L. (2001) 'Mapping and the spatial analysis of hazardscapes' in S. L. Cutter (ed) *American Hazardscapes: The Regionalization of Hazards and Disasters*, The Joseph Henry Press, Washington, DC, pp37–60

Jacob, G. (1990) *Site Unseen: The Politics of Siting a Nuclear Waste Repository*, University of Pittsburgh Press, Pittsburgh

Jaeger, C. C., Renn, O., Rosa, E. A. and Webler, T. (2001) *Risk, Uncertainty, and Rational Action*, Earthscan, London

Jernigan, J. A., Stephens, D. S., Ashford, D. A., Omenaca, C., Topiel, M. S., Galbraith, M., Tapper, M., Fisk, T. L., Zaki, S., Popovic, T., Meyer, R. F., Quinn, C. P., Harper, S. A., Fridkin, S. K., Sejvar, J. J., Shepard, C. W., McConnell, M., Guarner, J., Shieh, W., Malecki, J. M., Gerverding, G. L., Hughes, J. M., Perkins, B. A. and members of the Anthrax Bioterrorism Investigation Team (2001) 'Bioterrorism-related inhalational anthrax: The first 10 cases reported in the United States', *CDC Emerging Infectious Diseases*, vol 7, no 6 www.cdc.gov/ncidod/EID/vol7no6/jernigan.htm accessed in October 2002

Kasperson, J. X. and Kasperson, R. E. (eds) (2001) *Global Environmental Risk*, United Nations University Press and Earthscan, Tokyo

Kasperson, J. X., Kasperson, R. E. and Turner II, B. L. (1995) *Regions at Risk: Comparisons of Threatened Environments*, United Nations University Press, Tokyo

Kasperson, R. E. and Kasperson, J. X. (1996) 'The social amplification and attenuation of risk', *Annals of the American Academy of Political and Social Science*, vol 545, pp95–105

Kasperson, R. E., Renn, O., Slovic, P., Brown, H. S., Emel, J., Goble, R., Kasperson, J. X. and Ratick, S. (1988) 'The social amplification of risk: A conceptual framework', *Risk Analysis*, vol 8, no 2, pp177–187

Kates, R. W. (1985) 'Success, strain, and surprise', *Issues in Science and Technology*, vol II (fall), pp46–58

Kates, R. W. (1987) 'The human environment: The road not taken, the road still beckoning', *Annals of the Association of American Geographers*, vol 77, no 4, pp525–534

Kates, R. W., Clark, W. C., Corell, R., Hall, J. M., Jaeger, C. C., Lowe, I., McCarthy, J., Schellnhuber, H. J., Bolin, B., Dickson, N. M., Faucheux, S., Gallopin, G. C., Gruebler, A., Huntley, B., Jäger, J., Jodha, N. S., Kasperson, R. E., Mabogunje, A., Matson, P., Mooney III, H., Moore, B., O'Riordan, T. and Svedin, U. (2001) 'Sustainability science', *Science*, vol 292, pp641–642

Kolpin, D. W., Furlong, E. T., Meyer, M. T., Thurman, E. M., Zaugg, S. D., Barber, L. B. and Buxton, H. T. (2002) 'Pharmaceuticals, hormones, and other organic wastewater contaminants in US streams, 1999–2000: A national reconnaissance', *Environmental Science and Technology*, vol 36, pp1202–1211

Krimsky, S. (2000) *Hormonal Chaos. The Scientific and Social Origins of the Environmental Endocrine Hypothesis*, The Johns Hopkins University Press, Baltimore

Landrigan, P. J., Schechter, C. B., Lipton, J. M., Fahs, M. C. and Schwartz, J. (2002) 'Environmental pollutants and disease in American children: Estimates of morbidity, mortality, and costs for lead poisoning, asthma, cancer, and developmental disabilities', *Environmental Health Perspectives*, vol 110, no 7, pp721–728, http://ehpnet1.niehs.nih.gov/docs/2002/110p721-728landrigan/abstract.html

Meselson, M., Guillemin, J., Hugh-Jones, M., Langmuir, A., Popova, I., Shelokov, A. and Yampolskaya, O. (1994) 'The Sverdlovsk anthrax outbreak of 1979', *Science*, vol 266, no 5188, pp1202–1208

Mileti, D. (1999) *Disasters by Design: A Reassessment of Natural Hazards in the United States*, The Joseph Henry Press, Washington, DC

Miller, J., Engelberg, S. and Broad, W. (2001) *Germs: Biological Weapons and America's Secret War*, Simon and Schuster, New York

Mitchell, J. K. (1999) *Crucibles of Hazard: Mega-cities and Disasters in Transition*, United Nations University Press, Tokyo

Monmonier, M. (1997) *Cartographies of Danger: Mapping Hazards in America*, University of Chicago Press, Chicago

Montz, B., Cross, J. and Cutter, S. L. (2003) 'Hazards', in Gaile, G. and Willmott, C. (eds) *Geography in America at the Dawn of the 21st century*, Oxford University Press, Oxford, pp481–491

National Research Council (1989) *Improving Risk Communication*, National Academy Press, Washington, DC

National Research Council (1996) *Understanding Risk: Informing Decisions in a Democratic Society*, National Academy Press, Washington, DC

National Research Council (1999a) *Making Climate Forecasts Matter*, National Academy Press, Washington, DC

National Research Council (1999b) *Our Common Journey: A Transition Toward Sustainability*, National Academy Press, Washington, DC

National Research Council (2000) *Ecological Indicators for the Nation*, National Academy Press, Washington, DC

National Research Council (2001) *Grand Challenges in the Environmental Sciences*, National Academy Press, Washington, DC

National Research Council (2002) *Making the Nation Safer: The Role of Science and Technology in Countering Terrorism*, National Academy Press, Washington, DC

Oberg, J. E. (1988) *Uncovering Soviet Disasters: Exploring the Limits of Glasnost*, Random House, New York

Palm, R. (1994) *Earthquake Insurance: A Longitudinal Study of California Homeowners*, Westview Press, Boulder, CO

Palm, R. and Hodgson, M. E. (1992) *After a California Earthquake: Attitude and Behavior Change*, University of Chicago Press, Chicago

Perrow, C. (1984) *Normal Accidents: Living with High-risk Technologies*, Princeton University Press, Princeton, NJ

Platt, R. H. (1999) *Disasters and Democracy: The Politics of Extreme Natural Events*, Island Press, Washington, DC

Pulido, L. (2000) 'Rethinking environmental racism: White privilege and urban development in Southern California', *Annals of the Association of American Geographers*, vol 90, pp12–40

Radke, J., Cova, T., Sheridan, M. F., Troy, A., Mu, L. and Johnson, R. (2000) 'Application challenges for geographic information science: Implications for research, education, and policy for emergency preparedness and response', *URISA Journal*, vol 12, no 2, pp15–30

Revkin, A. C. (2002) 'FDA considers new tests for environmental effects', *New York Times*, 14 March, ppA20

Rosser, S. V. (2000) *Women, Science, and Society: The Crucial Union*, Teachers College Press, New York

Schettler, T., Solomon, G., Valenti, M. and Huddle, A. (1999) *Generations at Risk: Reproductive Health and the Environment*, MIT Press, Cambridge, MA

Schiebinger, L. (1999) *Has Feminism Changed Science?*, Harvard University Press, Cambridge, MA

Schneider, S. H., Turner II, B. L. and Morehouse Garriga, H. (1998) 'Imaginable surprise in global change science', *Journal of Risk Research*, vol 1, no 2, pp165–185

Sherbaniuk, R. (2001) *The Fifth Horseman*, Tom Doherty Associates Book, New York

Shrader-Frechette, K. S. (1991) *Risk and Rationality: Philosophical Foundations for Populist Reforms*, University of California Press, Berkeley, CA

Shrader-Frechette, K. S. (1993) *Burying Uncertainty: Risk and the Case Against Geological Disposal of Nuclear Waste*, University of California Press, Berkeley, CA

Sims, J. H. and Baumann, D. D. (1972) 'The tornado threat: Coping styles of the north and south', *Science*, vol 176, pp1386–1392

Slovic, P. (1987) 'Perception of risk', *Science*, vol 236, pp280–285

Slovic, P. (2001) *The Perception of Risk*, Earthscan, London

Slovic, P., Finucane, M., Peters, E. and MacGregor, D. G. (2002) 'The affect heuristic', in Gilovich, T., Griffin, D. and Kahneman, D. (eds) *Heuristics and Biases: The Psychology of Intuitive Judgment*, Cambridge University Press, New York, pp397–420

Smelser, N. J. (1998) 'The rational and the ambivalent in the social sciences', *American Sociological Review*, vol 63, pp1–16

Smith, K. R. (2001) 'Environment and health: Issues for the new US administration', *Environment*, vol 43, pp34–38

Snow, C. P. (1993) *The Two Cultures*, Cambridge University Press, Cambridge

Starr, C. (1969) 'Social benefit versus technological risk', *Science*, vol 165, pp1232–1238

Tenner, E. (1996) *Why Things Bite Back: Technology and the Revenge of Unintended Consequences*, Alfred A. Knopf, New York

Thomas, D. S. K. (2001) 'Data, data everywhere, but can we really use them?' in S. L. Cutter (ed) *American Hazardscapes: The Regionalization of Hazards and Disasters*, The Joseph Henry Press, Washington, DC, pp 61–76

Thomas, D. S. K., Cutter, S. L., Hodgson, M., Gutekunst, M. and Jones, S. (2002) *Use of Spatial Data and Geographic Technologies in Response to the September 11 Terrorist Attack*, Quick Response Report no 153, University of Colorado, Natural Hazards Research and Applications Information Center, Boulder, CO, www.colorado.edu/hazards/qr/qr153/qr153.html accessed in October 2002

Thomas, W. L. jr (ed) (1956) *Man's Role in Changing the Face of the Earth*, University of Chicago Press, Chicago, IL

Thomas, W. L. jr (1975) 'The use of herbicides in South Vietnam: Resultant economic stress and settlement changes', *Pacific Viewpoint*, vol 16, no 1, pp1–25

Thornton, J. (2000) *Pandora's Poison: Chlorine, Health, and a New Environmental Strategy*, MIT Press, Cambridge, MA

Turner II, B. L. (2002) 'Contested identities: Human-environment geography and disciplinary implications in a restructuring academy', *Annals of the Association of American Geographers*, vol 92, no 1, pp52–74

Turner II, B. L., Clark, W. C., Kates, R. W., Richards, J. F., Mathews, J. T. and Meyer, W. B. (eds) (1990) *The Earth as Transformed by Human Action: Global and Regional Changes in the Biosphere over the Past 300 years*, Cambridge University Press, Cambridge

UNDP (United Nations Development Programme) (2000) *Human Development Report 2000*, Oxford University Press, New York

Wargo, J. (1996) *Our Children's Toxic Legacy: How Science and Law Fail to Protect us from Pesticides*, Yale University Press, New Haven, CT

White, G. F. (1962) 'Critical issues concerning geography in the public service – Introduction', *Annals of the Association of American Geographers*, vol 52, no 3, pp279–280

White, G. F. (ed) (1974) *Natural Hazards: Local, National, Global*, Oxford University Press, Oxford

World Bank (2001) 'World Development Indicators. Environmental Indicators', www.worldbank.org/data/wdi2001/environment.htm accessed in October 2002

World Economic Forum (2000) *Pilot Environmental Sustainability Index*, Yale Center for Environmental Law and Policy, New Haven, CT

Part III

Societal Responses to Threats

10
Societal Responses
to Environmental Hazards

Susan L. Cutter

Introduction

On 1 January 1990 the United Nations General Assembly proclaimed the start of the International Decade of Natural Disaster Reduction (IDNDR) and, by all accounts, not a minute too soon. The first half of the decade was riddled with unprecedented disasters: earthquakes in Zanjan, Iran (1990), Northridge, California, US (1994) and Kobe, Japan (1995); tropical cyclones and flooding in Bangladesh (1991); volcanic eruptions (Mt Pinatubo in 1991); flooding during 1993 on the Mississippi River (US); and the most costly disaster to the US, Hurricane Andrew (1992), to name just a few.

The IDNDR is a multinational effort designed to shift social and political attention from post-disaster recovery to pre-disaster planning, preparedness and prevention. Through cooperative arrangements between national and international scientific committees, improved predictions of potential disasters are occurring. The IDNDR also promotes improvements in warning systems, community awareness and disaster preparedness at both the local and national levels. Disaster preparedness and mitigation are key elements in the IDNDR, strategies that are designed to lessen the impacts of disasters on society. The importance of natural disasters in the decline of the human condition is an implicit assumption behind the IDNDR's activities. The prevalence of geographical contributions to IDNDR activities is apparent since hazards research has always emphasized a desire to reduce human suffering. This chapter presents an overview of contemporary hazards research and its importance in understanding societal responses to environmental hazards.

Note: Reprinted, with permission, from the *International Social Science Journal*, vol 47, no 4, Susan L. Cutter, 'Societal Responses to Environmental Hazards', pp525–536. © Blackwell Publishing, 1996

Definitional Clarification

Historically, the terms risk, hazards and disasters have been used interchangeably although each has a very precise meaning. *Hazard* is the broadest term and reflects a source of danger or the potential for harm. *Risk* is the likelihood or probability of an event occurring. Hazards include risk (e.g. probability), impact (or magnitude) and contextual (socio-political) elements. In other words, hazards are threats to people and the things they value (Cutter, 1993). They are therefore socially constructed, where people contribute to, exacerbate and modify them. Hazards can vary by culture, gender, race, socio-economic status and political structure. *Disasters,* on the other hand, are singular hazard events (like those mentioned in the introduction above) that have a profound impact on local people or places either in terms of loss of life or injuries, property damages, or environmental impact. While geographers traditionally studied hazards, the newer generation of scholars is branching out to examine the spatial dimensions of risks and disasters as well.

Fundamental Questions

Despite 50 years of geographical research on hazards, we are still perplexed by a series of unanswered questions. These questions provide the foci for contemporary hazards research. Implicit in each of the following is the understanding of physical and social processes, as well as the spatial and temporal variations in the processes and outcomes:

1   Are societies becoming more vulnerable to environmental hazards and disasters?
2   What social/physical factors influence changes in human occupance of hazard zones?
3   How do societies perceive and estimate the occurrence of environmental risks and hazards?
4   How do people respond to environmental hazards and what accounts for differential adjustments (in the short term) and adaptation (in the longer term)?
5   How do societies mitigate the risk of environmental hazards and prepare for future disasters?
6   How do local risks and hazards become the driving forces behind global environmental changes?

Disaster Trends

There is no simple answer to the question: are societies becoming more vulnerable to environmental hazards? The frequency and magnitude of natural disasters have been steadily increasing for the last 30 years with a noticeable peak in 1991, the worst year for disasters in decades (Figure 10.1). The less developed countries suf-

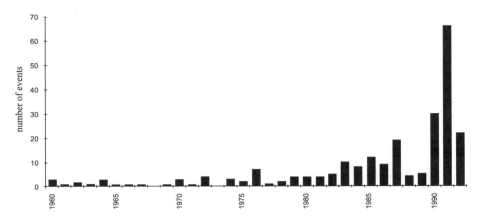

Source: Adapted from Tolba et al, 1992, with additional data from UNEP, 1993

Figure 10.1 *Frequency of major natural disasters, 1960–1993*

fered about 97 per cent of these disasters and account for around 99 per cent of the deaths attributed to natural disasters (UNEP, 1993). While numeric estimates of mortality and injury are often questionable, the loss of life from natural disasters is enormous (Table 10.1). Tropical cyclones and earthquakes are the primary source of fatalities from natural hazard events.

Economic losses from natural disasters are greatest in the developed world and have tripled during the last 30 years. During the 1960s, for example, disaster losses were estimated at US$40 billion and by the 1980s these losses had risen to $120 billion. In the first half of the 1990s, cumulative losses were already beyond $160 billion (Figure 10.2). In the US, losses from Hurricane Andrew ($30 billion) and the Northridge earthquake ($30 billion) make these the most disastrous

Table 10.1 *Top natural disasters, 1945–1990**

Year	Location	Type	Deaths
1970	Bangladesh	Tropical cyclone	300,000
1976	China	Earthquake	242,000
1991	Bangladesh	Tropical cyclone	132,000
1948	Soviet Union	Earthquake	110,000
1970	Peru	Earthquake	67,000
1949	China	Flood	57,000
1990	Iran	Earthquake	40,000
1965	Bangladesh	Tropical cyclone	36,000
1954	China	Flood	30,000
1965	Bangladesh	Tropical cyclone	30,000
1968	Iran	Earthquake	30,000
1971	India	Tropical cyclone	30,000

* Based on estimated number of fatalities.
Sources: Cutter, 1994; UNEP, 1993; Tolba et al, 1992.

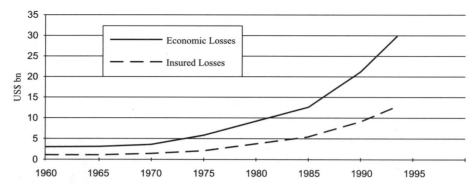

Source: Adapted from Domeisen, 1995

Figure 10.2 *Losses from natural disasters in billions of US dollars, 1960–1993*

events to affect the nation. In Japan, losses from the Great Hanshin-Awaji (Kobe) earthquake are running at $50 billion (Domeisen, 1995). It is ironic that economic losses from two of the top ten natural disasters since 1945 occurred in the beginning of the 1990s, the start of the IDNHR (Table 10.2).

Industrial accidents are a by-product of economic development and often have a much smaller catastrophic potential than natural hazards. Often they do not result in immediate fatalities, but pose longer-term threats to human health and ecosystem stability. Many industrial accidents are associated with energy produc-

Table 10.2 *Losses from natural disasters, 1985–1995*

Year	Location	Event	Economic losses (US$ billion)
1995	Kobe, Japan	Great Hanshin earthquake	50.00
1992	Florida, US	Hurricane Andrew	30.00
1994	California, US	Northridge earthquake	30.00
1993	Midwest, US	Mississippi floods	12.00
1989	Caribbean and US	Hurricane Hugo	9.00
1990	Europe	Winter storm, Daria	6.80
1989	California, US	Loma Prieta earthquake	6.00
1991	Japan	Typhoon Mireille	6.00
1993	Northeast, US	Blizzard	5.00
1987	Western Europe	Winter gale	3.70
1990	Europe	Winter storm, Vivian	3.25
1992	Hawaii	Hurricane Iniki	3.00
1995	Florida, US	Hurricane Opal	2.80
1990	Europe	Winter storm, Wiebke	2.25
1991	US	Forest fire	2.00
1990	Europe	Winter storm, Herta	1.90
1991	California, US	Berkeley–Oakland Hills fire	1.60

Sources: Domeisen, 1995; Showalter et al, 1994; *New York Times,* 1991, 1995.

Table 10.3 *Top industrial disasters, 1945–1990*[a]

Year	Location	Type	Deaths[b]
1984	Bhopal, India	Toxic vapour/methyl isocyanate	2750–3849
1982	Salang Pass, Afghanistan	Toxic vapour/carbon monoxide	1500–2700
1956	Cali, Colombia	Explosion/ammunitions	1200
1958	Kyshtym, Russia	Radioactive leak	1118[c]
1947	Texas City, TX	Explosion/ammonium nitrate	576
1989	Acha Ufa, Russia	Explosion/natural gas	500–575
1984	Cubatao, Brazil	Explosion/gasoline	508
1984	St Juan Ixhautepec, Mexico	Explosion/natural gas	478–503
1992	Zonguldak, Turkey	Mine explosion/gas	388
1983	Nile River, Egypt	Explosion/natural gas	317
1992	Guadalajara, Mexico	Sewer explosion/gas	210
1986	Chernobyl, Ukraine	Explosion/radioactivity	31–300[c]

[a] Based on estimated fatalities
[b] Estimates vary widely depending on the source(s) used, therefore ranges are provided where discrepancies exist.
[c] Reported fatality figures reflect immediate deaths only, not longer-term fatalities associated with the exposures.
Sources: Cutter, 1994; UNEP, 1993; Tolba et al, 1992.

tion and distribution such as oil tanker accidents (Exxon Valdez, Aegean Sea and Braer) and intentional spills (Persian Gulf conflict 1991) (Table 10.3). Chemical disasters have increased steadily since the 1960s (Figure 10.3) with a decline in industrial accidents during the 1990s. As was the case with natural disasters, two of the top industrial disasters occurred in 1992: the mine explosion and gas leak in Zonguldak, Turkey and the 1992 sewer gas explosion in Guadalajara, Mexico that killed 210 people.

Regionally, natural disasters are more prevalent in the less developed countries, where increasing urbanization and environmental degradation makes these areas more vulnerable to the impacts of natural events. Industrial disasters, on the other hand, are more common in the developed nations. Regionally, Southern and Eastern Asia have the greatest fatality rate from natural disasters, with Bangladesh being the extreme case.

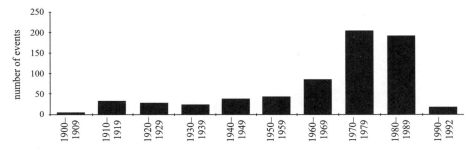

Source: Cutter, 1993

Figure 10.3 *Chemical accidents, 1900–1992*

Disaster-Proneness: Towards Measuring Vulnerability

In 1990, the UN Disaster Relief Organization (UNDRO) produced its first assessment of the vulnerability of nations to natural disasters. Working within the framework of economic impacts caused by natural disasters, UNDRO created its disaster-proneness index for individual countries. The index provides a measure of the total economic effect of disasters over a 20-year period as a percentage of the total annual gross national product (GNP). Only significant disasters, defined as those causing financial damages assessed at more than 1 per cent of the country's annual gross domestic product (GDP), were included (UNEP, 1993). While preliminary in nature and fraught with all types of assumptions, the disaster-proneness index does provide some global comparative statistics on the vulnerability of countries to disasters.

Not surprisingly, some of the most disaster-prone countries are those with hazards (such as tropical cyclones) with repeated frequencies and 'hits' during the last 20 years (the period of study). Thus Caribbean countries such as Montserrat, Dominica and St Lucia and the Pacific island nations of Vanuatu and Cook Islands rank among the top ten. Other countries had one disastrous event during the last 20 years, which inflated their ranking on the index. Figure 10.4 maps the disaster-proneness of countries. In addition to the island nations mentioned above, Central American nations (El Salvador, Honduras, Nicaragua), Sahelian countries (Burkina Faso, Ethiopia, Mauritania) and Asian countries (Bangladesh) are the most disaster-prone. The inverse relationship with national wealth comes as no surprise. Not only are these nations the most disaster-prone, they are among the least able to respond in the aftermath of a disaster and mitigate the impacts of future ones.

While provocative, the disaster-proneness index does not measure those factors that govern the increasing vulnerability of countries to hazards. We know that urbanization, industrialization and technology all influence the impact of hazards on places, often making the local residents more vulnerable overall. Population pressures, poverty and gender relations influence vulnerability by making certain segments of the population more susceptible to the impacts of disasters once they occur. These factors are not included in the disaster-proneness index, yet they are vital in understanding why some countries and certain populations within those countries are disproportionately affected by hazards. There are both spatial and temporal dimensions to this biophysical and social vulnerability that are not fully understood, nor incorporated into this index.

Complications

There are a number of confounding concerns that prohibit us from simply answering the questions posed earlier in this chapter. First and foremost, the very nature of hazards has changed from singular natural events ('acts of God') to more complex phenomena involving the interaction between natural, social and technological systems. The development of typologies based on the etiology of events no longer works, nor does the distinction between natural and technological hazards.

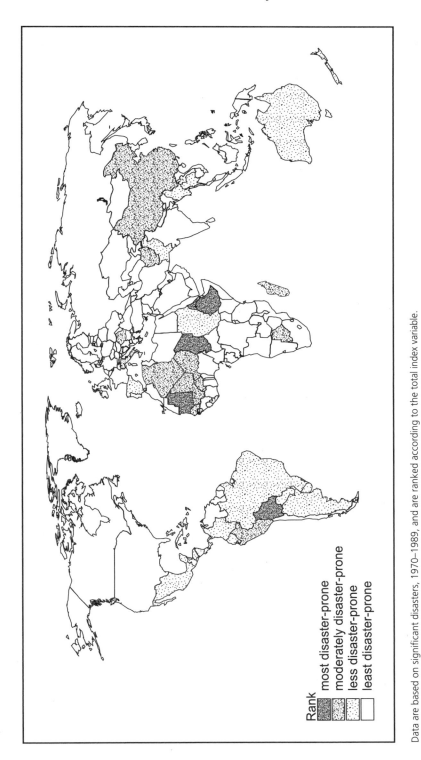

Data are based on significant disasters, 1970–1989, and are ranked according to the total index variable.

Source: UNEP, 1993

Figure 10.4 *UNDRO's disaster-proneness index*

Second, responses to hazards are now viewed as embedded within larger social and environmental milieus where it is increasingly impossible to separate the impacts of specific disasters or hazards from the broader-based social or environmental contexts. A direct result is the increased complexity of hazard management systems and the expanded range of management alternatives beyond the geotechnical. As risks and hazards become more politicized, management decisions will be made on the basis of social choices, not technical prowess (Mitchell, 1990; Kates, 1985).

Within this framework, geography plays a pivotal role. As I have suggested elsewhere (Cutter, 1994), scale is crucial in understanding hazards distribution, impact and reduction. Scale is an important parameter in detecting and monitoring the impacts and consequences of environmental hazards. The discovery of new hazards and the rediscovery of older ones with more dispersed and cumulative impacts necessitate the globalization of risk and hazard management systems. Yet, most hazard studies continue to be localized case studies. The articulation between global processes and local impacts will continue to challenge the hazards community.

Geography also provides the linkages between physical processes and human contexts and helps define the areal or spatial extent of the hazard. There are a number of geometric manifestations of hazards (Zeigler et al, 1983; Turner et al, 1990), but these have not been analysed in any systematic way. The application of geographic information processing techniques (such as remote sensing and GIS) can help delineate hazard zones, but it is not widely used at present.

Data difficulties also inhibit our understanding of the broad patterns of hazards distributions as well as societal responses. While some international comparative statistics are available, their reliability is often questionable due to inaccuracies and inconsistencies in reporting and record-keeping. The most basic disaster data such as location, magnitude and duration are often missing, incomplete, or withheld for national security purposes. Measuring the impacts of disasters is more problematic. Most databases concentrate on three main criteria: mortality, number of people affected and damage estimates (usually in US$), each with their own inherent biases in data collection. For example, most of the damage estimates are made in local currency and then adjusted to the US dollar standard. Fluctuations in exchange rates and inflation from year to year often render these estimates meaningless. For example, the United Nations Environment Programme (UNEP) maintains a disaster database, but only reports events when at least 30 immediate fatalities occur. In addition to the UN, the Centre for Research on the Epidemiology of Disasters (CRED) in Brussels, Belgium and the US Office of Foreign Disaster Assistance also maintain global databases on natural disasters (International Federation of Red Cross and Red Crescent Societies, 1995). As should be clear by now, all these efforts focus on disasters arising from extreme natural events. Rarely are multiple origins considered (e.g. cyclones and flooding) or hazards arising from more chronic conditions such as drought (which could facilitate a famine disaster or forest fires).

Human-induced hazards are increasing in importance, yet relevant global data are rare. Oil spills, chronic toxic contamination and pollution are good examples. Industrial accident data are collected (the Organisation for Economic Co-operation and Development (OECD) databases are among the best), as are statistics on oil spills (International Tanker Owners Pollution Federation Limited, Oil Spills Intelligence Report) and nuclear accidents (International Atomic Energy Agency – IAEA). Data on the trans-boundary movement of hazardous waste is difficult to acquire because of the lack of international agreement on what constitutes hazardous waste. The Basel Convention comes closest to a universal definition by providing a list of regulated categories of hazardous waste. Other sources of data include UNEP's International Register of Potentially Toxic Chemicals (IRPTC) and APELL (Awareness and Preparedness for Emergencies at Local Level) programme (Tolba et al, 1992).

Unfortunately, basic data on the range and extent of the hazards has not kept pace with the needs. Detailed information on the human occupance of the hazard zones and adjustments is generally available only at a very localized level. We can monitor and even model the physical systems' response to hazards and ultimately assess the biophysical impacts at both the global and local levels. However, there are few global databases on human occupance and societal adjustments to environmental hazards. Social data are unreliable in many world regions, further hampering our efforts to assess the social consequences of environmental hazards.

Just as we lack the basic data for determining the range, extent and response to environmental hazards, we also lack theoretical constructs that help us to understand the processes by which hazards are produced and the options for mitigation and recovery. Hazards research is a very active component of the nature–society emphasis within geography and has been for more than half a century. Most of the early research was practically driven, and interested in why people occupy hazardous environments and what policy outcomes would reduce the impacts of such locational decisions. In recent years, more emphasis has been placed on theory development: hazards in context (Palm, 1990; Mitchell et al, 1989; Kirby, 1990), social theories of risk (Krimsky and Golding, 1992; Johnson and Covello, 1987), social amplification of risks (Kasperson et al, 1988; Kasperson, 1992) and vulnerability (O'Riordan, 1986; Liverman, 1990; Blaikie et al, 1994). Despite these attempts there is still some frustration with the lack of an integrated theory on how people respond to and interact with the environment. For example, we still need to understand the linkages between macro-level processes and micro-scale impacts as well as the linkages between dynamic systems and static phenomena. Within the geographical community as well, we have not done much work on longitudinal analyses of localized environments nor on the temporal changes in residents' responses to single events or multiple hazards. While advancing our understanding of nature–society interactions, hazards research still requires some additional theoretical development to ascertain what makes places and people vulnerable to environmental hazards.

Reducing Vulnerability: Short-Term Adjustments

When a disaster strikes, the immediate societal adjustments are to rescue the survivors and re-establish lifelines to the ravaged community. These relief operations include medical supplies, food, shelter, water and power. In some instances, the rescue and relief operations are within the capabilities of the affected country. Often however, the disaster is just too large for the individual country, and international relief efforts are mobilized through international relief organizations such as the Red Cross/Red Crescent and through cooperative arrangements within UNDRO. Once the lifelines are re-established and the 'crisis' period is over, the recovery phase begins. Recovery adjustments are temporary in nature and provide for the beginning of normality after an event. The use of temporary shelters during the recovery period gives way to building permanent structures during the reconstruction phase. Throughout the recovery and reconstruction phases, hazard mitigation continues. Some of the mitigation options are structural in nature, such as the use of steel-reinforced construction materials in seismic areas, or the use of elevated pilings in flood-prone areas. Other mitigation strategies are non-structural in their emphasis and involve land use planning and management, insurance and pre-event preparedness including warning systems.

Differential Adjustments

While the range of potential adjustments to hazards has increased over time, individual access to adjustments is more restricted now than in the past as a function of social class, income and life circumstances. Increasingly, nations and societies are becoming polarized between rich and poor, powerful and powerless and divided by ethnic divisions or subcultures. The chasm between the 'haves' and the 'have nots' is widening within societies and between nations. Ultimately, the ability to respond to environmental hazards is constrained by these divisions, as we have seen time and time again during this decade.

Poverty and environmental degradation are linked and create an impoverishment degradation spiral (Mellor, 1988; Kates and Haarmann, 1992). The driving forces behind environmental degradation are development/commercialization along with population growth and poverty. Natural hazards accelerate the process and further restrict the use of those remaining natural resources, many severely degraded already.

Wealth plays an enormous role in fostering opportunities for adjustments to these deteriorating conditions and recovery from hazards. Poverty restricts one's ability to maintain the simplest of adjustments, such as protective works, because of lack of skill and labour to undertake the improvement, lack of needed inputs for rebuilding, or lack of access to education and thus knowledge of public programmes for recovery. Without capital or power, poor people who often live on marginal lands to begin with, eventually get displaced from them and begin a migratory odyssey as environmental refugees. In many countries, these refugees are the forgotten casualties: mostly women and children, a subgroup often least able to adjust to environmental hazards (Chapter 5).

Urbanization is one of the key processes that influence vulnerability to environmental hazards. Not only are the world's megacities becoming more populated, they are also situated in some of the most natural-hazard-prone areas of the world: along coastlines or in active seismic areas. Air pollution, toxic chemical contamination and poor water quality plague the world's megacities as well. The

Table 10.4 *Social trends affecting environmental risks and hazards*

Aggravating the impacts	Lessening the impacts
Occupancy of hazard zones	Improved building technology
Ageing populations	Better detection and warning systems
Ageing infrastructure	Improved health care
Increasing populations	Improved environmental regulations
Urbanization	Environmentally sound development
Migration	Better understanding of risks and hazards
Industrialization	Improved educational opportunities
Resource exploitation	
Increasing poverty	
Reliance on complex technological systems	

Source: Showalter et al, 1993

elderly and children are most susceptible to air pollution episodes, be they in cities of the developing or developed worlds. Los Angeles, Mexico City, Beijing, Seoul and Cairo fail to meet more than half of the World Health Organization's standards for air quality. Lead contamination (which contributes to learning disabilities in children) is on the rise in the developing world cities as the use of motor vehicles using lead-based fuel (lead-free is more expensive) rises. There are many other societal trends affecting the hazardousness of places and people that require further exploration by hazard geographers (Table 10.4).

Making the Tent Bigger: Expanding the Hazards Reduction Decade

Hazard reduction will come about only with profound changes in society. Geotechnical solutions (levees or seismic-proof buildings) will provide some short-term relief, but ultimately will exacerbate the hazard in the future. Nations must address why people live in hazardous environments in the first place, how they respond and adjust to environmental hazards, and what types of mitigation programmes are appropriate at the local and national level. Hazard reduction strategies will vary from region to region depending on the range of hazards that affect local places. Geographers are key players and have much to contribute to these ongoing discussions. Our understanding of the physical processes and societal responses gives us a unique perspective from which to examine the relationship between society and nature, and to work towards improving the human condition.

While disasters capture our immediate attention when they happen, we must be cautious and understand that hazards are part of our daily lives. It is not only the extreme natural event such as an earthquake or hurricane that we need to plan for, but we must take precautions against those hazards which we experience every day involving the air we breathe, the water we drink and the food we eat. Poor water quality and sanitation kill more people in developing countries than all natural disasters combined. Clearly, the International Decade of Natural Hazard Reduction is not focusing on these chronic everyday hazards, which may be more costly to societies in the long run in terms of loss of life, injury and reduced productivity than the periodic natural event. Now is the time to expand the International Decade to include an 'all-hazards' approach to understanding the vulnerability of societies to environmental risks and hazards. In so doing, improvements in the human condition will occur and the major goal of the decade will be achieved.

References

Blaikie, P., Cannon, T., Davis, I. and Wisner, B. (1994) *At Risk: Natural Hazards, People's Vulnerability, and Disasters*, Routledge, London

Cutter, S. L. (1993) *Living with Risk: The Geography of Technological Hazards*, Edward Arnold, London

Cutter, S. L. (ed) (1994) *Environmental Risks and Hazards*, Prentice-Hall, Englewood Cliffs, NJ

Domeisen, N. (1995) 'Disasters: Threat to social development', *Stop Disasters*, vol 34, winter, pp7–9

International Federation of Red Cross and Red Crescent Societies (1995) *World Disasters Report*, Nijhoff, Dordrecht

Johnson, B. B. and Covello, V. T. (eds) (1987) *The Social and Cultural Construction of Risk: Technology, Risk, Society*, D. Reidel, Dordrecht

Kasperson, R. E., Renn, O., Slovic, P., Brown, H. S., Emel, J., Goble, R., Kasperson, J. X. and Ratick, S. (1988) 'The social amplification of risk: A conceptual framework', *Risk Analysis*, vol 8, no 2, pp177–187

Kasperson, R. E. (1992) 'The social amplification of risk: Progress in developing an integrative framework' in S. Krimsky and D. Golding (eds) *Social Theories of Risk*, Praeger, Westport, CT, pp153–178

Kates, R. W. (1985) 'Success, strain, and surprise', *Issues in Science and Technology*, vol II, no 1, pp46–58

Kates, R. W. and Haarmann, V. (1992) 'Where the poor live, are the assumptions correct?', *Environment*, vol 34, no 4, pp4–11, 25–28

Kirby, A. (ed) (1990) *Nothing to Fear: Risks and Hazards in American Society*, University of Arizona Press, Tucson

Krimsky, S. and Golding, D. (eds) (1992) *Social Theories of Risk*, Praeger, Westport, CT

Liverman, D. (1990) 'Vulnerability to global environmental change' in R. E. Kasperson, K. Dow, D. Golding and J. X. Kasperson (eds) *Understanding Global Environmental Change: The Contributions of Risk Analysis and Management*, The Earth Transformed Program, Clark University, Worcester, MA, pp27–44

Mellor, J. W. (1988) 'The intertwining of environmental problems and poverty', *Environment*, vol 30, no 9, pp8–13, 28–30

Mitchell, J. K., Devine, N. and Jagger, K. (1989) 'A contextual model of natural hazard', *Geographical Review*, vol 79, no 4, pp391–409

Mitchell, J. K. (1990) 'Human dimensions of environmental hazards: Complexity, disparity, and the search for guidance' in A. Kirby (ed) *Nothing to Fear: Risks and Hazards in American Society*, University of Arizona Press, Tucson, pp131–175

New York Times (1991) 26 October, section II, p8:1; 22 October, pA1:1

New York Times (1995) 'Deadly Hurricane Opal loses power as it races north', 6 October, pA12

O'Riordan, T. (1986) 'Coping with environmental hazards', in Kates, R. W. and Burton, I. (eds) *Geography, Resources, and Environment, Volume II, Themes from the Work of Gilbert F. White*, University of Chicago Press, Chicago, pp272–309

Palm, R. I. (1990) *Natural Hazards: An Integrative Framework for Research and Planning*, The Johns Hopkins University Press, Baltimore

Showalter, P. S., Riebsame, W. E. and Myers, M. F. (1993) 'Natural hazard trends in the United States: a preliminary review for the 1990s', Working Paper no 83, Natural Hazards Research Center, University of Colorado, Boulder, CO

Tolba, M. K., El-Kholy, O. A., El-Hinnawi, E., Holdgate, M. W., McMichael, D. F. and Munn, R. E. (1992) *The World Environment 1972–1992*, Chapman and Hall, London

Turner II, B. L., Kasperson, R. E., Meyer, W. B., Dow, K. M., Golding, D., Kasperson, J. X., Mitchell, R. C. and Ratick, S. J. (1990) 'Two types of global environmental change: definitional and spatial-scale issues in their human dimensions', *Global Environmental Change*, vol 1, no 1, pp14–22

UNEP (United Nations Environment Programme) (1993) *Environmental Data Report 1993–94*, Blackwell, Cambridge, MA

Zeigler, D. J., Johnson, J. H. jr and Brunn, S. D. (1983) *Technological Hazards*, Association of American Geographers, Washington, DC

11

Risk Cognition and the Public: The Case of Three Mile Island

Susan L. Cutter

The accident at the Three Mile Island (TMI) nuclear power plant held the world's attention for over a week in March and April 1979. Nearly 1 million people were threatened by what was thought at the time to be a significant release of radioactivity. The status of the situation was so uncertain that, despite no formal evacuation order, over 100,000 people chose to leave the area (Cutter et al, 1979; Flynn and Chalmers, 1980; Flynn, 1982). Now, four years after the accident, Three Mile Island remains in the public's eye. Continued debates about the effects of the accident and the future of the plant as an energy producer are news items that appear frequently. It is perhaps most visible as a symbol of the technological hazards that threaten society's well-being.

The accident at Unit 2 provided a situation within which to study how an affected population estimated and evaluated risks, and the range of coping actions they took to mitigate any adverse impact to themselves or their family. Data from 1979, 1980, and 1982 are used to compare changes in the local residents' estimation of risk, shifts in their evaluation of risk over time, and changes in their level of preparedness to cope with future accidents of this nature.

There has been considerable governmental and scientific debate on the determination of risks posed by various technologies (Whyte and Burton, 1980) and the acceptability of such risks in modern society (Fischhoff et al, 1979; Schwing and Albers, 1980). Recent estimates, for example, calculate that technological hazards surpass natural hazards in terms of social and economic costs and may be the most pressing environmental problem of the 1980s (Harriss et al, 1978).

Even with our expanding knowledge of how much risk is associated with certain technologies, we are left with the question of how acceptable these risks are both to the individual and to society. The determination of risk acceptability can be accomplished through a number of different approaches, each of which is based

Note: Reprinted, with kind permission, from *Environmental Management*, vol 8, no 1, Susan L. Cutter, 'Risk cognition and the public: The case of Three Mile Island', pp15–20. © Springer Science and Business Media, 1984

(to varying degrees) on the subjective evaluations held by individuals, experts or society (Fischhoff et al, 1981). These evaluations are, in turn, judgemental and reflect individual and societal beliefs, values, mores and ethics (Goodwin, 1980). The decision-making processes resulting in acceptable risk decisions are quite complex and not completely understood. Often the risk acceptability decisions are based on contradictory assumptions about human behaviour (rational and perceptive versus irrational and unreasonable) (Fischoff et al, 1981; Otway et al, 1978).

The human factor is central in acceptable risk decisions. We have limited research experience involving risk cognition and are still uncertain as to how people cognize and respond to risks posed by technology (Slovic et al, 1980). This chapter seeks to add to the growing body of empirical research on risk cognition by illustrating how one segment of the population, residents of within 50 miles of the nuclear reactor at Three Mile Island, cognized the risks associated with the production of power from nuclear sources and the range of responses they took to mitigate these risks following the 1979 accident.

Methodology

Study design

Residents in the vicinity of Three Mile Island were surveyed in April 1979 using a mailed questionnaire. They were asked a series of open-ended and fixed-response questions on their knowledge of the accident, their opinion of the reliability of information sources, and their evaluation of risks, evacuation, and other behavioural responses and social characteristics. The sampling plan was based on stratified random procedures using distance and direction from the facility. The area was divided into five concentric zones (5, 10, 15, 20, and greater than 20 miles) and four quadrants (north, south, east, and west), resulting in 20 sampling units. A total of 922 questionnaires were delivered (approximately 50 per sampling unit). A total of 374 were returned, for a response rate of 40 per cent. Due to financial constraints, no follow-up letter was sent. The results of this first survey are summarized elsewhere (see Chapter 13; also Cutter et al, 1979; Cutter and Barnes, 1982).

Of the 1979 respondents, 66 per cent agreed to participate in a follow-up study at some unspecified future date. One year later, May 1980, another questionnaire was sent to these individuals. Three questions were repeated from the 1979 survey in order to assess changes in viewpoints over the year's time. The remaining questions focused on mitigation measures taken by the individuals and their views on the venting of the radioactive steam and water from the crippled reactor. A total of 170 (out of 240) questionnaires were returned, for a response rate of 71 per cent. A follow-up letter was sent. These same 240 individuals were resurveyed in April 1980 to again assess changes in their attitudes toward risk and their coping strategies for the clean-up operations of Unit 2 and the potential restart of Unit 1. A total of 212 questionnaires were delivered (24 residents had moved, died, or were otherwise unavailable) and 141 of these were returned, for a response rate of 67 per cent.

The sampling frame used in this study is consistent with those of other researchers studying the responses of the residents to the March 1979 accident (Flynn and Chalmers, 1980; Ziegler et al, 1981). The initial sample population represents a self-selected group, but the biasing resulting from self-selection is minimal, as their responses are consistent with and verified by the findings of other research groups (Flynn and Chalmers, 1980; Flynn, 1982; Ziegler et al, 1981). While the sample may not be representative of the views held by all residents in the area, it does provide longitudinal data on one segment of the population at risk and can be used to assess and monitor changes in their cognitions of risk and behavioural responses over the course of the three years.

Nuclear power: A question of public concern

National public opinion data from the last ten years provide us with a context in which to examine risk cognition by the local TMI residents. Production of power from nuclear sources has had tacit public approval. There is a general consensus among public opinion polls regarding the use of nuclear power – one-third of those queried strongly support its use, one-third strongly oppose its use, and the remaining third shift their opinions based on media reports and headlines (Schulman, 1979). Immediately after the accident at Three Mile Island, there was some divergence of opinion with 44–54 per cent of those sampled expressing opposition to the use of nuclear power to generate electricity (Kasperson et al, 1980). Three years later, the majority of the public still favours the use of nuclear power, but recognizes the need for improved safety features. This majority, however, is slowly eroding (Mitchell, 1980).

Nuclear power plants have generally been evaluated as safe, although there has been more concern about safety issues since the mid-1970s. This heightened concern appears to be linked to news coverage of accidents, closures due to system failures and design problems, and nuclear waste disposal. The acceptance of the technology without improved safeguards is diminishing, however, as anti-nuclear groups become more organized and vocal in their protest efforts (Barkan, 1979; Mitchell, 1981).

When the public is asked to personalize the issue ('Would you like a plant within five miles of your community?'), a different pattern of acceptance emerges. There has been increased opposition to the siting of nuclear power plants and other noxious facilities near communities. In 1976, for example, national opposition to siting a nuclear power plant within five miles of the respondents' homes was 45 per cent. Three years later, following the accident at Three Mile Island, 62 per cent of those sampled were against siting a nuclear power plant within five miles of their community (Mitchell, 1980). This opposition has been quite militant at times and has temporarily halted construction and systems testing at a number of plants – Seabrook, New Hampshire; Shoreham, New York; and Diablo Canyon, California.

Overall, there is moderate public support for the continued use of nuclear power, along with a recognition of the need for safety improvements at the facilities. Quite a different pattern of acceptability emerges when the public is asked about siting these facilities near their own communities. There is considerable opposition to the siting of facilities within five miles of the respondents' communities. The public says yes, we want and need nuclear power, but don't locate the plant near me. Given their experience with the March 1979 accident, how do the residents in the vicinity of TMI feel about these issues?

Results

Risk estimation and evaluation

There are minor shifts in residents' feelings about the frequency of nuclear power plant accidents over the three-year period (Table 11.1). Most respondents think that accidents are likely to occur once every ten years. Fewer people evaluated accidents as unlikely in 1982 than they did in 1979, and there is very little change in the once every three or four years category. The shift toward the moderate responses (one every ten years) may be a function of increased knowledge about nuclear power from media coverage of the accident and subsequent clean-up activities.

When respondents were asked to state their feelings on the future use of nuclear power stations, a slightly different pattern of answers appears. There are noticeable shifts over the three-year period, with respondents expressing more negative feelings about the continued use of nuclear power (Table 11.2). This could easily be a function of the dissatisfaction associated with the clean-up operations of the damaged reactor and the controversy surrounding the restart of Unit 1. There were no noticeable changes in the respondents' feelings from 1979 to 1980. Most feel that nuclear power stations should be modified to prevent the occurrence of accidents like the one at TMI. There was a sizeable minority opinion in both 1979 and 1980 that all nuclear power stations should be permanently closed as soon as possible. In 1982, however, these feelings became more negative. There was a significant drop in the modified-for-safety category from, 1980 to 1982, with subsequent increases in the percentage in the permanent closure categories. Of our respondents, 27 per cent felt that all nuclear power stations should be permanently closed as soon as possible (an increase of 10 per cent over

Table 11.1 *Frequency of nuclear power plant accidents (in %)*

	1979[a]	1980[b]	Δ79–80[c]	1982[d]	Δ80–82[c]
Unlikely	14.6	11.2	−3.4	9.9	−1.3
1–2 per lifetime	35.5	41.2	+5.9	34.8	−6.4
1 per 10 years	14.6	18.8	+4.2	25.5	+6.7
1 per 3–4 years	16.0	21.8	+5.8	20.6	−1.2
1 per year	12.2	4.7	−7.3*	6.4	+1.7
No answer	7.0	2.4	−4.6*	2.8	+0.4

[a] $n = 369$.
[b] $n = 170$.
[c] Difference of proportions test, *$p = 0.05$
[d] $n = 141$

Table 11.2 *Future use of nuclear power stations (in %)*

	1979[a]	1980[b]	Δ79–80[c]	1982[d]	Δ80–82[c]
Continue to use as is	3.0	4.1	+1.1	2.8	−1.3
Continue to use but modify for safety	64.2	70.0	+5.8	53.2	−16.8**
Close all TMI-like permanently	10.0	8.2	−1.8	17.0	+8.8*
Close all plants permanently	20.6	17.1	−3.5	27.0	+9.9*
No answer	2.1	0.6	+1.5	0.0	−0.6

[a] $n = 369$.
[b] $n = 170$.
[c] Difference of proportions test, $*p = 0.05$, $**p = 0.01$
[d] $n = 141$

1980), while an additional 17 per cent felt that nuclear power stations of the type installed at Three Mile Island (Babcock and Wilcox manufacturers) should be permanently closed (an increase of 9 per cent over 1980).

It has been suggested that the public is willing to accept risks at the societal level, yet when the issue is personalized, such as locating a power plant near them, the level of acceptability decreases. Respondents were asked in 1980 and 1982 to evaluate the future use of both reactors at the TMI site (Table 11.3). Unit 1, the undamaged reactor, was shut down prior to the accident for inspection and still remains closed. There are considerable shifts in the respondents' views toward the use of Unit 1 over the two-year period (Table 11.3). The majority of respondents in 1980 favoured reopening the plant after safety improvements had been made, with a minority (31 per cent) expressing a view of permanent closure. Two years later, the respondents were evenly divided in their views – 44 per cent favoured reopening after safety improvements had been made and 43 per cent favoured permanent closure. A recent (May 1982) ballot measure in the three counties around the damaged reactor found 67 per cent of the voters opposed to the restart of Unit 1.

When queried about Unit 2, the damaged reactor, the majority of our respondents favoured permanent closure. There were no significant changes in views over

Table 11.3 *Status of Three Mile Island (in %)*

	Unit 1 undamaged			Unit 2 damaged		
	1980[a]	1982[b]	Δ[c]	1980[a]	1982[b]	Δ[c]
Open immediately	22.4	9.2	−13.2***	0.6	0.0	−0.6
Reopen after clean-up or after safety improvements	41.7	44.0	+2.3	44.1	37.6	−6.5
Close permanently	30.6	43.3	+12.7**	48.2	56.0	+7.8
None of the above	5.3	3.5	−1.8	7.1	6.4	−0.7

[a] $n = 170$.
[b] $n = 141$.
[c] Difference of proportions test, $**p = 0.01$, $***p = 0.001$.

Table 11.4 *TMI benefit risk ratio (in %)*

	1980[a]	1982[b]	Change[c]
Benefits > risks	19.4	20.6	+1.2
Benefits = risks	20.6	17.7	−2.9
Benefits < risks	51.8	61.0	+9.2*
No answer	8.2	0.7	−7.5

[a] $n = 170$.
[b] $n = 141$.
[c] Difference of proportions test, *$p = 0.05$.

the two-year period. As part of the determination of risk cognition, respondents were asked (1980) in open-ended format to describe the ways in which TMI benefits the area. Of the sample, 44 per cent felt there were no benefits. Those who listed benefits included cheap electricity (23 per cent) and jobs (18 per cent). When asked to compare the benefits to the costs and risks, 52 per cent in 1980 and 61 per cent in 1982 replied that the benefits were less than the risks (Table 11.4). There were significant changes in this view over the course of the two years. The rest of the respondents were evenly split between benefits equalling risks and benefits exceeding risks.

Nine different aspects of everyday life were used to assess the personal consequences of TMI (Table 11.5). Respondents were asked to evaluate how the accident at TMI had changed each of these by indicating whether there was an increase, decrease or no change. This question was asked in 1979 and 1980, but was not repeated in 1982. One of the biggest casualties of the TMI accident was the respondents' trust of institutions (Table 11.5). Of the sample, 43 per cent listed a decline in their trust of government immediately after the accident and this rose to 65 per cent one year later. Trust in power companies declined similarly: 74 per cent of those sampled in both years expressed a decline in their trust of power companies. There was also very little change in the respondents' trust of science. Overall, they expressed a certain pessimism about the government's handling of the clean-up operations and seeming lack of willingness to adequately protect them from the risks associated with the clean-up, particularly the venting of radioactive gases.

Some of the early fears, such as loss of revenue from property, were not substantiated by our respondents a year after the accident. Initially, almost one in three of the respondents felt that the value of their house and/or property would decrease as a result of TMI, but this opinion was held by only 22 per cent of the sample the following year. An empirical analysis of residential property values and TMI failed to disclose any significant decline in property values as a result of the accident (Nelson, 1981). In contrast, 43 per cent of the respondents in 1979 listed that their faith in God had increased after the accident, but this dropped to 10 per cent the following year. It is apparent that, after the confusion and uncertainty subsided, residents were not as reliant on religious forces to help them cope with events at the plant.

One interesting aspect of the personal consequence evaluations is the change in the 'no answer' category. One year after the accident, respondents were more

Table 11.5 *Personal consequences of Three Mile Island*

	Decrease (%)			No change (%)			Increase (%)			No answer (%)		
	1979	1980	Δ^a	1979	1980	Δ^a	1979	1980	Δ^a	1979	1980	Δ^a
Value of house/property	31.7	21.8	−9.9*	55.6	74.1	18.5***	0.8	1.2	0.4	11.9	2.9	−9.0**
Residential desirability	19.0	22.9	3.9	69.9	74.1	4.2	0.8	1.2	0.4	10.3	1.8	−8.5**
Involvement in community affairs	2.2	2.9	0.7	73.7	81.8	8.1	12.5	12.9	0.4	11.7	2.4	−9.3***
Physical health	14.4	7.6	−6.8*	72.4	88.8	16.4***	1.6	3.5	1.9	11.7	3.5	−8.2**
Mental well-being	23.8	25.3	1.5	63.4	71.2	7.8	1.9	1.2	−0.7	10.8	2.4	−8.4**
Trust of power companies	74.3	73.5	−0.8	16.5	22.4	5.9	1.6	3.5	1.9	7.6	0.6	−7.0***
Trust of government	43.1	65.3	22.2***	42.5	32.4	−10.1*	4.3	1.2	−3.1	10.0	1.2	−8.8***
Trust of science	28.7	31.2	2.5	51.2	58.8	7.6	9.5	7.1	−2.4	10.6	2.9	−7.7**
Faith in God	1.6	1.2	−0.4	48.0	64.1	16.1**	43.1	32.9	10.2*	7.3	1.8	−5.5*

**p < 0.05, **p < 0.01, ***p < 0.001 difference of proportions test.

definitive in their answers. There was a higher degree of certainty and confidence about the impact of TMI on their daily lives. Immediately following the accident, there was a tremendous amount of confusion and uncertainty regarding both the long- and short-term impacts. This was reflected not only in their evaluations of risk but also in their behaviour in response to the accident.

Behavioural responses

How did the respondents' cognition of risk influence their behaviour? Nearly 39 per cent of our sampled households fully or partially evacuated in response to the accident. Another one-third of the sample made preparations to evacuate such as filling the car with gas, withdrawing money from the bank and packing suitcases. The major factors influencing the evacuation decision were: (a) the advisory statement issued by Governor Thornburgh; (b) spatial proximity to the plant; and (c) inability to confirm the hazard information (see Chapter 13).

The advisory statement issued by Governor Thornburgh applied only to pregnant women and pre-school-aged children living within a five-mile radius of the plant. It was clearly relied on by a much larger percentage of the population as a cue to evacuate. This relatively high percentage of voluntary evacuation, noted by other authors as well (Flynn, 1982; Ziegler et al, 1981), indicated a general tendency on the part of the local residents to assume the initiative in assessing the immediate danger and taking corresponding actions to cope with it. It should be stressed that the residents had no prior experience with the event and thus had to rely on secondary and tertiary sources of information, which were confusing: the 'experts' could not agree on the situation and this uncertainty was transmitted to the general public (Dynes et al, 1979).

With the wisdom of hindsight, 55 per cent of our respondents felt they would not have done anything differently than they had in 1979: 14 per cent responded they would have either left the area earlier or returned later then they actually did, or they would now undertake an evacuation although they had not left the area in 1979. A majority (82 per cent) replied they would leave the area immediately if another advisory statement were issued as a result of activities surrounding the clean-up of Unit 2 or the restart of Unit 1.

When residents were queried as to evacuation cues other than an advisory statement, uncertainty about events (12 per cent) and confusion over the reliability of information (12 per cent) were seen as factors encouraging evacuation: 13 per cent responded that the continual venting of radioactive gas and the release of contaminated water were enough to make them leave. The remaining 13 per cent replied that they would remain in the area regardless of what happened at the plant.

There is an even split in the residents' evaluation (a year later) of how prepared they were to deal with another TMI emergency – 37 per cent said they were not better prepared, 32 per cent felt they were better prepared and 28 per cent were not sure. Also, 44 per cent of the respondents have done nothing to improve their ability to cope with future accidents at the site. A few have taken the initiative to develop personal or family evacuation plans (20 per cent). Another 25 per cent said they have attended public meetings on nuclear hazards and have familiarized themselves with public evacuation or shelter plans, although three-quarters of our sample had not received copies of such plans at the time of the interview (May 1980).

While the residents may be more aware of the risk, they may not have improved their capacity to cope with it. There is an apparent inability on the part of our respondents to translate their cognition of risk into overt actions to minimize or mitigate the risks. There were only weak statistical associations between an individual's cognition of risk and evacuation behaviour ($r = 0.48$, $p = 0.003$ in 1979; $r = 0.131$, $p = 0.045$ in 1980).

Conclusion

The residents in the vicinity of Three Mile Island show a heightened cognition of risk when compared to national averages, and this increased awareness has not changed since the March 1979 accident. Our respondents also feel that the future use of nuclear power is assured and the facilities need only be modified for additional safety systems.

There is no discernible association between risk cognition and coping responses, specifically, evacuation. Whether this is due to discrepancies between risk cognition and overt behaviour, constraints on decision-making, constraints on behaviour, or other intervening variables is unclear at this time. The lack of congruence may be a function of the inadequacy of the risk cognition measure itself.

On a more pragmatic level, the loss of credibility that respondents registered with scientific, government and power company sources has the potential to cripple future response planning. The effectiveness of these plans is already being challenged. Given no perceived source of reliable information, evacuation decisions by local residents would be based on incomplete and inaccurate information. This could limit the effectiveness of evacuation procedures by county, state and federal emergency response personnel charged with implementing evacuation orders. To date, this type of information has not been included in emergency response plans.

This analysis should aid our understanding of how individuals cognize risks posed by the potential restart of Unit 1 and the clean-up operations at Unit 2 as well as the types of actions they are taking or will take in response to these risks. Further investigation is needed, however, before the full psychological impact of TMI on the residents is known.

Acknowledgements

Funding has been provided by the New Jersey Agricultural Experiment Station, publication D-26410-4-82, supported by state funds and by the Center for Coastal and Environmental Studies, Rutgers University.

References

Barkan, S. E. (1979) 'Strategic, tactical and organizational dilemmas of the protest movement against nuclear power', *Social Problems*, vol 27, pp19–27

Cutter, S. L., Brosius, J., Barnes, K. and Mitchell, J. K. (1979) 'Special session on Three Mile Island: Risk evaluation and evacuation responses', *Proceedings, Middle States Division*, Association of American Geographers, vol 13, pp80–88

Cutter, S. L. and Barnes, K. (1982) 'Three Mile Island: Risk assessment and coping responses of local residents', summary report, discussion paper no 20, Department of Geography, Rutgers University, New Brunswick, NJ

Dynes, R. R., Purcell, A. H., Wenger, D. E., Stern, P. S., Stallings, R. A. and Johnson, Q. T. (1979) *Report of the Emergency Preparedness and Response Task Force: The Presidents Commission on the Accident at Three Mile Island*, Government Printing Office, Washington, DC

Fischhoff, B., Slovic, P. and Lichtenstein, S. (1979) 'Weighing the risks', *Environment*, vol 21, pp17–20, 32–38

Fischhoff, B., Lichtenstein, S., Slovic, P., Derby, S. L. and Keeney, R. L. (1981) *Acceptable Risk*, Cambridge University Press, Cambridge

Flynn, C. B. and Chalmers, J. A. (1980) *The Social and Economic Effects of the Accident at Three Mile Island: Findings to Date*, US Nuclear Regulatory Commission (NUREG/CR-1215)

Flynn, C. B. (1982) 'Reactions of local residents to the accident at Three Mile Island' in D. L. Sills, C. P. Wolf and V. B. Shelanski (eds) *Accident at Three Mile Island: The Human Dimensions*, Westview, Boulder, CO, pp49–63

Goodwin, R. E. (1980) 'No moral nukes', *Ethics*, vol 90, pp417–449

Harriss, R. C., Hohenemser, C. and Kates, R W. (1978) 'Our hazardous environment', *Environment*, vol 20, pp6–15

Kasperson, R. E., Berk, G., Pijawka, D., Sharof, A. B. and Wood, J. (1980) 'Public opposition to nuclear energy: Retrospect and prospect', *Science, Technology and Human Values*, vol 5, pp11–23

Mitchell, R. C. (1980) 'Public opinion and nuclear power before and after Three Mile Island', *Resources (Resources for the Future)*, vol 64, pp5–8

Mitchell, R. C. (1981) 'From elite quarrel to mass movement', *Transaction/Society*, vol 18, pp76–84

Nelson, J. P. (1981) 'Three Mile Island and residential property values: Empirical analysis and policy implications', *Land Economics*, vol 57, pp363–372

Otway, H. J., Maurer, D. and Thomas, K. (1978) 'Nuclear power: The question of public acceptance', *Futures*, vol 10, pp109–118

Schulman, M. A. (1979) 'The impact of Three Mile Island', *Public Opinion*, June/July, pp7–9, 23–26

Schwing, R. C. and Albers, W. A. jr (eds) (1980) *Societal Risk Assessment: How Safe is Safe Enough?*, Plenum, New York

Slovic, P., Fischhoff, B. and Lichtenstein, S. (1979) 'Rating the risks', *Environment*, vol 21, pp14–20, 36–39

Slovic, P., Fischhoff, F. and Lichtenstein, S. (1980) 'Facts and fears: Understanding perceived risk' in R. C. Schwing and W. A. Albers jr (eds) *Societal Risk Assessment: How Safe is Safe Enough?*, Plenum, New York

Whyte, A. V. and Burton, I. (1980) *Environmental Risk Assessment*, Wiley, New York

Ziegler, D. J., Brunn, S. D. and Johnson, J. H. jr (1981) 'Evacuation from a nuclear technological disaster', *Geographical Review*, vol 71, pp1–16

12
En-gendered Fears: Femininity and Technological Risk Perception

Susan L. Cutter, John Tiefenbacher and William D. Solecki

Introduction

More than a decade has passed since the original research by Fischhoff, Lichtenstein and Slovic on perception of technological risks and benefits (Fischhoff et al, 1978; Lichtenstein et al, 1978). Critiques are now emerging leading to an overall reappraisal of the psychometric paradigm in particular (Renn and Swaton, 1984; Gardner and Gould, 1989; Hansson, 1989) and risk perception research in general (Douglas and Wildavsky, 1982; Johnson and Covello, 1987; Kasperson et al, 1988). While there is some work on cross-cultural comparisons of risk perceptions (Vlek and Stallen, 1981; Englander et al, 1986; Teigen et al, 1988; Bastide et al, 1989; Keown, 1989; Kleinhesselink and Rosa, 1989), research on social distinctions (race, ethnicity, gender) is virtually non-existent. Yet race, ethnicity and gender may be crucial in understanding the social acceptability of risk at both the local and national levels. In particular, the issues of social equity and the burdens of technological risk and hazards are now being raised (UCC, 1987; Bullard, 1990).

We argue for a feminist analysis of technological risk that addresses these social distinctions. Specifically, a pilot study of gender differences in the perception of technological risk is used to illustrate the shortcomings of the psychometric paradigm and the need for alternative approaches to extract gender-based differences in risk perception and behaviour toward technological hazards.

Note: Reprinted, with permission, from *Organization & Environment* (previously *Industrial Crisis Quarterly*), vol 6, no 1, Susan L. Cutter, John Tiefenbacher, William D. Solecki, 'En-gendered fears: Femininity and technological risk perception', pp5–22. © Sage Publications, 1992

Re-evaluating Nature, Society and Technology

If viewed on a continuum, the underlying industrialized world philosophies that govern nature–society interactions range from ecocentrism at one pole to technocentrism at the other. Ecocentrism views the world according to natural laws. The Earth's functioning involves a complex and sensitive balance between all parts of nature striving for stability through the principles of diversity and homeostasis (O'Riordan, 1981). Ecocentrism preaches responsibility and care, where humans are a part of the larger system, not apart from it. Smallness and low-impact technology are also governing principles.

Technocentrism, the dominant view since the Industrial Revolution, argues that nature exists to be used by societies through the application of rationality, science and professionalized managerial techniques. Progress, efficiency and control form the ideology that underpins technocentrism (O'Riordan, 1981). Human domination of nature through technology can be traced historically to the development of Western culture (White, 1967; Moncrief, 1970). Merchant (1980), for example, has shown that the domination mentality co-evolved with rationality and science during and since the Renaissance.

At the beginning of the 18th century, nature was the primary target of rationalism as Baconian thinking encouraged order, hierarchy, linearity and logic. These were traits of men, not nature. By distinguishing the duality of nature and man, and placing man at the pinnacle, the anthropocentric worldview was born. Rationalism also changed the belief that nature was the nurturing mother. Nature became threatening – a foe that needed conquering. Chaos, disorder, uncontrollability and unpredictability were anathema to this rationalized worldview. One way that man could overcome the antagonisms of nature was through technological innovation. Earth was no longer passive and 'her' wrath and fury justified the use of technology to tame and subdue her (Plant, 1990). Women were closely identified with nature because of their nurturing qualities and ability to reproduce (Merchant, 1980). Their provision of these services (mother, wife, homemaker, gardener) relegated them to a more passive role than men (hunter, provider, protector). Patriarchal systems soon developed, ultimately resulting in the domination of women. Many of the technologies that liberated men and empowered them over nature have subjugated women.

Natural hazards are often characterized as 'acts of God' or products of 'the wrath of nature'. Technology is employed to control nature and protect people from harm or mitigate adverse impacts. Not until very recently has an alternative framework been suggested (Hewitt, 1983). This political-economic perspective suggests that natural hazards are prompted by natural events, but their impacts and society's responses to them are largely governed by the failures of the political, economic and social systems. Therefore, technological fixes will not simply solve the problem or render the wrath of nature immutable.

Technological hazards, on the other hand, are viewed as acts of people. Technological systems fail because of their complexities and because of human fallibility. Accidents should be seen as normal, not extreme occurrences, at least in complex systems (Perrow, 1984). The idea that technological systems can be improved through bigger and better science and technology, better risk assessments and more management clearly represents the technocentric view.

Masculinity and Technology

Masculinity manifests itself clearly in nature–society interactions. Its effect on the technological world is less apparent. As Paehlke (1989) suggests, men in decision-making positions have traditionally undervalued the nurturing dimension that forms the central tenet of ecocentrism or what is now called environmentalism. Instead, these 'experts' feel more comfortable with a rational, scientific view embodied in such disciplines as engineering. Technology is a creation of science and engineering, where women traditionally have had limited access and professional acceptance. The growing sophistication of resource management meant the separation of the resource manager from the public. Policy-makers became dependent on 'scientific advisers' from a narrow range of specialities, most of whom were men. Women, if they were involved in resource decision-making, were most likely the citizen activists, or the 'bird, bug and bunny lovers' according to the professional managerial elite. In accordance with the moniker, women's views were ridiculed and discounted.

The separation of informed judgements (by experts) from those of an uninformed public fuels public debates on the acceptability of technological risks. Some feel the lay public does not have a valid understanding of, or constructive opinions on, technological risks (Lewis, 1990), and thus should simply defer judgements and management to the experts. It is, in fact, the creation and maintenance of the aura of expertise that establishes hierarchies that ultimately reduce the value of the opinion of the 'other', be they women, minorities or the poor (Hynes, 1989, 1991). Risk perceptions based upon anti-technocentric, anti-masculine or anti-progress modes of thought are not only ignored but disabled. Clearly, what the public views as acceptable risk is as important to the use of technology as what the expert thinks. Often the public view is more persuasive with lawmakers.

Numerous cases can be mentioned that emphasize the disparity between the acceptability of a technology or activity to experts and its unacceptability to the public. For example, the use of Alar (daminozide) on apples became an unacceptable activity to mothers based on evidence of the likely carcinogenic effects on children – the most apple-consuming cohort. Experts insisted that levels ingested even in this most vulnerable population were not enough to induce cancer. Likewise, the apple industry asserted their product was safe. Nevertheless, millions of parents boycotted red apples, sales plummeted, and apple growers withdrew the products from market as a sign of concern, losing millions of dollars in the process.

In contrast, the control of ozone-depleting substances like CFCs and halons is championed more by the experts and less by the general public, although it is the latter who would need to change their lifestyles to support the goal. In fact, most of the concern for global warming, greenhouse gases and ozone depletion is coming from scientists, large environmental organizations and other institutions that focus on global concerns. Thus far, the public has demonstrated little direct concern about this issue.

Ecofeminism and the Politics of Technology

Within the last decade, feminists and environmentalists have discovered one another, recognizing commonalities in their goals. The pragmatism of radical environmentalists (Foreman and Haywood, 1987; Manes, 1990; Scarce, 1990) and the critical nature of radical ecologies (like social ecology) provide support to feminist critiques of the anthropocentrism of technology and society. The nearest kindred spirits, deep ecology (Devall and Sessions, 1985) and bioregionalism (Sale, 1985) argue for a biocentric worldview, but it is a biocentrism built upon the foundations of masculinity-based science, the cause of the problem. The interaction between feminism and environmentalism provides a wide range of ecofeminisms that challenge the social, cultural and political zeal of masculine modern culture. The message is clear: when women suffer through social discrimination and the domination of nature, the planet is also threatened (King, 1989). There are a number of central tenets to ecofeminism that are pertinent to our discussion. Ecosystem malaise and abuse is rooted in androcentric (man-centred) values and institutions. Human liberation and its relationship to non-human nature requires a new ethic about the use of technology, since technology is the tool by which humans manipulate nature. Relations between society and nature, and between men and women, need reassessing to become more harmonizing and less dominating. Ecofeminists praise diversity and view it as enriching not confining, a strength rather than a weakness. The problems of relations and connections (human and non-human, male and female) will not be resolved until androcentric values and institutions are restructured (Oelschlaeger, 1991). Finally, as a social movement, ecofeminism supports harmony, diversity, decentralized communities and technologies based on sound ecological principles (King, 1989).

The politics of social control over the use of the environment is governed by public opinion. These collective views represent a wide range of individual perspectives that are ultimately masked by the creation of averages. The obscurity of the views of socially alienated groups is managed by their omission from telephone surveys, or their amalgamation into the average statistic to derive a 'typically American' view. Indeed, what is a typical American? A case in point is the social construction of sex roles. Sexual stereotypes often dictate the activities that may be performed, given the vagaries of social approvals and disapprovals – acceptance, ostracism, security, fear. Sex roles will, for example, create guidelines for acceptable activities revolving around ideas concerning body/mind strength, body/mind agility, body image and body size – that is, ideas merely based on sex or biological difference.

When individual personality is examined, perception can be regarded as a product of non-physical, 'emotional' development. 'Gender' is a term that describes the extent to which traits that are socially defined as masculine or feminine are present within an individual's personality. The dynamics of gender may be unseen and unknown, yet it conditions the individual's method of processing information, and ultimately his or her view of nature. Tracing the work of psychologists, Merchant (1981) says femininity stems from the woman's role as reproducer in Western culture and is imprinted upon offspring from birth. The female psyche is based on empathy, identification and wholeness, while the male psyche is rooted in separation, dualism and distinction. Each leads to a different view of nature and our place in it. This argument is further enhanced by Gilligan's (1982) different voice thesis. She argues that there are distinct differences in the psychological development of men and women that arise from the social construction of identity. Power, social status and reproductive biology all interact to shape the individual experiences of males and females as well as the interactions between them. Thus, if women perceive and experience the world differently from men, then it stands to reason that they would also perceive risks differently as well.

An examination of the perceptions of women versus those of men can provide insights into understanding the role gender plays within a society and the political processes occurring within that society. Is there a difference, for instance, between the levels of risk perceived by men and women automobile drivers? Would the presence of a nuclear power plant in a neighbourhood elicit more concern in a woman than in a man? Would the potential of handgun use produce the same perceptual and emotional response in men as in women?

Gender Perceptions

Some general distinctions between men's and women's responses to risks have already been identified (McStay and Dunlap, 1983; Stallen and Thomas, 1988). For example, studies have variously described women as more nurturing and concerned with health and well-being, interested in the fate of society as a whole, and desiring to limit destructive technologies. As such, they are more concerned about industrial hazards and more opposed to military spending, military intervention and war, especially nuclear war (Boulding, 1984; Silverman and Kumka, 1987; Bastide et al, 1989). Men are described as more self-interested, prone to more aggressive behaviours, and more willing to gamble and take risks (Levin et al, 1988). In other words, men may be viewed as risk-takers and women as risk-avoiders.

The above statements partially reflect some truisms and oversimplifications about gender differences. Unfortunately, we have very little empirical evidence to support or reject them, and the evidence that is available is inconclusive. Specific studies in the feminist literature, for example, examined gender differences in the perception of nuclear war and found that women were more concerned about the risk and more willing to work for peaceful solutions to conflict (Boulding, 1984; Jensen, 1987; Silverman and Kumka, 1987; Hamilton et al, 1988). In a study of acid rain, another technological hazard, men were found to be more concerned with the problem, and more knowledgeable than women (Arcury et al, 1987). Currently, it is virtually impossible to determine what kind of gender perception differences might exist.

Understanding the role of gender in risk perception is critical for several reasons. First, it is important to understand the socialization process and how sex roles influence risk perception. Women may bear a disproportionate share of the risks, thus they may have completely different views of the risks and avenues for ameliorating them. Second, it is crucial to understand differences for the improvement of risk communication. The reliance on risk perception studies based solely

on a male or mixed population points to the potential failure of risk communication, where the interests and beliefs of women, who might be disproportionately
more involved in a series of risk management issues, are largely ignored. Last, the
social acceptability of risk may vary widely between different gender, racial and
ethnic groups. The influence of women in the political and economic arena is
increasing along with their representation among policy analysts and decision-
makers (Holcomb et al, 1990; Regulska et al, 1991). Women in government, for
example, may favour radically different laws and regulatory strategies for technological hazards than their male counterparts, particularly if they feel that the laws
will differentially affect women and men. A political gender gap does exist, and it
is related not only to traditional women's concerns, but also to many other issues,
including risk assessment and the acceptability of such risks.

Pilot Study: Gender-Based Differences in Risk Perception

Many methods for studying technological risk perception have been used over the
years. They range from attitude theory and change (Ajzen and Fishbein, 1980;
Verplanken, 1989) to affective responses and judgements (Johnson and Tversky,
1983, 1984). The psychometric paradigm is the most widely used method and
the one selected for this pilot study. The survey instrument used in this research
is similar in design to the one described by Slovic et al (1985). The questionnaire
had four major sections: a rank-ordering of the perceived level of risk for 33 technologies and activities; a judgement on the acceptability of risk from each of these
(e.g. could it be made more or less risky?); an evaluation of the characteristics of
risk for each technology or activity; and finally the current and desired level of
regulation for each technology.

The survey was administered in April 1989 to a group of undergraduate students in five separate sections of an introductory geography course. A sample of
college students was also used in the original psychometric studies (Fischhoff et al,
1978; Slovic et al, 1985) in addition to a smaller group of respondents from the
League of Women Voters. Students were asked to complete the survey during a
regular 80-minute class period. A brief introduction and description of the survey
and its use in a research project was given. A total of 294 completed questionnaires
were returned.

Respondent characteristics

The average age of our respondents was 21. The sample had more men (56 per
cent) than women (40 per cent) (4 per cent failed to identify themselves). 32 per
cent of the students were in their senior year, with the remaining evenly distributed between the other years (Table 12.1). About 72 per cent of the sample were
Caucasian, making racial and ethnic comparisons impossible because of the small
sample size and unreliability of the self-reporting. 15 per cent of the respondents
were economics majors, followed by psychology and undecided. Finally, more
than three-quarters of the students were native to New Jersey. There were very
few differences between males and females in referent characteristics. Psychology

Table 12.1 *Sample population (in %)*

	Total	Female	Male
Number	294	119	166
Mean age	21.0	20.9	21.0
Year			
First year	21.8	20.2	24.1
Sophomore	20.1	25.2	17.5
Junior	20.1	15.1	23.5
Senior	32.0	36.1	30.7
No response	6.0	3.4	4.2
Race/ethnicity			
African American	4.8	5.0	4.8
Asian	6.5	7.6	6.0
Caucasian	72.4	76.5	72.3
Hispanic	3.1	4.2	2.4
Native American	3.1	0.8	4.8
Other	3.7	2.5	4.8
No response	6.4	3.4	4.9
US citizen			
Yes	89.5	92.4	91.0
No	5.8	4.2	7.2
No response	4.7	3.4	1.8
New Jersey native			
Yes	75.2	77.3	76.5
No	17.3	17.6	18.1
Non-citizen	4.1	5.0	3.6
No response	3.3	0.0	1.8

and economics majors were prevalent among the females in the sample, while economics was the most often listed major among males.

Risk rankings

Respondents were asked to rank the relative importance of each of the 33 items in terms of the risk of dying as a consequence of the technology, substance or activity (using 11 as the least risky and 43 as the most). There are a few statistically significant differences between males and females in their ranking of technological risks, although there is considerable agreement on the top five (Table 12.2). Females listed nuclear weapons, handguns, illegal drugs, smoking and sexually transmitted diseases as the most risky technologies/activities. Males, on the other hand, listed illegal drugs, handguns, nuclear weapons, motor vehicles and smoking. There were no differences in the evaluation of the least risky items; food colouring, high school/college football, vaccinations, contraceptives and home appliances were given a very low ranking of perceived riskiness.

Table 12.2 *Relative ranking of risks*

Activity/technology	Arithmetic means		
	Total	Men	Women
1. Illegal drugs	36.1	36.8	35.3*
2. Nuclear weapons	35.8	35.3	36.6
3. Handguns	35.6	35.5	35.8
4. Smoking	34.3	34.1	34.4
5. Motor vehicles	34.2	34.1	34.2
6. Sexual diseases	32.9	32.0	34.2*
7. Police work	32.5	32.6	32.1
8. Nuclear power	32.3	31.4	33.4
9. Alcoholic beverages	31.5	31.7	31.4
10. Motorcycles	31.3	31.6	30.6
11. Firefighting	30.9	31.4	30.4
12. CFCs	29.4	28.7	30.4
13. Pesticides	28.9	29.0	28.8
14. Surgery	28.7	28.6	29.0
15. Burning fossil fuels	27.4	27.6	27.1
16. Large construction	26.7	26.9	26.7
17. Commercial aviation	25.8	24.9	27.0*
18. Non-nuclear electric	25.1	24.4	26.1
19. Mountain climbing	25.0	25.8	24.2
20. Hunting	24.4	25.0	23.8
21. X-rays	23.6	23.7	23.5
22. Railroads	22.8	22.5	23.0
23. Prescription drugs	22.8	22.0	23.6
24. Food preservatives	19.4	18.9	20.1
25. Skiing	19.4	19.3	19.6
26. Power mowers	19.3	19.2	19.3
27. Swimming	19.3	19.3	19.2
28. Bicycles	18.9	19.2	18.2
29. Home appliances	17.8	18.3	17.1
30. Contraceptives	17.7	17.7	17.3
31. Vaccinations	17.2	17.6	16.5
32. High school football	16.4	17.2	15.2*
33. Food colouring	16.1	15.7	16.5

*Difference between male/female means (*t*-statistic) significant at $p > 0.05$.

Risk characteristics

Students were asked to evaluate risk characteristics for each of the 33 items using a seven-point bipolar scale. The nine dimensions, based on the psychometric approach, included: voluntary/involuntary; immediate effect/delayed effect; risk level known to the exposed/unknown to the exposed; risks known to science/ unknown to science; risks new and novel/old and familiar; chronic (kills one at a time)/catastrophic (kills large numbers at once); learn to live with or common/ dreaded or feared; fatal or severe consequences/no effects or not severe; risks are controllable/uncontrollable. To identify those risk characteristics that best illustrate and distinguish among the different types of technological hazards, a factor analysis was done (Slovic et al, 1985). This statistical procedure identified two factors that help define the dimensions and commonalities of risk among the 33 items.

The first factor (*Known*) describes a group of technological hazards whose risks are familiar, where people engage in the activities on a voluntary basis, whose effects are chronic, and the risks are more or less acceptable. This is in sharp contrast to the second factor (*Dreaded*), which highlights technologies that are perceived as newer, where risks are imposed involuntarily, with potential cata-strophic consequences, resulting in technology that is feared. Technological risks from sources such as pesticides, CFC use, nuclear power and nuclear weapons involuntarily expose people to risks and are relatively new hazards according to our sample. In addition, these risks are known to science and, to people exposed, catastrophic in their potential to cause death, and therefore highly feared.

Based on this statistical analysis and two-dimensional mapping, two different types of technological hazards emerge. The first grouping of hazards are what we might consider societal in origin. These are hazards that are new, to which we are involuntarily exposed, have an enormous catastrophic potential (i.e. may kill large numbers of people at one time), and where individuals have very little con-trol over the personal risk, thus making the consequences quite dreaded. Examples include the commercial use of nuclear power, nuclear weapons, pesticides, CFC use and food additives (preservatives and colouring). The second grouping of technological hazards are more individual in nature. This group is characterized by more voluntary exposures to familiar hazards, where the risks are well known to science, and where mishaps result in fatalities. Examples of these hazards include handguns, illegal drugs, smoking and motor vehicles.

While the overall classification of technological risks is similar between men and women, there are some clear distinctions in the evaluation of each of the nine attributes of risk. For example, we found that women were more likely than men to evaluate risks as more catastrophic in potential, more dreaded and more fatal (Table 12.3). Women consistently rated hunting, motor vehicles, firefight-ing, construction projects, mountain climbing, contraceptives and motorcycles as posing a more catastrophic risk potential than did men. Similarly, women were more inclined to evaluate motor vehicles, nuclear power, pesticides, X-rays, sexu-ally transmitted diseases, commercial aviation and the burning of fossil fuels as dreaded risks. Women were also more pessimistic than men in their evaluations of the severity of risks and the fatal consequences of alcoholic beverages, skiing, sexually transmitted diseases, CFCS, contraceptives and food additives.

Risk regulation

Students were asked to evaluate the current and desired level of regulation for each of the 33 different technologies and activities utilizing the same 0–5 scale employed by Slovic et al (1985). In that original work, nuclear power and spray cans (CFCs in our survey) were viewed as the activities/technologies where the most stringent regulations were desired, followed by pesticides, handguns and hunting. Our sam-ple is less interested in regulation, perhaps a result of the deregulation fervour of

Table 12.3 *Differences in female/male perceptions based on selected risk characteristics*

Activity/technology	Risk characteristics		
	Catastrophic	Dread	Fatality/severity
1. Illegal drugs	0.25	0.12	0.06
2. Nuclear weapons	−0.01	0.14	0.08
3. Handguns	0.32	0.29	0.03
4. Smoking	0.27	0.22	0.17
5. Motor vehicles	0.48*	0.51*	0.11
6. Sexual diseases	0.38	0.49*	0.76**
7. Police work	0.37*	0.32	0.26
8. Nuclear power	0.40*	0.43*	0.28
9. Alcoholic beverages	0.31	0.20	0.63**
10. Motorcycles	0.36*	0.17	0.00
11. Firefighting	0.73*	0.12	0.05
12. CFCs	0.15	0.44**	0.45*
13. Pesticides	0.43*	0.65**	0.35*
14. Surgery	0.14	0.29	0.29
15. Burning fossil fuels	0.19	0.56*	0.12
16. Large construction	0.61*	0.23	−0.13
17. Commercial aviation	0.32	0.53*	0.06
18. Non-nuclear electric	0.39	0.36	0.33*
19. Mountain climbing	0.36*	0.14	−0.21
20. Hunting	0.18*	0.04	−0.00
21. X-rays	0.24	0.54	0.27
22. Railroads	−0.11	0.35*	0.15
23. Prescription drugs	0.28	−0.08	0.36*
24. Food preservatives	0.49*	0.28	0.50*
25. Skiing	0.17	−0.03	0.48*
26. Power mowers	0.35*	0.04	0.20
27. Swimming	0.33*	0.03	0.01
28. Bicycles	0.23*	0.09	0.37*
29. Home appliances	0.15	−0.01	0.25
30. Contraceptives	0.23	0.26	0.57**
31. Vaccinations	0.31	−0.06	0.08
32. High school football	0.26*	−0.01	0.36*
33. Food colouring	0.48*	0.32	0.22

*Difference between female/male means (*t*-statistic) significant at $p > 0.05$.
**Difference between female/male means (*t*-statistic) significant at $p > 0.001$.

the 1980s. The mean score for desired regulation in our sample was consistently lower than the Slovic et al sample for all items with the exception of handguns, smoking and alcoholic beverages. Our respondents felt the most stringent regulation should be placed on illegal drugs (mean score 4.54) and nuclear weapons (mean score 4.34) (Table 12.4). Severe restrictions on product use were desired for handguns, smoking, nuclear power, CFCs, pesticides, commercial aviation and the burning of fossil fuels – all issues in the news at the time.

There are only a few important distinctions between men and women in their views of current levels of regulation. Men felt that alcoholic beverages were

Table 12.4 *Current and desired levels of regulation (mean scores)*

Activity/technology	Regulation		M/F differences	
	Current	Desired	Current	Desired
1. Illegal drugs	3.62	4.54	0.316	0.002
2. Nuclear weapons	3.22	4.34	0.135	−0.198
3. Handguns	2.76	3.80	0.065	−0.249
4. Smoking	1.98	3.43	−0.073	0.075
5. Motor vehicles	2.31	2.62	−0.141	−0.250
6. Sexual diseases	1.71	2.42	−0.284	−0.109
7. Police work	1.76	2.18	−0.003	0.140
8. Nuclear power	3.19	3.81	−0.023	−0.317*
9. Alcoholic beverages	2.41	2.90	−0.270*	−0.121
10. Motorcycles	1.70	2.24	0.013	0.095
11. Firefighting	1.61	1.85	0.118	−0.015
12. CFCs	2.16	3.66	−0.112	−0.231
13. Pesticides	2.15	3.40	0.064	−0.283*
14. Surgery	2.20	2.48	−0.003	0.236
15. Burning of fossil fuels	1.97	3.00	−0.120	−0.038
16. Large construction	1.76	2.28	0.117	0.060
17. Commercial aviation	2.31	3.01	−0.059	−0.151
18. Non-nuclear electric power	1.97	2.35	−0.224	0.070
19. Mountain climbing	0.76	1.03	0.120	0.026
20. Hunting	1.79	2.26	0.217	0.022
21. X-rays	1.98	2.50	0.021	−0.026
22. Railroads	1.77	2.25	0.127	−0.028
23. Prescription drugs	2.15	2.65	−0.142	−0.118
24. Food preservatives	1.73	2.65	−0.096	−0.210
25. Skiing	0.67	0.84	0.015	0.150
26. Power mowers	0.85	1.13	0.035	0.023
27. Swimming	0.83	0.93	0.048	0.127
28. Bicycles	0.76	1.04	0.028	0.002
29. Home appliances	1.12	1.40	0.116	−0.038
30. Contraceptives	1.25	1.59	−0.290*	−0.327
31. Vaccinations	1.72	2.06	0.123	0.189
32. High school football	0.91	1.22	0.104	0.085
33. Food colouring	1.62	2.46	−0.022	−0.202

Scale:
0 = do nothing
1 = monitor the risk and/or inform those exposed
2 = place mild restrictions on who, how, when and where something can be done or used
3 = place moderate restrictions on who, how, when and where something can be done or used
4 = place severe restrictions on who, how, when and where something can be done or used
5 = ban the product or activity
*Differences between male/female means is significant at $p > 0.05$.

mildly restricted at present, whereas women felt that more stringent restrictions existed. Similarly, men responded that contraceptive regulations simply informed the users, whereas women felt there were some minor restrictions imposed on their use. These differences may be partly explained by each group's access to and participation in the activity. As for desired regulation, there was considerable congruity between the two groups. The two main areas of disagreement were in the regulation of nuclear power and pesticides. In each instance, women wanted more restrictive regulations, whereas men only desired moderate regulation.

Discussion

This pilot study corroborates many of the generalized findings in the risk perception literature. The pattern of risk rankings, associated risk characteristics and desire for risk regulation in our sample reflect the findings of earlier studies utilizing the psychometric technique. Some of the changes in risk ranking and characteristics can be explained by the differences in the sample populations (location and background) and in the decade difference in the timing of the surveys (1976 versus 1989).

We expected to find greater differences between males and females than we actually did. Although there are some areas of disagreement between the two subpopulations in their views of risks and risk regulation, the magnitude of difference is not great. Perhaps age played a role, as students are not sufficiently aware of these technologies or activities to have formed an opinion on them. Perhaps the lack of difference was a function of the survey instrument we used, which did not explicitly address male/female differences. More likely, we can speculate that differences in risk perceptions are not as important as how these translate into overt actions or behaviours. Specifically, how does gender influence the ways in which people respond to these perceived risks?

A number of questions arise from this case study. First, how can we improve risk perception studies to more effectively reflect the perceptions of a heterogeneous sample population? Second, how can we improve the methodology to more effectively interpret the impact of spatial, temporal and compositional differences in the perception of risk? Last, how can a feminist analysis help in understanding risk perception and behaviour?

Future modifications to the psychometric design and other instruments must be more sensitive to subgroup differences and more adept at distinguishing between the perceptions of men and women. Many of the risks included in the original survey represent traditionally male-oriented activities such as motor-cycling, firefighting, construction, hunting and football, while only two technologies/activities (birth control devices and home appliances) can be considered as more female-oriented. Redesigned surveys should either include a more balanced number of male- and female-oriented risks or exclude all those that are gender-specific.

Classification of technologies/activities as male- or female-oriented will improve our understanding of how males or females will respond to these risks, but better identification of gender also must be done. In order to correlate perception with gender (not sex), the survey must provide a measure of the femininity or masculinity for each individual. How one feels about certain activities and situations (not necessarily risks) may provide enough insight to enable placement of the respondent along a femininity–masculinity continuum. It is necessary to determine how much masculinity and femininity is present in the individual's psychology to better understand the effect of gender on risk perception.

Comparative questions (gender, race, ethnicity) on risk can also be included, such as: Are women or men more aware of the risk from this activity/technology? Are women more voluntarily exposed to this risk than men? Who is more likely to be exposed to this risk, men or women? Do men take part in this activity or technology more than women? Similar questions could be developed for racial or ethnic comparisons.

Risk communication strategies attempt to incorporate the findings of the risk perception research and develop approaches to allay the fears of a concerned public. How effective can these strategies be when the public is defined as a homogeneous group rather than one with distinct gender, ethnic and racial characteristics that influence the interpretation of risk and its ultimate acceptability? This is particularly important in understanding citizen rejection of governmental and industrial risk management and communication policies. Since we found that women in our survey indicated a slightly stronger preference for less risky technologies and more stringent regulation on existing technologies than men, it is obvious that the efforts of *Mothers Against Pesticides*, *Mothers Against Drunk Driving*, and Lois Gibbs at *Citizens' Clearing House for Toxic Waste* are not aberrations, and may in fact be more representative of the general public than previously thought.

Risk perception surveys can be made more robust by including measures of behavioural responses to these risks. A matched sample of respondents – one drawn from activist groups, the other drawn from a more random public – might help to elicit the relative importance of perceived risk and its relation to proactive behaviour. Clearly, more understanding of the relationship between perception and behaviour is warranted as well.

Most importantly, a feminist analysis allows us to frame questions in a different light and to ultimately ask different questions. Rather than an absolute judgement of risks, perhaps a more comparative approach is warranted. How women cope with the myriad of risks they face in everyday life and their role in hazards decision-making needs to be further addressed.

Finally, an ecofeminist analysis can provide a critique of the ethics of technological innovation and invention. Once a clear determination has been made regarding gender division of risk, questions focusing on the unevenness of risk exposure, the disparity in the control of risks or the provision of operational and safety information to the involuntarily exposed can be examined with a moral and ethical ear turned toward the dominated. A re-evaluation of current technologies, not based on the 'average American', but on a range of gender, class and ethnic distinctions, will serve to enhance the assessment of current and future risks and policies to manage them.

Conclusions

Our pilot survey demonstrates that more regulation of technology and activities is desired by our respondents. This is consistent with current public opinion that also wants more environmental regulation and environmental laws. Our sample certainly expresses a strong desire to have many environmentally harmful technologies, such as nuclear power, CFCs, pesticides and the burning of fossil fuels, severely restricted.

Before we can definitely conclude the significance of gender differences in the perception of technological risks, however, much more work is needed. Gender differences certainly exist, as suggested by feminist analysis, but the empirical proof is weak. Furthermore, the causes of gender differences in risk perception and behaviour (individual personality, sex roles, socialization) are relatively unknown and not addressed in this study or any others. While this chapter provides some very preliminary data on the role of gender in the perception of technological risk, its value is in highlighting the need for more localized and population-specific analyses of risk perception, a continued reappraisal of the psychometric paradigm, a broadening of risk perception research to include behaviour, and a reassessment of the prevailing masculine-based view of nature, science and technology.

References

Ajzen, I. and Fishbein, M. (1980) *Understanding Attitudes and Predicting Social Behavior*, Prentice-Hall, Englewood Cliffs, NJ

Arcury, T. A., Scollay, S. J. and Johnson, T. P. (1987) 'Sex differences in environmental concern and knowledge: The case of acid rain', *Sex Roles*, vol 16, pp463–472

Bastide, S., Moatti, J. P., Pages, J. P. and Fagnani, F. (1989) 'Risk perception and social acceptability of technologies: The French case', *Risk Analysis*, vol 9, pp215–223

Boulding E. (1984) 'Focus on: The gender gap', *Journal of Peace Research*, vol 21, pp1–3

Bullard, R. D. (1990) *Dumping in Dixie: Race, Class, and Environmental Quality*, Westview Press, Boulder, CO

Devall, B. and Sessions, G. (1985) *Deep Ecology: Living as if Nature Mattered*, Gibbs Smith, Salt Lake City, UT

Douglas, M. and Wildavsky, A. (1982) *Risk and Culture: An Essay on the Selection of Technological and Environmental Dangers*, University of California Press, Berkeley, CA

Englander, T., Farago, K., Slovic, P. and Fischhoff, B. (1986) 'A comparative analysis of risk perception in Hungary and the United States', *Social Behavior*, vol 1, pp55–66

Fischhoff, B., Slovic, P., Lichtenstein, S., Read, S. and Combs, B. (1978) 'How safe is safe enough? A psychometric study of attitudes toward technological risks and benefits', *Policy Sciences*, vol 9, pp127–152

Foreman, D. and Haywood B. (eds) (1987) *Ecodefense: A Field Guide to Monkeywrenching*, 2nd edition, Ned Ludd Book, Tucson, AZ

Gardner, G. T. and Gould, L. C. (1989) 'Public perceptions of the risks and benefits of technology', *Risk Analysis*, vol 9, pp225–242

Gilligan, C. (1982) *In a Different Voice: Psychological Theory and Women's Development*, Harvard University Press, Cambridge, MA

Hamilton, S. B., Van Mouwerik, S., Oetting, E. R., Beauvais, F. and Keilin, W. G. (1988) 'Nuclear war as a source of adolescent worry: Relationships with age, gender, trait emotionality, and drug use', *The Journal of Social Psychology*, vol 128, pp745–763

Hansson, S. O. (1989) 'Dimensions of risk', *Risk Analysis*, vol 9, pp107–112

Hewitt, K. (ed) (1983) *Interpretations of Calamity*, Allen and Unwin, Boston, MA

Holcomb, H. B., Kodras, J. E. and Brunn, S. D. (1990) 'Women's issues and state legislation: Fragmentation and inconsistency' in J. E. Kodras and J. P. Jones III (eds) *Geographic Dimensions of United States Social Policy*, Arnold, London, pp178–199

Hynes, H. P. (1989) *Recurring Silent Spring*, Pergamon, New York

Hynes, H. P. (ed) (1991) *Reconstructing Babylon: Essays on Women and Technology*, Indiana University Press, Bloomington, IN

Jensen, M. P. (1987) 'Gender, sex roles, and attitudes toward war and nuclear weapons', *Sex Roles*, vol 17, pp253–267

Johnson, B. and Covello, V. (eds) (1987) *Social and Cultural Construction of Risk*, Reidel, Boston, MA

Johnson, E. J. and Tversky, A. (1983) 'Affect, generalization and the perception of risk', *Journal of Personality and Social Psychology*, vol 45, pp20–31

Johnson, E. J. and Tversky, A. (1984) 'Representations of perceptions of risk', *Journal of Experimental Psychology: General*, vol 113, pp55–70

Kasperson, R. E., Renn, O., Slovic, P., Brown, H. S., Emel, J., Goble, R., Kasperson, J. X. and Ratick, S. (1988) 'The social amplification of risk: A conceptual framework', *Risk Analysis*, vol 8, pp177–187

Keown, C. F. (1989) 'Risk perceptions of Hong Kongese vs. Americans', *Risk Analysis*, vol 9, pp401–405

King, Y. (1989) 'The ecology of feminism and the feminism of ecology' in J. Plant (ed) *Healing the Wounds: The Promise of Ecofeminism*, New Society, Philadelphia, PA, pp18–28

Kleinhesselink, R. R. and Rosa, E. A. (1989) *Cognitive Representation of Risk Perceptions: A Comparison of Japan and the United States*, paper presented at annual meeting of the Society for Risk Analysis, San Francisco, CA

Levin, I. P., Snyder, M. A. and Chapman, D. P. (1988) 'The interaction of experiential and situational factors and gender in a simulated risky decision-making task', *The Journal of Psychology*, vol 122, pp173–181

Lewis, H. W. (1990) *Technological Risk*, Norton, New York

Lichtenstein, S., Slovic, P., Fischhoff, B., Layman, M. and Combs, B. (1978) 'Judged frequency of lethal events', *Journal of Experimental Psychology: Human Learning and Memory*, vol 4, pp551–581

Manes, C. (1990) *Green Rage: Radical Environmentalism and the Unmaking of Civilization*, Little, Brown, Boston, MA

McStay, J. R. and Dunlap, R. E. (1983) 'Male-female differences in concern for environmental quality', *International Journal of Women's Studies*, vol 6, pp291–307

Merchant, C. (1980) *The Death of Nature: Women, Ecology and the Scientific Revolution*, Harper and Row, New York

Merchant, C. (1981) 'Earthcare', *Environment*, vol 23, pp6–13, 38–40

Moncrief, L. W. (1970) 'The cultural basis for our environmental crisis', *Science*, vol 170, pp505–512

Oelschlaeger, M. (1991) *The Idea of Wilderness*, Yale University Press, New Haven, CT

O'Riordan, T. (1981) *Environmentalism*, Pion, London

Paehlke, R. C. (1989) *Environmentalism and the Future of Progressive Politics*, Yale University Press, New Haven, CT

Perrow, C. (1984) *Normal Accidents: Living with High-Risk Technologies*, Basic Books, New York

Plant, J. (1990) 'Searching for common ground: Ecofeminism and bioregionalism' in I. Diamond and G. F. Orenstein (eds) *Reweaving the World: The Emergence of Ecofeminism*, Sierra Club Books, San Francisco, CA, pp155–161

Regulska, J., Fried, S. and Tiefenbacher, J. (1991) 'Women, politics, and place: Spatial patterns of representation in New Jersey', *Geoforum*, vol 22, no 2, pp203–221

Renn, O. and Swaton, E. (1984) 'Psychological and sociological approaches to the study of risk perception', *Environment International*, vol 10, pp557–575

Sale, K. (1985) *Dwellers in the Land: The Bioregional Vision*, Sierra Club Books, San Francisco, CA

Scarce, R. (1990) *Eco-Warriors: Understanding the Radical Environmental Movement*, Noble Press, Chicago, IL

Silverman, J. M. and Kumka, D. S. (1987) 'Gender differences in attitudes toward nuclear war and disarmament', *Sex Roles*, vol 16, pp189–203

Slovic, P., Fischhoff, B. and Lichtenstein, S. (1985) 'Characterizing perceived risk' in R. W. Kates, C. Hohenemser and J. X. Kasperson (eds) *Perilous Progress: Managing the Hazards of Technology*, Westview Press, Boulders, CO, pp91–124

Stallen, P. J. M. and Thomas, A. (1988) 'Public concern about industrial hazards', *Risk Analysis*, vol 8, pp237–245

Teigen, K. H., Brun, W. and Slovic, P. (1988) 'Societal risks as seen by a Norwegian public', *Journal of Behavioral Decision-Making*, vol 1, pp111–130

UCC (United Church of Christ Commission for Racial Justice) (1987) *Toxic Waste and Race in the United States*, United Church of Christ, New York

Verplanken, B. (1989) 'Beliefs, attitudes, and intentions toward nuclear energy before and after Chernobyl in a longitudinal within-subjects design', *Environment and Behavior*, vol 21, pp371–392

Vlek, C. and Stallen, P. J. (1981) 'Judging risks and benefits in the small and in the large', *Organizational Behavior and Human Performance*, vol 28, pp235–277

White, L. (1967) 'The historical roots of our ecological crisis', *Science*, vol 155, pp1203–1207

13

Evacuation Behaviour
and Three Mile Island

Susan L. Cutter and Kent Barnes

Introduction

A recent study of the Three Mile Island nuclear power plant accident of March 1979 (Zeigler et al, 1981) reports a number of generalizations about the evacuation behaviour of area residents. Unfortunately, they were unable to address fully the role of spatial proximity and the social correlates of evacuation due to the limitations in the size of their data set. What we would like to do in this chapter is to examine those correlates. Findings from our study of the responses of the affected population reveal some statistically significant associations between evacuation and socio-spatial variables.

Three Mile Island (TMI) was the first example in the US of a widespread, voluntary evacuation associated with a nuclear mishap, and thus it can be used as a case study of what prompts evacuation when residents have no clear knowledge of the consequences posed by the threat. Several factors influence individual coping responses to such threats, including prior experience with the hazard in question, the material wealth of the individual, personality variables, confirmation of hazard warning, age and stage in the life cycle, and the actions of friends and neighbours (Burton et al, 1978; Quarantelli, 1980; Quarantelli and Dynes, 1978). Other research on the spatial aspects of evacuation, on risk assessment and on evacuations following disasters has expanded our knowledge of what prompts voluntary evacuations under various conditions of uncertainty (Baker et al, 1976; Whyte et al, 1980; Perry, 1981).

Many generalizations found in the natural hazards and disaster literature may not be applicable to technological hazards. For example, limited experience cannot influence evacuation in unprecedented situations; no experience may also increase

Note: Reprinted, with permission, from *Disasters*, vol 6, no 2, Susan Cutter and Kent Barnes, 'Evacuation Behavior and Three Mile Island', pp116–124. © Blackwell Publishing, 1982

the fear of the unknown and prompt evacuation. There is uncertainty regarding impacts on health, and that could influence the choice of coping responses. Personality factors influence an individual's assessment of risk. The lack of prior knowledge regarding the extent and consequences of the hazard necessitates an immediate decision under extremely stressful conditions.

We suggest that four factors, as gleaned from our data and analysis are significant influences on voluntary evacuations from technologically hazardous situations:

1   confirmation of the hazard information;
2   spatial proximity to the hazard;
3   social status; and
4   social influence.

Ambiguous information, as it relates to the inability to confirm the hazard threat, and proximity to the hazard source are hypothesized as the most important influences prompting evacuation.

Study Design

Residents in the vicinity of TMI were surveyed in April 1979 using a mailed questionnaire. They were asked a series of questions relating to their knowledge of the event, reliability of information sources, risk assessment, coping responses and social characteristics. Of particular importance were the questions regarding the nature and extent of evacuation. If the respondents indicated they left the area during the crisis, evacuation information sought included:

1   time of departure;
2   specific cues leading to evacuation decision;
3   destination;
4   reasons for destination selection; and
5   date of return.

If the respondents did not evacuate they were asked to explain why.

The sampling plan consisted of a stratified random sample based on direction and distance from TMI (Figure 13.1). The area was divided into five-mile concentric zones around the reactor and four quadrants (north, south, east and west), resulting in 20 sampling units. Telephone directories were used to obtain the names and addresses of potential respondents. The initial sample size of 1000 was reduced to 922 because many questionnaires were undeliverable. A total of 359 questionnaires were returned, a response rate of 40 per cent. There was no follow-up letter. A more complete discussion of the survey design, including study limitations, can be found in a preliminary report on the responses of the affected populations to the accident (Barnes et al, 1979; Cutter et al, 1979).

Approximately 39 per cent (140) of the respondents in our sample evacuated themselves and/or their families from the area during the crisis. The majority

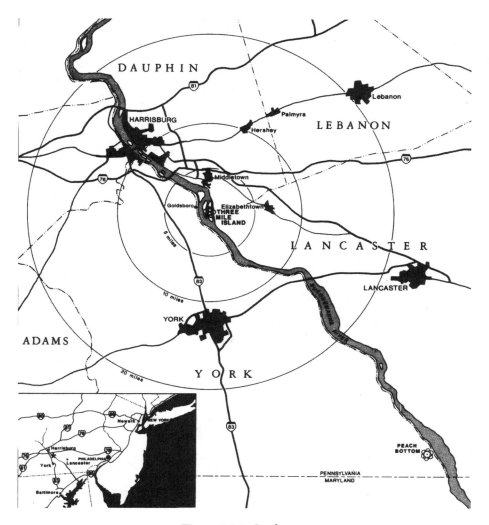

Figure 13.1 *Study area*

of evacuees (54 per cent) left the area on Friday, 30 March, following Governor Thornburgh's advisory evacuation statement. The advisory statement recommended that pregnant women and pre-school-age children within five miles of the reactor evacuate, and that all residents within ten miles remain inside with doors and windows closed.

Most evacuated families stayed with friends or relatives (74 per cent), although a significant minority (20 per cent) moved to second homes, commercial accommodations and other premises. None of our sample respondents used an official evacuation reception centre such as the one in Hershey, Pennsylvania (11 miles from TMI). This finding was also confirmed by Brunn et al (1979).

One-third of the evacuees remained in southeastern Pennsylvania, within 10 to 50 miles of the reactor site. Twenty-four per cent of the evacuees elected to

Table 13.1 *Reasons cited for voluntary evacuation**

Reason	No.	Percentage
Thornburgh's evacuation advisory	80	68
Anticipated consequences:	70	60
Safety of children		18
Possibility of meltdown		12
Fear and anxiety		13
Long-term health effects		7
Confusion:	57	41
Lack of leadership and		
conflicting information		21
Uncertainty		11
Anticipation of evacuation		8
Peer pressure to evacuate	13	9

Total number of households evacuated = 140.
*Multiple responses were possible.

remain within their counties of origin, still in the risk zone. They simply moved to places within these counties they considered safe or, more importantly, where they could find accommodation with friends and relatives. Some serious questions are raised as to whether evacuees removed themselves far enough from danger had a major catastrophe occurred.

The majority (53 per cent) of those who evacuated returned home within one week of the accident (4 April). An additional 37 per cent returned home two weeks later. Three weeks after the accident, 98 per cent of all evacuees had returned. A few residents took the opportunity for an extended vacation.

The evacuees in our sample were asked in an open-ended question to indicate their specific reasons for evacuating (Table 13.1). An overwhelming majority (68 per cent) stated that Governor Thornburgh's advisory statement was a major factor in their decision to depart. Twenty-one per cent of this group lived outside the five-mile radius and only 28 per cent of all evacuating families reported pre-school-aged children, the two target groups of the advisory statement. Approximately 46 per cent of the sample cited anticipated consequences, such as harm to children and family, or the possibility of a core meltdown, as reasons for their departures.

Emergency Response Planning

Responsibility for the welfare of residents during any emergency situation rests first with local officials. At the time of the accident, no community within five miles of the Three Mile Island plant had emergency response plans approved by the Nuclear Regulatory Commission (NRC), although communities within this radius of nuclear reactors are expected to have such plans (USNRC and USEPA, 1978; USGAO, 1979). The operating utility (Metropolitan Edison) had emergency plans for on-site releases of radioactivity as part of their requirements for licensing, although the utility and surrounding communities had no coordinated response plan for off-site releases. The communications link was poorly designed and only able to handle normal operations. With the exception of a direct link to the Pennsylvania Emergency Management Agency (PEMA) and the State Police, the off-site communication was through a manual switchboard, which, when unattended, could only handle one incoming call at a time (Dynes, 1979). This effectively prohibited access to the plant for verification of information by local and county officials who had to rely on the NRC, the state and the news media for information.

The only county plans in existence prior to the accident were for Dauphin County, in which the reactor is located, and that was because of NRC licensing requirements. The plan consisted of emergency evacuation procedures for a 5-mile zone around the reactor. The NRC requirements at the time were only a 2.2 mile radius, defined as the low population zone. The PEMA's function was to integrate local and county plans into an overall state plan and to oversee their implementation.

Six risk counties – Dauphin, Cumberland, Lancaster, Leganon, Perry, York – were designated by PEMA. All or part of the risk county lies within a 20-mile radius of TMI. Host counties were also designated to accommodate potential evacuees. The selection of host counties was based on direction from risk area, size of population centres, and number of major transportation arteries out of the risk area. Distance, other than outside the 20-mile radius, was not a factor (Crowe et al, 1979).

The NRC, as part of their general operating procedures, concurred with the utility's on-site plan despite the lack of detailed procedures. The NRC did not undertake a formal review of the plan and did not examine the links between the response plans of the utility and local communities. Existing plans thus were poorly conceived and lacked coordination and integration needed for managing any emergency that would transcend local, county or state jurisdictions (Dynes, 1979). This lack of coordination may have contributed to the confusion at the time of the accident; it most certainly contributed to the ambiguity of the information sent to residents.

Estimated Evacuees

Several other evacuation studies were done at Three Mile Island (Zeigler et al, 1981; Brunn et al, 1979; Flynn, 1979). Over half of the impacted population in the 20-mile radius remained in the area. Approximately 663,500 people (1975 population estimates) were at risk within 20 miles of TMI. Estimates of the number of evacuees range from 76,000 people within 10 miles of the plant, to 144,000 within 15 miles, and 195,000 within 20 miles (Cutter et al, 1979; Flynn, 1979). Not all evacuees left at the first mention of threat (Wednesday, 28 March 1979); many tried to confirm the seriousness of the situation and the potential, personal impact. Most evacuees left as family units and sought temporary accommodation with friends or relatives.

Confusion and Uncertainty

Confusion and uncertainty concerning events at the plant and the degree of risk involved were stated by 41 per cent of our respondents as grounds for evacuation (Table 13.1). Lack of leadership on the part of elected officials and Metropolitan Edison (the operating utility) and conflicting information were interpreted by 21 per cent of the sample as cues to leave the area.

Two-thirds of our respondents did not evacuate. More than half of those who stayed did so primarily because they felt the danger was not great enough to warrant an evacuation. Fourteen per cent cited fear of looting as a reason for not leaving. Although looting is rare during natural disasters, it is a common misconception of behavioural responses (Dynes, 1974). Looting was insignificant during the TMI crisis partly because the area was not completely emptied. Other reasons for not leaving were: waiting for an evacuation order (8 per cent); job constraints (7 per cent); lack of money (6 per cent); no place to go (3 per cent).

The remaining residents did undertake some precautionary measures either to minimize their risk of exposure to radioactive contamination or to begin preparations to evacuate. These actions included: staying indoors (18 per cent); packing suitcases (15 per cent); filling automobile gas tanks (4 per cent); and waiting for formal evacuation announcements (8 per cent).

Confusion and uncertainty were listed as reasons for evacuating and for remaining in place. Ambiguity by itself does not necessarily lead to a cognition of threat, but ambiguity has been shown to permit extreme latitude for individual interpretations of situations that are based on an individual's own psychological structure (Lazarus, 1966). Ambiguous information such as 'the situation is under control, however, please be prepared to leave the area if you hear a siren', contributed to an already confused understanding of what was happening at the reactor site.

Conditions at the reactor site were unclear and the options that officials could take were not clearly defined. Scientists and policy-makers were divided on the issue and on the appropriate courses of action. Residents also were confused by the extension of the evacuation planning radius and by some of the preparatory actions taken by county and state officials.

Statements issued by the utility were generally optimistic, conflicting with the messages issued by the NRC. It was not until Sunday, 1 April (day five of the crisis), that Governor Thornburgh designated the NRC as the sole source of technical information concerning the status of the reactor. Until that time conflicting reports were issued. Information was sent from the utility to the NRC, to state and PEMA officials, to county and local officials, and then to residents. Sizeable gaps existed in the linear flow of information and, in some instances, information from the state took days to reach local officials. The mayor of Royalton, a borough within 2 miles of the plant never received official notification of the accident (*The Harrisburg Evening News*, 1979a); while the Mayor of Middletown said he kept informed by listening to radio and television because no information was coming from the plant operators (*The York Sunday News*, 1979). Local and county officials had to depend totally on the state and the news media for direction.

The weakest link in emergency preparedness and response is the public (Mileti, 1975). Events at TMI support this. One of the main objectives of elected officials was to control panic, although disaster researchers have noted that panic during crises is rare and is a popular misconception about disaster behaviour (Dynes, 1974; Quarantelli and Taylor, 1977). There was no evidence of wide-spread panic on the part of TMI-area residents (Crowe et al, 1979). There was no single spokesperson or agency issuing information to the public, and there is some disagreement as to whose function this should have been. PEMA personnel felt it was the job of the Governor's press secretary. The press secretary had other views: 'The Governor was the one voice for decisions that impacted on the population. It wasn't me who was designated to be the single voice' (*The Harrisburg Bulletin*, 1979). Residents were forced to rely on second- and third-hand information (Sandman and Paden, 1979).

Extension of the emergency evacuation zone from 5 to 20 miles also contributed to the confusion. Emergency management officials had been assured by the NRC that their 5-mile plans were sufficient, but on Friday morning, 30 March (day three), the NRC told state and local officials to extend the radius to 10 miles; later they ordered the zone extended to 20 miles from the plant (Crowe et al, 1979). Within hours the number of potential evacuees rose from 27,000 to 700,000, and this caught emergency management officials without satisfactory emergency response plans.

All of the at-risk counties, excluding Dauphin, elected to accommodate most potential evacuees within their own boundaries, but outside of the 20-mile radius of TMI. These counties all had facilities and population centres to support mass care requirements. Any possible overflow of people would go to adjacent counties in Pennsylvania and Maryland. Dauphin was not so fortunate and was forced to seek emergency accommodation for its residents outside the county. Details concerning these arrangements, including evacuation routes and mass care sites, were announced to the public over the weekend (30 March – 1 April). News reports on the actions of hospitals and other institutions may have aggravated the situation. Reports of emergency admissions and release of non-critical patients emphasized the potential need to evacuate hospitals in order to provide emergency care for potential victims.

Governor Thornburgh ordered the closing of 23 schools within five miles of the plant for an unspecified length of time, effective 12:30pm, Friday, 30 March. Late Sunday night, he recommended that only those schools within the five-mile radius remain closed and encouraged school districts beyond this radius to open. The decision to open or close schools outside the five-mile radius was left to local school boards. Owing to the uncertainty of the situation, in light of Thornburgh's statements, risk county schools (beyond the five-mile radius) remained closed on Monday. Local planning officials were 'troubled by the pressure on schools to open, arguing the step would encourage families to return and also tie up buses that would be needed in the event of an evacuation' (*The Harrisburg Evening News*, 1979b).

Anticipation of an evacuation order and the perceived ensuing problems (traffic jams, money runs on banks, lines at gas stations) were cited by almost 8 per cent of the evacuees as reasons for leaving the area. This finding is consistent with the behaviour observed by Janis (1962) and with McGrath's views on psychological stress (1970).

Spatial Proximity

It is expected that as distance from the hazard source increases, residents will be less likely to evacuate voluntarily. There is significant association between evacuation and zonation outward from the plant (Table 13.2). The proportion of those respondents who evacuated decreases with distance, from approximately 47 per cent in the 5-mile zone to 12 per cent outside the 20-mile radius. The impact of Governor Thornburgh's advisory statement is clearly visible in the sharp break in the percentages within a 10-mile radius and those beyond this line. This advisory statement may have reassured some residents as to their relative safety, but it may have decreased the confidence of others, especially those within 11 miles of the plant. It also may have increased stress by making the likelihood of disaster seem more imminent.

Distance from the origin of a nuclear hazard can be viewed as a buffer protecting the individual from immediate and possibly long-term harm. It functions as an environmental counter-harm resource (Lazarus, 1966). Although persons close to the site might have been expected to show a more pronounced response by evacuating to a greater distance, this did not happen. Evacuees living near the site travelled shorter distances than those who lived further away. The mean distance of evacuation was 111.6 miles. One reason may be that there are few accomodations for evacuees beyond the 20-mile radius of TMI because of the rural nature of the area. One would have to travel greater distances (30 miles or more for example) to find sizeable population centres in this zone. Another reason may be a greater cognition of threat on the part of those evacuees further from TMI. Those who evacuated were self-selected respondents who might have represented the most frightened group; hence, they would try to get as far away as possible. Diggory (1956) found that individuals living further from the hazard zone were more apt to overestimate the extent of the threat than those living closer to the high-risk area.

Table 13.2 *Origin of evacuees by zones from TMI**

Zone	Distance from TMI	No. of evacuated households	Percentage of total in zone
I	0–5 miles	37	46.8
II	5–10 miles	42	45.2
III	10–15 miles	18	27.3
IV	15–20 miles	17	23.3
V	20 miles	6	12.2

Chi squared = 26.33, d.f. = 4, significance = 0.00, gamma = –0.3599.
*Only considers 120 households who evacuated.

Social Characteristics

The third hypothesized influence on evacuation behaviour is the social position of the household. Younger households in their childbearing years would be more likely to evacuate than older households with no children present. Size of the household might also be a consideration as the decision to leave is usually a family one and not solely up to one individual. Also, the household's ability or willingness to undertake a voluntary evacuation may also be influenced by social class (occupation, education).

Age

The proportion of those evacuated decreases with age (Table 13.3). Forty-five per cent of the respondents aged 20–49 evacuated, while only 14 per cent of those over age 50 left the area. Even proximity (five-mile zone) to the hazard could not overcome inertia among the older population.

This was not entirely unexpected. At the time of the crisis, information was conveyed to residents that the high-risk age groups were young children and pregnant women. The presence of pre-school-aged children was a strong factor in the decision to evacuate. Seventy households in our sample had pre-school-aged children; 40 of them (57 per cent) evacuated.

The consequences of exposure to the other age groups was never explained effectively. There was a lack of agreement among the experts as to the risks involved. Many of our older respondents expressed a lack of concern for themselves, but were relieved that their children and grandchildren left the area. The prevailing attitude among the middle-aged and elderly non-evacuees can best be summed up by one respondent who wrote: 'In 20 years, I'll be dead anyway, so why worry?'

Older persons often are reluctant or unable to respond to the possibility of evacuation (Friedsam, 1962; Kilijanek and Drabek, 1979). Several factors may account for this, including the inability of the elderly to leave home in response to warnings because of infirmity or because they did not receive the warning information, a desire not to be separated from familiar surroundings, a fear of a

Table 13.3 *Age characteristics of sample evacuees*

Age groups in years	No. in sample	No. of evacuees	Evacuees as % of age group
20–29	47	22	46.8
30–39	92	40	43.5
40–49	75	34	45.3
50–59	70	10	14.3
60 and over	65	9	13.8
Unknown	10	5	–
Totals	359	120	

Chi squared = 35.70, d.f. = 4, significance = 0.00, gamma = –0.4124.

loss of independence and/or being separated from remaining friends and relatives, and the perceived futility of evacuation at their ages. Subjective losses in a disaster are more acute for the elderly, particularly the loss of various symbolic objects, including the home itself. Despite the unknown degree of risk, the elderly may find a greater sense of security at home rather than with relatives or friends or at an emergency centre. This may well contribute to inertia concerning evacuation.

We hypothesized that age would influence early knowledge of the accident, but cross-tabulation of the data failed to find any noteworthy association between age and early warning or knowledge of the Three Mile Island accident. This may not be the case for the elderly individuals in the sample. Comparison of evacuees and non-evacuees over age 65 (n = 34) with those under 65 (n = 325) indicates that the elderly may have been less likely to have early knowledge of the accident. Sixty-two per cent of those respondents under 65 years of age first learned of the accident on Wednesday 28 March, while only 47 per cent of the respondents over age 65 heard about the accident on that day. This difference is statistically significant (p = 0.016). An additional 29 per cent of those over age 65 learned on Thursday, while another 21 per cent learned on Friday.

Several factors may account for the lag between the time elderly respondents heard of the accident and when others heard. Homebound elderly people have limited daily interaction with neighbours, friends and family. The retired or semi-retired have little or no access to information from co-workers. Both of these are important factors determining early knowledge of an emergency. Eighteen per cent of our respondents indicated that their first source of information was neighbours, family, friends and co-workers (Barnes et al, 1979). The validity of making inferences from these percentages to the general population is questionable, yet the elderly were the only age group in which less than half of the total number of respondents reported learning of the accident on Wednesday, the first day of the crisis.

Household size

Previous researchers have found that families evacuate as units and remain together even if disagreement exists as to whether evacuation is the proper course of action (Moore et al, 1963; Drabek, 1969), Voluntary evacuation from TMI during the crisis appears to confirm this thesis. Eighty-four per cent of the sampled households with evacuees reported complete evacuation. Those individuals remaining generally did so because of job constraints, fear of looting of personal property, or the need to care for livestock.

The number of individuals living in a household was cross-tabulated with evacuation behaviour. A significant direct association was revealed (chi squared = 9.23, d.f. = 3, significance = 0.050, gamma = 0.2942, n = 350). When distance from TMI is controlled, associations between household size and evacuation become insignificant beyond the five-mile radius. Respondents living within five miles of the plant were a little more prone to evacuate if there were more persons residing in the household, particularly if pre-school-aged children were present (chi squared = 11.28, d.f. = 3, significance = 0.025, gamma = 0.3156, n = 101).

Individuals living alone (n = 23) tended to remain in place regardless of age or proximity to TMI. Only 21 per cent of these individuals reported that they evacuated. Age was a major factor influencing evacuation in households with two or more persons. There was also an association between evacuation and education of respondents in households of three to five persons (chi squared = 8.55, d.f. = 3, significance = 0.50, gamma = 0.2772, *n* = 187). Households of this size where one or two members were pre-school-aged children, with a well-educated household head between 30 and 39 years of age, were the most likely evacuees. No associations were revealed when controlling for smaller and larger households. This suggests that larger families were unlikely to have undertaken a complete household evacuation beyond a five-mile radius of TMI regardless of the respondent's education level.

Although households with two members *(n = 115)* were more apt to leave than individuals living alone, only 26 per cent of these households reported one or both members evacuating. Forty-one per cent of those households with three or more members *(n = 212)* reported that some or all members left. Interaction between other members of the household appears to be an important factor influencing evacuation.

Social class

The influence of social class on evacuation was examined using occupation and education as indicators. No significant association was discerned between the occupation of the head of household and evacuation (chi squared = 6.53, d.f. = 3, significance = 0.089, gamma = 0.1496). Even when controlling for age, education and zone, no relationship was noted. Education levels of the respondents were weakly associated with evacuation behaviour – the more educated the individual, the greater the propensity for that individual to undertake evacuation (Table 13.4). There was no difference between median years of education for the non-evacuees and evacuees (12.2 and 12.4 years, respectively). When controlling for age, differences in education do not account for differences in adaptive behaviour. This is consistent with some of the previous research concerning education and evacuation. Mack and Baker (1961) found that individuals with high school educations were more apt to evacuate than persons with more or less education. Lachman et al (1961), however, found no association between education and pre-impact evacuation.

Controlling for proximity to the nuclear power plant clarifies the relationship between education and evacuation (Table 13.5). The association is spatially incon-

Table 13.4 *Education and evacuation*

Years of education	No. in sample	No. of evacuees	Evacuees as % of education group
Less than high school (<12)	49	9	18.4
High school (12)	164	55	33.5
Some college (13 to 15)	49	13	26.5
College (16+)	82	40	48.7
Totals	344	117	

Chi squared = 14.56, d.f. = 3, significance = 0.005, gamma = 0.2779.

Table 13.5 *Summary statistics of education and evacuation behaviour by zone*

Zone		Chi squared	d.f.	Significance	Gamma
I	0–5 miles	1.52	3	0.750	+0.1374
II	5–10 miles	13.72	3	0.003	+0.5820
III	10–15 miles	3.27	3	0.351	+0.0330
IV	15–20 miles	11.54	3	0.010	+0.6470

sistent. Evacuation is strongly associated with education in the 5–10 and 15–20 mile zones. This is not the case in the 0–5 or 10–15 mile zones. The intensity of the threat was greatest in the 0–5 mile zone and residents here tended to evacuate regardless of educational background. Proximity to the hazard and the spatial dimension of Thornburgh's prompt were sufficient to overcome any inertia on the part of most residents to leave. This suggests that proximity to hazard and warnings were the most important prompting factors in the immediate impact zone.

There was no association between education and evacuation in the 10–15 mile zone. Several factors may account for this phenomenon. The major urban centres of Harrisburg and York, and their immediate suburbs, are located in this zone, and the majority of the zone's population live in these cities. It has been suggested that urbanism is a significant factor in assessing hazard warnings (Mack and Baker, 1961). Urbanism would influence individuals' assessments of their ability to cope with the act of evacuating (e.g. traffic jams, route specifications). There is also a greater exposure to the actions of local officials and neighbours, and to the news media. People were encouraged (or at least were not discouraged) to leave the area. The headlines of the 1 April 1979 *Harrisburg Sunday Patriot-News* read, 'Those uncomfortable urged to leave'. Once again, people tended to evacuate from this zone regardless of educational background.

In the 5–10 and 15–20 mile zones, differences in education were important social characteristics discriminating evacuees from non-evacuees. The former zone constitutes a transition between the zone of immediate impact and that of urban influences; the latter was the outermost zone being considered for possible evacuation by emergency management officials. It may be that more educated individuals relied less on prompts or cues, and more on their own initiative in undertaking evacuation.

Social Influence

Evidence of increased social conformity in intensified fear settings has been noted (Darley, 1966). We hypothesized that social influence prompted evacuation. Social influence refers to the impact of the responses of friends, neighbours and others upon individual behaviour. Reasons cited for voluntary evacuation from TMI (Table 13.1) indicate that fear and confusion were pervasive among evacuees and may have contributed to a heightened susceptibility to social influence.

Respondents were asked whether their neighbours left the area during the TMI crisis. The cross-tabulation of evacuation and neighbours' behaviour (Table 13.6)

Table 13.6 *Respondent behaviour and reported neighbour behaviour*

	Respondents (total no.)	Non-evacuees (%)	Evacuees (%)
Neighbours stayed	129	50.0	9.7
Neighbours left	184	39.7	74.0
Neighbours' behaviour unknown	44	10.3	16.3

Chi squared = 56.83, d.f. = 2, significance = 0.000, Goodman and Kruskal Tau = 0.1592.

suggests a significant association between the respondent's behaviour and the reported behaviour of neighbours. Individuals evacuating the area reported others undertaking the same behaviour (74 per cent). For the non-evacuees, 50 per cent reported that their neighbours did not leave, while 40 per cent replied that their neighbours did leave. An individual who reported that his neighbours left the area was more likely to have evacuated than one who did not. When controlling for proximity to TMI, this association is significant for all zones.

Social influence has been observed by researchers investigating individuals' responses to hurricanes (Baker et al, 1976). In addition, predispositions to evacuate in response to hurricane warnings are affected by what the individual believes his or her neighbours think or will do about the situation (Carter et al, 1979). Opinion is divided over the role of social influence in prompting evacuation, and further research is needed (Christensen and Ruch, 1980). The results of this analysis suggest, but do not confirm, that social influence is an important factor in pre-impact evacuation decision-making.

Summary

The behaviour of Three Mile Island residents serves as a case study highlighting some of the contextual, spatial and social factors influencing voluntary evacuations from technologically hazardous situations. The inability of residents to confirm hazard information resulted in decision-making based on confusion cues and ambiguous information. A sizeable percentage of evacuees left, not because there was consistent information on which to base their decisions, but because of a lack of such information. The individual interpretation of events at the plant and the actions of institutions resulted in two different responses – evacuation and remaining in place.

Proximity to hazard was found to be related to evacuation. Those residents who lived closer to the plant were more likely to undertake an evacuation than those living further away, regardless of occupational or educational levels. A household's stage in the life cycle also influenced the evacuation decision. Older households were less apt to evacuate that were younger households, especially if those younger households had children. There is also some evidence that social influence enhanced the evacuation decision by reinforcing individual behaviour through the actions of friends and neighbours.

Thornburgh's advisory statement had a contagious or spillover effect. Its impact on evacuation decisions extended beyond those individuals in the recommended five-mile radius from TMI, and it prompted more than those individuals in the two target groups to leave. This contagion must be considered in emegency situations regarding future technological hazards. Emergency management officials may find themselves having to cope with greater numbers of evacuees and larger volumes of traffic than otherwise intended or expected, particularly if a selective, rather than a general, advisory or evacuation order is issued.

A number of future research questions arise from this analysis. What is the applicability of the model of responses to a range of technological hazards, not just nuclear power plants? Are there similarities between pre- and post-impact responses regardless of the source of the hazard? How applicable is natural hazard research to the study of technological hazards? Recent events (Love Canal, NY; Seveso, Italy; Mississauga, Ontario; Three Mile Island, PA; natural gas leak in San Francisco) point to the vulnerability of populations to these types of hazards, and questions the emergency preparedness to mitigate the adverse impacts of these hazards on the local residents.

It behoves all of us to direct some of our research efforts to these pragmatic concerns, especially the assessment of individual risk from technological hazards; the examination of the nature of technological hazards and their distribution; the range of coping responses that may be undertaken and the emergency planning for such actions; and last, the spatial implications of these coping activities. This line of enquiry represents a growing commitment within the social sciences to socially responsive research and is an area within which we can make substantial contributions.

References

Baker, E. J. et al (1976) *The Social Impact of Hurricane Eloise on Panama City*, The Florida State University, Tallahassee, FL

Barnes, K., Brosius J., Cutter S. L. and Mitchell, J. K. (1979) *Responses of Impacted Populations to the Three Mile Island Nuclear Reactor Accident: An Initial Assessment*, Department of Geography Discussion Paper no 13, Rutgers University, Brunswick, NJ

Brunn, S. D., Johnson, J. H., jr and Zeigler, D. J. (1979) *Final Report on a Social Survey of Three Mile Island Area Residents*, Department of Geography, Michigan State University, East Lansing, MI

Burton, I., Kates, R. W. and White, G. F. (1978) *The Environment as Hazard*, Oxford University Press, New York

Carter, T. M., Clark J. P. and Leik, R. K. (1979) *Organizational and Household Response to Hurricane Warnings in the Local Community*, NHWS Report Series no 79-01, Department of Sociology, University of Minnesota, MN

Christensen, L. and Ruch, C. E. (1980) 'The effects of social influence on response to hurricane warnings', *Disasters*, vol 4, no 1, pp205–210

Crowe, C., Hetz, R. jr and Emerich, H. (1979) 'PEMA Officials', personal interview, Harrisburg, PA, 15 September

Cutter, S. L., Brosius, J., Barnes, K. and Mitchell, J. K. (1979) 'Risk evaluation and evacuation responses', *Proceedings, Middle States Division, Association of American Geographers*, vol 13, pp80–88

Darley, J. M. (1966) 'Fear and social comparison as determinants of conformity behavior', *Journal of Personality and Social Psychology*, vol 4, no 1, pp73–78

Diggory, J. C. (1956) 'Some consequences of proximity to a disease threat', *Sociometry*, vol 19, pp47–53

Drabek, T. E. (1969) 'Social processes in disaster: Family evacuation', *Social Problems*, vol 16, pp336–349

Dynes, R. R. (1974) *Organized Behavior in Disaster*, The Disaster Research Center Series, The Ohio State University, Columbus, OH

Dynes, R. R. (1979) *Report of the Emergency Preparedness and Response Task Force*, The President's Commission on the Accident at Three Mile Island, Government Printing Office, Washington, DC

Flynn, C. B. (1979) *Three Mile Island Telephone Survey*, Nuclear Regulatory Commission, Washington, DC

Friedsam, H. J. (1962) 'Older persons in disaster' in G. W. Baker and D. W. Chapman (eds) *Man and Society in Disaster*, Basic, New York, pp151–184

The Harrisburg Bulletin (1979) cover story, Harrisburg, PA, 22 April, p1

The Harrisburg Evening News (1979a) 'N-incident warning gaps are questioned', Harrisburg, PA, 29 March, p1

The Harrisburg Evening News (1979b) 'Cautious approach advised in signs of easing TMI crisis', Harrisburg, PA, 3 April, p1

Janis, I. I. (1962) 'Psychological effects of warning' in G. W. Baker and D. W. Chapman (eds) *Man and Society in Disaster*, Basic, New York, pp55–92

Kilijanek, T. S. and Drabek, T. E. (1979) 'Assessing long-term impacts of a natural disaster: A focus on the elderly', *The Gerontologist*, vol 19, no 6, pp555–566

Lachman, R., Tatsuoka, M. and Bonk, W. (1961) 'Human behavior during the tsunami of May 1960', *Science*, vol 133, pp1405–1409

Lazarus, R. S. (1966) *Psychological Stress and the Coping Process*, McGraw-Hill, New York

McGrath, J. E. (1970) *Social and Psychological Factors in Stress*, Holt, Rinehart and Winston, New York

Mack, R. W. and Baker, G. W. (1961) *The Occasion Instant*, National Research Council Disaster Study no 15, National Academy of Sciences, Washington, DC

Mileti, D. S. (1975) *Natural Hazards Warning Systems in the United States: A Research Assessment*, Institute of Behavioral Science, NSF-RA-E-013, University of Colorado, Boulder, CO

Moore, H. E. (1963) *Before the Wind: A Study of the Response to Hurricane Carla*, National Academy of Sciences, National Research Council, Washington, DC

Perry, R. W. (1981) *Citizen Evacuation in Response to Nuclear and Non Nuclear Threats*, Battelle Human Affairs Research Centers, BHARC-400/81/013, FEMA contract-EMW-C-O296, Seattle

Quarantelli, E. L. (1980) *Disasters: Theory and Research*, Sage, London

Quarantelli, E. L. and Dynes, R. R. (1978) 'Response to social crisis and disaster', *Annual Review Sociology*, vol 3, pp23–49

Quarantelli, E. L. and Taylor, V. (1977) *Some Views on the Warning Problem in Disasters as Suggested by Sociological Research*, Disaster Research Center Preliminary Paper no 45, Ohio State University, Columbus, OH

Sandman, P. M. and Paden, M. (1979) 'At Three Mile Island', *Columbia Journalism Review*, July/August, pp45–58

USGAO (US General Accounting Office) (1979) *Areas Around Nuclear Facilities Should be Better Prepared for Radiological Emergencies*, Government Printing Office, Washington, DC

USNRC (US Nuclear Regulatory Commission) and USEPA (US Environmental Protection Agency) (1978) *Planning Basis for the Development of State and Local Government Radiological Emergency Response Plans in Support of Light Water Nuclear Power Plants*, NUREG-0396/EPA520/1-78-016, Government Printing Office, Washington, DC

Whyte, A. V. T., Liverman, D. and Wilson, J. P. (1980) *Preliminary Report on Survey of Households Evacuated During the Mississauga Chlorine Gas Emergency, November 10–16 1979*, Institute for Environmental Studies, Working Paper ERR-7, University of Toronto, Toronto

The York Sunday News (1979) 'Residents tell TMI panel of fears, lies', York, PA, 20 May, p1

Zeigler, D. J., Brunn, S. D. and Johnson, J. H. jr (1981) 'Evacuation from a nuclear technological disaster', *Geographical Review*, vol 71, no 1, pp1–16

14

Crying Wolf: Repeat Responses to Hurricane Evacuation Orders

Kirstin Dow and Susan L. Cutter

Hurricanes provide a constant reminder to coastal residents of the precarious nature of living in these high-risk areas. Between 1984 and 1994 in the US, for example, more than 200 lives were lost to hurricanes (storm surge and winds), and property losses totalled about $40 billion (US Bureau of the Census, 1996). In terms of federal disaster relief costs, Hurricane Andrew (1992) was the costliest at $1.8 billion, followed by Hurricane Hugo (1989) at $1.3 billion and the 1995 Hurricane Marilyn ($542 million), which struck Puerto Rico and the US Virgin Islands in 1995 (FEMA, 1997).

When a hurricane threatens the east coast of the US, comparisons with Andrew and Hugo are inevitable, especially in the Southeast. However, less frequently mentioned are the smaller hurricanes that threaten the region, many of them prompting protective actions but making landfall elsewhere. In the 1996 hurricane season, two of these hurricane events, Bertha and Fran, prompted the governor of the state of South Carolina to issue evacuation orders along the entire South Carolina coast. In each case, the edge of the hurricane nicked the northern coast of the state – making landfall in North Carolina, thus creating a 'near miss' for South Carolina.

These two hurricane events offer a unique opportunity to study the impact of repeated false alarms – 'unnecessary evacuations' ordered based on expectations of a hurricane landfall that ultimately proved to be wrong. The influence and credibility of forecasters and local officials, important factors in the evacuation response, could be affected by this recent history of repeated 'misses', 'near-misses' and 'hits'. The impact of false alarms on future evacuations, often referred to as the 'crying wolf syndrome' (Breznitz, 1984), is a widespread source of speculation and concern in the emergency management community. Repeated false alarms reduce the credibility of warning information, yet very little research has directly

Note: Reprinted, with permission, from *Coastal Management*, vol 26, Kirstin Dow and Susan L. Cutter, 'Crying wolf: Repeat responses to hurricane evacuation orders', pp237–252. © Taylor & Francis Group, 1998

studied them and their impact on evacuation behaviour. Using South Carolina as the study area, this chapter examines the impact of 'crying wolf' through three specific research questions:

1   Were there differences in the evacuation responses of residents for Hurricanes Bertha and Fran?
2   Was there an action or a specific piece of information that convinced people to evacuate and did this vary between the two hurricane events?
3   What was the major source of 'reliable' information influencing the decisions to evacuate and did this differ in the two hurricane events?

Responses to these questions also raised more general issues about the role of local disaster culture and the perceived relationships among residents, government officials at various levels, and information sources such as the Weather Channel. These topics are addressed in the chapter as well.

Evacuation Behaviour

The influx of new residents (many with little or no hazard experience), large seasonal tourist populations and rapid development in coastal communities have increased the vulnerability of coastal populations not only to hurricane threats but to other coastal hazards as well. This has placed enormous burdens on emergency management professionals and elected officials, many of whom struggle with the need to minimize loss of life and property, (short-term issues) and develop more sustained policies of reducing hazard vulnerability (Pielke, 1997). The escalating demand for, and the economic realities of, coastal development worsen the emergency management situation. One outcome is the increase in the number of seemingly premature evacuations in response to impending hurricane threats. Unlike other natural hazards, hurricanes have not produced a distinctive disaster mitigation culture (Sheets, 1995), so preparedness is emphasized over mitigation. Thus, the timing of storm warnings and evacuation messages becomes one of the most salient issues faced by emergency management officials.

Decades of research on natural hazards include a substantial body of empirical evidence on how people respond to hazard warnings in general, while behaviours in response to hurricanes are less studied (Schneider, 1995). Reports on individual hurricane events and the comparisons across findings comprise much of this existing literature. Post-hurricane case studies often examine the factors influencing perception of hurricane hazards, such as experience with a hurricane, residence in a hurricane-prone area and interpretation of hurricane probability data.

Sorenson and Mileti (1988) reviewed a variety of evacuation events (including hurricanes) and found that evacuation rates vary from 32–98 per cent depending on the level of warning and perception of personal risk. For hurricanes, evacuation rates were around 90–95 per cent in geographically defined high-risk areas compared to 25–35 per cent in lower risk areas. In his review of evacuation behaviour in over a dozen hurricanes during the last three decades, Baker (1991) provided the following generalizations about how people respond to these threats.

- The definition of the risk area and actions of public officials are the most important variables affecting public response.
- More than 90 per cent of residents of high-risk barrier islands and open coasts will evacuate in response to strong, clear warnings from officials.
- General knowledge of hurricanes and hurricane safety is a poor predictor of hurricane evacuation behaviour.
- Variation in hurricane evacuation is largely accounted for by the hazardousness of the area, action by public authorities, type of housing, prior perception of personal risk and storm-specific threat factors.

These findings provide some initial understanding of how residents respond to the hurricanes, but they consistently overlook tourist populations, an increasing concern of coastal emergency managers. Largely because of the methodological difficulties in locating transient populations, such as tourists, these groups are under-represented in most evacuation studies. One exception is Drabek's (1996) study of tourists and other transients in five disaster events – Hurricanes Bob (1991), Andrew (1992), and Iniki (1992) and the earthquakes in Big Bear (1992) and Northridge (1994). Approximately 75 per cent of the tourists and the business people responded to warnings by evacuating to a safer place, while only about 58 per cent of the homeless people evacuated.

Efforts to understand differences in responses to hurricane evacuation warnings and support for mitigation have taken several approaches to the problem. Studies regularly include analyses of socio-demographic characteristics of respondents and exposure to hurricane risks in their investigation of patterns of evacuation warning response. Factors such as age, gender, and past experience of a hurricane are consistently found to be poor predictors of risk perception and evacuation behaviour (Aguirre, 1991; Baker, 1991; Cross, 1990).

In general, the stronger predictors of evacuation behaviour are tied to personal risk perception. Evacuation warnings that are timely, personally relevant and provided by a credible source are more effective (Sims and Baumann, 1985). Severity of the storm and damage expectations are also among the better predictors, although they are confounded by officials' tendency to increase warning efforts for stronger storms (Baker, 1991). Other research points to the role of officials in increasing evacuation response rates; however, the relative significance of actions by local officials and the governor vary in the reports.

Additional factors influencing personal risk evaluation include evaluation of housing safety, use of probability information, and communication linkages. Mobile-home owners are more likely to evacuate than occupants of other types of housing, particularly in medium-risk and lower-risk areas (Baker, 1991). Personal assessment of the quality of construction materials and workmanship influenced evacuation decisions for residents of Cancun when they faced Hurricane Gilbert's arrival in 1988 (Aguirre, 1991). Based on a comparison of two communities, one directly hit by a hurricane and another community that experienced the storm mostly via media coverage, Beatley and Brower (1986) reported that residents of the community hit by the hurricane had a more accurate assessment of the impact, increased belief in the strength of structures and increased support for mitigation activities.

Probabilistic information factors into hazard perception over the long and short term, playing an important role in hurricane emergency management efforts. In a rare longitudinal study of residents of a coastal Florida community, Cross (1990) found that as time since the last hurricane lengthened, more residents (24 per cent) became increasingly concerned about the hurricane hazard. The most common explanation for this increased concern was the sense that a hurricane was due, followed by belief that increased population in the area would result in more difficult evacuations and possibly more injuries. Residents who reported a decrease in concern also cited probabilities; 55 per cent noted that there have not been any major hurricane impacts in decades.

Release of probability calculations on the path and landfall location of individual hurricanes was a controversial matter before it was first implemented in 1983 (Baker, 1995). Emergency personnel were unsure how this type of information would influence evacuation behaviour. A study using hypothetical hurricane approach scenarios found that people were fairly sophisticated in their use of probability information. This study also tested the role of warnings by local officials and concluded that 'local officials' advice or orders regarding evacuation remain, by far, the most important element in affecting evacuation, regardless of whether probabilities are included in people's information or not' (Baker, 1995, pp146–147).

Finally, the credibility of information that people receive and rely on is an important factor in the evacuation decision. Sources of information on the physical aspects of the storm and warnings are available from a wide variety of media as well as through informal networks and direct communications with response personnel. Recent work suggests that mass media (especially television) are among the most credible sources of hazard information (Driscoll and Salwen, 1996). Technological advances in the communications field and the increasing importance of cable television (especially the Weather Channel) suggest an increased need to focus more attention on the ways different media sources, including internet access and cable television, influence decision-making (Aguirre, 1991; Emani and Kasperson, 1996).

Hurricanes Bertha and Fran in the Carolinas

The 1996 Atlantic hurricane season was certainly one for the record books. There were 13 named storms, with 4 making landfall in the US or its territories (Mayfield, 1996). Loss estimates are still coming in, but the latest figures place losses well above $1.6 billion in insured property damage. The National Hurricane Center estimates total damages from a hurricane based on a conservative ratio of 2 to 1 total damage to insured property damage. Their estimates of total losses for Bertha and Fran equal $4.3 billion (Lawrence, 1996; Mayfield, 1996). As of May 1997, Federal Emergency Management Agency (FEMA) relief costs for the 1996 hurricane season were around $746 million (FEMA, 1997).

Hurricane Bertha passed through the Caribbean on 6–10 July with winds up to 105 mph (Figure 14.1). The U.S. Virgin Islands was declared a federal disaster area with approximately 2500 homes damaged (Lawrence, 1996). The Bahamas

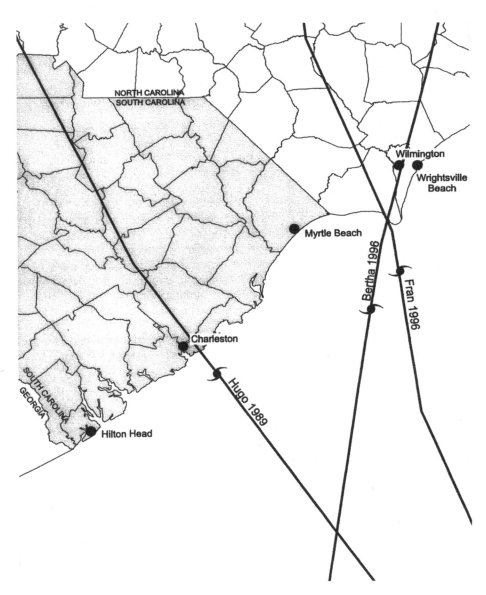

Figure 14.1 *Hurricane storm tracks*

and the Dominican Republic were affected by the weak side of the hurricane, but no loss figures are available (Lawrence, 1996).

Bertha made landfall at Wrightsville Beach, NC, as a Category 1 hurricane on 12 July at 4:45pm with hurricane force winds of 105 mph (FEMA, 1996; Figure 14.1). Tropical force winds extended 230 miles outward from the centre. Approximately 750,000 people evacuated from North and South Carolina (Lawrence, 1996). Damages in North Carolina included power outages, downed trees and power lines. In North Carolina, there was considerable beach erosion at Carolina Beach and Wrightsville Beach and structural damage in Kure Beach and Surf City. In South Carolina, damage was minimal and included some downed trees and power lines in Horry and Georgetown counties. On 18 July a federal disaster declaration was issued for seven North Carolina counties based on storm, wind and flood damages associated with Bertha. Total US damage from the storm is estimated at $270 million (Lawrence, 1996).

Two months later, on 5 September, Hurricane Fran made landfall over Cape Fear just south of Wilmington, NC, as a weak Category 3 storm (Fran's maximum sustained winds were 115 mph or 100 knots) with a storm surge of 12–15 ft. Tropical force winds extended 290 miles seaward of the storm's centre and inland up to 100 miles. Twenty-six deaths were attributed to the storm. The primary damage was in North Carolina, with wind and storm damage ranging from Corncake Inlet in the south to New River Inlet in the north. The hardest hit barrier island communities included Carolina Beach, Wrightsville Beach, Topsail Beach, and North Topsail Beach. Inland flooding from the already swollen rivers and saturated ground was extensive throughout the state.

In South Carolina, damage from Hurricane Fran was limited to downed trees, flooding damage, power outages and some roof damage to structures. A federal disaster declaration was issued on 6 September for North Carolina, Virginia, and four counties in South Carolina. As of May 1997, FEMA relief costs associated with Hurricane Fran total $496 million for the six affected states (North Carolina, South Carolina, Virginia, West Virginia, Maryland, and Pennsylvania) (FEMA, 1997). South Carolina's expenditures were more than $8 million in the immediate aftermath for debris clearance, utility restoration and protective measures.

Precautionary Measures: The Official Response

In South Carolina, the governor holds sole authority to issue evacuation orders for all counties. The Office of Emergency Preparedness and local authorities offer advice and consult with the governor's office, but the timing and geographic extent are determined by the governor. For Hurricane Bertha, South Carolina's Governor Beasley activated the state emergency operations plan on 10 July. At that time he called for a voluntary evacuation of barrier islands, beachfront areas, and residents in low-lying coastal areas. A mandatory evacuation order covering all persons east of the intercoastal waterway throughout the state was issued on 11 July. The intercoastal waterway lies oceanside of Highway 17 (Figure 14.2).

On 4 September 1996 at 2:40pm South Carolina's governor issued a mandatory evacuation order in anticipation of Hurricane Fran's landfall in South Carolina. The evacuation order was for Georgetown and Horry counties east of US 17, all barrier islands, all beachfront properties, all low-lying areas and all property bordering waterways in Jasper, Beaufort, Colleton and Charleston counties. In other words, the evacuation order covered all of coastal South Carolina (Figure 14.2).

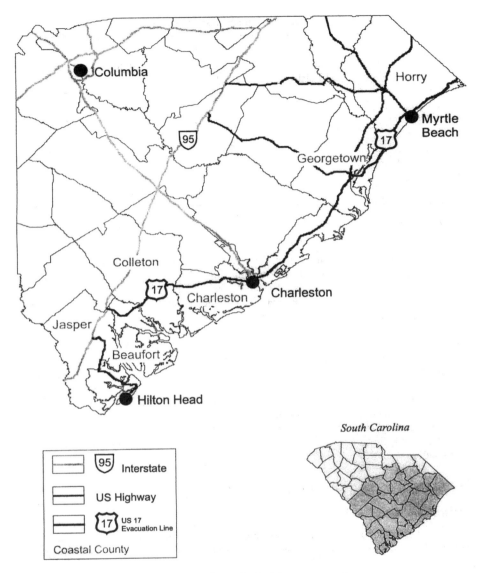

Figure 14.2 *Coastal South Carolina evacuation zones*

Assessing Evacuation Behaviour

Three communities were selected for interviewing to determine the behaviour of residents and to identify a range of experiences in the hurricane threat from hurricanes Bertha and Fran. All are distributed along coastal Carolina (from south to north). The communities include Hilton Head and Myrtle Beach, South Carolina, and Wilmington, North Carolina.

Table 14.1 *Survey responses on specific dates in 1996*

Total surveys	Hilton Head 13–14 Sep	Myrtle Beach 14–15 Sep	Wilmington 28 Sep	Total 13–28 Sep
Not in area	32	177	4	213
Completed	128	143	52	323
Refusals	79	76	24	179
Total contacts	238	396	80	714
Response rate (%)	67.2	80.8	70.0	74.9
Completed survey response rate (%)	53.7	36.1	65.0	45.2

Although the entire South Carolina coast was evacuated for each hurricane, the actual risk was in the northern part of the coastline at the border between the Carolinas. Wilmington experienced both hurricanes.

The surveys involved face-to-face interviews with respondents at the entry to major stores (grocery and discount) in each community. The surveys included both open-ended and closed questions and required from five to ten minutes to administer. This design was selected in order to focus on the residential populations of these heavily touristed communities. Less than two weeks after Hurricane Fran, survey teams were in the field in South Carolina (13–15 September 1996). Because of the extent of damage, we were unable to get into the Wilmington area for interviewing until two weeks later (28 September). Our overall response rate was 75 per cent. However, we used a screening question to target residents and those who were in the area for Fran and Bertha. A total of 323 interviews was completed (Table 14.1).

To identify and explain the effects of what might be called 'false alarms' on evacuation behaviour we will only examine the responses from our South Carolina residential sample. This permits us to compare residents following two hurricane events, none of whom experienced a direct hit from the hurricane. Three main factors are described: differences in evacuation responses between the two storms; key decision-making criteria, such as a specific source or piece of information that contributed to the evacuation decision; and the major source of 'reliable' information influencing the decisions to evacuation.

Evacuation Decisions and Responses

Evacuation rates

More people evacuated for Hurricane Fran than Bertha in both South Carolina study communities. A total of 41 per cent of residents evacuated for Bertha, while 59 per cent evacuated for Fran. There were, however, considerable differences between the two communities in rates of evacuation (Table 14.2). The highest evacuation rates (for both events) were in Hilton Head, the community furthest from the landfall. This can be partially explained by the island location of Hilton Head (compared to the mainland location of the Myrtle Beach area) and a sin-

Table 14.2 *Evacuation rates by study site*

Location	Number evacuated prior to Bertha (% of community sample)	Number evacuated prior to Fran (% of community sample)	Total interviews
Hilton Head	64 (50%)	83 (65%)	128
Myrtle Beach	48 (34%)	76 (53%)	143
Total	112 (41%)	159 (59%)	271

gle evacuation route off the island. Hilton Head is also a wealthier community and has a very proactive planning and emergency response team with significant public education/outreach efforts, especially during hurricane season. Both factors might help explain some of these differences. Previous experience with a hurricane did not differentiate between evacuees and non-evacuees, with 74 per cent, responding they had gone through a hurricane before. Evacuation rates for 1989's Hurricane Hugo ranged from 62 to 81 per cent in selected coastal communities, while for Hurricane Diana (1984) the range was between 10 and 48 per cent (Hazards Management Group, 1985). Table 14.3 summarizes recent findings on hurricane evacuation rates in South Carolina. The discrepancies between the Baker (1997) survey and ours may be related to the timing of interviews (September 1996 for ours, January 1997 for Baker) and the different survey methods (face-to-face interviews versus telephone surveys).

Despite the difference in the storms, however, there was a considerable degree of consistency in individuals' decisions to evacuate. Of the 264 respondents to this question, the majority either evacuated (39 per cent) for both hurricanes or stayed (37 per cent) for both. The remaining respondents did not evacuate for Bertha (21 per cent) but did for Hurricane Fran. Only 3 per cent evacuated for Bertha but not Fran.

Table 14.3 *South Carolina's prior experience with hurricane evacuations*

Year/hurricane/ category	Reference	Locale	% evacuated	Sample size
1996/Fran/CAT 3	This chapter	Myrtle Beach	53	143
		Hilton Head	65	128
1996/Bertha/CAT 1	This chapter	Myrtle Beach	34	143
		Hilton Head	50	128
1996/Bertha/CAT 1	Baker (1997)	Myrtle Beach	27	370
1989/Hugo/CAT 4	Baker (1990)	Beaufort	72	90
		Charleston	62	99
		Mt. Pleasant/ Sullivan's Island	81	85
		Myrtle Beach	79	113
1984/Diana/CAT 2	Hazards Management Group (1985)	Georgetown	10	107
		Myrtle Beach	48	102

Triggering action or information

In investigating possible changes in evacuation behaviour between events, we asked respondents in an open-ended format, 'What convinced you to leave the area?' Respondents who evacuated were asked to rank the top three factors that influenced the decision to evacuate. Approaching the evacuation decision from other angles, respondents who stayed were asked why, and respondents who evacuated for one hurricane and not the other were asked to explain the difference. Our analysis of the decision-making criteria revealed no dramatic shifts in factors convincing people between Bertha and Fran. Unlike previous evacuation studies, no single factor dominated responses; rather, the residents provided multiple reasons for their decision-making (Table 14.4).

The ranking of factors suggests less emphasis on advice and warnings from authorities and more reliance on media and assorted household considerations (included in the 'other' category) as prompts for an evacuation. Among those who evacuated, a basic cross-tabulation table of the first (most) important factor in convincing them to leave for Bertha versus that for Fran identified the following tendencies: the Governor's order and media reports were almost equal in their influence on the decision to evacuate. The large category of 'other' factors included a number of individual or household considerations, such as safety of children and pets, vacation plans, work obligations and potential flooding. In addition, during Hurricane Fran, the severity of the storm also prompted many residents to flee from the coastal areas.

What is interesting to note is the decline in the reliance on government officials as the most salient information source in triggering evacuation between the two storms. This is partially explained by the frustrations of the Hilton Head residents over traffic jams and difficulties with emergency operations that they encountered during the Bertha evacuation, two months earlier. In fact, 57 per cent of the respondents reported problems in trying to leave the area for Bertha, while only 15 per cent reported similar problems for Fran.

Among the 55 people who did not evacuate prior to Bertha but evacuated for Fran, evacuation prompts were not significantly different among the sites (chi-square probability for Bertha = 0.487, chi-square probability for Fran = 0.398). At Hilton Head, the majority of respondents, 50 per cent, were convinced to leave based on

Table 14.4 *What convinced you to leave the area?*

First reason given	Bertha (% of evacuees, n = 106)	Fran (% of evacuees, n = 153)
Governor's order/advice	24.5	22.9
Local officials/local emergency responders	11.3	5.2
Weather Channel/National Weather Service/ local news	26.4	26.8
Actions/advice from friends or family	6.6	7.8
Severity of storm/probability of a 'hit'	6.6	13.1
Other	24.5	24.2

Table 14.5 *Reasons for non-evacuation for both hurricanes*

Reason	Hilton Head (% of non-evacuees, n = 57)	Myrtle Beach (% of non-evacuees, n = 85)
Severity of storm/probability of a 'hit'	24.5	14.0
Low risk based on information from the Weather Channel	24.5	3.5
Perception of safety of home and/or location	8.8	36.5
Job requirements	7.0	8.2
Other (contains no category greater than 5%)	24.6	37.6
Traffic delayed departure from Hilton Head, storm track changed, or waited too long to leave	10.5	0

orders/advice from state and local officials and the National Weather Service. At Myrtle Beach, 58 per cent reported taking into account advice from friends, family, the media and a combination of 'other' individual factors. Of those few residents who evacuated for Bertha but not for Fran, explanations included proximity to Fran's landfall, changes in health status, or perceived greater safety at home.

Reasons given for non-evacuation centred on the perceived probability and severity of a 'hit' followed by the perception of safety of the housing unit and/or location relative to the danger (Table 14.5). Non-evacuees in Hilton Head also specifically mentioned the low probability of landfall and risk information from the Weather Channel as reasons for staying.

Whether they stayed or evacuated, our data suggest that people are considering a wide variety of factors in their decision-making. More so than in previous hurricane evacuation studies, individual evaluation of risks (largely derived from media reports and from the Weather Channel) seems to have played a larger role in evacuation decision making during these two hurricane events. The role of media coverage of storm characteristics and how individuals utilize this information in their personal risk calculations in evacuation decisions is an important area for further research.

Reliable sources of information

The perceived most reliable source of information was the media in general (37 per cent for Bertha, 51 per cent for Fran). While we expected local radio and television to be perceived as credible sources, we were surprised by the specific mentioning of the Weather Channel as one of the most reliable sources (Table 14.6). Despite its importance as a prompt for 'convincing' people to evacuate, the governor's orders were not evaluated as the most reliable source of information about evacuation. The percentages of people reporting all types of media as the most reliable increased between the two storms. There were no significant differences between our two sites in these evaluations.

Table 14.6 *Reliability of information sources*

Source	Bertha (% of responses, n = 116)	Fran (% of responses, n = 155)
Governor's order	7.8	5.8
Media – total	84.5	86.4
Media general	54.3	52.3
Local media	8.6	9.0
The Weather Channel	15.5	18.1
Radio	6.0	7.1
Actions of friends/neighbours	2.6	2.6
Personal experience	2.6	1.9
Other	2.6	2.6

For evacuees who left for Fran and not Bertha, media sources were more widely used. In order of descending importance, the most reliable sources of information for Fran were the media – general (51 per cent), the Weather Channel (19 per cent), the radio (13 per cent), local media (6 per cent) and the governor's order (6 per cent), followed by actions of family and friends and personal experience (2 per cent). Direct advice from local officials is absent from these reports, although residents following the news would have heard their warnings.

The broader response of listening to the media, coupled with specific references to the Weather Channel, again indicated people considered a variety of types of information. Unsolicited comments such as 'I watched the Weather Channel for information' suggest that individuals are judging information more independently than previously thought. Several respondents reported logging onto the internet to get information. Local emergency managers reported receiving phone calls, however, asking for assistance in interpreting the statistics respondents found there.

This difference sheds some light on the distinction between the reliability of information sources and actions and information that convinced people to evacuate. The most reliable sources (media) provided data on hurricane characteristics such as magnitude and direction of landfall. Advice or orders from officials sometimes convinced people to evacuate, but the advisories were not reported as particularly reliable. These findings suggest that access to basic data and experts' evaluations through sources such as the Weather Channel and the internet provided a necessary confirmation for a more independent and personally relevant evaluation of hurricane risks by local residents.

If another hurricane approached

The impact of unnecessary evacuations can be considered by asking a hypothetical question, 'If another hurricane approached the coast, would you evacuate? And why?' While hypothetical questions can pose difficulties, in the context of this discussion, asking residents about future actions was based on their recent, past decision-making in the face of potential danger. The majority of our respondents

(48 per cent) answered 'It depends' to the question, while 21 per cent responded 'No.' The remaining third said yes, they would evacuate if another hurricane approached.

For those who replied yes, concerns over personal and family safety were paramount. Statements such as 'I'm afraid', 'Better safe than sorry' or 'I'd be crazy not to evacuate' illustrate this view. Other respondents gave specific reasons including past experience with hurricanes, and living in a mobile home or near water. The experience with 'false alarms' did not seem to sway their perception of risk. Furthermore, these responses were consistent with actions taken for both Bertha and Fran.

Among those respondents who replied 'No', a few, less than 2 per cent of all respondents, mentioned they would not evacuate because the last few forecasted hurricanes did not hit their area. Comments included, 'Government leaders cried wolf too often' and 'The last few didn't hit' as reasons for non-evacuation. The largest group, however, was residents who believed their home was a safe place or at least safer than anywhere else. Others cited job requirements as a reason for staying. There were only a few respondents who mentioned concern about being able to return home as a reason for not leaving. The majority of these future non-evacuees (81 per cent) also did not evacuate for either Bertha or Fran.

The indirect effects of these seeming 'unnecessary evacuations' are more apparent in the group of respondents who replied that their future actions would 'depend' on the situation. The reasons respondents gave differed substantially from the factors that convinced them to evacuate for Bertha and Fran. The largest group replied that their future evacuation would depend on the severity of the storm, but gave no indication of what specific magnitude would prompt their departure. A few said they would leave for storms classified as Category 4 or higher. Others responded that it would depend on a variety of storm conditions such as the path, probability of a hit, and potential for flooding. In sum, most residents were using risk heuristics based on storm characteristics as their decision-making criterion. Less than 2 per cent answered that their evacuation would depend on an order from the governor. The advice of public officials is accorded only a minor role in future decision-making.

Between our study sites, there is some inconsistency in the number of respondents who would definitely undertake an evacuation for future hurricanes (39 per cent in Hilton Head; 27 per cent in Myrtle Beach), yet those who replied 'It depends' are quite similar (50 per cent in Hilton Head; 46 per cent in Myrtle Beach). However, there are significant differences between the 'No' and 'It depends' groups. More than a quarter of the Myrtle Beach residents (27 per cent) were adamant in their refusal to evacuate for future hurricanes. In Hilton Head, it was less than half of this (11 per cent). We speculate on the existence of a strong reluctant population in Myrtle Beach with very strong bipolar views toward evacuation. Some of this reluctance may be a function of the backlash from the 'crying wolf' syndrome, a reflection of local emergency preparedness attitudes, a sense that evacuations are intended to protect tourists, lack of recent experience, a mainland rather than an island location, or all of these.

Crying Wolf Too Often

The influence of 'premature evacuations' for Bertha played only a minor role in evacuation decisions for Hurricane Fran in South Carolina. Evacuation rates increased in Myrtle Beach and Hilton Head for the stronger Hurricane Fran, despite the 'false alarms' for Bertha only two months earlier. South Carolina residents anticipate little change in their future evacuation activities, although there is some semblance of a resistant evacuation population emerging, with more than a third of our residents stating they would not evacuate under any conditions. The 'premature evacuations' did not result in any dramatic shifts in reasons residents gave for their evacuation or the sources they found most reliable. We found that the reported role of official advisories and mandatory orders was limited as people sought a wider variety of information for their decisions.

Personal assessment of the storm characteristics and its risks played a larger role in evacuation behaviour than reported in previous studies. Individuals considered the quality of home construction, location, family safety and needs, and data on storm tracks, strength and probabilities in their evacuation decision-making. Reliance on the media, and the Weather Channel in particular, was more pronounced than in prior research. Those who evacuated for one storm and not the other (mostly for Fran and not Bertha) did so largely on the basis of storm characteristics as the evacuation warnings were nearly identical. Differences in evacuation rates among communities were not based on demographics or community hurricane history. The diversity of 'reliable' and 'convincing' sources of information provide evidence to confirm that the 'premature evacuations' ordered by the governor were not deemed highly credible or particularly reliable. Instead, residents sought other confirmatory data on the nature of the threat before making the decision to evacuate or not.

Implications and Future Research Directions

This research has a number of implications for coastal planners, emergency managers and researchers. It is clear that our previous models of evacuation decision-making and behaviour are not in keeping with technological advances and increasing diversity of warning and risk information systems. A first step is to re-examine the role of hazard information in the decision-making process. We found that evacuation decisions were based on multiple sources of risk information. There was a greater reliance on risk assessments derived from the physical parameters of the storms themselves (wind speed, forward motion, path, category), rather than an assessment of what other people were doing. Confirmation of the risk information was sought from the electronic media (e.g. the Weather Channel) rather than from emergency management officials. This suggests that coastal residents in South Carolina are becoming more sophisticated in their risk calculations and exhibiting more independence in their assessment relying on widely available technology such as cable television, weather radios, the internet and so forth. Clearly, additional research is needed on the role of increased media coverage, improved technological access and greater breadth of information in public decision-making.

A second avenue for continued research is based on the false alarms. While precautionary evacuations are necessary, the timing and longer-term implications require detailed study in other locales. One of the reasons residents chose to stay was because of the delay in re-entry to the area after the storm's passage. Perhaps a re-examination of procedures to facilitate the repopulation of the area after the storm (or after the false alarm) will help assuage the fears of residents that once they leave, it will take quite a while to be able to return to their properties. These cautious evacuation orders do not seem to influence the decision-making of residents as to whether to evacuate or not. However, we see significant reduction in the credibility of governmental officials, so much so that official advisories are not perceived as reliable or personally relevant for individuals.

One practical implication is a change in how residents obtain risk information and, more importantly, their view of emergency management officials. In the past, emergency management officials had a paternalistic relationship with the residents – it was their job to provide hazard information and help protect the community from harm. Perhaps due to more aggressive educational programmes, this paternalistic relationship is weakening and people are building on their understandings of hurricane threats to collect and evaluate relevant information. Emergency managers seem to have little effect on the evacuation decisions of local residents, according to our survey. Instead, they are now being viewed as traffic control officers, caretakers for tourists and major obstacles to re-entry after the storm; they ultimately influence a decision to stay and ride out the storm. It is clear that the electronic media information is often inconsistent with official warnings from the governor. One alternative derived from our results is to have coordinated advisories so that there is 'one voice' and thus one set of information that is being transmitted to the public. The placement of official hurricane evacuation advisories and orders on the Weather Channel (for example) may help alleviate some of the confusion and improve the credibility of state-elected and emergency response officials. A second alternative is to provide more detailed explanations of the rationale behind evacuation orders and their implementation so that those considerations are more fully incorporated into decision-making processes.

A final area for future research involves the notion of a local disaster culture. Despite more aggressive coastal and hurricane education programmes, we still see a significant evacuation-resistant population varying among locations. A more detailed study of these reluctant evacuees might help determine the existence of a local disaster culture that either enhances the movement of people out of harm's way or thwarts attempts to do so. The differences between our study sites suggests that geographic site and situation may also be important in the formation of local disaster culture and the perceived relationships among residents, authorities at different levels of government and information sources such as the Weather Channel. Clearly, more localized studies of evacuation decision-making and behaviour will help determine either the uniqueness of the South Carolina experience or its generalization to all coastal communities and residents.

Acknowledgements

This research was funded, in part, by the Quick Response Program of the Natural Hazards Research and Applications Information Center at the University of Colorado with support from the National Science Foundation. We are also indebted to our great field assistants who helped administer the interviews at Hilton Head, Myrtle Beach, and Wilmington – Jerry Mitchell, Valerie Kudes, Cindy Kirkconnell, Channel Menzel, and Megan Warner. Lastly, Jerry Mitchell and Paul Whitten (Horry County Emergency Preparedness Department) provided insightful comments on the draft of the manuscript.

References

Aguirre, B. E. (1991) 'Evacuation in Cancun during Hurricane Gilbert', *International Journal of Mass Emergencies and Disasters*, vol 9, no 1, pp31–45

Baker, E. J. (1990) *Evacuation Decision-Making and Public Response in Hurricane Hugo in South Carolina*, Quick Response Report, Natural Hazards Research and Applications Information Center, Boulder, CO

Baker, E. J. (1991) 'Hurricane evacuation behavior', *International Journal of Mass Emergencies and Disasters*, vol 9, no 2, pp287–310

Baker, E. J. (1995) 'Public response to hurricane probability forecasts', *Professional Geographer*, vol 47, no 2, pp137–147

Baker, E. J. (1997) *Hurricanes Bertha and Fran in North and South Carolina: Evacuation Behavior and Attitudes Toward Mitigation*, report prepared for the Charleston and Wilmington Districts, US Army Corps of Engineers, Hazards Management Group, Tallahassee, FL

Beatley, T. and Brower, D. (1986) 'Public perception of hurricane hazards: Examining the differential effects of hurricane Diana', *Coastal Zone Management Journal*, vol 44, no 3, pp241–269

Breznitz, S. (1984) *Cry Wolf: The Psychology of False Alarms*, Lawrence Erlbaum Associates, Hillsdale, NJ

Cross, J. A. (1990) 'Longitudinal changes in hurricane hazard perception', *International Journal of Mass Emergencies and Disasters*, vol 8, no 1, pp31–47

Drabek, T. E. (1996) *Disaster Evacuation Behavior: Tourists and Other Transients*, Program on Environment and Behavior Monograph no 58, Institute of Behavioral Science, University of Colorado, Boulder, CO

Driscoll, P. and Salwen, M. B. (1996) 'Riding out the storm: Public evaluations of news coverage of Hurricane Andrew', *International Journal of Mass Emergencies and Disasters*, vol 14, no 3, pp293–303

Emani, S. and Kasperson, J. X. (1996) 'Disaster communication via the information superhighway: Data and observations on the 1995 hurricane season', *International Journal of Mass Emergencies and Disasters*, vol 14, no 3, pp321–342

FEMA (Federal Emergency Management Agency) (1996) 'Final Situation Report for Hurricane Bertha', http://www.fema.gov/hu96/besrp6.html

FEMA (1997) 'Top Ten Hurricane Disasters Ranked by FEMA Relief Costs', http://www.fema.gov/hu_arch/top10hu.html

Hazards Management Group, Inc. (1985) *South Carolina Hurricane Evacuation Study: Behavioral Analysis*, report prepared for the Charleston District, US Army Corps of Engineers, Hazards Management Group, Inc., Tallahassee, FL

Lawrence, M. B. (1996) 'National Hurricane Center, Preliminary Report, Hurricane Bertha: 5–14 July, 1961', http://www.nhc.noaa.gov/bertha,html

Mayfield, M. (1996) 'National Hurricane Center, Preliminary Report, Hurricane Fran: 23 August– 8 September, 1996', http://www.nhc.noaa.gov/fran.html

Pielke, R. A. jr (1997) 'Reframing the US hurricane problem', *Society and Natural Resources*, vol 10, no 5, pp485–499

Schneider, S. K. (1995) *Flirting with Disaster: Public Management in Crisis Situations*, M. E. Sharpe, Armonk, NY

Sheets, R. C. (1995) 'Stormy weather', *Forum for Applied Research and Public Policy*, vol 10, no 1, pp5–15

Sims, J. H. and Baumann, D. D. (1985) 'Natural hazards research and policy: Time for a gadfly', *American Statistician*, vol 39, pp358–362

Sorensen, J. H. and Mileti, D. S. (1988) 'Warning and evacuation: Answering some basic questions', *Industrial Crisis Quarterly*, vol 2, pp195–209

US Bureau of the Census (1996) *Statistical Abstract of the United States: The National Data Book*, Government Printing Office, Washington, DC, p240

15

Public Orders and Personal Opinions: Household Strategies for Hurricane Risk Assessment

Kirstin Dow and Susan L. Cutter

Introduction

The challenges of hurricane preparedness have changed dramatically over recent decades. Most public attention goes to the striking physical manifestations of these changes, the growth in population and investment along the hurricane-exposed coasts. Equally dramatic, although subtle in physical expression, is the significant increase in information availability that affects public response to hurricane warnings.

Evacuation decision-making among residents of coastal areas is changing, becoming a more complex process influenced by shifting circumstances at the local and state levels. The combination of greater potential hurricane activity and heightened vulnerability is addressed by emergency managers and the public in a social information context that is richer and more diverse than ever before, yet still characterized by persistent scientific uncertainties. Sources of information, including the Weather Channel and numerous private and governmental websites, provide forecasts as well as detailed current and background information around the clock. The new information context is contributing to a reduction in public reliance on emergency management officials in making hurricane evacuation decisions.

The extensive criticism of the Floyd evacuation and past research findings showing a reduced reliance on government orders in evacuation decisions suggest a growing separation between individual views and governmental responses to hurricane risks (Chapter 14). Yet residents are still very supportive of the process

Note: Reprinted, with permission, from *Environmental Hazards*, vol 2, no 4, Kirstin Dow and Susan L. Cutter, 'Public orders and personal opinions: Household strategies for hurricane risk assessment', pp143–155. © Elsevier, 2001

of calling for evacuations. In order to better understand this changing relationship, we first examine coastal residents' responses to and support for the hurricane evacuation process in Hurricane Floyd. A case study of Horry County residents' evacuation practices over the past four years provides a detailed view of local decision-making strategies. We use the case study to evaluate the emergence of a hurricane-savvy population where judgements about hurricane risks and evacuation have become less dependent on governmental advisories. Finally, we document the broader priorities and criteria for evaluating evacuation success held by local elected officials as well as residents in order to identify points of difference and shared concern between these two constituencies.

Hurricane Floyd Evacuation in South Carolina

When Hurricane Hugo, a Category 4 hurricane and the worst storm in the state in recent history, made landfall in 1989, between 62 per cent and 81 per cent of South Carolina communities evacuated (Baker, 1994, p204). Hurricane Floyd (September 1999) was also a powerful hurricane with nearly Category 5 winds as it passed the Bahamas and its cloud bands covered much of the coastal Southeast. Floyd weakened considerably. However, it remained a hurricane with the potential to intensify as it moved northward towards landfall in North Carolina. The governor of South Carolina ordered a mandatory evacuation of low-lying areas along the entire coast (Figure 15.1). Although Hurricane Floyd was a Category 2

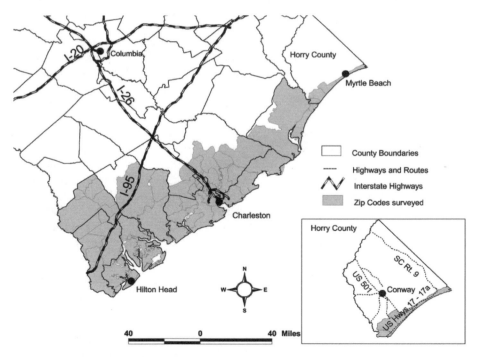

Figure 15.1 *Map of evacuation area of South Carolina*

storm at landfall, approximately 64 per cent of the population near the coast evacuated. By all accounts, the evacuation for Hurricane Floyd was unprecedented in this state and the region. Approximately half a million South Carolinians joined residents of Florida and Georgia in an evacuation that resulted in bumper-to-bumper traffic on the Interstate highways. Under these conditions, a distance of 100 miles sometimes took over 15 hours by car. It was not until late in the day of the first wave of evacuation that state agencies succeeded in transforming a major stretch of Interstate 26 between Charleston and Columbia into a one-way route away from the coast. Despite the traffic jam, evacuees were off the road by the time Hurricane Floyd neared landfall.

The Hurricane Floyd evacuation was also different from previous storms in terms of communication. Since Hurricane Hugo (1989), the internet, cell phones and the cable TV Weather Channel have all become part of the coastal hurricane information system. The cell phones were used to communicate drivers' frustration with the traffic to state and emergency management officials and radio stations, which broadcast problems. The internet and the Weather Channel set new records for viewers and visits to the websites.

Advances in Hurricane Warnings, Risk Perception and Public Response

Over the past 20 years, there have been many advances in warning systems for hazards in general. Among hazards, hurricane-warning systems are exemplary for improvements in forecasting and presentation of scientific warnings and information (Elsner and Kara, 1999; Sheets, 1995; Sorensen, 2000). Hazard warning systems, including those for hurricanes, are limited by hazard-specific issues such as detection, emergency management and public response (Mileti, 1999). Improved monitoring capabilities have lengthened the lead time for hurricane forecasts and, with the aid of computer graphics, contributed to the widespread availability of storm imagery, often days in advance of physical changes along the shore (AMS, 2000). Emergency management is making great progress as geographic information systems (GIS) and other computer-aided models improve the ability to manage large amounts of data, and a greater variety of media sources are involved in the dissemination of information. However, if evacuation rates associated with mandatory evacuation orders are the measure of public response, then this dimension of hurricane emergency management has not advanced as quickly as other areas.

Currently, warnings given 24 hours before hurricane landfall cover an average of 400 miles of the coastline, while the damage swath typically covers about one-quarter of that area (AMS, 2000). As the American Meteorological Society (AMS) Council notes in its policy statement on hurricane forecasting, this relationship means that three-quarters of the coastal area is 'overwarned'. Due to the way the track of Hurricane Floyd paralleled the coast, warnings covered the Atlantic seaboard from Florida to Virginia, a distance of 1000 miles. The uncertainty in the hurricane path is expressed to the public in maps of landfall probability and hurricane watch/warning areas as well as verbal communication by mass media and governmental sources. Despite the concern over the impact of 'overwarning' or 'crying wolf' (ordering an evacuation that proves with hindsight to be unnecessary), as long as the rationale for evacuation orders is understood, these cases are unlikely to reduce willingness to evacuate in the future (Chapter 14; see also Sorensen and Mileti, 1988).

Factors influencing household assessments of risk

Households' decision-making about whether or not to evacuate draws on an increasingly diverse set of information sources. The internet and the Weather Channel, relatively recent additions to the radio and television news sources, are playing larger roles in public tracking of hurricane risks (Chapter 14; see also Emani and Kasperson, 1996; Zimmerman, 1999). Floyd was 'the most closely tracked hurricane of the internet Age' (Zimmerman, 1999). Internet industry analysts report that daily page views for weather.com, the website of the Weather Channel, increased from approximately 2.7 million on 6 September to 23.5 million on 14 September, as evacuations started (Cheng, 1999). In contrast, during Hurricane Dennis (Category 1), the week of 5 September, the activity of the weather. com site was less than half of that during Floyd (Cheng, 1999). Other top internet weather sites, including accuweather.com, weather.yahoo.com, weather. com, intellicast.com and weatherunderground.com, all experienced at least a threefold increase in traffic during the height of the storm (Zimmerman, 1999). Peak cable ratings were also set for the Weather Channel on the evening of 14 September, as 2.5 million people tuned in to check on Floyd as it moved north along the Atlantic coast (Trigoboff, 1999).

These information sources discuss hurricane development, influences on the hurricane track, the history of past hurricanes and seasons, and increasingly, preparedness measures. The information is addressed to audiences ranging from grade school children to practising professional meteorologists. As Drabek (1999) observes:

> *The pace of technological innovation has quickened and future populations at risk may receive disaster warning messages and confirmation information through a variety of channels that were not available to people when earlier studies were conducted. **How these technologies, both home-based and those adopted by governmental and non governmental organizations will alter the future response patterns will comprise important niches of the research agenda.*** (Drabek, 1999, pp521–522; emphasis in original)

Factors influencing public response

Public response to information about risks is the outcome of a rather complex communication process among various groups, individuals and institutions. As Kasperson and colleagues (1988, 1996) point out, public concern over risk can be amplified or attenuated over time. This communication process extends well beyond the one-way delivery of an evacuation order by officials, although that specific message and credibility of the information source are very influential components of hurricane evacuation decision-making. For a recurrent hazard, like hurricanes, collective experiences (trials and tribulations) remain in the public and institutional consciousness long after the storm has ended.

Research confirms that public perceptions of risks differ from those of experts, with experts tending to use narrower, technical definitions of risk (Otway, 1992; Cutter, 1993). While the public concerns range into social dimensions of risks, such as fairness or the indirect consequences of disruptions, risk experts tend to focus on measures such as the probability of mortality or morbidity. These comparative studies suggest that parallel differences may exist between publics and experts in their perception of hurricane risks. However, this point has not been addressed explicitly.

Research on evacuation warnings has focused mostly on identifying the characteristics of an effective warning message. Years of research have confirmed that the most effective evacuation warnings are timely, personally relevant and delivered by a credible source (Mileti, 1999). While the topic of 'trust' in government and in experts delivering risk information has received considerable attention in recent years by the research community, the credibility of the information source and the cognitive process used to assess risks may be more important (Trettin and Musham, 2000). Research involving community groups exposed to environmental hazards suggests that better access to understandable information is the greatest priority in collective efforts to assess credibility and reliability (Trettin and Musham, 2000). The advice of state officials and local emergency response personnel has been among the top factors cited in households' decisions to evacuate, yet the severity of the hurricane, likelihood of a nearby landfall and past experience are among those most important considerations reported in post-event behavioural surveys (Chapter 14; see also Baker, 1991). The scope of what is 'personally relevant' continues to differ among publics and experts. Individual assessments of risk, increasing awareness of scientific uncertainty, diversity of information sources, and past experiences are emerging as more significant aspects of household response than previously documented (Chapter 14).

Additional studies examine the relationships between evacuation participation rates and household composition, and with direct and indirect hurricane impacts (Sorensen, 2000). The highest evacuation response rates are realized in high-risk areas, among mobile home owners, and in response to stronger storms (Baker, 1991). Households that include children are also more likely to evacuate than those without (Sorensen, 2000). Because of the difficulty in reaching tourists and other transient populations in coastal areas, little research has addressed their concerns specifically. Drabek (1996) conducted interviews with tourists and other transient groups following three hurricanes and two earthquakes. His data indicate that approximately 75 per cent of tourist/transient populations evacuated, but variation among individual events is not discussed in detail.

In contrast non-evacuation is frequently justified by the feeling that one's home is 'safe' (Chapter 14; see also Baker, 2000; HMG, 1985). Concerns about access to homes after evacuation, protecting property, job obligations and the well-being of pets are also among the indirect concerns that prompt some households to stay despite mandatory evacuation orders (Chapter 14; see also Baker,

2000). These broader sets of concerns about the indirect impacts of evacuation can outweigh official advice on safety.

The reporting of, and confidence in, scientific knowledge play important, although not determining, roles in public response. Since 1983, probabilistic information has become an increasingly large part of hurricane risk communication (HMG, 1985). There is ample advance notice for the specific warning messages, but these timely warnings do not have great accuracy due to forecast limitations. A discrepancy between timely and more accurate warnings has received considerable attention. The result is an evacuation policy that is, by design, precautionary, but raises concerns about credibility of the information and its source.

Despite expanded information, past experience will continue to play a major role in household decision-making, influencing both increases and decreases in evacuation participation rates (Sorensen, 2000; Gladwin, 1999). Evacuation rates vary among storms and locations (Pielke and Pielke, 1997). Often, the local variability in evacuation rates reflects the range of possible experiences with a hurricane, from personal relief to empathy to devastation. Personal experience significantly alters the salience of a hazard, the sense of uncertainty and vulnerability, as well as the amount and concreteness of available information about a hazard (Weinstein, 1989). Experiences can be better or worse than expected, while damages might be more or less extensive and expensive. Experience may also be direct or indirect if, for instance, a family member suffers losses. Gladwin's (1999) preliminary discussion of a survey of Florida residents following Floyd suggests other dimensions of experience incorporated into evacuation decision-making. The Floyd experience lessened the willingness of people to say that they will evacuate for the next big hurricane, but it is not clear whether this 'experience' effect reflects complacency or a more realistic assessment of a hypothetical question (Gladwin, 1999). The significance of experience does not necessarily diminish over time (Cross, 1990).

Methodology

Three different surveys were conducted to document the evacuation responses and perspectives of residents and public officials in South Carolina towards evacuation. The methodology for each of these is described below.

Coastal South Carolina phone survey

In cooperation with University of South Carolina (USC) Institute of Public Affair's Survey Research Lab, we conducted a telephone survey of residents throughout ten coastal South Carolina counties. Phone numbers were randomly selected from the complete sets of phone numbers for all zip code areas completely or partially included in the governor's mandatory evacuation order. The survey took approximately ten minutes to complete and was administered in the evenings between 25 October and 9 November 1999. Responses totalled 536, which included 513 completed interviews and 19 partial completions. The response rate for this survey was 63.5 per cent and the sampling is accurate to within ±4.2 per cent for South Carolina.

Horry County mail survey characteristics

In the past four years, six hurricanes have threatened Horry County, SC. Our 1998 research examining Hurricane Bonnie (Dow et al, 1999) took place in September and drew on a convenient sample of Horry County residents for a ten-minute face-to-face survey. At that time, residents were asked their evacuation decisions for Hurricane Bonnie, as well as the Hurricanes Bertha and Fran, which occurred two years earlier. We contacted this previously sampled group (n = 166) through a mailed survey sent on 29 October 1999, six weeks after Hurricane Floyd and concurrent with the coastal population phone survey. The response rate for this non-representative sample of 'experienced' respondents was 74 per cent (n = 123).

Elected officials

The ongoing biannual survey of elected officials conducted by the USC Institute of Public Affairs is a broad survey sent to local elected officials (response rate = 81 per cent, n = 431) throughout the state on a variety of issues and concerns for local government. In addition to the regular questions asked on the survey, we were allowed to include a question on hurricane emergency planning and response. This question was: 'What is the most important factor to consider in preparing an evacuation for a hurricane?' We received up to three answers from 427 local elected officials.

Findings

The following discussion considers evacuation decisions and support for official actions along the South Carolina coast following Hurricane Floyd. We then examine fours years of longitudinal information about hurricane evacuation among our group of experienced Horry County residents. These findings provide more detailed information on households' hurricane strategies. The differences, as well as the similarities, in households 'expectations and local officials' priorities in evacuation are summed up in the final section.

Heeding and supporting evacuation orders

Sixty-four per cent of the respondents, sampled from among residents of the entire mandatory evacuation area, left in anticipation of Hurricane Floyd (Table 15.1). This is the highest coastal average reported for the state since Hurricane Hugo, a 1989 Category 4 storm (Chapter 14).

On a regional basis (Table 15.2), evacuation rates are consistently lower than Baker's findings for the South Carolina part of his four-state study of the Hurricane Floyd evacuation (Baker, 2000). Some of this is due to differences in sampling design, especially the geographic delimitation of the sampling areas. The sampling areas used in each study cannot be completely reconciled because the surge zones, county boundaries and mandatory evacuation areas do not corre-

Table 15.1 *Hurricane Floyd evacuation response*

Did you evacuate?	Horry County mail survey (%) (n = 123)	Coastal South Carolina phone survey (%) (n = 536)
No	17 (20)	34 (183)
Yes	83 (102)	64 (344)
Tried to evacuate, but was unsuccessful	NA	2 (9)

Table 15.2 *Summary of South Carolina regional evacuation rates*

Baker 2000[a] (n = 1862)	Combined surge zones (%)	All coastal county area (%)	Non-coastal counties only (%)	USC survey mandatory evacuation areas within counties	USC phone survey[b] (%) (n = 513)
Southern SC region includes Beaufort	84	80	26	Beaufort, Jasper, Colleton, and Hampton	73
Northern SC region includes Myrtle Beach	64	59	21	Georgetown and Horry	60
Charleston and adjacent central counties	71	71	49	Charleston, Berkeley, Dorchester	55

[a] Error estimate was not provided. Baker (2000) notes that the error varies among each individual table.
[b] Error estimate is ±4.2% for the sample.
Sources: Baker (2000); this study

spond exactly. Despite this, there is some overlap in the sampling areas making comparisons possible. Second, differences may be attributed to the timing of the surveys – 6 weeks after the event, and months later. Finally, differences in the responses may be due to differences in the wording of questions, although care was taken to replicate wording from previous surveys to the greatest extent.

Among the 'experienced' Horry County respondents surveyed by mail, the evacuation rate was 83 per cent, almost 20 per cent higher than the state-wide average. However, when we compared our experienced respondents to those Horry County residents contacted in the coastal South Carolina phone survey, considerably fewer of the phone survey respondents evacuated, only 62 per cent. The differences in the evacuation rate may be due to self-selection by people particularly concerned with hurricanes in Horry County. This group constitutes our experienced population, one that clearly has a heightened sense of concern about evacuation. While the Horry County sample may not be broadly representative, it does reflect an important subset of the population involved, and can provide some valuable insights into evacuation decision-making.

Table 15.3 *Hurricane Floyd evacuation approval ratings*

Question	Coastal South Carolina phone survey (%)
A. Given what you knew about the storm before it made landfall, was evacuation the proper response to Hurricane Floyd?	
Yes	86
No	10
Don't know	4
B. On another issue … given the uncertainties about the hurricane track, was evacuation the appropriate response to Hurricane Floyd?	
Yes	84
No	8
Don't know	4

Although not all residents complied with the evacuation order, over 80 per cent agreed that calling an evacuation was appropriate (Table 15.3). The non-evacuees were more likely to disapprove of the evacuation than evacuees (chi-square results for Question $b = 0.009$; Question A sample distribution was too small for statistical analysis). This broad support for precautionary action coupled with individual decision-making is not uncommon. Gladwin (1999) reported similar findings among Florida residents surveyed following Floyd. A state-wide sample, part of a larger annual effort, found that while only 12.6 per cent (or approximately 782, 000 households) *throughout* Florida evacuated, 79 per cent of respondents said the official decisions concerning Hurricane Floyd were completely or mostly correct (Gladwin, 1999).

The factors households considered in their personal decision-making are quite diverse (Table 15.4). The severity of the storm was a top concern among respondents all along the coast. Overall, around 17 per cent of respondents throughout coastal South Carolina gave past experience as their most important reason to evacuate. The perceived safety of the home was the major factor in residents deciding to stay in an area despite evacuation orders. Responses also indicate that residents consider a variety of indirect costs in their evaluation. Evacuating entails travel costs, potential problems with re-entry to the evacuated area, care for pets (either left behind or brought along) and time away from other responsibilities. In addition, there are some differences along the coast that cannot be clearly assessed in light of the small samples. For instance, in Horry County adjacent to North Carolina, around 24 per cent of mail survey respondents cited landfall location as their primary reason to evacuate in contrast to only 6 per cent of the state-wide respondents.

Development of a hurricane-savvy resident population

Surveys in 1998 and 1999 recorded the evacuation decisions of Horry County residents for Hurricanes Bertha (1996), Fran (1996), Bonnie (1998), Dennis (1999), Floyd (1999) and Irene (1999). After six evacuations in four years, hurricane response is not an entirely hypothetical situation for residents of Horry County. Rather, longitudinal surveys indicate that some residents have developed a fairly

Table 15.4 *Explanations for evacuation behavior for Hurricane Floyd*

Did you evacuate?	Most important factor which convinced people to leave	Horry County mail (%) (n = 76)	Horry County subset of Coastal South Carolina (%) (n = 44)	Coastal South Carolina phone (%) (n = 344)
Yes	Landfall location	23.7	14.5	5.5
	Severity of the storm	36.8	18.2	23.1
	Governor's advice/order	15.8	20.5	18.8
	Past experience	5.3	18.2	17.3
	Local TV, National Weather Service, the Weather Channel	7.9	18.8	13.6
	Other (work, fear of floods, advice/actions of friends/relatives)	10.5	20.5	21.7
	Most important factor which convinced people NOT to leave	Horry County mail (%) (n = 15)	Horry County subset of Coastal South Carolina (%) (n = 22)	Coastal South Carolina phone (%) (n = 192)
No	Landfall location	6.7	4.5	6.5
	Home is safe	33.3	18.2	14.1
	Past experience	26.7	0	7.1
	Work obligations	0	0	12.4
	Didn't think anything would happen	0	9.1	7.6
	Didn't want/plan to leave	0	18.2	5.9
	Other (includes traffic concerns, work, pets, all less than 5% each in Coastal Carolina survey)	33.3	50.0	46.4

robust personalized approach to making evacuation decisions. 'Hurricane savvy' is more dependent on individuals' household circumstances and preferences than on official orders, involves diligent case-by-case monitoring of a variety of information sources and incorporates evaluations of past experiences.

Table 15.5 outlines the four-year evacuation history among our Horry County respondents. The table is arranged according to wind speed at landfall. This series allows comparison of responses to different conditions and increasing levels of experience. Considered as a temporal sequence, the relatively small changes in evacuation rates for Hurricanes Bertha, Bonnie and Fran generally seem to suggest that the so-called 'crying wolf' factor does not have a major impact on evacuation rates. Although evacuation orders accompanied each of these hurricanes, Hurricane Floyd evacuation rates were significantly higher than rates for other hurricanes that made landfall at Category 2 strength. This simple summary suggests that evacuation rates are better correlated with the maximum

Table 15.5 *Horry County longitudinal survey hurricane evacuation responses*

	Dennis	Irene	Bertha	Floyd	Bonnie	Fran
Strength at landfall	Tropical storm Aug–Sep 1999	Tropical storm Oct 1999	Category 2 hurricane July 1996	Category 2 hurricane Sep 1999	Category 2/3 hurricane Aug 1998	Category 3 hurricane Aug–Sep 1996
Max. wind speed (mph)	104	109	115	155	115	121
Evacuated	17%	7%	38%	84%	44%	46%
Did not evacuate	82%	93%	62%	16%	56%	54%

wind speeds of the hurricanes at the time the evacuation is ordered than with landfall strength.

The longitudinal study conducted by Whitehead et al (2000) of North Carolina residents' evacuations for Hurricanes Bonnie, Dennis and Floyd also indicated that evacuation rates are correlated with storm strength. In comparison with Hurricane Bonnie evacuation rates, North Carolina residents were more likely to evacuate for Floyd (Whitehead et al, 2000). As our data on Hurricanes Bertha and Bonnie illustrate, the relationship to storm intensity does not hold in all situations. Wind speed is only one dimension of the risk posed. The flood potential and probability of nearby landfall were also mentioned.

The diversity in these evacuation rates may more closely reflect sets of factors that residents consider in the evacuation decision. For Hurricane Bonnie, primary reasons for evacuating were the governor's evacuation order (10 per cent) followed by the strength of the storm and past experience (7 per cent each) (Dow et al, 1999). The governor's order was mandatory and residents can legally be forced to leave their homes. However, recent enforcement has not been that strict. In contrast, 22 per cent reported that the strength of the storm was the top reason for evacuating prior to Hurricane Floyd. The probability of a nearby landfall provided motivation for another 14 per cent of the respondents and the governor's evacuation order was the main motivation for 9 per cent.

The evacuation responses of Horry County residents are consistent with household criteria expressed in previous surveys. Following Hurricane Bonnie, in 1998, we asked these residents what they would do if another hurricane threatened the South Carolina coast. Table 15.6 reports respondents' 1998 beliefs about their future decisions against their actual 1999 evacuation for Floyd, a year later.

The largest group, 60 per cent, responded that their decision to evacuate would 'depend on ...' specified decision criteria. At least 75 per cent of this group expected they would take into account the strength of the storm, proximity to the anticipated landfall location and the governor's evacuation order (Table 15.6). Among the group that said they would evacuate in the future, 97 per cent did so. Among the group that said they would not evacuate in the future, 70 per cent did evacuate for Hurricane Floyd. Statistical analysis of these data confirms a strong relationship between anticipated and actual evacuations (chi squared = 6.81, p = 0.03), despite the changes in opinions of the respondents who had not planned to evacuate.

Table 15.6 *Anticipated and actual evacuations*

Will you evacuate in the future?	Did you evacuate for Floyd?	
Depends on	Yes (%)	No (%)
Landfall location (n =16)	75	25
Severity of the storm (n = 47)	85	15
Governor's orders (n = 8)	87	13
Yes (n = 30)	97	3
No (n = 20)	70	30

To further account for hurricane strength, the evacuations for the two Category 1 hurricanes, Dennis and Irene, were analysed. Hurricanes Dennis and Irene were also part of the 1999 hurricane season that brought Floyd. Neither of these storms showed the early strength of Floyd, although both were strong Category 1 storms while they were offshore of the Carolinas. These hurricanes generated much less concern. In late August–early September 1999, Dennis developed Category 2 strength, then weakened to Category 1 as it moved north offshore past South Carolina. Once off Cape Hatteras, North Carolina, Dennis reversed course and moved south again, making landfall in North Carolina as a tropical storm (Beven, 2000). Hurricane Irene came north along the Atlantic coast in October 1999 with Category 1 wind speeds and strengthened briefly to a weak Category 2 for the North Carolina coast. Although the eye did not make landfall, it brought heavy rainfall to the areas already flooded during Floyd (Avila, 1999). For these weaker hurricanes, the relationship between anticipated evacuation and actual actions was not as strong as we expected (Table 15.7). Even among the people who had said they would evacuate if another hurricane approached, only 35 per cent and 16 per cent, respectively, evacuated for Dennis and Irene. Of those that thought they might evacuate, only 11 per cent did so for Dennis. Similarly, these storms did little to change the minds of those who did not plan to evacuate. More specific questions on response to hurricanes of different intensity may reveal more consistent decision-making and is clearly an avenue for future research.

Our findings of robust decision strategies have been observed in North Carolina. In their longitudinal study of evacuation following Hurricanes Bonnie, Dennis and Floyd in North Carolina, Whitehead et al (2000) asked residents, in

Table 15.7 *Evacuations for Category 1 storms**

Will you evacuate in the future?	Did you evacuate for Dennis?		Did you evacuate for Irene?	
	Yes (%)	No (%)	Yes (%)	No (%)
Depends (n = 72)	11	89	4	86
Yes (n = 31)	35	65	16	84
No (n = 20)	10	90	0	100

Note: * Because of the small number of responses in some cells chi-square analysis was not conducted.

January 1999, how they would respond to future hurricanes of different intensities. They found that 83 per cent of the residents acted as they said they would for a hypothetical storm similar to Dennis (p = 0.01) and 64 per cent of the responses to the stronger hypothetical storm corresponded with the actual evacuation behaviour for Floyd (p = 0.01). Multivariate probit analysis provided further evidence that current evacuation decisions are related to past evacuation decisions and that it is inappropriate to evaluate evacuation decisions independent of the history of personal experience with hurricanes in general and evacuations in particular (Whitehead et al, 2000).

Despite limitations in asking people to anticipate their future behaviour under undefined circumstances, the consistency between behavioural intent (in 1998) and actual evacuation decisions (in 1999) is quite strong. According to the widely available Saffir-Simpson scale, Category 1 hurricanes are not associated with extreme levels of damage, away from the immediate shoreline. Under those circumstances, non-evacuation can be viewed as a rational judgement about the individual risks, albeit less precautionary than that suggested by emergency management community. It appears that, in the case of stronger hurricanes, people who do not expect to evacuate will, in fact, change their minds and leave. Our results suggest that respondents may be developing fairly robust criteria for evacuation decision-making with respect to stronger hurricanes. While there are many questions to explore here, it is clear that respondents' decisions are developing independently and drawing on information other than official emergency management sources.

A closer look at the types of information and experience that underlie the judgement reveals a variety of potential sources. The respondents in Horry County actively seek additional information from a variety of sources and have an unusual amount of experience with hurricanes. In the first survey of this group (following Hurricane Bonnie in 1998), residents identified the most reliable sources of information as the Weather Channel, local television stations and local radio. Responses to open-ended questions revealed that the assessment of reliability was based on the degree to which these sources provided current information, local information, accuracy, extensive coverage and expert staff, and also on respondents' trust in the individuals named as sources in press coverage (Dow et al, 1999). In the 1999 post-Floyd survey, this set of preferences was confirmed, as the combination of local television and the Weather Channel were identified as the most credible source of information by 70 per cent of respondents and the second most credible by 55 per cent of respondents. Less than one percent of these respondents relied on local officials or emergency managers for information. Table 15.8 summarizes their information-gathering strategies.

As a group, these Horry County residents have considerable experience with hurricanes (Table 15.9). Statistical analysis suggests that longer-term residents are more likely to remain (chi squared = 13.04, p = 0.001, note that 33 per cent of the cells are less than 5). They also invest a great deal of time staying well informed on hurricane issues.

The public's judgement of hurricane risks appears more sensitive to indirect costs and risks associated with hurricane evacuation. As indicated by responses in Table 15.4, within households, risk evaluations consider indirect costs and thus

Table 15.8 *Learning about and monitoring hurricanes (Horry County, SC)*

Measures of learning/monitoring effort associated with hurricane evacuations (n = 123)	Percentage of respondents
Leave a news source on **all day** once they are aware that a hurricane is within 2–3 days of the East Coast and might threaten South Carolina	58
Check a news source **every hour** once they are aware that a hurricane is within 2–3 days of East Coast and might threaten South Carolina	53
Consult the internet for information	30
Consult the Weather Channel	89
Want more media coverage addressing specific information such as hurricane formation and steering process, impact calculations and mitigation strategies	67
Report learning the most about hurricanes through watching the Weather Channel	38
Respond that they did not learn anything about hurricanes from the events surrounding Hurricane Floyd	61

Table 15.9 *Characteristics of past experience (Horry County, SC)*

Measures of past experience with hurricane evacuations (n = 123)	Percentage of respondents
Have been advised to evacuate over 5 times	63
Have been advised to evacuate over 10 times	19
Suffered hurricane-related damage in Floyd	44
Believe their general knowledge of hurricane processes is very good to excellent (4% believe their general knowledge of hurricane process is very limited to poor)	59
Believe their general knowledge of hurricane impacts is very good to excellent (2% believe their general knowledge of hurricane impacts is very limited to poor)	53
Have experienced over 10 hurricane seasons along the Carolina Coast	82
Have experienced over 20 hurricane seasons along the Carolina Coast	67

are not solely responses to the direct safety risks posed by a hurricane. A household's determination of an 'appropriate' level of precautionary action for themselves does not necessarily correspond to their view of an appropriate response at community levels.

Judging a successful evacuation

In the context of increased independence of public decision-making, we sought better understanding of what was expected of a successful evacuation and how that related to planning priorities among elected officials. While the governor of South Carolina has the power to 'mandate and compel' evacuation for hurricanes, in practice, evacuation is a choice that is made under pressure from officials. There is strong encouragement to leave, but police and other service personnel do not force residents from their homes. As a choice, participation depends to some extent on public confidence in the evacuation process.

Recognition of the need to maintain confidence is apparent in the response to the tremendous criticism of the Hurricane Floyd evacuation. While the evacuation succeeded in moving all of the evacuees out of harm's way, it failed to meet the expectations of many South Carolina residents. The governor apologized and promptly created a state-level task force to make recommendations for immediate improvements. That task force was the first of several public gestures designed to reassure residents that they could rely on evacuation planning, including a well-publicized trial of the lane reversal system for the most congested sections of Interstate 26.

Coastal residents were asked to evaluate the importance of ten evacuation procedures and goals. In a separate survey, we asked local elected officials to identify their priorities in evacuation planning. The results identified clear priorities and topics of mixed levels of concern as well as contrasts between public and officials' priorities.

Assuring that lives were not lost was clearly the most important goal for residents. Seventy-eight per cent of coastal residents ranked that as extremely important (Table 15.10). Responses from Horry County residents were largely consistent with those of the coastal South Carolina survey respondents. Ninety-four per cent of Horry County residents said this is extremely important. A total of 57 lives were lost during Floyd, mostly due to riverine flooding.

As discussed earlier, keeping traffic flowing and making information on evacuation routes readily available over the radio were seen as very or extremely important to approximately 90 per cent of respondents. These concerns reflect problems strongly associated with the Floyd evacuation and may not remain among the top concerns over time. The strength of support for making protecting lives a priority, however, reinforces the public endorsement of a precautionary stance towards calling evacuations. Other goals varied more in the level of importance assigned, but all characteristics were identified as extremely or very important by at least 60 per cent of respondents, with the exception of the timing of tourist evacuation.

Requiring tourists to evacuate first received the least overall support. It was not too or not at all important to 29 per cent of the total set of respondents and only extremely important to 19 per cent. In Horry County, which is dominated by Myrtle Beach, 48 per cent of residents think evacuating tourists first is extremely important.

Given the significance of concerns about traffic congestion and the uncertainties of forecasts, respondents were also asked for more detail about their expectations of timing actions during an evacuation. For an evacuation to be judged successful, most people (40 per cent) believed that the mandatory and voluntary evacuation orders should be spaced by at least 24 hours, with about 20 per cent suggesting that 12 hours would be a sufficient interval. In addition, the largest group, 67 per cent, believed that the travel delays should be no more than two

Table 15.10 *Importance of evacuation characteristics among coastal South Carolina respondents**

	Extremely important	Very important	Not too important or not important at all
Goals			
Making sure that lives are not lost (n = 519)	77.5	20.4	0.6
Providing readily available disaster assistance for rebuilding when people first return (n = 514)	46.1	41.1	1.8
Evacuating all people to safe inland areas (n = 511)	43.1	41.3	3.3
Allowing people to return home no later than three days after landfall (n = 501)	30.1	39.1	8.2
Restoring services, such as electricity, before return to their homes (n = 513)	30.0	33.9	12.3
Process considerations			
Keeping traffic flowing out of the area (n = 519)	68.6	28.3	0.8
Providing readily available information on evacuation routes on the radio (n = 518)	55.4	37.6	2.3
Conducting the evacuation in phases, from the barrier islands inward (n = 508)	44.3	43.3	2.8
Being able to change the evacuation plans based on the size and direction of the hurricane (n = 510)	36.3	47.6	3.6
Requiring tourists to evacuate first (n = 505)	19.0	28.1	29.3

* Percentages based on the number of valid responses out of a total sample of 536 respondents.

times the normal length of the trip and that they should be able to return home within one to two days (29 per cent), although the restoration of services might take an additional two to three days (48 per cent).

Residents were also asked an open-ended question regarding the types of information that should receive more coverage by the media. The question elicited a relatively low response rate of 63 per cent, perhaps because it followed two other open-ended questions near the end of the survey or because respondents did not have specific ideas. Still, 50 per cent of respondents said they wanted more information. Topics mentioned included floodplain maps of flood potential, hurricane tracks, recovery times and evacuation routes. Fifteen per cent said that current coverage was adequate.

Perhaps influenced by the Hurricane Floyd evacuation, the concerns of local elected officials intersected with those of the public on the topics of evacuation

Table 15.11 *South Carolina local elected officials' hurricane preparedness priorities*

Responses (n = 427)	%
Evacuation routes	17
Ensure public safety	11
Notify citizens	9
Planning/preparedness	9
Traffic and transportation	9

routes, traffic and transportation. The most frequently mentioned among the number one priorities for elected officials are reported in Table 15.11. The main area of difference between the officials and the public is in the emphasis placed on providing information. The public identified receiving transportation-related information as a priority as well as a desire for broader coverage of other evacuation issues. Local elected officials included notification of citizens among their top priorities. But even when all of their top three priorities, a total of 864 responses, are considered, there were only 46 mentions (5.3 per cent) of the importance of providing other kinds of information to the public during an evacuation.

Conclusions

Under a mandatory evacuation order from the governor, only 64 per cent of South Carolinians in the evacuation zones left to go somewhere safer as Hurricane Floyd approached; that is the highest rate of compliance in years. These residents actively considered the vast array of information available, particularly storm intensity and landfall, as well as their past experiences and understanding of hurricane risks to make independent decisions about how to respond to the hurricane threat. The complex matrix of information that South Carolinians rely on for evacuation decision-making only partially relies on officials for information; the role of the governor's mandatory orders seems to be diminishing.

Despite the uncertainties inherent in evacuations, over 80 per cent of the respondents agreed that calling an evacuation is an appropriate precautionary action. But, questions on how to measure success in an evacuation revealed some differences between the public and local officials, the former desiring more information on the risk and evacuation routes. This desire for risk information for independent decision-making needs to be recognized as another significant dimension of hurricane management efforts.

Estimates of tolerable disruptions due to hurricane risks yield fairly consistent results. For example, most respondents wanted at least 24 hours (or a minimum of 12 hours) between a voluntary and mandatory evacuation order. These expectations may be difficult to implement, yet they enter into evacuation decisions (directly or indirectly) and ultimately influence how people respond (i.e. leave before the mandatory warning, wait for traffic to thin out, don't leave at all). As noted earlier, the 'public' outrage over the Hurricane Floyd traffic problems did not appear to diminish support for strong precautionary actions including evacuation. But, as explanations of decisions to evacuate or stay indicate, in addition to hurricane characteristics and loss potential, individuals are considering how the evacuation process, specifically travel logistics, have worked and are working for them, especially as they develop household plans.

As surveys of Horry County residents demonstrated, some of the population along the coast is becoming hurricane savvy. This segment of the population is a new sort of audience for warnings that may require fresh strategies in risk communication and emergency management planning. As the National Research Council (1989, p8) observed in its volume *Improving Risk Communication*:

> *Because risk communication is so tightly linked to the management of risks, solutions to the problems of risk communication often entail changes in risk management and risk analysis.*

In the case of hurricane hazards, the desire for more information may be accommodated in many ways and management can be improved by preparing the desired kinds of information well in advance. For instance, as residents are monitoring the storm approach, advanced coverage by the media could provide reminders of hurricane evacuation routes, more information on the range of flooding-related risks, and enhanced coverage of the uncertainties in predicting hurricane processes that quickly alter hurricane direction and intensity. While past experience is an important factor in response, residents also report that they are actively seeking information on hurricanes to inform personal risk assessments. Risk assessment and communication could address the broader range of concerns that influence evacuation decisions, such as job responsibilities, ability to return home, or care for pets. The 2001 hurricane season preparedness activities have begun to address some of these issues. Keeping pace with the changes in information technology and anticipating their implications for risk communication and management will be one of the important measures of success in future hurricane seasons.

Acknowledgements

This research was funded by the Quick Response Program of the Natural Hazards Research and Applications Information Center at the University of Colorado with support from the National Science Foundation, and the Department of Geography, University of South Carolina. We wish to acknowledge the help of Dr Robert Oldendick, Director of the Institute of Public Affairs' Survey Research Lab, University of South Carolina and Patrice Burns, Wilson Brown, Arleen Hill, and Dr Deborah S. K. Thomas for their assistance in this research. We would also like to thank the three anonymous reviewers for their helpful suggestions. Any errors, of course, are ours.

References

AMS (American Meteorological Society) (2000) 'Policy statement: Hurricane research and forecasting', *Bulletin of the American Meteorological Society*, vol 81, no 6, pp1341–1346

Avila, L. A. (1999) 'Preliminary report Hurricane Irene, 13–19 October 1999', National Hurricane Center, Miami, FL, available at www.nhc.noaa.gov/1999irene_text.html

Baker, E. J. (1991) 'Hurricane evacuation behavior', *International Journal of Mass Emergencies and Disasters*, vol 9, no 2, pp287–310

Baker, E. J. (1994) 'Warning and response' in National Research Council (ed) *Hurricane Hugo*, National Academy Press, Washington, DC, pp202–210

Baker, E. J. (2000) *Southeast US Hurricane Evacuation Traffic Study Behavioral Analysis*, Hazards Management Group, Tallahassee, FL

Beven, J. (2000) 'Preliminary report Hurricane Dennis 24 August–7 September 1999', National Hurricane Center, Miami, FL, http://www.nhc.noaa.gov/1999dennis_text.html

Cheng, K. (1999) 'Weather.com reigned over Floyd', *Brandweek*, vol 40, p72

Cross, J. A. (1990) 'Longitudinal changes in hurricane hazard perception', *International Journal of Mass Emergencies and Disasters*, vol 8, no 1, pp31–47

Cutter, S. L. (1993) *Living with Risk*, Edward Arnold, London

Dow, K., Burns, P. and Cutter, S. L. (1999) 'To stay or leave: Residents' evaluation of hurricane evacuation orders' in A. F. Schoolmaster (ed) *Applied Geography, Vol 22*, Applied Geography Conferences, Inc., Charlotte, NC, pp107–114

Drabek, T. E. (1996) *Disaster Evacuation Behavior: Tourists and other Transients*, Program on Environment and Behavior Monograph no 58, Institute of Behavioral Sciences, University of Colorado, Boulder, CO

Drabek, T. E. (1999) 'Understanding disaster warning responses', *The Social Sciences Journal*, vol 36, pp515–523

Elsner, J. B. and Kara, A. B. (1999) *Hurricanes of the North Atlantic*, Oxford University Press, New York

Emani, S. and Kasperson, J. X. (1996) 'Disaster communication via the information superhighway: Data and observations on the 1995 hurricane season', *International Journal of Mass Emergencies and Disasters*, vol 14, no 3, pp321–342

Gladwin, H. (1999) 'Hurricane Floyd Evacuation, vol 2000', Institute for Public Opinion Research, www.fiu.edu/orgs/ipor/foydevac/index.htm

HMG (Hazards Management Group, Inc.) (1985) *South Carolina Hurricane Evacuation Study: Behavioral Analysis*, Hazards Management Group, Inc., Tallahassee, FL

Kasperson, R. E. and Kasperson, J. X. (1996) 'The social amplification and attenuation of risk', *Annals of the American Academy of Political and Social Science*, vol 545, pp95–105

Kasperson, R. E., Renn, O., Slovic, P., Brown, H. S., Emel, J., Goble, R., Kasperson, J. X. and Ratick, S. (1988) The social amplification of risk: A conceptual framework', *Risk Analysis*, vol 8, no 2, pp177–187

Mileti, D. (1999) *Disasters by Design*, Joseph Henry Press, Washington, DC

National Research Council (NRC) (1989) *Improving Risk Communication*, National Academy Press, Washington, DC

Otway, H. (1992) 'Public wisdom, expert fallibility: Toward a contextual theory of risk' in S. Krimsky and D. Golding (eds) *Social Theories of Risk*, Praeger, Westport, CT, pp215–228

Pielke, R. A. jr and Piekle, R. A. sr (1997) *Hurricanes: Their Nature and Impacts on Society*, Wiley, New York

Sheets, R. C. (1995) 'Stormy weather', *Forum for Applied Research and Public Policy*, vol 10, no 1, pp5–15

Sorensen, J. H. (2000) 'Hazard warning systems: Review of 20 years of progress', *Natural Hazards Review*, vol 1, no 2, pp119–125

Sorensen, J. H. and Mileti, D. S. (1988) 'Warning and evacuation: Answering some basic questions', *Industrial Crisis Quarterly*, vol 2, pp195–209

Trettin, L. and Musham, C. (2000) 'Is trust a realistic goal of environmental risk communication?', *Environment and Behavior*, vol 32, no 3, pp410–426

Trigoboff, D. (1999) 'Frantically following Floyd', *Broadcasting & Cable*, vol 129, p16

Whitehead, J., Edwards, B., Van Willigen, M., Maiolo, J. and Wilson, K. (2000) 'Hurricane evacuation behavior: A preliminary comparison of Bonnie, Dennis and Floyd', report for North Carolina Department of Crime Control and Public Safety, April

Weinstein, N. D. (1989) 'Effects of personal experience on self-protective behavior', *Psychological Bulletin*, vol 105, no 1, pp31–50

Zimmerman, C. (1999) 'In the eye of the storm: Floyd's lessons help sites brace for traffic spikes', *Internet Week*, p1

Part IV

Environmental Justice

16

Race, Class and Environmental Justice

Susan L. Cutter

The growth of the environmental justice movement in the US surprised even the most seasoned of policy-makers by its speed and the magnitude of its impact on US national policy (Russell, 1989; Inhaber, 1990; Grossman, 1991; Goldman, 1992). Responding to intense public pressure from environmental and civil rights activists for close to a decade, the US Environmental Protection Agency (EPA) established an Environmental Equity Workgroup in 1990. The workgroup had two primary tasks:

1 to evaluate the evidence that racial minority and low-income groups bore a disproportionate burden of environmental risks; and
2 to identify factors that contributed to different risk burdens and to suggest strategies for improvement.

In 1992 their signature report was released (USEPA, 1992a), partially reaffirming earlier studies that found a strong correlation between the location of commercial hazardous-waste facilities in communities and the percentage of minority residents in those same communities. By February 1994, President Clinton signed Executive Order 12898, requiring every federal agency to achieve the principle of environmental justice by addressing and ameliorating the human health or environmental effects of the agency's programmes, policies and activities on minority and low-income populations in the US (Bullard, 1994a).

How much of the new policy is based on solid evidence of discrimination and how much is a direct response to the pressure-politics activist groups? This progress report reviews some of the recent literature on environmental equity and the empirical evidence supporting claims of environmental injustice in the US. While the review focuses on the North American experience, the issue of environmental justice in other regions will intensify in the years to come as nations implement international accords for sustainable development.

Note: Reprinted, with permission, from *Progress in Human Geography*, vol 19, no 1, Susan L. Cutter, 'Race, class and environmental justice', pp107–118. © Hodder Arnold Journals, 1995

What is Environmental Justice?

A healthy environment is a basic right of all the Earth's inhabitants, a right reaffirmed by the Rio declaration (UN, 1992). Yet we know that environmental risks are unevenly distributed within and between societies, and we know that these risks affect populations differently. Inequities in risk exposure, risk reduction and risk compensation are crucial elements in contemporary management issues, so much so that the concepts of fairness and equity are now regular components in decision-making for all remedial actions (National Academy of Engineering, 1986; Cutter, 1993).

Environmental equity versus environmental justice

Environmental equity is a broad term that is used to describe the disproportionate effects of environmental degradation on people and places. There are many ways to view environmental equity. For example, most of the social science literature examines either the causal mechanism of inequity or the spatial-temporal distribution of benefits and burdens (Greenberg, 1993; Kasperson, 1994). The former is referred to as process equity and the latter as outcome equity.

Environmental equity originates from three major sources of dissimilarity – social, generational, procedural. Social equity refers to the role of social and economic factors (class, race, gender, ethnicity, political power) in environmental degradation and resource consumption. The juxtaposition of economic activities, largely determined by locational criteria (property values, transportation access) and the social geography of places creates the landscape of risk. Classism, racism and sexism all contribute to social inequalities. Generational equity (Weiss, 1989, 1990) is a framework of legal norms to bring justice to future generations from current and past practices. In other words, public policy decisions are governed by the concept of fairness to future generations, so that our children and grandchildren will have the same access to resources and the same quality of life as we do. Generational equity ensures that society does not mortgage the environmental future for a present short-term economic gain. Procedural equity is the extent to which governmental rules and regulations, enforcement and international treaties and sanctions are applied in a non-discriminatory way.

For many, the phrase 'environmental equity' implies an equal sharing of risk burdens, not an overall reduction in the burdens themselves (Lavelle, 1994). Environmental justice is a more politically charged term, one that connotes some remedial action to correct an injustice imposed on a specific group of people, mostly people of colour in the US (Bullard, 1994b). The principle of environmental justice guarantees:

1 the protection from environmental degradation;
2 prevention of adverse health impacts from deteriorating environmental conditions before the harm occurs, not afterwards;
3 mechanisms for assigning culpability and shifting the burden of proof of contamination to polluters not residents; and
4 redressing the impacts with targeted remedial action and resources.

For aggrieved parties, environmental justice guarantees three basic rights: the right to information, the right to a hearing and the right to compensation (Capek, 1993).

Environmental justice according to whom?

The term environmental racism was coined in 1982 by Benjamin Chavis, then head of the United Church of Christ's Commission for Racial Justice (Mushak, 1993). He states:

> *Environmental racism is racial discrimination in environmental policy-making and enforcement of regulations and laws, the deliberate targeting of communities of color for toxic waste facilities, the official sanctioning of the presense of life threatening poisons and pollutants in communities of color, and the history of excluding people of color from leadership of the environmental movement.* (Chavis, 1994, pxii)

Within the activist community, environmental justice is now the preferred term and the one that I will use. Environmental racism is part of a historical system of discriminatory exploitation, but is too restrictive a term for the current movement. Environmental justice on the other hand, moves beyond racism to include others (regardless of race or ethnicity) who are deprived of their environmental rights, such as women, children and the poor. Environmental justice is political action and social mobilization that marshals public and private commitment to change. By merging environmental, social equality and civil rights movements into one potent political force, environmental justice advocates have considerable influence on public policy at all levels.

The environmental justice movement redefined and expanded the dominant environmental paradigm during the last decade and partially reduced the elitism that permeates modern environmental organizations and their causes. The shifting in focus from the 'white upper-class environmental rhetoric' surrounding the preservation of distant pristine habitats to a more localized strategy on environmental improvements in the quality of life closer to the homes of affected residents is one tangible outcome. For example, locally based activism against toxics now includes working-class people, inner-city residents and people of colour all working towards a cleaner and safer environment. Since the production of toxics and exposure to industrial hazards coincides with low income, working class and communities of colour, it is not unexpected that the toxics movement has its greatest success in urban areas. Politically, the Black Congressional Caucus has the best environmental voting record in Congress reflecting the plight of constituents who are victimized by poor environmental quality.

In theory, the principle of environmental justice means that we can no longer ignore who benefits and loses in the environmental game or in whose backyard the unwanted facility is located (Wenz, 1988). The increasing salience of environmental degradation to urban residents and people of colour means a broader-based constituency for action (Bullard and Wright, 1990), resulting in a new form of 'ecopopulism' (Szasz, 1994). For the US, it means that the NIMBY (not in my back yard) syndrome has been eclipsed by the BANANA (build absolutely nothing anywhere near anybody) syndrome (Knox, 1993). Unfortunately, this attitude and its political manifestation often result in the relocation of toxic industries from developed to developing countries, thereby continuing the patterns of environmental injustice only at a different spatial scale (Taliman, 1989).

The Environmental Justice Movement

By most accounts, the environmental justice movement began in 1982 in Warren County, North Carolina, when the state selected a site (Afton) to host a hazardous waste landfill containing 30,000 cubic yards of PCB-contaminated soil (Geiser and Waneck, 1983). Residents, mostly African American, rural and poor, were joined in their protests by national civil rights groups, environmental groups, clergy and members of the Black Congressional Caucus. Although unsuccessful in halting the landfill construction, the Warren County demonstrations marked the first time that African Americans mobilized a national broad-based coalition in response to an impending environmental threat. The Warren County demonstrations were the first of many community of colour struggles over toxic substances.

The publication of two studies, one by the government (USGAO, 1983), and the other by the United Church of Christ's Commission for Racial Justice (UCC, 1987), galvanized the movement and provided some much-needed empirical support for the claims of environmental racism. Bullard's *Dumping in Dixie* (1990) added further empirical support for the disproportionate burden of toxic waste on minority communities.

In January 1990, the University of Michigan's School of Natural Resources sponsored a conference on race and the incidence of environmental hazards, bringing together scholar-activists interested in the issues and providing some national visibility to the debates on environmental equity (Bryant and Mohai, 1992). Later the same year, the EPA established its Workgroup on Environmental Equity. By October 1991, the First National People of Color Environmental Leadership Summit took place, organized and attended by more than 650 grass roots and national leaders representing more than 300 environmental groups. Many of the delegates, participants and observers shared their experiences and early struggles and offered networking tips on surviving 'environmental sacrifice zones' (Bullard, 1994b).

By 1992, the EPA formally established its Office of Environmental Equity and the Workgroup on Environmental Equity had finished its report (USEPA, 1992a). Critics of the report contend that EPA did not go far enough in examining its current activities, including its own role in re-enforcing environmental inequalities through its own decision-making procedures (Collin, 1993; Mohai, 1993; Roque, 1993). Legislatively, a number of bills were introduced into Congress, most notably the Environmental Justice Act 1992, first sponsored by Senator Albert Gore (Tennessee) and Congressman John Lewis (Georgia). Individual states also introduced legislation to address environmental justice concerns, with Arkansas and Louisiana enacting the first environmental justice laws at the state level. Finally, President Clinton signed Executive Order 12898 (federal actions to address environmental justice in minority populations and low-income populations) into law on 11 February 1994.

Proving Environmental Discrimination: Outcome Equity

The empirical evidence for environmental discrimination is mixed. The ambiguity in the research results is a consequence of four factors:

1   the environmental threat chosen for analysis;
2   the geographic scale or areal unit chosen for measurement;
3   the subpopulation selected; and
4   the time frame.

For example, most of the recent empirical work examines hazardous waste and other toxic substances. During the 1970s, however, air pollution was the more thoroughly investigated environmental hazard (Mohai and Bryant, 1992a, 1992b).

Unfortunately, poor environmental quality is associated with economically depressed regions wherever they are located. Hall and Kerr (1991) illustrate this quite graphically in their *Green Index* which maps the regional disparities in environmental quality. The environmental pillaging of the Deep South is quite apparent with every state in the region (Louisiana, Mississippi, Alabama, South Carolina, Georgia) clustered at the bottom of the list on most of the 256 environmental indicators. Is it coincidental that these states also have the highest percentages of African American residents as well?

As mentioned previously, the original USGAO (1983) study examined racial inequalities in communities surrounding four of the largest hazardous waste landfills in the south. Only four sites were selected (one in Alabama, two in South Carolina and the Warren County, NC, facility) and, of those four, three had a majority of African American residents in the surrounding communities (e.g. 90 per cent in the Alabama site, 38 per cent in the Sumter County, SC site, 52 per cent in the Chester County, SC site, and 66 per cent in Warren County, NC facility). While the study was the first of its kind, the statistical validity of the results is questionable. There is no way of comparing these sites to other places in the country, nor to other communities without hazardous waste facilities within the region. Just how representative are these communities and the findings? Despite these problems, the USGAO study did point to a potential problem regarding race and the incidence of hazardous waste sites.

The other oft-cited study is the United Church of Christ's Commission for Racial Justice (UCC, 1987). This study was more systematic, focusing on commercial hazardous waste facilities and uncontrolled waste sites as the environmental threats. Using a national sample based on the five-digit zip code, this study found that '... race proved to be the most significant among variables tested in association with the location of commercial hazardous waste facilities,' (UCC, 1987, pxiii). In fact, communities with one or more commercial facilities had twice the percentage of minority residents than those communities without commercial hazardous waste facilities. They also found that three out of five African

American and Hispanic residents lived in communities with one or more uncontrolled toxic waste sites.

National perspectives

Recent research highlights additional ambiguities in the empirical support for environmental justice. In their investigation of the siting of hazardous waste treatment, storage and disposal facilities (TSD), Anderton et al (1994) used census tracts within a national sample of metropolitan areas (SMSA) as their areal unit for measurement. They found no statistically significant differences in the racial composition of tracts that contained TSD facilities and those that did not. When they changed scale (aggregating to large spatial units within a three-mile radius of the site or examining only the largest SMSAs), dramatically different results were produced. It was at the aggregation level that the association between race and TSD facilities location was most pronounced. Regional variations in the findings were also acknowledged.

The distribution of Superfund National Priority List (NPL) sites by county for the entire US shows no statistical link between poorer counties and the number of Superfund sites (Hird, 1993). On the other hand, counties with NPL sites do have a slighter higher percentage of minority residents (holding other factors such as income constant). Another study (Zimmerman, 1993) also examined about 800 NPL sites in the process of being cleaned up. Locationally, Zimmerman found that racial and ethnic minorities were over-represented in communities (determined by minor civil division designations) for sites in large urban areas, otherwise they are under-represented with respect to the national average. In looking at clean-up decisions, she found a more pronounced relationship between minority status and clean-up status with predominately African American communities having relatively fewer remediation plans than other communities.

Greenberg (1993) conducted a national analysis of waste-to-energy facilities (WTEFs) comparing the towns where the facilities were located and their service areas. In a series of tests he illustrated the effect of town size and facility capacity, geographic unit and subpopulations in determining outcome inequity. He found that '... inequity in the case of WTEFs depends not only on the geography of LULUs [locally unwanted land uses], but also the geography of the characteristic being tested for inequity' (Greenberg, 1993, p235). Greenberg also found the strongest inequity was not based on income or race/ethnicity but on age. A disproportionate number of these facilities are located in communities with high percentages of elderly residents. In the same article he also provides a detailed case study of WTEF in New Jersey, where the results were also mixed.

Using a related measure for equity in incinerator-siting practices, Costner and Thornton (1990) found that the percentage of minorities in the US communities with existing incinerators was 89 per cent higher than the national average. In their analysis of the siting of new incinerators, Costner and Thornton found that the proposed host communities had minority populations 60 per cent higher than the national average.

Finally, Lester et al (1994) also produced ambiguous results. In examining a number of environmental stressors (nuclear sites, NPL sites, military sites, landfills, toxic air pollutants, etc.) by state, they found only slight support for the environmental racism hypothesis. This is largely a function of the scale (state level) of their analysis.

State surveys

While there is some indication of environmental inequity at the national level, it is by no means definitive. What about at a more localized scale? Greenberg (1994) examined New Jersey's 113 NPL (Superfund sites) located in 90 municipalities in order to find out if priority ratings were associated with race and ethnicity. Using the federal Hazard Ranking System (HRS) as a measure of severity, Greenberg found higher rankings were not associated with percentage of minority residents in municipalities; in fact, quite the opposite was true although these differences were not statistically significant. His primary explanation is that remediation (as a function of priority ratings) in New Jersey is driven by the threat to potable groundwater supplies. Most of the lower-income minority communities rely on surface-water drinking sources, hence NPL sites in these areas often result in lower priorities for clean-up. The question that was not asked, of course, is whether the federal HRS itself is equitable.

In another state-wide analysis, Cutter (1994) examined three risk indicators – number of acute airborne toxic releases, amount of toxic releases and amount of hazardous waste generated – for the 46 counties in South Carolina. Based on the geography of emissions, she found that the most affected residents lived in racially mixed, more urbanized counties with average incomes. In a more detailed analysis of South Carolina, Holm (1994) tested the correlation between location of hazardous treatment, storage and disposal (TSD) facilities, and race and income. She used census tracts and block groups as her spatial unit. According to Holm, TSD facilities are clustered around urbanized areas with high population densities, but are not disproportionately located in minority or economically disadvantaged communities.

Local domains

In one of the first metropolitan-level studies, Bullard (1983) found that solid waste sites were not randomly scattered throughout metropolitan Houston, but were more often found in largely African American neighbourhoods. According to Bullard, this 50-year pattern is a result of Houston's lack of zoning as well as the institutional racism that permeated the region.

In metropolitan Detroit, Mohai and Bryant (1992b) examined racial biases in the location of commercial hazardous waste facilities. The conclusion is that race is a better predictor of proximity to these sites than income. In fact, if you were a minority resident your chance was four times greater that you lived within a mile of a hazardous waste facility than if you were white.

Municipal solid-waste landfills and petrochemical plants are the environmental focus of Adeola's (1994) study of the Baton Rouge metropolitan area. Using self-reported measures of proximity and race based on a random sample of residents in the metropolitan region, he found statistically significant results that race and proximity to the environmental threats were related. African Americans were more likely to reside near hazardous waste facilities than other racial or ethnic groups.

Burke's (1993) analysis of Toxic Release Inventory (TRI) sites in Los Angeles shows a clear relationship between minority percentage and number of facilities within census tracts. Her study found that the number of TRI facilities increased with higher percentages of minority residents, lower per capita incomes and lower population densities. Hispanics are the most disproportionately exposed subpopulation in Los Angeles. Although Burke found race, ethnicity and class important predictors, she could not conclude which of them had greater significance.

Threats to Barrios, Ghettos and Reservations: Process Equity

Process equity, as distinguished from outcome equity, refers to some of the underlying causes of environmental inequities such as basic social inequalities, siting decisions, clean-up or differential enforcement of laws and regulations. The issue posing the greatest difficulty in environmental justice research is which came first. Were the LULUs or sources of environmental threats sited in communities because they were poor, contained people of colour and/or were politically weak? Or were the LULUs originally placed in communities with little reference to race or economic status and, over time, the racial composition of the area changed as a result of white flight, depressed housing prices and a host of other social ills? In other words, did the residents come to the nuisance or was the nuisance imposed on them (voluntarily or involuntarily) (Jones, 1993; Mitchell, 1993)?

Little of the environmental justice research examines causality except in very broad terms. For example, racism, economic inequality and economic segmentation are often cited as the root cause of environmental inequalities (Colquette and Robertson, 1991; Lazarus, 1993; Mitchell, 1993). Ong and Blumenberg (1993) describe in a very general way the environmental and occupational risks to Latinos in southern California, who bear a disproportionate share of exposures to industrial lead pollution, air pollution and hazardous waste sites. Gedicks (1993, 1994), on the other hand, places the cause on resource colonialism and multinational corporate greed, particularly as it affects indigenous peoples and their land. A recent example is the controversy surrounding the establishment of a private nuclear waste and storage facility on Apache territory in New Mexico. It should be noted that the facility is being actively sought by the Apache nation as a source of revenue. Unfortunately, none of these studies provides any empirical support for causality.

In his exposé of environmental change in Gary, Indiana, Hurley (1988) traces the historical demographic changes in that city over three decades. He found little correlation between particulate pollution and minority residents prior to 1950 but, since then, higher pollution levels were increasingly associated with poor minority areas of the city. Hurley suggests that increasing exposures were a function of increasing African American migration into the city, into those areas where white resistance to integration was the lowest (primarily adjacent to industrial areas). He admits, however, that the causes of such migrations and locational decisions are not well understood.

In an attempt to address the 'which came first?' question, Been (1994) examined causality at the time of the siting decision. She examined the market dynamics and their influence in the disproportionate siting of LULUs and found that the role of market dynamics was uneven. To clarify further, Been re-examined the neighbourhood demographics at the time of the original siting of the LULUs in the USGAO (1983) and Bullard (1983) studies and traces these demographic changes over time. She found some evidence that the siting process was flawed and differentially affected minority residents in both studies. However, Been found no evidence that host communities became increasingly populated by minority residents, or that the landfills changed neighbourhood desirability. In the Bullard study, market dynamics did play a small role – property values and rents did decline and the percentage of minority residents increased as a result of the lack of opportunities to move elsewhere. Neither study is definitive and we are still left with the issue of which came first, the people of colour and/or the poor or the LULU.

Finally, a 1992 study by the *National Law Journal* (Lavelle and Coyle, 1992) examined the relationship between race and enforcement of environmental laws by the EPA. They found that the EPA discriminates against minority communities with respect to clean-up decisions and enforcement of existing environmental laws. In examining every environmental lawsuit from 1985 to 1991 and every residential NPL site (1777) since the Superfund programme came into existence (1980), the research found that financial penalties were around 500 per cent higher for violations affecting predominately white communities as opposed to minority ones. Furthermore, it took 20 per cent longer to get hazardous waste sites listed on the federal priority system for clean-up if those sites were located in communities of colour (Lavelle, 1994). Community income levels made no difference.

Righting the Wrong

Regardless of specific causality, there is substantial evidence that people of colour in the US bear a disproportionate burden of environmental hazards. I suspect this is true in other nations as well. But what can be done about it?

Enforcement and regulation

A primary focus of the environmental justice movement is differential enforcement of environmental protection statutes (USEPA, 1992b). The use of existing environmental laws to challenge construction and operating permits, siting decisions, discharge permit violations and under-enforced environmental statutes such as the Lead Contamination Control Act is one strategy in a hierarchy of legal options (Brown, 1993; Chase, 1993; Lazarus, 1993; Cole, 1994). Community-based advocacy and representation (Cole, 1992) and land-use planning law (Collin, 1992) are two additional mechanisms that can be used to overcome decades of exclusionary zoning ordinances. The development of new legislation targeted to environmental justice concerns such as the Environmental Justice Act

1992 (HR5326), the Environmental Equal Rights Act 1993 (HR1924) or the Environmental Risk Reduction Act (S2132) (Harding and Holdren, 1993) is another avenue.

Toxic torts and judicial remedies

Case law on environmental justice is sparse, but rapidly growing. It covers two areas: toxic tons and equal protection doctrines. The principal remedies for racial discrimination are the equal protection clause of the Fourteenth Amendment and Section 1983 of the Civil Right Act 1866. Under both statutes, the establishment of racial intent is required, a burden of proof that is hard to accomplish in environmental justice claims. Illustrating the disparate impact of governmental action does not show racial animus and as such does not meet the 'intent' provision in case law (Godsil, 1991). Thus far, civil rights law has not been an effective mechanism for achieving environmental justice nor is it likely to be as effective as environmental and public health laws (Cole, 1994).

Toxic torts are a more successful judicial remedy. In seeking monetary damages, people claim injuries to their health, property or environment as a result of criminal or negligent conduct or failure to act by an industrial firm. Increasingly, the courts are asked to resolve claims against industry by local residents or the federal government. Some have been successfully settled, others are more ubiquitous.

Grass roots activism

Another alternative is direct social change. Much of the social science literature examines the development of the people of colour grass roots environmental movements and their effectiveness in garnering social change (Brown and Mikkelsen, 1990; Heiman, 1990; Piller, 1991; Brown and Masterson-Allen, 1994) or mobilizing the black community for environmental justice (Bullard and Wright, 1990, 1992; Almeida, 1994; Bullard, 1993, 1994b). Still other studies simply foster awareness of the issues (Fitton et al, 1993; Link, 1993) providing information, contacts and maps of affected communities (Goldman, 1991). The use of litigation, demonstrations, regulatory/zoning hearings, etc. are part and parcel of the bag of tricks local organizers can use (Austin and Schill, 1991). Because of the duality of the environmental-economic agenda, many groups argue for the right to a clean industry and the right to assist in pollution prevention policies as they affect the community (Austin and Schill, 1991).

The Next Step

The empirical claims for environmental racism are not definitive, as this review has shown. The debates currently underway are not about the salience of concern, but rather how we define, classify and measure inequity (Zimmerman, 1994). Specifically, much more research is needed on what thresholds constitute an equity problem, what spatial unit is most appropriate for exploring equity issues and over what time frame. We obviously need better and more robust data to support inequity claims one way or the other, especially if those claims form the basis for litigation or public policy decisions. Geographers can make a major contribution to the formulation of equitable public policies by producing the methodological support for equity analyses. Scale is a central issue as I have shown, as is the ability to manipulate social and environmental data. Environmental equity is an inherently geographic problem, yet we are noticeably absent from the literature. We need more involvement by our research community to ensure that public policies are based on sound social science, not hyperbole. Only then can we truly ensure environmental justice for everyone.

References

Adeola, F. O. (1994) 'Environmental hazards, health, and racial inequality in hazardous waste distribution', *Environment and Behaviour*, vol 26, pp99–126

Almeida, P. (1994) 'Network for environmental and economic justice in the southwest: Interview with Richard Moore', *Capitalism, Nature, Socialism*, vol 5, pp21–54

Anderton, D. L., Anderson, A. B., Rossi, P. H., Oakes, J. M., Fraser, M. R., Webber, E. W. and Calabrese, E. J. (1994) 'Hazardous waste facilities: "Environmental equity" issues in metropolitan areas', *Evaluation Review*, vol 18, pp123–140

Austin, R. and Schill, M. (1991) 'Black, brown, poor and poisoned: Minority grass roots environmentalism and the quest for eco-justice', *Kansas Journal of Law and Public Policy*, summer, pp69–82

Been, V. (1994) 'Locally undesirable land uses in minority neighborhoods: Disproportionate siting or market dynamics?', *Yale Law Journal*, vol 103, pp1383–1422

Brown, A. L. (1993) 'Environmental justice: New civil rights frontier', *Trial*, July, pp48–53

Brown, P. and Masterson-Allen, S. (1994) 'The toxic waste movement: A new type of activism', *Society and Natural Resources*, vol 7, pp269–287

Brown, P. and Mikkelsen, E. J. (1990) *No Safe Place: Toxic Waste, Leukemia, and Community Action*, University of California Press, Berkeley, CA

Bryant, B. and Mohai, P. (eds) (1992) *Race and the Incidence of Environmental Hazards: A Time for Discourse*, Westview Press, Boulder, CO

Bullard, R. D. (1983) 'Solid waste sites and the black Houston community', *Sociological Inequity*, vol 53, pp273–288

Bullard, R. D. (1990) *Dumping in Dixie: Race, Class, and Environmental Quality*, Westview Press, Boulder, CO

Bullard, R. D. (ed) (1993) *Confronting Environmental Racism: Voices from the Grassroots*, South End Press, Boston, MA

Bullard, R. D. (1994a) 'Overcoming racism in environmental decision-making', *Environment*, vol 36, pp10–20, 39–44

Bullard, R. D. (ed) (1994b) *Unequal Protection: Environmental Justice and Communities of Color*, Sierra Club Books, San Francisco, CA

Bullard, R. D. and Wright, B. H. (1990) 'Mobilizing the black community for environmental justice', *Journal of Intergroup Relations*, vol 17, pp33–43

Bullard, R. D. and Wright, B. H. (1992) 'The quest for environmental equity: Mobilizing the African-American community for social change' in R. E. Dunlap and A. G. Mertig (eds) *American Environmentalism: The US Environmental Movement 1970–1990*, Taylor and Francis, Philadelphia, PA, pp39–49

Burke, L. (1993) 'Race and environmental equity: A geographic analysis in Los Angeles', *Geo Info Systems*, October, pp44–50

Capek, S. M. (1993) 'The "environmental justice" frame: A conceptual discussion and an application', *Social Problems*, vol 40, pp5–24

Chase, A. R. (1993) 'Assessing and addressing problems posed by environmental racism', *Rutgers Law Review*, vol 45, pp335–369

Chavis, B. F. jr (1994) 'Preface' in R. D. Bullard (ed) *Unequal Protection: Environmental Justice and Communities of Color*, Sierra Club Books, San Francisco, CA, ppxi–xii

Cole, L. W. (1992) 'Empowerment as the key to environmental protection: The need for environmental poverty law', *Ecology Law Quarterly*, vol 19, pp619–683

Cole, L. W. (1994) 'Environmental justice litigation: Another stone in David's sling', *Fordham Urban Law Journal*, vol 21, pp523–545

Collin, R. W. (1992) 'Environmental equity: A law and planning approach to environmental racism', *Virginia Environmental Law Journal*, vol 11, pp495–546

Collin, R. W. (1993) 'Environmental equity and the need for government intervention: Two proposals', *Environment*, vol 35, pp41–43

Colquette, K. and Robertson, E. B. (1991) 'Environmental racism: The causes, consequences, and commendations', *Tulane Environmental Law Journal*, vol 5, pp153–207

Costner, P. and Thornton, J. (1990) *Playing with Fire: Hazardous Waste Incineration, a Greenpeace Report*, Greenpeace, Washington, DC

Cutter, S. L. (1993) *Living with Risk: The Geography of Technological Hazards*, Edward Arnold, London

Cutter, S. L. (1994) 'The burdens of toxic risks: Are they fair?', *Business and Economic Review*, vol 41, pp3–7

Fitton, L. J., Choe, J. and Regan, R. (1993) *Environmental Justice: Annotated Bibliography*, Center for Policy Alternatives, Washington, DC

Gedicks, A. (1993) *The New Resource Wars: Native and Environmental Struggles Against Multinational Corporations*, South End Press, Boston, MA

Gedicks, A. (1994) 'Racism and resource colonization', *Capitalism, Nature, Socialism*, vol 5, pp55–76

Geiser, K. and Waneck, G. (1983) 'PCBs and Warren County', *Science for the People*, July/August, pp13–17

Godsil, R. D. (1991) 'Remedying environmental racism', *Michigan Law Review*, vol 90, pp394–427

Goldman, B. A. (1991) *The Truth about Where you Live: An Atlas for Action on Toxins and Mortality*, Random House, New York

Goldman, R. D. (1992) 'Polluting the poor', *The Nation*, 5 October, pp348–349

Greenberg, M. R. (1993) 'Proving environmental inequity in siting locally unwanted land uses', *4 Risk – Issues in Health and Safety*, vol 4, pp235–252

Greenberg, R. D. (1994) 'Separate and not equal: Health-environmental risk and economic-social impacts in remediating hazardous waste sites', draft of chapter subsequently published in 1996 in S. K. Majumdar, F. J. Brenner, K. W. Miller and L. M. Rosenfeld (eds) *Environmental Contaminants, Ecosystems and Human Health*, Pennsylvania Academy of Sciences, Philadelphia, PA

Grossman, K. (1991) 'Environmental racism', *The Crisis*, vol 98, pp14–17, 31–32

Hall, B. and Kerr, M. L. (1991) *1991–1992 Green Index: A State-by-State Guide to the Nation's Environmental Health*, Island Press, Washington, DC

Harding, A. K. and Holdren, G. R. (1993) 'Environmental equiry and the environmental professional', *Environmental Science and Technology*, vol 27, pp1990–1993

Heiman, M. (1990) 'From "not in my backyard" to "not in anybody's backyard": Grass roots challenge to hazardous waste facility siting', *Journal of the American Planning Association* summer, pp359–362

Hird, J. A. (1993) 'Environmental policy and equity: The case of Superfund', *Journal of Policy Analysis and Management*, vol 12, pp323–343

Holm, D. M. (1994) 'Environmental inequities in South Carolina: The distribution of hazardous waste facilities', unpublished Master's thesis, Department of Geography, University of South Carolina, Columbia, SC

Hurley, A. (1988) 'The social biases of environmental change in Gary, Indiana, 1945–1980', *Environmental Review*, vol 12, pp1–19

Inhaber, H. (1990) 'Hands up for toxic waste', *Nature*, vol 347, pp611–12

Jones, S. C. (1993) 'Inequities of industrial siting addressed', *Natural Law Journal*, vol 15, p.20

Kasperson, R. E. (1994) 'Global environmental hazards: Political issues in societal responses' in G. J. Demko and W. B. Wood (eds) *Reordering the World: Geopolitical Perspectives on the 21st Century*, Westview Press, Boulder, CO, pp141–166

Knox, R. J. (1993) 'Environmental equity', *Journal of Environmental Health*, vol 55, pp32–34

Lavelle, M. (1994) 'Environmental justice' in World Resources Institute (ed) *The 1994 Information Please Environmental Almanac*, Houghton-Mifflin, Boston, MA, pp103–192

Lavelle, M. and Coyle, M. (1992) 'Unequal protection: The racial divide in environmental law', *National Law Journal*, 21 September, supplement

Lazarus, R. J. (1993) 'Pursuing "environmental justice": The distributional effects of environmental protection', *Northwestern University Law Review*, vol 87, pp787–857

Lester, J. P., Allen, D. W. and Milburn-Lauer, D. A. (1994) 'Race, class, and environmental quality: An examination of environmental racism in the American states', unpublished manuscript

Link, T. (1993) 'Environmental racism/environmental equity: A bibliography', *Green Library Journal*, winter, pp17–22

Mitchell, C. M. (1993) 'Environmental racism: Race as a primary factor in the selection of hazardous waste sites', *National Black Law Journal*, vol 12, pp176–188

Mohai, P. (1993) 'Commentary: Environmental equity', *Environment*, vol 35, pp2–4

Mohai, P. and Bryant, B. (1992a) 'Environmental racism: Reviewing the evidence' in B. Rosenfeld and P. Mohai (eds) *Race and the Incidence of Environmental Hazards: A Time for Discourse*, Westview Press, Boulder, CO, pp163–176

Mohai, P. and Bryant, B. (1992b) 'Environmental injustice: Weighing race and class as factors in the distribution of environmental hazards' *University of Colorado Law Review*, vol 63, pp921–932

Mushak, B. (1993) 'Environmental equity: A new coalition for justice', *Environmental Health Perspectives*, vol 101, pp478–483

National Academy of Engineering (1986) *Hazards: Technology and Fairness*, National Academy Press, Washington, DC

Ong, P. M. and Blumenberg, E. (1993) 'An unnatural trade-off: Latinos and environmental justice' in R. Morales and F. Bonilla (eds) *Latinos in a Changing US Economy*, Sage, Beverly Hills, CA, pp207–225

Piller, C. (1991) *The Fail-safe Society: Community Defiance and the End of American Technological Optimism*, University of California Press, Berkeley, CA

Roque, J. A. (1993) 'Environmental equity: Reducing risk for all communities', *Environment*, vol 35, pp25–28, 'Commentary and reply', *Environment*, vol 35, p4

Russell, D. (1989) 'Environmental racism', *The Amicus Journal*, spring, pp22–32

Szasz, A. (1994) *Ecopopulism: Toxic Waste and the Movement for Environmental Justice*, University of Minnesota Press, Minneapolis, MN

Taliman, V. (1989) 'Toxic waste dumping in the Third World', *Race and Class*, vol 30, pp47–56

UCC (United Church of Christ Commission for Racial Justice) (1987) *Toxic Wastes and Race in the United States*, United Church of Christ, New York

UN (United Nations) (1992) *Agenda 21: Programme of Action for Sustainable Development*, United Nations, New York

USEPA (US Environmental Protection Agency) (1992a) *Environmental Equity: Reducing Risk for all Communities*, Government Printing Office, Washington, DC

USEPA (1992b) 'Environmental protection: Has it been fair?', *EPA Journal*, vol 18, pp1–64

USGAO (US General Accounting Office) (1983) *Siting of Hazardous Waste Landfills and their Correlation with Racial and Economic Status of Surrounding Communities*, Government Printing Office, Washington, DC

Weiss, E. B. (1989) *In Fairness to Future Generations: International Law, Common Patrimony, and Intergenerational Equity*, Transnational Publishers and the United Nations University, New York

Weiss, E. B. (1990) 'In fairness to future generations', *Environment*, vol 32, pp6–11, 30–31

Wenz, P. S. (1988) *Environmental Justice*, State University of New York Press, Albany, NY

Zimmerman, R. (1993) 'Social equity and environmental risk', *Risk Analysis*, vol 13, pp649–666

Zimmerman, R. (1994) 'Issues of classification in environmental equity: How we manage is how we measure', *Fordham Urban Law Journal*, vol 21, pp633–669

17

Issues in Environmental Justice Research

Susan L. Cutter

Introduction

Environmental equity – preventing disproportionate effects of environmental degradation on people and places – has been a federal concern for at least three decades (see Chapter 16; also Berry, 1977; USGAO, 1997). In the early 1990s, coalitions of civil rights and environmental activists transformed environmental equity concerns into the environmental justice movement, ostensibly because of concerns about the placement of toxic waste facilities in low-income and minority communities (UCC, 1987; Bullard, 1990, 1994, 1996; Bryant, 1995). The First National People of Color Environmental Leadership Summit was held in 1991 and immediately was followed by the establishment of the US Environmental Protection Agency's (EPA's) Office of Environmental Equity. In 1994, environmental justice was institutionalized within the federal government through Executive Order 12898, which focused federal attention on human-health and environmental conditions in minority and low-income communities. It also provided for greater public participation and access to environmental information in these impacted communities.

While the environmental justice movement has been successful in bringing the issue to the attention of policy-makers and the public, there is some scepticism as to whether or not injustices do, in fact, exist. In other words, there is a federal policy in place despite little empirical verification of the true extent of the problem. While we may see a correlation between the presence of facilities and the demographic composition of places in the late 1990s, we have little knowledge

Note: Reprinted from *Proceedings, Third National Conference on GIS and Public Health*, San Diego, CA, Susan L. Cutter, 'Issues in environmental justice research', pp525–531, www.atsdr.cdc.gov/gis/conference98/proceedings/proceedings.html#volume3, 1999.

of how this situation arose. The outcome is important, but the process behind it is equally relevant in environmental justice considerations (Yandle and Burton, 1996; Been and Gupta, 1997). Were these sources of environmental threats intentionally located in communities that were poor, minority and/or politically weak? Or is there an alternative explanation, one suggesting that facilities were located without any reference to the race and economic status of communities, and that the demographics of communities with facilities simply changed over time, producing the inequity that we see today?

This chapter examines some of the geographic factors involved in proving or disproving environmental justice claims. Six issues are highlighted as the most salient.

Precise Locations of Threats

The vast majority of social science studies of environmental justice use a standard correlation methodology to examine the relationship between toxic facilities and the demographics of their locations. There is an implicit assumption that the reported locations are correct. While many of the studies comment on some of the reliability issues of the EPA's Toxic Release Inventory (TRI) – the database most often used – there is rarely comment on the locational accuracy of the sites (McMaster et al, 1997). In a state-wide study of South Carolina using EPA databases (TRI, the National Priorities List – NPL – and the Biennial Reporting System – BRS) for the 1987–1992 time period, we found that nearly 60 per cent of the facilities listed were located in the wrong census block group (Scott et al, 1997). Comparing inaccurately recorded locations with accurately recorded locations can lead to widely different conclusions about the racial make-up of the surrounding community. For example, Westinghouse Nuclear Fuels Division (in Columbia, South Carolina) was improperly located on an EPA website that illustrated the use of geographic information systems (GIS) in environmental justice.

Table 17.1 *Differences in socio-economic characteristics before and after correcting for the location of the Westinghouse nuclear fuels facility in Columbia, SC*

	Block Group		0–1 mile		0–3 miles		0–5 miles	
	Old[a]	New[b]	Old[a]	New[b]	Old[a]	New[b]	Old[a]	New[b]
% non-white	0	91	25	61	36	56	38	41
% poverty	11	38	19	21	19	15	16	13
Total population	536	2051	15,804	190	74,076	5099	148,660	26,964
Total minority population	0	1873	3300	143	27,026	4308	61,206	11,377
Density (per square mile)	1703	14	2043	21	1562	185	1366	564

[a] Demographic characteristics according to an EPA Region 4 website illustrating the use of GIS in environmental justice
[b] Revised demographic characteristics based on the correct location of the facility. Conducted by the Hazards Research Lab, University of South Carolina

When the site was located correctly and the concentric zones redrawn, the profile of the community changed from completely white (according to EPA) to 91 per cent non-white. As Table 17.1 shows, there was very little percentage change in the 0- to 5-mile range, although the absolute number of potentially affected residents was lessened significantly.

Choice of the Environmental Threat

The potential for scientific replication and generalization of findings is often thwarted by the lack of comparability between empirical studies. Depending on the type of threat examined (e.g. a landfill, a TRI facility, a Superfund site, actual emissions), very different patterns can be observed, leading to conflicting results in the literature. Hird (1994) found that affluent counties were more likely to host NPL sites than non-affluent counties. On the other hand, no relationship between poverty and host/non-host counties was found when hazardous waste treatment, storage and disposal facilities were examined (CleanSites, 1990).

Very few studies have been conducted comparing two different sources of threats and their spatial manifestations for particular places. In a study of the Southeast comparing acute releases (reported by the federal Emergency Response and Notification System) with more chronic releases (reported under TRI), little association with race was found (see Chapter 19). Wealth indicators, on the other hand, were positively correlated with releases, with TRI releases being dominant in urban areas. In an earlier study of the same region, considering only TRI emissions, Stockwell et al (1993) developed a GIS-based profiling method to delineate high-risk from low-risk counties and found that high-risk counties were correlated with population density and more urbanized places. Depending on the nature of the environmental threat, we can see radically different conclusions from the empirical literature.

Geographic Scale of Analysis

This issue of geographic or spatial scale is perhaps one of the most important issues in environmental justice research. While the scale of research studies varies widely (census block, tract, metropolitan area, county), there is no assessment or uniform opinion as to which scale is the most appropriate for proving or disproving environmental justice claims (Zimmerman, 1993). Because of the aggregation bias and the modified areal unit problem (well-known spatial considerations in geography), the selection of the enumeration unit is critical in the proof. A number of studies demonstrate that the statistical results change as the geographical unit of analysis is varied (Zimmerman, 1994; Anderton, 1996). For example, there was no association between any of the three indicators examined (TRI, BRS, NPL) and the racial or economic composition of host census tracts or blocks for a study of South Carolina. However, when data were aggregated to the county level, larger numbers of facilities were associated with higher-income white counties – just the opposite of what most people expected (see Chapter 18).

A secondary scale issue involves the methods for stratifying the population around the facilities and the resulting classification problems. The host/non-host methodology (i.e. using statistical analyses – such as difference of means and difference of proportions tests – to compare host and non-host communities, thus ascertaining the statistical significance of facility distribution) is the most common way to differentiate the local geography. Recent research is moving toward using buffers (at varying distances from the source) as the classification tool (Opaluch et al, 1993; Glickman and Hersh, 1995; Chakraborty and Armstrong, 1997; Neumann et al, 1998). However, major questions arise concerning the actual interval distance to use (0.5 miles, 1 mile, etc.) and the basis for that selection (worst-case events, modelled effects, convenience). Obviously, the choice of buffer distance is an important variable in determining whether inequities exist or not.

Subpopulation Selected

Thus far, most environmental justice research has targeted two subpopulations, delineated by race/ethnicity and income levels. There are few studies that examine the disproportionate effects on subpopulations delineated by gender or age, despite very real differences in susceptibility, vulnerability, and ability to cope with and recover from environmental threats (see Chapter 5; also Swanston, 1994) including disasters (Fothergill, 1996).

The following example illustrates why other subpopulations should be considered in addition to those based on race/ethnic and wealth indicators. Again drawing on the experience with South Carolina, the state's block groups were categorized based on the percentage of children under 18 in each block group, compared with the state-wide average for the same percentage. The comparisons were expressed as ratios. Once they were categorized as either high (>1.1), medium (0.9–1.1) or low (<0.9) regions, the block groups were mapped and statistically compared with the block group locations of all TRI facilities in South Carolina, and also those TRI facilities in the state that emitted heavy metals, using a host/non-host methodology. The differences between each group were statistically significant (based on chi-square tests), as shown in Table 17.2. More

Table 17.2 *Children and the location of toxic facilities in South Carolina, 1990*

Block group characterization for children <18 years*	Percentage of top 100 TRI releasers in block group category	Percentage of TRI heavy metal emitters in block group category	Number of TRI heavy metal emitters in block group category
High	44%	45%	61
Medium	31%	28%	38
Low	25%	27%	36
Chi-square (significance)	6.08 (0.0478)	10.09 (0.0064)	

* Block group characterization (high, medium, low) is calculated as the percentage younger than 18 in a block group, divided by the percentage younger than 18 for the state. 'High' indicates block groups with a ratio of children <18 years greater than 1.1:1, 'medium' indicates a ratio between 0.9:1 and 1.1:1, and 'low' indicates a ratio lower than 0.9:1.

importantly, when the sites were desegregated, we found that nine out of the top ten heavy emitters were located in block groups with greater than the state-wide average of children under 18. How this relates to potential health outcomes is unclear at this time, but it does provide another perspective on who bears the burdens of toxic releases.

Time Frame

As noted earlier in this chapter, environmental justice research needs to address the fundamental issue of 'which came first', so that we more accurately understand the processes that gave rise to the patterns that are observed today. As Greenberg (1993) suggests, it is important that environmental justice research focuses on both outcome (current patterns) and process. However, the process-oriented studies require detailed time-series analyses of demographic change in communities. These are difficult to perform because of limitations in historical databases, knowledge of facility start dates and, most importantly, matching historical census boundaries. However, a number of studies (see Chapter 21; also Anderson et al, 1994 and Yandle and Burton, 1996) have conducted these time-series analyses with inconclusive results. While inequities may currently exist, they came about by a process more likely explained by regional and state migration patterns, market dynamics, and unique and localized socio-spatial contexts. For example, in an attempt to solve income and employment disparities within a region, states may embark on economic development plans that promote economic growth but may also promote environmental inequities. This may help to explain some of the disparities found in rural, southern states, for example, though this explanation may not address the processes giving rise to inequities in northern urban-industrial areas.

Relative Hazardousness of Spatial Units

The late 1990s have seen an increasing sophistication of environmental justice research. There is movement away from the static indicators of injustices – mere presence or absence in a community – to more consideration of the underlying processes and potential impacts of facilities and their emissions. Of critical concern are the quantity and toxicity of emissions from facilities. Secondary concerns are the spatial variability of emissions and their potential impact on local populations. While many of the existing databases (such as TRI) provide estimates of releases or emissions, there is no consistent source of data regarding the toxicity or potential health impact of these emissions. One of the biggest stumbling blocks to this line of enquiry is the lack of a consistent measure of toxicity that the social science community can use in comparing risk.

Only a handful of studies have tried to incorporate toxicity measures into environmental justice research (Stockwell et al, 1993; Bowen et al, 1995; Perlin et al, 1995; McMaster et al, 1997; Neumann et al, 1998). While each study used TRI data, they employed different toxicity measures, so comparability between them and generalizations from them are difficult. Much more work needs to be done in this area to develop a representation of relative risk and thus a prioritization or action.

Conclusions

This chapter has described the evolution of environmental justice policy. Based on the research and empirical work to date, a number of issues or lessons have been highlighted. First, there is a critical need for spatial accuracy in the location of toxic facilities. Second, geographical scale is important because injustices may statistically exist at one scale, but disappear when using another. The optimal scale depends on the initial questions asked of the research and/or policy. Third, the choice of environmental threat, subpopulation and time frame affect the comparability of findings and their replication. A number of important subgroups are missing from much of the research (e.g. the elderly, children). Thus far, there is little replication of results, largely due to the differences mentioned. Fourth, the current physical distribution of environmental threats may not lead to differences in potential exposures. Just because a facility is located in a minority tract, for example, does not mean that there is more potential exposure to that tract's residents. Fifth, the spatial delineation of toxicity indicators can help to define the relative hazardousness of places. Last, and perhaps most important, the empirical 'proof' of an injustice may be less important than the local perception of and sensitivity to the issue. Demanding complete certainty in the existence of environmental injustice before policy initiatives are undertaken may pose greater risks to the well-being and functioning of communities than simply responding to the perception of the threats.

References

Anderson, A. B., Anderton, D. L. and Oaks, J. M. (1994) 'Environmental equity: Evaluating TSDF siting over the past two decades', *Waste Age*, vol 25, no 7, pp83–100

Anderton, D. L. (1996) 'Methodological issues in the spatiotemporal analysis of environmental equity', *Social Science Quarterly*, vol 77, no 3, pp508–515

Been, V. and Gupta, F. (1997) 'Coming to the nuisance or going to the barrios? A longitudinal analysis of environmental justice claims', *Ecology Law Quarterly*, vol 24, pp1–56

Berry, B. J. L. (1977) *The Social Burdens of Environmental Pollution*, Ballinger, Cambridge, MA

Bowen, W. M., Salling, M. J., Haynes, K. E. and Cryan, E. J. (1995) 'Toward environmental justice: Spatial equity in Ohio and Cleveland', *Annals of the Association of American Geographers*, vol 85, pp641–63

Bryant, B. (ed) (1995) *Environmental Justice: Issues, Policies, and Solutions*, Island Press, Washington, DC

Bullard, R. D. (1990) *Dumping in Dixie: Race, Class, and Environmental Quality*, Westview Press, Boulder, CO

Bullard, R. D. (1994) *Unequal Protection: Environmental Justice and Communities of Color*, Sierra Club Books, San Francisco

Bullard, R. D. (1996) 'Environmental justice: It's more than waste facility siting', *Social Science Quarterly*, vol 77, no 3, pp493–499

Chakraborty, J. and Armstrong, M. P. (1997) 'Exploring the use of buffer analysis for the identification of impacted areas in environmental equity assessment', *Cartography and Geographic Information Systems*, vol 24, no 3, pp145–157

CleanSites (1990) *Hazardous Waste Sites and the Rural Poor: A preliminary Assessment*, Clean Sites, Inc., Alexandria, VA

Fothergill, A. (1996) 'Gender, risk and disaster', *International Journal of Mass Emergencies and Disasters*, vol 14, no 1, pp33–56

Glickman, T. S. and Hersh, R. (1995) *Evaluating Environmental Equity: The Impact of Industrial Hazards on Selected Social Groups in Allegheny County, Pennsylvania*, Discussion Paper 5–13, Resources for the Future, Washington, DC

Greenberg, M. R. (1993) 'Proving environmental equity in siting locally unwanted land uses', *Risk – Issues in Health and Safety*, vol 4, pp235–252

Hird, J. A. (1994) *Superfund: The Political Economy of Environmental Risk*, Johns Hopkins University Press, Baltimore

McMaster, R. B., Leitner, H. and Sheppard, E. (1997) 'GIS-based environmental equity and risk assessment: Methodological problems and prospects', *Cartography and Geographic Information Systems*, vol 24, no 3, pp172–189

Neumann, C. M., Forman, D. L. and Rothlein, J. E. (1998) 'Hazard screening of chemical releases and environmental equity analysis of populations proximate to Toxic Release facilities in Oregon', *Environmental Health Perspectives*, vol 106, no 4, pp217–226

Opaluch, J. J., Swallow, S. K., Weaver, T., Wessells, C. W. and Wichelns, D. (1993) 'Evaluating impacts from noxious facilities: Including public preferences in current siting mechanisms', *Journal of Environmental Economics and Management*, vol 24, pp41–59

Perlin, S. A., Setzer, R. W., Creason, J. and Sexton, K. (1995) 'Distribution of industrial air emissions by income and race in the United States: An approach using the Toxic Release Inventory', *Environmental Science and Technology*, vol 29, pp69–80

Scott, M. S., Cutter, S. L., Menzel, C., Ji, M. and Wagner, D. F. (1997) 'Spatial accuracy of the EPA's environmental hazards databases and their use in environmental equity analyses', *Applied Geographic Studies*, vol 1, no 1, pp45–61

Stockwell, J. R., Sorenson, J. W., Eckert, J. W. jr and Carreras, E. M. (1993) 'The US EPA geographic information system for mapping environmental releases of Toxic Chemical Release Inventory (TRI) chemicals', *Risk Analysis*, vol 13, pp155–164

Swanston, S. F. (1994) 'Race, gender, age, and disproportionate impact: What can we do about the failure to protect the most vulnerable?', *Fordham Urban Law Journal*, vol 21, pp577–604

UCC (United Church of Christ Commission for Racial Justice) (1987) *Toxic Wastes and Race in the United States*, United Church of Christ, New York

USGAO (US Government Accounting Office) (1995) *Hazardous and Nonhazardous Waste: Demographics of People Living Near Waste Facilities*, GAO/RCED-95-84, Government Printing Office, Washington, DC

Yandle, T. and Burton, D. (1996) 'Reexamining environmental justice: A statistical analysis of historical hazardous waste landfill siting patterns in metropolitan Texas', *Social Science Quarterly*, vol 77, pp477–492

Zimmerman, R. (1993) 'Social equity and environmental risk', *Risk Analysis*, vol 13, pp649–666

Zimmerman, R. (1994) 'Issues of classification in environmental equity: How we manage is how we measure', *Fordham Urban Law Journal*, vol 21, pp633–669

18

The Role of Geographic Scale in Monitoring Environmental Justice

Susan L. Cutter, Danika Holm and Lloyd Clark

Introduction

The issue of fairness in the distribution and impact of environmental risks and hazards continues to generate headlines. Concern about the disproportionate impact of environmental hazards on people of colour and economically disadvantaged groups led to the formation of the environmental justice movement – a coalition of environmental, civil rights, and social equality activists. In 1987 the United Church of Christ's Commission on Racial Justice published their landmark study on toxic waste and race, offering some empirical support for environmental discrimination claims (UCC, 1987). On 11 February 1994, President Clinton signed Executive Order Number 12898, requiring each federal agency to adopt the principle of environmental justice in programmatic decisions. Yet, two years after this new directive, there still is little consensus on the definition, classification and measurement of inequity.

Most of the social science literature on environmental equity either examines the spatial and/or temporal distribution of benefits and burdens (called outcome equity) or identifies the causal mechanisms that give rise to these differences in the first place (process equity). As suggested elsewhere (Chapter 16; see also Bullard, 1994 and Kasperson, 1994), inequity originates from three major sources of dissimilarities: social, generational and procedural. To test for outcome equity, one examines the disproportionate effect of environmental degradation on places or people arising from these dissimilarities (Greenberg, 1993).

To fully examine equity issues we need a more systematic analysis of what constitutes an equity problem (what parameter we measure), what the appropriate

Note: Reprinted, with permission, from *Risk Analysis*, vol 16, no 4, Susan L. Cutter, Danika Holm and Lloyd Clark, 'The role of geographic scale in monitoring environmental justice', pp517–526. © Blackwell Publishing, 1996

scale is for examining equity (which spatial unit of measurement) and what time frame should be considered in looking at causes of equity or its spatial consequences (Chapter 16; see also Zimmerman, 1994 and Perlin et al, 1995). Two of these considerations (parameter measured and scale) are addressed in this chapter. Using 1992 hazards and 1990 social data, three different risk sources and three different spatial units are used to test the following hypothesis: hazardous waste or toxic facilities are disproportionately located in economically disadvantaged and minority communities within South Carolina.

South Carolina is one of the primary dumping grounds for hazardous and radioactive waste for the entire nation (Bullard, 1990; Hall and Kerr, 1991; Hall, 1994). It is a poor, rural state with a relatively high percentage of residents who are people of colour. Given that South Carolina is 'dumped on' in the national context, are the facilities within the state also dumping on minority, poor and disempowered communities? A number of specific questions guide our analysis. First, what is the nature of the distribution of hazardous waste and toxic facilities/sites throughout the state and what is the relationship between race, economic status and location of these facilities? Second, do these associations differ when varying spatial scales are employed as the unit of analysis? Third, are the relationships between race, economic status, and location of facilities consistent between different types of hazardous facilities/sites?

The Social Burdens of Environmental Pollution

The suggestion that the poor residents of inner-city neighbourhoods bear the greatest burden of environmental contamination is nothing new. As early as 1971, the US Environmental Protection Agency (EPA) commissioned a number of studies on the topic (USEPA, 1971a, b; Kruvant, 1974; Berry, 1977). Currently, research on the social burdens of pollution is being addressed within the environmental justice framework.

Environmental justice

Most people consider the environmental justice movement began in Warren County, North Carolina, in 1982 (Geiser and Waneck, 1983; Bullard and Wright, 1990; Bryant and Mohai, 1992; Bullard, 1993, 1994). Civil rights activists and political leaders joined area residents to block, unsuccessfully, the construction of the PCB landfill. An investigation of hazardous landfill siting practices followed, which found a strong relationship between the siting of four hazardous waste landfills in the Southeast and the race and socio-economic status of the surrounding communities (USGAO, 1983). The accumulating evidence and increasing public awareness prompted the United Church of Christ's Commission for Racial Justice to initiate a national study of toxic waste sites and race (UCC, 1987). Communities with commercial hazardous waste facilities had greater numbers of minority residents living in close proximity to hazardous waste facilities than other communities in the same county without facilities. Race, more than any other demographic variable, most strongly correlated with the location of waste facilities, prompting many activists to claim 'environmental racism' in describing the inequality resulting from corporate economic and governmental regulatory decisions (Goldman, 1992).

Do inequities exist?

Despite the fact that environmental justice is a major social issue, the empirical support for inequity remains mixed (see Chapter 16; also Mohai and Bryant, 1992). There is little consistency in the research findings as to the source of the inequity (e.g. the specific environmental threat), the spatial scale, targeted subpopulations (people of colour, elderly, children) or time frame (longitudinal or snapshot approaches). For example, the United Church of Christ study (UCC, 1987) compared demographic patterns and the location of hazardous waste sites using zip code areas as the unit of analysis. In a 1994 update (Goldman and Fitton), the initial UCC results were reaffirmed and the strength of the associations increased. For example, the concentration of people of colour living in communities with commercial hazardous waste facilities increased from 25 per cent in 1987 to 31 per cent in 1993. This was largely due to manipulating statistical averaging procedures, not necessarily as a consequence of demographic shifts. In the 1987 report, unweighted statistics were utilized while the 1994 update used weighted averages based on the total population in each zip code area. When controlling for regional variations, income, not race, turns out to be the key determinant of differences in the locations of facilities.

As a consequence of different units of analysis (zip codes, census tracts, etc.), and the use of different sources of environmental threats (National Priority List – NPL sites, treatment, storage and disposal – TSD – facilities), the findings on differential burdens cannot be compared and thus do not offer definitive proof of environmental justice claims one way or the other (Table 18.1). Clearly, the methodological units employed directly impact the conclusions. For example, proponents of zip codes as the unit of measurement (UCC, 1987; Goldman and Fitton, 1994; Hamilton, 1995) claim zip codes offer more detailed analyses for national comparisons than county coverages. There are about 3100 counties nationwide versus 30,000 5-digit zip codes, and the areal coverage of zip codes is less. Zip codes are more inclusive than census tracts, for example, which do not always cover rural areas. Furthermore, for national comparisons, census tract data are more expensive to acquire for the entire US, a consideration that might limit comparative assessments for the entire US. Studies using census tract divisions (Burke, 1993; Anderton et al, 1994a, b; Glickman, 1994; Holm, 1994) offer more detailed localized analyses. Census tracts are relatively homogeneous in terms of population size (around 4000) while zip code populations are highly variable, thus necessitating standardization when computing percentages, a problem addressed by Goldman and Fitton (1994) in their use of weighted averages. Also, census tracts are a better approximation for 'neighbourhood' than zip codes because of their smaller areal coverage. Other spatial units used in previous empirical studies include counties (Hird, 1993; Crew-Meyer, 1994; Cutter, 1994; Perlin et al, 1995), minor civil divisions (MCDs) (Zimmerman, 1993; Greenberg, 1994), and undifferentiated metropolitan areas (Bullard, 1983; Adeola, 1994).

Table 18.1 *Empirical support for environmental justice claims*

Reference	Coverage	Spatial unit	Environmental threat
Perlin et al (1995)	national	county	TRI emissions
UCC (1987)	national	zip codes	hazardous waste landfills
Goldman and Fitton (1994)	national	zip codes	hazardous waste landfills and facilities
Hamilton (1995)	national	zip codes	TSD facilities
Greenberg (1993)	national	towns	waste-to-energy facilities
Zimmerman (1993)	national	minor civil div.	NPL sites
Anderton et al (1994a)	25 SMSAs	census tract	TSD facilities
Anderton et al (1994b)	25 SMSAs	census tract	TSD facilities
Berry (1977)	13 SMSAs	census tract	air and water pollution, noise, solid waste
Crew-Meyer (1994)	state/SC	county	TSD facilities
Cutter (1994)	state/SC	county	toxic emissions
Greenberg (1994)	state/NJ	minor civil div.	NPL sites
Holm (1994)	state/SC	census tract	TSD facilities
Mohai and Bryant (1992)	SMSA/Detroit	1.5-mile zones	commercial hazardous waste facilities
Glickman (1994)	SMSA/Pittsburgh	census tract	TRI, extremely hazardous substance facilities
Bullard and Wright (1990)	SMSA/Houston	neighbourhood	incinerators and landfills
Adeola (1994)	SMSA/Baton Rouge	entire area	environmental hazards
Burke (1993)	county/Los Angeles	census tract	TRI emissions
USGAO (1983)	Southeast/4 locales	zip codes	hazardous waste landfills
Been (1994)	Southeast/4 locales	census tract	hazardous waste landfills
Bullard and Wright (1990)	SMSA/Houston	census tract	incinerators and landfills

The discrepancy in the choice of areal units affects the comparability of studies and ultimately the strength of the statistical associations. Within geography, this is known as the modifiable areal unit (MAU) problem (Openshaw, no date). Scale differences or the variation in results obtained when data are aggregated into fewer and larger units is one manifestation of the MAU problem. The ecological fallacy, ascribing aggregate data (such as per cent minority) to all individuals who form that aggregate, is another example of the MAU problem. Correlation coefficients tend to increase with aggregation (Openshaw, no date). Thus, it should be no surprise that different spatial units of analysis will produce different correlations, and that the larger the unit of measurement, the stronger the correlation. Unfortunately, these methodological issues have not been adequately addressed in the literature, as Zimmerman and others point out (Zimmerman, 1994; see also Chapter 16 and Perlin et al, 1995). To illustrate these methodological concerns, we will test the robustness of the equity hypothesis using three different spatial scales and three different environmental parameters.

South Carolina's Social Geography

South Carolina is a relatively small state with a diverse physical and human landscape (Kovacik and Winberry, 1987). It is characterized by its poor and rural populace. The state is below the national and regional averages for median household income and educational attainment, and above the national average for percentage of residents living in poverty. Less than 55 per cent of the state's population is defined as urban, and only 16 of the state's 46 counties are labelled metropolitan according to the US Census.

The state's four major regions represent a different settlement history that typifies the social mosaic found within the state. The Upstate region is the historical centre of manufacturing and has the smallest percentage of both African American residents and persons below the poverty line (Figure 18.1a, b). The Upstate has more than a third (1.3 million) of the state's population, yet has moderate population densities (50 persons per square mile). More than 70 per cent of the population is white and more than 85 per cent live above the poverty line with median household incomes greater than $24,000 (State of South Carolina, 1993).

The Midlands region is more densely populated than the Upstate (61 people per square mile), yet has fewer people (600,000). With the exception of the Columbia metropolitan area, most of the Midlands is rural. The population is generally more affluent and more educated than state-wide averages (Figure 18.1b).

The Inner Coastal Plain is rural with average densities of 28 persons per square mile. The population is poor (25 per cent below the state average for median household income), African American (53 per cent), and less educated than the rest of the state. More than one-quarter of the population lives below the poverty line and the region has the highest unemployment rate in the state (averaging more than 8 per cent) (Figure 18.1c). The regional economy is dominated by agriculture.

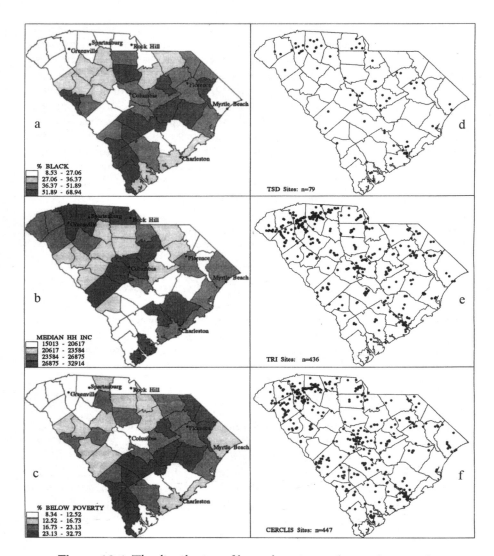

Figure 18.1 *The distribution of hazardous sites and socio-demographic characteristics in South Carolina*

The Low country, South Carolina's coastal region, contains some of the steepest socio-economic gradients within the state. For example, one of the wealthiest communities in the state (Hilton Head with a median household income of $42,995) as well as some of the poorest (Ridgeland with a median household income of $16,029) are found within close proximity. The Low country has one-quarter of the state's population, mostly concentrated in the Charleston metropolitan area and in Myrtle Beach, yet the rest of the Low country is very rural. Population densities mirror the state-wide average. Median household income is below the state average, while the percentage of non-white residents is slightly above (35 per cent). Tourism and forestry dominate the regional economy, with the exception of an industrialized core in metropolitan Charleston.

Risk Mosaic

Three parameters were used to measure inequities in hazardous waste/toxic burdens on state residents: hazardous waste treatment, storage, and disposal (TSD) facilities; Toxic Release Inventory (TRI) facilities; and inactive hazardous waste sites (CERCLIS). The state has 79 treatment, disposal and storage (TSD) sites that are concentrated in the three largest metropolitan complexes – Spartanburg-Greenville, Charleston and Columbia – although more than half the counties in the state (26 of 46) are sites for these permitted hazardous waste facilities (Figure 18.1d). In 1992, 46 states sent hazardous waste to South Carolina (South Carolina DHEC, 1993), and the majority of this out-of-state waste was sent to seven facilities: two hazardous waste incinerators (Rock Hill, Roebuck), a commercial hazardous waste land disposal facility (GSX-Laidlaw) in Pinewood, two cement kiln incinerators (Harleyville, Holly Hill), and two recycling facilities in Greer and Sumter (Lynn, 1993).

The second risk indicator is TRI sites. TRI is a national database of industrial facilities that release toxic and hazardous chemicals. The current reporting threshold is for facilities generating more than 25,000 pounds of toxics in manufacturing and processing uses, and 100,000 pounds for other uses. The TRI includes on-site releases (air, water, land, underground injection), and off-site transfers (to treatment or disposal facilities). In 1991, the TRI was expanded to include new data on off-site transfers of wastes for recycling and energy recovery as well as on-site recycling, energy recovery and treatment as mandated by the Pollution Prevention Act of 1990. In 1992 there were 436 TRI-reporting facilities in South Carolina (USEPA, 1993, 1994) (Figure 18.1e). These were concentrated primarily in the Upstate, especially in Greenville and Spartanburg counties. Outliers are found in the Midlands metropolitan counties and in the Charleston metropolitan region.

The last indicator of toxic hazards is the location of inactive hazardous waste sites that are candidates for remediation. These abandoned hazardous waste sites litter the South Carolina landscape, as they do elsewhere. In 1992, there were 23 South Carolina sites on the National Priority List (NPL) in the process of being cleaned up, and another 424 were identified by the state for priority clean-up under the Superfund programme. The 23 NPL sites were located predominately in Greenville, Lexington, Richland and Beaufort counties. The remaining CERCLIS sites (identified by the state and listed for eventual remediation under the national Superfund programme) are more evenly distributed, although some clustering occurs in the Greenville-Spartanburg area and in the Columbia and Charleston metropolitan regions (Figure 18.1f).

Scale Differences in Measuring Inequity

To begin our analysis, we examined the relationship between the location of hazardous/toxic facilities and the social profiles of counties. There are strong and

Table 18.2 *County comparisons of the frequency*
of sources of environmental threats

Social indicator	TSD	CERCLIS	TRI	Total
Population	0.81***	0.90***	0.83***	0.90***
Population density	0.78**	0.86***	0.83***	0.88***
% black	−0.39**	−0.42**	−0.43**	−0.44***
% below poverty	−0.45**	−0.46**	−0.45**	−0.48***
Med HH income	0.57***	0.55***	0.47***	0.54***
% under 18	−0.33*	−0.42**	−0.38*	−0.41**
% over 55	−0.41**	−0.26	−0.17	−0.24
% < 12 yrs educ	−0.61***	−0.54***	−0.38**	−0.50***
% college degree	0.63***	0.64***	0.51***	0.61***
% mfg employ	0.63***	0.66***	0.51**	0.61***
% labourers	−0.58***	−0.51***	−0.29*	−0.43**
% unemployed	−0.47***	−0.44**	−0.41**	−0.45**
Total *n*	79	447	436	962
% counties	56.5	95.6	93.5	97.8

*** $p < 0.001$
** $p < 0.01$
* $p < 0.05$

statistically significant associations between the number of facilities per county and a number of our social indicators (Table 18.2). For example, the strongest correlation was with population and population density. Counties with larger populations and higher population densities were associated with greater numbers of these facilities. More surprising was the negative association with percentage black and the percentage below poverty levels. Higher frequencies of facilities per county were associated with higher income ($r = 0.54$, $p = 0.001$), white ($r = 0.45$, $p = 0.01$), college-educated residents ($r = 0.58$, $p = 0.001$). There is no significant difference between each risk indicator (TSD, CERCLIS or TRI) and direction of the social indicators correlations (positive or negative), but there were minor differences in the relative strength of the associations.

Based on this initial statistical test, we conclude that inequities do exist within South Carolina, but they do not involve counties that one thought were the most obvious, (i.e. low income counties with high percentages of minority residents). Rather, it appears from this county-level analysis that it is the more urbanized, white, middle-income counties that bear a disproportionate burden of hazardous waste/toxic facilities.

Because of the state's developmental history, South Carolina counties are not homogeneous and exhibit wide variations in social characteristics within each county. The rural nature of much of the state and the lack of localized zoning means that socio-economic gradients within and between counties are quite steep. To test whether hazardous waste facilities are located in the economically disadvantaged or minority sections within counties required an examination of the state's sub-county geography. There are 821 census tracts in South Carolina, each containing approximately 4000 people. In replicating the county correlation

Table 18.3 *Correlations between frequency of facilities and spatial unit*

Social indicator	County	Tract	Block Group
Population	0.90***	0.20***	0.10***
Population density	0.88***	−0.20***	−0.14***
% black	−0.44**	0.00	0.03
% below poverty	−0.48***	−0.00	0.02
Med HH income	0.54***	−0.05	−0.06**
% under 18	−0.41**	0.11***	0.06***
% over 55	−0.24	−0.10**	−0.07***
% < 12 yrs educ	−0.50***	0.12***	0.07***
% college degree	0.61***	−0.17***	−0.11***
% mfg employ	0.61***	−0.16***	−0.11***
% labourers	−0.43**	0.18***	0.10***
% unemployed	−0.45**	0.05	−0.06***
Total *n*	46	832	3185
% with Sites	97.8	46.9	18.8
Mean # Sites	20.56	1.15	0.29
Range	0–106	0–13	0–7

*** $p < 0.001$
** $p < 0.01$
* $p < 0.05$

analysis we found little or no correlation between frequency of sites and social indicators at the tract level (Table 18.3). Race and income had no association with the presence or absence of hazardous waste/toxic facilities at this spatial scale. Even when controlling for the effect of population and population density, there was no association between race and income and the number of facilities. This can be partially explained by the lack of any facility in 53 per cent of all tracts. It is also partially explained by the disaggregation of the data.

We also used this statistical procedure at the block group census level. Here, even fewer block groups contained sites (only 19 per cent contained one or more facilities). Again, there was no association between the number of facilities, race or income at the block group unit of analysis. Even when controlling for population density and populations, the income or racial composition of block groups had no bearing on the presence or absence of facilities.

Because of the high correlations with population and population density discovered in our first test, we ran a sensitivity analysis on the data to see if there was an urban bias. Only MSA-designated counties were selected (*n* = 16), and the Pearson correlation analysis was repeated at the county, tract and block group levels. There are no statistically significant associations between race or income and the presence of hazardous waste/toxic facilities in urban counties. This conclusion also holds true for tracts and block groups within urban counties as well.

As a result of the weak associations in the correlation test, we ran a t-test procedure to examine socio-economic differences between tracts with and without a hazardous waste/toxic facilities. Census tracts with toxic/hazardous waste facilities averaged 2.5 sites per tract (ranging from 1 to a high of 13). There are no significant

Table 18.4 *Difference of means test between areas with and without sites*

Social indicator	Tracts[a] W/sites n = 385	Tracts[a] W/O sites n = 436	Difference	Block group[b] W/sites n = 600	Block group[b] W/O sites n = 2585	Difference
Population	4725	3808	917***	1256	1053	203***
Population density	255	560	305***	255	599	344***
% non-white	33.5	32.4	1.1	33.6	31.4	2.2
% below poverty	16.2	15.9	0.3	16.5	15.9	0.6
Med HH income ($)	25,324	26,644	1320*	25,137	26938	1801***
% under 18	26.8	25.1	1.7***	26.9	25.3	1.6***
% over 55	19.8	21.7	1.9***	20.4	22.5	2.1***
% < 12 yrs educ	34.2	30.1	4.1	36.2	32.0	4.2
% college degree	12.4	16.9	4.5***	11.3	15.7	4.4
% mfg employ	17.8	21.7	3.9***	16.7	20.8	4.1***
% labourers	22.7	18.6	4.1	24.1	19.8	4.3
% unemployed	6.3	5.8	0.5	6.6	5.9	0.7

*** $p < 0.001$
** $p < 0.01$
* $p < 0.05$

[a] DF 435, 384
[b] DF 2864, 599

differences in the racial composition of tracts that host and those that do not host a hazardous waste/toxic producing facility (Table 18.4). With respect to economic indicators, there are no differences based on our poverty indicator but there is a distinction between tracts with sites and those without when one looks at median household income. In other words, the median income for tracts with a site is 5 per cent lower ($1320) than those without a site. Tracts hosting hazardous waste/toxic facilities generally are more populated but have lower population densities. Census tracts with facilities also have a higher percentage of residents under 18, residents who are less educated, and a higher percentage of residents employed as labourers than tracts without facilities. Similar findings were found when the block group spatial unit was used (Table 18.4). At this level, race was also insignificant. Median household income discrepancies were slightly greater (7 per cent or around $1801). Block groups hosting facilities are characterized by higher populations, higher percentages of children, poorer educational levels (36 per cent do not even have a high school diploma) and higher percentages of residents working in labouring professions.

Since we found differences in the social profile of tracts and block groups with and without hazardous/toxic sites, our final test of the equity hypothesis involved a classification procedure. A discriminant analysis was run first for tracts (dichotomized as those with and those without sites) to see if we could predict membership in either category based on the social profile of the tract. In the first procedure, the discriminant analysis correctly classified only 60 per cent of the tracts using these social indicators. Type of employment (labour, manufacturing) and educational levels were the most significant variables in differentiating tracts and block groups with toxic facilities from those without. In the second procedure, block groups were used, and we were able to correctly classify 81 per cent of the block groups using these social indicators. We can conclude that neither race nor economic status in and of them, predict whether or not a community hosts a hazardous waste or toxic facility. In South Carolina, those social indicators best able to differentiate are percentage employed in labour occupations, percentage of residents with college degrees and percentage employed in manufacturing occupations. There is no spatial pattern to those census tracts or block groups that were correctly or incorrectly classified.

Proving Environmental Injustice

There are a number of important findings of this research. First, the distribution of hazardous facilities within South Carolina is clustered in the Upstate industrial core and in the metropolitan complexes of Charleston and Columbia. Second, there is general consensus on the relationship between race, income, and the locations of our three different risk indicators (TSD, TRI and CERCLIS sites). Where correlations differed it was due to minor variations in the strength of correlations not the direction (Table 18.5). Third, in using three different spatial units (county, census tract, block group), we found conflicting evidence in support of our inequity hypothesis. At the county level, there was an association between race and economic status and the presence of hazardous waste/toxic facilities. In South Carolina, this association meant that white, relatively affluent residents in

Table 18.5 *Correlation coefficients of race and income by spatial scale and source of environmental risk*

	RCRA		CERCLIS		TRI	
	With sites	All	With sites	All	With sites	All
County						
% black	−0.39**	−0.39**	−0.42**	−0.42**	−0.43**	−0.42***
% below poverty	−0.45**	−0.46**	−0.46*	−0.48**	−0.45**	−0.46**
Median income	0.57**	0.57**	0.55**	0.56**	0.47**	0.47**
Tract						
% non-white	−0.04	−0.01	0.02	0.02	−0.05	−0.01
% below poverty	−0.09	−0.05	0.02	0.02	−0.02	−0.00
Median income	0.09	0.03	−0.04	−0.06	−0.00	−0.04
Block Group						
% non-white	−0.03	−0.00	−0.05	−0.04*	−0.02	−0.02
% below poverty	−0.06	−0.02	0.06	0.03	0.01	0.01
Median income	0.05	−0.00	−0.03	−0.05**	−0.02	−0.02

*** $p < 0.001$
** $p < 0.01$
* $p < 0.05$

Note: County $n = 46$ for all, $n = 45$ with sites only; tract $n = 821$ for all, $n = 385$ with sites only; block group $n = 3185$ for all, $n = 600$ for sites only.

metropolitan areas were disproportionately affected more than rural, low-income minority residents. When these patterns are examined at the census tract and block group levels, there is no discernible difference in the racial composition of tracts (or block groups) that have or do not have one or more of these facilities. There are only slight differences in economic levels.

These results challenge the conclusions reached by Goldman and Fitton (1994) for the South. This suggests that aggregation at regional scales masks both inter-state and intra-state variations. In South Carolina, the bulk of the state's industrial sector is located in the upper Piedmont, a region that has a relatively low African American population. This may help explain why race is not associated with the presence of these facilities. Manufacturing plants produce a range of toxic substances in varying amounts with different toxicity levels, yet our analysis grouped them all together. For example, one of the region's largest and most toxic hazardous waste facilities (GSX-Laidlaw in Pinewood) is, in fact, located in one of the poorest communities in the state. If we were to look at those facilities that generated the most toxic of emissions (in both quantity and toxicity) we may find a very different pattern of inequity than the one presented here.

Whether or not this current analysis provides conclusive support of the inequity hypothesis is difficult to say. Because our analysis focused on political divisions (e.g. census-defined areas) there are some caveats to our conclusions. The geographic area may not be representative of the impact area, which might extend beyond the boundary of the census unit. Second, the facility may not be located in the centre of the spatial unit, and thus the representativeness of the socio-demographic data may be questionable as pointed out earlier in this chapter. This edge effect is a consistent problem in census geography and one that could easily be remedied using the analytical capabilities in a GIS. While not the focus of this current study, this is a direction for future research.

We also chose to examine associations between the presence or absence of sites and socio-economic characteristics. This was deliberate as we wanted to compare our findings to others in the literature. Again, a more robust analysis could take a linear, predictive approach using probit or regression analyses, or a non-linear approach utilizing neural network analysis. Both methodologies, however, are beyond the scope of this chapter and the questions we posed.

The next step is to focus on potential exposures to hazardous substances from these facilities (as mentioned above), not simply their presence or absence in the community. From our perspective, this is the most important consideration for environmental justice research, as communities of colour might have greater potential exposure levels to environmental contaminants even though the number of hazardous waste/toxic sites is relatively small. This type of analysis moves the debate from a static dimension (e.g. the original siting decision and the current demographic composition of communities) to a more dynamic system involving both qualitative and quantitative estimates on the amount of contaminants discharged from facilities and the potential pathways of exposure. These can then be generalized to estimate which communities might be most affected, by what type of contamination, and thus determine the appropriate mitigation or policy responses. This localized ecology of hazards and potential exposures could be expanded to include other non-industrial sources of risk such as those from agricultural use of pesticides or the transportation of hazardous substances. A secondary line of research should focus on the historical development of the toxic landscape, and the need to identify which came first (the facility or the people) as we track the original siting of facilities and changes in community composition over time. Both are needed as we focus on the hazards of places and the implementation of environmental justice principles.

Finally, our results suggest that tracts and block groups are the most appropriate spatial scale for assessing inequities because of wide intra-county and intra-zip code variations in risks and socio-economic indicators. Empirical verification of environmental justice must be conducted on a state-by-state basis to ensure the robustness of the findings, thus building the evidential support from the local context to the national pattern. County-level analyses are useful as a first cut to provide a comparative assessment at the national or regional level, but to adequately measure and monitor environmental justice concerns, we must look to our own backyards and our knowledge of the local setting. It may be that the most appropriate scale lies beyond our ability to manipulate statistical information (e.g. local neighborhoods or blocks). Specific site-level visits may be required to determine whether locational decisions, do, in fact, lead to greater potential exposures for people of colour. In moving beyond the activist rhetoric, we must have, a better social scientific understanding of the complexities of environmental threats, locational patterns, spatial scale and the social geography of local places. A geographical understanding of all these dimensions is absolutely critical in the implementation of environmentally just public policies.

Acknowledgements

We wish to thank Minhe Ji for his assistance in the preparation of the graphics for this chapter. This research was partially supported by grants from the South Carolina Universities Research and Education Foundation (#30–90, #62–95).

References

Adeola, F. O. (1994) 'Environmental hazards, health, and racial inequity in hazardous waste distribution', *Environment and Behavior*, vol 26, no 1, pp99–126

Anderton, D. L., Anderson, A. B., Rossi, P. H., Oakes, J. M., Fraser, M. R., Weber, E. W. and Calabrese, E. J. (1994a) 'Hazardous waste facilities: "Environmental equity" issues in metropolitan areas', *Evaluation Review*, vol 18, no 2, pp123–140

Anderton, D. L., Anderson, A. B., Oakes, J. M. and Fraser, M. R. (1994b) 'Environmental equity: The demographics of dumping', *Demography*, vol 31, no 2, pp229–248

Berry, B. J. L. (ed) (1977) *The Social Burdens of Environmental Pollution: A Comparative Metropolitan Data Source*, Ballinger, Cambridge

Bryant, B. and Mohai, P. (eds) (1992) *Race and the Incidence of Environmental Hazards: A Time for Discourse*, Westview Press, Boulder, CO

Bullard, R. D. (1983) 'Solid waste sites and the black Houston community', *Sociological Inequity*, vol 53, pp273–288

Bullard, R. D. (1990) *Dumping in Dixie: Race, Class, and Environmental Quality*, Westview Press, Boulder, CO

Bullard, R. D. (ed) (1993) *Confronting Environmental Racism: Voices from the Grassroots*, South End Press, Boston, MA

Bullard, R. D. (1994) *Unequal Protection: Environmental Justice and Communities of Color*, Sierra Club Books, San Francisco, CA

Bullard R. D. (1994) 'Overcoming racism in environmental decisionmaking', *Environment*, vol 36, no 4, pp10–20, 39–44

Bullard R. D and Wright, B. H. (1990) 'Mobilizing the black community for environmental justice', *Journal of Intergroup Relations*, vol 17, no 1, pp33–43

Burke, L. M. (1993) 'Race and environmental equity: A geographic analysis in Los Angeles', *Geo Info Systems*, October, pp44–50

Crew-Meyer, K. (1994) 'Hazardous waste and race in South Carolina', *The South Carolina Policy Forum* vol 5, no 3, pp25–28

Cutter, S. L. (1994) 'The burdens of toxic risks: Are they fair?', *South Carolina Business and Economic Review*, vol 41, no 1, pp3–7

Geiser, K. and Waneck, G. (1983) 'PCBs and Warren County', *Science for the People*, July/August, pp13–17

Glickman, T. S. (1994) 'Measuring environmental equity with geographical information systems', *Renewable Resources Journal*, vol 12, no 3, pp17–21

Goldman, B. A. (1992) 'Polluting the poor', *The Nation*, 5 October, pp348–349

Goldman, B. A. and Fitton, L. (1994) *Toxic Wastes and Race Revisited*, Center for Policy Alternatives, New York

Greenberg, M. R. (1993) 'Proving environmental inequity in siting locally unwanted land uses', *Risk Issues in Health and Safety*, vol 4, pp235–252

Greenberg, M. R. (1994) 'Separate and not equal: Health-environmental risk and economic-social impacts in remediating hazardous waste sites', draft of chapter subsequently published in 1996 in S. K. Majumdar, F. J. Brenner, E. W. Miller and L. M. Rosenfeld (eds) *Environmental Contaminants, Ecosystems and Human Health*, Pennsylvania Academy of Sciences, Philadelphia, PA

Hall, B. (1994) 'Gold and green', *Southern Exposure*, fall, pp3–24

Hall, B. and Kerr. M. L. (1991) *1991–1992 Green Index: A State-by-State Guide to the Nation's Environmental Health*, Island Press, Washington, DC

Hamilton, J. T. (1995) 'Testing for environmental racism: Prejudice, profits, political power?', *Journal of Policy Analysis and Management*, vol 14, no 1, pp107–132

Hird, J. A. (1993) 'Environmental policy and equity: The case of Superfund', *Journal of Policy Analysis and Management*, vol 12, no 2, pp323–343

Holm, D. M. (1994) 'Environmental inequities in South Carolina: The distribution of hazardous waste facilities', unpublished Master's thesis, Department of Geography, University of South Carolina, Columbia, SC

Kasperson, R. E. (1994) 'Global environmental hazards: Political issues in societal responses' in G. J. Demko and W. B. Wood (eds) *Reordering the World: Geopolitical Perspectives on the 21st Century*, Westview Press, Boulder, CO, pp141–166

Kovacik, C. F. and Winberry, J. J. (1987) *South Carolina: The Making of a Landscape*, University of South Carolina Press, Columbia, SC

Kruvant, W. (1974) *Incidence of Pollution Where People Live in Washington*, Center for Metropolitan Studies, Washington, DC

Lynn, L. B. (1993) 'Environmental equity in South Carolina: Hazardous waste issues impacting the African American community' in K. Campbell (ed) *The State of Black South Carolina: An Action Agenda for the Future*, The Columbia Urban League, Columbia, SC

Mohai, P. and Bryant, B. (1992) 'Environmental racism: Reviewing the evidence', in B. Bryant and P. Mohai (eds) *Race and the Incidence of Environmental Hazards: A Time for Discourse*, Westview Press, Boulder, CO, pp163–176

Openshaw, S. (no date) 'The modifiable areal unit problem', *Concepts and Techniques in Modern Geography 38*, Geo Books, Norwich

Perlin, S. A., Setzer, R. W., Creason, J. and Sexton, K. (1995) 'Distribution of industrial air emissions by income and race in the United States: An approach using the Toxic Release Inventory', *Environmental Science and Technology*, vol 29, no 1, pp69–80

South Carolina DHEC (1993) *Hazardous Waste Activities Reported in South Carolina for 1992*, South Carolina Department of Health and Environmental Control, Columbia, SC

South Carolina State (1993) *South Carolina Statistical Abstract*, South Carolina State Budget Control Board, Columbia, SC

UCC (United Church of Christ Commission for Racial Justice) (1987) *Toxic Wastes and Race: A National Report on the Racial and Socioeconomic Characteristics of Communities with Hazardous Waste Sites*, United Church of Christ, New York

USEPA (US Environmental Protection Agency) (1971a) *Our Urban Environment*, USEPA, Washington, DC

USEPA (1971b) *Improving the Inner City Environment*, USEPA, Washington, DC

USEPA (1993) *1991 Toxics Release Inventory*, EPA 745-R-92-003, USEPA, Washington, DC

USEPA (1994) *1992 Toxics Release Inventory State Fact Sheets*, EPA 745-F-94-001, USEPA, Washington, DC

USGAO (US General Accounting Office) (1983) *Siting of Hazardous Waste Landfills and their Correlation with Racial and Economic Status of Surrounding Communities*, Government Printing Office, Washington, DC

Zimmerman, R. (1993) 'Social equity and environmental risk', *Risk Analysis*, vol 13, no 6, pp649–666

Zimmerman, R. (1994) 'Issues of classification in environmental equity: How we manage is how we measure', *Fordham Urban Law Journal*, vol 21, pp633–669

19

Setting Environmental Justice in Space and Place: Acute and Chronic Airborne Toxic Releases in the Southeastern United States

Susan L. Cutter and William D. Solecki

The development of the environmental justice movement – a coalition of environmental, civil rights and social equality activists is one of the most significant new
social movements in recent decades (Szasz, 1994; Gottlieb, 1993). Throughout
the 1980s, the number of local environmental groups concerned with and protest-
ing against sources of local environmental risk and hazards rose dramatically. During this period as well, the first of a number of studies (USGAO, 1983) provided
some initial evidence on the disproportionate impact of environmental hazards
on people of colour and economically disadvantaged groups. This coalescence of
governmental data and local activism led to the formation of the environmental
justice movement (Geiser and Waneck, 1983; Bryant and Mohai, 1992; Bullard,
1993, 1994a, b; Schwab, 1994). At the local, state and national levels, this movement injected a new set of questions into the political discourse.

Following from this initial social activism were a series of reports and studies
attempting to verify the existence of environmental inequities. Perhaps the most
famous was the 1987 United Church of Christ's Commission on Racial Justice
study on toxic waste and race, which offered partial empirical support for environmental discrimination claims (UCC, 1987). Most of these early studies used a case
study or comparative case study methodology and focused on specific communities or selected environmental contaminants (Kruvant, 1974; Berry, 1977; Bullard,
1983; McMaster, 1988; Adeola, 1994). There is some evidence of environmental
racism in this literature (Bullard, 1990; Mohai and Bryant, 1992), yet it is far from

Note: Reprinted, with permission, from *Urban Geography*, vol 17, no 5, Susan L. Cutter and William D. Solecki, 'Setting environmental justice in space and place: Acute and chronic airborne toxic
releases in the Southeastern United States', pp380–399. © V. H. Winston & Son, Inc., 360 South
Ocean Boulevard, Palm Beach, FL 33480, 1996. All rights reserved.

conclusive (see Chapter 16). For example, the issue of spatial scale is emerging as a critical element in the evaluation and assessment of environmental inequities (see Chapter 18). Correlations between race and the sources of risk and hazards show strength and significance at the county level, but these same correlations may decline and ultimately disappear at finer spatial scales such as census tracts. Other critiques highlight methodological deficiencies in how inequities are defined, classified and measured (Perlin et al, 1995; Zimmerman, 1994; Greenberg, 1993).

In addition to these methodological critiques of the early environmental justice literature are commentaries about the lack of theoretical rigour. One key concern is the failure of the literature to formally theorize about the nature and role of racism within the political decision-making process (Lake, 1995), and the underlying social and economic processes that create the patterns of inequity in the first place (Chapter 16). Another critique is that a more formal theory of hazards and risk production is not yet present within much of the environmental justice literature, and composite measures of hazard and risk exposure are not fully articulated. More significantly, much of the existing literature does not incorporate the geographic context into the evaluation of the environmental risk burdens. Urban geographers and hazards geographers focusing on community-based hazards, have long recognized the significance of place-specific context in the social construction of the human experience, in general, and population vulnerability to hazards and risks, more specifically (Cutter, 1993; Liverman, 1986; Mitchell, 1990; Krimsky and Golding, 1992).

This chapter attempts to overcome some of the emerging critiques of the environmental justice literature and more formally root it within the theoretical constructs of hazards geography using the hazardousness of place and hazards-in-context conceptual frameworks. In this chapter we compare the character and spatial distribution of these two categories of risk for the southeastern US for a four-year period (1987–1990) with the purpose of identifying whether lower income, minority counties are disproportionately at risk from these airborne releases of extremely hazardous substances. Risk exposure events are defined here in terms of two categories: acute, large-scale, short-term events and chronic, small-scale, long-term exposures. Two specific questions are posed. First, is there a difference in the spatial pattern of toxic releases that is a function of their acute or chronic nature? Second, do predominately African American counties in the Southeast bear a disproportionate burden of exposures to airborne releases, generally, and to chronic releases more specifically?

We deliberately chose to conduct this analysis at a regional level to see whether Bullard's (1990) 'Dumping in Dixie' hypothesis held true when different risk indicators were used. We also wanted a basis of comparison with the only other regional study conducted for the Southeast (defined as US Environmental Protection Agency (EPA) Region 4) (Stockwell et al, 1993). Our rationale was to use the region-wide analysis to uncover the spatial intricacies of toxic exposures which in turn reveal the complexities of the social production of environmental inequities. In this way we want to link hazards geography and environmental justice research in such as way as to make it more robust, empirically and theoretically.

Incontrovertible Proof?

On 11 February 1994, President Clinton signed Executive Order Number 12898, requiring federal agencies to adopt the principle of environmental justice in their programmatic decisions. One of the key elements in the executive order is the need for research, data collection and data analysis that assesses and compares environmental and human health risks to populations according to race, national origin or income. Unfortunately, there are few analytical tools for monitoring or measuring the differential impact of environmental conditions and regulations on poor and/or minority communities. An interagency working group on environmental justice was formed to assist in the development of environmental justice policies for each federal agency as well as establishing communication links with local residents. Public input is being solicited in order to share concerns and recommend changes in existing strategies. Local knowledge on hazardous waste exposures, lead poisonings, Superfund issues, and so on are also being solicited by the interagency working group in an effort to help local communities address these issues.

Currently, the empirical support for injustice claims is varied and is confounded by differences in the parameters used to define injustice and the scale of measurement as noted earlier. Most of the research to date falls into two broad categories: single scale, single parameter analyses, and multiple scale, multiple parameter studies. With a rare exception or two, the research focuses exclusively on locations of industries producing hazardous substances, not the quantity, frequency or toxicity of the releases. This chapter provides a unique contribution to environmental justice literature for it uses two different data sets of actual events and releases rather than only relying on inequities resulting from industrial location.

The by-products of industry: Hazardous waste and Toxic Release Inventory sites

Comparisons between the location of hazardous waste sites and the characteristics of communities that host them dominate the environmental justice literature. National analyses of site locations of Superfund (National Priority List or NPL) sites and the demography of communities were done for a number of different spatial units: zip codes (Goldman and Fitton, 1994), counties (Hird, 1993) and minor civil divisions (Zimmerman, 1993) among others. Goldman and Fitton, for example, revisited the original UCC (1987) study and calculated that roughly 30 per cent of African Americans in this country live in a zip code with at least one NPL site. This is confirmed by Hird at the county level where he found higher percentages of minority residents associated with higher numbers of NPL sites, holding other socio-economic characteristics (such as income) constant. Zimmerman also found some association between NPL sites and the racial characteristics of communities, although her study only examined three-quarters of the NPL sites, mainly those in metropolitan regions.

In addition to examining the relict burdens of industrialization using these inactive waste sites, a number of researchers are providing the contemporary context by examining current hazardous waste burdens using the location of hazardous waste treatment, storage and disposal (TSD) sites. Nationally, Anderton et al (1994a, b) found no differences in the racial characteristics of census tracts and the presence or absence of a TSD facility.

Although the majority of studies provide a national perspective, there are some detailed level analyses at the state and sub-state levels. Again the focus has been on the relationship between TSD or NPL site location and the racial composition of host communities (see Chapter 18; also Greenberg, 1994; Holm, 1994; Crew-Meyer, 1994). In the case of New Jersey and South Carolina, race and income are not associated with site locations at the census tract level.

Metropolitan studies using the location of Toxic Release Inventory (TRI) facilities have been done for Los Angeles, where a pattern of injustice did appear among lower-income Hispanic census tracts (Burke, 1993), and in Pittsburgh where they did not (Glickman, 1994). A range of other locality studies using TRI data have been produced by local or state environmental groups. Using the total pounds of toxic releases, most of these case studies suggest evidence of racial or income injustices. Although critically important for locally based advocacy groups, typically these studies are limited methodologically and fail to set their findings within a larger geographic or theoretical context.

Moving beyond locational inequities

There is a dearth of empirical evidence on the actual pollution burdens or potential exposures arising from these locational sources and which segments of society are differentially affected by these. One of the first geographical research efforts in this area provided a comparison of 13 US metropolitan areas and the distribution of pollution burdens and social impacts (Berry, 1977). That study found that poor residents in inner-city locations, many of whom were African American, had the greatest exposure to air pollutants. Another regional exposure study mapped the spatial distribution of TRI releases in pounds of emissions per year for the Southeast by county (Stockwell et al, 1993). The study not only examined the magnitude of releases, but also attempted a characterization of the emissions according to toxicity. Their analysis did not include demographic analyses other than a preliminary estimate of population density by county. Finally, in a pilot study of South Carolina, Cutter (1994a) examined three risk measures at the county level: number of acute airborne toxic releases; quantity of TRI emissions; and quantity of hazardous waste generated for 1992. Based on the geography of emissions, she found that most affected residents lived in racially mixed, more affluent, and urbanized counties within the state.

Sources of Toxic Releases Data

For this analysis, data on toxic releases came from two different sources. The EPA's TRI provides data that measures longer-term more chronic exposures of airborne toxic releases. The Airborne Chemical Release Inventory Data set (ACRID) developed by the authors, provides measures of acute exposures, exposures that cause bodily harm, injury, or even death within minutes to hours of exposure. The chronic releases are from stationary facilities such as manufacturing plants, while the acute releases reflect both stationary and transportation sources.

Acute releases

ACRID is a national database of acute airborne toxic releases that are geo-referenced by county. ACRID covers the time period from 1980–1990 and includes approximately 11,000 incidents. Data for ACRID were gathered from existing federal databases (e.g. US Department of Transportation's – DOT's – Emergency Response Notification System, EPA's Acute Hazardous Events (AHE) database, published articles and newspaper accounts). Most of the ACRID, however, consists of records obtained through fieldwork and site visits to individual states. ACRID only includes incidents involving Superfund Amendments and Reauthorization Act (SARA) Title III, Section 302 chemicals (EPA's list of Extremely Hazardous Substances and Their Threshold Planning Quantities as defined in the Federal Register 52:77, Wednesday 22 April 1987, p13397). However, non-SARA chemicals were included when releases/spills were large or when it was suspected that a SARA chemical might be a by-product of reactions among existing chemicals. Incidents involving oil, gasoline and natural gas were specifically excluded from our data collection.

For each incident ACRID contains up to 45 different variables describing it. These include measures of where (state, county, city/town, metropolitan designation), when (date and time of release), what (up to three chemicals, CAS numbers, SARA Title III or Section 304 designation, quantity released, verification of airborne release), how (in transit or stationary; transport mode such as truck, train, barge; transport location such as parking lot or railyard; fixed mode and fixed location), why (causes of the incident such as crash or human error), who (responsible party such as corporation or private citizen), to whom (injuries, deaths, evacuations, area evacuated, damage estimates, other impacts) and sources of the information (state files, newspaper, AHE database).

There are some variations in the quality and quantity of data for each state as record keeping was inconsistent between states and between federal regions. The temporal coverage is also inconsistent for the same reason. The Southeast has good quality data with the exception of Tennessee, where our access to state records on releases was restricted.[1] The Tennessee ACRID data that we possess (a total of 40 incidents, none covering the 1987–1990 time period) come from other sources. Extensive quality control studies were performed on the ACRID database. These included cross-checking with existing databases (such as EPA's Acute Hazardous Events database, DOT's Emergency Release Notification System) to eliminate redundancies and overlap. In addition, a 10 per cent sample of ACRID records was selected and manually verified against original field data to check consistency and accuracy. Three types of errors were found: misspellings; omission errors caused by differences in interpretation or incomplete data entry; and inconsistent definitions for data collection including chemical names. Most of the errors were corrected for all records. We estimate that ACRID has no more than a 6 per cent error rate. Despite these limitations, ACRID is the most comprehensive national database of acute airborne toxic releases and more than likely underestimates the number of incidents at the national level during the last decade.

Chronic releases

Chronic air releases were derived from the TRI, a national database of industrial facilities that release toxic and hazardous chemicals (USEPA, 1994). Under SARA's Emergency Planning and Community Right-to-Know Act of 1986 (EPCRA), manufacturing facilities (Standard Industrial Code (SIC) classification codes 20–39 with more than ten full-time employees) must report their estimated toxic releases and transfers on an annual basis to the EPA. The inventory covers more than 300 chemicals and 20 categories of chemicals (USEPA, 1993). The current reporting threshold is for facilities generating more than 25,000 pounds of toxics in manufacturing and processing uses, and 100,000 pounds for other uses. The TRI includes on-site releases (air, water, land, underground injection), and off-site transfers (to treatment or disposal facilities). Nationally, more than 23,000 facilities report annual releases of TRI substances. In addition to the location of facilities, the magnitude (pounds of emissions by media of release – air, water, land, off-site), type and frequency of emissions are available as well.

Although the TRI represents a significant data source for this type of analysis, these data have several limitations. Most obvious is that not all industrial facilities are required to submit toxic release data. Facilities generating small amounts of pollution are exempt from the regulations, as are selected types of industries such as mineral processing facilities and US military installations. A second caveat is that facilities are only required to report releases of those chemicals or compounds listed in the EPCRA or Right-to-Know regulations. Although many more chemicals were recently added to the list of those currently monitored, many other potentially hazardous materials remain off the list. Finally, the facilities self-report the type and volume of releases to state regulatory agencies and then to the EPA and are, for the most part, not independently verified. When these limitations are considered in the aggregate, it becomes apparent that the TRI database underestimates the absolute volume of toxic materials released within any locale. It does serve, however, as one of the most reliable approximations of chronic toxic releases currently available.

Southern Places and Toxic Exposures

Patterns of potential exposure

Our study area is the Southeast which coincides with the EPA's Region 4. Roughly 80 per cent of the 736 counties in the Southeast recorded airborne toxic releases during the study period (Table 19.1). Releases varied considerably between states with South Carolina registering the highest percentages of counties with both acute and chronic releases. In comparing ACRID and TRI releases we can see the clustering of ACRID releases in the Carolinas, Florida and Alabama (Figure 19.1). Georgia is noticeable by the absence of any significant number of

Table 19.1 *Releases in Southeastern US counties*

State	Counties	Counties with TRI releases (%)	Counties with acute releases (%)	Counties with total releases (%)
Alabama	67	80.6	35.8	92.5
Florida	67	88.1	47.8	89.4
Georgia	159	65.4	6.9	66.7
Kentucky	118	66.9	28.0	68.6
Mississippi	81	81.5	28.4	84.0
N. Carolina	100	90.0	33.0	90.0
S. Carolina	46	95.7	73.9	95.7
Tennessee	95	87.4	NA	NA[1]
SOUTHEAST	733	79.8	29.8[2]	29.8[2]

[1] At least 87.4% based on the TRI release data
[2] Base of 638 counties because of the missing Tennessee data.

ACRID releases with the exception of the greater metropolitan Atlanta region. Acute releases for Tennessee were recorded as 'no data' as a result of the limitations in the ACRID database. The distribution of TRI releases (Figure 19.2) is more uniform throughout the region, although there are noticeable gaps in Georgia and in eastern Kentucky. What is apparent from the maps is the clustering of toxic releases in metropolitan counties within the Southeast. This is no real surprise, as previous studies have indicated a distinct metropolitan bias in toxic releases (Chapter 2), although not as pronounced as those suggested here.

Social Burdens

The first step in the analysis was to evaluate the association between the number of airborne toxic releases and county-level socio-demographic characteristics. A basic assumption driving this analysis is that a higher frequency of releases (an estimate of the magnitude of potential exposure) is typical of those counties with higher proportions of residents exposed to the processes of environmental injustice. In other words, these are counties with poorer residents, more vulnerable (aged/young) populations and high percentages of minority residents. Residents of these countries would bear the burden of toxic exposure to a greater extent than counties with more affluent and largely white populations. Three sets of variables were collected to test these assumptions. In order to avoid the obvious problems with multicollinearity and to focus more precisely on the question of the socio-spatial context for environmental inequities, most of the demographic variables were standardized as percentages of the total population (Table 19.2).

The first data set consisted of information on a set of urban-related variables. On the basis of the existing literature, it was hypothesized that increased population and urban density would be associated with higher numbers of releases. A second data set focused on the social characteristics of the counties' residents. Again, based on the literature, it was hypothesized that counties with higher percentages of minority populations would be exposed to higher numbers of releases. It was also believed that, because such a high number of young children in the

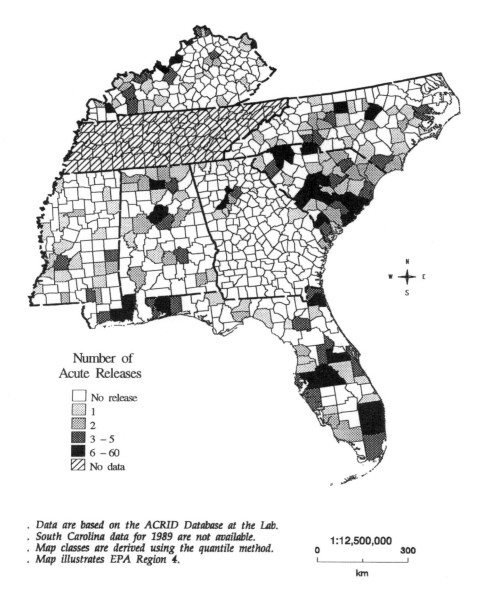

Number of
Acute Releases

☐ No release
▨ 1
▨ 2
▨ 3 – 5
■ 6 – 60
▨ No data

. *Data are based on the ACRID Database at the Lab.*
. *South Carolina data for 1989 are not available.*
. *Map classes are derived using the quantile method.*
. *Map illustrates EPA Region 4.*

1:12,500,000
0   300
km

Source: Based on the ACRID database developed by Dr Susan Cutter and housed at the University of
South Carolina.

Figure 19.1 *Acute airborne releases, 1987–1989*

US live in poverty, the percentage of residents under the age of five would be
positively associated with the number of releases. Several other variables, including gender and the elderly, were included for exploratory reasons, even though
the literature has not defined explicit links between percentage female and elderly,

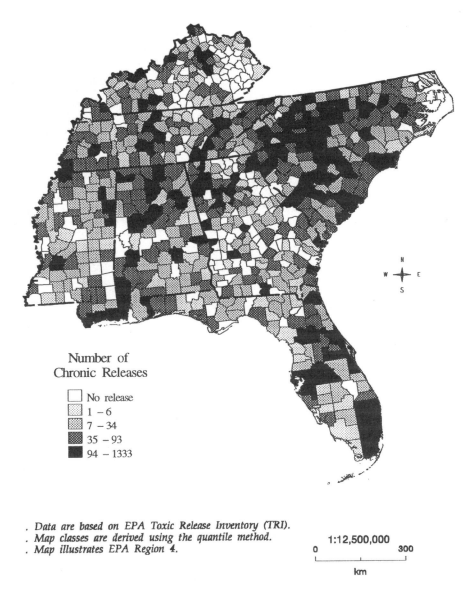

Number of
Chronic Releases

☐ No release
▨ 1 – 6
▨ 7 – 34
▨ 35 – 93
■ 94 – 1333

. Data are based on EPA Toxic Release Inventory (TRI).
. Map classes are derived using the quantile method.
. Map illustrates EPA Region 4.

1:12,500,000
0   300
km

Source: Based on the EPA's Toxic Release Inventory.

Figure 19.2 *Chronic airborne releases, 1987–1990*

and the number of releases. A third set of variables analysed the issue of income. In general, the expected relationship is that the number of releases decreases as income increases. The relationship between number of releases and poverty level is somewhat unclear, particularly with respect to the American rural South (Solecki, 1992). Relatively few source locations for airborne releases are present in the

Table 19.2 *County-level data used in the analysis and the expected relationship with the frequency of airborne toxic releases*

Data	Expected relationship
Urban	
Residential population, 1990	+
Population per square mile, 1990	+
Percentage of total population, urban residents	+
Race/Gender/Age	
Percentage of total population, African American	+
Percentage of total population, other minorities	+
Percentage of total population, non-white – total	+
Percentage of total population, white	+/–
Percentage of residents under the age of 5	+
Percentage of residents over the age of 65	NA
Percentage of total population, female	NA
Income	
Percentage of total population below poverty levels	+/–
Income per capita	–
Median value of housing	–

Source: All data from the US Census of Population, 1990, County CD-ROM.

poorest rural counties of the region (one of the reasons the poverty rate is high in some counties is because of a lack of manufacturing or processing facilities), and therefore, one would expect there to be few releases in such places.

A Pearson correlation test was performed to test the hypotheses and ascertain the association between the social indicators and the airborne toxic release data. Because of the temporal variability between the TRI and ACRID coverages, the release data were also standardized by year. Three county-level release variables were used in the correlation analysis: the number of chronic (TRI) releases per year; the number of acute (ACRID) releases per year; and total number of releases per year.

In general the correlation analysis failed to indicate any substantial association between the racial composition of the county and the frequency of airborne toxic releases. The only significant association was with the variable, percentage other minority, and that correlation was very weak. Wealth indicators (percentage living below the poverty line, median house value, per capita income) demonstrated some statistical significance and were moderately associated with the number of toxic releases, but not in the direction we anticipated (Table 19.3). Counties with higher frequencies of releases are those with lower percentages of residents below the poverty level, higher per capita incomes and higher median values of housing. Clearly, these initial findings are counter-intuitive to the arguments developed in the environmental justice literature, although not with respect to the poverty indicator.

Variables reflecting the urban nature of counties (population density, absolute size, percentage urban) had the strongest positive correlation with number

Table 19.3 *Correlation matrix (Pearson's* r*)*

Variable	TRI releases/year	Acute releases/year	Total releases/year
Population	0.63***	0.32***	0.61***
Population density	0.62***	0.31***	0.59***
% urban	0.52***	0.27***	0.51***
% African American	−0.00	−0.06	−0.03
% other minority	0.11**	0.05	0.11**
% non-white	0.02	−0.05	−0.01
% white	−0.01	−0.06	−0.02
% under age 5	−0.20***	−0.07	−0.21***
% over 65	−0.16***	−0.04	−0.14***
% female	0.08*	0.02	0.06
% below poverty	−0.29***	−0.13***	−0.30***
Per capita income	0.46***	0.20***	0.44***
Median housing value	0.35***	0.14***	0.34***

* $p < 0.05$
** $p < 0.01$
*** $p < 0.001$

of releases. In general then, highly urbanized counties were more likely to have a greater frequency of releases, especially TRI releases, than less urbanized counties. Therefore, we can suggest broadly that chronic releases are correlated with heavily populated counties with high population densities, higher per capita incomes and higher housing values. Acute releases are more associated with less urbanized counties, those with lower populations and population densities and whose residents have lower per capita incomes than those exposed to chronic releases.

Underlying Processes Contributing to Differential Releases

Although the correlation analysis illustrated the weakness of the association between the frequency of releases and many variables in question, it was determined that a secondary analysis highlighting the role of the socio-spatial context in the production of risk was warranted. Literature on the social construction of risk recognizes the importance of contextual variables in the overall riskscape mosaic, and since the counties were analysed as a single group, significant intra-group variation could be masked. The issue of scale or aggregation bias also was a consideration. Finally, it is possible that the association between the frequency of releases and the socio-economic variables addressed is non-linear and that specific subsets of counties are more highly associated with the number of releases.

In order to test the relevance of the county subsets assertion, three hypotheses were developed, which are basic extensions of our earlier ones. The first hypothesis is that the highly urbanized counties are positively correlated with high frequency of releases. This is based on the assumption that urbanized locations have higher proportions of potential sources of releases, in the form of both fixed facilities and transportation networks. A second hypothesis is that the counties with the highest percentage African American population are the most positively correlated with higher frequency of releases. The assumption here is that race becomes an issue when a greater than average percentage of the population is African American. A third hypothesis examines the association between the number of releases and income with the highest correlations found in the middle-income counties. Based on the economic reality of the South, the poorest counties in the region have relatively few sources for releases. We assumed here that the working class, mill counties of the South experience the greatest number of releases.

In order to test these three hypotheses, we divided our data into quantiles with three equal categories based on urbanization, percentage African American and per capita income levels. Separate correlations were run for each category resulting in a total of nine additional correlation analyses. Four socio-economic variables were included in each analysis: percentage urban, percentage African American, per capita income and population. The latter variable was included because it is strongly associated with the frequency of releases.

The analyses produced some interesting results (see Tables 19.4, 19.5 and 19.6). Of the three, the race-based analysis proved to be the most meaningful (Table 19.5). The level of association between population and frequency of releases increased dramatically when comparing the counties with the highest percentage

Table 19.4 *Analysis of sub-samples of Southeast counties (correlation matrix: urban)*

Variable	TRI releases/year	Acute releases/year	Total releases/year
Top third of counties			
Population	0.58***	0.37***	0.55***
% urban	0.48***	0.31***	0.45***
% African American	−0.01	−0.12	−0.05
Per capita income	0.37***	0.21**	0.36***
Middle third of counties			
Population	0.57***	−0.01	0.55***
% urban	0.14*	0.06	0.14*
% African American	−0.11	−0.10	−0.15
Per capita income	0.35***	0.02	0.35***
Bottom third of counties			
Population	0.50***	0.19**	0.49***
% urban	0.35***	0.23**	0.35***
% African American	−0.02	0.17*	−0.04
Per capita income	0.24***	0.04	0.22**

* $p < 0.05$
** $p < 0.01$
*** $p < 0.001$

Table 19.5 *Analysis of sub-samples of Southeast counties*
(correlation matrix: African American)

Variable	TRI releases/year	Acute releases/year	Total releases/year
Top third of counties			
Population	0.92***	0.55***	0.90***
% urban	0.54***	0.30***	0.53***
% black	−0.12	−0.06	−0.12
Per capita income	0.54***	0.22***	0.53***
Middle third of counties			
Population	0.55***	0.40***	0.53***
% urban	0.53***	0.33***	0.52***
% African American	0.06	0.00	0.05
Per capita income	0.48***	0.24**	0.46***
Bottom third of counties			
Population	0.36***	0.06	0.29***
% urban	0.40***	0.20**	0.33***
% African American	0.26***	−0.04	0.24**
Per capita income	0.33***	0.12	0.31***

* $p < 0.05$
** $p < 0.01$
*** $p < 0.001$

African American with those with the lowest. In the group of counties with the highest percentage African American, the correlation was $r = 0.90$, indicating that more so than in any other test, population size was highly correlated with the frequency of releases. The income-based hypothesis also was shown to have some validity. High correlation ($r = 0.78$) was found between the number of releases and population in counties with intermediate range per capita income values. It is interesting to note that in this same case the variable, percentage African American, showed no association with the number of releases. Overall, the separation of the counties in three urban groups failed to improve the understanding of the relationship between the variables.

A Hierarchy within the Southern Riskscape

The division of the sample into equal quantiles illustrates the importance of sub-sample sets of counties, a procedure designed to promote an understanding of the character of these subsets and assist in the identification of patterns of environmental injustice for the region. A principal components analysis was conducted in order to identify such subgroupings and to develop a typology of county toxic exposures. Many of the variables used in our earlier tests (Table 19.2) were dropped from this statistical test because of multicollinearity problems among the independent variables. Eleven variables were included in the final iteration of the procedure: two release variables (ACRID per year, TRI per year); and nine of the

Table 19.6 *Analysis of sub-samples of Southeast counties*
(correlation matrix: income)

Variable	TRI releases/year	Acute releases/year	Total releases/year
Top third of counties			
Population	0.57***	0.32***	0.54***
% urban	0.45***	0.26***	0.42***
% African American	0.17**	−0.05	0.12
Per capita income	0.29***	0.13	0.28***
Middle third of counties			
Population	0.77***	0.35***	0.78***
% urban	0.46***	0.20**	0.46***
% African American	0.002	−0.04	−0.004
Per capita income	0.16*	0.12	0.15*
Bottom third of counties			
Population	0.62***	0.25***	0.62***
% urban	0.38***	0.07	0.36***
% African American	0.12	0.03	0.12
Per capita income	0.32***	0.07	0.31***

* $p < 0.05$
** $p < 0.01$
*** $p < 0.001$

social indicators (total population, percentage female, percentage African American, percentage other minority, percentage rural, median house value, income per capita, percentage below poverty and percentage under age 5).

The principal components analysis identified four factors with eigenvalues greater than 1.0, and when taken together, these factors explain 84 per cent of the variation among the counties. We identified four types of toxic release counties in the Southeast:

1 high release, highly urbanized counties;
2 high release intermediate sized African American counties;
3 low release other minority counties; and
4 high acute release counties.

High-exposure urban counties

Factor 1 is characterized by large numbers of toxic releases in a group of relatively wealthy, white, heavily populated urbanized counties, a group not clearly identified in the second set of correlation analyses (Table 19.7). This factor reflects previously described dimensions of the spatial distribution and the patterns of urbanism in the American South. Historically, the South was a region without extensive urban settlements. During the past half-century, however, several large-scale metropolitan complexes developed. Most of the industrialization in the Southeast also occurred in these metropolitan complexes. Illustrative coun-

Table 19.7 *Factor loadings*

	Factor 1	Factor 2	Factor 3	Factor 4
TRI releases/year	0.63055	0.51413	−0.18842	0.31756
Acute releases/year	0.37701	0.44724	−0.26573	0.64523
Total releases/year	0.71050	0.39405	0.28804	0.06387
% rural	−0.69918	−0.36945	−0.07127	0.18932
% African American	−0.37014	0.65195	0.22443	−0.33242
% other minority	0.41809	−0.01706	0.81532	0.09786
% under age 5	−0.65379	0.43473	0.21900	0.04729
% female	−0.19248	0.59283	−0.37334	−0.44859
% below poverty	−0.77128	0.40729	0.19142	0.07977
Per capita income	0.85582	0.03280	−0.12255	−0.31715
Median housing value	0.83035	−0.11832	0.03679	−0.29258
Variance explained	43.3%	19.0%	11.5%	10.7%
Total explained – 84.5%				

ties with high loadings on this factor include Jefferson County (Louisville), KY; Fulton County (Atlanta), GA; and Mecklenburg County (Charlotte), NC. The racial composition of counties had no effect in the construction of Factor 1, while income measures did.

High-exposure African American counties

The second county type is characterized by high numbers of both acute and chronic releases, and medium size populations of mostly African American origin. These counties are characterized by high percentages of female residents and moderate percentages of residents in poverty. This factor is important in that it identified a subset of high-exposure counties, especially those counties with higher numbers of TRI releases. Geographically, these high-exposure counties are found throughout the region, but there is a clustering of these communities along the Gulf and Atlantic Coastal Plain. The most notable examples of the non-metropolitan counties identified by Factor 2 are Greene, AL, and Washington, MS, each with large pulp and paper mills located in predominately African American areas.

Low-release counties

The third factor identified low-release counties. Most of these counties are associated with high percentages of other minority residents (e.g. non-African American). Counties identified by this factor are less populated and not located along major cross-country transportation corridors – one reason why acute releases are so low. Most of the counties identified by this factor are in southern Florida – typically with large Hispanic populations. In addition to these, the other types of counties identified are those with sizeable Native American populations (Swain, NC) and those counties with military installations (Chattahoochee, GA, home of

Fort Benning). Hispanics are often over-represented in military towns (Winsberg, 1994), which may account for the high loadings on this factor.

High acute-release counties

The fourth factor identified high acute-release counties, which are essentially rural in character. These counties are largely white, lower income (but not poverty) counties and fall into two categories. First, they have major regional or trans-continental transportation nodes or corridors that cross their borders. Examples include Greenville, SC (Interstate 85 bisects the county), Madison, KY (Inter-state 75), and Meade and Carroll counties in KY (along a major rail line). The other category encompasses counties with multiple large generators such as Polk County, FL, which hosts four very large agricultural chemical and fertilizer pro-duction facilities. In fact, a larger amount of ammonia is released into the air than any other chemical.

Towards a Broader Understanding of Environmental Justice

We began our analysis with two primary questions. First, are there differences in the spatial distribution of airborne releases? Second, are these releases concen-trated in lower-income African American counties? We provide mixed evidence in support of the 'Dumping in Dixie' hypothesis. Clearly, we have shown that the distributional patterns of chronic and acute exposures to airborne toxic releases are varied, and under certain conditions they disproportionately affect African American communities. However, high numbers of releases also were found in other socio-economic settings. One conclusion is that the story of environmental injustice in the Southeastern US is more complicated than simple correlations between race, income and toxic exposures. It is a narrative that must be examined within the context of the underlying socio-spatial processes that gave rise to the production of airborne toxic releases that created the riskscape. As identified here, these socio-spatial processes included regional urban-industrial growth, rural underdevelopment, the structure of industrial production (small facilities versus large ones), proximity to transportation corridors *and* racism. In effect, racism seems to account for only part of the process of the social production of risk.

During the past two decades, considerable research in the social sciences was devoted to understanding the impact of human response and adjustments to hazards and risks in society. Questions on how individuals and organizations respond to events, the psychological impact of the events, and the role of risk and hazards in local and national policy and planning are now part of active research agendas within the social science community (Mayo and Hollander, 1991; Cutter, 1994b). Geographers developed conceptual models on the hazardousness of places that help explain why certain locations are affected more strongly by toxic releases than others (Pijawka and Radwan, 1985; Cutter and Solecki, 1989). Critical to a full understanding of the 'context' in which a hazard occurs are the circumstances surrounding and influencing the severity of the event and the broader economic, political and social conditions in which the technology is used (Mitchell et al, 1989; Kirby, 1990; Mitchell 1990; Palm, 1990).

Equally important is the concept of vulnerability (Blaikie et al, 1994), a concept embedded in both the hazardousness-of-place and hazards-in-context models. Vulnerability is the likelihood that an individual or group will be exposed to or adversely affected by a hazard (Cutter, 1993). It examines the potential for harm based on socio-structural characteristics of the population and biophysical or technological sources of risk. The biophysical/technological risk combines with the social and political structures to identify vulnerable places and vulnerable people within those places. As a dynamic process, vulnerability links the environmental risk sources (which spatially manifest themselves in the hazards of place), to the societal impact and response. It is within this broad conceptual framework that the distribution of airborne toxic releases and their differential impact on poor communities or communities of colour is situated.

There is an established literature on the kinds of conditions most associated with industrial pollution and toxic releases. Taken at a regional level, many of the expectations developed from this literature are reflected in the data presented here. While the hazards literature seems to restrict the analysis to a broad regional level of analysis, the theoretical constructs about the social construction of hazards permits a shift from broad spatial patterns to more place-specific contexts. While we are interested in broad spatial patterns at the regional level, a multitude of processes are at work producing the differential toxic releases that reflect the Southern riskscape. As a result of different societal processes, the poorest and wealthiest southern counties experience relatively low levels of releases in comparison to lower- to middle-income counties, regardless of race, and to counties with high percentages of African American residents. The exceptions are the central city counties associated within the larger metropolitan complexes.

Although the issue of race obviously is important, the issue of economic development must also be examined in order to understand fully the evolution of riskscapes. It seems that those counties at the economic development–toxic release margin – outliers identified in Figures 19.1 and 19.2 – are the most vulnerable. Bullard (1992) described these places as experiencing a kind of 'environmental blackmail'. Without these large facilities, the counties would reduce their toxic burdens, yet become more economically impoverished. They would join the ranks of other, increasingly depopulated and deindustrialized counties in the Southeast such as those found in southern Georgia and in Alabama's 'black belt' region (Colcough, 1988). Furthermore, it is unlikely that these counties will experience a rapid influx of new, potentially less polluting, economic development opportunities. Facility operators and other local elites – typically those individuals who make the economic development decisions in such communities – resist the introduction of new economic opportunities into the community because they may drive up local wages and other operating expenses (Cobb, 1984).

Although the examination of these sociospatial processes is present within the environmental justice literature, often it is not the main focus of the research. We now have partial evidence of environmental inequities, but we need to learn much more about the social construction of hazardous places. How do environmental inequities develop, how are they perpetuated, and how can they be eliminated? It is clear the environmental justice research agenda is moving away from its early conceptual and empirical roots, and is advancing toward this set of deeper theoretical and methodological questions. We contend, based on the arguments and empirical support in this chapter, this is an advancement long overdue.

Note

1   Acquisition of information in Tennessee was a particularly challenging task. We needed to make individual Freedom of Information Act (FOIA) requests for each record we wished to examine. This required that we have previous knowledge of the incidents in question, because state officials would only allow us to request specific information. Because we did not have prior information on incidents, we were unable to obtain the relevant data.

Acknowledgements

We wish to thank Minhe Ji for his assistance in the preparation of the graphics for this chapter. This research was partially supported by grants from the South Carolina Universities Research and Education Foundation (#30–95, #62–95) and the National Geographic Society (#3917–88).

References

Adeola, F. O. (1994) 'Environmental hazards, health, and racial inequity in hazardous waste distribution', *Environment and Behavior*, vol 26, no 1, pp99–126
Anderton, D. L., Anderson, A. B., Rossi, P. H., Oakes, J. M., Fraser, M. R., Weber, E. W. and Calabrese, E. J. (1994a) 'Hazardous waste facilities: "Environmental equity" issues in metropolitan areas', *Evaluation Review*, vol 18, no 2, pp123–140
Anderton, D. L., Anderson, A. B., Oakes, J. M. and Fraser, M. R. (1994b) 'Environmental equity: The demographics of dumping', *Demography*, vol 31, no 2, pp229–248
Berry, B. J. L. (ed) (1977) *The Social Burdens of Environmental Pollution: A Comparative Metropolitan Data Source*, Ballinger, Cambridge, MA
Blaikie, P., Cannon, T., Davis, I. and Wisner, B. (1994) *At Risk: Natural Hazards. People's Vulnerability and Disasters*, Routledge, New York
Bryant, B. and Mohai, P. (eds) (1992) *Race and the Incidence of Environmental Hazards: A Time for Discourse*, Westview Press, Boulder, CO
Bullard, R. D. (1983) 'Solid waste sites and the Black Houston community,' *Sociological Inequity*, vol 53, spring, pp273–288
Bullard, R. D. (1990) *Dumping in Dixie: Race, Class, and Environmental Quality*, Westview Press, Boulder, CO
Bullard, R. D. (1992) 'Environmental blackmail in minority communities' in B. Bryant and P. Mohai (eds) *Race and the Incidence of Environmental Hazards: A Time for Discourse*, Westview Press, Boulder, CO, pp82–96
Bullard, R. D. (ed) (1993) *Confronting Environmental Racism: Voices from the Grassroots*, South End Press, Boston, MA
Bullard, R. D. (1994a) 'Overcoming racism in environmental decision-making', *Environment*, vol 36, no 4, pp10–20, 39–44
Bullard, R. D. (1994b) *Unequal Protection: Environmental Justice and Communities of Color*, Sierra Club Books, San Francisco, CA

Burke, L. M. (1993) 'Race and environmental equity: A geographic analysis in Los Angeles,' *Geo Info Systems*, October, pp44–50

Cobb, J. C. (1984) *Industrialization and Southern Society, 1877–1984*, University Press of Kentucky, Lexington, KY

Colclough, G. (1988) 'Uneven development and racial composition in the Deep South: 1970–1980', *Rural Sociology*, vol 53, pp73–86

Crew-Meyer, K. (1994) 'Hazardous waste and race in South Carolina', *The South Carolina Police Forum*, vol 5, no 3, pp25–28

Cutter, S. L. (1993) *Living with Risk: The Geography of Technological Hazards*, Edward Arnold, London

Cutter, S. L. (1994a) 'The burdens of toxic risks: Are they fair?,' *Business and Economic Review*, vol 41, no 1, pp3–7

Cutter, S. L. (ed) (1994b) *Environmental Risks and Hazards*, Prentice-Hall, Englewood Cliffs, NJ

Cutter, S. L. and Solecki, W. D. (1989) 'The national pattern of airborne toxic releases', *The Professional Geographer*, vol 41, no 2, pp149–161

Geiser, K. and Waneck, G. (1983) 'PCBs and Warren County', *Science for the People*, July/August, pp13–17

Glickman, T. S. (1994) 'Measuring environmental equity with geographical information systems', *Renewable Resources Journal*, vol 12, no 3, pp17–21

Goldman, B. A. and Fitton, L. (1994) *Toxic Wastes and Race Revisited*, Center for Policy Alternatives, New York

Gottlieb, R. (1993) *Forcing the Spring: The Transformation of the American Environmental Movement*, Island Press, Washington, DC

Greenberg, M. R. (1993) 'Proving environmental inequity in siting locally unwanted land uses', *4 Risk – Issues in Health and Safety*, vol 235, Summer, pp235–252

Greenberg, M. R. (1994) 'Separate and not equal: Health–environmental risk and economic–social impacts in remediating hazardous waste sites' in S. K. Majumdar, F. J. Brenner, E. W. Miller and L. M. Rosenfeld (eds) *Environmental Contaminants and Health*, Pennsylvania Academy of Sciences, Philadelphia, PA

Hird, J. A. (1993) 'Environmental policy and equity: The case of Superfund', *Journal of Policy Analysis and Management*, vol 12, no 2, pp323–343

Holm, D. M. (1994) 'Environmental inequities in South Carolina: The distribution of hazardous waste facilities', unpublished master's thesis, Department of Geography, University of South Carolina, Columbia, SC

Kirby, A. (ed) (1990) *Nothing to Fear: Risks and Hazards in American Society*, University of Arizona Press, Tucson, AZ

Krimsky, S. and Golding, D. (eds) (1992) *Social Theories of Risk*, Praeger, Westport, CT

Kruvant, W. (1974) *Incidence of Pollution Where People Live In Washington*, Center for Metropolitan Studies, Washington, DC

Lake, R. W. (1995) 'Volunteers, NIMBYs, and environmental justice: Dilemmas of democratic practice', paper presented at the Annual Meeting of the Association of American Geographers, March, Chicago, IL

Liverman, D. (1986) 'The vulnerability of urban areas of technological risks', *Cities*, May, pp142–147

Mayo, D. G. and Hollander, R. D. (eds) (1991) *Acceptable Evidence: Science and Values in Risk Management*, Oxford University Press, New York

McMaster, R. B. (1988) 'Modeling community vulnerability to hazardous materials using GIS' in *Proceedings: Third International Symposium on Spatial Data Handling IGU*, Department of Geography, University of Ohio, Columbus, OH, pp143–156

Mitchell, J. K. (1990) 'Human dimensions of environmental hazards: Complexity, disparity, and the search for guidance' in A. Kirby (ed) *Nothing to Fear: Risks and Hazards in American Society*, University of Arizona Press, Tucson, AZ, pp131–175

Mitchell, J. K., Devine, N. and Jagger, K. (1989) 'A contextual model of natural hazard', *Geographic Review*, vol 79, pp391–409

Mohai, P. and Bryant, B. (1992) 'Environmental racism: Reviewing the evidence' in B. Bryant and P. Mohai (eds) *Race and the Incidence of Environmental Hazards: A Time for Discourse*, Westview Press, Boulder, CO, pp163–176

Palm, R. I. (1990) *Natural Hazards: An Integrative Framework for Research and Planning*, Johns Hopkins University Press, Baltimore, MD

Perlin, S. A., Setzer, R. W., Creason, R. W. and Sexton, K. (1995) 'Distribution of industrial air emissions by income and race in the United States: An approach using the Toxic Release Inventory', *Environmental Science and Technology*, vol 29, pp69–80

Pijawka, K. D. and Radwan, A. E. (1985) 'The transportation of hazardous materials: Risk assessment and hazard management', *Dangerous Properties of Industrial Materials Report*, September/October, pp2–11

Schwab, J. (1994) *Deeper Shades of Green: The Rise of Blue-Collar and Minority Environmentalism in America*, Sierra Club, San Francisco, CA

Solecki, W. D. (1992) 'Rural places and the circumstances of acute chemical disasters', *Journal of Rural Studies*, vol 8, no 1, pp1–13

Stockwell, J. R., Sorenson, J. W., Eckert, J. W. jr and Carreras, E. M. (1993) 'The USEPA geographic information system for mapping environmental releases of toxic chemical release inventory (TRI) chemicals', *Risk Analysis*, vol 13, no 2, pp155–164

Szasz, A. (1994) *Ecopopulism: Toxic Waste and the Movement for Environmental Justice*, University of Minnesota Press, Minneapolis, MN

UCC (United Church of Christ Commission for Racial Justice) (1987) *Toxic Wastes and Race: A National Report on the Racial and Socioeconomic Characteristics of Communities with Hazardous Waste Sites*, United Church of Christ, New York

USEPA (United States Environmental Protection Agency) (1993) *1991 Toxics Release Inventory*, EPA745-R-92-003, USEPA, Washington, DC

USEPA (1994) *1987–1992 Toxics Release Inventory*, EPA 749/c-94-001 (CDU-ROM), USEPA, Washington, DC

USGAO (United States General Accounting Office) (1983) *Siting of Hazardous Waste Landfills and their Correlation with Racial and Economic Status of Surrounding Communities*, Government Printing Office, Washington, DC

Winsberg, M. (1994) 'Specific Hispanics', *American Demographics*, February, pp44–53

Zimmerman, R. (1993) 'Social equity and environmental risk', *Risk Analysis*, vol 13, no 6, pp649–666

Zimmerman, R. (1994) 'Issues of classification in environmental equity: How we manage is how we measure', *Fordham Urban Law Journal*, vol 21, pp633–669

20
Using Relative Risk Indicators to Disclose Toxic Hazard Information to Communities

Michael S. Scott and Susan L. Cutter

Introduction

Recently, the US Environmental Protection Agency (EPA) announced a plan to provide pollution profiles of selected industries (automobile, steel, metals, oil refining and paper-making) via the internet (Cushman, 1997). These profiles would include releases and spills, pollution-to-production ratios, as well as data on inspections, non-compliance, and enforcement actions. In addition, the EPA plans on providing a hazard indicator for each plant based on the relative toxicity of the chemicals released and some demographic data on residents within three miles of the plant.

The issue of deriving a relative measure of risk to compare individual facilities or different types of contaminants is not new and has been part of EPA's agenda for many years. The risk assessment paradigm (describing the detrimental effects of industrial toxins on people and ecosystems that support human activity) has dominated most of these discussions. The methods used to conduct risk assessments include four steps: hazard identification, dose-response assessment, exposure assessment and risk characterization (National Research Council, 1983, 1994). However, as Nyerges et al (1997) discussed earlier, the practices of risk assessment are coming under attack. The primary points of contention include data needs, data compatibility and data uncertainty (National Research Council, 1994), the nature of acceptable risks and acceptable evidences (Mayo and Hol-

Note: Reprinted, with permission, from *Cartography and Geographic Information Systems*, vol 24, no 3, Michael S. Scott and Susan L. Cutter, 'Using relative risk indicators to disclose toxic hazard information to communities', pp158–171. © American Congress on Surveying and Mapping, 1997

lander, 1991; Kunreuther and Slovic, 1996), prioritizing and comparing risks (Davies, 1996), and communication of technical results to decision-makers and the public (National Research Council, 1996).

A central issue in characterizing and communicating risks is the representation of those risks graphically and in an accessible manner. Risk information varies across space, and the variability in risk perception is partially dependent on the quality of data received. Geographic information systems (GIS) and digital cartography will play a large role in risk assessment and communication in the future as we move away from strict deterministic models of risk to more socially constructed approaches to risk assessment. This shift was recognized by the National Center for Geographic Information and Analysis (NCGIA) as part of Initiative 19 – GIS and Society. Central to this initiative are key questions on how GIS influences the perception of risk, how GIS can empower or disempower community groups, and how equity issues can be examined within a socio-spatial context (Harris and Wiener, 1996).

Related to the empowerment question is the analysis of the disproportionate distribution of risk on people and places. The idea of environmental inequities has captured the attention of many activists and researchers following the publication of the watershed study by the United Church of Christ (UCC, 1987) and Bullard's *Dumping in Dixie* (1990). Concern about the correlation between race and hazardous facility location has prompted a surfeit of research on environmental justice topics (see Chapter 16). Differences in the environmental threat examined, the scale of measurement, the subpopulations sampled and the time frames have led to ambiguous conclusions in the empirical support for or against environmental (in)justice.

This chapter describes the development of a comparative measure of environmental risk in order to contrast facilities and spatial units at the state and local levels. Our primary purpose is twofold:

1   to illustrate a simplified methodology for conducting comparative risk assessments; and
2   provide a tool for risk visualization and communication to the public, using a GIS and digital cartography framework.

We contend that to develop relative risk measurements at the community level, one must be cognizant of the accuracy of the database, the differences in the magnitude and toxicity of industrial toxins, the transport and fate of these toxins, and the degree to which community activists, business leaders and decision-makers understand risk visualizations.

The Context of Comparative Risk

Since the publication of the EPA's *Unfinished Business* (USEPA, 1987), locally based risk assessments are burgeoning. Through EPA support, more than three dozen regions, states and municipalities have conducted some form of comparative risk study (Minard, 1996). The EPA has also established its Community-

Based Environmental Protection (CBEP) programme in an effort to support local risk projects (Wernick, 1996), realizing that national comparisons often mask locally important risks. While providing a good baseline of data, most of these efforts only rank risks along a variety of dimensions; they do not spatially represent them (Wernick, 1997).

Correlating risks: The spatial domain

Some of the earliest comparative risk projects were conducted in the 1970s. Berry (1977), for example, mapped pollution indicators (water, air, solid waste, noise) for 13 metropolitan areas in an effort to understand the social burdens of environmental pollution. More recently, Goldman (1991) examined the relationship between demographic characteristics, health outcomes and multiple risks (industrial toxins, pesticides, water quality, air quality). Using county-level data, Goldman depicted regional variation in risk exposure and mortality.

Using multiple indicators of toxic releases, Cutter and Solecki compared the spatial distribution of airborne toxic releases by county in the Southeast in an effort to define the relative hazardousness of places based on these acute and chronic emissions (see Chapter 19). They also questioned whether lower-income, minority counties were disproportionately at risk and found no conclusive evidence of socio-demographic inequities. In another example using South Carolina (Chapter 18), three indicators of industrial toxins were mapped at three different spatial scales. There were distinct geographic variations in risks across the state, although the pattern of socio-demographic impacts was not as well defined. Finally, Stockwell et al (1993) utilized GIS to delineate the spatial patterning of potential risk exposures from Toxic Release Inventory (TRI) facilities for the Southeast. Utilizing magnitude estimators for this single risk indicator, they found the largest TRI releases were near the most densely populated areas.

Contrasting impacts: The social domain

Another approach to comparative risk assessment is to take a single risk indicator (such as Superfund sites or TRI facilities) and examine potential exposures of areas based on their socio-demographic profiles. These studies provide empirical data on the social inequalities of potential impacts. However, much of this research is more statistically than spatially oriented (see Chapters 16 and 18 for a review). The use of GIS in illuminating spatial equity has been demonstrated in a number of recent studies (Burke, 1993; Bowen et al, 1995; Glickman, 1994; Glickman et al, 1995; McMaster et al, 1997; and Sui and Giardino, 1995).

In this chapter, we have opted to concentrate on comparing risks and communicating these to the public, rather than providing a spatial equity study (see the remaining chapters in this volume). However, it is an easy translation to move from the delineation and communication of relative risk to the incorporation of social and demographic indicators of potentially affected populations.

Methodology

Data for this research were taken from three of the EPA's national databases on hazardous waste and toxic releases: the Comprehensive Environmental Responsibility, Cleanup, and Liability Act's (CERCLA's) National Priorities List (NPL); the Emergency Planning and Community Right-to-Know Act's (EPCRA's) Toxic Release Inventory (TRI); and RCRA's Biennial Reporting System (BRS). For more detailed descriptions of these databases see Scott et al (1997a). This chapter utilizes 1992 data because at the time this research was launched (1996), these data were the most current. It is important to be cognizant, however, that the data for each of these hazard indicators varies year to year because of changes in reporting releases and in the listing and/or delisting of facilities.

Developing the hazard source inventory

When developing a catalogue of hazardous facilities, it is erroneous to simply tabulate records in separate databases because some facilities appear in several databases due to reporting requirements. Moreover, single facilities can and do produce multiple exposures. The EPA recognizes this and assigns a unique facility identifier in the TRI, BRS and CERCLIS databases. Unfortunately, the EPA identification number did not prove to be unique in all cases. We therefore developed a procedure for creating a unique identifier or key field (Scott et al, 1997a). In this way, we were able to ensure a many-to-one correspondence between South Carolina facility listings and their characteristics across the three databases. Finally, the positions of many of the facilities were incorrect. Procedures for error estimation and correction protocols are reported elsewhere (Scott et al, 1997b).

Magnitude/toxicity indicators

Not only is the locational accuracy of hazardous facilities an important consideration in comparative risk assessments, so is an estimate of the magnitude of potential chemical exposure from those facilities. Unfortunately, there are some inherent obstacles in the chemical information reported in the databases that, at this time, prevent us from accurately estimating hazard magnitudes from all our risk sources. Specifically, RCRA's Biennial Reporting System summarizes the hazardous waste generated and treated not by chemical but by the generation and treatment process. This means that the majority of wastes are reported as 'soups' consisting of several different, often unknown, chemicals. Determining the hazardousness of CERCLIS sites is not possible because most of the sites in our state have not had a preliminary assessment or site inspection. The National Priority List sites may have had land and water samples taken and tested for the concentration of chemicals, but the actual amounts of toxins present at a site are not known.

Given the problems in the chemical information found in the BRS, CERCLIS and NPL databases, we concentrated on TRI data to estimate the hazardousness of industrial facilities. When creating a magnitude estimator, it is important to take into account both the magnitude (amount of chemicals released) and the toxicity of the release. Fortunately, the magnitude of the TRI releases is standardized to pounds per year. Unfortunately, there is no universally accepted measure of environmental hazardousness, largely due to insufficient toxicological studies on the behaviour of many chemicals in a natural setting. While there has been a plethora of research on the toxicity of chemicals in industrial or workplace settings, data on many of the more than 600 regulated chemicals' properties in the open environment are still sparse. Therefore, we borrowed the industrial hygiene measurements of toxicity as our relative measurement of environmental toxicity (ACGIH, 1991). Our reasoning is that while the exact levels of dangerous exposure are bound to change in an outdoor environmental setting, the relative hazardousness of a chemical should remain constant. Our relative measure is based on the threshold limit value – time-weighted average (TLV-TWA) or the maximum average amount in mg/m^3 to which a worker can be exposed in a given eight-hour workday. These TLVs were converted to their inverse values (1/TLV), so that the greater the number, the higher the relative toxicity.

While we feel that using TLVs as a relative measure of toxicity is reasonable, it is important to point out a few caveats. First, not all of the chemicals reported by TRI facilities in 1992 have TLVs, although the vast majority (89 per cent) do. Second, the medium of exposure often determines the level of toxicity, but we have assigned one number per chemical, regardless of physical state (vapour, liquid, solid). Fortunately, most of the releases we classified with the environmental TLVs are airborne, the medium on which most occupational TLVs are based. Finally, it has been suggested that chemicals with high TLVs may not be more toxic than others, just more closely studied. There is little we can do to remedy this potential bias, except to echo calls for more research into the toxicity of industrial and environmental toxins. Incidentally, Bowen et al (1995) reached the same conclusion, adopting threshold limit values as their measure of toxicity, however their creation of a composite toxicity index was significantly different from the weighted average toxicity index described here.

Once a measure of relative toxicity for each chemical was created, there was the need to relate that toxicity to a given facility. However, because most facilities release more than one chemical, a system for combining several toxicity values was required. We created an index called a weighted average toxicity (WAT) value (Appendix). The WAT allows us to construct a measure of relative risk when comparing two facilities in terms of the magnitude and toxicity of their releases. For example, the WAT helps differentiate low emissions of highly toxic substances from high emissions of relatively non-toxic ones. In this way, we are able to move beyond the quantity of releases, which is what is routinely reported to the EPA, to a more realistic assessment of the risk which includes both quantity released and toxicity.

To calculate a WAT value for a given facility, we summed the total number of pounds of chemicals the facility releases in a year. Second, we found what proportion each chemical adds to the total (i.e. if the total pounds equals 10,000, then releasing 1000 pounds of a given chemical would represent 10 per cent of the total). Third, we multiplied each proportion by the relative toxicity of respective chemicals. Finally, we added the products together to get a weighted average toxicity for each facility for a given year. The mathematical notation used is:

$$WAT_f = \sum_{i=1}^{n} \frac{C_i}{C_t \cdot TLV_i}$$

(1)

where:

WAT_f = weighted average toxicity value for a given facility
n = number of chemicals released by a given facility
C_i = amount of chemical i (in pounds)
C_t = total amount of chemicals released (in pounds)
TLV_i = threshold limit value of chemical i.

Table 20.1 gives an example of the computation of the WAT for two different facilities in Lexington County (part of the Columbia metropolitan area). Once calculated, the weighted average toxicity (WAT) for each facility can be compared to others in the county or state. For example, the WATs could be ranked from most toxic to least (Table 20.2). For the 1992 TRI facilities, the WAT values range from 0.0001 to 100.0.

Table 20.1 *Reported releases and computation of weighted average toxicity*

Chemicals	Pounds released	% Total	1/TLV
Trichloroethylene	1300	0.54	0.0037
Methanol	1100	0.46	0.0038

Example 1: Cooper Power Tools.
0.54 × 0.0037 = 0.0020
0.46 × 0.0038 = 0.0017
WAT = 0.0020 + 0.0017 = 0.0037

Chemicals	Pounds released	% Total	1/TLV
Chromium compounds	851	0.0070	2.00
Manganese compounds	45,078	0.3699	0.20
Lead	8522	0.0699	6.67
Copper	938	0.0077	5.00
Zinc (fume or dust)	66,250	0.5434	100.00
Nickel	63	0.0005	1.00
Barium	172	0.0014	2.00

Example 2: Owen Electric Steel Company
0.070 × 2 = 0.0140
0.3699 × 0.2 = 0.0740
0.0699 × 6.67 = 0.4662
0.007 × 5 = 0.0385
0.5434 × 100 = 54.34
0.0005 × 1 = 0.0005
0.0014 × 2 = 0.0028
WAT = 0.0140 + 0.0740 + 0.4662 + 0.0385 + 54.34 + 0.0005 + 0.0028 = 54.94

Table 20.2 *Ranking of most toxic TRI facilities in South Carolina based on weighted average toxicity in 1992*

Rank	Facility name	City	County	Number of chemicals	Amount (lb)	WAT	Majority chemical	Majority % of total
1	Nucor Steel Co.	Darlington	Darlington	1	22,438	100.00	Zinc	100
2	Profession Medical Products Co.	Greenwood	Greenwood	2	5650	95.58	Zinc	96
3	ACM Corp.	Summerville	Dorchester	2	4203	82.12	Zinc	82
4	Georgetown Steel Co.	Georgetown	Georgetown	4	29,589	68.63	Zinc	68
5	Owen Electric Steel Co.	Cayce	Lexington	7	21,874	54.94	Zinc	54
6	Southern States Galvanizing Co.	Traveller's Rest	Greenville	3	2570	47.92	Zinc	48
7	B. L. Montague Co.	Sumter	Sumter	3	22,862	45.94	Methyl ethyl ketone	53
8	Gaston Copper Recycling Corp.	Gaston	Lexington	7	108,855	40.69	Zinc	37
9	Hitachi Electronic Devices	Greenville	Greenville	7	72,698	24.14	Lead	47
10	AVM Inc.	Marion	Marion	5	2500	20.83	Chromium	20

Table 20.3 *Ranking of most toxic TRI facilities in South Carolina based on total pounds released in 1992*

Rank	Facility name	City	County	Number of chemicals	Amount (lb)	WAT	Majority chemical	Majority % of total
1	Westvaco	W. Charleston	Charleston	14	5,353,180	0.11	Methanol	77
2	Westinghouse Electric Co.	Hampton	Hampton	11	4,756,120	0.01	Methanol	84
3	Bowater Inc.	Catawba	York	14	3,948,992	0.28	Methanol	52
4	Stone Container Corp.	Florence	Florence	6	3,044,712	0.08	Methanol	47
5	Hoechst-Celanese Corp.	Rock Hill	York	19	2,965,008	0.037	Acetone	76
6	Anchor Continental	Columbia	Richland	2	2,948,702	0.012	Toluene	99
7	Carolina Eastman	Columbia	Lexington	16	2,888,153	0.222	Acetaldehyde	25
8	Nicca USA Inc.	Fountain Inn	Laurens	2	2,235,790	0.999	Ammonia	99
9	International Paper Inc.	Georgetown	Georgetown	10	2,060,155	0.055	Methanol	65
10	Teepak Inc.	Swansea	Calhoun	2	1,708,000	0.085	Ammonia	97

In and of itself, WAT rankings provide only limited information. Adding infor- mation on the amount released, the number of different chemicals released, and the dominant chemical as a percentage of the total releases provides a more complete profile of the facility. Facilities can be differentiated based on high emissions of lower toxicity (HE/LT), such as Hitachi Electronic Devices, from those with lower emissions but higher toxicity (LE/HT), such as Professional Medical Products (Table 20.2).

The majority of high-WAT facilities emit heavy metals such as zinc, lead and chromium. However, if one ranks by total emissions, a different listing is produced (Table 20.3). This ranking shows that the state's largest emitters which (according to Livingston, 1996) have consistently been listed as the worst in the state, release relatively low-toxicity substances such as methanol. The examination of Tables 20.2 and 20.3 in tandem illustrates the high magnitude/low toxicity (HE/LT) and low magnitude/high toxicity (LE/HT) continuum. The dichotomy points to the critical need to examine both magnitude and toxicity indicators in any comparative risk assessment for individual facilities or county-wide comparisons. Once we created the relative risk components, we explored ways to represent the risk graphically and to make these visualizations readily available to the general public.

Visualizing Risk

The visualization of risk was the most challenging part of this research. Magnitude and toxicity maps using graduated circles were produced for the entire state. We then created a series of maps showing pounds released classified by weighted average toxicity. In this way, we present the interaction between magnitudes and toxicities at the individual facility level and how this varies from site to site across the state.

Figure 20.1 illustrates this visualization using 1992 data. In South Carolina, the majority of facilities (241) fall into the lowest toxicity class and have moderate amounts of releases (Figure 20.1a). Most of these facilities are clustered in the Upstate region, the most industrialized portion of the state. Facilities with the largest emissions generally have either low or moderate toxicities (Figure 20.1b). They tend to be located in smaller mill towns throughout the state and in the state's major metropolitan centres. Highly toxic emissions are released by only a few facilities (89), but they normally are at very low quantities (Figure 20.1c). The one exception is the Union Camp paper/pulp mill in lower Richland County, which had a total mission of 1,324,725 pounds in 1992 and a WAT of 1.48. The emissions (by percentages of the total) were methanol (57 per cent), hydrochloric acid (28 per cent) and sulphuric acid (5 per cent), as well as several other chemicals released in small amounts.

Moving beyond a composite facility-based indicator, we next attempted to visualize risk from an aggregate perspective by comparing all 46 counties within the state. Counties were classified by WAT and total pounds released and placed into a three-by-three matrix (Figure 20.2). As can be seen, there were no counties with large releases in the medium to high toxicity range. The riskiest counties

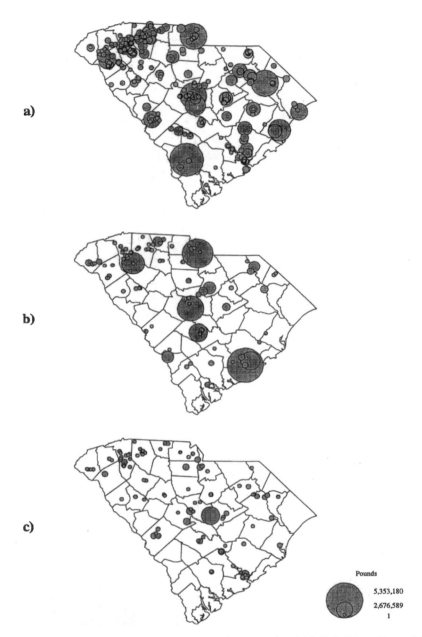

Note: a) facilities with a weighted average toxicity less than 0.099 (n = 241); b) facilities with a weighted average toxicity greater than or equal to 0.01 and less than 0.99 (n = 87); c) facilities with a weighted average toxicity greater than 1.0 (n = 89). The greater the weighted average toxicity, the higher the relative toxicity level.

Figure 20.1 *Pounds of chemical released from Toxic Release Inventory facilities in South Carolina during 1992*

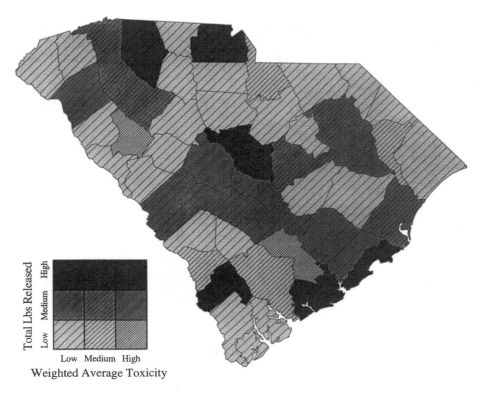

Figure 20.2 *Relative risk from Toxic Release Inventory facilities,*
given total pounds of chemicals released and weighted average toxicity
per county in South Carolina, 1992

had moderate to low amounts of emissions with high toxicity (LE/HT) or high amounts of emissions with low toxicity (HE/LT). With one exception, all of these counties are metropolitan areas adjacent to the state's urban centres in Charleston, Columbia, Greenville and Rock Hill, SC-Charlotte, NC. The one anomaly is Westinghouse Electric located in rural Hampton county in the southern portion of the state along the South Carolina/Georgia border.

Locally relevant information on risks was provided as well. This involved presenting the toxicity and magnitude indicators at a more detailed scale such as census enumeration districts. One example is Lexington County, located in the middle of the state (Figure 20.3). Lexington County was selected because it has moderate levels of emissions, yet these are rather high in toxicity. Mapping both the pounds released (Figure 20.3a) and weighted average toxicity (Figure 20.3b) furnished an interesting pattern at the local level.

The majority of releases in the county come from one plant, Carolina Eastman (2.9 million pounds in 1992), but the WAT of the emissions is rather low (0.22). In contrast, the highest toxicity releases come from the Owens Electric Steel and the Gaston Copper plant (now defunct), even though the quantities emitted were less than 5 per cent of the total releases from Carolina Eastman.

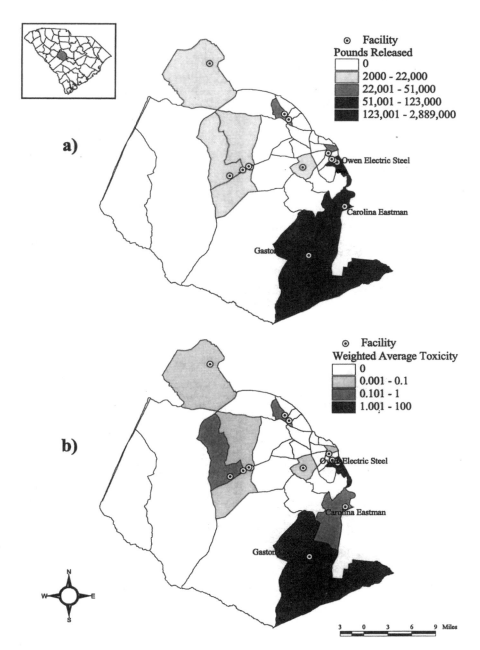

Figure 20.3 *Pounds of chemicals released (a) and weighted average toxicity (b) of census tract divisions in Lexington County, South Carolina, 1992*

Most of the emissions at the Owens Steel plant are from electroplating processes involving the release of heavy metals such as zinc (Table 20.1) with an extremely high WAT. Gaston Copper's high relative toxicity was also due to the release of heavy metals, but from a recycling process.

Finally, we experimented with a technique for visualizing the risks which involves representing individual chemicals and their toxicity by facility. The technique is illustrated in Figure 20.4, where the areas of the circles represent the total pounds released, while the divisions signify what proportion different chemicals contributed to the total pounds released. The shading of the pie-chart wedges indicates each chemical's relative toxicity.

It is difficult to compare chemicals from facility to facility because each uses different manufacturing processes resulting in different products and chemical releases. However, we can depict how important (in terms of quantity released) and how toxic a contributing chemical is in the overall computation of the WAT. This generalization can then be portrayed spatially to illustrate the differing hazard profiles of facilities within a community or county.

Figure 20.4 serves to illustrate this representation for Lexington County. One can see that while Carolina Eastman released almost 3 million pounds of

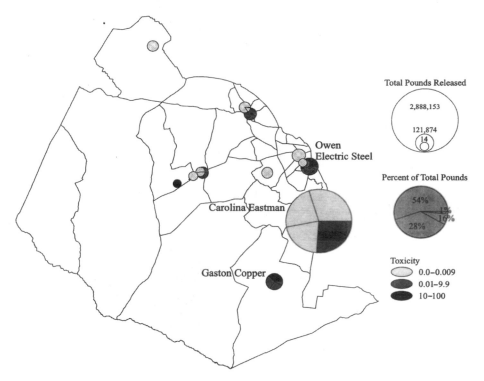

Note: The size of each graph represents the magnitude of the amount released, the graph divisions represent a chemical's percentage of the total released, and the shading represents the level of toxicity for a given chemical.

Figure 20.4 *Graphical depiction of weighted average toxicity calculation for Toxic Release Inventory facilities in Lexington County, South Carolina, 1992*

chemicals in 1992, almost 75 per cent had a relatively low toxicity. This plant can be compared to Gaston Copper or Owen Electric Steel which released highly toxic chemicals in relatively small amounts. This type of visualization allows one to move beyond one or two numbers representing hazardousness and begin to extract the complex and conflicting information about magnitudes and toxicities for given facilities.

Communicating Risks to the Public

Following the database creation and magnitude analysis, a means of communicating these risks to the public was sought. We were concerned about how to communicate a complicated set of data to a general public not familiar with evaluating toxic risk. Our primary consideration was to provide the information to as many people as possible in a form that would be easily understood. A second priority was to locate a computer system for the visual representation of the information. Libraries are a natural location for such information but not all libraries have the same computer capabilities, such as graphical user interfaces or internet access.

A vital decision in communicating any information to the public, particularly in digital form, is the selection of an appropriate data/user interface. In selecting a given interface, system designers can either empower users with unprecedented possibilities for understanding, or they can channel user interaction so that a limited amount of information can be retrieved (Kuhn, 1992). An interface can overwhelm a user with exploration possibilities or release information in manageable amounts, thus enhancing understanding and facilitating the risk communication process.

We had several design goals for our risk communication system. First, it had to provide text, maps and graphs at a level suitable for general public consumption. Second, the interface had to be easy to learn with minimal expert interaction. Third, a level of interactivity was necessary, given that the communication of personal neighbourhood information was the objective. Fourth, it had to be inexpensive or free so that wide dissemination throughout the state would be possible. Finally, it had to be accessible to most computer users, regardless of operating system or hardware capabilities.

When we were searching for a suitable risk communication system (in early 1996), several options were available to us. First, a customized user interface could be created from scratch, using a high-level programming language. While this would provide the maximum amount of control over the interface properties and capabilities, the cost of development was too high. Second, we could use an existing mapping package, such as ArcView 2.1. The interface can be customized to limit user choices while retaining a high level of interactivity. However, this option also posed problems since it is not free, not completely cross-platform-compatible, nor is it compact.

We concluded that a web browser interface (such as Netscape Navigator 2.0™) would be the most accessible and best understood by all levels of potential users. The web browser allows easy point-and-click access to the information within the system via its hypertext conceptual model. In addition, this browser and data can be compacted onto disks and transferred to another personal computer. The software was free, meaning that the disks could be distributed to libraries and others interested in hazards assessment. Unfortunately, a level of interactivity was lost when moving to this solution, because creating dynamic map displays was extremely difficult at that time.

South Carolina Toxic Risk Atlas Prototype (SCTRAP)

The first step in system development was to create a prototype. Our goal regarding the prototype was to explore the various options for revealing risks to the community. This involved interactive maps, tables, lists, static maps, text and hypertext. In the beginning of the development processes, we realized that the audience would need some general knowledge about environmental risks and hazards, so a fair amount of background information was encoded and made available to the user on demand. This included prototype goals, federal regulations, a glossary, and factsheets on the effects of chemicals on human health produced by the Agency for Toxic Substances and Disease Registry (ATSDR). To simplify construction, only one county in South Carolina – Richland – was used as a proof of concept.

The second and most time-consuming portion of prototype construction was the creation of interactive maps. The word 'interactive' is used loosely here because while the user can choose which neighbourhood maps to view, the scale, positioning and the information presented on the maps is fixed. Before mapping the risk information, considerable discussion took place as to the nature of the ancillary information that would be provided to the user. Finally, it was decided that the maps would include easily recognized landmarks – schools, fire stations, Interstate highways, US highways, major water bodies and incorporated area boundaries – as well as the sources of risk. Both the risk and the ancillary information was then visualized in ArcView 2.1 at three scales: the state (which shows only county name); the county (which shows only risk sources, Interstate highways, water bodies and incorporated areas); and the community level.

Each community-level map, of which there are 28 in Richland County, covers approximately 36 square miles. This size was chosen as a compromise between visualizing the neighbourhood, the community and the surrounding communities (Figure 20.5). The county index map is linked to the community-level maps through a common gateway interface (CGI) script called Imagemap. The Imagemap application allows the definition of an area of a GIF image as being linked to another HTML resource. Thus, when a user clicks on a given map square, he or she is taken to the page with that map.

The third task in constructing our risk communication tool was to encode the risk information for individual facilities. This risk information included a picture of the facility (when available), the facility's address, the latitude/longitude position and the emissions information given under different regulations (see above). The information varies by database. For example, TRI release listings contain the pounds released from the smokestack (or equivalent), the pounds released from fugitive sources, the chemical released and the chemical's relative toxicity. In the prototype, each of the column headings as well as the chemical names themselves

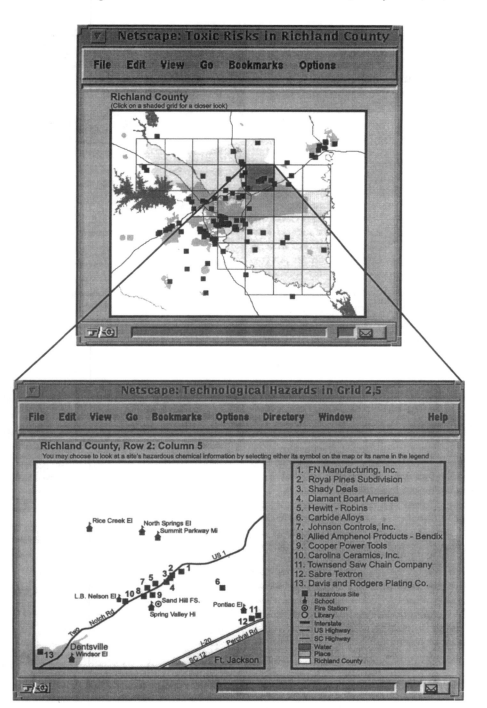

Figure 20.5 *The community mapping portion of the South Carolina Toxic Risk Atlas Prototype*

are linked via hypertext to the appropriate listings in the glossary or the ATSDR chemical fact sheets. The user can select the facility's symbol on the community level map, its name from the map legend, or its name from a text-based listing of all risk sources per county to access the individual facility pages.

The fourth and final piece of the prototype were the static maps of risk. In order to explore the public reaction to different types of risk visualization and to give users a comparative state-wide perspective, we used static maps of magnitude and toxicity. These maps (Figure 20.1) were displayed separately from the community risk source maps to keep from confusing users; the community maps have three different sources of risk, the static maps show only TRI magnitude and toxicity.

Discussion

One conclusion that can be drawn from this research is that while an indication of the amount of relative risk an industrial facility poses can be determined using total pounds released and a toxicity index, we are far from discussing the risk potential of environmental releases of toxic chemicals with any certainty. After decades of research, scientists still have little knowledge of the way chemicals affect living organisms in the environment. Between differences in transport media, varying chemical properties, lack of toxicological research, and the importance of individual's risk factors (age, weight, sex, etc.), a true measure of risk continues to be elusive. Unfortunately, we cannot wait for science to catch up with political reality. Every day, citizens and their leaders are making important decisions regarding personal and neighbourhood exposure to toxic chemicals. Surrogate and incomplete measures of risk must not only be calculated, they must also be communicated to the public in an efficient and illuminating way.

The South Carolina Toxic Risk Atlas Prototype (SCTRAP) represents an initial foray into the visualization and communication of toxic risks to the public. As is the case with all prototypes, we will change a number of the features when the system is implemented, using improved software and comments from users. First, we will expand and update the prototype to include all counties in the state as well as more recent data (1995 TRI, 1995 BRS and 1997 CERCLA data). We will add other environmental risk data such as hazardous materials (hazmat) accidents; extremely hazardous and/or criteria air pollutants regulated under the Clean Air Act (i.e. ozone, sulphur dioxide, etc.); water quality indicators; and so forth.

The use of more and different visualizations based on user feedback would be beneficial. It has become clear that many of our users lack the geographical sophistication to adequately interpret many of the visualizations (graduated circle, choropleth maps) that we take for granted as geographers. In future versions, we will include more charts, graphs and text descriptions to expedite map interpretation. Expanding the interactivity of the prototype is another goal. Recently released software can facilitate this interactivity (i.e. ESRI's Map Objects™). Web users can now type addresses, perform queries and manipulate visualizations on-line and in real time. This level of interactivity will help us solve some of the limitations identified by users.

The development of a risk visualization tool can assist local communities in making geographic comparisons of risk. It can also enhance access to and understanding of environmental data. The delivery mechanism supports the community right-to-know disclosure provisions of many environmental laws and will certainly help inform residents of risks in their community. Once armed with this information, it will be up to the residents and community leaders to decide on an acceptable level of risk from toxic chemicals in their community.

Acknowledgements

We would like to thank Charmel Menzel, Dan Wagner, Minhe Ji and Lloyd Clark for their initial work on this project. Also thanks to Deborah S. K. Thomas, and Jerry T. Mitchell for contributing critical and editorial comments on this manuscript. Finally, we are grateful to the South Carolina Universities Research and Education Foundation (#30-95, 62-96) for providing funding for the risk atlas prototype.

References

ACGIH (American Conference of Governmental Industrial Hygienists) (1991) *Documentation of the Threshold Limit Values and Biological Exposure Indices*, 6th edn, ACGIH, Cincinnati, OH

Berry, B. J. L. (1977) *The Social Burdens of Environmental Pollution*, Ballinger, Lexington, MA

Bowen, W. M., Sailing, M. J., Haynes, K. E. and Cyran, E. J. (1995) 'Toward environmental justice: Spatial equity in Ohio and Cleveland', *Annals of the Association of American Geographers*, vol 85, no 4, pp641–63

Bullard, R. D. (1990) *Dumping in Dixie: Race, Class, and Environmental Quality*, Westview Press, Boulder, CO

Burke, L. (1993) 'Race and environmental equity: A geographic analysis in Los Angeles', *Geo Info Systems*, October, pp44–50

Cushman, J. H. (1997) 'EPA is pressing plant to publicize pollution data', *The New York Times*, 12 August, ppA1, C20

Davies, J. C. (ed) (1996) *Comparing Environmental Risks: Tools for Setting Government Priorities*, Resources for the Future, Washington, DC

Glickman, T. S. (1994) 'Measuring environmental equity with geographical information systems', *Renewable Resources Journal*, vol 12, no 3, pp17–21

Glickman, T. S., Golding, D. and Hersh, R. (1995) 'GIS-based environmental equity analysis: A case study of TRI facilities in the Pittsburgh area' in G. E. G. Beroggi and W. A Wallace (eds) *Computer Supported Risk Management*, Kluwer Academic, Dordrecht, pp95–114

Goldman, B. A. (1991) *The Truth About Where You Live*, Random House, New York

Harris, T. and Weiner, D. (1996) 'GIS and society: The social implications of how people, space, and environment are represented in GIS', *Technical Report 96-7*, NCGIA

Kuhn, W. (1992) 'Paradigms of GIS use' in P. Bresnahan, E. Corwin and D. Cowen (eds) *Proceedings, 5th International Symposium on Spatial Data Handling*, vol 1, pp91–103

Kunreuther, H. and Slovic, P. (eds) (1996) 'Challenges in risk assessment and risk management', *The Annals of the American Academy of Political and Social Science*, vol 545, pp8–183

Livingston, M. (1996) 'EPA: SC industry polluted less in '94', *The State*, June 27, ppB1, B7

Mayo, D. G. and Hollander, R. D. (eds) (1991) *Acceptable Evidence: Science and Values in Risk Management*, Oxford University Press, New York

McMaster, R. B., Leitner, H. and Sheppard, E. (1997) 'Risk assessment in the Twin Cities using geographic information systems', *Cartography and Geographic Information Systems*

Minard, R. A. (1996) 'CRA and the states: History, politics, and results' in J. C. Davies (ed) *Comparing Environmental Risks: Tools for Setting Government Priorities*, Resources for the Future, Washington, DC, pp23–62

National Research Council (1983) *Risk Assessment in the Federal Government: Managing the Process*, National Academy Press, Washington, DC

National Research Council (1994) *Science and Judgment in Risk Assessment*, National Academy Press, Washington, DC

National Research Council (1996) *Understanding Risk: Informing Decisions in a Democratic Society*, National Academy Press, Washington, DC

Nyerges, T., Robkin, M. and Moore, T. J. (1997) 'Geographic information systems for risk evaluation: Perspectives on applications concerning human and ecological impacts', *Cartography and Geographic Information Systems*, vol 24, no 3, pp123–144

Scott, M., Menzel, C. and Cutter, S. L. (1997a) 'Relative risk profiles: A methodology for assessing community risk', Discussion Paper no 9, Hazards Research Lab, Department of Geography, Columbia, SC

Scott, M., Cutter, S. L., Menzel, C., Ji, M. and Wagner, D. (1997b) 'Spatial accuracy of the EPA's environmental hazards databases and their use in environmental equity analyses', *Applied Geographic Studies*, vol 1, pp45–61

Stockwell, J. R., Sorenson, J. W., Eckert, J. W., jr and Carreras, E. M. (1993) 'The USEPA geographic information system for mapping environmental releases of toxic chemical release inventory (TRI) chemicals', *Risk Analysis*, vol 13, pp155–164

Sui, D. Z. and Giardino, J. R. (1995) 'Applications of GIS in environmental equity analyses: A multi-scale and multi-zoning scheme study for the city of Houston, Texas, USA', *Proceedings, GIS/LIS '95*, vol 2, ACSM and ASPRS, Bethesda, MD, pp950–959

UCC (United Church of Christ Commission for Racial Justice) (1987) *Toxic Wastes and Race: A National Report on the Racial and Socioeconomic Characteristics of Communities with Hazardous Waste Sites*, United Church of Christ, New York

USEPA (United States Environmental Protection Agency) (1987) *Unfinished Business: A Comparative Assessment of Environmental Problems*, Report Number EPA 230-2-87-025a, USEPA, Washington, DC

Wernick, I. K. (1996) 'Editorial: Better risk information for communities', *Risk Analysis*, vol 16, no 5, pp601–603

Wernick, I. K. (1997) 'Community risk profiles: Background', available at http://phe.rockefeller.edu/comm_risk/

Appendix

Weighted Average Toxicity Calculation Procedure

1. Create file of facility releases containing unique facility number, name of chemical released, CAS number of chemical released, amount released.
2. Create file of chemical toxicities (available from http://www.cla.sc.edu/geog/hrl/sctrap/toxfaqs/toxicity.html).
3. Join facility release file to toxicity file.
4. Create file of total releases per facility.
5. Relate file of total releases per facility to facility release file.
6. Calculate the proportional amount each chemical contributes to the total.
7. Calculate the weighted toxicity for each release.
8. Sum the proportional toxicities for each facility.
9. Combine the total amount per facility file and the weighted average toxicity per facility file. The result is a file with unique facility numbers and each facility's magnitude and toxicity of releases.

Arc/INFO Example

Note that this process takes place at the Arc: prompt and within Tables. These two programs will be differentiated by A: and T:, respectively.

```
T:  DEFINE facfile
        FAC_ID,4,5,b
        CHEM_NAME,30,30,c
        CAS_NO,15,15,c
        AMT,10,10,i
        T_AMT, 10,10,i < – These items
        P_AMT,4,6,f,2< – will be
        P_TOX,4,7,f,3< – calculated later
T:  (Add facility information)
T:  DEFINE toxfile
        HEM_NAME,30,30,c
        CAS_NO,15,15,c
        TOXICITY,4,7,f,3
T:  (Add toxicity information)
A:  JOINITEM facfile toxfile facfile
        FAC_ID AMT
A:  FREQUENCY facfile amt_per_fac
        Freq Item:          FAC_ID
        Sum Item:           AMT
```

T: RELATE ADD
    Relation name: templ
    Table Identifier: amt_per_fac
    Database name: INFO
    INFO Item: FAC_ID
    Relate Column: FAC_ID
    Relate Type: LINEAR
    Relate Access: RO
T: SELECT facfile
T: CALCULATE P_AMT = AMT/temp 1//AMT
T: CALCULATE P_TOX = TOXICITY *
    P_AMT
A: FREQUENCY facfile wat_per_fac
    Freq Item: FAC_ID
    Sum Item: P_TOX
A: JOINITEM amt_perfac wat_perfac
    amtwat_perfac FAC_ID FAC_ID

21

Dumping in Dixie Revisited: The Evolution of Environmental Injustices in South Carolina

Jerry T. Mitchell, Deborah S. K. Thomas and Susan L. Cutter

The South has been tagged as a 'sacrifice zone' for the rest of America's toxic waste (Schueler, 1992; Bullard, 1990). More pointedly, the assertion is that racial minorities and the lower-income classes within this sacrifice zone bear a disproportionate burden of the region's environmental problems. A serious research effort has been undertaken to legitimize this claim, nationally and regionally, with results ranging from an unequivocal 'yes' (UCC, 1987; Bullard, 1990; Mohai and Bryant, 1992; Pollock and Vittas, 1995) to several more recent studies suggesting 'maybe' or 'maybe not' (Chapters 18 and 19; see also Yandle and Burton, 1996; Anderson et al, 1994; Been, 1994; Been and Gupta, 1997). Past scholarly efforts, however, have focused on *current* outcomes with little regard to *process* – how the inequitable situation came into existence in the first place. Been (1994) notes that in some instances poor and minority residents living near locally unwanted land uses came to the area after the land-use siting decision had been made. Regardless of process or outcome mechanisms, blanket statements of environmental racism, certainly as applied to an entire region such as the South, demand critical review.

This chapter thus addresses the ambiguities in environmental justice research by examining the question of which came first: Did the residents come to the nuisance or was the nuisance imposed on them? In other words, were the sources of environmental threats (e.g. hazardous waste or Toxic Release Inventory sites) located in communities because they were poor, minority or politically weak? Or were the facilities originally placed in communities with little reference to race or economic status, and, over time, did the composition of the area change due to migration, market dynamics or some other factor? We present a systematic

Note: Reprinted, with permission, from *Social Sciences Quarterly*, vol 80, no 2, Jerry T. Mitchell, Deborah S.K. Thomas and Susan L. Cutter, 'Dumping in Dixie revisited: The evolution of environmental injustices in South Carolina', pp229–243. © Blackwell Publishing, 1999

appraisal of process inequity in South Carolina and use this research as an illustration of some of the difficulties common to equity studies, such as geographic scale, population migration trends, economic development and the uncertainties associated with data sources.

Determining Process Inequity

A longitudinal review of the circumstances that led to today's environmental picture requires the consideration of several factors. First and perhaps most troublesome is the scale of enquiry – that is, identifying the appropriate geographic unit of analysis (Chapter 18; see also Perlin et al, 1995). The United Church of Christ (UCC) study (1987) utilized zip code areas, while others have used minor civil divisions (Zimmerman, 1993) or census tracts (Anderton et al, 1994; Been and Gupta, 1997; Burke, 1993). Inherent within all these studies is the assumption of a spatially uniform population distribution. In addition, the enumeration units inform us only about 'night' conditions – where people sleep – but provide little insight into daytime risk. This is important in considering those who benefit from employment at a site but who may not carry the environmental burden because they reside elsewhere. Still, census tracts remain attractive due to their relatively stable nature, availability, and comparability of population size (Been, 1995). A third assumption is that tracts reflect the area around the facility, and that the area closest to the facility will therefore bear the worst impact. Although Pollock and Vittas (1995) discuss exposure as a function of distance, people living closest to a facility do not always face greater exposure than people further away. This assumption neglects the importance of toxicity and magnitude, method of pollutant dispersal and the physical dispersal processes themselves, all of which contribute to the potential exposure (Glickman, 1994).

The utility of census tracts for longitudinal analysis is helpful only as far back as 1980 for South Carolina (when the delineation first appeared state-wide, not just in selected urban areas). This is a significant limitation. If we are to follow the premise established by Bullard (1994), that the present risk landscape, or riskscape, results from the past social and economic 'backwardness' of the region, limiting our investigation to dates based on census tract availability misses several opportunities. Environmental threats in the South did not just appear on the scene after 1960 with the rise of the 'New South' and its accompanying rapid industrialization, but may have manifested themselves much earlier. To fully appreciate the injustice process, then, we must explore older established facilities, accepting that census tract enumeration, while optimal as a spatial unit of analysis, should not be the limiting factor in our investigation. This research thus uses incorporated areas and counties as the spatial unit of analysis.

Methods

To conduct a state-wide historical analysis, we selected Toxic Release Inventory (TRI) sites in South Carolina as our risk indicator. Although considerable controversy surrounds the reporting accuracy of industrial emissions in general (Air and Waste Management Association, 1997), and TRI releases specifically (Lynn and Kartez, 1994), TRI data are used widely in equity analyses (Perlin et al, 1995; Cohen, 1997). In using TRI data, we can compare results to existing studies and also replicate our methods for other places.

The TRI facilities included in this study met three criteria:

1   emissions were reported by the facility for each of the six years of the study (1987–1992);
2   facility emissions exceeded an average of 100,000 pounds for the six-year period; and
3   income and racial demographic data were available for the area in which the facility was located.

Between 1987 and 1992, 89 facilities in South Carolina reported more than 100,000 pounds of annual emissions; 17 of these reported more than 1,000,000 pounds of emissions. Census data were not available for the areas surrounding 7 facilities, so the total number of TRI facilities serving as point sources of environmental threats in this research is 82.

Establishing accurate locations and facility start dates

Thirty of South Carolina's 46 counties (about 65 per cent) host at least one of the 82 facilities used in this analysis. Our previous research found that almost half (48 per cent) of the locations of South Carolina's TRI facilities were in the wrong block group, which required correction (Scott et al, 1997).

Facility establishment dates were confirmed using *The South Carolina Industrial Directory* (South Carolina Department of Commerce, 1941–1996). Entries in this directory include the following information: establishment dates, locations, employment totals and product descriptions. The 1996 edition contains listings for more than 3600 manufacturers with Standard Industrial Codes of 20 to 39. Determining plant start dates was a little more problematic than expected, as several facilities changed corporate ownership or were renamed under another division; often the establishment dates on record reflected the time of that corporate change, not the date the plant was originally opened.

To maintain quality control over the establishment date identification, we implemented a four-step date-confirmation procedure that included cross-checking earlier directories and local newspapers, consulting local economic development boards for host towns and counties, and contacting the companies directly. First, industrial directories were compared against each other to detect changes or inconsistencies in listings. Then local newspapers were researched for articles pertaining to plant openings. When establishment date confirmation was unavailable using these sources, economic development boards were contacted for tax information that could point to a facility opening date. Direct firm contact was initiated as the last option if the other sources were unsuccessful. The industrial directory provided confirmation for 59 start dates, and 5 more were identified through researching newspaper articles and making calls to economic develop-

ment boards. The remaining 18 facility start dates were confirmed via direct contact with the firms.

Demographic characteristics

We collected data for incorporated areas and counties from the US Census of
Population and Housing in order to have a consistent geographic unit across all
decades. The facility point locations and political boundaries were geo-referenced
and entered into a geographic information system (GIS). A one-mile buffer was
constructed around each incorporated area (1990 boundary), so we could examine facilities located on the fringes of towns that might potentially affect those
towns' populations. The incorporated areas were labelled as urban locations in
our analysis. Suburban locations were defined by the one-mile buffer around
the incorporated area, but did not include the urban core (i.e. the incorporated
area). Rural locations were defined as everything beyond the one-mile buffer.
Twenty-five sites were defined as urban, 28 as suburban and 29 as rural. Data for
incorporated areas were used for both the urban and suburban locales and county
data were used for the rural places. The demographic data were collected for the
period from the decade preceding the earliest establishment date of the facility to
1990. For example, if a facility start date was 1961, we collected socio-economic
data for that location starting with 1950.

The variable percentage black is used in this analysis since the state populace
has been overwhelmingly either African American or white. The 1990 census
reflects this, as 98.8 per cent of the state's population is either African American
or white. In other words, to speak of this state's racial minorities in a historical
sense is synonymous with discussing its African American population. Median
family income was used as the economic variable because of its availability in the
historic censuses.

Data source limitations

Creating a historical profile using census data posed several challenges. First, the
variables reported in the census were not always uniform over time or geographic
space. For example, the definition of certain variables changed, or they were
reported differently from decade to decade – such as percentage Negro changing
to percentage black, changing to percentage non-white – with subtle definitional
changes. Also, we were unable to collect data for towns with populations smaller
than 1000 people for any decade. Finally, the geographic boundaries of incorporated areas changed over time. Facilities that were located in rural areas at start-up
may now be located within a town boundary (e.g. in an urban area) because of
population growth, annexation or suburbanization. Unfortunately, most of the
earlier incorporated boundaries are unavailable, a casualty of the large number of
small towns in this investigation and the lack of historic geographic data about
them. As such, the incorporated areas described in this chapter refer to the 1990
boundaries.

Using the TRI as a measure of environmental threat also presents some limitations. First, the TRI represents only one of many potential environmental risks

that communities face. Furthermore, it could be viewed as both an economic good (a source of jobs) and an environmental bad (a source of toxic releases). In addition, it is impossible to ascertain the quantity and toxicity of emissions prior to the implementation of the TRI reporting. Thus, we have made an assumption in our analysis that toxic chemicals were produced from the establishment date forward.

A final data concern is the establishment of a baseline with which to compare demographic changes in the TRI host communities over time. At least two possible solutions exist: paired community comparisons or comparisons to a larger standardized unit. Paired comparisons would allow changes to be followed between TRI and non-TRI host communities. This requires, however, a level of comparability between places that is difficult to achieve in South Carolina due to the varied spatial distribution of its population, economy and industry. Instead, we have chosen to analyse demographic changes using the state means for each decade in which a facility has been operating.

Results

The census data and the information on the TRI facilities were input into a geographic information system (GIS) for management, analysis, and display purposes. We examined three relationships:

1   regional variations in facilities' locations and start-up dates;
2   racial and economic differences between the state and the facility host area at the time of the facility's establishment; and
3   racial and economic differences between the state and the facility host area in 1990.

Regional variations

Most of South Carolina's largest emitters were established in the 1960s and 1970s, a period coinciding with the rapid industrialization of the state as well as the South in general. Notable exceptions include a number of facilities established in old mill towns at the turn of the century. The oldest facility in our study (a phosphate producer) was founded in 1880 in Charleston. In contrast, the three newest facilities were built in 1987.

The geographic distribution of TRI facilities closely follows the historical industrial development of South Carolina (Kovacik and Winberry, 1987). Facilities are concentrated in the Upstate region around the cities of Spartanburg and Greenville, both along the Interstate 85 corridor. Smaller clusters exist in Columbia, which is the state capital, and Charleston (see Figure 21.1). The facilities established earliest are scattered throughout the state and are located primarily within incorporated or urban areas. Beginning in the 1950s and continuing through the 1960s, most facilities were located in the Upstate region. Also during this period a transition occurred in the location of the facility relative to the town (see Table 21.1). Beginning in the 1950s, the location of greater numbers

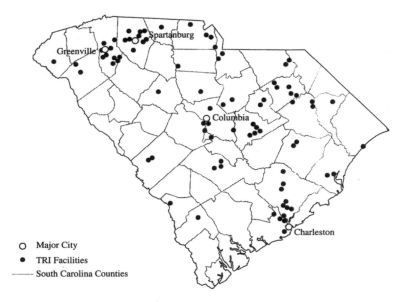

Figure 21.1 *Major emitters of TRI chemicals, 1987–1992*

of facilities shifted to the periphery of incorporated areas. By 1960, many were being situated in rural areas. This trend continued into the 1980s. The average facility establishment date for each category – urban (1952), suburban (1962) and rural (1969) – further demonstrates this trend of locating facilities farther from incorporated areas over the last few decades.

Table 21.1 *Average establishment dates of TRI facilities, by type of area*

Decade	Urban (no. within incorporated area)	Suburban (no. within one mile of incorporated area)	Rural
1880s	1880 (1)	*	*
1890s	*	1899 (1)	*
1900s	1904 (1)	*	*
1910s	*	*	*
1920s	1920 (1)	*	1928 (1)
1930s	1936 (4)	1937 (2)	*
1940s	1944 (3)	1948 (2)	*
1950s	1953 (3)	1954 (5)	1959 (1)
1960s	1963 (5)	1964 (6)	1964 (12)
1970s	1975 (5)	1974 (8)	1975 (10)
1980s	1986 (2)	1983 (4)	1982 (5)
n = 82	1952 (25)	1962 (28)	1969 (29)

*No facilities established

Race and income of facility host area at establishment

Generally, the host areas with facilities in the Upstate region were predominantly white. In the Coastal Plain, however, the reverse was true. These communities tended to be above the state average for the black population. The Midlands region was mixed. These demographic patterns in racial composition parallel both the historic and contemporary social geography of the state.

The average minority-population percentage for each host area by establishment decade was compared to the state minority-population percentage for the same decade (see Table 21.2). For instance, ten facilities were established in rural host areas in the 1970s, with an average minority population of 35.9 per cent compared to the state's average minority population of 30.7 per cent. The differences between minority-population averages for host areas and the minority-population average for the state were analysed through a t test. No significant differences were found to exist for urban or rural host-area minority populations at establishment date as compared to the overall state minority average. Only in the suburban host areas in the 1950s and 1960s do we find minority percentages that differ significantly from the state mean. In this instance, however, the relationship is negative, indicating that on average, the populations of host facility areas were significantly more white than the state average.

The average income level for each host area by establishment decade was also compared to the state average income level for the same decade (see Table 21.3). For example, ten facilities established in rural host areas in the 1970s had an average income level of $6000, compared to a state average income level of $7621.

Table 21.2 *Minority population at facility establishment date, by host area and state*

Host area	Decade established	No. of facilities	Average host area % minority	Average state % minority	t test
Urban (n = 22)	1930	4	44.7	45.7	−1.60
	1940	2	30.9	42.9	−1.03
	1950	3	44.5	38.9	1.52
	1960	5	25.5	34.9	−2.19
	1970	5	39.5	30.7	1.28
	1980	2	41.7	31.2	1.25
Suburban (n = 25)	1930	2	51.3	45.7	0.89
	1940	2	28.9	42.9	−1.84
	1950	4	32.5	38.9	−3.67*
	1960	5	19.3	34.9	−4.55*
	1970	8	25.9	30.7	−0.83
	1980	4	41.6	31.2	3.12
Rural** (n = 27)	1960	12	40.0	34.9	1.01
	1970	10	35.9	30.7	1.14
	1980	5	38.3	31.2	1.57

*significant at $p < 0.05$; ** county data.

Table 21.3 *Income level at facility establishment date, by host area and state*

Host area	Decade established	Number of facilities	Average host area income level ($)	Average state income level ($)	t test
Urban (n = 15)	1950	3	1664	1647	0.12
	1960	5	4740	3821	3.41*
	1970	5	7927	7621	0.93
	1980	2	16,500	16,978	−1.34
Suburban (n = 17)	1950	4	2121	1647	8.38*
	1960	2	4774	3821	45.38*
	1970	7	8399	7621	4.51*
	1980	4	15,443	16,978	−2.41
Rural**(n = 27)	1960	12	2858	3821	−3.77*
	1970	10	6000	7621	−5.83*
	1980	5	17,053	16,978	0.089

*significant at $p < 0.05$; **county data.

The differences between the average income levels of the host areas and the average income level for the state were also analysed through a *t* test. The average income levels for urban host areas in the 1960s and for suburban host areas in the 1950s, 1960s and 1970s were found to be significantly higher than the state averages at those times. Only for rural host areas in the 1960s and 1970s were the average income levels significantly lower than the state average. Both Tables 21.2 and 21.3 only portray those instances where significance testing was possible; the absence or small number of facilities in previous decades precluded their analysis. It appears that for South Carolina, TRI facilities were located quite equitably so that low-income and minority populations bore no disproportionate burdens.

Race and income of facility host area in 1990

There were few significant differences in income levels or minority-population percentages between host areas and the state at the time the facilities were established. In all but two instances the differences that are significant point to the establishment of facilities in host areas that had higher income levels and a smaller minority-population percentage than the state.

In examining the same host areas in 1990, however, we see that demographic patterns have changed dramatically. By 1990, all urban and suburban host areas had minority-population percentages that were significantly higher than the state-wide average (see Table 21.4). In contrast, minority-population percentages for rural host areas continued to show no significant differences when compared with the state average in 1990.

Regarding income levels, by 1990 suburban host areas had income levels significantly lower than the state average (see Table 21.4). These same host area income levels either were not significantly different or were significantly higher than the state average at the time the facilities were established. Overall, rural host-area income levels remained significantly lower than the state average in 1990; urban host-area income levels showed no significant changes.

Table 21.4 *Minority population percentage and average income level in 1990 for host area and state*

Host area	No. of facilities	Mean host area % monitory	Mean state % minority	Minority t test	Mean host area income ($)	Mean state income ($)	Income t test
Urban	25	40.3	30.9	4.01*	29,122	30,797	−1.73
Suburban	28	39.6	30.9	3.31*	28,342	30,797	−3.40*
Rural**	29	36.5	30.9	1.97	25,221	30,797	−7.04*

*significant at $p < 0.05$; ** county data

Discussion

We began this chapter addressing the following question: Did the residents come to the nuisance or was the nuisance imposed on them? Our results seem to indicate the former. When these facilities were established, there was no significant differentiation in host communities by race or income. It would appear that these facilities were not located in communities because they were poor or minority but instead were situated with little reference to race or economic status. Yet over time the socioeconomic composition of the areas in which they were located changed. Admittedly, however, the scale used here is too coarse to determine whether facilities are situated within predominantly minority neighbourhoods in the host areas.

Several broad processes help to explain these changes. First, the percentage of the overall population that is black has decreased substantially over time. Additionally, while black populations in urban and suburban areas are growing, the reverse is taking place in rural areas. Last, the economics associated with the siting of industrial facilities influenced a shift of facility locations from urban areas to more rural locales.

While utilizing the local level as the scale of analysis is important for examining environmental equity, each area has unique characteristics that may create ambiguities in the analysis, thus making environmental equity claims more difficult. For example, contextual factors like state-wide and regional migration and economic factors add to our understanding of the racial composition of areas around environmental threats. Simply relying on a time series census analysis overlooks these important factors.

South Carolina's racial migration trend

The shifts in the demographic composition of incorporated areas from white to black likely has more to do with state-wide migration trends than the actual siting of TRI facilities. South Carolina experienced a steady decline in its black population relative to the total population as a consequence of a mass exodus of blacks during the 1960s (see Table 21.5). This decline slowed beginning in the 1980s. The initial black migrants were from the rural farm areas, with most leaving South Carolina for perceived better employment and social equality in northern cities.

Table 21.5 *South Carolina black population change*

Census year	Black population	Total population	% Black
1880	604,472	995,577	60.7
1890	689,141	1,151,149	59.8
1900	782,509	1,340,316	58.3
1910	836,239	1,515,400	55.1
1920	865,186	1,683,724	51.3
1930	794,725	1,738,765	45.7
1940	815,496	1,899,804	42.9
1950	823,622	2,117,027	38.9
1960	831,572	2,382,594	34.9
1970	796,086	2,590,516	30.7
1980	974,596	3,121,820	31.2
1990	1,079,729	3,486,703	30.9

Apparent dissatisfaction with the North and a changing political and economic climate in South Carolina caused a reversal of the migration trend. Blacks were not returning to rural areas, however, but rather turning towards urban centres for work. The shift of more blacks into metropolitan areas (such as Charleston) and the rapid suburbanization of whites (as in Berkeley and Dorchester Counties, adjacent to Charleston) dramatically altered the demographic profiles of host areas. Thus, the racial composition of TRI host areas with large black populations may have been caused by state and regional migration trends, not necessarily by environmental injustices.

Inequity or economic development?

Although TRI represents facilities releasing toxic chemicals into the environment, arguably benefits exist as well. Depressed local economies can be uplifted by employment generated by the plants and strengthened by an increase in corporate tax dollars. Lobbying by local areas for these plants can be intense even when it is known that hazardous by-products are part of the deal (Bourke, 1994). Indeed, the promise of financial benefits arising from the establishment of new facilities may have led to siting facilities closer to white communities in order to provide jobs. The pattern of facility siting in the predominantly white Upstate region during the 1950s and 1960s potentially reflects this goal. The subsequent siting of post-1960 facilities in rural areas – those areas with an average income level significantly lower than the rest of the state – attempted to reverse this trend by bringing economic development to impoverished areas; this effort was a response to changing racial and social attitudes within South Carolina.

Familiarity with the local context

Broad-based state, regional or national studies of empirically based indicators designed to uncover inequity patterns make attractive, neat packages to hand policy-makers, but they neglect several issues related to the local context. One example of the importance of understanding local factors is the Baxter Healthcare facility in Kingstree, South Carolina, which was established in 1961 and closed in 1996. Census data for 1990 shows Kingstree's population to be 64 per cent black with an income level only 60 per cent of the state average. On the surface, the site of the Baxter Healthcare facility appears to be a strong candidate for an equity investigation. The facility, however, is actually removed from the town and its residents, and instead is situated among vast acreages of farmland; the company only uses a Kingstree address. Thus Kingstree residents may not be at risk when compared to another community downwind from the facility. Further, the composition of the plant's work force and the location of workers' residences would determine whether those who live near the facility actually benefit from employment by its location. Only through this type of individual, local investigation can we truly understand the context and processes that produce inequities.

Conclusion

This research examined the issue of which came first: Were toxic facilities initially located in areas irrespective of racial or economic factors, and over time did community demographics change so that inequities appear to exist in 1990? Or were the facilities located in communities that were initially poor or minority and remained so during the intervening years? Our results suggest that the former mechanism was true for the state of South Carolina. The outcome of inequity that we see manifested in 1990 reflects socio-demographic processes of population change and not inequitable siting practices, at least at this scale of analysis. It appears that larger economic and social processes such as land cost and migration are more likely determinants of the current outcomes visible today, rather than when the industrial facilities were initially sited.

While this study cannot provide indisputable answers to the question of environmental equity, it does point to the necessity of undertaking process-equity analyses in order to substantiate current claims of environmental inequity. It suggests three directions for future research. First, it would be useful to develop paired comparisons of communities with and without facilities to test for differences in socio-demographic changes. A second line of enquiry should detail the siting process as much as possible, including minutes from public hearings, tax records, government incentives, and a review of property values and changes over time. Finally, a third important research area involves differentiating between emission types, toxicity, magnitude and disposal methods. An example of the utility of such research is provided by the following case: a particular social group resides near few facilities, and yet those facilities adjacent to it have the highest emission rate of toxic releases. It should be understood, however, that since the present research only examined one type of environmental threat, these conclusions therefore address only one part of the equity debate.

References

Air and Waste Management Association (1997) 'Are inaccurate emission measurements clouding pollution control planning?', *EM*, September, pp16–17

Anderson, A. B., Anderton, D. L. and Oakes, J. M. (1994) 'Environmental equity: Evaluating TSDF siting over the past two decades', *Waste Age*, vol 25, pp83–100

Anderton, D. L., Anderson, A. B., Oakes, J. M. and Fraser, M. R. (1994) 'Environmental equity: The demographics of dumping', *Demography*, vol 31, pp229–248

Been, V. (1994) 'Locally undesirable land uses in minority neighborhoods: Disproportionate siting or marker dynamics?', *Yale Law Journal*, vol 103, pp1383–1422

Been, V. (1995) 'Analyzing evidence of environmental justice', *Journal of Land Use and Environmental Law*, vol 11, pp1–36

Been, V. and Gupta, F. (1997) 'Coming to the nuisance or going to the Barrios? A longitudinal analysis of environmental justice claims', *Ecology Law Quarterly*, vol 24, pp1–56

Bourke, L. (1994) 'Economic attitudes and responses to siting hazardous waste facilities in rural Utah', *Rural Sociology*, vol 59, pp485–496

Bullard, R. D. (1990) *Dumping in Dixie: Race, Class, and Environmental Quality*, Westview Press, Boulder, CO

Bullard, R. D. (1994) 'Overcoming racism in environmental decision-making', *Environment*, vol 36, no 4, pp10–20, 39–44

Burke, L. M. (1993) 'Race and environmental equity: A geographic analysis in Los Angeles', *Geo Info Systems*, vol 3, October, pp44–50

Cohen, M. J. (1997) 'The spatial distribution of toxic chemical emissions: Implications for non-metropolitan areas', *Society and Natural Resources*, vol 10, pp17–41

Glickman, T. S. (1994) 'Measuring environmental equity with geographical information systems', *Resources*, vol 116, pp2–6

Kovacik, C. F. and Winberry, J. J. (1987) *South Carolina: The Making of a Landscape*, University of South Carolina Press, Columbia, SC

Lynn, F. and Kartez, J. (1994) 'Environmental democracy in action: The Toxic Release Inventory', *Environmental Management*, vol 18, pp511–521

Mohai, P. and Bryant, B. (1992) 'Environmental racism: Reviewing the evidence' in B. Bryant and P. Mohai (eds) *Race and the Incidence of Environmental Hazards: A Time for Discourse*, Westview Press, Boulder, CO, pp163–176

Perlin, S. A., Setzer, R. W., Creason, R. W. and Sexton, K. (1995) 'Distribution of industrial air emissions by income and race in the United States: An approach using the Toxic Release Inventory', *Environmental Science and Technology*, vol 29, pp69–80

Pollock, P. H. and Vittas, M. E. (1995) 'Who bears the burdens of environmental pollution? Race, ethnicity, and environmental equity in Florida', *Social Science Quarterly*, vol 76, pp294–310

Schueler, D. G. (1992) 'Southern exposure', *Sierra*, vol 77, no 6, pp42–49

Scott, M. S., Cutter, S. L., Menzel, C., Ji, M. and Wagner, D. F. (1997) 'Spatial accuracy of the EPA's environmental hazards databases and their use in environmental equity analyses', *Applied Geographic Studies*, vol 1, pp45–61

South Carolina Department of Commerce (1941–1996) *South Carolina Industrial Directory*, South Carolina Department of Commerce, Columbia, SC

UCC (United Church of Christ Commission for Racial Justice) (1987) *Toxic Wastes and Race in the United States: A National Report on the Racial and Socioeconomic Characteristics of Communities with Hazardous Waste Sites*, United Church of Christ, New York

Yandle, T. and Burton, D. (1996) 'Re-examining environmental justice: A statistical analysis of historical hazardous waste landfill siting patterns in metropolitan Texas', *Social Science Quarterly*, vol 77, pp477–492

Zimmerman, R. (1993) 'Social equity and environmental risk', *Risk Analysis*, vol 13, pp649–666

Part V

From Theory to Practice

22

Emergency Preparedness and Planning for Nuclear Power Plant Accidents

Susan L. Cutter

Introduction

The threat of closure of nuclear power plants in the US due to inadequate emergency response plans still exists despite the recent Nuclear Regulatory Commission (NRC) decision concerning the Indian Point, New York, power plant located just outside New York City. In April 1983, the NRC challenged state, local and utility planning efforts and gave them until June 1983 to provide for substantial improvements; otherwise the NRC would close the reactor. Although the NRC did not close Indian Point for inadequate plans, it certainly scared licensees and state and local governments. This issue also highlighted the need for and problems inherent in planning for nuclear power plant accidents in the US.

At the time of the March 1979 accident at Three Mile Island (TMI), Pennsylvania, only 11 out of 31 states with operating reactors had NRC concurred plans (USFEMA, 1980). Submission of plans by the licensee was voluntary and implied that they had met the NRC regulations. There was no evaluation of the quality of the plans. Pennsylvania was not among this group of 11 and the level of preparedness for the subsequent Three Mile Island accident was less than adequate. If there had been a major off-site release of radioactivity from the plant endangering the public, most people, including the Presidential Commission investigating the accident, felt that the state and local emergency response plans would not have been sufficient to ensure the protection of the health and safety of local residents.

As the events at the plant unfolded, emergency response planning was reactive in nature and done very much on an ad hoc basis. For example, the NRC ordered risk counties and the state to prepare evacuation plans for a 20-mile radius *while the accident was in progress*. Initially, local officials were assuming a 10-mile

Note: Reprinted, with permission, from *Applied Geography*, vol 4, Susan Cutter, 'Emergency preparedness and planning for nuclear power plant accidents', pp235–245. © Elsevier, 1984

evacuation zone involving 27,000 people. Within minutes this escalated to a 20-mile zone involving 700,000 people (see Chapter 13). Fortunately, these hastily derived plans never had to be implemented.

Since Three Mile Island, emergency response planning has been slowly evolving, yet there are still sites where there is no formally approved plan. There are constant challenges to evacuation plans, in particular, during licensing hearings such as those underway for Indian Point. Citizens, scientists and public advocates question the reliability of such plans. This reliability question is crucial as all emergency response planning depends, first and foremost, on the unknown human factor, yet the potential range of responses by the public are not incorporated into the plans. What will the residents in the vicinity of a nuclear power plant do when the sirens go off or when they are told of an accident at the facility? Will they follow the dictates of the emergency management officials or make their own plans? No one really knows for sure.

This chapter focuses on the unknown human factor and examines emergency response planning for nuclear power plant accidents, particularly those assumptions about the responses of the local residents. The purpose is to demonstrate the inherent weaknesses of the plans due to the exclusion of this behavioural information.

The Planning Process

There are currently 73 licensed reactors in 31 states in the US which require some form of emergency response planning, and formal approval of these plans is now a condition for granting and maintaining operating licences of nuclear facilities. The planning effort includes on-site preparations by the licensee (the utility company operating the reactor) as well as off-site plans developed by state and local governments. The local government planning effort is usually done at the county level with the assistance of consultants and state personnel.

The Federal Emergency Management Agency (FEMA) is the lead federal agency for the coordination of all off-site radiological emergency preparedness efforts and, in conjunction with the NRC, evaluates state and local plans. Interim planning guidelines developed jointly by these two agencies provide a checklist for state and local officials and the licensee as to what should be included in their plans (USNRC and USFEMA, 1980). These guidelines are divided into 16 topical headings, and within each there are a number of evaluative criteria which must be present (Table 22.1). In the case of the state plans, 98 evaluative criteria must be present, while 81 are needed for the local plans.

Planning area

The areal extent of planning is designated as the emergency planning zone (EPZ). These zones are based on short- and long-tem radiation exposures including airborne (plume) pathways and environmental (ingestion) pathways. The actual area of these zones is determined by the need to assure adequate response measures in order to protect human health and safety in the event of an accident at the

Table 22.1 *Planning elements*

Administrative	Public safety
Support and resources	Notification method and procedures
Organization and responsibilities	Public information
Planning effort responsibilities	Protective response options
On-site emergency organization	Medical and public health support
	Recovery and re-entry
Technical	
Emergency classification	**Evaluation**
Communications	Exercises and drills
Equipment	
Accident assessment	
Exposure control	
Emergency response training	

Source: Adapted from USNRC and USFEMA, 1980

site. A 10-mile primary zone and a 50-mile secondary zone were established as baseline distances for planning by the NRC and FEMA (USNRC and USEPA, 1978). This was done to ensure that all plans encompass all accident sequences and incorporate consequences of all types of accidents, including core melt and containment failure, regardless of their probability of occurrence. The 10- and 50-mile zones were based on standardized meteorological conditions, time-dependent characteristics of potential releases and exposures including the duration of each, and the types of radioactive materials released including their persistence in the environment (half-lives). States were to adjust the size and shape (not necessarily circular) of these zones to account for local variations in topography, meteorology, population density and distribution, land use, transportation access routes and jurisdictional boundaries.

Public safety

The three protective measures which are recognized as vital elements in any radiological emergency planning are sheltering, medical prophylactics (thyroid blocking agents) and evacuation. There is very little research on the effectiveness of each of these options in protecting public health and safety and even less on the acceptance of each by the public. Both the NRC and FEMA assume they will work.

Currently, there is no federal guideline on sheltering as a protective action that is of practical use by state and local officials although there are a number of research reports on the subject (Anno and Dore, 1979; USNRC, 1979). Yet, many states are adopting sheltering as an appropriate response. The wooden walls of a house or basement afford some protection against the short-term immediately released radionuclides.

The use of potassium iodide (a thyroid blocking drug) is a second protective option. During the accident at Three Mile Island, neither the federal government, Commonwealth of Pennsylvania, nor the utility operating the plant had any potassium iodide on hand nor did they have a policy for its use (USFEMA,

1980, part III, p30). A St Louis, Missouri, firm produced 237,000 1-ounce vials of liquid potassium iodide but the shipment did not arrive in Harrisburg until 4 April, six days after the first sign of trouble at the plant. There are still no federal guidelines on the use of medical prophylactics, although there are numerous recommendations for and against the use of potassium iodide as a protective response for the general public (Aldrich and Blond, 1980; USNRC, 1982). Undaunted, the state of Tennessee selected to use potassium iodide as a protective measure. It has been distributed to 7000 residents within five miles of the Sequoyah nuclear power plant near Soddy-Daisy, Tennessee, as part of the state's radiological emergency response plan.

The third and most widely recommended protective action is evacuation. Here there is considerable federal guidance. For example, all state and local plans are required to have evacuation elements including total amount of time required to implement and confirm an evacuation. In addition, there are regulations requiring prompt notification of the public in the event of any unusual activity at the plant. Utilities, as a condition for licensing, must be able to notify all (100 per cent) of the affected population in the 10-mile EPZ 15 minutes after they notify state and local officials.

Rapid public alert in the event of an accident is a key element in prompting the public to respond to warning measures. Given the cost of some of these warning systems ($1 million per site), their usefulness has been and is being challenged by state and local governments as well as the utilities operating the plants. As a consequence, one recommendation from FEMA after a review of state response plans in 1980 was to:

> ...*engage behavioural scientists in an immediate effort to resolve issues related to the time, nature and testing of public response to emergency alerting and notification around fixed nuclear facilities.* (USFEMA, 1980, part VI, p14)

To date, only one such study has been completed (Sorenson, 1982).

Drills and exercises

If implemented, how well will the plans work? As part of the NRC/FEMA approval process, drills and exercises must be conducted on an annual basis to test the equipment and other elements of the plans. This testing involves simulated scenarios and includes on-site and off-site personnel. Unfortunately, all the drills are announced beforehand, and local and state agencies are in a 'ready-to-respond' posture rather than in situations of normal operations. In many instances, state and local officials have cleared their desks and await notification of the 'accident'. While public officials acknowledge that these drills are held under somewhat ideal conditions they are quick to point out that they are better than no drill at all.

These drills rarely involve field activity or active public participation, although the public is notified of a drill in progress. During a 1979 drill at the Salem nuclear power plant in southern New Jersey, officials termed their responses to the drill a success. At a debriefing session, however, they were immediately confronted by local residents who queried how the drill could be considered successful when few members of the public knew what to do when the sirens went off. In a March 1982 drill at the Indian Point 3 reactor outside New York City, most of the 88 newly installed warning sirens failed to operate (*New York Times*, 1982a). This drill, like most, is primarily an exercise in command functions with limited field experience. This lack of field activity poses a number of potential problems. In reference to the Indian Point drill:

> *A single mock evacuation involving tens of thousands was ordered, but because of a typographical error, county information officers contradicted each other on which numbered zones were to be evacuated.* (*New York Times*, 1982b, pB1)

Underlying Assumptions of Radiological Emergency Plans

There are two major assumptions inherent in the development of radiological emergency response plans which should be questioned, as they point to potential deficiencies in the planning process and may ultimately prove the plans unworkable in the event of an accident. First, it is assumed that states will adjust their planning unit (EPZ) according to local variations in population, topography, land use, transportation access and so on, rather than using the generic 10- and 50-mile zones suggested by the NRC and FEMA. This is not the case. In a preliminary examination of four completed state plans (California, New Jersey, Virginia and Arkansas), only one had modified the generic EPZ to conform to topographic variations.

There may be good reasons for not modifying these zones. State and local governments, in particular, are in an unfortunate position of having limited financial and technical resources upon which to draw for plan development. This not only accounts for the minimum planning effort, but also accounts for the lack of adherence to deadlines for completed plans. For example, Westchester County, New York, one of eight counties in the state within a 10-mile radius of an operating reactor, estimates that their radiological emergency response plan alone will cost $1.5–2 million (*New York Times*, 1982b). Under these circumstances state and local officials simply assume a compliance posture and only incorporate those elements that will ensure NRC approval of their plans without any site-specific corrections or any evaluation of their effectiveness. The financial constraint, however, may not be solely due to federal regulations. Both NRC and FEMA thought that the radiological plans would simply be additions or appendices to the states' general emergency response plans (US Congress, 1981). For some states, this is not the case and the new regulations are providing the stimulus for the development of general emergency response plans as well as those for radiological emergencies.

The second underlying assumption in these planning efforts provides the focus for the rest of this chapter: namely, all of the plans are based on a 'military model of authority' (Dynes et al, 1979, p26). They assume the public will do as it is told, will respond in a rational manner, will follow directions or orders, and will comply with the protective actions officials have planned. Research in the social and behavioural sciences suggests that this may not be the case (Perry, 1981; Perry et al, 1981).

Major Deficiencies

There are five major criticisms of these plans which should be stressed, for they illustrate major deficiencies in the emergency response plans as currently developed. These include evacuation behaviour, evacuation in high-density areas, evacuation as the sole protective response, evacuation timing and inter-state coordination.

Evacuation behaviour

Most plans assume the public will respond to orders and evacuation routes suggested by the planning document, including the time frame specified and the specific routes. Criticism of this assumption was also made by the Three Mile Island task force in a review of Pennsylvania's plans (Dynes et al, 1979, p26). Planners assume the public possesses the necessary information to respond to authoritative cues in a logical and orderly fashion. While panic may not be the issue, residents not following orders might be. Residents may choose alternative routes and destinations or simply not evacuate. Contingency plans for coping with these potential behaviours are necessary and are not found in most state plans.

Approximately 196,000 people evacuated in response to the accident at Three Mile Island although *no formal evacuation order* was given (see Chapter 13; also Flynn 1982). Those factors which influenced the evacuation decision were proximity to the plant, inability to confirm the risk information, age of household head and actions of friends and neighbours (Chapter 13). There is no provision in any state plan for this spontaneous type of evacuation which occurred at Three Mile Island. While the message from the governor was quite specific – 'pregnant women and pre-school-aged children residing within five miles of the plant are *advised* to evacuate, and those within ten miles from the plant are *advised* to remain indoors' – reactions to the message were quite varied. Most of the targeted individuals (pregnant women and pre-school-aged children) complied with the advice but so did many other individuals, many of whom lived farther than five miles from the plant. This advice, as well as confusion and uncertainty at the plant, were viewed as cues to evacuate by some, and cues to remain in place by others.

It should be noted there is no such thing as forced compliance by members of the general public. Residents have the freedom of choice to select the most appropriate protective measure based on their own decision-making. There is no legal basis for the federal government, state or local authorities to forcibly remove people from their own homes. Every effort must be made, therefore, to increase voluntary compliance to recommended actions suggested by emergency management officials. This requires extensive pre-planning information dissemination and public awareness campaigns.

There is no mention in radiological emergency plans of the level of risk and threat that would prompt individuals to comply with the actions being recommended by emergency management personnel. Social science research found individuals have a heightened awareness and fear of radiation and have many misconceptions about reactors themselves, equating radiological releases with mushroom-type clouds (Slovic et al, 1979, 1980). If individuals perceive the personal risk as high then this is likely to induce evacuation behaviour. If, however, individuals are unable to confirm the risk information (as was the case with Three Mile Island) then there is less likelihood of evacuation. If the warning messages are given by credible sources (there were some doubts during Three Mile Island), then this will also increase an individual's likelihood of evacuation (Perry, 1981; Perry et al, 1981; Sorenson, 1982). Content and credibility of warning messages were recognized as factors determining evacuation after Three Mile Island and resulted in new regulations specifying communication centres (Emergency Office Centers) where accurate information could be quickly disseminated to state and local officials and then transmitted to the general public. There was also one individual who was designated as the spokesperson to the public.

Most theoretical and pragmatic research on evacuation found that families evacuate as units (Drabek, 1969; Dynes et al, 1979; Perry et al, 1981). State plans do not include provisions for individuals moving into the hazard zone in an attempt to reunite their family, nor do they incorporate mechanisms for information acquisition about where family members might be, such as a family message centre. The assumption is that schoolchildren will be taken care of while at school, parents will make no attempt to locate them, and employees coming back from the workplace will not attempt to find spouses and children. This may be a faulty assumption, particularly if the individuals perceive loved ones to be exposed to high risks.

State and county plans are much better in describing special evacuation problem populations such as patients in hospitals, inmates in federal or state confinement and so on. Very few plans mention 'reluctant' populations that may pose particular problems in evacuation such as mobility-poor subgroups, including inner-city poor and the elderly, and farmers with livestock. Virginia's plan mentions protective actions for livestock, while California's plan mentions specific reluctant subgroups. There is also no provision in any of the plans examined for the evacuation of family pets.

There is a substantial body of literature which concludes that the public will not use planned shelters and will find accommodation with friends, neighbours or in motels (Dynes et al, 1979). This was true with the majority of evacuees from Three Mile Island (Chapter 13; see also Ziegler et al, 1981). There are also a variety of problems encountered in evacuation such as gasoline allocation, and a run on local banks for withdrawal of money. None of these situations is mentioned in the plans. Second, in the case of Three Mile Island, some evacuees did not move far enough away from the zone of danger and would have had to evacuate a second or perhaps a third time, which could result in cascading relocations.

As a final comment about evacuation behaviour, there is no provision for population convergence on the area. The influx of media personnel, emergency officials from all levels of government, and curiosity seekers was one of the main problems that caught emergency officials off guard at Three Mile Island. As the Presidential Task Force stated:

The convergence of individuals and information is a common problem in many emergencies; this incident was no exception. Telephone exchanges may become overloaded and the distribution of critical emergency information hindered or blocked. Those who arrive on the scene require a number of services. These needs range from such basic elements as food and shelter to the provision of work space and communication facilities to access to decision-makers and emergency person-nel. None of the plans references these problems or includes any provisions for ameliorating them. (Dynes et al, 1979, p25)

Evacuation and high-density areas

Evacuation is an unlikely protective response in high-density population areas due to limitations on the emergency management system, including timing and noti-fication of all affected residents. There are over 100,000 people living within ten miles of each of the highest-density reactor sites with current operating licences (Indian Point, NY; Zion, IL; Beaver Valley, PA; Three Mile Island, PA; Millstone, CN). There are 289,000 people living within ten miles of the Indian Point reac-tors (35 miles north of midtown Manhattan) alone. The total number of people living within ten miles of reactors with operating licences nationwide is 3.3 mil-lion (USFEMA, 1980, part EX, p2).

There is no way that all of these individuals can be safely evacuated. Urbanik (1981) conducted an analysis of evacuation time estimates. Data were based on utility responses to an NRC enquiry asking the utility to estimate how long it would take to evacuate residents within ten miles of their sites. The median evacu-ation time given for all sites (52) was 5.3 hours under good weather conditions, and 6.4 hours under adverse weather conditions. For reactors with more than 100,000 people within the ten-mile radius, the median evacuation time was 5.8 hours for good weather and 7.3 hours for adverse weather. The report stated that the median was a much better indicator of the true nature of evacuation times as many utilities projected lengthy evacuations (a range of 4.8 to 21 hours for good weather, and 5.3 to 27 hours for adverse weather). Unfortunately, these higher estimates may reflect a truer estimate of the time. The utilities were also asked to provide a confidence rating for these: 33 per cent responded that they had little or no confidence in their estimates.

Evacuation as sole protective response

A third criticism involves the recommendation of evacuation as the only protec-tive response rather than as part of a combination of methods such as shelter-ing, evacuation and medical prophylactics. One of the assumptions of voluntary evacuation is the detection of the hazard in sufficient time to warn and evacuate the affected population prior to the release of the radiation. The NRC provides guidance on initiation and duration of radioactive releases (Table 22.2) but, in some situations, officials may have one hour from the time of an initiating event to the time at which a major portion of the release occurs. With these types of rapid releases, evacuation is completely out of the question. Sheltering and air-filtering devices may be the only realistic protective actions available. Large-scale evacuations under the most ideal conditions normally take from 12 to 24 hours, depending on the number of potential evacuees, although utility estimates are considerably lower. Evacuation, if used as the only protective action, may increase

Table 22.2 *Guidance on initiation and duration of release*

Time from the initiating event to start of atmospheric release	0.5 hours–1 day
Time period over which radioactive material may be continuously released	0.5 hours–several days
Time at which major portion of release may occur	0.5 hours–1 day after start of release
Travel time for release to exposure point (time after release)	5 miles – 0.5–2 hours 10 miles – 1–4 hours

Source: USNRC and USFEMA, 1980, p14

rather than decrease exposure levels by forcing residents into their cars, which afford less protection against airborne radiation than do concrete basements and wooden walls of houses.

Evacuation timing

Similarly, the timing of the evacuation order is important and could be delayed to allow passage of the plume through the affected area. There are longer-term impacts which can occur as a result of releases of radioactivity such as Caesium-137 which have longer half-lives (750 days) than do some of the radioactive iodines (8 days or less). Few of the plans include this concept. While it is important to protect for short-term exposures, the longer-term impacts may in fact be the most damaging. A hastily called evacuation may expose the public to more radiation than if they were to shelter in place.

The California Office of Emergency Services has examined the effectiveness of protective actions in direct-exposure EPZs. They modelled the effects of evacuation, sheltering and relocation on acute fatalities and delayed cancers. As expected, they found the highest numbers of hypothesized early fatalities occurred when no protective action was taken and when the plume travelled over major population centres such as Sacramento, the state capital. Evacuation reduced the number of fatalities, but required 23 hours for the most densely populated zone. Evacuation reduced, but did not eliminate, the impact of delayed cancers. Because the evacuation over the 30-mile zone took nearly a day, people would be caught in their cars as the plume passed overhead. The principal effect, then, would have resulted in exposure to larger doses than if the people stayed put (State of California, 1980).

A selective evacuation, usually done in sectors according to the plume direction, may also not work. First, it assumes that residents know which sector they reside or work in. Second, and more importantly, it assumes people will remain in place until they are told to leave. Again, common sense and research on evacuation behaviour suggests that this may also not be true.

Inter-state coordination

The accident at Three Mile Island pointed to the need for inter-state cooperation in emergency response planning. Currently, there are no regional response
plans although states do have memoranda which define their roles and coordinate
responses of all levels of government in the affected area. There are a number of
instances where integrated inter-state plans are necessary given the size of the state
and the site and situation of the reactor itself. For example the EPZs for Three
Mile Island and Peach Bottom not only include Pennsylvania, but New Jersey
and Maryland. An accident at Beaver Valley, in western Pennsylvania would also
involve personnel from Ohio and West Virginia, while an accident at the Salem,
New Jersey, plant would involve New Jersey, Delaware and Maryland.

Cooperative agreements are not integrated into overall response plans at either
the state or regional level. This could pose potential problems. During the accident at Three Mile Island, for example, New Jersey officials notified Pennsylvania
authorities that cars would be turned back at the border unless Pennsylvania set
up decontamination centres at all border crossings into New Jersey. This call was
ignored and could have resulted in disastrous effects (Fischer, 1981).

There is also no federal master plan on responses to radiological emergencies
at fixed locations which defines and delineates the federal role and what states
might expect from the federal government. FEMA is currently working on such a
master plan called the National Radiological Emergency Preparedness Plan. The
plan is supposed to cover all the procedures for federal assistance and response at
an accident at a nuclear power plant. The plan is not yet completed, nearly four
years after the accident at Three Mile Island.

Where Do We Go from Here?

While emergency response planning has come a long way in just four years, it
is still far short of ensuring maximum protection of the public around these
fixed nuclear power plant sites. State and local authorities must go beyond the
simple compliance mentality and incorporate knowledge from research in the
social and behavioural sciences, in order to upgrade and improve planning efforts.
This includes information on geographical variation, in order to determine the
true nature of the emergency planning zone, as well as the range of behavioural
responses by the public that might be expected in response to recommended protective actions. The development of regional response plans by federal authorities
may help alleviate inter-state disputes during times of crisis.

One obvious solution to the planning problem is to educate the public and
instil confidence in the planning efforts. Brochures to local residents and publication of evacuation plans in local telephone books is one such method.

To date, the financial burden of planning has rested with local municipalities and states. This accounts for many of the shortcomings in the plans. The
plans need to anticipate the extraordinary and be flexible enough to handle
unexpected problems. This cannot be accomplished when the plans are hastily
drawn and incorporate only the minimal amount of information necessary to gain

NRC approval. If the federal government wishes to have radiological emergency response plans which may work, then they should allocate money to the states to undertake such planning.

The reliability of emergency response plans depends on the unknown human factor. What will residents do when the sirens blow? Social scientists have much to offer to these planning efforts, yet their research is underutilized. More effort on the part of the academic community should be made to apply its training and skills to help local and state governments ensure the safety and welfare of the residents in the event of an accident at a nuclear power plant in their community. If we become complacent, our applied research will have been done in vain.

Acknowledgement

This work was supported in part by the New Jersey Agricultural Experiment Station, Publication Number 0-26410-3-82, supported by State funds and by a Faulty Academic Study Program (FASP) grant from The Research Council, Rutgers University.

References

Aldrich, D. C. and Blond, R. M. (1980) *Examination of the Use of Potassium Iodine (KI) as an Emergency Protective Measure for Nuclear Reactor Accidents*, NUREG/CF-1433, Government Printing Office, Washington, DC

Anno, G. H. and Dore, M. A. (1979) *Protective Actions Against Nuclear Accidents Involving Gaseous Releases*, EPA 520/1-78-001B, Government Printing Office, Washington, DC

Drabek, T. E. (1969) 'Social processes in disaster: Family evacuation', *Social Problems*, vol 16, pp336–349

Dynes, R. R., Purcell, A. H., Wenger, D. E., Stern, P. S., Stallings, R. A. and Johnson, Q. T. (1979) *Report of the Emergency Preparedness and Response Task Force, the President's Commission on the Accident at Three Mile Island*, Government Printing Office, Washington, DC

Fischer, D. W. (1981) 'Planning for large-scale accidents: Learning from the Three Mile Island accident', *Energy*, vol 6, pp93–105

Flynn, C. B. (1982) 'Reactions of local residents to the accident at Three Mile Island' in D. L. Sills, C. P. Wolf and V. B. Shelanski (eds) *Accident at Three Mile Island: The Human Dimensions*, Westview Press, Boulder, CO, pp49–64

New York Times (1982a) 4 March 1982, pB1

New York Times (1982b) 25 May 1982, ppB1, B6

Perry, R. W. (1981) *Citizen Evacuation in Response to Nuclear and Non-nuclear Threats*, BHARC-400/81/013, Battelle Human Affairs Research Centers, Seattle, WA

Perry, R. W., Lindell, M. K. and Greene, M. J. (1981) *Evacuation Planning in Emergency Management*, Lexington Books, Lexington, MA

Slovic, P., Lichtenstein, S. and Fischhoff, B. (1979) 'Images of disaster: Perception and acceptance of risks from nuclear power' in G. Goodman and W. Rowe, (eds) *Energy Risk Management*, Academic Press, London, pp233–245

Slovic, P., Fischhoff, B. and Lichtenstein, S. (1980) 'Facts and fears: Understanding perceived risk' in R. C. Schwing and W. A. Albers, jr (eds) *Societal Risk Assessment: How Safe is Safe Enough?*, Plenum Press, New York, pp181–216

Sorenson, J. H. (1982) *Evaluation of the Emergency Warning System at the Fort St Vrain Nuclear Power Plant*, TM-8171, Oak Ridge National Laboratory, Oak Ridge, TN

State of California, Office of Emergency Services (1980) *Emergency Planning Zones for Serious Nuclear Power Plant Accidents*, Office of Emergency Services, Sacramento, CA

US Congress (1981) 'Radiological emergency planning and preparedness', hearing before the Senate Committee on Environment and Public Works, Subcommittee on Nuclear Regulation, 97th Congress, First Session, 27 April, Serial No. 97-H13

USFEMA (United States Federal Emergency Management Agency) (1980) 'Report to the President: State radiological emergency planning and preparedness in support of commercial nuclear power plants', Government Printing Office, Washington, DC

USNRC (United States Nuclear Regulatory Commission) (1979) *Examination of Off-site Radiological Emergency Protective Measures for Nuclear Reactor Accidents Involving Core Melt*, NUREG/CR-1131, SAND-78-0454, Government Printing Office, Washington, DC

USNRC (1982) *1981 Annual Report*, Government Printing Office, NUREG-0920, Washington, DC

USNRC and USEPA (United States Environmental Protection Agency) (1978) *Planning Basis for the Development of State and Local Government Radiological Emergency Response Plans in Support of Light Water Nuclear Power Plants*, NUREG-0396, EPA 520/1-78-016, Government Printing Office, Washington, DC

USNRC and USFEMA (1980) *Criteria for Preparation and Evaluation of Radiological Emergency Response Plans and Preparedness in Support of Nuclear Power Plants*, NUREG-0654, FEMA-REP-1, Government Printing Office, Washington, DC

Urbanik, T. (1981) *An Analysis of Evacuation Time Estimates Around 52 Nuclear Power Plant Sites*, NUREG/CR-1856, Government Printing Office, Washington, DC

Ziegler, D. J., Brunn, S. D. and Johnson, J. H. (1981) 'Evacuation from a nuclear technological disaster', *Geographical Review*, vol 71, pp1–16

23

Airborne Toxic Releases:
Are Communities Prepared?

Susan L. Cutter

In the wake of hazardous chemical accidents like that in Bhopal, India, governments at all levels have become keenly aware of the potential for toxic hazards in
their own jurisdictions and of the necessity for contingency planning for possible
airborne toxic releases (Bowonder et al, 1985). The concern of the US Congress
was reflected in its enactment in October 1986 of the Superfund Amendments
and Reauthorization Act (SARA), a portion of which addresses this need for
improved emergency response planning. SARA now mandates a comprehensive
planning effort for hazardous chemical releases, involving coordination between
local, state and federal governments and industry (see Box 23.1).[1]

By their nature, airborne toxic releases are troublesome to prepare for: the
onset of these technological emergencies is rapid and the substances involved
present immediate acute health effects; such releases can occur anywhere and can
originate from both stationary, or fixed, sites (like industrial plants) and mobile
sites (for example, trains); there is a higher likelihood that public evacuation will
be necessary than there would be with similar releases into the soil and water;
and the population at risk cannot be identified because it varies according to the
substance released, time of day, location of the release, prevailing meteorological
conditions and other factors.

The value of contingency planning for natural hazards has been well documented (Rubin, 1986), yet the same level of documentation on contingency planning for technological hazards is virtually non-existent. The example of nuclear
accidents shows that, even where contingency plans do exist, many are seriously
flawed (see Chapter 22; also Jaske, 1983; Sylves, 1984). Despite the enormous
amounts of money that have been spent, the massive drills that have been conducted and the public debate that has ensued over nuclear plant safety, events
such as Chernobyl illustrate how truly unprepared we are for these large-scale
emergencies and their geographic impacts.

Note: Reprinted, with permission, from *Environment*, vol 29, no 6, Susan L. Cutter, 'Airborne toxic
releases: Are communities prepared?' pp12–17, 28–31. © Heldref Publications, 1987

This chapter examines the current status of contingency planning for technological accidents involving airborne releases of non-radioactive toxic substances in the US. The purpose is to demonstrate the lack of preparedness of some communities and to highlight the obstacles they face in trying to plan effectively for these accidents. Four actual airborne toxic releases are described in the chapter in terms of how local residents and emergency management personnel handled them. The chapter also suggests some ways in which communities can improve contingency planning for such accidents in their own areas.

The disaster at Bhopal highlighted the public health dangers associated with non-nuclear airborne toxic substances, but there is still a lack of research on local community preparedness for releases of these substances.[2] Several how-to booklets have been written to facilitate planning for accidents involving hazardous materials (USFEMA, 1981; DePol and Cheremisinoff, 1984; USDOT, 1984, 1985; USEPA, 1985a; Hushon, 1986; US Congress OTA, 1986), but few of these are specific to airborne toxic releases.[3]

There are three main obstacles that thwart contingency planning for airborne toxic releases:

1   lack of data and basic information on toxic hazards in the community;
2   little or no prior experience with these types of incidents; and
3   incomplete knowledge about the likely responses of residents and emergency managers.

The background and severity of each obstacle are described in the following sections.

Knowledge of Local Hazards

There is little information on how chemicals are transported, stored, used and disposed of in communities. In the aftermath of the accident at Bhopal, state legislation has been trying to rectify this basic lack of data (Ajamie, 1985). 'Bhopal bills' have been passed in states such as New Jersey, which is currently conducting site-specific inventories of industrial chemical use (see Box 23.1). Over 23 states have passed right-to-know laws (US Congress OTA, 1986). While many of the provisions differ, all of these laws require public access to information on hazardous materials present in the state or municipality, inventories and surveys of chemical use, computerized record keeping on locations of chemical use, and exposure-reporting systems. At present, little of this essential information has been compiled, let alone released to local officials, to fire and police personnel, or to the public.

In those communities with major fixed-site industrial users, there is often little coordination between on-site and off-site responses to possible accidents. The situation with transportation corridors is even more nebulous. State officials may be aware of hazardous materials transportation through the issuance of permits or registration of carriers; yet all too often, the local municipal leaders are not notified. Local officials need better data on toxic materials storage and transportation

---

Box 23.1 *New Jersey's Bhopal bill*

The New Jersey State Assembly introduced the 'Toxic Catastrophe Prevention Act' (TCPA) on 9 September 1985, and it was signed into law on 8 January 1986.* The law (the first of its kind in the US) is designed to mitigate and prevent future toxic releases like that at Bhopal through a series of measures including definitions of hazardous substances, registration of substances, risk assessment, management and reduction programmes, and penalties for violations.

TCPA identifies 11 substances as extraordinarily hazardous substances – hydrogen chloride, allyl chloride, hydrogen cyanide, hydrogen fluoride, chlorine, phosphorus trichloride, hydrogen sulphide, phosgene, bromine, methyl isocyanate (the substance released at Bhopal) and toluene. Owners or operators of facilities that generate, store or handle any of these substances are required to complete a registration form that includes the quantities and locations of the substances on site, the risks involved and the insurance carriers underwriting the facility's liability insurance.

Facilities are required to provide and review an on-site safety evaluation for a risk management programme involving the extraordinarily hazardous substances. If necessary facilities must also provide an off-site plan for risk reduction and a timetable for its implementation. The risk reduction plan is essentially a contingency plan.

How well is the law working? There are a series of statutory deadlines for implementing various provisions of the law that the state Department of Environmental Protection has failed to meet. The complexity of the bill and the enormity of the task have to date overwhelmed the department. Industry has begun to adhere to the new registration and reporting requirements, although compliance has been slow. There are no regulations yet on implementing the risk management aspects of the law, but the state is diligently working to establish them. The state is nowhere near the point of establishing regulations for the risk reduction plans.

Both New Jersey's Bhopal bill and the newer federal Title III are attempting to rectify decades of lax record keeping. If they succeed in determining where toxic materials are generated, stored, used and transported, the laws will be a significant step forward in the battle against community unpreparedness.

* N.J. Slat. Ann, § 13:1K-19 (West 1987 Supp.).

---

that specify the type and hazards of those toxic substances they are most likely to encounter.[4]

Prior Experience

Accidents are local in nature. They happen so quickly that local officials must take the lead role in mitigation efforts. But until technological accidents occur in their jurisdictions, most local officials do not know where the primary industrial users are, and they are not aware of potential hazards that could occur from these sites.

Relatively few local officials have prior experience with accidental releases from plants, fewer still with releases from transportation accidents. Since the officials rarely have experience on which to draw, their crisis planning or damage control approach to the event relies heavily on state and federal agencies for guidance. All too often, however, state and federal plans and directives are generic and do not take into consideration site or local specificity. While some communities (in California and New Jersey, for example) send local fire, police and public health officials to specialized training sessions on hazardous materials accidents, most communities do not enjoy the benefit of such practical experience.

Contingency planners will find few statistics on actual accidents involving airborne releases of toxic substances. The US Department of Transportation (DOT) says that an average of 11,462 reported transportation accidents occur yearly involving hazardous materials. DOT also suggests that three to four times that amount go unreported (US Congress OTA, 1986, p4). Not all of these accidents, however, involve toxic releases into the air. A preliminary analysis by DOT and other data suggest that there are about 1000 accidents a year involving airborne toxic releases from either fixed or mobile sites (Solecki et al, 1986).

The Acute Hazardous Events (AHE) database of the US Environmental Protection Agency (EPA) includes over 3000 records representing about 6900 incidents between 1980 and 1986 (Industrial Economics, 1985). Originally developed to provide a historical record of acutely toxic events, these data helped in assessing selection criteria for EPA's priority list of acutely hazardous substances. The AHE database is limited: it does not represent a complete inventory of incidents (only reported incidents are included); it is regionally biased; it does not distinguish between in-plant and off-site releases; and it provides little information on the human consequences of such events. Despite these caveats, the AHE database is one of the few compilations of incidents involving acutely toxic releases.

Not all of these accidents were deemed serious enough to require evacuations of local residents. From 1978 to 1986, more than 60 cases were documented in the US in which more than 100 people were evacuated in direct response to airborne toxic releases (see Figure 23.1). All but 3 of these cases occurred between 1980 and 1986. The number of residents evacuated ranged from 100 to more than 40,000 (Miamisburg, Ohio). The substances most often released included hydrochloric acid, anhydrous ammonia and chlorine, and most of the accidents involved stationary facilities.

Behavioural Responses

People react differently to technological emergencies than they do to natural disasters, in part because there is often less warning and people have less knowledge of how to proceed in technological emergencies (Burton et al, 1978; Kates, 1978; Perry et al, 1981; Perry and Mushkatel, 1984; Kasperson and Pijawka, 1985; Kates et al, 1985). A considerable amount of practical experience and research has shown how people respond to natural hazards, but public awareness of and responses to emergencies involving airborne toxic releases are not as well known (Gray, 1981; Helms, 1981; Tierney, 1981).

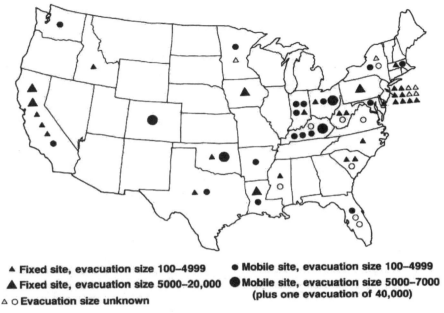

▲ Fixed site, evacuation size 100–4999　　● Mobile site, evacuation size 100–4999

▲ Fixed site, evacuation size 5000–20,000　● Mobile site, evacuation size 5000–7000

△ ○ Evacuation size unknown　　　　　　　　(plus one evacuation of 40,000)

Note: Three accidents, in New York, Montana and Ohio, were omitted because of lack of data.
Locations of symbols reflect state only and not actual site of accident.

Source: Data compiled by the author from a variety of sources.

Figure 23.1 *Known non-radioactive airborne toxic releases involving large evacuations of US residents, 1978–1986*

Residents are usually even less aware of the potential for toxic hazards in their communities than are local officials. With little or no information on which to make judgements, residents can unpredictably over- or underreact in emergencies of this type. Fear and lack of faith in local officials may also affect their responses. The planning process may be hampered by institutional and legal constraints on funding and educational needs, and may be complicated by the uncertainty of determining the populations at risk and their likely responses to such emergencies. As a result of all of these factors, the emergency response is reactive and crisis oriented; it is not usually the result of adherence to a well-formulated contingency plan.

Four case studies illustrate the extent, type and range of responses to accidents by affected residents and emergency management personnel. These case studies are:

- the North York, Ontario, gasoline leak (1979);
- the Mississauga, Ontario, derailment and chlorine leak (1979);
- the Somerville, Massachusetts, tank car accident involving phosphorous trichloride (1980); and
- the Taft, Louisiana, acrolein tank explosion (1982).

These events were chosen for discussion because of the size and extent of their evacuations and the availability of published data on emergency response and recovery efforts.

North York Gasoline Leak

During the early morning hours of 21 February 1979, a gasoline valve malfunctioned at the Imperial Oil terminal in North York, Ontario (Hazen et al, 1980). The leak occurred outside the dyked storage area and reached the catchment area around the loading docks. A design flaw allowed spillage from one catchment to reach the sewers without going through a separator that would have skimmed off the petroleum product. As a result, between 800 and 2000 gallons of gasoline leaked into the sewer system underlying an industrial area dense with chemical and petroleum plants, and the fumes percolated upward into the surrounding buildings. The leak occurred sometime between 5:00am and 6:00am, with first reports of gasoline odour at 8:00am. An evacuation of 5000 people began at 10:30am, and they were allowed back into the area about 4:00pm. This evacuation only involved personnel in the industrial and commercial facilities. Rapid response in isolating the area and preventing entrance to it kept the number of people evacuated to a minimum.

Four factors led to a successful evacuation (that is, with neither serious injuries nor widespread panic). First, the metropolitan Toronto police became the de facto commanders at the scene because of their statutory authority to protect life and property, and because there was no contingency plan specifying the primary response agency. Rapid police action permitted other response agencies to move about unimpeded and facilitated a quick departure for evacuees. Second, the area was primarily industrial and commercial; people are always more willing to leave their places of work than they would be their homes. No delay to locate other family members occurred as it might have in a residential area. Third, the odour of gasoline fumes provided an easy clue as to the potential danger of the incident. Finally, emergency agencies quickly converged on the area.

At the same time, a number of elements complicated the evacuation. With the exception of the police, the roles of the other response agencies were not clearly defined, resulting in interagency conflicts over management responsibilities during the early part of the accident. There was also initial difficulty in ascertaining the magnitude of the event, including the exact quantity of gasoline spilled.

Mississauga Tank Car Derailment

The derailment of a freight train at Mississauga, Ontario, and the subsequent orderly evacuation of 250,000 people for almost a week have been widely discussed in the hazards literature (Timmerman, 1980; Whyte et al, 1980; Liverman and Wilson, 1981). On 10 November 1979, a freight train of 106 cars derailed. Thirty-eight cars were carrying hazardous materials, and a BLEVE (boiling liquid expanding vapour explosion) occurred. One of the cars contained 90 tons of chlorine, which vaporizes on contact with air. This car had been damaged and chlorine was leaking from it.

A regional disaster plan was promptly activated. Approximately 97 minutes after the derailment, local officials decided to evacuate an adjacent residential area because of the chlorine hazard. The initial number of evacuees was 8000, but reevaluations of the danger and changing meteorological conditions prompted a series of evacuations involving 61,500 households in an area of 50 square kilometres. Nearly 92 per cent of the residents evacuated. Of these, 17 per cent nearest the site left before being ordered to. The nearest group had perceptual clues (for example, seeing the derailed train or hearing sirens), warnings from police and fire personnel, and had received instructions during the darkness. Those farther from the site relied on second-hand media reports. Without perceptual clues, residents farther from an emergency often overestimate the danger, and the 22 per cent of the evacuees farthest from the Mississauga accident also left before being told to do so. But many residents delayed evacuation for hours.

Nearly 80 per cent of the evacuees went to homes of friends and relatives within a 50-kilometre radius of the accident, and many had to evacuate a second time to a safer distance. Few of the evacuees used the official evacuation centre, and a third of those who did left after one day. Lastly, fewer than 43 per cent of the respondents to a post-accident survey (some of whom had been evacuees) knew beforehand that hazardous chemicals were being transported through Mississauga (Liverman and Wilson, 1981). Of those who knew, only 11 per cent said it worried them. This attitude changed markedly after the accident.

The evacuation was facilitated by the existence and implementation of a regional disaster plan, good coordination among agencies, and clear lines of agency authority and responsibility. The timing of the accident (late Saturday night) was favourable because many families were home together and had time to contact friends and relatives to arrange shelter. The nature of the accident provided clues that an evacuation was imminent, as did warning messages delivered by police and fire personnel door to door. Finally, the relative affluence of the residents meant they had their own means of transportation (private automobiles) for evacuation and could afford hotels if necessary.

On the negative side, the designated area of the initial evacuation was too small (50 square kilometres). As a result, the residents were forced to evacuate a second and, in some cases, a third time. This unnecessarily complicated the emergency management response.

Somerville Tank Car Rupture

At approximately 9:00am on the morning of 3 April 1980, in the Mystic Junction Yards of the Boston and Maine Railroad in Somerville, Massachusetts, a switching locomotive struck a tank car and ruptured it. The tank car contained 13,600 gallons of phosphorous trichloride that began flowing down an embankment (USFEMA, 1980). After initial notification of the Somerville fire department (15 minutes after the accident began), the Chemical Transportation Emergency

Center (CHEMTREC) was contacted and asked for mitigation advice.[5] Other emergency management officials were also notified.

Phosphorous trichloride vaporizes on contact with air and forms a cloud of hydrochloric and phosphoric acids on contact with water. When the substance hit the soil, damp with morning dew, a toxic cloud formed. At 9:30am the fire department ordered an evacuation 1.5 miles downwind (in the path of the plume) of the site. Additional areas were evacuated at 2:30pm, and residents were able to return to their homes 24 hours later. There is no definitive number on the size of the evacuation, but media accounts suggest it was in the thousands. Slightly more than 700 people were evacuated to shelters.

Three factors helped make this evacuation work. First, the weather was dry, slowing the vaporization of the chemical, and the ground was unfrozen, allowing a detention pit to be dug to prevent the spilled material from reaching the storm drains. Second, the chemical was quickly identified by the fire department with the help of CHEMTREC, prompting the initial evacuation order half an hour after the spill. Finally, the event occurred at a time when children were at school and many people were at work. While this is often a complication because of the desire of families to act as a unit, the situation in this case served to get one of the most vulnerable populations (children) out of the area quickly.

On the negative side, no disaster plan was in effect at the time of the incident, and no state plan for chemical emergencies existed. Therefore, emergency management was ad hoc, and even the participating agencies attributed much of their success to favourable conditions and luck (USFEMA, 1980). Although the toxic material was identified early, many of the response personnel were not properly equipped and suffered from chemical exposures.

While the tank rupture had the potential for catastrophic consequences, it did not become a major disaster. Despite the size of the evacuation, only 100 people were treated for inhalation of acid fumes. People who stayed indoors appeared to have been less affected than those who evacuated, suggesting that evacuation was not the most appropriate protective course of action.

Taft Chemical Tank Explosion

In the early hours of 11 December 1982, a chemical tank containing acrolein exploded at the Union Carbide plant in Taft, Louisiana, 30 miles north of New Orleans. Approximately 17,000 residents were evacuated within a five-mile zone around the plant (Quarantelli et al, 1984). The evacuation took place at least in partial accordance with a local emergency plan for accidents like nuclear power plant releases and hurricanes. Police officials (the first responders), for example, knew to ask plant management for the name of the chemical, to check its properties in an available handbook, and to monitor meteorological readings during the event.

The first evacuation order came at 4:30am, more than 3.5 hours after the explosion and after plant personnel had been evacuated. Local officials accepted Union Carbide's five-mile evacuation zone, yet issued warnings of decreasing urgency as distance from the site increased. Residents within one mile were 'ordered' to evacuate, although it is unclear whether the police could have enforced the order. Residents from one to two miles away were warned of the danger and strongly urged to evacuate. Beyond two miles, officials did not make any special effort to persuade people to leave and issued a number of ambiguous warnings suggesting that residents leave, but that if they did not, they should stay indoors. In addition to the evacuation area, the Coast Guard established a 12-mile safety zone along the Mississippi River and barred all shipping through the area.

No households within one mile of the plant resisted evacuation, although many were reluctant to leave. Farther away, however, some families did resist because the warning messages were so ambiguous. Most of the people in the evacuated area were familiar with or at least aware of the presence of dangerous chemicals in facilities like Union Carbide's or in transit along the area's river, road and rail corridors. In the year before the accident, at least six events involving technological agents had necessitated evacuations, although much smaller in scale.

The factors contributing to the success of the evacuation included an in-place plan in the event of technological failures. This resulted in a better-than-average level of preparedness by local responders. In addition, residents' prior experience led to the formation of a disaster subculture: individuals and organizations knew what to do before any official action was taken. For example, the sheriff's office received calls asking for evacuation routes and the whereabouts of shelters prior to the evacuation order. Another contributing factor was the time of the accident (very early Saturday morning). The early morning hour meant that families were already together and could more quickly leave the area. There was also minimal convergence on the area by residents trying to reach family members.

The evacuation was complicated, however, by poor communication between plant and emergency response officials. Cross-jurisdictional activities were also not as well coordinated as they could have been. Still, the evacuation of a larger-than-anticipated number of people took place rapidly and without injury in darkness and heavy rainfall.

Lessons Learned

It was a combination of unique factors, including the timing of the incidents, that prevented a disaster in each of these cases. In comparing each site (see Table 23.1), a number of generalizations emerge. The existence of a plan with clear lines of agency authority does contribute to the success of the emergency response both by officials and local residents. Cooperation between on-site and off-site emergency management officials is also essential.

In the case of Taft, a lack of such cooperation may have exacerbated the situation. We know from the hazards literature that residents respond favourably and comply with evacuation messages that are delivered door to door. Fortunately, most of these accidents occurred in smaller municipalities where this type of notification was possible.

The Somerville case study illustrates two important issues for emergency preparedness. One is that evacuation may not be the most appropriate response to a toxic cloud. The other concerns the size and geometry of the evacuation zone:

Table 23.1 *Comparison of case study accident characteristics*

	North York gasoline	Mississauga chlorine	Somerville phosphorous trichloride	Taft acrolein
Population evacuated	5000	250,000	1000	17,000
Time for evacuation	2.25 hours	24 hours	6 hours	2.5 hours
Duration of evacuation	5.5 hours	36 hours–6 days	29 hours	7.5 hours
Type of evacuation	forced	forced	forced	forced
Evacuation zone geometry	unknown	50 sq. km. circular	1.5 miles downwind	5 miles circular
Population at risk	5000	250,000	17,000	37,259
Special needs population	yes	no	yes	unknown
Contingency plan in place	no	yes	no	yes

Sources: Author's derivation from various sources, including journal and newspaper articles and case studies.

the Somerville case appears to be the only one in which residents were evacuated downwind rather than in a simple circular evacuation geometry based on distance from the source. This was a wise decision.

Residents and emergency managers responded to each of these accidents in a variety of ways. In some instances, residents evacuated the area; in others, they did not (for differences between population at risk and population evacuated, see Table 23.1). At Mississauga those residents with perceptual clues immediately left the area before an evacuation order, while many others, relying on second-hand warning information, delayed evacuation for hours. This variability in human response is a function of four general factors: notification (issuance and timeliness of warnings, and compliance with directives); chemical danger; preparedness (prior experience with toxic accidents, in situ plans and agency coordination); and geographic characteristics (location, timing and population at risk).

Improvement of Contingency Plans

Contingency planning for airborne toxic releases is not totally in disarray around the country. Many areas, such as the Twin Cities, Minnesota, and Staten Island, New York, routinely conduct response drills for mock accidents involving airborne releases (*New York Times*, 1986). Others have developed and actually tested contingency plans for specific types of toxic substances and industries in their locality (Elizabeth and Newark, New Jersey). In addition, a number of nation-wide industry-sponsored outreach programmes, the Community Awareness and Emergency Response (CAER) programmes, have been developed.[6] It is too soon to tell how successful CAER has been in facilitating emergency-response planning efforts.

The Emergency Planning and Community Right-to-Know Act of 1986, Title III of SARA, should help all communities overcome the largest obstacle to improving municipal contingency plans – the lack of baseline data on the storage, use and transportation of toxic materials within municipal borders. The primary purpose of Title III is to:

> encourage and support emergency planning efforts at the state and local level and provide residents and local governments with information concerning potential chemical hazards present in their communities. The emergency planning requirements of this Act recognize the need to establish and maintain contingency plans for responding to chemical accidents which can inflict health and environmental damage as well as cause significant disruption within a community.[7]

There are four main areas covered by Title III: emergency planning, emergency notification, community right-to-know and reporting requirements, and reporting of emissions or of chemical releases (see Box 23.2). The planning elements are designed to ensure cooperation among various levels of government and industry in the development of community response plans. The community right-to-know elements allow for public disclosure about the presence of toxic substances in the community as well as about actual releases into the environment. Because SARA was recently enacted, it is impossible to evaluate the impact and effectiveness of Title III. It certainly is a step in the right direction, however.

For Title III to succeed, financial resources must be distributed to municipalities to undertake these extensive planning efforts. But financial resources must also be accompanied by data on the potential population at risk and the most vulnerable population subgroups, such as children, the elderly and people with respiratory problems. Site-specific assessments of the toxic hazards potential, coupled with data on the location, density and vulnerability of residents, will provide the initial groundwork for the development of viable contingency plans.

Some assessment of residents' likely responses to airborne toxic releases is also needed. The use of public forums and educational brochures explaining hazards and appropriate responses to an accident is perhaps the best strategy. Local officials cannot dictate how residents will respond; they can only anticipate. To reduce the potential range of likely actions, emergency managers should ensure that residents have as much information as possible on which to make their own informed decisions (see Box 23.3).

Planning for airborne toxic releases is an important social and environmental issue that is most appropriately addressed at the local level. Unfortunately, most communities currently lack the expertise and resources to undertake extensive planning efforts. But with the support of Title III, citizen activism and some innovative planning efforts, local municipalities can become more prepared for that possible toxic cloud. Despite the reluctance of local planning authorities to develop them, contingency plans can and do make a difference.

Box 23.2 *Main elements in Title III: The Emergency Planning and Community Right-to-Know Act of 1986*

Emergency planning

- Defines local emergency-planning districts (to be developed by state commissions)
- Establishes local emergency-planning committees and specifies broad-based membership
- Requires the planning committees to develop an emergency response plan by fall 1988
- Provides guidance and technical assistance for planning efforts including the Environmental Protection Agency (EPA) list of 402 extremely hazardous substances and the threshold planning quantities for each substance
- Requires that all facilities notify the state commissions of their coverage under Title III

Notification

- Requires immediate notification of a release of a hazardous substance included on EPA's 402 list and/or subject to reporting requirements under the Comprehensive Environmental Response, Compensation, and Liability Act of 1980 (Superfund)
- Specifies the method of initial notification including information on the release (chemical, acute toxicity, quantity, time, duration, health risks, precautionary measures, contact person, phone number and facility where release occurred)
- Requires a follow-up written notice with more specific information on response actions, known or anticipated health risks, and any updates to the initial verbal report

Community right-to-know

- Requires facilities to maintain material safety data sheets and submit these to the planning committee, local fire department and state commission
- Requires facilities to submit an emergency and hazardous chemical inventory form to the planning committee providing estimates of the quantity of all chemicals on site and their general locations
- Allows committees to request additional information from facilities on specific substances

Emissions and release reporting

- Requires EPA to develop an inventory of toxic chemical releases from certain facilities with 10 or more full-time employees and with Standard Industrial Classification Codes 20 to 39
- Requires EPA to establish a toxic chemical release form consisting of name, location, type of business, general category of chemical use, quantities present, waste treatment, quantity entering the environment annually and certification of accuracy of the report
- EPA is to also maintain a national inventory of toxic chemical releases

Sources: EPA Journal (1987); Pub. L. No. 99–499 (1986); Part III Emergency Planning and Community Right to Know Programs, 40 C.F.R. Part 300 (1986); 51 *Federal Register* 41570–94 (1986).

Box 23.3 *What you can do in your community*

There are many ways you can assist in developing contingency plans for your community. The most important activity is to ask questions of your local officials:

- Do they know what toxic substances are generated, used, stored in, or transported through the community?
- Have they properly defined the populations at risk and identified particularly vulnerable subgroups (children, the elderly, the infirm) who are highly sensitive to chemical releases? Where are these vulnerable residents located? Do evacuation plans reflect their needs?
- Are there adequate warning or notification measures to alert the public of an evacuation? The US Nuclear Regulatory Commission requires a 15-minute notification of the public in the event of an accident at a nuclear power plant. What are the timing and methods of warnings (sirens, door-to-door messages) for local non-radioactive toxic releases that also require immediate notification?
- What are the geographic extent and geometry (circular or sectoral) of the planned evacuation area? Does the area account for specific meteorological and topographic conditions and the nature of the substance released, all factors that will affect the path of a plume?
- Are there monitoring stations located downwind of facilities to measure airborne releases and determine potential human exposures?
- What provisions have been made for population convergence on the affected area?
- What provisions have been made to get families together when children are at school, parents at work and pets at home, given people's desire to evacuate as a family unit?
- How will the media and the curious be kept away from the site?
- In cases where evacuation is not the best response, particularly in densely populated areas, what other protective actions – for example, remaining sheltered or using masks or air-filtering devices – may be taken?
- How is the public likely to respond to an accident? What types of educational materials will instil public confidence in planning efforts? Are the plans available to local residents?
- Have the plans been tested? What level of cooperation has been established between on-site and off-site officials or among state officials when toxic substances cross state lines?
- Are local officials aware of Title III and its implications?

Next, become an expert yourself on the provisions of Title III. The emergency planning provision mandates the establishment of local planning committees that must include elected state and local officials; police, fire, emergency management, public health, environmental, hospital, and transportation professionals; community groups; and the media. Get yourself appointed to the local contingency-planning committee.

Also, become an expert on the nature of your community. While chemical inventories will best be handled by professionals, local citizens can serve as watchdogs to ensure that the inventories are done. You can also help define the populations at risk and vulnerable subgroups by drawing up maps representing the community block by block.

Finally, you can help to organize informational meetings on contingency planning and on appropriate resident response in the event of an airborne toxic release. The more that residents are informed of the potential hazards and what they should do, the easier the job becomes for emergency managers during a crisis.

In general, we know that contingency plans work. By helping your community develop a viable plan, you may make all the difference when a toxic cloud passes overhead.

Acknowledgement

This research was supported by The National Science Foundation Industry/University Cooperative Center for Research in Hazardous and Toxic Substances, at the New Jersey Institute of Technology, an Advanced Technology Center of the New Jersey Commission on Science and Technology.

Notes

1. *EPA Journal* (1986); Pub. L. No. 99-499 (1986); Part III Emergency Planning and Community Right to Know Programs, 40 C.F.R. Part 300 (1986); 51 *Federal Register* 41570-94 (1986).
2. The exceptions are the post-accident community case studies of chemical emergencies by E. L. Quaranteli and his colleagues at the Disaster Research Center (Quarantelli, 1981, 1984; Quarantelli et al, 1979).
3. The exception is the EPA's Chemical Emergency Preparedness Program, which provides training and technical assistance to local and state governments in preparing for and responding to chemical incidents (see USEPA, 1985b).
4. A good start at state-level analyses of transportation-related incidents is found in Pijawka and Radwan, 1985.
5. CHEMTREC is the Chemical Manufacturers Association 24-hour hotline, designed as an emergency public service programme where callers can receive immediate advice on the nature of the chemical spilled and steps to ensure safe handling of it.
6. The Community Awareness and Emergency Response (CAER) programmes are designed to provide the public with information on chemicals used at local plants and to help improve off-site emergency plans. Not all companies participate, however. CAER programmes are currently underway in California, Illinois, Michigan, New Jersey, Ohio and Texas (see Alford, 1987).
7. *Federal Register* 41570-94 (1986).

References

Ajamie, T. R. (1985) 'Emergency Planning for hazardous chemical accidents: Elements of a legislative solution', *Journal of Legislation*, vol 12, pp195–212
Alford, P. N. (1987)'An industry that CAERs: Chemical manufacturers help communities prepare for hazardous chemical emergencies', *Hazard Monthly*, vol 8, spring, pp8–10
Bowonder, B., Kasperson, J. X. and Kasperson, R. E. (1985) 'Avoiding Future Bhopals', *Environment*, September, p6
Burton, I., Kates, R. and White, G. F. (1978) *The Environment as Hazard*, Oxford University Press, New York

DePol, D. R. and Cheremisinoff, P. N. (1984) *Emergency Response to Hazardous Materials Incidents*, Technomic, Lancaster, PA

EPA Journal (1986) 'Title III: Emergency planning and community right-to-know', *EPA Journal*, vol 13, pp28–30

Gray, J. (1981) 'Characteristic patterns of and variations in community response to acute chemical emergencies', *Journal of Hazardous Materials*, vol 4, 357–365

Hazen, S. B., Myers, H. and Timmerman, P. (1980) 'The North York Gasoline Leak, February 21, 1979: Emergency Response and Impact Assessment', working paper ERR-5, Institute for Environmental Studies, University of Toronto, Canada

Helms, J. (1981) 'Threat perceptions in acute chemical disasters', *Journal of Hazardous Materials*, vol 43, 2l–29

Hushon, J. M. (1986) 'Response to chemical emergencies', *Environmental Science and Technology*, vol 20, pp18–21

Industrial Economics (1985) *Acute Hazardous Events Data Base*, interim final report for the Office of Toxic Substances, EPA 560-5-85-029, Industrial Economics, Cambridge, MA

Jaske, R. T. (1983) 'Emergency preparedness – Status and outlook', *Nuclear Safety*, vol 24, ppl–11

Kasperson, R. E. and Pijawka, K. D. (1985) 'Societal response to hazards and major hazard events: Comparing natural and technological hazards', *Public Administration Review*, vol 45, pp7–18

Kates, R. (1978) *Risk Assessment of Environmental Hazard*, John Wiley, New York

Kates, R. W., Hohenemser, C. and Kasperson, J. X. (1985) *Perilous Progress: Managing the Hazards of Technology*, Westview Press, Boulder, CO

Liverman, D. and Wilson, J. P. (1981) 'The Mississauga train derailment and evacuation, 10–16 November 1979', *Canadian Geographer*, vol 25, pp 365–375

New York Times (1986) 'Just in case: SI drills in mock spill', *New York Times*, 14 April, pB2

Perry, R. W., Lindell, M. K. and Greene, M. R. (1981) *Evacuation Planning in Emergency Management*, Lexington Books, Lexington, MA

Perry, R. W. and Mushkatel, A. H. (1984) *Disaster Management*, Quorum Books, Westport, CT

Pijawka, K. D. and Radwan, A. E. (1985) 'The transportation of hazardous materials: Risk assessment and hazard management', *Dangerous Properties of Industrial Materials Report*, vol 5, pp2–11

Quarantelli, E. L. (1981) *Sociobehavioral Responses to Chemical Hazards*, Disaster Research Center, Ohio State University, Columbus, OH

Quarantelli, E. L. (1984) 'Chemical disaster preparedness at the local community level', *Journal of Hazardous Materials*, vol 8, pp239–249

Quarantelli, E. L., Hutchinson, D. C. and Phillips, B. (1984) 'Evacuation behavior: Case study of the Taft, Louisiana chemical tank explosion', miscellaneous report no 34, Disaster Research Center, Ohio State University, Columbus, OH

Quarantelli, E. L., Lawrence, C., Tierney, K. and Johnson, T. (1979) 'Initial findings from a study of socio-behavioral preparations and planning for acute chemical hazard disasters', *Journal of Hazardous Materials*, vol 3, pp79–90

Rubin, C. B. (1986) 'Comprehensive emergency planning and management' in F. S. So, I. Hand and B. D. McDowell (eds) *The Practice of State and Regional Planning*, American Planning Association, Chicago, IL, pp613–626

Solecki, W. D., Lotstein, E. L. and Cutter, S. L. (1986) 'Passing gas: The geography of acute toxic releases', paper delivered at the annual meeting of the Society for Risk Analysis, Boston, MA, November

Sylves, R. T. (1984) 'Nuclear power plants and emergency planning: An intergovernmental nightmare', *Public Administration Review*, vol 44, pp393–401

Tierney, K. J. (1981) 'Community and organizational awareness of and preparedness for acute chemical emergencies', *Journal of Hazardous Materials*, vol 4, pp331–342

Timmerman, P. (1980) 'The Mississauga train derailment and evacuation, November 10–17, 1979: Event reconstruction and organizational response', working paper ERR-6, Institute for Environmental Studies, University of Toronto, Canada

US Congress OTA (Office of Technology Assessment) (1986) *Transportation of Hazardous Materials; State and Local Activities*, OTA-SET-301, Government Printing Office, Washington, DC

USDOT (United States Department of Transportation) (1984) *Emergency Response Guidebook*, DOT P5800.3, Government Printing Office, Washington, DC

USDOT (1985) *Patterns and Trends for National Response Center Hazardous Releases,* DOT-TSC-EPA-S-I, Government Printing Office, Washington, DC

USEPA (United States Environmental Protection Agency) (1985a) *A Strategy to Reduce Risks to Public Health from Air Toxics,* Government Printing Office, Washington, DC

USEPA (1985b) *Chemical Emergency Preparedness Program Interim Guidance,* Government Printing Office, Washington, DC

USFEMA (United States Federal Emergency Management Agency) (1980) *Case Study: Hazardous Material Spill Somerville, MA, April 3, 1980,* FEMA, Boston, MA

USFEMA (1981) *Planning Guide and Checklist for Hazardous Materials Contingency Plans,* FEMA-10, Government Printing Office, Washington, DC

Whyte, A. V. T., Liverman, D. M. and Wilson, J. P. (1980) 'Preliminary survey of households evacuated during the Mississauga chlorine gas emergency, November 10–16, 1979', working paper ERR-7, Institute for Environmental Studies, University of Toronto, Canada

24

Geographers and Nuclear War: Why We Lack Influence on Public Policy

Susan L. Cutter

The deployment of nuclear weaponry and preparation for nuclear war have not only altered geopolitics at the regional and global scale, but have transformed our social institutions and changed our perceptions of the global environment and our future existence in it. The geographical effects of this transformation are increasingly apparent and provide a focus for a burgeoning new topical area within the discipline. The overall theoretical basis for geographical enquiry into nuclear war and peace is vague. Thus the 'problem' becomes one of definition: political geographers look for political and spatial theories to explain international conflicts and non-nuclear war behaviour; natural hazards researchers apply known and familiar concepts to a new hazard, nuclear war; economic geographers examine the differential impacts of military spending on regional economies. This fragmentation results in little cross-fertilization of ideas from geographic subfield to subfield, limited explanations of the geographical effects of nuclear war and peace, and little influence on the scientific and policy debates on nuclear war and its ultimate consequences.

Through a review of the recent geographical work on nuclear war and peace issues, I illustrate the contributions the discipline can make to address this most pressing global threat to human existence. While some may claim that all geographical work has relevance, this review is restricted to those works explicitly focusing on the question of nuclear war and nuclear peace, and those non-geographic works so fundamentally important to our understanding of these issues that they cannot be ignored. A number of questions guide the analysis. First, what are the moral, ethical and educational responsibilities of geographers as global citizens living in the nuclear era? Second, how has geography contributed to the

Note: Reprinted, with permission, from the *Annals of the Association of American Geographers*, vol 78, no 1, Susan L. Cutter, 'Geographers and nuclear war: Why we lack influence on public policy', pp132–143. © Blackwell Publishers, 1988

public's understanding of nuclear war and peace issues? Third, what new avenues of geographical enquiry and research are necessary to prevent the ultimate technological catastrophe, nuclear war? Last, why hasn't the discipline been effective in influencing the public policy debates on this issue?

The Geographer's Responsibility

One of the earliest calls on the perils of radioactivity and its role in the potential eradication of our species is Bunge's (1973a) work on the geography of human survival. Bunge argues for a future geography where humans can come to terms with nature and live in harmony with it. He continues on this theme of human survivability in another article where he calls for the elimination of national geographies where students are taught to love the land at the expense of the people inhabiting it; to love their particular nation-state and hate and fear others (Bunge, 1973b). In order to achieve human survivability, Bunge argues, 'We must stop using geography to purge, to distort the earth's surface to please the state' (Bunge, 1973b, p334). While laudable in their intentions, these two pieces apparently had little effect on the discipline's ethical and moral positions regarding nuclear war and peace.

Not until ten years later did another geographer, Richard Morrill, speak on the responsibility of geography and geographers. In his 1983 presidential address to the Association of American Geographers, Morrill (1984) chastised the discipline for its failure to live up to its intellectual and ethical responsibilities for public and professional education on the effects of nuclear war and the economic and social costs of a nuclear deterrent. He argues that geographers, whose understanding of the interdependence between human systems, environmental processes and urban structures places them in a unique position to educate the public, have in large measure abdicated this responsibility. Geography can play a major role and provide intellectual leadership in the public policy debates on nuclear war and peace, yet has not. Some reasons for this neglect are discussed in later sections.

While Morrill provides the intellectual rationale for geography's role in nuclear war and peace issues, a more pragmatic approach for getting geographers involved is offered by White (1984, 1985). He identifies three specific ways in which geographers might contribute to the reduction of the probability of nuclear war:

1   studies on the impacts and effects of nuclear attacks on places;
2   environmental effects of global exchanges; and
3   professional and public education.

White notes that geographers are particularly well suited to focus their efforts on the third, public and professional education. In making public and professional education a first priority, White (1984, p4) argues for the introduction of information on the potential effects of nuclear war into our courses, textbooks, atlases and other teaching materials.

The educational role for geography in the emerging field of peace studies also has been described by others (Bunge, 1983; Isard and Smith, 1982; Jenkins,

1985; Kofman, 1984; Pepper and Jenkins, 1983; van der Wusten, 1984; van der Wusten and O'Loughlin, 1986; Wisner, 1986). While largely polemical in nature, these articles provide little concrete information on how to teach war and peace issues or sources of educational materials. There is, however, a steady and growing interest in the geography of nuclear war and peace (Brunn, 1987; Pepper, 1985; Pepper and Jenkins, 1985). Colleagues within the discipline now include sections on nuclear war in a number of their courses, and a session at the 1986 National Council for Geographic Education annual meetings examined innovative ways to teach nuclear war and peace issues. In addition, teaching modules and teaching guides have been developed to facilitate instruction (Jenkins and Pepper, 1986; Ringler, 1985; Solecki and Cutter, 1987; Wien, 1984).

The lack of educational materials and innovations may reflect a dichotomy between personal concern and activism on the one hand and professional involvement on the other. White and Morrill both argue for a merger between our personal beliefs in a peaceful, non-nuclear world and the use of our research and teaching to foster that attitude among ourselves, our students, and the public. This convergence between private and public personas is already underway. For example, a working group of North American geographers recently drafted a statement on nuclear war which was signed by more than 100 members of the Association of American Geographers (AAG). In its annual meeting in May 1986 this resolution was passed, thus making the AAG one of a growing number of professional organizations to publicly condemn the deployment and use of nuclear weapons.

The need to take one's vocation and use it to influence public policy is crucial to the discipline's survival and the realization of its full potential as a social science. Perhaps the seeming importance of 'scientific objectivity' has prevented us from tackling nuclear war and peace issues and constructively providing geographical input into public policy debates. This might well explain the minute and passive role of the discipline in the nuclear war area instead of the active leadership stance it should rightfully occupy.

In addition to our moral and ethical responsibilities, geographical concepts are conspicuously absent in the overall literature, yet these same concepts are essential in understanding the local, national, regional and global effects of nuclear war and peace. Why is there such an absence? Is it the paucity of geographical work, the lack of recognition of such work, or some other factor? In order to address this question, a number of topical areas where geographers already have contributed to our understanding of the effects of nuclear war and nuclear deterrents are examined.

Environmental Effects of Nuclear War

The centre of the recent scientific research on nuclear war examines the environmental consequences of a large-scale detonation of nuclear weapons (Crutzen, 1983; Crutzen and Birks, 1982; Dotto, 1986; Grover, 1984; Grover and White, 1985; Turco et al, 1983; US Office of Technology Assessment, 1979). A symposium held in 1983 at the American Association for the Advancement of Science

(AAAS) annual meeting reviewed the current state of knowledge (and ignorance) on the environmental effects of a nuclear exchange, drawing upon a diverse group of scientists (London and White, 1984). The topics ranged from estimates of the effects of human casualties from radiation and blast effects to the impairment of the physical, biological and social environments. London and White (1984) also provided a chapter on the need for further research in order to narrow some of the uncertainties regarding the environmental consequences of nuclear war. These research areas include: lack of knowledge regarding 'nuclear war scenarios', specifically when, where, how and the magnitude of weapons exchanges; lack of verification of models on the effects of smoke and dust clouds; problems involving atmospheric models and their inability to incorporate feedback processes; inability to model and predict biospheric effects including the fallout effects on freshwater systems; estimating human casualties with any degree of confidence; and finally, unresolved questions on the scale of analysis and the synergistic relation between the physical, biological and social environments. As one can read from this list, there are many areas in which geographical work is needed, yet only one geographer (Gilbert White) contributed to this collaborative effort.

The two-volume SCOPE report on the environmental consequences of nuclear war is the most comprehensive treatment of the subject to date (Harwell et al, 1985; Pittock et al, 1985). Geographers contributed material for the chapter on 'Experience and Extrapolations from Hiroshima and Nagasaki.' Using natural hazards research as a base, this group (Walter Isard, Diana Liverman, James K. Mitchell, William Riebsame and Gilbert White) speculated on the societal impacts of a prospective nuclear exchange. In addition, several other sections of the SCOPE monograph report on geographical implications where geographers did not directly contribute material but where their perspective is warranted. Volume 1, for example, addresses the physical and atmospheric effects of nuclear war, while volume 2 looks at the impact of a nuclear weapons exchange on the global ecology. The vulnerability of the ecological system to climatic perturbations resulting in impacts on agricultural productivity, food availability and human survival was specifically addressed. Here again, geographers are conspicuously absent from the scientific and public debates.

In addition to the work by the SCOPE group, geographers have commented in a general fashion on a variety of environmental issues related to nuclear war. Elsom (1985), for example, reviews the scientific studies on the climatological effects of a nuclear exchange and concludes that climatologists were in error. He claims that researchers underestimated the effect of a large-scale nuclear exchange in causing profound climatological changes, resulting in large-scale environmental disturbances, and calls for continued research by scholars on the implications of a severe nuclear winter for survivors.

There has been little, if any, place-specific work on the environmental consequences of nuclear war. Larimore (1984) provides general speculation on the ecological effects of nuclear exchanges in developing countries. A second, more place-specific analysis, examined the atmospheric, hydrologic, biologic, geomorphic and agricultural impacts on Boulder County, CO, resulting from the detonation of three nuclear warheads in Denver, some 40km to the southeast (Bennett et al, 1984). In addition to agricultural crop contamination and loss of animal life, the study also predicts flooding, increased sedimentation as a result of geomorphic changes in hillslope stability, ground shaking, displacement along faults and extensive soil erosion as a result of changes in vegetative cover. Recovery times for the environmental systems in question are not given because of the unknown synergistic effects and potential changes in atmospheric conditions. This article is one of a few that aptly illustrates the use of physical geography to understand the localized effects of a nuclear exchange.

A number of geographers reviewed the controversy surrounding the theory of nuclear winter, but have added little new information (Bach, 1986; Perry, 1985; Smith, 1985). The governing ideology behind nuclear winter including its foundations in literature, philosophy and science is also critiqued (Curry, 1985, 1986a). In his attack of the empirical nature of many of the present scientific studies, Curry (1986a) argues that literary works may be just as illustrative and useful in explaining the environmental consequences of a nuclear holocaust. He argues for a more diversified discourse reaching beyond science and the need for alternative perspectives in the public policy debates regarding nuclear deterrence.

Currently, the scientific debate focuses on the severity of the nuclear winter problem. In a series of articles appearing in *Foreign Affairs,* Thompson and Schneider (1986a, b) reveal new data using global atmospheric models, suggesting a lower estimate of temperature reductions following a nuclear exchange – nuclear fall, rather than nuclear winter. There remain a number of unanswered questions including the amount of smoke that might be released into the troposphere and stratosphere as a result of detonations over urban areas; the extent, magnitude and duration of changes in temperature, light and precipitation resulting from urban and forest fires; the likely effect on crop production resulting from the first two questions; and finally the relevance of these findings to national and international policies. This last question has raised the most serious concerns and challenges by the scientific community (Rathgens and Siegel, 1986; Sagan, 1986; Turco, 1986). A re-examination of the SCOPE estimates of physical and biological stresses concludes that the original estimates are still valid, the findings of Thompson and Schneider notwithstanding (Harwell and Harwell, 1987).

Human Consequences: Place Annihilation and Post-Nuclear Landscapes

Some of the more innovative work done by geographers is their empirical and phenomenological research on place annihilation and the post-nuclear landscape. Hewitt's (1983, 1984) work on place annihilation and defenceless space provides a framework for the study of the effects of war on urban places. Although this work describes the effects of aerial bombing of German cities during World War II, the relevance of this type of enquiry to nuclear destruction is obvious.

Openshaw, Steadman and Greene either separately or as a team have published a series of works on the spatial aspects of a nuclear attack on Britain, in which they discuss the resulting number of casualties and damage to the nation's infrastructure (Greene et al, 1982; Openshaw and Steadman, 1982, 1983a, b, c, 1985; Openshaw et al, 1983). These computer-simulation studies further illustrate geography's role in describing the destruction of places and landscapes resulting from nuclear war. Using an empirical approach, this research depicts post-nuclear landscapes in the UK: many residential casualties because of the high population concentration in the country, close proximity of population to nuclear targets, the spatial range of the weapons and the excessive explosive power of the weapons. As Openshaw and Steadman comment:

> *For the UK, nuclear war means national suicide ... The next step is to ensure that politicians and decision-makers are left in no doubt whatsoever about the likely outcome.* (Oppenshaw and Steadman, 1985, p123)

A non-empiricist perspective on the post-nuclear landscape is provided by Renwick (1982, 1986). She compares the post-nuclear landscapes of science fiction writers to the US governmental reports from 1950 to the present and finds little difference between the 'science' and the 'science fiction'. Similarly, Curry (1985, 1986b) criticizes the future geographies evident in the scientific literature. He stresses the limitations of individual scientists and scientific attitudes in their attempts to objectively plan for the future.

Hazards Research: Emergency Management and Planning for the Inevitable

Hazards research has a long tradition within geography and is used to help explain human–environment interactions. First used to delineate and mitigate the effects of natural events such as floods, droughts and coastal erosion, this line of enquiry has been extended to include technological hazards such as nuclear power plant accidents and chemical explosions. Mitchell (1984) highlights the role and importance of natural hazards research in contributing to our understanding of the effects of nuclear war on the global environment and society. He distinguishes between emergency management perspectives (the before, during and after of the emergency or disaster) and hazard mitigation (the underlying processes that contribute to the hazard's creation and attempts to reduce human susceptibility) in studying nuclear war.

One geographical manifestation of the emergency management perspective is population evacuation or relocation planning which attempts to temporarily remove people from the place-specific source of the threat (e.g. low-lying coastal areas subject to flooding, nuclear power plant, strategic target site) to a perceived safer place. Zeigler (1985) provides a good overview of civil defence and evacuation planning in the US but offers little substantive geographical analysis. A more comprehensive view of the US civil defence programme is found in Winkler (1984).

Crisis relocation planning for nuclear war poses significant moral problems for geographers which Platt (1984) raises. Realizing our skills and expertise in emergency response planning, we are faced with the dilemma of contributing to plans which foster the image of survivability of war, knowing full well that the entire planning effort, if implemented, would be a catastrophe. Geographers are in the best position to undertake such planning efforts, but are morally reluctant to do so.

There have been a number of place-specific evaluations and critiques of crisis relocation planning. Katz (1982) and Leaning and Keyes (1984), for example, focused on Massachusetts and highlighted the futility of such planning efforts. Specific case studies on host communities were done by Anderson (1984a, b) on Spokane, WA; Platt (1986) on Greenfield, MA; and Zeigler (1986) on Hampton Roads, VA. The conclusions of all three studies are the same: crisis relocation planning places extraordinary burdens on the local community and is far worse than no planning at all. As Platt comments:

> *The illusion of security which it seeks to foster is far more dangerous in terms of national willingness to risk nuclear war than the chilling acceptance of the reality that the meaning of life, if not life itself, would be utterly destroyed.* (Platt, 1986, p198)

Mitigating the Hazard Threat: Waging Peace

Instead of planning for the inevitable, geographers can use their skills in a constructive manner to help mitigate the threat of nuclear war and alter public policies. Within the last few years there has been an increase in geographical research on peace movements. In an overview of international and US peace movements, Brunn (1985) provides a summary of the diversity, extent, purposes and activities of these groups. Little is mentioned on their role in formulating nuclear deterrent policies or their importance in determining a non-nuclear future. In the same volume, Gerasimov (1985) provides a Soviet perspective in the peace/nuclear war dichotomy, arguing for a special branch of geography to examine the geographical aspects of the problems of peace and war. Again, this essay conveys little new information. Finally, Barnaby (1985) provides a cursory review of the nuclear-free zone concept and its role in fostering worldwide nuclear disarmament. While providing an adequate historical analysis of the concept, Barnaby ignores the use of nuclear-free zones as a grass-roots-inspired disarmament strategy both in the US and in the South Pacific.

More detailed analyses of political activity aimed at mitigating the threat of nuclear war focus on the national and regional scale. Some preliminary observations on the geographical patterns of support for a nuclear weapons freeze were presented in 1984 (Holcomb et al, 1984) and subsequent work provides a more detailed analysis of public support for a nuclear weapons freeze within the United States (Cutter et al, 1986; Shatin, 1987). They conclude that state-level support for a nuclear weapons freeze is related to the number of freeze/peace groups per state and the political attitude and innovativeness of the state. At a more local level, the analysis of election results in New Jersey and South Dakota showed a strong correlation between ethnicity/race, party affiliation (Democrat) and support for a weapons freeze (Cutter et al, 1987). This study also found little evidence to support the contention that the pro-freeze voting was limited to municipalities and counties with predominantly white, highly educated, upper-income constituents. Their conclusion: grass roots political action embodied in the freeze concept has now become part of the agenda for partisan politics.

Society and Space: Political, Social and Economic Transformations

Recently there has been a call for political geographers to strive toward more geopolitically relevant research and address the question of 'human survival' (van der Wusten and O'Loughlin 1986). Pepper and Jenkins (1984) in particular argue that nuclear weaponry and global militarization have brought 'territorial anarchy' which disrupts many of the classical notions of geopolitics. These notions therefore must be re-evaluated and new theories constructed, particularly those involving spatial models of international conflict (O'Loughlin, 1986; van der Wusten, 1985), deterrence as a policy option (O'Sullivan, 1982, 1985; Pepper, 1986), and the geographical dimensions of defence against nuclear and non-nuclear attacks (Bateman and Wiley, 1987). Resurgent interest in questions on conflict resolution and nuclear as well as conventional warfare was evident at the 1986 annual meeting of the Association of American Geographers with several special sessions examining the research agenda of political geography and the peace sciences. O'Loughlin and van der Wusten's (1986) progress report on political geography further illustrates these renewed interests which only recently began to examine the geographic aspects of nuclear weapons treaties, the role of resource dependency on the proliferation of weapons and conflict, and of regional and local conflict as a cause of limited or extensive nuclear weapons exchange.

Research on the militarization of world and national economies has also recently appeared in the geographic literature (Anderton and Isard, 1985; Ives, 1985; Malecki, 1984; Williams, 1982). Despite enormous contributions by economists (Gordon and McFadden, 1984; Melman, 1985; Mosley, 1985), geographers have added a spatial dimension to understanding the effects of the militarization of economies. For example, Rees (1982) examined the patterns of defence spending and its role in fostering regional change. Anderton and Isard (1985) focused on US regional disparities in defence contracting and the number of jobs created. They found a significant regional dependence on arms manufacturing in the US. Malecki (1984) on the other hand examined the regional patterns of military contracts and subcontracts, noting a geographical concentration of defence production in the US, notably in the Pacific Coast, New England and Mountain West regions. There has been little additional work despite the strong regional science emphasis within the discipline. It has long been shown that US defence spending is economically inefficient and that the monies could be better spent through a programme of economic restructuring involving a movement away from a military-based economy to a civilian-based one. While this truism is widely held, economic convergence and its spatial manifestations, thus far, have not been thoroughly examined by the geographic community.

Location theory, including the patterns of industrial location and relocation and the processes promoting restructuring, is an area of interest as well. Here the most significant contributions include Ann Markusen's work on high-tech industries (Markusen et al, 1986) and the obscuring of the military connection in the industrial restructuring of the country (Markusen, 1986; Markusen and Bloch, 1984). Malecki's (1981, 1982, 1986) work on Research and Development, a component of the defence industry, shows a significant difference between the location of industrial research and development (R&D) and federal (largely defense-related) R&D. The latter are highly concentrated in urban areas with little industrial research, such as Albuquerque, NM, and Knoxville, TN.

At the international scale, Ives (1985) presents a preliminary piece on the geography of weapons transfers and the reasons and methods behind such transfers. In total the volume of geographic work in the area of the militarization of economies is quite limited. An intensive analysis of the geography of the international weapons trade and its role in the perpetuation of armed conflict in both the developing and developed countries is still unavailable.

One Tool of Our Trade: Cartography

One of the first efforts to cartographically illustrate the effects of nuclear war was Bunge's (1982) *Nuclear War Atlas*. Despite some failings, this pamphlet showed the value of cartography in helping others to learn about nuclear war and peace. Burnett (1985), in a less polemical piece, provides an excellent review of propaganda cartography. He analyses how propaganda maps relating to nuclear weapons are used to promote perceptions of threat, aggression, military superiority and peace. Burnett classifies maps into armament categories – those that argue for nuclear arms proliferation, and disarmament maps, which have been produced to promote the cause of nuclear disarmament. He points out that the traditional methods of propaganda cartography are employed, such as the judicious use of certain colours and careful choice of size and distribution of symbols, to convey the desired message. Burnett argues that nuclear mapping is flourishing and that cartographers have not been involved in nuclear war/peace studies despite the need for their input. Selected thematic maps on nuclear war and peace issues such as women's peace camps are occasionally found in specialized atlases (Seager and Olson, 1986).

Non-geographers have been the most active in graphically portraying the geography of nuclear war and peace. Shortly after Bunge's 1982 publication, Kidron and Smith's (1983) *War Atlas* was published. Despite the lack of geographic input, this atlas is the most comprehensive cartographic treatment to date of issues relating to nuclear war and peace.

Future Geographies: Doom and Gloom, Apathy, Activism

Despite the contributions reviewed here the question of why geography is not playing a major intellectual role in the policy debates on nuclear war and peace remains. I suggest there are a number of possible explanations. First, we currently have no comprehensive geographical theory which helps us to understand nuclear war and peace issues. The lament on lack of theory permeates the entire discipline and is most pronounced in human geography. As O'Loughlin comments in a progress report on political geography:

> *Like the discipline as a whole, political geographers have tended to give short shrift to theoretical and philosophical issues. One must continually ask for whom and why is geography applied. By its nature, political geography cannot be neutral: it can, however, be aware of its societal setting.* (O'Loughlin, 1987, p250)

There are, however, a number of new and perhaps not so new avenues of enquiry that may help stimulate interest in the geography of nuclear war and peace and help the discipline achieve a clear leadership role within peace studies. Geography's contribution lies in the discipline's understanding of the synergistic effects of alterations in the physical and environmental systems and their resulting spatial impact on social systems, including the scale at which these interactions and alterations occur. Rather than a unified theory, perhaps the best we can hope for is a synthesis of subfields within the discipline which can guide our formulation of research questions. Yet it is precisely this notion of synthesis which is a fundamental problem for geography. While we may claim to 'synthesize', this review clearly illustrates the fragmented nature of the discipline in addressing a particular problem. One prevailing view is that geography lacks a coherent focus and thus has little to offer in understanding nuclear war issues that is not already being done better by some other discipline. Unfortunately, this review tends to support this contention.

One solution is a return to the central focus of the discipline or its 'core'. Geographers are fundamentally concerned with landscapes and places. Whether this focus is termed chorology, regional geography, areal differentiation, regionalism or the new regional geography is of no consequence. If we concentrate our efforts on places and the understanding of the events and relationships in and between places, then we can achieve the synthesis that we claim and also provide the needed expertise that is not found in other disciplines. This call for a return to geography's regional and locational core is not new; it recently has been most forcefully argued by Abler (1987).

Fundamentally, geographers can contribute to the nuclear war policy debates through their examination of the effects of nuclear war and war preparation on specific places. The need for micro-level analyses is already clear within the broader scientific community. While the scientific work to date has concentrated on global effects, there is already dissatisfaction with the global scale of analysis. For example, the original SCOPE group is currently preparing case studies at the national level in order to provide more detailed data on climate changes and other physical disturbances and their impact on environmental systems (Harwell and Harwell, 1987). Their goal is to provide a clear picture about the quality of life in individual countries after nuclear war. These national geographies will increase public policy relevance as they will bring the issue much closer to home and thus make it more salient to the decision-makers.

Geography can have its most significant impact on policy through this place-specific research detailing how physical, environmental and social processes differentiate and affect the use of space. Physical geographers, who thus far have been relatively silent on this issue, can play an important role in understanding the potential effects of nuclear war on the landscape. While atmospheric scientists are busily determining the global climatic effects of nuclear detonations, micro-level studies may also yield useful results. Microclimatological analyses on the local impact of nuclear war can be developed, either based on a strategic site with a scenario-based detonation, or more practically, on an examination of the microclimatic effects of nuclear detonations in peace time. For example, what if there was an accidental detonation and radioactive release at a storage site such as Dover Air Force Base in Delaware? What local changes would occur and how would these induce other longer-term environmental changes in vegetation, soils and the hydrologic cycle? Biogeographers seem equally disinterested despite the need to understand the potential disruptions in ecosystems as a result of a nuclear catastrophe. Granted that the issue is somewhat speculative and empirical studies hard to generate at this time, we do have a number of incidents (Chernobyl comes to mind), where large-scale radioactive contamination of vegetation and soil has occurred. Perhaps these data can be used to develop detailed studies of vegetative change. The source of the contamination may be slightly different, but the results could shed some light on the extent of human disturbance and recovery in specific ecosystems. Are there specific types of ecosystems which are likely to recover while others are not? In addition to temporal variations in recovery rates, are there spatial dimensions as well? There is an obvious need for a cross-fertilization of ideas and approaches as the climatological impacts are necessary in understanding vegetative responses.

In human geography, a number of questions should be addressed. What is the role of the militarization of economies in the social transformation of space? What is the spatial manifestation of the relationship between defence spending, social spending and political activity? If there is a restructuring of industrial America, as some suggest, what is the role of the military–industrial complex in this process? How have high-tech-defence-related industries fostered geographical dispersion or concentration of local and regional economies? Ann Markusen's recent work is a step in the right direction, yet more is needed on the spatial patterns of regional growth and decline and the role of the military and disarmament activities in fostering such patterns. Since peace is often thought of as a feminist issue, social geographers have the potential for enormous input. Questions relating to the feminization of poverty and the increased numbers of minority women in the military can best be answered by social geographers. What social forces have caused this shift and where is it most pronounced? What role have women taken in response to the threat of nuclear war and how have these efforts manifested themselves politically and geographically?

Finally, cartography and geographic information systems provide us with the technical ability to analyse the environmental, physical and social information at the local and regional scale. GIS provides the integrating tool and cartography permits us to graphically display the variations in the effects of nuclear war from place to place. We should not be afraid to use one of the most powerful tools of our trade, maps.

Place-specific analyses on the impacts of nuclear war and war preparation are not the only contribution geography can make in understanding the nuclear threat. Integrating micro-level analyses into broad-based theories of human–environment interaction is equally as important. A number of questions come to mind. For example, what are the causes of war? Why do we have a nuclear arms race in the first place? How can nuclear war be prevented? While these questions are of concern, many disciplines address them. I still contend that our greatest impact on public policy will derive from place-specific analyses.[1]

By raising these issues I do not want to imply either implicitly or explicitly that nuclear war or war preparation is acceptable. It is not. Our contributions can be great if we stick to what we do best, study places and the interaction between the physical and human systems, and if we are careful about how our science is used by policy-makers. Ignoring our moral and ethical responsibilities will not make the threat of nuclear war go away or seem more palatable. Rather, we must actively get involved in nuclear war and peace issues because our skills and training require us to do so. We ultimately have no choice if we seek a liveable future world.

Note

1. An anonymous reviewer suggested the need for macro-level analyses and would probably disagree with this statement. He further suggested that the geographical theories of territoriality and spatial interdependence are key in understanding and resolving the nuclear war threat. While I agree that we must also search for broad theories which help explain the human condition and the need to link micro-level observations to macro-level theories (Palm, 1986), I remain sceptical that we can advance theory on this issue at this time. Instead, I argue for a more pragmatic approach as an immediate and viable means of ensuring our participation in the public policy debates on nuclear war and war preparation.

References

Abler, R. (1987) 'What shall we say? To whom shall we speak?', *Annals of the Association of American Geographers*, vol 77, pp511–524

Anderson, J. (1984a) 'Ashfall and fallout: Lessons from Mount St. Helens for nuclear crisis relocation planning', paper presented at the annual meeting of the Association of American Geographers, Washington, DC

Anderson, J. (1984b) 'Lessons from the Mount St. Helens ashfall', *Transition*, vol 13, pp24–25

Anderton, C. H. and Isard, W. (1985) 'The geography of arms manufacture' in D. Pepper and A. Jenkins (eds) *The Geography of Peace And War*, Blackwell, Oxford, pp90–104

Bach, W. (1986) 'Nuclear war: The effects of smoke and dust on weather and climate', *Progress in Physical Geography*, vol 10, no 4, pp315–363

Barnaby, F. (1985) 'Nuclear weapon free zones' in D. Pepper and A. Jenkins (eds) *The Geography of Peace And War*, Blackwell, Oxford, pp165–177

Bateman, M. and Wiley, R. (eds) (1987) *The Geography of Defense*, Rowman and Littlefield, Totowa, NJ

Bennett, J. O., Johnson, P. S. C, Key, J. R., Pattie, D. C. and Taylor, A. H. (1984) 'Foreseeable effects of nuclear detonations on a local environment: Boulder County, CO', *Environmental Conservation*, vol 11, pp155–165

Brunn, S. D. (1985) 'The geography of peace movements' in D. Pepper and A. Jenkins (eds) *The Geography of Peace And War*, Blackwell, Oxford, pp178–191

Brunn, S. D. (1987) 'A world of peace and military landscapes', *Journal of Geography*, vol 86, no 6, pp253–262

Bunge, W. W. (1973a) 'The geography of human survival', *Annals of the Association of American Geographers*, vol 63, pp275–95

Bunge, W. W. (1973b) 'The geography', *The Professional Geographer*, vol 25, pp331–337

Bunge, W. W. (1982) *The Nuclear War Atlas*, The Society for Human Exploration, Victoriaville, Quebec

Bunge, W. W. (1983) 'Geography is a field subject', *Area*, vol 15, pp208–210

Burnett, A. (1985) 'Propaganda cartography' in D. Pepper and A. Jenkins (eds) *The Geography of Peace And War*, Blackwell, Oxford, pp60–89

Crutzen, P. J. (1983) 'The global environment after nuclear war', *Environment*, vol 27, pp6–11, 34–37

Crutzen, P. J. and Birks, J. (1982) 'The atmosphere after a nuclear war: Twilight at noon', *Ambio*, vol 11, pp114–125

Curry, M. (1985) 'In the wake of nuclear war: Possible worlds in an age of scientific expertise', *Environment and Planning D*, vol 3, pp309–321

Curry, M. (1986a) 'Beyond nuclear winter: On the limitations of science in political debate', *Antipode*, vol 18, pp244–267

Curry, M. (1986b) 'On possible worlds: From geographies of the future to future geographies' in L. Guelke (ed) *Geography and Humanistic knowledge: Waterloo Lectures in Geography*, vol 2, Department of Geography Publication Series no 25, University of Waterloo, Ontario, pp87–101

Cutter, S. L., Holcomb, H. B. and Shatin, D. (1986) 'Spatial patterns of support for a nuclear weapons freeze', *The Professional Geographer*, vol 38, pp42–52

Cutter, S. L., Holcomb, H. B., Shatin, D., Shelley, F. M. and Murauskas, G. T. (1987) 'From grassroots to partisan politics: Nuclear freeze referenda in New Jersey and South Dakota', *Political Geography Quarterly*, vol 6, no 4, pp287–300

Dotto, L. (1986) *Planet Earth in Jeopardy: Environmental Consequences of Nuclear War*, John Wiley, New York

Elsom, D. (1985) 'Climatological effects of a nuclear exchange: A review' in D. Pepper and A. Jenkins (eds) *The Geography of Peace And War*, Blackwell, Oxford, pp126–47

Gerasimov, I. P. (1985) 'Geography of peace and war: A Soviet view' in D. Pepper and A. Jenkins (eds) *The Geography of Peace And War*, Blackwell, Oxford, pp192–201

Gordon, S. and McFadden, D. (eds) (1984) *Economic Conversion: Revitalizing America's Economy*, Ballinger, Cambridge, MA

Greene, O., Rubin, B., Turok, N., Webber, P. and Wilkinson, G. (1982) *London After the Bomb: What a Nuclear Attack Really Means*, Oxford University Press, New York

Grover, H. D. (1984) 'The climatic and biological consequences of nuclear war', *Environment*, vol 26, pp6–13

Grover, H. D. and White, G. F. (1985) 'Toward understanding the effects of nuclear war', *Bioscience*, vol 35, pp552–556

Harwell, M. A. and Harwell, C. C. (1987) 'Updating the "nuclear winter" debate', *Bulletin of the Atomic Scientists*, vol 43, pp42–44

Harwell, M. A., Harwell, C. C. and Hutchinson, T. C. (1985) *Environmental Consequences of Nuclear War*, SCOPE 28, Volume II, John Wiley, New York

Hewitt, K. (1983) 'Place annihilation: Area bombing and the fate of urban place', *Annals of the Association of American Geographers*, vol 73, pp257–284

Hewitt, K. (1984) 'Defenseless space? Civil protection in war', paper presented at the annual meeting of the Association of American Geographers, Washington, DC

Holcomb, B., Shatin, D. and Cutter, S. (1984) 'Geographical aspects of the nuclear weapons freeze movement', paper presented at the annual meeting of the Association of American Geographers, Washington, DC

Isard, W. and Smith, C. (1982) *Conflict Analysis and Practical Management Procedures: An Introduction to Peace Science*, Ballinger, Cambridge, MA

Ives, T. (1985) 'The geography of arms dispersal' in D. Pepper and A. Jenkins (eds) *The Geography of Peace And War*, Blackwell, Oxford, pp42–59

Jenkins, A. (1985) 'Peace education and the geography curriculum' in D. Pepper and A. Jenkins (eds) *The Geography of Peace And War*, Blackwell, Oxford, pp202–213

Jenkins, A. and Pepper, D. (1986) *The Geography of War and Peace – Geography Section Module 2635*, Oxford Polytechnic, Oxford

Katz, A. M. (1982) *Life After Nuclear War: The Economic and Social Impacts of Nuclear Attack on the United States*, Ballinger, Cambridge, MA

Kidron, M. and Smith, D. (1983) *The War Atlas*, Simon and Schuster, New York

Kofman, E. (1984) 'Information and nuclear issues: The role of the academic', *Area*, vol 16, p166

Larimore, A. E. (1984) 'Geographical terms of discourse used in assessing the environmental effects of nuclear war', paper presented at the annual meeting of the Association of American Geographers, Washington, DC

Leaning, J. and Keyes, L. (eds) (1984) *The Counterfeit Ark*, Ballinger, Cambridge, MA

London, J. and White, G. F. (eds) (1984) *The Environmental Effects of Nuclear War*, AAAS Selected Symposium No. 98, Westview Press, Boulder, CO

Malecki, E. J. (1981) 'Government funded R&D: Some regional economic implications', *The Professional Geographer*, vol 33, pp72–82

Malecki, E. J. (1982) 'Federal R&D spending in the United States of America: Some impacts on metropolitan economies', *Regional Studies*, vol 16, pp19–35

Malecki, E. J. (1984) 'Military spending and the US defense industry: Regional patterns of military contracts and subcontracts', *Environment and Planning C: Government and Policy*, vol 2, pp31–44

Malecki, E. J. (1986) 'Research and development and the geography of high-technology complexes' in J. Rees (ed) *Technology, Regions, and Policy*, Rowman and Littlefield, Totowa, NJ, pp51–74

Markusen, A. (1986) 'Defense spending and the geography of high tech industries' in J. Rees (ed) *Technology, Regions, and Policy*, Rowman and Littlefield, Totowa, NJ, pp94–119

Markusen, A. and Bloch, R. (1984) 'Defensive cities: Military spending, high technology, and human settlements' in M. Castells (ed) *Technology, Space, And Society: Emerging trends*, Sage Urban Affairs Annual Reviews, Beverly Hills, CA, pp106–120

Markusen, A., Hall, P. and Glasmeier, A. (1986) *High Tech America*, Allen and Unwin, Boston, MA

Melman, S. (1985) *The Permanent War Economy: American Capitalism in Decline*, Simon and Schuster, New York

Mitchell, J. K. (1984) 'Nuclear war and hazards research', paper presented at the annual meeting of the Association of American Geographers, Washington, DC

Morrill, R. L. (1984) 'The responsibility of geography', *Annals of the Association of American Geographers*, vol 74, pp1–8

Mosley, H. C. (1985) *The Arms Race: Economic and Social Consequences*, D. C. Heath and Company, Lexington, MA

O'Loughlin, J. (1986) 'Spatial models of international conflicts: Extending current theories of war behavior', *Annals of the Association of American Geographers*, vol 76, pp63–80

O'Loughlin, J. (1987) 'Political geography: Marching to the beats of different drummers', *Progress in Human Geography*, vol 11, pp247–263

O'Loughlin, J. and van der Wusten, H. (1986) 'Geography, war and peace: Notes for a contribution to a revived political geography', *Progress in Human Geography*, vol 10, pp484–510

Openshaw, S. and Steadman, P. (1982) 'On the geography of a worst case nuclear attack on the population of Britain', *Political Geography Quarterly*, vol 1, pp263–278

Openshaw, S. and Steadman, P. (1983a) 'The geography of two hypothetical nuclear attacks on Britain', *Area*, vol 15, pp193–210

Openshaw, S. and Steadman, P. (1983b) 'The bomb: Where will the survivors be?', *Geographical Magazine*, vol 55, pp293–296

Openshaw, S. and Steadman, P. (1983c) 'Predicting the consequences of a nuclear attack on Britain: Models, results, and implications for public policy', *Environment and Planning C*, vol 1, pp205–228

Openshaw, S. and Steadman, P. (1985) 'Doomsday revisited' in D. Pepper and A. Jenkins (eds) *The Geography of Peace And War*, Blackwell, Oxford, pp107–125

Openshaw, S., Steadman, P. and Greene, O. (1983) 'Doomsday' in *Britain After Nuclear Attack*, Blackwell, Oxford

O'Sullivan, P. (1982) 'Antidomino', *Political Geography Quarterly*, vol 1, pp57–64

O'Sullivan, P. (1985) 'The geopolitics of deterrence' in D. Pepper and A. Jenkins (eds) *The Geography of Peace And War,* Blackwell, Oxford, pp29–41

Palm, R. (1986) 'Coming home', *Annals of the Association of American Geographers,* vol 76, pp469–479

Pepper, D. (1985) 'Introduction: Geographers in search of peace' in D. Pepper and A. Jenkins (eds) *The Geography of Peace And War,* Blackwell, Oxford, pp1–12

Pepper, D. (1986) 'Political geography of contemporary events IX: Spatial aspects of the West's deep strike doctrine', *Political Geography Quarterly,* vol 5, pp253–266

Pepper, D. and Jenkins, A. (1983) 'A call to arms: Geography and peace studies', *Area,* vol 15, pp202–208

Pepper, D. and Jenkins, A. (1984) 'Reversing the nuclear arms race: Geopolitical bases for pessimism', *The Professional Geographer,* vol 36, pp419–427

Pepper, D. and Jenkins, A. (eds) (1985) *The Geography of Peace and War,* Blackwell, Oxford

Perry, A. H. (1985) 'The nuclear winter controversy', *Progress in Physical Geography,* vol 9, pp76–81

Pittock, A. B., Ackerman, T. P., Crutzen, P. J., MacCracken, M. C., Shapiro, C. S. and Turco, R. P. (1985) *Environmental Consequences of Nuclear War,* SCOPE report, John Wiley, New York

Platt, R. H. (1984) 'The planner and nuclear crisis relocation', *Journal of the American Planning Association,* vol 50, pp259–260

Platt, R. H. (1986) 'Nuclear crisis relocation: Issues for a host community – the case of Greenfield, Massachusetts, USA', *Environmental Management,* vol 10, pp189–198

Rathgens, G. W. and Siegel, R. H. (1986) 'Comment and correspondence: The Nuclear winter debate', *Foreign Affairs,* vol 65, pp169–171

Rees, J. (1982) 'Defense spending and regional industrial change', *Texas Business Review,* vol 56, pp40–44

Renwick, H. L. (1982) 'The post-nuclear-holocaust landscape', paper presented at the annual meeting of the Association of American Geographers, San Antonio, TX

Renwick, H. L. (1986) *The Post-nuclear Landscape: How Science Fiction Compares with Official and Scientific Scenarios,* Discussion Paper no 24, Department of Geography, Rutgers University, New Brunswick, NJ

Ringler, D. (1985) 'Nuclear war: A teaching guide', *Bulletin of the Atomic Scientists,* vol 40, pp2s–32s

Sagan, C. (1986) 'Comment and correspondence: The nuclear winter debate', *Foreign Affairs,* vol 65, pp163–168

Seager, J. and Olson, A. (1986) *Women in the World: An International Atlas,* Touchstone, Simon and Schuster Press, New York

Shatin, D. (1987) 'The spatial pattern of support for the nuclear weapons freeze in the United States, 1980–1984', Masters thesis, Department of Geography, Rutgers University, New Brunswick, NJ

Smith, K. (1985) 'Environmental issues', *Progress in Human Geography,* vol 9, pp82–87

Solecki, W. D. and Cutter, S. L. (1987) 'Living in the nuclear age: Teaching about nuclear war and peace', *Journal of Geography,* vol 86, pp114–120

Thompson, S. L. and Schneider, S. H. (1986a) 'Nuclear winter reappraised', *Foreign Affairs,* vol 64, pp981–1005

Thompson, S. L. and Schneider, S. H. (1986b) 'Comment and correspondence: The nuclear winter debate', *Foreign Affairs,* vol 65, pp171–178

Turco, R. P. (1986) 'Comment and correspondence: The nuclear winter debate', *Foreign Affairs,* vol 65, pp168–169

Turco, R. P., Toon, O. B., Ackerman, T., Pollack, J. P. and Sagan, C. (1983) 'Nuclear winter: Global consequences of multiple nuclear explosions', *Science,* vol 222, pp1283–1292

US Office of Technology Assessment. (1979) *The Effects of Nuclear War,* Government Printing Office, Washington, DC

van der Wusten, H. (1984) 'Geography and war/peace studies' in P. J. Taylor and J. House (eds) *Political Geography: Recent Advances and Future Directions,* Croom Helm, London, pp191–201

van der Wusten, H. (1985) 'The geography of conflict since 1945' in D. Pepper and A. Jenkins (eds) *The Geography of Peace and War,* Blackwell, Oxford, pp13–28 van der Wusten, H. and O'Loughlin, J. (1986) 'Claiming new territory for a stable peace: How geographers can contribute', *The Professional Geographer*, vol 38, pp18–28

White, G. F. (1984) 'Notes on geographers and the threat of nuclear war', *Transition*, vol 14, pp2–4

White, G. F. (1985) 'Geographers in a perilously changing world', *Annals of the Association of American Geographers*, vol 75, pp10–16

Wien, B. (1984) *Peace and World Order Studies: Curriculum Guide*, World Policy Institute, New York

Williams, S. W. (1982) 'Pieces in the global war game', *Geographical Magazine*, vol 54, pp373–375

Winkler, A. M. (1984) 'A 40-year history of civil defense', *Bulletin of the Atomic Scientists*, vol 40, pp16–22

Wisner, B. (1986) 'Geography: War or peace studies?', *Antipode*, vol 18, pp212–217

Zeigler, D. J. (1985) 'The Geography of civil defense' in D. Pepper and A. Jenkins (eds) *The Geography of Peace And War*, Blackwell, Oxford, pp148–164

Zeigler, D. J. (1986) 'Evacuation from a nuclear attack: Prospects for population protection in Hampton Roads', *Virginia Social Science Journal*, vol 21, pp22–31

25
Emerging Hurricane Evacuation Issues: Hurricane Floyd and South Carolina

Kirstin Dow and Susan L. Cutter

Introduction

There is a new urgency in hurricane preparedness efforts and the challenges faced by the emergency management community (Pielke and Landsea, 1998; Jamieson and Drury, 1997; Sheets, 1995). Forecasters are concerned that recent storms signal the return to a period of greater hurricane activity (Goldenberg et al, 2001; Landsea et al, 1999). Researchers offer compelling documentation of the increased vulnerability of coastal residents due to tremendous population growth and investment along the coast (Pielke and Pielke, 1997; Elsner and Kara, 1999; Heinz Center, 2000a, b). In some areas, tourism-based economic growth has been so rapid that traffic infrastructure does not even adequately accommodate the usual summer (and hurricane season) crowds. Researchers estimate that the aggregate value of insured property in coastal counties grew 48 per cent between 1988 and 1993 to reach a total of about \$21.4 trillion (Pielke and Pielke, 1997). Concurrently, clearance times for some coastal communities exceed reasonable expectations of present and projected forecast accuracy and the perceived willingness of communities to begin evacuation earlier when uncertainty levels are higher (AMS Council, 2000). The unprecedented scale of 1999's Hurricane Floyd evacuation in the Southeast highlighted the potential pressures on the transportation system at both the state and regional levels. These transportation difficulties are emerging as a more common factor in residents' decisions not to evacuate.

In mid-September 1999, as Hurricane Floyd threatened the Atlantic coast, South Carolina Governor Jim Hodges ordered a mandatory evacuation in the state's six coastal counties, including the cities of Charleston and Myrtle Beach.

Note: Reprinted, with permission, from *Natural Hazards Review*, vol 3, no1, Kirstin Dow and Susan L. Cutter, 'Emerging hurricane evacuation issues: Hurricane Floyd and South Carolina', pp12–18.

This was the sixth evacuation order for the state's coastal counties in three years. Unofficial estimates indicated that more than half a million South Carolinians left their homes for inland areas, making it the largest evacuation in the state's history. These South Carolinians joined approximately two million other coastal residents from Florida, Georgia, North Carolina and Virginia who left their homes to escape the potential impacts of Hurricane Floyd (Baker, 2000). It has been called the largest evacuation in US history.

The threat posed by Floyd tested hurricane-planning efforts (especially transportation) all along the Atlantic coast. The miles of crawling traffic associated with Hurricane Floyd were due, in part, to a unique combination of physical characteristics of the storm – size, intensity and trajectory. The size of Floyd was dramatically communicated by satellite images of spiral cloud bands overlaying several southeastern coastal states at once. The maximum wind speeds as the hurricane neared the Florida coast were just below Category 5 on the Saffir-Simpson scale. Lastly, the coastal-parallel path of Floyd threatened the eastern portion of Florida, then Georgia, before approaching South Carolina and continuing north. As a result of the trajectory, Florida and Georgia evacuees heading north along Interstate 95 (I-95), which parallels the coast, were met by evacuees from coastal South Carolina evacuating west and north. In South Carolina, this evacuation resulted in a lengthy traffic jam on Interstate 26 (I-26) westbound out of Charleston and the implementation of an unplanned lane reversal along a 161km segment of I-26 to Columbia. Despite this radical alteration in plans, some evacuees still experienced a tenfold increase in normal travel times. However, according to emergency management officials, all evacuees were off the roads prior to landfall.

The history of recent evacuations in South Carolina and the concerns over hurricane preparedness in more populated and rapidly urbanizing coastal areas prompted a post-Hurricane Floyd survey of coastal South Carolina residents. This chapter examines aspects of household evacuation decision-making that potentially influences transportation planning for future evacuations. Four specific issues are considered:

1. number of vehicles taken by a household;
2. the timing of evacuees' departures;
3. distances travelled in the evacuation; and
4. the role of information in the selection of specific evacuation routes.

Transportation Considerations in South Carolina

For years, hurricane emergency managers have watched with concern as the Atlantic and Gulf shores coastal populations have grown and property values increased over 200 per cent in some counties (Pielke and Pielke, 1997). The implications of this tremendous growth affects all aspects of hurricane preparedness, from implementation of mitigation strategies in new construction to the complexity and capacity of recovery operations. In evacuation planning, the growth in absolute numbers has focused attention on infrastructure capacity issues, such as departure times, destinations and shelters, rather than evacuees' decisions about routes or details of the mode of transportation (Sorensen and Mileti, 1988). Despite the surge of interest in contraflow proposals, there are still many considerations involved in making these plans function safely and efficiently (Wolshon, 2001). The latter are especially critical as they can multiply and accelerate the demand on transportation infrastructure during crucial times. For example, South Carolina's coastal counties accounted for 22 per cent of the state-wide population increase between 1990 and 2000. Beaufort, Jasper and Horry counties registered more than a 33 per cent population increase making them the top three growth counties in the state.

Transportation-demand investigations focus largely on engineering-based studies of clearance times to inform the timing of evacuation decisions. The reported clearance times have increased substantially in many coastal areas (AMS Council, 2000). However, the transportation models, such as the model in the Army Corps of Engineers (ACOE) *Evacuation Travel Demand Forecasting System* (USACOE, 2000b), are often community, county or regionally based and incorporate several assumptions about behaviour in evacuations that warrant further examination. For example, evacuation transportation models incorporate the expectation that between 20 and 30 per cent of households may take a second vehicle (Don Lewis, personal email communication, 7 August 2000), yet the rationale behind this household practice has not been examined in a way that allows any differentiation among households in different communities. Also receiving little systematic attention, by both planners and the evacuees themselves, is the evacuees' selection of travel routes (and alternatives). Historically, evacuation route planning was concentrated within a state because the evacuation destinations of evacuees tended to be relatively local. However, the experience with Hurricane Floyd illustrates the need for greater attention to several aspects of evacuation decision-making. This includes the regional (or inter-state) impact of local transportation plans and the potential convergence of evacuees on capacity-limited Interstate highways (USACOE, 2000a).

In addition to the number of vehicles on the road, other factors contributed to high traffic levels during Hurricane Floyd, specifically shadow and tourism evacuations. In many hurricanes, some residents living in counties not adjacent to the coast and outside the zone of mandatory evacuation orders also evacuate. Hurricane Floyd was no exception. This 'shadow evacuation' population contributed to the congestion on the highways along the coast from Florida to North Carolina (Baker, 2000). In South Carolina, the evacuation rate from non-coastal counties ranged from 21 per cent in the northern part of the state to 49 per cent in the central area around Charleston and averaged 28 per cent along the entire coast (Baker, 2000). Unfortunately, consistent data and household surveys of this shadow evacuation population are not widely reported nor analysed with respect to the risk perception or decision-making process that prompted this response.

Another factor contributing to the traffic congestion is the tourist population. In 1997, approximately 15 million people visited coastal South Carolina. This number is bound to increase in the future as the state promotes tourism more aggressively (SCPRT, 1999a). The peak tourism season unfortunately corresponds closely with hurricane season (SCPRT, 1999b). Drabek (1996), in one of the few studies involving tourists and other transient populations, reported that approximately 48 per cent of the hurricane evacuees who responded to this question evacuated in their own vehicles and another 24 per cent took rental cars. Drabek's percentages may be an underestimate for South Carolina, given the nature of tourist development along the coast. 98 per cent of the tourists to South Carolina are based in the US, and for that group, cars or recreational vehicles (RVs), rather than airlines, are the primary transportation for 84 per cent (SCPRT, 1999a). These vehicles will probably be the preferred mode of transport out the evacuation area.

Methodology

In cooperation with the University of South Carolina's Institute of Public Affairs' Survey Research Lab, we conducted a telephone survey of residents given mandatory evacuation orders throughout coastal South Carolina (Figure 25.1). Our sample does not address the topic of shadow evacuations. Phone numbers from zip code areas, either completely or partially covered by the mandatory evacuation order, were randomly selected from the complete set of randomly generated phone numbers representing all possible combinations. The sampling is accurate to within ±4.2 per cent for South Carolina. The survey included both open-ended and closed question formats on the topics of departure time, planned and ultimate destination, duration of trip, number of cars taken, choice of route, availability and use of road maps, what convinced them to leave, and importance of various measures of success in an evacuation. The survey took approximately ten minutes to complete. It was administered in the evenings between 25 October and 9 November 1999, about six weeks after the hurricane. There were 513 completed

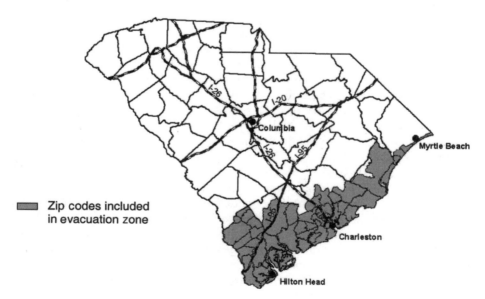

Figure 25.1 *Survey area sampled in South Carolina*

interviews and another 19 interviews were partially completed for a survey total of 536 households. The response rate for the survey, 63.5 per cent, represents the total number of fully and partially completed interviews divided by the sum of the number of fully and partially completed interviews plus the total number of contacts that were unable or unwilling to respond to the survey during the fielding period.

Behavioural Influences Stressing Transportation Systems

Evacuation traffic

On average, 65 per cent of the residents of the mandatory evacuation zone surveyed reported leaving for Hurricane Floyd. This evacuation compliance rate is the highest reported state-wide since Hurricane Hugo in 1989 (see Chapter 14). While the Hurricane Floyd evacuation was a test of dealing with large numbers of evacuees, those numbers easily could have been larger since 35 per cent of the potential evacuees chose not to leave.

Evacuation rates are influenced by the governor's orders as well as residents' personal evaluations of a wide variety of risk factors (see Chapter 14). Evacuees report that storm severity, landfall locations and the governor's mandatory orders are top influences in their decisions. Among those who stayed, traffic concerns were the second most commonly mentioned factor (12 per cent), right after the safety of their home. Other major categories were work responsibilities (11 per cent) and probability that the landfall will be nearby (8 per cent). The number of traffic concerns reported may have been elevated by media reporting, which began to comment on traffic before all evacuees were on the road. However, in our four years of research on hurricane evacuations in South Carolina, this is the first time that traffic concerns were among the top three reasons to stay at home despite an evacuation warning. This concern has also been identified in previous evacuations. In a 1998 sample of Hurricane Bonnie evacuees in South Carolina, 12 per cent of respondents mentioned traffic as a significant consideration for not evacuating (Dow et al, 1999). In a survey following Hurricanes Bertha and Fran in 1996, 1.2 per cent and 1.6 per cent respectively mentioned traffic as a reason for staying (Dow et al, 1999).

Vehicles per household

Some of the traffic volume for the Hurricane Floyd evacuation was related to the number of households taking more than one vehicle. Because existing research clearly identifies the importance of having the household together as a condition for evacuating, it might be presumed that households will also evacuate together (Sorenson, 2000). Although transportation models account for households taking more than one vehicle, the rationale for the household decisions is not well documented. Among our South Carolina respondents, approximately 25 per cent of all evacuating households used more than one vehicle. This average corresponds with the 20–30 per cent estimates used in transportation planning. Chi-square analysis indicates a significant relationship between number of cars per household and household size (chi squared = 33.08; p = 0.00). The average size of a multi-vehicle household was approximately 4.5 people. The greater the size of the household, the more likely the household was to take more than one car, as expected. In three- and four-person households, for example, 31 per cent took two or more cars. Nonetheless, 21 per cent of two-person households took two vehicles during the evacuation. Although the significance level was not as high, chi-square tests also indicate that higher household income was related to taking more vehicles in the evacuation (chi squared = 6.92; p = 0.07). Despite these statistical relationships, it is still unclear whether households take two or more cars because job respon- sibilities might require one member to return sooner than others, or the vehicles are very valuable, or residents took too many possessions with them, or they want the flexibility to allow one member to return to clean up while others stay with children. The importance of keeping the household together remained a strong factor in evacuation. Despite splitting up during the initial journey, 92 per cent of all households reported that all members went to the same destination.

Evacuation traffic flow can be less than normal daily commute conditions. Highway flow under evacuation conditions is reduced because of evacuees' ten- dency to heavily load vehicles or to pull trailers (Wolshon, 2001). The South Carolina Department of Transportation (SCDOT) conducted vehicle counts on nine major egress routes during the hurricane (SCDOT, unpublished data on file with the authors, 1999). These counts showed that, at all locations except those in Charleston, traffic flow under evacuation conditions on Tuesday 14 September 1999 totalled 25 per cent less than it had on the previous Tuesday. In compar- ing the peak hour of evacuation traffic on 14 September to the peak hour of the previous Tuesday, reports from five of the nine count sites indicate that the peak evacuation hour had less traffic than the peak commuting hour. In addition to considering the number of vehicles, it may be prudent to consider the vehicle equivalents represented by heavily loaded vehicles and trailers.

Timing of evacuation

Research on past evacuations shows that departure patterns are quite consistent among hurricane events with the majority of evacuation trips beginning during normal waking hours on the two days prior to anticipated landfall (Baker, 2000). South Carolina residents had ample warning of the possibility of an evacuation order as national news networks were covering the track of the storm and evacu- ation in Florida. The South Carolina voluntary evacuation was called at 7:00am on Tuesday, 14 September 1999, and the mandatory evacuation order followed five hours later at noon. South Carolina's traffic jam was attributed, in part, to the close spacing of the governor's voluntary and mandatory evacuation orders. The spacing of evacuation orders was addressed in the recommendations of the committee appointed by the South Carolina governor to study evacuation prob- lems (Ravenel, Columbia, SC, unpublished memo to Governor James Hodges, September 1999). According to our survey findings, the majority of residents (61 per cent) left on Tuesday between 6:00am and 9:00pm followed by a second large group of 31 per cent during the daylight hours of Wednesday. Hurricane Floyd made landfall in North Carolina early in the morning on Thursday, 16 September.

Only a small percentage left Monday (5 per cent) prior to any South Carolina official advisories or evacuation orders. In actual numbers, evacuees totalled between 520,000 and 624,000. An estimated 317,000 to 381,000 people left the coastal areas of South Carolina on Tuesday, 14 September followed by another 161,000 to 193,000. The vast majority (48 per cent or 250,000–300,000) left in one of two periods, either between 9:00am and noon (25.4 per cent) or from noon to 3:00pm (22.6 per cent). Traffic counts from SCDOT verify this compact window of evacuation (SCDOT, unpublished data on file with the authors, 1999). For no immediately apparent reason, this 9:00am to 3:00pm window, narrower than even the daylight travel hours available on Tuesday, was strongly preferred. While the compactness of evacuation response is well documented, the concentration of people on the roads in the middle of the day is not completely explained by the 7:00am and noon timing of the governor's orders. The number of people leaving before noon and soon afterwards indicates that many residents left or prepared to leave well before the governor's mandatory order was given – thus suggesting that the order affirmed, rather than motivated, their decision. It is also likely that many of those who left in the 9:00am to noon time period also made some preparations well in advance of the voluntary order.

Route selection

According to our survey, evacuees relied heavily on the Interstate system while traffic on smaller highways and roads was reportedly much lighter. I-26, between Charleston and Columbia, was the most heavily used route during the evacuation with 19 per cent of our respondents taking it during some part of their evacuation journey. I-95, the second most commonly used route, carried about 10 per cent of our respondents. In addition, I-95 bore considerable traffic from Florida and Georgia (Baker, 2000), more than 27,000 vehicles on 14 September alone (South Carolina Department of Transportation, unpublished data on file with the authors, 1999).

This preference for the Interstate seems to be based on more than simple lack of knowledge about alternative routes. Approximately 65 per cent of respondents had maps in their cars, yet only 51 per cent of that group used them to select their evacuation routes. While maps provided information on the availability of alternate routes, anecdotal information on radio call-in programmes at the time suggests that some evacuees were looking for assurance that services would be available along the route. Others expressed concern about being isolated on a rural road in case of an emergency, and those who wanted to maintain wireless communication worried about cell phone coverage away from the Interstate corridor. With 49 per cent of the evacuees who had easy access to maps not using that information, it is apparent that more work is needed on this aspect of decision-making and issues of services, communications and security on alternate routes.

Distance of evacuation destinations

Of the evacuees in our survey, 56 per cent left South Carolina, 32 per cent stayed in state and 9 per cent stayed in their county of origin. The number of evacuees travelling out of state is significantly higher and the percentage of respondents evacuating within their local areas is lower than observed in past studies of South Carolina hurricane evacuation. Surveys of South Carolina residents who evacuated from Hurricanes Bertha and Fran in 1996 found that 15 and 28 per cent, respectively, evacuated out-of-state (Hazard Management Group, 1985; Baker, 1997). Evacuation in the local area was more common in these earlier hurricane events, with approximately half of the evacuees remaining in the 'local', or same county area for Hurricane Diana in 1984, while 22 per cent evacuated in the same county for Bertha and 19 per cent for Fran, both in 1996 (Hazard Management Group, 1985; Baker, 1997). In the case of Hurricane Floyd, respondents to a survey conducted on behalf of Federal Agencies involved gave three main reasons for going outside the county in their evacuation:

1 friends and family that they could stay with lived outside the county;
2 evacuees wanted to get far away from Floyd because it was a strong storm; and
3 they travelled that far to find available lodging (USACOE et al, 2000a).

Table 25.1 provides a comparison of evacuated distances of South Carolina residents from previous hurricanes. As can be seen, evacuees from Hurricane Floyd took significantly longer trips than did evacuees from previous storms. As a consequence, traffic congestion and flow problems extended well beyond the coastal areas of the state.

Figure 25.2 shows the destinations of respondents broken down into three population centres – Beaufort, Charleston and Myrtle Beach (Horry County) – running from South to north along the coast. All nearby states, including the more distant Tennessee, were destinations. Baker (2000) and Gladwin (1999) also report significant levels of out-of-state travel for residents of other states (particularly Florida and Georgia) in the potential path of Hurricane Floyd. It is important to note that some evacuees travelled to North Carolina, moving into areas also at risk due to the uncertainties in landfall location. In this case, North Carolina not only received the impacts of landfall and much of the heavy rainfall and associated flooding, but also had to contend with evacuees from neighbouring states as well.

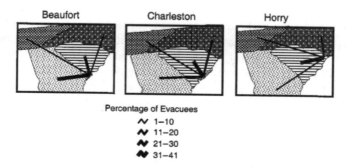

Figure 25.2 *Out-of-state destinations of South Carolina evacuees by county*

Table 25.1 *Historic comparisons of South Carolina evacuation distances*

Hurricane	Destination distances (approximate)[a,b]	Percentage of evacuees	Approximate vehicle kilometres assuming 100 vehicles total	Estimated total evacuation kilometres for 100 cars
Diana in Myrtle Beach area (1984) (Hazard Management Group, 1985)	Local (in county) (24km)	50	1208	–
	Out of town (in state) (242km)	50	12,075	13,283
	–	–	–	–
Bertha in Myrtle Beach area (1996) (Baker, 1997)	Local (in neighbourhood) (8km)	22	177	–
	In county (24km)	20	322	–
	In state (242km)	43	10,385	–
	Out of state (402km)	15	6038	16,922
Fran in Myrtle Beach (1996) (Baker, 1997)	Local (in neighbourhood) (8km)	19	153	–
	In county (24km)	12	193	–
	In state (242km)	41	9901	–
	Out of state (402km)	28	11,270	21,517
	–	–	–	–
Floyd in South Carolina (1999) (Chapter 15)	In county (24km)	9	145	–
	In state (242km)	32	7728	–
	Out of state (402km)	56	22,540	30,413
Floyd in Myrtle Beach (1999) (Chapter 15)	In county (24km)	19	306	–
	In state (242km)	57	13,766	–
	Out of state (402km)	38	15,295	–
	–	–	–	29,367

[a] Local distances are estimated at 24km from Myrtle Beach as the nearest large inland city located in the centre of Horry County. Conway, is 22.5km away. In-state travel distance is estimated at 242km, based on the distance from Myrtle Beach to Columbia (a very common destination), which is 242km. Out-of-state travel distances are estimated at 402km based on the approximate distance to Raleigh, NC (298km) or Atlanta, GA (576km) from Myrtle Beach.
[b] The original survey questions asked respondents for distances in miles, although distances are reported here in SI units.

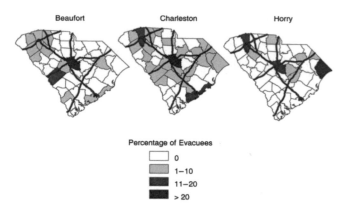

Figure 25.3 *In-state destinations of South Carolina evacuees by county*

For those respondents who evacuated but remained within the state, Columbia, Augusta and Greenville were favoured destination points. Figure 25.3 indicates another dimension of the regional variability of evacuation practices among residents in the state. None of the evacuees in the southernmost part of the state (Beaufort) stayed in their counties of origin. In the Charleston area and particularly in the Horry County/Myrtle Beach region, residents evacuated to other destinations, yet stayed within their home county. These sub-state differences reflect the amount of inland area in the county, the availability of other desirable shelters, or the residents' level of familiarity with other parts of their county. Clearly, regional and sub-state variations in evacuation travel will need greater attention in future hurricane planning.

Conclusions

Coastal development and population growth combined with hurricane threats and evacuation choices resulted in the largest evacuation in South Carolina's history, with all of its attendant difficulties. The massive public outcry brought traffic concerns to the forefront of emergency preparedness issues for elected officials and emergency managers. In addition to the sheer number of evacuees along the Southeast seaboard, multiple cars from single households, a narrow window of preferred evacuation times, marked preferences for Interstate routes, and longer trips added to the traffic problems associated with Hurricane Floyd. The behaviour of coastal residents indicates that the severity of the storm was the most important factor in decisions to leave. In deciding to stay, the sense that the home was safe was the first consideration. For the first time in our observations, concern about traffic was among the top three reasons not to evacuate. Evacuation rates for future hurricanes may well be more heavily influenced by these transportation concerns.

Our findings suggest there is more behind the traffic issues than simply the number of people leaving an area and infrastructure capacity. About 25 per cent of households took two or more cars. Approximately half of the evacuees left between 9:00am and 3:00pm on the day evacuation orders were announced, creating traffic pressures on the Interstate system, particularly I-26. About 63 per cent of respondents carried road maps, yet only half used them to determine their course while others decided to stay on the Interstate despite the crowding. The majority of South Carolinians travelled out of state, much farther than necessary for safe sheltering.

Specific components of the behavioural response – number of vehicles per household, timing of evacuation, route selection and evacuation distances – highlighted in this study will become important as the demand on coastal infrastructure grows. The questions needed to inform transportation planning have not been asked often or answered fully. Specific questions that could aid in future planning efforts are raised below.

What makes crowded Interstates preferable to alternative routes? The traffic jam on I-26 illustrated the immediate need for greater attention to decisions made during the course of evacuation once households have decided to leave. It is unclear why the majority of frustrated and nearly motionless evacuees remained on the Interstate when a large percentage had information on alternative parallel routes nearby.

Why did so few evacuees leave before 9:00am or after 3:00pm? The timing of residents' evacuation trips followed the general pattern of evacuations with larger groups of evacuees leaving during the daylight hours on the two days prior to the predicted landfall. However, about 25 per cent left between 9:00am and noon and 23 per cent between noon, the time of the mandatory evacuation order, and 3:00pm. The five-hour interval between the governor's voluntary (7:00am) and mandatory order (noon) was pointed to as a cause of traffic problems; however, that factor alone is not adequate to explain why so few left before 9:00am or after 3:00pm. With more daylight hours available and the most severe traffic problems affecting one major east–west route, there were other options available. Perhaps the earlier departures in the afternoon were linked to more distant destinations, or those leaving after the voluntary evacuation order expected a greater interval before the mandatory orders. But as behavioural and social solutions become more important in coping with the limitations of crowded infrastructure, potentially expanding the preferred evacuation window merits consideration.

How are decisions about keeping the family together and taking multiple cars reconciled? On first consideration, the practice of taking two or more cars appears to run counter to other expectations about evacuation behaviour since having the family united is generally established as an important factor, which increases the probability of evacuation (Sorensen, 2000). While this pair of observations is not necessarily contradictory, it is uncertain how these decisions relate to one another and what implications they hold for future evacuations. There are also many cases where two-person households take two cars, thus understanding the rationale behind this choice could help improve estimates of evacuation traffic. It would also be instructive to examine regional and sub-state differences in vehicle usages. Given the relative wealth of the Charleston area, for example, we could hypothesize that the multi-vehicle caravans were used to pack more belongings (rather than people) and get possessions, including the expensive vehicles, out of harms way. This behavioural pattern might be anticipated for other wealthy coastal communities as well.

Why has distance travelled during evacuations increased over recent years? While destinations are usually homes of friends and family, these longer trips contribute to increased traffic problems and evacuation costs. More investigation is needed to understand the range of options residents have (besides sheltering) and what specific factors are influencing the selection of longer journeys.

As population and investment along the Atlantic coast continues to increase, accommodating the extreme demands on transportation during hurricane evacuations will become more difficult. Creating additional capacity by road building and developing lane reversal strategies offers one approach. The results of our behavioural survey suggest that improving our understanding of the demand offers opportunities to explore non-structural and more sustainable approaches to this problem.

Acknowledgements

Thanks to the other members of the research team, Dr Robert Oldendick of the University of South Carolina Institute of Public Affairs, Patrice Burns, Melanie Baker and Dr Deborah Thomas. This research was conducted with financial support by the National Science Foundation through the Quick Response Grant from the Natural Hazards Research and Applications Information Center at the University of Colorado, and from the Department of Geography, University of South Carolina.

References

AMS (American Meteorological Society) Council (2000) 'Policy statement: Hurricane research and forecasting', *Bulletin of the American Meteorological Society*, vol 81, no 6, pp1341–1346

Baker, E. J. (1997) *Hurricanes Bertha and Fran in North and South Carolina: Evacuation Behavior and Attitudes Toward Mitigation*, Hazards Management Group, Tallahassee, FL

Baker, E. J. (2000) *Southeast US Hurricane Evacuation Traffic Study Behavioral Analysis*, Hazards Management Group, Tallahassee, FL

Dow, K., Burns, P. and Cutter, S. L. (1999) 'To stay or leave: Resident's evaluations of hurricane evacuation warnings', *Proceedings of the Applied Geography Conference*, Applied Geography Conferences, Charlotte, NC, pp107–114

Drabek, T. E. (1996) *Disaster Evacuation Behavior: Tourists and Other Transients*, Monograph No. 58, Program on Environment and Behavior, Institute of Behavioral Sciences, University of Colorado, Boulder, CO

Elsner, J. B. and Kara, A. B. (1999) *Hurricanes of the North Atlantic*, Oxford University Press, New York

Gladwin, H. (1999) 'Hurricane Floyd evacuation', Institute for Public Opinion Research, available at www.fiu.edu/orgs/ipor/floydevac/index.htm

Goldenberg, S. B., Landsea, C. W., Mestas-Nuñez, A. M. and Gray, W. M. (2001) 'The recent increase in Atlantic hurricane activity: Causes and implications', *Science*, vol 273, pp474–479

Hazard Management Group (1985) *South Carolina Hurricane Evacuation Study: Behavioral Analysis*, Hazards Management Group, Tallahassee, FL

Heinz Center for Science, Economics, and the Environment (2000a) *The Hidden Costs of Coastal Hazards: Implications for Risk Assessment and Mitigation*, Island Press, Covello, CA

Heinz Center for Science, Economics, and the Environment (2000b) 'Evaluation of erosion hazards (summary)', The Heinz Center, Washington, DC, available at www.heinzcenter.org/publications/erosion/erosnrpt pdf

Jamieson, G. and Drury, C. (1997) 'Hurricane mitigation efforts at the US Federal Emergency Management Agency' in H. F. Diaz and R. S. Pulwarty (eds) *Hurricanes: Climate and Socioeconomic Impacts*, Springer, Berlin, pp51–272

Landsea, C. W., Pielke, R. A. J., Mestas-Nuñez, A. M. and Knaff, J. A. (1999) 'Atlantic Basin hurricanes: Indices of climatic changes', *Climatic Change*, vol 42, pp89–129

Pielke, R. A. J. and Landsea, C. N. (1998) 'Normalized hurricane damages in the United States: 1925–95', *Weather and Forecasting*, vol 13, no 3 (part 2), pp621–631

Pielke, R. A., jr and Pielke, R. A., sr (1997) *Hurricanes: Their Nature and Impacts on Society*, John Wiley, New York

SCPRT (South Carolina Department of Parks, Recreation, and Tourism) (1999a) 'Visitation to South Carolina by geographic area' available at www.scprt.com/programs/statistics...t/visitation%20to20south%20carolina.htm (27 November 2000)

SCPRT (1999b) 'Visitation to South Carolina' available at www.scprt.com/programs/statistics...t/visitation%20to20areas%20of%20SC.htm (27 November 2000)

Sheets, R. C. (1995) 'Stormy weather', *Forum for Applied Research and Public Policy*, vol 10, no 1, pp5–15

Sorensen, J. H. (2000) 'Hazard warning systems: Review of 20 years of progress', *Natural Hazards Review*, vol 1, no 2, pp119–125

Sorensen, J. H. and Mileti, D. S. (1988) 'Warning and evacuation: Answering some basic questions', *Industrial Crisis Quarterly*, vol 2, pp195–209

USACOE (United States Army Corps of Engineers and Federal Emergency Management Agency) (2000a) *Hurricane Floyd Assessment*, Post, Buckley, Schuh, & Jernigan, Tallahassee, FL

USACOE (2000b) *Evacuation Travel Forecasting System*, technical memorandum no 2, Post, Buckley, Schuh, & Jernigan, Tallahassee, FL

Wolshon, B. (2001) 'One-way-out: Contraflow freeway operation for hurricane evacuation', *Natural Hazards Review*, vol 2, no 3, pp105–112

26

GIScience, Disasters
and Emergency Management

Susan L. Cutter

Introduction

Globally, it is estimated that more than 535,000 people were killed by natural disasters during the past decade with more than $684 billion in losses from direct damages to infrastructure and crops (IFRCRCS, 2002). In the US every state in the union (except Alaska) has experienced at least $1 billion weather disaster in the past two decades (NCDC, 2003). The longer-term economic impact of these disasters, both domestically and internationally, continues to affect economies at all scales (local to global).

Disasters normally are singular large-scale, high-impact events. They are different from hazards and risks (Cutter, 2001). Hazards (defined as the potential threats to people and the things they value) arise from the intersection of human systems, natural processes and technological systems. Examples include earthquakes, tornadoes, blizzards, floods, drought, industrial plant failures, terrorism and air pollution. Hazard zones can be spatially delineated (such as the floodplain) and have a risk (the probability of a hazard or event occurring) estimator attached to them, such as the 1 per cent chance flood (often called the 100-year flood). Disasters, on the other hand are an outcome of the risk and the hazard, and are difficult to spatially delineate beforehand, let alone assign a probability and magnitude estimator. Historically, sociologists and engineers studied disasters, primarily focusing on failures in the infrastructure and built environment, and societal responses to the extreme event. Geographers, planners and natural scientists studied hazards and risks, examining the underlying social and physical processes that produced the hazards and which precipitated the disaster event.

Note: Reprinted, with permission, from *Transactions in GIS*, vol 7, no 4, Susan L. Cutter, 'GIScience, disasters, and emergency management', pp439–445. © Blackwell Publishing, 2003

Emergency Management

There is a prescribed system of how societies respond to disasters, which often is referred to as the emergency response cycle (Figure 26.1). This cycle includes actions immediately following an event such as rescue and relief, to longer-term stages in the recovery process. As communities recover and rebuild in the aftermath of the disaster, the cycle moves into the mitigation phases where reconstruction is undertaken in ways that aim to reduce vulnerability and improve preparedness for the next unexpected event. GIScience has been used throughout all phases of the emergency response cycle, although in some phases more than others. In this chapter, the term GIScience is used in its broadest sense to include the suite of geographical information methods, models, processing and visualization techniques such as global positioning systems (GPS), geographic information systems (GIS), remote sensing and spatial analysis. This chapter highlights some of these applications and offers some suggestions for improving the utilization of GIScience in disasters research and emergency management.

Through technological advancements, GIScience tools and techniques have improved our identification of hazard events, especially in real or near-real time. Examples include the use of NEXRAD (Doppler Radar) to identify the hook echo in a thunderstorm supercell containing a violent tornado, to the range of satellite sensors (Aster, MODIS, TOMS) that monitored the 1997 fires in Southeast Asia or the western forest fires in 1998 (Jensen, 2000; King and Herring, 2000). Monitoring global drought conditions (Kogan, 1995) or examining the spatial extent of drought severity in the US on a weekly basis (LeComte, 2003) are additional examples that show how GIScience can help policy-makers in anticipating drought conditions and developing mitigation alternatives before the drought becomes a disaster. Perhaps the most recognizable use of GIScience in threat detection is the use of remote sensing to monitor the development and progression of hurricanes in the Atlantic and Caribbean basins and typhoons in the Pacific Rim.

Once the event occurs (Figure 26.1), the initial response involves rescue (hours to days) and relief operations (days to weeks). GIS-based incident command systems and consequence analysis tools help emergency managers in the immediate response phase. In heavily damaged areas, such as hurricane-affected coasts or cities damaged by earthquakes, it is often difficult to assess precise loca-

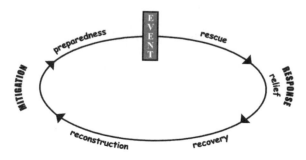

Figure 26.1 *Schematic representation of the emergency response cycle*

tions as most buildings and landmarks have been destroyed. The use of GPS (for coordinates), coupled with GIS and remote-sensing data have been employed to assist in compiling quick damage estimates (Ramsey et al, 2001).

During the reconstruction phase (months to years), communities are rebuilt after a disaster, and often their spatial data and information management systems are reconfigured or at a minimum, updated. GIScience is used to guide and monitor land use, delineate transportation routes for potential evacuations, and re-delineate hazard zones based on new knowledge or changes in the natural or human use systems (Greene, 2002). Finally, in the pre-impact planning or preparedness phase, GIS-based vulnerability assessments are now emerging, applications that integrate both social and biophysical indicators of vulnerability at specific places (see Chapter 7; also Wu et al, 2002). Other uses of GIScience in the pre-impact preparedness phase include the development of E-911 systems to facilitate emergency response and public notification of impending dangers such as a chemical spill or wildfire.

Disaster Response

The terrorist events of 11 September 2001 demonstrated in unmistakable ways the value and utility of GIScience in emergency management. As has been noted elsewhere (e.g. Cahan and Ball, 2002; Thomas et al, 2002; Bruzewicz, 2003), the use of GIS was extensive during the initial rescue and relief operations. Applications ranged from the positioning of logistical support and resources (such as the Urban Search and Rescue (USAR) teams) to public maps of the damage (by the mass media, both print and electronic). Remote sensing and GIS were used to develop preliminary damage assessments – at gross scales and by individual building and/or infrastructure. One of the noteworthy uses of GIScience was communication to the public on the availability of services (electricity, subway, telephone), information that was visualized in the form of daily maps published in the *New York Times* and in other outlets. Whether or not it was realized by emergency responders, spatial decision support systems were used routinely in the rescue and relief operations in the World Trade Center disaster. These ranged from micro-level risk assessments (shifts in the debris pile and temperature hot spots at the site) to the spatial status of lifelines (electric, water, telephone, transportation networks), all of which changed almost daily.

GIScience Issues

Previous researchers have outlined some of the applications and challenges of GIScience in disasters and emergency management (Alexander, 1991; Carrara and Guzzetti, 1996; Radke et al, 2000; Goodchild, 2003a, b; Kwan, 2003). From the viewpoint of the GIScientist these can be classified as follows:

- spatial data acquisition and integration;
- distributed computing;
- dynamic representation of physical and human processes;

- cognition of geographic information;
- inter-operability;
- scale, spatial analysis and uncertainty; and
- decision support systems.

From the perspective of the local responder or emergency management practitioner, the questions are quite different:

- What data need to be collected and where or who has it?
- Is there a ready-made model or software program that I can plug my data into that will provide the answers to my questions and where do I get it?
- Can my computer talk to yours?
- What features need to be analysed and at what locations?

Not surprisingly, there is a large disconnect between the language used and needs of the research and the applications communities.

The vast majority of first responders (such as police, fire, emergency medical personnel) is not that familiar with GIS, nor are they likely to use these systems in the immediate response or rescue phase. The development of advanced spatial decision support systems for disaster management is an important application element for GIScience, but how does this really help the local firefighter in his or her search and rescue operation in the minutes to hours after an event occurs? The decision support system must be transparent with output that is easy to understand to the non-technical manager, and more importantly, not filtered through vast bureaucratic layers of 'technical support' personnel. In the case of the World Trade Center collapse, New York City lost its Emergency Operations Center (and its GIS capabilities) due to the collapse of the building (Galloway, 2003). Fortunately, it took a little more than a day to rebuild the system. At present, practitioner preferences are oriented towards paper maps, not digital ones; and human intelligence information, not information derived from remote-sensing systems. For first responders, the major constraint to utilizing GIScience technology is an understandable user interface and willingness to adopt new technologies.

A second key issue is the development of baseline data to support GIScience applications in emergency management. Data quantity, quality and integration continue to plague the community. For example, the Federal Emergency Management Agency (FEMA) has developed its GIS-based disaster modelling and loss estimation model, HAZUS (FEMA, 1997), which currently includes earthquake hazards (hurricane wind and flood modules are under development).Touted as an 'off the shelf' application, the default inventory of buildings and structures, geology and economic values included in the model is derived from very general national overviews and inventories and has not been populated with local-level data. Local emergency managers can glean a general picture of potential losses from scenario events, but cannot detail expected losses for specific places (communities or counties) without updating and providing data on local building inventories, geology and critical infrastructure. This is a very data-intensive exercise, one that is often beyond the economic and human resource capacities of emergency management agencies. There is a growing recognition of the need for a national spatial data infrastructure such as the National Map (USGS) or the federal government's GeoSpatial One Stop. More importantly, local communities are using 11 September 2001 funds to develop foundation data such as high-resolution orthophotos and multipurpose cadastral maps.

Finally, there is a critical need for real-time data and information, a temporal requirement that often cannot be met in the field. For example, the pre- and post-processing time for remote-sensing images may negate their use in immediate response activities. There was certainly ample evidence from the 11 September 2001 events that time dependence, scale and even organizational issues (including inter-operability, connectivity and agency cooperation) thwarted the use of remote-sensing imagery (Bruzewicz, 2003).

GIScience Research Needs

There are many GIScience research areas that would enhance the disasters and emergency management research and practitioner communities. In the interest of brevity, only a few of these will be discussed here. First, the community needs better temporal and spatial estimates of tourists, homeless people and undocumented workers. Seasonal tourists occupy many hazardous regions (Atlantic and Gulf coasts during hurricane season) and getting more definitive seasonal and diurnal estimates of this population would enhance evacuation planning in these regions. Similarly, improved estimates of homeless people or undocumented workers in urban areas would assist preparedness efforts for responding to building collapses (either by human-induced threats such as bombs, or natural events such as earthquakes), or establishing sheltering and mass care needs in the preparedness phases of the emergency response cycle. The daily and diurnal occupancy of high-rise buildings is another important data need especially for planning evacuations (due to fires, bomb threats, and so on) (Kwan, 2003).

Second, and this point echoes one made by Radke et al (2000), we need better integration of physical processes and social models to enhance the prediction of hazard impacts. In this way we can examine the exposure to such risks and hazards with a population at risk over time and across space utilizing spatial analytic tools (Cutter et al, 2001). A practical example of these dynamic models is the coupling of hurricane forecast tracks (and likely landfall positions) with near real-time demographic data in order to narrow the length of the coastal area that should be evacuated and thus reduce the clearance times necessary to safely evacuate the area. At present, these physical models have so much uncertainty in them, let alone the paucity of data on population daytime distributions, that emergency managers are forced to take a precautionary approach to evacuation – ordering a greater area earlier than what might be necessary, just to err on the side of safety.

Third, the community needs better representations of risk and vulnerability, visual images that capture the spatial and temporal shifts in the risks and local vulnerability, but also the uncertainty inherent in the information being presented. For example, how good are the data that are used to make the evacuation decisions? The users of this information, more often than not, lack any formal geographical training and have varying abilities to understand complex spatial information. Maps and other visualizations of data (either hard copy or digital) must be simple and easy to interpret by an educated public. Unfortunately, this is not often the case.

Finally, the infrastructure for GIScience technology and data during emergencies is often non-existent or pieced together in an ad hoc fashion using a combination of local, county, state, federal and private providers and assets. The technical issues of data sharing, inter-operability, power sources and human resources often are insurmountable and pose major constraints on the use of GIScience for rapid response. Similarly, behavioural and social issues such as inadequate training, aversion to technology, and the 'culture' of the response community itself limits the adoption of GIScience techniques in disaster and emergency management.

Conclusions

We have witnessed how essential GIScience was during the Coalition War in Iraq where spatial decision support systems were used to identify command and control structures and movements of opposing forces, positioning of assets, and the identification of targets. In other words, spatial information-based responses were just as vital as spatial information-based destruction. The precision targeting was derived from very detailed spatial information, and when such targets were destroyed, the 'before' and 'after' images were proudly displayed for the anxious public to view on the nightly news.

While it may seem as though there is an optimistic future for the utilization of GIScience for disaster and emergency management, there is reason for some pessimism, especially if the commercial and research GIScience communities do not fully understand the limitations and constraints of the practitioner community, and the lack of fundamental data in some of the most hazardous places. The most significant research questions will be derived from the everyday experiences of the practitioners, 'Why is this community more vulnerable than the one next door? How many people are on the beach on 4 July that I might have to potentially evacuate?' While these questions originate from very practical concerns, some of the most critically important theoretical issues are embedded within them, issues that the GIScience community can help address. Closer collaborations with this user community (a bottom-up approach versus the top-down approach most often taken by non-applied scholars) will help inform GIScience researchers on the nature and scope of spatial information problems faced by the emergency management community. GIScience can and should make a difference in emergency preparedness, response, recovery and mitigation activities. It should become ubiquitous within the practitioner community, but it currently is not for many of the reasons outlined above. As researchers it is important to maintain the scientific challenges inherent in our geographical information science, but it is also the responsibility of the GIScience community to make the science and its application accessible, usable, and relevant to the emergency management practitioners.

Acknowledgements

This is the written version of an invited paper presented at the GIScience 2002 conference held in Boulder, Colorado, in September 2002. The author would like to thank David Cowen, Bryan Boruff, Melanie Gall and John Wilson for their helpful comments on an earlier draft of this paper.

References

Alexander, D. (1991) 'Information technology in real-time for monitoring and managing natural disasters', *Progress in Physical Geography*, vol 15, pp238–260

Bruzewicz, A. J. (2003) 'Remote sensing imagery for emergency management' in S. L. Cutter, D. B. Richardson and T. J. Wilbanks (eds) *Geographical Dimensions of Terrorism*, Routledge, New York, pp87–97

Cahan, B. and Ball, M. (2002) 'GIS at Ground Zero: Spatial technology bolsters World Trade Center response and recovery', *GEOWorld*, vol 15, no 1, pp26–29

Carrara, A. and Guzzetti, F. (eds) (1996) *Geographical Information Systems in Assessing Natural Hazards*, Kluwer, Dordrecht

Cutter, S. L. (ed) (2001) *American Hazardscapes: The Regionalization of Hazards and Disasters*, Joseph Henry Press/National Academy Press, Washington, DC

Cutter, S. L., Hodgson, M. E. and Dow, K. (2001) 'Subsidized inequities: The spatial patterning of environmental risks and federally assisted housing', *Urban Geography*, vol 22, pp29–53

FEMA (Federal Emergency Management Agency) (1997) *Multi Hazard Identification and Risk Assessment*, Government Printing Office, Washington, DC

Galloway, G. E. (2003) 'Emergency preparedness and response: Lessons learned from 9/11' in S. L. Cutter, D. B. Richardson and T. J. Wilbanks (eds) *Geographical Dimensions of Terrorism*, Routledge, New York, pp27–34

Goodchild, M. F. (2003a) 'Geospatial data in emergencies' in S. L. Cutter, D. B. Richardson and T. J. Wilbanks (eds) *Geographical Dimensions of Terrorism*, Routledge, New York, pp99–104

Goodchild, M. F. (2003b) 'Data modeling for emergencies' in S. L. Cutter, D. B. Richardson and T. J. Wilbanks (eds) *Geographical Dimensions of Terrorism*, Routledge, New York, pp105–109

Greene, R. W. (2002) *Confronting Catastrophe: A GIS Handbook*, ESRI Press, Redlands, CA

IFRCRCS (International Federation of Red Cross and Red Crescent Societies) (2002) *World Disasters Report: Focus on Reducing Risk*, Kumarian Press, Bloomfield, CT

Jensen, J. R. (2000) *Remote Sensing of the Environment: An Earth Resource Perspective*, Prentice-Hall, Upper Saddle River, NJ

King, M. D. and Herring, D. D. (2000) 'Monitoring Earth's vital signs', *Scientific American*, vol 282, no 4, pp92–97

Kogan, F. (1995) 'How drought looks from space', *Geocarto International*, vol 10, pp51–56

Kwan, M.-P. (2003) 'Intelligent emergency response systems' in S. L. Cutter, D. B. Richardson and T. J. Wilbanks (eds) *Geographical Dimensions of Terrorism*, Routledge, New York, pp111–116

NCDC (National Climatic Data Center) (2003) 'Billion dollar US weather disasters, 1980–2002', available at www.ncdc.noaa.gov/oa/reports/billionz.html

LeComte, D. (2003) 'US drought monitor', available at http://drought.unl.edu/dm/monitor.html

Radke, J., Cova, T., Sheridan, M. F., Troy, A., Mu, L. and Johnson, R. (2000) 'Application challenges for geographic information science: Implications for research, education, and policy for emergency preparedness and response', *URISA Journal*, vol 12, no 2, pp15–30

Ramsey, E. W., Hodgson, M. E., Sapkota, S. K., Laine, S. C., Nelso, G. A. and Chappell, D. K. (2001) 'Forest impact estimated with NOAA AVHRR and Landsat TM data related to a predicted hurricane windfield distribution', *International Journal of Remote Sensing*, vol 77, pp279–292

Thomas, D. S. K., Cutter, S. L., Hodgson, M. E., Gutekunst, M. and Jones, S. (2002) 'Use of spatial data and technologies in response to the September 11 terrorist attack', Quick Response Bulletin no 153, Natural Hazards Research and Applications Information Center, University of Colorado, Boulder, CO, available at www.colorado.eduhazards/qr/qr153/qr153html

Wu, S.-Y., Yarnal, B. and Fisher, A. (2002) 'Vulnerability of coastal communities to sea-level rise: A case study of Cape May County, New Jersey', *Climate Research*, vol 22, pp255–270

Index